Frommer's®

S0-AFI-707

Thailand

10th Edition

by Ron Emmons

WILEY

John Wiley & Sons, Inc.

Published by:
JOHN WILEY & SONS, INC.

Copyright © 2012 John Wiley & Sons Ltd, The Atrium, Southern Gate, Chichester, West Sussex PO19 8SQ, UK

Telephone (+44) 1243 779777

Email (for orders and customer service enquiries): cs-books@wiley.co.uk. Visit our Home Page on www. wiley.com

Publisher: Kelly Regan
Production Manager: Daniel Mersey
Editors: Mark Henshall & Jill Emeny
Content Editor: Sarah Pavey
Cartography: Andrew Murphy
Photo Editor: Richard H. Fox

Front cover photo: Front Credit: Buddhas in Ayutthaya Temple, Thailand / © Art Kowalsky / Alamy Images
Back Cover photo: Long-tail boats at Laem Phra Nang Beach, Krabi, Thailand / © parasola.net / Alamy Images

For information on our other products and services or to obtain technical support, please contact our Customer Care Department within the U.S. at 877/762-2974, outside the U.S. at 317/572-3993 or fax 317/572-4002.

British Library Cataloguing in Publication Data

A catalogue record for this book is available from the British Library

ISBN 978-1-118-11998-3 (pbk), ISBN 978-1-118-22456-4 (ebk), ISBN 978-1-118-26272-6 (ebk), ISBN 978-1-118-23800-4 (ebk)

Typeset by Wiley Indianapolis Composition Services

Printed and bound in the United States of America

5 4 3 2 1

CONTENTS

1 THE BEST OF THAILAND 1

2 THAILAND IN DEPTH 9

3 SUGGESTED ITINERARIES IN THAILAND 35

4 ACTIVE TRIP PLANNER 48

LIST OF MAPS

ACKNOWLEDGMENTS

Updating this guidebook has been a collaborative effort involving input from several people whose help has been invaluable. First and foremost, the editorial teams of Jennifer Reilly and Maureen Clarke in the USA as well as Mark Henshall and Jill Emeny in the UK have worked tirelessly to bring the project to completion, while Andrea Kahn in the USA did a great job of co-ordinating the mass of data that required processing. In Thailand, I am indebted to several travel trade professionals who contributed vital information about developments in the various regions of the country. These include Lee Sutton, Jittranuch Mingkwan, Marion Walsh-Hedouin, Korawee Sapmanee, Mark Shrives, Ken Scott, Nicholas Downing, Benjawan Sudhikham and Phatthawut Wutthipraphanphong; thank you all.

HOW TO CONTACT US

In researching this book, we discovered many wonderful places—hotels, restaurants, shops, and more. We're sure you'll find others. Please tell us about them, so we can share the information with your fellow travelers in upcoming editions. If you were disappointed with a recommendation, we'd love to know that, too. Please write to:

Frommer's Thailand, 10th Edition
Wiley Publishing, Inc. • 111 River St. • Hoboken, NJ 07030-5774

ABOUT THE AUTHOR

Ron Emmons taught English in Africa and the Americas before moving to Thailand, where he now works as a freelance writer/photographer. He is the author and photographer of *Portrait of Thailand* and *Walks Along the Thames Path* (New Holland, U.K.), as well as the writer of *Top Ten Bangkok* (Dorling Kindersley, U.K.) and *Spiral Guide to the Dominican Republic* (Automobile Association, U.K.). Ron has also made major contributions to several other guidebooks, such as the *Rough Guide to Vietnam* and *National Geographic Traveler Vietnam*.

FROMMER'S STAR RATINGS, ICONS & ABBREVIATIONS

Every hotel, restaurant, and attraction listing in this guide has been ranked for quality, value, service, amenities, and special features using a **star-rating system.** In country, state, and regional guides, we also rate towns and regions to help you narrow down your choices and budget your time accordingly. Hotels and restaurants are rated on a scale of zero (recommended) to three stars (exceptional). Attractions, shopping, nightlife, towns, and regions are rated according to the following scale: zero stars (recommended), one star (highly recommended), two stars (very highly recommended), and three stars (must-see).

In addition to the star-rating system, we also use **eight feature icons** that point you to the great deals, in-the-know advice, and unique experiences that separate travelers from tourists. Throughout the book, look for:

Special finds—those places only insiders know about

Fun facts—details that make travelers more informed and their trips more fun

Best bets for kids and advice for the whole family

Special moments—those experiences that memories are made of

Places or experiences not worth your time or money

Insider tips—great ways to save time and money

Great values—where to get the best deals

Warning—traveler's advisories are usually in effect

The following **abbreviations** are used for credit cards:

AE	American Express	**DISC**	Discover	**V**	Visa
DC	Diners Club	**MC**	MasterCard		

TRAVEL RESOURCES AT FROMMERS.COM

Frommer's travel resources don't end with this guide. Frommer's website, **www.frommers. com,** has travel information on more than 4,000 destinations. We update features regularly, giving you access to the most current trip-planning information and the best airfare, lodging, and car-rental bargains. You can also listen to podcasts, connect with other Frommers.com members through our active-reader forums, share your travel photos, read blogs from guidebook editors and fellow travelers, and much more.

THE BEST OF THAILAND

From the temples of Wat Pho and The Grand Palace through to Thailand's Khao Yai and Doi Inthanon national parks and Ko Hong rock, to scuba diving in Ko Pha Ngan and the white, sandy beaches of Hua Hin, Thailand is a land of variety. The country has plenty to satisfy single travelers, couples, or families, from Bangkok's shopping and nightlife to adventure sports in the northern hills or a pampering spa at a beach resort. All topped off with the famous Thai hospitality; their smiles and irresistible, laid-back attitude.

CITIES & TOWNS   Begin in **Bangkok,** with its chaotic mix of ancient temples and modern glass towers, street markets and stylish shopping malls, tuk-tuks, and river taxis. Then head north to the venerable, walled city of **Chiang Mai** for a peek at the capital of the region once known as "the Kingdom of a Million Rice Fields," but leave at least a few days to sprawl on a beach on **Ko Samui** or **Phuket.**

COUNTRYSIDE   Go trekking or white-water rafting in the **northern hills** that are home to brightly dressed hill-tribes, cycle round the ancient cities of **Ayutthaya** and **Sukhothai** in the Central Plains, pick from over a hundred **national parks** to explore, or cruise along the **Andaman** or **Gulf coast** in search of stunning dive sites.

EATING & DRINKING   Thai cuisine is enough reason to visit the country in itself, and whether you crave the brow-mopping challenge of a fiery *tom yam* or an aromatic bowl of noodles in broth, you'll find it all here. Learn to eat like the Thais, squatting on low stools at street-side food stalls, but treat yourself at least once to a gourmet feast served on starched tablecloths by waiters in traditional dress.

THE COAST   Thailand's long coastline is peppered with beautiful beaches, and presents some tough choices for visitors. Do you head for one of the mainstream beaches, like **Patong Beach** on Phuket, where you'll find a huge choice of hotels, restaurants, shopping, and nightlife, or do you look for somewhere quiet that's off the tourist radar, like **Prachuap Khiri Khan** on the Gulf coast or **Ko Kradan** near Trang? The decision rests with you.

THE most unforgettable
THAI EXPERIENCES

○ **Speaking Thai for the first time:** You'll probably feel like an idiot, and your hosts will probably roll around laughing as you splutter out your first "sawasdee" (hello) or "khop khun" (thank you). Yet you'll notice how much your effort is appreciated, and you'll be encouraged to try it again. See p. 390.

○ **Seeing the sun rise over a sea of mist:** It's only possible in the north and during the cool season, but it's a sight to remember—the sun emerging from a sea of mist in the valley below. Spectacular sights include the Mae Hong Son loop (p. 331) and from the summit of Doi Luang Chiang Dao (p. 324).

○ **Going eye to eye with a parrotfish:** Diving is one of the most popular activities in Thailand, but even snorkelers will be blown away by the colorful wonderland that lies just below the surface of the Andaman Sea and the Gulf of Thailand. Best place to learn to dive? Ko Tao (p. 206). Best spot for snorkeling? Ko Surin (p. 248).

○ **Riding an elephant:** It may be corny, but there's an inescapable thrill at being transported by such a huge creature, and any time spent with elephants will confirm all you've heard—they're gentle, sensitive, and intelligent animals. Rides are available in tourist areas countrywide; check out the Thai Elephant Conservation Center near Lampang. See p. 322.

○ **Chatting with monks:** Thai temples rank high on most people's hit list, but few expect to have a meaningful conversation with the resident monks. Fortunately the Thais' outgoing, friendly nature means many monks are eager to practice their English, and some temples even have set times when visitors can visit for a "monk chat." See p. 309.

○ **Watching a bout of Thai boxing (muay thai):** If you'd like to see Thais acting passionately about something, attend any Thai boxing contest. You'll probably watch the audience more than the boxers themselves, as they flail their fists in the air and scream encouragement for their chosen fighter. See p. 117.

THE best CITY EXPERIENCES

○ **Riding the Skytrain in Bangkok:** It was built as an attempt to alleviate Bangkok's traffic problems, but it could just as easily have been designed to help visitors get to know Bangkok. Grab a window seat and watch the city sail by from 20m (65 ft.) above ground. See p. 64.

○ **Getting lost in Chiang Mai's Old City:** Not all experiences need an itinerary, and it's fun to take an improvized stroll through Chiang Mai's Old City. Start at any corner and wander along narrow lanes, through peaceful temple compounds and squares, until you reach the moat on the other side. Then get a tuk-tuk to take you back to your hotel. See p. 288.

○ **Watching a cabaret in Pattaya:** Thailand is famous for its lady-boys (transsexuals), and Pattaya has a reputation as the country's sex capital, so why not see what all the fuss is about by attending one of the cabaret shows in town? Don't forget the camera—you'll be faced with a clutch of sumptuously dressed, over-eager models who pose on stage and after the show. See p. 145.

- **Imagining how Ayutthaya used to be:** The former capital of Siam, Ayutthaya was razed by the Burmese in the 17th century and was never rebuilt. Fortunately, enough remains of the ruins to imagine how it looked to early European emissaries, who reported the city more beautiful than Paris or London in its heyday. See p. 133.
- **Exploring Lampang in a horse and carriage:** Put on your best Stetson and hop aboard for a canter round town in one of Lampang's colorful horse and carriages. An hour's tour of the main temples costs around $10 and you might just feel like the Lone Ranger as there are rarely any other tourists in town. See p. 321.

THE best FOOD & DRINK EXPERIENCES

- **Eating at a food stall for the first time:** Many Westerners are reluctant to squat on a low stool and eat at a street-side food stall, but once you've done it, you'll find this is one of the tastiest (and cheapest) ways to enjoy Thai food. Don't worry about language problems—just point to an appealing dish, settle down, and dig in. See p. 27.
- **Discovering noodle dishes:** Thai cuisine is lauded for its stir-fries and curries, generally eaten with rice, but there are hundreds of exquisite noodle dishes, too. Try a *phad thai* (literally "Thai fry"), a delicious combination of rice noodles, beansprouts, peanuts, egg, and shrimp, or *rat na*, a plate of flat noodles topped with vegetables, meat of your choice, and a thick gravy. See p. 24.
- **Eating in food courts:** For a crash course in Thai cuisine head to one of the food courts that are found in every department store and shopping mall. Buy a fistful of coupons (200B should be plenty) and choose something tasty from one of the many stalls that specialize in different dishes. See p. 24.
- **Tasting durian for the first time:** The range of tropical fruits in Thailand is enormous, but don't miss the chance of tasting durian, which to most Thais is simply "the king of fruits." It might smell like a pair of old socks, but the creamy taste and smooth texture is nothing short of heavenly. See p. 24.
- **Joining a cookery class:** Once you've got a taste for Thai food, you'll probably want to learn how to prepare it yourself, and fortunately there are hundreds of places throughout the country where you can try your hand and taste the results. In Bangkok, head for the **Blue Elephant** (p. 93), or in Chiang Mai, the **Chiang Mai Thai Cookery School** (p. 310).

THE best WAYS TO EXPERIENCE THAILAND LIKE A LOCAL

- **Respecting elders:** Though Thais are very easy-going people in general, they abide by a fairly rigid social code that affords great respect to seniority, and you will accrue much merit with the locals by showing respect to anyone older than you. Give them a *wai* (bow), open a door for them, let them go first, and be rewarded with a broad grin of thanks. See p. 20.

- **Shopping in local markets:** Early morning is the best time to visit local markets, when there's a bustle in the air and all the produce is fresh. As a visitor, you may be more interested in taking photos than actually shopping, but keep your eyes open for a bunch of bananas for a snack or some fresh-cut flowers. In Bangkok, check out **Pak Klong Talad.** See p. 124.

- **Bargaining:** Many Western visitors are shy about offering a lower price than advertised for goods, but bargaining is the norm in Thailand. Start by offering 50–70% of the item's stated price and increase your offer as the vendor decreases the sale price to reach an agreement, but don't haggle about just a few baht.

- **Riding in a tuk-tuk:** Thais do it out of necessity, while foreigners do it for the thrill of roaring round town in these screaming, open-sided, brightly decorated vehicles. Savvy drivers know there's money to be made from foreigners, so bargain to get a reasonable price. See p. 370.

- **Getting stuck in Bangkok traffic:** It may not be the most thrilling experience, but if you want to live like a local, you just have to get caught in gridlock at least once. If it happens, don't panic, just sit back and take it like a Thai would by saying "*Mai pen rai*" ("It doesn't matter"), even if it does.

- **Taking an overnight train:** Given the number of low-cost airlines around, it perhaps doesn't make good economic sense to travel great distances by train. Yet the experience of heading somewhere new, being rocked to sleep by the chugging train and waking to views of misty paddy fields makes for a memorable experience. Good rides are from Bangkok to Chiang Mai, Nong Khai, and Had Yai. See p. 370.

THE best FAMILY EXPERIENCES

- **Relaxing on a sandy beach:** If there's one thing that kids and adults have in common, it's a love of being on a sandy beach by the sea, though parents should beware of bays with steep drop-offs. Two of the gentlest beaches in Thailand that also have roving vendors selling snacks are **Patong Beach** on Phuket (p. 217) and **Chaweng Beach** on Ko Samui (p. 179).

- **Befriending restaurant staff:** In fact, you won't need to befriend them as they'll befriend your kids first, and they'll probably amuse the children while you enjoy your dinner in peace. This simple feature of Thailand makes so much difference to many family holidays, and a small token of your appreciation in the form of a tip would not be amiss.

- **Visiting the Siam Museum:** Kids are often bored silly by museums, but Bangkok's newest offering is not so much about ancient history as what it means to be a Thai, and as such is interesting to all ages. There are lots of hands-on exhibits, plus chances to dress up in period costume and see how accurately you can fire a cannon. See p. 109.

- **Visiting a floating market:** In bygone days, much of Thailand's commerce took place on canals, and floating vendors sold everything from farming implements to bowls of noodles. These vendors' skills have not been lost, and though floating markets such as the one at **Damnoen Saduak** (p. 129) are now geared mostly to tourists, a ride round the canals looking at the fruits and flowers on sale is a great adventure for kids.

- **Watching a festival parade:** If possible, time your visit to coincide with one of Thailand's national or local festivals. These are inevitably accompanied by spectacular parades with elaborate floats and locals dressed up in their best. See p. 29.
- **Watching wildlife:** It's worth making the effort to visit the national parks and see wildlife as it should be; I recommend signing up for a tour in **Khao Yai National Park.** See p. 30.

THE best FESTIVALS

- **Songkran:** Thailand's traditional New Year festival is a celebration that lasts for a week or more, though it's officially only April 12 to 14. Often called the Water-Splashing Festival, it involves lots of playful fun with spray guns and buckets. Kids love it and it's worth planning a holiday around this event. See p. 28.
- **Loy Krathong:** Thailand's second-biggest festival, usually in November, involves floating candle-lit *krathong* on rivers and waterways throughout the kingdom. Without doubt the most visually beautiful of all Thai festivals, it marks the end of the rains and beginning of the cool season, a great time to be there. See p. 331.
- **Visakha Bucha:** Celebrating the Buddha's birth, death, and enlightenment, this countrywide festival is celebrated in May in temple compounds, where locals walk three times clockwise round the stupa carrying candles, incense, and flowers. Feel free to join in. See p. 330.
- **Phuket Vegetarian Festival:** The highlight of this eye-popping spectacle is when devotees parade the streets with skewers, swords, and drill bits stuck through their cheeks. Don't attend if you'd be disturbed by such scenes; do attend if you've got a strong stomach and want to see some unforgettable sights. See p. 220.
- **Chiang Mai Flower Festival:** Taking place in February, when the maximum number of flowers is in bloom in North Thailand, this festival features floats smothered with bright-colored and sweet-smelling flowers, accompanied by proud representatives from local schools and businesses dressed in elaborate costumes. See p. 330.
- **Surin Elephant Roundup:** A can't-miss event for elephant lovers, this pachyderm party sees hundreds of elephants converge on Surin in Isan in November for a weekend of parades, mock battles, and a blow-out buffet. Humans are welcome, too. See p. 366.

THE best BEACH EXPERIENCES

- **Dining on Chaweng Beach** (Ko Samui): Good for sunbathing, jogging, swimming, and partying, Chaweng isn't Samui's most popular beach for nothing. If you don't want to be kept awake by rowdy night owls, pick a spot at the north or south end of the beach. There's good snorkeling off the south end and about a hundred venues for a romantic, beachfront dinner. See p. 179.
- **Partying at Had Rin** (Ko Pha Ngan): The now-infamous Full Moon parties on Ko Pha Ngan's Had Rin have been attracting crowds of raving revelers for years, though many of the revelers have had their fun curtailed by drug busts or monster hangovers. There are also half-moon and black-moon (no moon) parties in case you can't make it for the full moon one. See p. 202.
- **Relaxing on Nai Thon Beach** (Phuket): Patong may be Phuket's best-known strip of sand, but Nai Thon gets this beach bum's vote for prettiest on the island (and

there's some stiff competition!). It's a perfect, 500-m (1,640-ft.) arc of golden sand lapped by turquoise waters and protected by two rocky headlands. Oh, and I almost forgot the best thing about it—there's hardly anyone there. See p. 231.

o **Wading at Loh Dalam Beach** (Ko Phi Phi): The north-facing beach of Phi Phi Don's two back-to-back beaches forms a perfect horseshoe and is fringed by blinding white sands. It's very shallow, so not too good for swimming, but if you take a walk out in the bay as the sea recedes at low tide, you'll enter a wonderland of corals, sea urchins, and sea anemones, without even needing a mask and snorkel. See p. 258.

o **Taking boat trips from Ao Nang** (Krabi): Though it's known to most people as a jumping-off pier for nearby Railay Beach, Ao Nang is much less crowded and has more options for dining and shopping, so is better suited to families. The beach itself is fine and safe for kids, but it's also easy to take boat trips to the many islands in Phang Nga Bay from here. See p. 251.

o **Watching sunsets on Had Sai Khao** (White Sand Beach, Ko Chang): This west-facing beach, with its gorgeous powder-soft sand and fringe of palm trees, fits anyone's notion of paradise, particularly when there's a sinking sun setting the sky ablaze. There's a wide choice of places to stay and eat, and it's long enough to get away from the crowds. See p. 152.

THE best GIFTS TO BRING HOME

o **Textiles:** Thai silk has a reputation for high quality, and different regions of the country are famed for different weaving styles and designs; tailored items of clothing make great souvenirs. Don't overlook garments made of local cotton and hemp, which is more comfortable to wear in a hot climate.

o **Home decor:** Thai designs display a flair that is admired worldwide, and small, packable items of home decor make ideal gifts. Pick up a bamboo and *sa* paper lantern that weighs next to nothing, a set of table mats in a striking design, or a compact set of coasters that will slip in any bag.

o **Lacquerware:** Though the process of making lacquerware is long and laborious, the finished product is both distinctively Thai and very light to carry. Bowls and plates, trays, jewelry boxes, and decorative animals are just a few top picks.

o **Silverware:** Thai silverware, particularly that made by the northern hill-tribes, is highly valued for its comparative purity and quality workmanship. Common items include jewelry (earrings, pendants, and bracelets, and even belts) and embossed bowls showing scenes from Thai history.

o **Woodcarvings:** While woodcarvings are generally too bulky and heavy to consider taking home, you'll see a huge variety of items on sale, including Buddha images and cute, palm-sized elephants. Also keep your eyes open for attractively designed picture and photo frames that pack easily and weigh little.

o **Ceramics:** Like woodcarvings, ceramics are bad news when it comes to baggage allowance, but some items are so beautiful that you may be tempted to take them home. Look out in particular for vases, plates, and trays made of celadon, which has a distinctive pale-green color and a cracked glaze. If you can't resist buying, I'd suggest you pay to have them shipped home.

THE best HISTORIC EXPERIENCES

○ **Visiting Thailand's origins:** Few visitors get to visit **Ban Chiang,** in a remote corner of Isan, but this is the country's oldest archaeological site. Remains of an advanced civilization which made metal tools and pottery with haunting spiral patterns are on display in the local museum. See p. 361.

○ **Stepping into the courtyard of a Khmer temple:** Parts of modern-day Thailand, including vast tracts of Isan, once belonged to the Khmer Empire. If you need proof, go and look at the superbly restored temples at **Pimai** (p. 358) and **Phanom Rung** (p. 367), which, incidentally, are in direct alignment with Angkor Wat. The Khmer style and craftsmanship is unmistakable, and the stone carvings in a class of their own.

○ **Gazing at illuminated Ayutthaya:** Just a hop and a skip from Bangkok, Ayutthaya is Thailand's most visited historical sight, and this former capital of the kingdom doesn't disappoint; its crooked stupas and broken Buddha images evoke a long-lost era. The main ruins are illuminated after dark, when they are particularly impressive. See p. 264.

○ **Arriving at the Dawn of Happiness:** Capital of the first true Siamese kingdom, Sukhothai (meaning "the dawn of happiness") is an inspiring place to visit. Slender stupas pierce the sky and graceful, jointless Buddhas are sculpted in mid-stride. Don't miss Wat Sri Chum and time your visit to coincide with the Loy Krathong Festival, when the clock seems to wind back almost 800 years. See p. 278.

○ **Exploring the ruins at Chiang Saen:** Sprawling beside the banks of the Mekong River, the ancient ruins at Chiang Saen are spread over a vast area, dwarfing the modern town. There has been a settlement here since the 7th century, and in the 13th century it was the birthplace of King Mengrai, who went on to found the Kingdom of Lanna. See p. 351.

○ **Walking round the walls of Chiang Mai:** Originally the capital of the Lanna Kingdom, Chiang Mai is steeped in over 700 years of history, and a stroll round its ancient city walls, gates, and moat gives a sense of how things used to be. For a bit of an extra challenge, see if you can track down the outer ring of earthen ramparts (*kamphaeng din*), some parts of which still exist. See p. 288.

THE best SMALL-TOWN EXPERIENCES

○ **Looking down over Mae Hong Son from Wat Phra That Doi Kong Mu:** From this temple on a hill, the entire town of Mae Hong Son, including Jong Kham Lake and the Burmese-style temples on its shores, as well as the main road and the airport, is spread below you. That is, when the town isn't socked in by cloud; its nickname is *muang sam mork* ("City of three mists"). See p. 340.

○ **Exploring Thailand's oldest town: Lamphun,** just south of Chiang Mai in the north, claims to be Thailand's oldest continually inhabited town. Wander round the largely intact city wall, pay your respects to the statue of city founder Queen Chamadhevi, and visit the temple named after her that has a couple of stupas built in the Dharavati period, over 1,000 years ago. See p. 320.

o **Hiding out in Loei:** If you want to give tourists the slip, make a bee-line for **Loei** (p. 362), a sleepy but friendly town in Isan without any big attractions. If you get fed up with nothing to do, get on your bike for a ride along the Mekong Valley to Nong Khai (p. 364) or put on your hiking boots and trek to the top of Phu Kra-dung (p. 362).

o **Monkeying around in Lopburi:** Situated just north of Ayutthaya, Lopburi was a favorite summer residence of former kings, particularly King Narai (r. 1656–88). It's worth visiting King Narai's Palace as well as Khmer-inspired Phra Prang Sam Yot, which is a favorite hang-out for the hordes of macaques that live here. See p. 272.

o **Crossing the bridge over the River Kwai at Kanchanaburi:** Before you cross the bridge on a special train to Hellfire Pass, pay your respects at the town's immacu-lately maintained Allied War Cemetery. You'll work out from the gravestones that many of those who died building the "Death Railway" were only teenagers. Take a tour of the Thailand–Burma Railway Center to learn more about what happened here. See p. 131.

o **Kicking back at Prachuap Khiri Khan:** It's getting more and more difficult to find a deserted beach in Thailand, but this little place south of Hua Hin attracts little interest apart from a few Thai weekenders. Wiggle your toes in the sand of local beaches, stuff yourself with seafood, and practice your Thai with the locals. See p. 169.

THAILAND IN DEPTH

*S*anuk mai? (Is it fun?) is a question frequently asked of for-eigners in Thailand, and the choice of question says a lot about the priorities of this fun-loving place. Basically, for Thais, anything that is not *sanuk* (fun) is not worth doing, so a positive response to the query ("*Sanuk, krup*" for men or "*Sanuk, ka*" for women) is bound to be met with a beaming smile, showing pleasure that outsiders are able to enjoy Thai culture. This concern for the wellbeing of *farang* (foreigners) manifests itself in all aspects of visitors' experience; at the hotel, in the restaurant, at the bus station, or in a temple compound, you are likely to come across Thais eager to make your experience smoother and more enjoyable, if they possibly can.

Thailand is no longer as undiscovered or as cheap as it was a decade ago, and recent political infighting along with global economic instability have tarnished the country's image as a tropical paradise that is immune to the rest of the world's worries. Yet the fact that Thailand remains Southeast Asia's most popular destination shows that the magnetic attraction of its sparkling temples, idyllic beaches, mountain trails, spicy cuisine, and glitzy shopping malls is as strong as ever.

In this chapter, we provide essential background information about the country's history, culture, and people, and the best time to visit the country.

THAILAND TODAY

Most of Thailand's 67 million people live in the countryside or in rural villages, where they earn a living in agriculture, predominantly by rice farming. However, as in many developing nations, there is a constant drift of people from the country to the city, and Bangkok, the nation's capital, is now home to over 8 million. The city's inhabitants are divided between wealthy Thais, often of Chinese ancestry, who are educated and hold formidable positions, and mostly uneducated workers, who came from the rural hinterland (termed "upcountry" by Thais). Hierarchy, or class, is an important distinction to Thais, who, like many of the region's nations, follow a loose version of India's caste system. When a Thai meets some-one, he or she can instantly size that person up and, depending on that individual's social status, will treat the person accordingly. Interestingly, as a foreigner, you are automatically awarded a position of stature, regardless of your social standing back home, just as long you don't flout Thai eti-quette (see "Thai etiquette" box later in this chapter).

So, who exactly are the Thai people? It's hard to say. There really are no historically "ethnic" Thais, but understanding some of Thailand's history helps to understand how it operates in the present day. Today's Thais (about 75% of the population) emerged from waves of various immigrants going back around 10 centuries. "The Making of Thailand," below, explains these waves in greater detail, but, by and large, the main bloodline is infused with indigenous people from the Bronze Age, southern Chinese tribes, Mons from Myanmar (Burma), Khmers from Cambodia, Malays, Arabs, and Europeans, plus more recent immigrants from China, Laos, Cambodia, and Myanmar. Central Thailand is a true mix of people; however, southern Thais have a closer ancestral affinity with Malays, while Thais in the north are more closely related to the Chinese, Laotians, and Burmese. The north is also home to small groups of Akha, Lisu, Lahu, Hmong, and Yao (p. 328)—brightly dressed hill-tribes who migrated south from China and Tibet during the past century. In the northeast province of Isan, Laotian influence prevails. The remaining 25% of the population are divided between Chinese (14%) and Indians, Malays, Karens, Khmer, and Mons (11%).

Despite this diversity of ethnic origin, when it comes to religion, over 95% of Thailand's inhabitants are Buddhist, and there are over 40,000 temples scattered around the country. There are small pockets of Christians, particularly in the north, where missionaries have had limited success in converting hill-tribes. Muslim communities tend to be concentrated in the south, where unpredictable attacks by separatists on schools and government buildings have made the southern provinces off-limits to tourists for some years now.

Unlike its neighbors, Thailand was never colonized, a fact which has helped to keep its rich culture undiluted and has undoubtedly contributed to the country becoming Southeast Asia's most popular tourist destination. The well-developed infrastructure makes it easy to make a hotel booking; get around by plane, train, or bus; or get connected by phone or online. The 18 million or so visitors who arrive every year have made tourism the nation's biggest foreign exchange earner, an honor held not so long ago by rice, the staple food of the region. Thailand has a high number of return visitors, though exactly what endears them to the place varies according to individual taste. For some it's the glittering temples, for others it's a laid-back resort overlooking a tranquil beach, while for others it's the chance to go on a shopping spree, or to study meditation or Thai cooking. For many, the most memorable moments are encounters with the Thai people, who are generally warm and welcoming. Locals delight in any foreigner who takes an interest in their heritage, learns a little bit of the language, eats Thai food, and follows Thai customs. Above all, the Thai people have an incredible sense of humor—a light-hearted spirit and a hearty chuckle go a long way toward making friends.

Since the economic crash of 1997, which started in Thailand but affected all Southeast Asian countries, the country has faced a string of problems. Some of these were natural disasters, such as the tsunami of 2004 and floods of 2011, while political conflict has accounted for others. Since the coup of 2006 that ousted Prime Minister Thaksin Shinawatra, fragile alliances have come and gone and Thailand is currently led by Yingluck Shinawatra, Thaksin's sister, at the head of the Pheua Thai ("For Thai") Party.

Recent years have been characterized by the conflict between the People's Alliance for Democracy (PAD), better known as the "yellow shirts," whose archenemy is the similar-sounding United Front for Democracy against Dictatorship (UDD), better known as the "red shirts"—supporters of Thaksin. Both groups have held frequent rallies, at which scuffles often break out and occasionally boil over, as in Bangkok during the Songkran Festival in April 2009 and again in 2010, when the red shirts eschewed the traditional water-splashing festivities in favor of hurling rocks and petrol bombs at the military. Tourists are never targeted in these conflicts, but it's best to steer clear of rallies where red and yellow shirts are in evidence.

These problems have inevitably had a negative effect on the economy; inflation is moving into double figures, and the cost of living is rising noticeably (so gone are the days of the 100B bungalow on the beach!). Moreover, the currency (the baht) has remained strong, so exchange rates have become less favorable for visitors.

Given the vagaries of Thai politics and unpredictable weather patterns, it is difficult to foretell what is in store for the country, but the Thais' resilience has held firm through these ups and downs and most of them are upbeat about the future.

THE MAKING OF THAILAND

EARLY HISTORY   Archaeologists believe that Thailand was a major thoroughfare for *Homo erectus* en route from Africa to China and other parts of Asia. Stone tools, dating back some 700,000 years, have been excavated around Lampang in northern Thailand. Cave paintings, found throughout the country, are believed to originate as early as 2000 B.C.; these show people dancing and hunting, as well as domesticated and wild animals in grasslike settings that appear to be rice paddies. There are also images of different forms of marine life, dolphins (in the south), and catfish (in the north). Human remains have been excavated at many sites, the most famous of which, **Ban Chiang,** in the northeastern province of Udon Thani (p. 361), contained copper and bronze items dating back to 2500 B.C., said to be the earliest examples of the Bronze Age in Thailand. A visit to this remote village is well worth the effort, both for the finds on display in the local museum and for a strong taste of rural Thailand.

It is generally thought that many of the peoples of Southeast Asia migrated south from areas in both central and southern China. These people, known as the *Tai,* settled in what are now Vietnam, Laos, and Thailand, and shared a similar culture and language. Their descendants are the core bloodline of the Thai people of today: the Shan of northern Myanmar, the Tai people of northern Laos, and the Lu of Yunnan province in southern China, as well as groups in Vietnam, on the Chinese island of Hainan, and others in northeastern India. The total number of Tai people today is estimated at 70 million.

The early Tais lived in lowland valleys in groups of villages called *muang* that were ruled over by a *chao* or feudal lord. They lived in stilted houses, making a living from subsistence agriculture; in fact, little has changed in rural areas and adventurous travelers can still witness this bucolic lifestyle today. In times of threat, either to their economic stability or from outside aggression, many *muang* would forge alliances and what developed were loosely structured feudal states where both lord and villager benefited—the lord from manpower and the villager from stability.

THE DVARAVATI (MON) PERIOD   From the 6th century, Southeast Asia underwent a gradual period of Indianization. Merchants and missionaries from India introduced Brahmanism and Buddhism to the region, as well as Indian political and social values—and art and architectural preferences. Many Tai groups adopted Buddhism, combining its doctrine with their own animistic beliefs. But the true significance of

India's impact can be seen in the rise of two of the greatest Southeast Asian civilizations—the Mon and Khmer.

The **Mon** were the earliest known inhabitants of Lower Burma, and it was they who introduced writing to the country as well as Buddhism. Around the 6th century A.D., their sphere of influence expanded, and they established Theravada Buddhism in Thailand. Mon settlements can be found at Lamphun, near Chiang Mai; Lopburi; Nakhon Pathom; Nakhorn Ratchasima (also called Khorat); and into Cambodia and northern Laos. Sadly, this once-proud race now numbers only around a million, most of whom are struggling to retain their culture in Myanmar (Burma) in the face of military oppression, though many have fled to Thailand and live, mostly in refugee camps, near the border west of Kanchanaburi.

THE SRIVIJAYA EMPIRE   In the southern peninsula, the **Srivijaya Empire,** based in Java, Indonesia, began to play an important role in cultural affairs. Before the 9th century A.D., southern port cities had drawn traders from all over the region and beyond. However, the Srivijayas, who had assimilated their own unique brand of Buddhism from India, would leave a lasting impression on these cities, linking them with other parts of Southeast Asia by importing Buddhism and Buddhist art. While the empire never actually conquered the area, its cultural influence is still evident in **Nakhon Si Thammarat** (p. 210) and from the southern art of this period. Some historians argue that **Chaiya,** near Surat Thani (p. 174), could have been the capital of the empire for a time, but the claim is largely disputed. Srivijaya power, ground down by endless warring with southern India, headed into decline and disappeared from Thailand by the 13th century.

THE KHMERS   By the early 9th century A.D., the **Khmer Empire** had risen to power in Cambodia, and spread deep into modern-day Thailand. Indravaraman (r. 877–89) saw the kingdom reach Nakhorn Ratchasima (Khorat) in northeastern Thailand. **Suryavarman I** (1002–50) extended the kingdom to the Chao Phraya River valley and north to Lamphun, driving out the Mons. **Suryavarman II** (1113–50) pushed the kingdom even farther, forcing the Mons still deeper into Myanmar (Burma) until his death in 1150.

With each conquering reign, magnificent Khmer temples honoring Hindu deities were constructed in outposts, thus expanding the Cambodian presence in the empire. Brahmanism, having been brought to Cambodia with traders from southern India, influenced not only Khmer religion and temple design (with the distinct corncob-shaped *prang*, or tower), but also government administration and social order. Conquering or forcing villages into their control, the Khmers placed their own leaders in important centers and supplied them with Khmer administrative officers. The empire was extremely hierarchical, with the king exerting supreme power and ruling from his capital.

Angkor, Cambodia's great ancient temple city, was built during the reign of Suryavarman II. It is believed the temples of **Pimai** (p. 358) and **Phanom Rung** (p. 367), in the Isan province, predated the Khmers' capital temple complex, thus influencing its style. For visitors who have not been to Angkor Wat, a trip to these beautifully restored temples is a memorable experience, and for admirers of Khmer architecture they are unmissable.

The last great Khmer ruler, **Jayavarman VII** (1181–1219), extended the empire to its farthest limits—north to Vientiane in Laos, west to Myanmar (Burma), and down to the Malay peninsula. It was he who finally shifted Khmer ideology away from

Hindu-based religion toward Buddhism, which inspired him to build extensive highways (portions of which are still evident today), plus more than 100 resthouses for travelers, and hospitals in the outer provinces. Jayavarman VII's death in 1220 marks Thailand's final break from Khmer rule. The last known Khmer settlement in Thailand is at **Wat Kamphaeng Laeng** in Phetchaburi (p. 169).

THE LANNA KINGDOM: THE NORTHERN TAIS   By A.D. 1000, the last of the Tai immigrants had traveled south from China to settle in northern Thailand. Several powerful centers of Tai power—Chiang Saen, in northern Thailand; Xishuangbanna, in southern China; and Luang Prabang, in Laos—were linked by a common heritage and the rule of extended families. In the region, *muang* grew stronger and better organized, but internal conflict remained a problem. In 1239, a leader was born in Chiang Saen who would conquer and unite the northern Tai villages and create a great kingdom, which came to be known as Lanna, or "a million rice fields." Born to the king of Chiang Saen and a southern Chinese princess, **Mengrai** ascended the throne in 1259 and established the first capital of his new kingdom at Chiang Rai in 1263. He then conquered and assimilated what remained of Mon and Khmer settlements in northern Thailand, and, in 1296, shifted his base of power to **Chiang Mai** (p. 288), which translates as "New City."

The Lanna Empire would strengthen and ebb over the following centuries; at its height, in the late 15th century, it extended into Burma (now Myanmar); Luang Prabang, in Laos; and Yunnan province, in China. Lanna society mixed animistic beliefs with Mon Buddhism. The Lanna era saw the rise of a scholarly Buddhism with strict adherence to orthodox doctrines. Its kings were advised by a combination of monks and astrologers and ruled over a well-organized government bureaucracy. By and large, the people were only mildly taxed and were allowed a great deal of autonomy.

SUKHOTHAI: THE DAWN OF SIAMESE CIVILIZATION   While Mengrai was busy building Lanna, a small southern kingdom was simultaneously growing in power. A tiny kingdom based in Sukhothai remained in obscurity until the rise of founding father King Indraditya's second son, Ram, who helped to defeat an invasion from neighboring Mae Sot, on the Burmese border. He proved a powerful force, winning the respect of his people, and upon his coronation in 1279, **Ramkhamhaeng,** or "Ram the Bold," set the scene for what is recognized as the first truly Siamese civilization.

In contrast to the Khmers' authoritarian approach, Ramkhamhaeng established himself as an accessible king. It is told he had a bell outside his palace for any subject to ring in the event of a grievance. The king himself would come to hear the dispute and would make a just ruling on the spot. He was seen as a fatherly and fair ruler who allowed his subjects immense freedoms. His kingdom expanded rapidly, it seems; through voluntary subjugation, it reached as far west as Pegu in Myanmar (Burma), north to the Laotian cities of Luang Prabang and Vientiane, and south beyond Nakhon Si Thammarat, to include portions of present-day Malaysia.

After centuries of divergent influences from external powers, we see for the first time an emerging culture that is uniquely Siamese. A patron of the arts, King Ramkhamhaeng commissioned many great Buddha images. While few sculptures from his reign remain today, those that do survive display a cultivated creativity. For the first time, physical features of the Buddha are Siamese in manner. Images have graceful, sinuous limbs and robes, insinuating a radiant and flowing motion; examples can be seen today in the **Sukhothai Historical Park** (p. 279). Ramkhamhaeng initiated the many splendid architectural achievements of Sukhothai and nearby **Si Satchanalai** (p. 283). He is also credited with developing the modern Thai written language, derived from Khmer and Mon examples of an archaic South Indian script. Upon Ramkhamhaeng's death in 1298, he was succeeded by kings who would devote their attentions to religion rather than affairs of state. During the 14th century, Sukhothai's brilliant spark faded almost as quickly as it had ignited.

AYUTTHAYA: SIAM ENTERS THE GLOBAL SCENE   In the decades that followed, the nation faltered with no figurehead, until the arrival of U Thong—the son of a wealthy Chinese merchant family. Crowning himself **Ramathibodi,** he set up a capital at **Ayutthaya,** on the banks of the Lopburi River (p. 264). From there, he set out to conquer what was left of the Khmer outposts, eventually engulfing the remains of Sukhothai. The new kingdom combined the strengths of its population—Tai military manpower and labor, Khmer bureaucratic sensibilities, and Chinese commercial talents—to create a strong empire. Ayutthaya differed greatly from its predecessor. Following Khmer models, the king rose above his subjects atop a huge pyramid-shaped administration. He was surrounded by a divine order of Buddhist monks and Brahman sanctities. During the early period of development, Ayutthaya rulers created strictly defined laws, caste systems, and labor units. Foreign traders from China, Japan, and Arabia were required to sell the first pick of their wares to the king for favorable prices. Leading trade this way, the kingdom was buttressed by great riches. Along the river, a huge fortified city was built with temples that equaled those in Sukhothai. This was the **Kingdom of Siam** that the first Europeans, the Portuguese, encountered in 1511.

But peace and prosperity would be disrupted with the coming Burmese invasion that would take Chiang Mai (part of the Lanna kingdom) in 1557, and finally Ayutthaya in 1569. The Lanna kingdom that King Mengrai and his successors built was never to regain its former glory. Fortunately, Ayutthaya had a better fate with the rise of one of the greatest leaders in Thai history. **Prince Naresuan,** born in 1555, was the son of the puppet Tai king—placed in Ayutthaya by the Burmese. Although Naresuan was a direct descendent of Sukhothai leaders, it was his early battle accomplishments that distinguished him as a ruler. Having spent many years in Burmese captivity, he returned to Ayutthaya to raise armies to challenge the Burmese. His small militias proved inadequate, but in a historic battle scene in 1593, Naresuan, atop an elephant, challenged the Burmese crown prince and defeated him with a single blow.

With the Tais back in control, Ayutthaya continued through the following 2 centuries in grand style. Foreign traders—Portuguese, Dutch, Arab, Chinese, Japanese, and English—not only set up companies and missions, but some also attained positions of power within the administration. Despite numerous internal conflicts over succession and struggles between foreign powers for court influence, the kingdom managed to proceed steadily. While its Southeast Asian neighbors were falling under colonial rule, the court of Siam was extremely successful in retaining its own sovereignty. It has the distinction of being the only Southeast Asian nation never to have been colonized—a point of great pride for Thais today.

The final demise of Ayutthaya would be brought about by two more Burmese invasions. The first, in 1760, was led by **King Alaunghpaya,** who would fail, retreating after he was shot by one of his own cannons. But 6 years later, two Burmese contingents, one from the north and one from the south, would besiege the city. The

Burmese raped, pillaged, and plundered the kingdom—capturing fortunes and laborers for return to Burma. The Thai people still hold a bitter grudge against the Burmese for these atrocities.

THE RISE OF BANGKOK: THE CHAKRI DYNASTY The fall of Ayutthaya forced the Siamese to move their capital. **Taksin,** a provincial governor of Tak in the northern central plains, rose to power on military excellence and charisma. Taksin was crowned king in 1768 and moved the capital to **Thonburi** (p. 62, Bangkok's waterways), an already well-established settlement on the western bank of the Chao Phraya River, now a suburb of modern Bangkok. Within 3 years he'd reunited the land from the previous kingdom, but his rule would not last. Over time he was able to successfully propagate the false notion that he was in fact divinely appointed as ruler. Legend tells that Taksin suffered from paranoia and his claims to divinity offended many, including the monastic order. His own wife, children, and monks were purported to have been murdered on his orders. Regional powers acted fast. He was swiftly kidnapped, placed in a velvet sack, and beaten to death with a sandalwood club—so no royal blood touched the soil. He was then buried secretly in his own capital. These same regional powers turned to the brothers Chakri and Surasi, great army generals (*phraya*), who had recaptured the north from Burma, to lead the land. In 1782, Phraya Chakri ascended the throne as **King Rama I,** founder of today's Chakri dynasty.

The Thai capital was relocated by King Rama I across the Chao Phraya River to the settlement of **Bangkok** (p. 102), where he built the Grand Palace, royal homes, administrative buildings, and great temples such as Wat Phra Kaew. The city teemed with canals as the river played a central role in trade and commerce. Siam was now a true confluence of cultures, no longer limited to the Tai, Mon, and Khmer descendants of former powers, but now including Arab, Indian, European, and powerful Southern Chinese clans. Rama I's first priorities involved reorganizing the Buddhist monkhood under an orthodox Theravada Buddhist doctrine and reestablishing the state ceremonies used during the Ayutthaya period, with less emphasis on Brahman and animistic rituals. He revised all laws so they were based upon the notion of justice. He also wrote the Ramakien, based upon the Indian Ramayana, which has become a beloved Thai tale and a subject for many Thai classical arts, such as dance and shadow theater.

Despite military threats from all directions, the kingdom continued to grow through a succession of kings from the new royal bloodline. Rama I and his successors expanded the kingdom to the borders of present-day Thailand and beyond. Foreign relations in the modern sense were developed during this early era with formal ties to European powers.

King Mongkut, Rama IV (r. 1851–68) had a unique upbringing. During 27 years as a monk (joining the monkhood at some stage of their life is a tradition all Thai men are expected to follow, even today), he developed an avid curiosity, which, throughout his reign, led to enormous innovation, dynamism, and appreciation for the West. It was King Mongkut who employed Anna Leonowens (who was the inspiration behind the character Anna, in *The King and I*) as an English tutor for his children. Her account of court life is still considered grossly inaccurate and offensive by Thais; indeed anyone found with copies of the book, or the movies—all of which are banned—can be tried for *lèse-majesté*.

Mongkut's eldest son, **King Chulalongkorn, Rama V** (r. 1868–1910), led Siam into the 20th century as an independent nation, by establishing an effective civil service, formalizing global relations, and introducing industrialization. It was during his reign that all of Siam's neighbors fell under the colonial yoke, while Chulalongkorn managed to play the European powers off against each other and thus maintain Siam's independence.

THAILAND IN THE 20TH & 21ST CENTURIES The reign of **King Prajadhipok, Rama VII** (r. 1925–35), saw the growth of the urban middle class, and the increasing discontent of a powerful elite. By the beginning of his reign, economic failings and bureaucratic bickering weakened the position of the monarchy, which was severely affected by the Great Depression. To the credit of the king, there had been a call to instate a constitutional monarchy, but, in 1932, a group of midlevel officials went ahead and instigated a coup d'état. Prajadhipok eventually abdicated in 1935.

The current king, **HM King Bhumibol Adulyadej, Rama IX,** has played an active role in stabilizing the nation. He has been the nation's figurehead since 1946 and now, in his 80s, is the world's longest reigning monarch. A compassionate man, he commands enormous loyalty from the Thai people by promoting cultural traditions and supporting rural reforms, especially among the poor.

Democracy was slow to take hold on Siam; in fact, many would argue that it has still not taken hold today. The country's original constitution, written in 1932, was more a tool for leaders to manipulate than a political blueprint. Over the following decades, government leadership changed hands fast and frequently. The army has always had an imposing influence, most likely the result of its ties to the common people as well as its strong unity. In 1939, the nation adopted the name "Thailand"— land of the free.

During World War II, the fledgling democracy was stalled in the face of the Japanese invasion in 1941. Thailand speedily submitted, choosing collaboration over conflict, even going so far as to declare war against the Allied powers. But at the war's end, no punitive measures were taken against Thailand, thanks to the Free Thai Movement organized by Ambassador Seni Pramoj in Washington, D.C., who had placed the declaration of war in his desk drawer rather than delivering it.

Thailand avoided direct involvement in the Vietnam War but assisted the Americans by providing runways for their B-52s and storage for the toxic defoliant Agent Orange. In turn, it benefited enormously from U.S. military-built infrastructure. The United States pumped billions into the Thai economy, bringing riches to many but further impoverishing the rural poor, who were hit hard by the resulting inflation. Communism became an increasingly attractive political philosophy to the poor as well as to liberal-minded students and intellectuals. A full-scale insurrection seemed imminent, and this naturally fueled further political repression by the military rulers.

In June 1973, thousands of Thai students demonstrated in the streets, demanding a new constitution and a return to democratic principles. Tensions grew until October, when armed forces attacked a demonstration at Thammasat University in Bangkok, killing 69 students and wounding 800, paralyzing the capital with terror.

The constitution was restored and a new government was elected. Many students, however, were not yet satisfied and continued to complain that the financial elite were still in control and resisting change. In 1976, student protests again broke out, and there was a replay of the grisly scene of 3 years before at Thammasat University. The army seized control in an effort to impose order, and another brief experiment with democracy was at an end. **Thanin Kraivichien** was installed as prime minister of a new right-wing government, which suspended freedom of speech and of the press, further polarizing Thai society.

In 1980, **Prem Tinsulanonda** became prime minister, and during the following 8 years he managed to bring remarkable political and economic stability to Thailand. The Thai economy grew steadily through the 1980s, fueled by Japanese investment and the departure of Chinese funds from Hong Kong.

Things changed dramatically in July 1997, when Thailand became the first victim of the Asian Economic Crisis. Virtually overnight, the Baht lost 20% of its value, followed by similar downturns in money markets throughout other major Asian nations. A legacy of suspicious government activity is linked to industry, massive overseas borrowing, inflated property markets, and lax bank lending practices. In November of 1997, **Chuan Leekpai** was elected to power to lead the country out of crisis, but 3 years later Thais were still unsatisfied.

In January 2001, the Thai people elected Populist candidate **Thaksin Shinawatra.** A self-made telecom tycoon, ex-police officer, and member of one of the nation's wealthiest families, Thaksin came into office promising economic restructuring and an end to widespread corruption and cronyism. Thaksin's popularity grew from aggressive reforms that brought the country out of debt. In November 2003, Thailand paid back its $12 billion loan to the International Monetary Fund, money borrowed during the 1997 currency crisis. The popular prime minister also waged a "War on Poverty and Dark Influence," cracking down on mafia activity and bribery; however, his tactics were often heavy-handed and wholly ignored human rights. Most glaringly, he is held responsible for the on-the-spot killing of suspected drug traffickers (estimates claim that as many as 3,000 people were shot dead with no legal process during his reign). Similarly, Thaksin's aggressive response to Muslim unrest in the far south came under international criticism.

In September 2006, the Royal Thai army, backed by the King, staged a bloodless coup d'état. Thaksin, who was preparing to address the United Nations in New York, was ousted overnight. During 2007, under the military junta, democratic reforms were stalled, press freedoms were curbed, and Thaksin's own Thai Rak Thai party was dissolved and its members banned from politics for 5 years. Meanwhile, the tycoon and his family have been convicted in absentia for fraud.

THAILAND–PRESENT DAY Elections held in December 2007 passed without much disturbance, but the surprising outcome gave the People's Power Party (PPP)— run by followers of former Prime Minister Thaksin—victory. However, without a clear majority, the party was forced into an uneasy coalition with five other parties, headed by **Samak Sundaravej.** In September 2008, Samak was replaced by **Somchai Wongsawat,** but after the occupation of Suvarnabhumi Airport by yellow-shirted People's Alliance for Democracy (PAD) supporters in November 2008, Somchai also had to step down, and the PPP was dissolved, to be replaced by the Pheua Thai, or "For Thai" party. The head of the Democratic Party, **Abhisit Vejjajiva,** managed to form a coalition to take the reins of government, though riots in Bangkok, in April 2010, by the United Front for Democracy against Dictatorship (UDD; supporters of Thaksin who wear red shirts) represented a further step in the polarization of politics in Thailand between the red shirts and yellow shirts—UDD vs. PAD. In the most recent general election (July 2011), **Yingluck Shinawatra** (Thaksin's sister) of the Pheua Thai Party was voted into power as Thailand's first female prime minister, though whether she will retain her position for the regulation 4 years is far from certain.

RELIGION IN THAILAND

Thai culture cannot be fully appreciated without some understanding of Buddhism, which is practiced by 95% of the population. The Buddha was a great Indian sage who lived in the 6th century B.C. He was born **Siddhartha Gautama,** a prince who was carefully sheltered from the outside world. When he ventured beyond the palace walls, he encountered an old man, a sick man, a corpse, and a wandering monk. He concluded that a never-ending cycle of suffering and relief exists everywhere. Sensing that the pleasures of the physical world were impermanent and the cause of pain, he shed his noble life and went into the forest to live as a solitary ascetic. Nearing starvation, however, he soon realized this was not the path to happiness, so he turned instead to the "Middle Way," a more moderate practice of meditation, compassion, and understanding. One night, while meditating under a Bodhi (fig) tree after being tormented by Mara, the goddess of death, Siddhartha Gautama became enlightened. With his mind free of delusion, he gained insight into the nature of the universe and viewed the world without defilement, craving, or attachment but as unified and complete. He explained his newfound ideology, **The Dhamma,** to his first five disciples, at Deer Park in India, in a sermon now known as "The Discourse on Setting into Motion the Wheel of the Law."

After the death of Buddha, two schools were formed. The oldest, **Theravada** (Doctrine of the Elders), is sometimes referred to, less accurately, as Hinayana (the Lesser Vehicle). This school of thought prevails in Sri Lanka, Myanmar (Burma), Thailand, Laos, and Cambodia. It focuses on the enlightenment of the individual with emphasis on the monastic community and the monks who achieve nirvana in this lifetime. The other methodology, **Mahayana** (the Greater Vehicle), is practiced in China, Korea, and Japan, and subscribes to a notion of all of mankind attaining enlightenment at the same time.

The basic document of Thai, or Theravada, Buddhism is the **Pali canon,** which was documented in writing for the first time in the 1st century A.D. The doctrine is essentially an ethical and psychological system in which no deity plays a role in the mystical search for the intuitive realization of the *oneness* of the universe. While it is a religion without a god, Theravada traditions follow a certain hierarchy based on age among monks and practitioners. The practice requires individuals to find truth for themselves through an inward-looking practice cultivated by meditation and self-examination. Although interpretation varies, the Buddha's final words are said to be "strive on with diligence."

If there is no deity to worship, then what, you might ask, are people doing in temples prostrating themselves before images or statues of the Buddha? Worshipers bow three times before the image: Once for the Buddha himself, once for the *sangha* (the order of monks), and once for the *dhamma* (truth). Prostrations at the temple are also a way to honor Buddhist teachers and those who pass on the tradition, to show respect for the Buddha's meditative repose and equanimity, and to offer reverence for relics (most temples house important artifacts, especially in the stupa).

Buddhism has one aim only: To abolish suffering. Buddhist practice offers a path to rid oneself of the causes of suffering, which are desire, malice, and delusion. Practitioners eliminate craving and ill will by exercising self-restraint and showing kindness to all sentient beings. Monks and members of the Buddhist Sangha, or community, are revered as those most diligently working toward enlightenment and the attainment of wisdom.

Other aspects of the philosophy include the law of karma, whereby every action has an effect and the energy of past action, good or evil, continues forever and is "reborn." (Some argue, though, that the Buddha took transmigration quite literally.) As a consequence, *tam bun* (merit making)—basically performing any act of kindness no matter how small—is taken very seriously.

Merit can be gained by entering the monkhood, which most Thai males do for a few days or months to study Buddhist scriptures and practice meditation. But these days it can equally be gained by transferring Frequent Flyer points to a charity.

When monks in Thailand go on their alms round each dawn, they are not seen as begging, but as giving Buddhist devotees an opportunity to make merit; similarly, those who sell caged birds, which people purchase and then set free, are allowing them to gain merit by freeing the birds. When making merit, it is the motive that is important—the intention in the mind at the time of action—which determines the karmic outcome, not the action itself. Buddhism calls for self-reliance; the individual embarks alone on the Noble Eightfold Path to Nirvana with the aim "to cease to do evil, learn to do good, cleanse your own heart."

Theravada Buddhism does not seek converts, nor does it ask practitioners to believe in any truths but those they learn themselves through experience and meditation. Opportunities to study Buddhism or practice meditation in Thailand with an English-speaking teacher are limited, though some programs are designed particularly for foreigners, such as at **Wat Suan Mokkh** in Chaiya (p. 174) and **Wat Rampoeng** in Chiang Mai (p. 311).

Most Chinese and Vietnamese living in Thailand follow Mahayana Buddhism, and several temples and monasteries in the country support this tradition as well. Other religions and philosophies are also followed in Thailand, including Islam, Christianity, Hinduism, and Sikhism. Sunni Islam is followed by more than two million Thais, mostly in the south. Most are of Malay origin and are descendents of the Muslim traders and missionaries who spread their teachings in the southern peninsula in the early 13th century. There are approximately 2,000 mosques in Thailand.

Christianity was first introduced in the 16th century by generations of Jesuit, Dominican, and Franciscan missionaries from Europe and later Protestant missionaries from America, yet even after centuries of evangelism, there are only a quarter of a million Christians living in the country, suggesting that most Buddhists have no interest in changing their belief system. Nevertheless, Thais have accepted much that has come from Christian missionaries, particularly ideas on education, health, and science.

ART & ARCHITECTURE

The **Sukhothai period** (13th–14th c.) is regarded as a period of notable achievement in Thai culture, with big advancements made in art and architecture. One of the lasting legacies of the Sukhothai period is its sculpture, characterized by the graceful aquiline-nosed Buddha either sitting in meditation or, more strikingly, walking contemplatively. These Buddha figures are considered to be some of the most beautiful representations ever produced of this genre. The city of Sukhothai itself is said to be an expansion of the decorative style typified by Khmer works. With the inclusion of Chinese wood-building techniques, polychromatic schemes, and elegant lines from Japanese-influenced carvings, the *wat*, or temple—with its murals, Buddha sculptures, and spacious design—is defined as the first "pure" Thai Buddhist style. During this period came the mainstays of Thai temple architecture: The *chedi* (stupa), *bot*, *viharn*, *prang*, *mondop*, and *prasat*.

THAI etiquette

Thai customs can be a bit confusing; foreigners are not expected to know and follow local etiquette to the letter, but good manners and appropriate dress will earn you instant respect. A few small gestures and a general awareness will help foster a spirit of good will. First-time visitors are sure to make a few laughable mistakes; read below carefully in order to avoid the more offensive faux pas.

Thais greet each other with a graceful bow called a **wai.** Palms and fingers are pressed flat together, fingers pointing up; the higher they are held, the greater the respect, with fingertips touching the top of the forehead forming the most respectful *wai.* Younger people are expected to *wai* an elder first, who will usually return the gesture. Foreigners are more or less exempt from this custom, though many new arrivals, eager to show their familiarity with Thai culture, *wai* everyone they meet, which is inappropriate. In hotels, doormen, bellhops, and waitresses will frequently *wai* to you. It's not necessary to return the greeting; a simple smile of acknowledgment is all that's necessary. In situations where a *wai* is appropriate, such as when meeting a person of obvious status, a friend's mother or father, or a monk, don't fret about the position of your hands. To keep them level to your chest is perfectly acceptable. Two exceptions—never *wai* a child, and never expect a monk to *wai* back (they are exempted from the custom).

An important aspect of the Thai character is that they expect a certain level of **equanimity, calm, and light-heartedness** in any personal dealings. If you are prone to temper, aggravation, and frustration, Thailand can be a challenge. Displays of anger and confrontational behavior, especially from foreign visitors, get you nowhere. Thais don't just think such outbursts are rude but believe them to be an indication of a lesser-developed human being. Getting angry and upset is in essence "losing face" by acting shamefully in front of others, and Thai people will walk away or giggle, to spare revealing their embarrassment. Travelers who throw fits often find themselves ignored or abandoned by the very people who could help.

So what do you do if you encounter a frustrating situation? The Thai philosophy advocates **jai yen,** meaning, "Take it easy. Chill." If it's a situation you can't control, such as a traffic jam or a delayed flight—*jai yen.* If you find yourself at loggerheads with the front desk, arguing with a taxi driver, or in any other truly frustrating situation, keep calm, try a little humor, and find a nonconfrontational, compromising solution that will save face for all involved.

The dome-shaped **chedi**—better known in the West as stupa—is the most highly regarded edifice here. It was originally used to enshrine relics of the Buddha, but later included holy men and kings. A stupa consists of a dome or tumulus, constructed atop a round base (drum), and enveloped by a cubical chair, representing the seated Buddha, over which is the *chatra* (umbrella) in one or several (usually nine) tiers. There are many types of stupas in existence in Thailand: The tallest, oldest, and most sacred is the golden *chedi* of Nakhon Pathom (p. 130).

The **bot** (*ubosoth* or *uposatha*) is the ordination hall, which is generally off-limits to women. It consists of either one large nave or a nave with lateral aisles built on a rectangular design with Buddha images mounted on a raised platform. At the end of each ridge of the roof are graceful finials, called *chofa* (meaning "sky tassel"), which are reminiscent of animal horns but are thought to represent celestial geese or the

The Thais hold two things sacred: Their religion and their royal family. In temples and royal palaces, **strict dress code** is enforced. Wear long pants or skirts, with a neat shirt, and tops with shoulder-covering sleeves. Remove shoes and hats before entering temple buildings and give worshipers their space. Young Thai society may seem very liberal, but it is in fact remarkably conservative and sartorially prudish. You will notice that most Thai women cover their shoulders and wear knee- or ankle-length hemlines. Men tend to wear a mix of casual-smart gear with collared shirts and would never be unkempt. In the city, it is considered extremely improper to dress in cutoff shorts, skimpy tops, or postage-stamp miniskirts. This may look good for a night's clubbing, but is regarded by locals as unacceptable attire—unless you are working in a go-go bar, or want to give that impression. On beaches, topless sunbathing is never accepted by locals, many of whom are Muslim.

While **photographing** images is generally allowed, do not climb on anything or pose near it in a way that could be seen as showing disrespect. Women should be especially cautious around monks, who are not allowed to touch members of the opposite sex. If a woman needs to hand something to a monk, she should either hand it to a man to give to the monk, or place the item in front of him.

Never, ever, say anything critical or improper about the **royal family,** past or present, not even in jest. Never deface images of royalty (on coins, stamps, or posters); this will result in a hefty prison sentence. In movie theaters, everyone is expected to stand for the national anthem, which is played before every screening.

Thais avoid **public displays of affection.** While straight members of the same gender often hold hands, or walk arm in arm (this includes men), you'll rarely see a Thai man and woman acting this way. Thai women who date foreign men flaunt these rules openly but, as a rule of thumb, Thais frown upon lovers who touch, hug, or kiss in public.

Buddhists believe **the feet** are the lowliest part of the body, so using the foot to point or touch an object in Thailand is unbelievably insulting. Do not point your feet at a person or a Buddha image, or use your foot to tap a runaway coin (it bears the king's image).

In contrast, **the head** is considered the most sacred part of the body. Don't touch a Thai on the head or tousle a child's hair, but rather offer a friendly pat on the back. Even barbers have to ask permission to touch a customer's crown.

Garuda (a mythological animal ridden by the god Shiva). The triangular gables are adorned with gilded wooden ornamentation and glass mosaics.

The **viharn** (*vihaan* or *vihara*) is the assembly hall where the abbot conducts sermons. The design is similar to that of the *bot*, and the hall is also used to house Buddha images, but it is generally a larger building. The **prang,** which originated with the corncob tower of the Khmer temple, is a form of stupa that can be seen in many temples at Sukhothai and Ayutthaya. The **mondop** may be made of wood or brick. On a square pillared base, the pyramidal roof is formed by a series of receding stories, enriched with elaborate decoration, and tapering off to a pinnacle. It may be used to enshrine holy objects, or it may serve as a library for religious ceremonial objects, as it does at Wat Phra Kaew (p. 346) in Bangkok.

The *prasat* (castle) is a direct stylistic descendent of the Khmer temple, with its round-topped spire and Greek-cross layout. At the center is a square sanctuary with a domed *sikhara* (tower) and four porchlike antechambers that project from the main building, giving the whole temple a multileveled contour. The *prasat* serves either as the royal throne hall or as a shrine for venerated objects, such as the *prasat* of Wat Phra Kaew in Bangkok, which enshrines the statues of the kings of the present dynasty.

Less recognized architectural structures include the *ho trai* (library), which houses palm-leaf books; the *sala*, an open pavilion used for resting; and the *ho rakhang*, the Thai belfry.

The Ayutthaya and Bangkok periods further cultivated the Sukhothai style by refining materials and design. The **Ayutthaya period** saw a Khmer revival, when Ayutthayan kings built a number of neo-Khmer-style temples and edifices. The art and architecture evident in early Bangkok allude to the dominant styles of the former capital. After the demise of Ayutthaya in the 18th century, the capital was established briefly at Thonburi before being moved across the Chao Phraya River to Bangkok, where replicas of some of Ayutthaya's most distinctive buildings were constructed. Khmer, Chinese, northern Thai, and Western elements were fused to create temples and palaces in what is now known as the **Rattanakosin style,** of which the key features are height and lightness, best exemplified at Wat Phra Kaew and the Grand Palace (p. 106) in Bangkok.

Over time, Thailand's architectural and artistic development has become increasingly diluted, somewhat compromisingly, by the West. During the latter days of the Ayutthaya period, Jesuit missionaries and French merchants brought with them distinctly baroque fashions. Although Thailand was initially reluctant to foster relations with the West, these European influences eventually became evident in architecture. **Neoclassical devices** were increasingly apparent, notably in the Marble Temple (p. 113), in Bangkok, which was started by King Chulalongkorn in 1900 and designed by his half-brother, Prince Naris. This style can also be seen in the splendid riverside façade of Siam Commercial Bank (1908), near the River City shopping complex. Thanks to a number of Italian engineers, Art Deco became an important style in Bangkok and is seen today at the arched Hua Lampong Rail Station, the Governor's House, and along Ratchadamnoen Avenue. In fact, the style is so ubiquitous that many writers use the term **Thai Deco** to describe certain buildings.

Today's Bangkok is almost indistinguishable from other Asian capitals; a mix of Thai classical, modernist, neo-Greco, Bauhaus, and Chinese shophouse styles all meld into a unique, urban mishmash. Sadly, vernacular styles, such as old Thai wooden houses, are rapidly being cleared and the *klongs* (canals) filled to give way to high-rise offices and apartments. Happily, efforts are now being made by a new generation of educated Thais to bring architectural integrity to the city, and some of the most interesting results can be seen in new shopping malls such as CentralWorld (p. 122) and Siam Paragon (p. 123).

THAILAND IN POPULAR CULTURE

Books

Tiziano Terzani's book *A Fortune-Teller Told Me* may not be exclusively about Thailand, but the late Italian journalist offers a well-crafted portrait of the interlocking cultures of Asia. The book tells of the superstitions and rituals affecting all aspects of

Southeast Asian culture in an autobiography detailing a year of overland travels in a bid to outdo a fortune-teller's premonition of his death.

Carol Hollinger's *Mai Pen Rai Means Never Mind* is a personal history of time spent in the kingdom some 50 years ago, but the cultural insights are quite current.

For help in understanding what the heck is going on around you in Thailand, pick up Philip Cornwel-Smith's *Very Thai*; it's a bit obvious in parts but does make for colorful and fun entertainment (don't expect any deep intellectual insights). It will, however, explain some peculiar habits of the host country. Or there's the more practical *Culture Shock! Thailand*, by Robert and Nanthapa Cooper.

The hilariously funny 2004 book *Bangkok Inside Out*, by Daniel Ziv and Guy Sharrett, gets under the skin of the Thai capital by exploring such fascinating topics as motorbike taxis, wet face cloths, and 7-Eleven stores. This is a witty, informative no-holds-barred, tell-it-how-it-is book.

Phrase books and Thai–English dictionaries are sold everywhere; for a comprehensive study of Thai, pick up a copy of *Thailand for Beginners*, by Benjawan Becker.

Books on Buddhism and Thai Theravada traditions are endless: Look for works by Buddhadasa Bhikkhu, founder of an international meditation center in the south of Thailand, and author of the *Handbook for Mankind* and *The ABCs of Buddhism*. Also look for writings by Jack Kornfield, an American who writes about meditation practices in such works as *A Path with Heart*. Phra Peter Parrapadipo's *Phra Farang*, literally "the foreign monk," tells the story of an Englishman who chose to go into the Buddhist monkhood; it makes for an unusual read.

These days, there are plenty of big glossy tomes covering all aspects of Thai design, old and new. *Modern Thai Living*, by Devahastin na Ayudhaya, is a great example of how modern interiors can combine rustic and contemporary elements. In the book, the author collaborates with Thai floral designer Sakul Intakul, who is celebrated in Bangkok for bringing a radical postmodernist approach to Thai floral arrangements. For a great insight into Thailand's northern Lanna history, pore over a copy of Ping Amranand and William Warren's exemplary *Lanna Style*, or the more academic guide to temple design in the north, the sumptuously illustrated *Lanna, Thailand's Northern Kingdom*, by photographer Michael Freeman.

Films

Since 1974, when a debonair Roger Moore—playing the irrepressible secret agent James Bond—was seen speeding across a turquoise Phang Nga Bay in *The Man with the Golden Gun*, Thailand has attracted moviemakers. Alex Garland's novel *The Beach* (and the much maligned film of the same name, featuring Leonardo DiCaprio) tells the seedy story of young backpackers in search of the perfect hideaway. They swim to a remote island (the filmmakers shot at Maya Bay on Ko Phi Phi Le), where they join a community of marijuana-stoked dropouts living in supposed bliss. Surprise, surprise, things go awry. Environmentalists might suggest that there are some pretty stark parallels in reality. After filming finished in 1998, locals accused the moviemakers and ensuing tourists of ruining the site. True enough, to this day, dozens of longtails oozing oil into the turquoise seas rock up on what is now called "The Beach," and heaps of litter are left in their wake. Is it a case of "art reflecting real life," or perhaps vice versa?

Despite such problems, Thailand remains one of the most sought-after locations for big-budget films, not only for its appealing landscapes but also for its developed infrastructure. One of the most recent examples is *The Hangover—Part II*.

Music

Thais love music, and Thailand has a long musical tradition dating back to at least the 7th century, especially in the rural hinterland. Most smart hotel lobbies are the stage for a Thai couple in gorgeous silks who play slow, rhythmic tunes on classical stringed instruments such as a *saw sam sai* (a vertically held, 3-string fiddle) or on a circular set of gongs called a *khong wong*. Country music is a more lively and raucous alternative; like in the U.S., it's become popularized in the last decade.

Jazz is increasingly popular among old and young as well. Thailand's king (who is an accomplished composer and musician) has been especially helpful in exposing Thais to jazz. Thailand has a number of homegrown pop stars who pump out Thai-language hits and have a huge teen following, too.

EATING & DRINKING

Food is one of the true joys of Thailand. If you are not familiar with Thai cuisine, imagine the best of Asian food ingredients combined with the sophistication of fragrant spices, sweet coconut or citrus, and topped off with ripe red and green chilies. You can find all styles of Thai (and international) cooking in Bangkok, from southern fiery curries to smooth northern cuisine. Where restaurants serve a variety of regional dishes, they are marked in this guide as Thai cuisine, though in a few cases where they specialize in Northern Thai or Royal Thai cuisine (dishes that were formerly eaten only by royalty), they are marked as such. Basic ingredients range from shellfish, fresh fruits, vegetables—asparagus, beansprouts, morning glory (water spinach), baby eggplant, bamboo shoots, and countless types of mushrooms—and spices, including lemongrass, mint, chili, garlic, and cilantro (coriander). Thai cooking also incorporates coconut milk, curry paste, peanuts, and a large variety of noodles and rice.

Among the popular dishes you'll find are *tom yum goong*, a Thai hot-and-sour shrimp soup; *satay*, charcoal-broiled chicken, beef, or pork strips skewered on a bamboo stick and dipped in a peanut-coconut sauce; spring rolls (similar to egg rolls but thinner); *larb*, a spicy chicken or ground-beef salad with mint-and-lime flavoring; spicy salads, made with a breadth of ingredients, but most have a fiery dressing made with onion, chili pepper, lime juice, and fish sauce; pad Thai, rice noodles fried with shrimp, eggs, peanuts, and fresh beansprouts; *khao sawy*, a northern-style Burmese soup with light yellow curry and layers of crispy and soft noodles; a wide range of explosive curries; and *tod man pla*, fried fish cakes with a sweet honey sauce. If you're feeling adventurous, pick up a snack of fried crickets, bamboo grubs, or red ant eggs that are sold in markets countrywide (see the "Anyone for Cricket?" box, on p. 97).

Seafood is a great treat in Thailand and is served at a fraction of the cost one would pay elsewhere. In the south, Phuket lobster (a giant langoustine) has no pincers and a firm trunk, and is generally different from the cold water variety you'll get in Maine or Brittany.

A word of caution: Thais enjoy incredibly spicy food, much hotter than is tolerated in even the most piquant Western cuisine. Protect your palate by saying "*Mai khin phet*," meaning "I do not take it spicy." Also note that most Thai and Chinese food, particularly in the cheaper restaurants and food stalls, is cooked with a lot of MSG (known locally as *phong churot*), and it's almost impossible to avoid. If you don't want MSG, say "*mai sai phong churot*." However, if you're dining in restaurants where foreign clientele are regulars, the kitchen usually will have made allowances for this.

Traditionally, Thai menus don't offer fancy desserts. The most you'll find are coconut milk-based desserts or a variety of fruit-flavored custards, but the local fruit is luscious enough for a perfect dessert. Familiar fruits are pineapple (sometimes served with salt and chili powder), mangoes, bananas, guava, papaya, coconut, and watermelon. Less familiar options are durian (in season during May and June, this Thai favorite has an exquiste taste, but smells like old socks); mangosteen (a purplish, hard-skinned fruit with delicate, white segments that melt in the mouth but stain your hands and clothes, and is available Apr–Sept); and jackfruit (large and green with a thick, thorny skin that envelops tangy-flavored flesh and is available in June and July). The pink litchi, which ripens in April, and the smaller tan-skinned longan, which comes in season in July, have very sweet white flesh. Other unusual fruits include tamarind (a sour, pulpy seed in a pod that you can eat fresh or candied); rambutan (small, red, and hairy with transparent sweet flesh clustered around a woody seed, available May–July); and pomelo (similar to a sweet and thirst-quenching grapefruit, available Aug–Nov). Some of these fruits are served as salads; pomelo and raw green papaya salads, for example, are excellent.

Thai families usually have an early breakfast of *khao tom*, a rice soup to which chicken, seafood, or meat may be added. Typically, it's served with a barely cooked egg floating on top and a variety of pickled vegetables, relishes, and spicy condiments to add flavor.

Thais take eating very seriously and also love to snack nonstop. Business lunches consist of several dishes, and some hotels offer blowout buffets at very reasonable prices, but most casual diners settle for a one-course rice or noodle dish at lunchtime. Most restaurants throughout the country offer lunch from 11am to 1pm; in Bangkok, street eateries, markets, and food stalls are packed during this busy time.

Thais usually stop at one of the country's many street-side food stalls for a large bowl of noodle soup (served with meat, fish, or poultry), or dine at a department store food court where they can buy snacks from many different vendors and have a seat in an air-conditioned environment. A note on etiquette: You won't see Thais walking down the street munching. Take a seat while you eat.

Dinner is the main meal, and for a Thai family this usually consists of a soup (*gaeng jued*); a curried dish (*gaeng phet*); a steamed, fried, stir-fried, or grilled dish (*nueng, thod, paad,* or *yaang*); a side dish of salad or condiments (*krueang kiang*); steamed rice (*khao nueng*); and some fruit (*ponlamai*). Thais always share a variety of dishes (typically balanced as sweet, salty, sour, bitter, and spicy), helping themselves to a spoonful at a time (to avoid being wasteful). All dishes are served together and are sampled by diners in no particular order. Thai cuisine has no concept of "courses," though restaurants that cater to foreigners generally manage to serve a soup before main course if Western food is ordered.

In Thailand men enjoy a strong drink; the majority of well-educated women and many practicing Buddhists abstain from alcohol. Liquor, beer, and soft drinks are widely available—from 11am to 2pm and 5pm to midnight—at 7-Eleven stores and supermarkets. Most bars serve alcohol until around 1am, except on Buddhist holidays, though a few with special dispensation in tourist areas stay open until the small hours. Thailand brews several beers; the best known is Singha, though Leo and Chang are cheaper, popular brands that still have a kick. Imported beers, such as Heineken, are also widely available. Despite high costs, wine is becoming a favorite among the country's middle class; local Thai and regional vintages are increasing in quality, too.

Mekong and Sang Som are two of the more popular local "whiskeys," even though the latter is more like rum (fermented from sugarcane). Thais will either buy a bottle or bring one to a restaurant where they can buy ice and mixers—usually Coke or soda water. Beware that some of the cheaper varieties are reputedly laced with some nasty chemicals.

Carbonated drinks, such as Fanta, Coke, and Pepsi, are sold everywhere. Fruit-shake vendors make fruit smoothies on the street, but diabetics should know that, at these street stalls, even fresh carrot or watermelon juice is heavily sweetened with thick syrup; insist on no syrup ("*mai sai naam waan*") and keep an eye on the beverage being made. *Gek huey* (chrysanthemum juice) is another popular treat.

Water is served at most meals, although you may have to ask for ice (*nam khaeng*). Many shops sell affordable bottled or filtered water. Do not purchase the inexpensive water in light-blue plastic bottles (sold on the street), as it contains no sodium or minerals and will not remedy dehydration. If you suffer from the heat, stock up on electrolyte drinks such as Gatorade, or inexpensive rehydration powders, sold in sachets. Both items are available from 7-Eleven stores.

Tips on Eating

One of the greatest joys of visiting Thailand is the plethora of dining options in any area. From high-class hotel restaurants with elegant buffet luncheons to simple, friendly diners, you'll find it all, and I list the whole range. To give an idea of how much it will cost, restaurants are divided into categories: **Very expensive** means that a meal for one without drinks will probably cost more than 1,000B; in **expensive** places, expect to pay from 500B to 1,000B; **moderate** covers the range from 200B to 500B; and **inexpensive** means you'll pay less than 200B per person.

Storefront restaurants and street vendors, apart from those in a specified night market area, are open early morning to late at night. To ease congested streets though, food vendors are now banned in Bangkok on Mondays (or rather this is the day when the rule is most enforced). Restaurants catering to tourists also open from morning until late. You're not expected to tip at most Thai restaurants, but rounding up the bill or leaving 20B on top of most checks is much appreciated. (A 15%–20% tip will shock and awe in smaller restaurants, but will be readily expected at fine-dining outlets.)

Thais are very practical about table manners. If something is best eaten with the hands, then feel free. If there are seeds or bones, you can spit them out onto the table or into a tissue. Single-serve noodle soups are usually eaten with chopsticks and a Chinese spoon. Rice dishes are eaten with a spoon and fork; the spoon is commonly held in the right hand, and the fork in the left is used only to load the spoon for delivery. Follow local customs if you wish, but do whatever you're comfortable with.

Note: In small towns featured throughout this guide, many dining (and nightlife) spots don't have working land lines; in those cases, cellphone numbers are provided wherever possible.

WHEN TO GO

It's wise to study the weather information below, as an ill-timed trip can mean pouring rain, debilitating humidity, or seas too rough for diving or beach activity. The high season for tourism throughout the kingdom is the North American/European winter period, mid-October through mid-February. Prices skyrocket and hotels fill up then, particularly around Christmas/New Year, so be sure to make advance reservations.

OVERCOMING A FEAR OF food STALLS

Considering the fact that, in Western countries, most people judge the potential quality of a restaurant's food by the smartness of its decor, it's hardly surprising that many visitors to Thailand can never bring themselves to order food from a street-side food stall. Typically, they suspect that hygiene will be poor and, with such cheap prices, surely the cooks must use inferior ingredients? The fact that most of these stalls have no English menu also dissuades potential customers.

Breaking through this fear of food stalls is a major step toward appreciating the fantastic variety of Thai cuisine. For a start, try to forget the hygiene concerns, as all Thais are meticulous about cleanliness in food preparation. (To be certain, check all ingredients for freshness, and make sure that anything you eat is prepared fresh and hasn't been languishing on liquefied ice for ages.) Also, because most stalls sell a single dish, they need to select the best ingredients to gain a competitive edge. As for the lack of a menu, you can overcome this by simply pointing at a dish you would like to sample. So next time you feel peckish as you walk past a food stall giving off an appealing aroma, do as the Thais do—sit down and eat!

Off-season weather, however, is not intolerable, and some travelers report joyfully trading the crowded beaches and high prices of high season for a bit of off-peak discomfort. Low season is generally composed of the odd rainy afternoon, significant savings, and a lot more elbowroom. Because this coincides with school holidays in the U.S. and Europe, there is a mini high season in July/August when families head for the kingdom.

Thailand has two distinct climate zones: **Tropical** in the south and **tropical savanna** in the north. The northern, northeastern, and central areas of the country (including Bangkok) experience three distinct seasons. The **hot season** lasts from March to May, with temperatures averaging in the upper 90s Fahrenheit (mid-30s Celsius), with April being the hottest month. Normally, this period sees sporadic rain. March is not the best time to visit the north, as in recent years it has been blanketed by dense haze at this time, blocking out views and causing respiratory problems.

Another recent shift in weather patterns is that the **rainy season** now often begins in April and lasts, on and off, until late October, even November. The average temperature is 84°F (29°C) with 90% humidity. While the rainy season brings heavy downpours, it is rare to see an all-day episode. From June to September, daily showers usually come in the late afternoon or evening for 3 to 4 hours, often bringing floods and forcing traffic to a standstill. In November 2011 much of Bangkok was under water for several weeks. Trekking in the north is not recommended during this time, due to slippery trails and rampant leeches. In Bangkok, expect smog from April to August.

The **cool season,** from November to February, has temperatures from the high 70s°F to low 80s°F (26°C–29°C), with infrequent showers. Daily temperatures can drop as low as 60°F (16°C) in Chiang Mai and 41°F (5°C) in the hills; 1 or 2 nights may even see frost.

The **Southern Thai Peninsula** has intermittent showers year-round and daily downpours during the rainy season (temperatures average in the low 80s Fahrenheit/30s Celsius). If you're traveling to Phuket or Ko Samui, it would be helpful to note that the two islands' peak seasons are not the same. Optimal weather on Phuket occurs between November and April, when the island welcomes the highest numbers of travelers. Ko Samui's best weather lasts from about December to February, though it's usually very pleasant until October when tropical storms arrive. It's wise to check weather patterns before heading to Samui, as occasional storms in recent years have left vacationers stranded for days.

Holidays

Many holidays are based on the Thai lunar calendar, falling on the full moon of each month; check with the Tourism Authority of Thailand (TAT; www.tat.or.th) for the current year's schedule. Chapter 12, "Exploring the Northern Hills," includes a list of festivals and events specific to the north.

On National and Buddhist holidays and on polling days, government offices, banks, small shops, and offices—as well as some restaurants and bars—usually close. By law, bars cannot serve alcohol on HM Queen Sirikit's birthday in August, nor on HM King Bhumibol's birthday in December, nor on the day before an election. *Note:* In most cases there will be little advance warning given to shop, restaurant, or bar customers. Public transport still runs on holidays, though.

JANUARY TO MARCH

Thailand celebrates New Year's Day the same as the rest of the world. In **late February** or **early March** (depending on the lunar cycle) is **Makha Bucha Day,** one of three annual Bucha festivals, this one celebrating a spontaneous gathering of 1,250 disciples to hear the Buddha preach. At all Bucha festivals, Thais walk mindfully three times round the stupa at their local temple carrying flowers, candles and incense as offerings, and foreigners are welcome to join in.

APRIL

Chakri Memorial Day (Apr 6) commemorates the founding of the current Chakri dynasty.

Songkran is the New Year according to the Thai calendar, and it's an event that begins officially on April 13 and lasts 3 days, though water splashing begins about a week before in the countryside. After honoring local monks and family elders, folks hit the streets for massive water fights. Be warned—foreigners are the Thais' favorite target and such areas as Khao San Road become messy war zones where everyone gets soaked (police included) and then covered in flour or colored powder. Truck-mounted power hoses can cause damage, and cellphones, cameras, and valuables should be kept in Ziploc bags. Wear thin, quick-drying clothes—anyone expecting to stay dry will be sorely disappointed!

MAY

National Labor Day falls on the 1st, while **Coronation Day,** celebrating the coronation of HM King Bhumibol in 1946, is on the 5th. **Visakha Bucha Day,** marking the birth, enlightenment, and death of the Buddha, falls around mid- to late **May,** depending on the lunar calendar.

JULY

Thais celebrate **Buddhist Lent** immediately following **Asarnha Bucha Day** in mid-July (depending on the lunar calendar), signaling the beginning of the rains' retreat and the 3-month period of meditation for all Buddhist monks—this was the day that the Buddha delivered his first sermon to his first five disciples. It is a favorite time for laymen to enter the monkhood for a period.

AUGUST

August 12 honors the birthday of HM Queen Sirikit and is also **Mother's Day.**

OCTOBER

On **October 23, Chulalongkorn Day,** the country's favorite king, Rama V, is remembered.

NOVEMBER

Loy Krathong, in late October or November, is Thailand's most romantic festival, although it's not usually a public holiday. After dark, handmade banana-leaf vessels are launched down rivers, and lanterns are hoisted into the sky in order to symbolize the release of sins. The most spectacular celebrations are in Sukhothai and Chiang Mai.

Watch out for fireworks and firecrackers in the street in the build-up to this festival.

DECEMBER

December 5 marks HM King Bhumibol's birthday and is also **Father's Day.** December 10 is **Constitution Day** and recognizes Thailand's first constitution in 1932.

Thailand Calendar of Events

Check with the **Tourist Authority of Thailand** (© **1672;** www.tourismthailand.org, and listings in each chapter) for more information on the events listed below as well as for other holidays celebrated throughout the country. Also see specific chapters for local information and schedules. For an exhaustive list of events beyond those listed here, check http://events.frommers.com, where you'll find a searchable, up-to-the-minute roster of what's happening in cities all over the world.

JANUARY/FEBRUARY

Chinese New Year, nationwide. Head for any Chinatown to see the vivid parades, firecrackers, and Lion Dances associated with this holiday. Things get most raucous on Bangkok's Yaowarat Road, in the heart of Chinatown. It falls anytime from mid-January to mid-February, during which many businesses close for the week.

FEBRUARY

Flower Festival, Chiang Mai. When all of the north is in bloom, Chiang Mai springs to life with parades, floats decorated with flowers, and beauty contests. First weekend of the month.

APRIL

Pattaya Festival, Pattaya. Parades and fireworks accompany a food festival and lots of partying, during the first week of the month.

JUNE

Hua Hin Jazz Festival, Hua Hin. Local and international musicians perform on the beach at Hua Hin. It's usually held on a weekend in June, though not always, so check www.huahinafterdark.com/events.

JULY

Koh Samui Regatta, Koh Samui. Late July brings yachtsmen and partygoers from all over to enjoy a week of fiercely competitive ocean races.

SEPTEMBER

King's Cup Elephant Polo Tournament, Hua Hin. Mahouts and madcap international polo players meet to battle it out in a hilarious but worthy week-long tournament that raises money for Thailand's main elephant charities. See www.anantaraelephantpolo.com for more details.

OCTOBER

Vegetarian Festival, Phuket. In this bizarre religious ritual, devotees spear, pierce, and percolate themselves while in a trance. It's not for the fainthearted! It takes place the second week of the month, and lasts for 9 days.

Naga Fireballs, Nong Khai, Isan. During this event, crowds gather along the river hoping to witness red glowing balls rising from the waters; they're thought to be methane bubbles released from the riverbed. The second or third week of the month.

NOVEMBER

Elephant Roundup, Surin. Elephant parades and cultural performances take place during the third weekend of November.

DECEMBER

King's Cup Regatta, Phuket. Global competitors race yachts, in this exciting international event, which takes place the second week of December.

NATURAL WORLD

Thailand's Ecosystems

Thailand's different geographical regions provide a large variety of ecosystems, which support a great diversity of animal and plant life. Most of the country's forests are deciduous or montane, such as those in the northern hills, where the summit of **Doi Inthanon** forms the highest point in Thailand at 2,565m (8415 ft.). There are a few pockets of primary rainforest on the southern peninsula, in places such as **Khao Sok National Park.** Other ecosystems that predominate on the southern peninsula and eastern seaboard are coastal forests, mangrove swamps, and coral reefs. Around half of these reefs are under the nominal protection of marine national parks, such as **Ko Similan** and **Ko Tarutao,** both off the Andaman Coast. Several regions of the country, most notably Phang Nga Bay, are characterized by karst outcrops—islands or mountains of porous limestone that conceal caves and pristine lagoons.

Flora & Fauna

Thailand boasts a fantastic range of plant and animal life, though many species are under threat due to loss of habitat. There are around 15,000 vascular plants, including over 500 types of trees and 1,000 types of orchids. Most of these plants are typical of tropical climates, such as **palms, teak,** and **bamboo,** though at higher elevations in the north, it is not uncommon to find such things as pines, ferns, and rhododendrons, which are more familiar in temperate zones. The country is particularly well-blessed with birds, many of which winter in the country, and almost 1,000 species have been sighted to date. These include common species, such as **bulbuls** and **mynahs,** but also rarities, such as **great hornbills** and **sarus cranes.** As for mammals, around 260 species have been recorded, including **primates, deer, civets, tigers,** and **elephants,** most of which survive under national park protection, but all are under constant threat from poachers. For information on sustainable issues in the country, see below.

Watching Wildlife

The best place to watch wildlife in Thailand is in the country's national parks. Since the first one was established at Khao Yai in 1962, more than 100 have been opened, and they now occupy around 13% of Thailand's land area—more than most countries. Most have log-cabin-style accommodation and campsites that can be reserved through the Department of National Parks, Wildlife and Plant Conservation website (http://web3.dnp.go.th/parkreserve/nature.asp?lg=2).

Khao Yai National Park, just 120km (75 miles) from Bangkok, is one of the best places to see wildlife, and on a typical trail, visitors are likely to see gibbons, macaques, deer, and hornbills, especially in the company of guides who know the habits of these creatures and where they are likely to be at a certain time of day. **Doi Inthanon National Park** in the north is particularly popular with birders, while divers looking for coral reefs teeming with tropical fish usually head for the marine national parks in the Andaman Sea, such as **Similan** and **Surin.**

RESPONSIBLE TRAVEL

Given the rapid deterioration of the global environment, it's not surprising that more and more people feel an obligation to act responsibly when they travel to reduce their impact on their chosen destination. Visitors who choose to spend their time cycling, trekking, or kayaking in the Kingdom of Thailand inevitably have less detrimental impact on the country than those who breeze around in tour buses churning out carbon dioxide. However, choosing a responsible tour operator is not easy, as just about all of them these days use the buzzword "eco-tourism" in their sales pitches. Ask them exactly what they are doing to reduce their carbon footprint and to benefit the local community in the areas that their tours visit. For a list of local green operators, contact the **Thai Ecotourism and Adventure Travel Association** (✆ **02642-5465;** www.teata.or.th).

Some hotel groups, such as the **Banyan Tree** resorts in Bangkok and Phuket, have made huge efforts over the past decade to implement sustainable projects, including a pledge to reduce their carbon footprint in all their resorts by 10% each year. To see a list of green hotels, contact the **Green Leaf Foundation** (✆ **02652-8321-2;** www.greenleafthai.org).

When booking hotels, particularly on the beach, consider carefully whether you really need a room with air-conditioning and other power-draining equipment such as wine coolers, TVs, and DVD players. These days many eco-friendly, luxury resorts do not offer air-conditioning; instead, they provide well-designed, wooden bungalows with balconies that attract a delicious breeze, allowing you to appreciate your surroundings more than in an enclosed room, and mosquito nets over the beds can save you from nighttime discomfort. You can also sleep more soundly knowing your stay is making minimal impact on the environment.

In more than 110 national parks, visitors can see the local wildlife species in residence, as well as appreciate the delicate balance of each habitat. The more popular parks have clearly displayed interpretation facilities at their visitor centers, as well as trails with bridges and catwalks, and markers explaining the important elements of the environment and its inhabitants. They also provide log-cabin-style bungalow accommodation, plus tents and supplies for campers. Get in touch with the **Department of National Parks** at ✆ **02562-0760,** or visit its website (http://web3.dnp.go.th/parkreserve/nationalpark.asp?lg=2), where you can find information about the parks and also make online reservations.

Unfortunately, Thailand is way behind much of the world in general eco-awareness; conflicts between economic and ecological interests generally work out in favor of the former. Environmental problems include deforestation, air and water pollution, flooding, habitat loss, and consequent species loss. Among the mammals in danger of extinction in Thailand are tigers, leopards, and elephants. The last of these is a particular shame, as the elephant was once revered (and still is in some quarters) as a creature of great spiritual significance; the few thousand that remain spend their time either entertaining tourists at elephant camps or searching for food in a shrinking forest.

Fortunately, several nongovernment organizations (NGOs), such as the World Wildlife Fund, have an active presence in the country, attempting to draw attention to the most serious problems. Thai authorities are also finally taking tiny steps to preserve the nature and wildlife of Thailand's many different ecological zones, from swamp jungles in the south, to mountain forests in the north, to the many marine parks in the Gulf of Thailand and the Andaman Sea.

As the world's leading exporter of rice, Thailand is at the forefront of research into new strains of the crop that are both more nutritious and less harmful in terms of use of pesticides. More and more restaurants are serving brown rice as well as white rice.

GENERAL RESOURCES FOR green TRAVEL

In addition to the resources for Thailand listed above, the following websites provide valuable wide-ranging information on responsible travel.

o **Responsible Travel** (www. responsibletravel.com) is a great source of sustainable travel ideas and lists of those engaging with travel responsibly. **Sustainable Travel International** (www. sustainabletravelinternational.org) promotes ethical tourism practices, and manages an extensive directory of sustainable properties and tour operators around the world.

o **Carbonfund** (www.carbonfund. org), **TerraPass** (www.terrapass. com), and **Carbon Neutral** (www. carbonneutral.org) provide info on

"carbon offsetting," or offsetting the greenhouse gas emitted during flights. For information on environment-friendly issues throughout the world, visit **Tread Lightly** (www.treadlightly.org).

o **Tourism Concern:** A highly recommended travel resource which works to make sure tourism benefits local communities.

o **Volunteer International** (www. volunteerinternational.org) has a list of questions to help you determine the intentions and the nature of a volunteer program. For general info on volunteer travel, visit **www.goabroad.com/ volunteer-abroad** and **www.idea list.org.**

Also, look out for **Doi Kham** brand fruits, vegetables, juices, and preserves (on sale in many airports). These are products of the King's royal projects, which provide work for rural people while following organic farming principles.

In addition to the resources for Thailand listed above, see www.frommers.com/ planning for more tips on responsible travel.

SPECIAL-INTEREST TRIPS

Escorted Tours

Escorted tours are structured group tours with a group leader. The price usually includes everything from airfare to hotels, meals, tours, admission costs, and local transportation. Here are some of the best operators for Thailand.

o **Absolute Asia** (15 Watts St., Fifth Floor, New York, NY 10013; © **800/736-8187;** fax 212/627-4090; www.absoluteasia.com): Founded in 1989, Absolute Asia offers an array of innovative itineraries, specializing in individual or small group tours customized to your interests, with experienced local guides and excellent accommodation. Talk to them about tours that feature art, cuisine, religion, antiques, photography, wildlife study, archaeology, and soft adventure—they can plan a specialized trip to see just about anything you can dream up for any length of time.

o **Asia Transpacific Journeys** (2995 Center Green Court, Boulder, CO 80301; © **800/642-2742** or 303/443-6789; fax 303/443-7078; www.asiatranspacific. com): Coordinating tours to every corner of South and Southeast Asia and the Pacific, Asia Transpacific Journeys deals with small groups and custom programs that include luxury hotel accommodation. They have specific tours for Thailand, such as the Best of Thailand, a 14-day trip that takes in Bangkok, the north, and the southern beaches. Asia Transpacific tours are fun, promote cultural understanding and sustainable tourism, and are highly recommended.

o **Diethelm** (Kian Gwan Building II, 12th Floor, 140/1 Wireless Rd., Bangkok 10330, Thailand; ✆ **02660-7000;** fax 02660-7020; www.diethelmtravel.com): The folks at this Swiss-based tour company, with offices throughout the region, are friendly and helpful, and a popular choice for European tour groups. Diethelm has full tour programs and can provide details for travelers in-country, arrange car rental or vans for small groups, and offer discount options to all destinations.

o **Intrepid** (Level 3, 380 Lonsdale Street, Melbourne, VIC 3000, Victoria, Australia; ✆ **1800/970-7299** in the U.S.; www.intrepidtravel.com): This popular Australian operator is a reliable choice to get off the beaten path on a tour of Asia. Intrepid caters for the culturally discerning, those with humanitarian goals, and adventure travelers on a budget looking for a group-oriented tour of off-the-map locations. They live up to their name, and with some of the best guides in Asia, these folks will take you to the back of beyond safely and in style.

Voluntourism

If you really want to give as well as you get during your trip, then consider signing up for volunteer work, though you'll need to commit yourself for more than a couple of weeks in most cases. People who experience the country in this way are guaranteed closer contact with Thais than those on the tourist circuit. The most common opportunities in Thailand involve teaching English, but computer skills and any other expertise might be employed to good effect. Below are some organizations that offer the chance to do voluntary work in Thailand; most require a donation to cover expenses such as accommodation and food.

A good place to start is by browsing the website of **Volunteer Work Thailand** (www.volunteerworkthailand.org), an umbrella group that provides links to a host of organizations looking for volunteers in the country, ranging from the Thai Society for the Conservation of Wild Animals to United Nation Volunteers.

If you know how to dot your Is and cross your Ts, you might have what it takes to be an **English teacher.** Contact **Lemon Grass Volunteering,** in Bangkok (✆ **081977-5300;** www.lemongrass-volunteering.com), or **Travel to Teach** (www.travel-to-teach.org/thai), an international organization with some teaching projects in the kingdom. If you've already qualified in this field, or would like to get qualified, check out **Dave's ESL Café** (www.eslcafe.com) for listings of courses and jobs available.

Global Experience Thailand (www.thai-experience.org), with a base in Nong Khai in Thailand's remote northeast, has requirements for English teachers and people with computer skills, but will try to place anyone with a sincere desire to help the underprivileged.

If you're an animal lover, you might prefer to expend your energy caring for some of the many endangered species in Thailand. Check out the **World Wildlife Fund's** website (www.wwf.or.th) for a summary of the country's many problems. There are organizations trying to protect animals like gibbons from exploitation and extinction, such as the **Gibbon Rehabilitation Project,** on Phuket (see "Back to Nature," on p. 243).

Those seriously interested in marine conservation can join the volunteer team at Ko Phra Thong north of Phuket, where an Italian-led organization called **Naucrates**

SHOPPING scams

Gems, fake goods, illegal betting: Every year naive tourists take the bait and get caught in a scam. To beat the cheats, follow these simple rules:

- If anyone approaches you on the street and offers to take you to a shop (or anywhere, for that matter), refuse.
- If a tuk-tuk or taxi driver wants to take you shopping say, "No thanks" (or *Mai ao, khop khun"*).
- Be suspicious of strangers who flash TAT, Tourist Police, or any other "badge" in order to get something from you.

- Know that there is no such thing as a government auction, government clearing-house, or anything "government"-related to the gems industry.
- There is no such thing as a tax-free day for gemstone purchases.
- Do not agree to let any gem purchases be shipped to your home address.
- As with any purchase you make, if you use a credit card, keep the card in your sight at all times and watch the store assistant make one print of it

(see "Nai Thon & Nai Yang Beaches," on p. 231) has spent over a decade educating local communities on ecological issues and monitoring the decline of local turtles. It also runs a mangrove revitalization scheme.

TIPS ON SHOPPING

While Thais love bargaining, they do not appreciate haggling over a few baht. Sometimes such tourists will be impolitely referred to as *kee neow* (meaning "stingy" or "cheapskates" in Thai). On the other hand, if the initial asking price is more than twice what you are prepared to pay, it probably isn't worth entering negotiations.

Customs officers in many countries are now actively searching bags of tourists returning from Thailand and confiscating any pirated CDs and DVDs, designer knockoffs, and copy watches. In places like the U.S., U.K., and Australia, the import of counterfeit merchandise is a crime and you, as the buyer, will have your vacation purchases confiscated. A purchase may be "low dollar" to you, but when thousands of copies are sold, it damages the businesses that create and pay for the copyright of these models. Every year, media reports also confirm that earnings from these underground counterfeit industries go toward money laundering, drug production, prostitution, and child trafficking. By not buying fake brands, you are not just abiding by the law, but helping stamp out racketeering that ruins lives.

SUGGESTED ITINERARIES IN THAILAND

Thailand has something for everyone; it's a great place to explore, learn, or connect with a decidedly rewarding local culture. In this laid-back country, though, planned itineraries work well to give way to spontaneity. Most trips begin in Bangkok—the country's capital and commercial center—and travelers' itineraries tend to include some beach time mixed in with a bit of history and adventure.

If at all possible, plan your trip around a passion or interest. Like Thai food. Start at the **Blue Elephant** cooking school in Bangkok ★★, or try the rural-based **Chiang Mai Thai Cookery School** ★ in the north, to learn how to prepare food the Thai way. Or simply discover local specialties by exploring the country's markets and many upmarket Thai restaurants. Interested in massage? Upscale **Chiva-Som Academy** ★★, in Bangkok, teaches the art of this fascinating ancient tradition. If adventure is more your thing, head to Chiang Mai for some **white-water rafting,** or watch wildlife in **Khao Yai National Park** ★, north of Bangkok, or **Khao Sok,** in the south.

Curious about Thailand's history and architecture? Bangkok's many temples and museums will enchant, while the ancient cities of **Ayutthaya** ★★ and **Sukhothai** ★★★ will transport you to a bygone era. Want to get enlightened or learn about Buddhism? Consider taking a meditation course; the "Middle Way" is not as easy as you may think. Try the **House of Dhamma,** in Bangkok; **Wat Ram Poeng,** near Chiang Mai; or **Wat Suan Mokkh,** near Surat Thani. These are just a few of the many special activities possible in Thailand. Find what suits you and go for it.

When flying directly to Thailand from the U.S. or Europe, watch out for **jet lag;** it takes some time to adjust to the abrupt climatic and culinary changes. It is best to go easy at the start. Arrival in frenetic Bangkok, with its intense traffic, heat, and humidity, can be a bit overwhelming—it all takes some time to get used to, and if you're doing a 1-week tour, you might just be settling in and starting to enjoy things by the time you leave. So do yourself a favor and factor in some rest days, even if it's just 1 or 2, at the beginning of your trip.

Multiple-week stays allow more opportunities to both explore the hills up north and lie on a white sandy beach. With shorter itineraries, you might want to limit yourself to Bangkok, plus a short visit to rural northern reaches near Chiang Mai, or a few days on one of the beaches in the south. Weather plays an important part in planning, too. The cool, dry season—November to February—is the best time to go, but this is also high season, which pushes up prices and makes bookings difficult. For these months, the north is much cooler than the rest of the country, while the monsoon season (June–Oct) brings heavy rain and floods almost everywhere. The best time to visit Phuket and areas on the Andaman coast is from November to April. For Ko Samui and other beach destinations on the east coast of the Gulf of Thailand, the optimal time to visit is from February to October (the result of opposing monsoonal systems). Check "When to go" (p. 26) and destination chapters for more weather specifics.

You also might want to plan your trip around a Thai holiday, such as **Songkran,** the Thai New Year. The celebration officially lasts 3 days, but often goes on for a week or more, depending on the region, climaxing on April 13. **Loy Krathong,** celebrated at the full moon in late October or November, is another magical holiday throughout Thailand (though the best celebrations are in the north at Sukhothai or Chiang Mai); during this holiday, small banana-stem floats are floated on rivers and paper lanterns are released into the sky to absolve the previous year's sins.

THE REGIONS IN BRIEF

The Thais compare their land to the shape of an elephant's head, seen in profile, facing the West, with the southern peninsula representing the dangling trunk. Thailand is roughly equidistant from China and India, and centuries of migration from southern China and trade with India brought tremendous influences from each of these Asian nations. Thailand borders Myanmar (Burma) to the northwest, Laos to the northeast, Cambodia to the east, and Malaysia to the south. Its southwestern coast stretches along the Andaman Sea, its southern and southeastern coastlines perimeter the Gulf of Thailand, and every coast boasts a myriad of islands. Thailand covers roughly 514,000 sq. km (198,450 sq. miles)—about the size of France or California—and spans over 1,600km (over 1,000 miles) from north to south. It is divided into six major geographic zones, within which there are 76 provinces.

BANGKOK Located on the banks of the Chao Phraya River—Thailand's principal waterway—Bangkok is more or less in the geographical heart of the country on both a north–south and east–west axis. It seems to exert a magnetic attraction on both rural Thais and foreign visitors, as it is home to more than 10% of the Thai population, as well as plenty of expats, who bustle along with the commuter crowd, glad to be based in this crazy metropolis. Its congested streets and infamous gridlock can be frustrating for visitors, though its glittering temples, colorful markets, and carefree inhabitants can be endearing in equal measure.

THE EASTERN SEABOARD The coastline east of Bangkok—sometimes referred to as the Eastern Gulf—is home to Pattaya, Rayong, and Trat. These are popular weekend destinations among Thai families and expats alike. For the best beaches, however, you'll need to hop on a boat to Ko Samet, Ko Chang, or Ko Kood, all of which offer luxury resorts and superb scuba diving. The region is also home to Thailand's greatest concentration of sapphire and ruby mines at Chanthaburi (known as Muang Chan). Chanthaburi has been a gem trading center for centuries and its so-called weekend "gem" market is fun, but certainly not for treasure seekers; the standards of the precious stones sold here are infamously low.

THE SOUTHERN PENINSULA   A long, narrow peninsula protrudes south to the Malaysian border with the Andaman Sea on the west and the Gulf of Thailand to the east. The gulf coastline (from Bangkok to Narathiwat) extends more than 1,000km (621 miles), while the western shoreline (from Ranong to Satun) runs about 500km (311 miles). Due to the high number of popular destinations in the south, this guide divides the region into two chapters—one focusing on the east coast and another focusing on the west coast.

Off the Gulf coast, Ko Samui has gone from sleepy hideaway to heaving tourist magnet, while Ko Pha Ngan and Ko Tao are following in its wake. Farther south, the three southernmost provinces of Yala, Narathiwat, and Pattani are home to a considerable Muslim population. Take extreme care in this region: Regular, violent attacks by insurgents target public markets as well as transport and Buddhist centers. Off the Andaman coast, the islands of Phuket, Ko Phi Phi, and Ko Lanta, as well as the peninsula of Krabi, boast some of the country's most beautiful beaches.

THE CENTRAL PLAINS   Thailand's central plains are an extremely fertile region: Its abundant jasmine rice crops are exported worldwide. The main attractions of the region, however, are the atmospheric ruins at the historic cities of Sukhothai and Ayutthaya, both former capitals of the Kingdom of Siam. To the west of the central plains, Kanchanaburi, on the River Kwai, is the site of the infamous World War II "Death Railway," where an estimated 16,000 Allied prisoners of war and around 100,000 Asians died during its construction for the Japanese. Other significant towns in this region are Lopburi, a favorite haunt of former kings of Siam; Phitsanulok, a major crossroads in the northern plains; and Mae Sot, a remote outpost near the Myanmar border and jumping-off point for a trip to Ti Lor Su Waterfall, in the Umphang Wildlife Reserve.

NORTHERN THAILAND   The north is a mountainous region and coolest from November to February, when conditions are ideal for trekking to visit the region's brightly dressed hill-tribes. This is also elephant country, but now that logging has been banned, there is little for them to do but provide entertainment for tourists in elephant camps. The cool hills in the north are well suited for farming, particularly for strawberries, asparagus, peaches, and litchis. Today, agricultural programs and charities, such as the Mae Fah Luang Foundation, are retraining hill-tribe villagers whose main crop used to be opium poppies. Settlements around Doi Tung have gallantly implemented crop replacement schemes, propagating coffee and macadamia nuts.

The major towns in the north are Chiang Mai, Chiang Rai, Lampang, and Mae Hong Son. The best way to enjoy the region's scenic beauty is by taking a motorbike or car around the Mae Hong Son Loop; or, for those with less time, a quick trip to Thailand's highest point in Doi Inthanon National Park, or to the infamous Golden Triangle, where the borders of Thailand, Laos, and Myanmar meet, can be great fun.

ISAN   The broad and relatively infertile northeast plateau that is Isan is the least developed region in Thailand. Bordered by the Mekong River, it separates the country from neighboring Laos, though the people of Isan share linguistic and cultural similarities with their neighbors. The region's attractions include the remains of a Bronze Age village at Ban Chiang, as well as major Khmer ruins at Pimai and Phnom Rung, near Nakhorn Ratchasima, also known as Khorat. Other than potash mining and subsistence farming, the region has enjoyed little economic development.

BANGKOK IN 3 DAYS

The Thai capital has a lot to offer but can be rather daunting at first, what with its chaotic traffic and hectic pace. Visitors who remain calm and curious will experience the exoticism of the East without too much discomfort, though.

Tack this short itinerary onto the beginning—or the end—of any trip to Thailand. You can also split it up: Spend time touring the city sites at the start of the journey and then use a day at the end to fill your suitcase with gorgeous handicrafts, silk fashions, or souvenirs.

Day 1: Bangkok's Riverside Sites

Start your tour of Bangkok at **Central Pier,** next to Saphan Taksin BTS, where you can hop on a fast river taxi or the more comfortable wide-berth Chao Phraya Tourist Boat.

Heading north along the S-curve of the river, you can hop off to visit many of the city's historical sites. The first stop should be Tha Tien, for **Wat Po** ★★★ (p. 113) and the Giant Reclining Buddha. From there, it's a short walk to the famed **Wat Phra Kaew,** the temple of the celebrated Emerald Buddha, and the **Grand Palace** ★★★ (p. 106).

Take a lunch break to rest your legs and eyes; then you can carry on upstream to visit the **National Museum** ★★ (p. 110), where you can easily spend a couple of hours delving into this proud nation's past. After visiting the museum, for a different type of sightseeing, wander north to Banglampoo and nose around **Khao San Road,** the vibrant backpacker strip. You can return to Central Pier by boat from Phra Arthit Pier before 6pm, or settle down for dinner at **Hemlock** (p. 99) and take a cab to your hotel later.

This is a lot to see in a day—but it does cover the city's unmissable sights and avoids traffic delays by using river transport. If you enjoy traveling on the river, you may want to end the day by taking a **dinner cruise** (see p. 100 for options), on which you can see the city by night.

Day 2: Bangkok Shopping & Eating

Start your second day in Bangkok at **Jim Thompson's House** ★ (p. 109), the beautiful wooden home on stilts of the American who rejuvenated the Thai silk industry. It's right in the city center (near the National Stadium BTS).

The shimmering silks on display in the shop at Jim Thompson's should put you in the mood for a full-frontal attack on the city's shops: About a 10-minute walk away from Jim Thompson's House is **Mah Boon Krong** (**MBK;** p. 122), a giant mall catering to Thai teenagers and bargain hunters alike. Adjacent to the Siam BTS is **Siam Paragon** (p. 123), a center filled with super-luxury boutiques and a huge choice of restaurants. If you still haven't found that special something, continue on to the funky, trendy clothing stores found in the maze of lanes in **Siam Square** (p. 62).

Have lunch at either **Taling Pling** or **Crystal Jade** ★, both on the ground floor of Siam Paragon, and then drop off your shopping bags at the hotel before indulging yourself in a spa treatment. All top-end hotels in Bangkok have excellent spas, but if yours doesn't have one, head for **Healthland** (p. 116), on Sathorn Road.

You should be feeling as light as a feather after this, but you'll feel even lighter when you ride up to the 54th floor of the State Tower, on Silom Road, to knock back a sundowner at the **Sky Bar** (p. 127) while drinking in the city views in every direction.

For dinner, if you want a sense of occasion, head around the corner to **Le Normandie** ★★★ (p. 87) or any of the Mandarin Oriental Hotel's fine dining restaurants. If you'd rather keep it simple and inexpensive, drop by **Harmonique** ★★ (p. 90), a few steps farther, in a lane off Charoen Krung Road.

Both these dining options are just a few blocks away from the city's most famed streets for go-go bars—**Patpong 1** and **2** (p. 127). Take a stroll around the bustling Night Market, and if you're curious, check out the bars (stick to downstairs bars, as those upstairs bring grief) and buy the girls a drink. When you've had enough, hop in a cab back to the hotel.

Day 3: Day Trip from Bangkok

To get a broader sense of the country, take a day trip out of town on your third day in Bangkok. Options include a visit to the **Ancient City** (p. 129), which has reproductions of the nation's best-known buildings; a wonderful bus and boat trip to the former capital of **Ayutthaya** ★★ (p. 264); a train ride to **Kanchanaburi** (p. 131), home of the "Death Railway"; or a trip to **Khao Yai National Park** ★ (p. 133), which offers welcome greenery.

ANCIENT CAPITALS TOUR IN 1 WEEK

This 1-week itinerary, heading north from Bangkok, enables you to trace the nation's legacy back to its ancient seats of power. First, you'll head north to Ayutthaya—the capital of Siam until the late 18th century—and then you'll carry on via Phitsanulok to Sukhothai and Si Satchanalai, the very origins of the Kingdom of Siam, before finally ending up in the ancient Lanna capital of Chiang Mai, which became a part of Siam/Thailand only in the early 20th century. The journey can be done by a combination of bus and train, though I'd recommend renting a car (and driver, if you're not confident of driving yourself), which offers more comfort and flexibility. Most rental agencies will allow you to pick up the vehicle in Bangkok and drop it off in Chiang Mai, and the daily rate should be cheaper for a week's rental.

Day 1: Bangkok to Ayutthaya

You can make the short trip north from Bangkok to Ayutthaya (see "Side Trips from Bangkok," in chapter 6) in about an hour and a half, leaving most of the day for sightseeing.

In Ayutthaya, check into **Kantary Hotel** ★ (p. 270), the town's newest and best lodgings. You can drive around the sights, though it's fun to rent a bicycle. Short elephant rides are also available. The main museums are the **Ayutthaya Historical Study Center** (p. 268) and the **Chao Sam Phraya National Museum** ★★ (p. 269); both contain good historical info and artifacts. Don't miss **Wat Phra Mahathat** ★★★ (p. 269), in the city center, the most striking of the Ayutthaya ruins, and **Wat Phra Si Sanphet** ★★ (p. 270), with its three

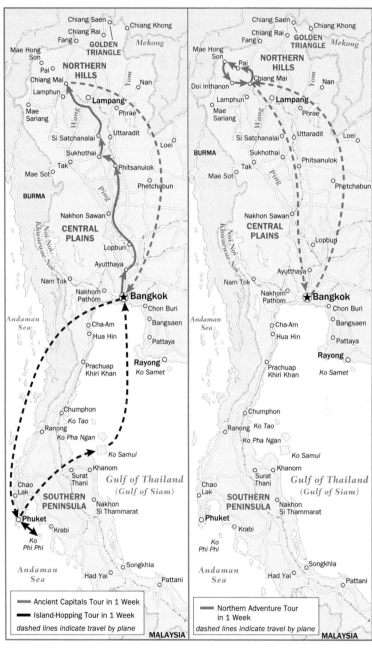

slender stupas. If you have time, take a late-afternoon tour by longtail boat around the city island to see the more far-flung ruins.

In the evening, catch a meal at the colorful **Chao Phrom Night Market** (p. 272) or at one of the many **floating restaurants** at the riverside. The ruins are illuminated in the evening, so a **night tour** is another option.

Day 2: Bang Pa-In, Lopburi, & Ayutthaya

Today you'll drive (or be driven) to two interesting destinations near Ayutthaya, allowing half a day for each site. **Bang Pa-In** (p. 272) is not an ancient Siamese capital, but it is a royal retreat that was particularly popular in the reign of King Chulalongkorn (r. 1868–1910); the curious mix of Thai and Western colonial architecture makes a striking contrast to the ruins at Ayutthaya.

Grab a bowl of rice or noodles for a roadside lunch as you head north to **Lopburi** (p. 272), another favorite royal retreat in the era of King Narai. Visit **King Narai's Palace** and the museum on the grounds. Take a look at **Ban Vichayen,** once home of King Narai's Western advisor, Constantine Phaulkon; and visit the town's mischievous macaques at **Phra Prang Sam Yot** before heading back to **Ayutthaya.**

In the evening, take a stroll along **Naresuan Road Soi 2,** where you'll find several places serving Western food, and some providing free Internet access and live music.

Day 3: Ayutthaya to Phitsanulok

Check out early and drive to **Phitsanulok** (p. 274). Most of the day will be spent looking out over endless rice paddies during the 300-km (186-mile) journey. Check in at **Grand Riverside** ★★ (p. 276), and then cross the river and stroll upstream to **Wat Yai** ★★ (p. 278), the town's only must-see attraction. In the evening, take a stroll back downstream beside the Nan River to the **Night Market** (p. 272); order some flying vegetables (fried morning glory vegetables) and have your camera ready to catch them being thrown some distance by the chef onto plates.

Day 4: Phitsanulok to Sukhothai

Call ahead to the **Tharaburi Resort** ★★ (p. 280), in Sukhothai, to book a room, then drive the short distance from Phitsanulok. Once you've checked in, spend the rest of the day exploring **Sukhothai Historical Park** ★★★ (p. 282). As in Ayutthaya, it's fun to explore the central area by rented bicycle, though for the furthest temples you'll need the car. Start at the **Ramkhamhaeng National Museum** to get clued up on this remarkable site, and then head for the most important ruins at **Wat Phra Mahathat** ★★, **Wat Traphang Tong,** and **Wat Si Chum.**

Ask at the resort if there is any **light and sound show** presentation at the historical park in the evening. If there is, it's a sight to remember; if not, settle for a satisfying dinner and drinks at the uniquely eccentric **Dream Café** ★ (p. 281).

Day 5: Sukhothai to Si Satchanalai & Chiang Mai

Most of this day is spent wending your way north from the central plains into the northern hills, with a welcome break at the ruined temples of **Si Satchanalai** ★ (p. 283). The main temples to see here are **Wat Chang Lom** and **Wat**

Phra Si Ratana Mahathat ★. On leaving the site, look out for another roadside lunch stop, and then sit back and watch the landscape become more dramatic as you make your way through the hills to **Chiang Mai** (p. 288), capital of the north. This ancient but hip city has a great range of places to stay, so check out the listings (p. 292) to find somewhere that suits your budget.

You'll want to stretch your legs after a day in the car, so make for the **Night Bazaar ★** (p. 316), and be prepared for some furious bargaining as you shop for souvenirs. If hunger pangs overtake you while shopping, pop into **Anusarn Market** (p. 302), and follow the most appealing aroma. If you can wait, cross the river to **Riverside ★★** (p. 303), where you can eat, drink, and dance to live music till late.

Day 6: Chiang Mai

For the last full day of this trip, you get to make a choice. If you'd like to get a sense of the city's long history, take a walk from the northeast corner to the southwest corner of Chiang Mai's Old City, winding through the back streets and taking in the principal temples (**Wat Chiang Man ★**, **Wat Chedi Luang ★★★**, and **Wat Phra Singh ★★★**) (p. 306). Stop off for lunch at either **Ruen Tamarind ★** (p. 304) or **Huen Phen ★★** (p. 304) along the way, and sit for a while in **Buak Had Park** at the end.

If, on the other hand, you've had enough history for one trip, you might like to spend the day learning how to prepare some tasty Thai dishes at the **Chiang Mai Thai Cookery School ★** (p. 310). Other options include **boat trips** on the river, a visit to an **elephant camp,** a (brief) visit to a **hill-tribe village,** or a drive up Doi Suthep to visit the north's most famous temple—**Wat Phra That Doi Suthep ★★★**.

In the evening, book tickets for the cultural show at the **Old Chiang Mai Cultural Center ★** (p. 319), where you can dine on northern specialties and watch traditional dancing. The show finishes at 9:30pm, allowing time for any last-minute shopping at the Night Bazaar, more drinking and dancing at the riverside bars, or packing your bags and getting an early night.

Day 7: Chiang Mai to Bangkok

If you have time before your flight leaves, try to do some last-minute shopping in Chiang Mai. If there's no time, then bon voyage.

ISLAND-HOPPING TOUR IN 1 WEEK

This itinerary offers a glimpse at three of Thailand's most lauded beach destinations—Phuket, Ko Phi Phi, and Ko Samui. If you like what you see, you may be tempted to stay longer than suggested here—but don't overstay your visa!

Day 1: Bangkok to Phuket

A short flight and transfer from Bangkok will bring you to **Phuket ★★** (p. 214), which has a range of accommodation from luxurious resorts to simple guesthouses; go for a room at the **Amari Coral Reef Resort ★★★** (p. 227), at Patong Beach, if you want to be near the action, or **Anantara Villas Phuket ★★★** (p. 233), on Mai Khao Beach, if you want somewhere away from it all.

Make dinner reservations at **La Gritta** ★★ (p. 237) if you're at the Amari, or at **Sea Fire Salt** if you're at the Anantara, then enjoy a lazy meal and soak up the sunset while plotting a week's island hopping.

Day 2: Phuket

Time for some serious rest and relaxation. Give yourself a day on the beach of your choice or by the pool, snacking from the pool bar or passing vendors on the beach. Read a novel, take a snooze, or indulge in a spa treatment in a beachfront pavilion.

In the evening, if you have kids in tow, sign up for the dinner and show at **Phuket Fantasea** (p. 247), on Kamala Beach. If not, eat your fill at **Patong Seafood Restaurant** (p. 237), then check out the raunchy bars and discos along **Bangla Road** in the heart of Patong.

Day 3: More of Phuket

Today you'll explore the island by car (and driver if necessary). Begin by exploring the west coast beaches (Karon, Patong, Kamala, etc.) and rating them all. See if any score higher than Nai Thon, near the northern end of the west coast.

Stop off somewhere with scenic views, such as **On the Rock** ★★ on Karon Beach (p. 236), for a lazy lunch. From here head to the island's northeast to visit the **Gibbon Rehabilitation Project** (p. 244), then go back south through the center of the island, pausing at Thalang to admire the **Heroines' Monument** (p. 220), and, if time allows, **Wat Phra Thong** (p. 221).

As dusk falls, park up in **Phuket Town** and take a stroll around the colonnaded streets of Sino-Portuguese houses before dining at **Ka Jok See** ★★ (p. 239). The after-dinner dance might make you ready for bed, but if you want more, head for **Timber Rock** bar (p. 246) and check out the local live bands before heading back to base.

Day 4: Day Trip to Ko Phi Phi

Just about every tour operator on Phuket runs day trips to **Ko Phi Phi** ★, so check the schedule of a few and sign up for one that appeals.

After a boat ride of a couple of hours, in which time you should see plenty of karst outcrops of the kind that typify Phang Nga Bay, you'll probably be taken to **Phi Phi Leh** (p. 257) first (the smaller, uninhabited island), where you'll have the chance to snorkel and explore Maya Bay, made famous by the movie *The Beach* (p. 23).

From here you'll go to **Phi Phi Don** (p. 257), which, depending on the season, might be heaving with vacationers. Lunch is usually included in these day trips, and a clamber up to the viewpoint over the back-to-back horseshoe bays brings a sight to treasure. Once back on Phuket, spruce yourself up and treat yourself to a meal to remember at **The Boathouse Wine & Grill** ★★★, on Kata Beach (p. 223).

Day 5: Phuket to Ko Samui

Hop on a flight from Phuket to **Ko Samui** ★★★ (p. 175), and you'll be able to compare the sand and sea color at Thailand's two most popular beach destinations. The fun begins at Samui airport, where you'll feel like you've landed in Disneyland.

If it's peace and quiet you're after, book into the **Six Senses Hideaway** ★★★ (p. 186), in the northeast corner of the island, where you can be sure nobody will disturb you except your personal butler. If you're more into partying, go for the **Centara Grand Beach Resort** ★★ (p. 187), which is right in the heart of the action on Chaweng Beach.

Spend the rest of the day relaxing and settling into your resort, which will have plenty of activities on offer if you feel restless. Dine at your chosen resort as well, and get a sound night's sleep before the last full day of this tour.

Day 6: Ko Samui

There are three attractive options for today, from which you'll have to choose just one. The first is to hire a car (with driver if necessary) to explore the island's ring road. Along the way you can take in such sights as phallic rocks, mummified monks, snake and monkey shows, waterfalls, and elephants. The second alternative is to sign up for a tour of the **Ang Thong National Marine Park** ★★ (p. 198), a cluster of rugged islands where you get to paddle a kayak through turquoise waters and scramble to the top of a hill for a breathtaking view.

The third choice is to indulge in a spa treatment, either in your resort or at **Tamarind Springs** ★★ (p. 197), at the northern end of Lamai Beach.

However you spend the day, treat yourself to a celebratory meal in the evening, at **Prego** ★★★ (p. 194), on Chaweng Beach—accompanied by a matching wine (just ask the sommelier for advice). If you still have energy to burn, check out Chaweng's cool bars like **Bar Solo** (p. 198), or the even cooler (in fact, sub-zero) **Ice Bar** (p. 198), where you'll run into hundreds of other party-minded people.

Day 7: Ko Samui to Bangkok

Put on your best white shirt to show off your suntan, take a cab to the airport, and zip back to Bangkok.

NORTHERN ADVENTURE TOUR IN 1 WEEK

Here's a good way to get to see a huge tract of the northern hills, as well as the ancient temples of Chiang Mai. You'll follow the Mae Hong Son Loop out to the northwest border with Myanmar. On the return leg, the route detours from the Loop to the highest point in Thailand, where you might even need a jacket or sweater.

Day 1: Bangkok to Chiang Mai

After a flight or an overnight train journey from Bangkok, arrive in Chiang Mai. Reasonable, centrally located guesthouses like the legendary **Gap's House** (p. 299) dot the **Old City** here. Alternatively, there are upscale old-world gems, such as the **Rachamankha** ★★★ (p. 298), or modern boutique properties like the **Ping Nakara** ★★ (p. 295).

After checking into your hotel, take a stroll round the narrow lanes of the **Old City.** Don't miss **Wat Phra Singh** ★★★ (p. 308) or **Wat Chedi Luang** ★★★ (p. 306), two of the city's most revered places of worship. If you have time, shop for fabulous home wares and fashions along chichi **Nimmanheimin**

Road. Then get ready for dinner at the fantastic Thai-fusion restaurant **The House** ★★★ (p. 303).

Day 2: Chiang Mai to Pai

Book a car and driver for 5 days, during which you will explore the north. Set out early and catch a show at an **elephant camp** in the **Mae Sa Valley,** before continuing north on Route 107, then branching left at Mae Malai onto Route 1095. The road follows switchbacks over an attractive range of hills before arriving at **Pai** ★ (p. 332). Check into the gorgeous **Belle Villa** ★★ (p. 335) outside of town. Take a stroll around town and soak up its laid-back atmosphere. If you need some exercise, walk up to **Wat Mae Yen** (p. 334), on a small hill to the east of town. In the evening, enjoy a tasty Thai meal at **Baan Benjarong** ★ (p. 336), and then check out the live music in the surrounding area.

Day 3: Pai to Mae Hong Son

It takes about half a day to negotiate the steep, narrow road through the mountains to **Mae Hong Son** ★ (p. 337), and a full day if you stop off to explore **Spirit Cave** (p. 336), located near Soppong.

In Mae Hong Son, check into the **Imperial** ★★ or **Fern Resort** ★★★ (p. 340), and then take a stroll around **Jong Kham Lake** and grab a few pictures of the Burmese-style temples of **Wat Jong Kham** and **Wat Jong Klang** (p. 338). Dine at **Fern Restaurant** ★★ (p. 342) and get an early night, as tomorrow is a long day's drive.

Day 4: Mae Hong Son to Doi Inthanon

Today's journey starts out on the southern (and longest) part of the Mae Hong Son Loop, passing through Khun Yuam and Mae Sariang before branching off to Thailand's highest peak—Doi Inthanon. The long journey doesn't leave much time for sightseeing, but it's a good idea to take frequent, short breaks to stretch your legs. One such stop could be at the **Japanese War Museum,** in **Khun Yuam** (p. 343), while the **Riverhouse Resort,** in **Mae Sariang** (p. 343), is a good choice for lunch. About 80km (50 miles) east of Mae Sariang, turn left onto Route 1088, and then at the small town of **Mae Chaem,** turn right and climb to the peak of **Doi Inthanon** ★★★ (p. 322). Stay in the log cabins at the national park headquarters, and eat at the neighboring cafe.

Day 5: Doi Inthanon to Chiang Mai

It takes only a couple of hours to drive from the summit of Doi Inthanon to Chiang Mai, so you can spend the morning exploring the upper reaches of the mountain, where it's much cooler than down in the valley. Walk the Kaew Mae Pan trail, near the park headquarters, and notice the wealth of plant and bird life. On the way down, stop at the Wachirathan and Sirithan Falls for some photos, and at the Mae Klang Falls for a grilled chicken and sticky rice lunch on the fly.

Once back in Chiang Mai, unwind with a spa session, either at your hotel or at **Oasis Spa** ★ (p. 314), in the town center.

For dinner, track down the stylish **W by Wanlamun** ★★, which still remains unknown to many locals (p. 303).

Day 6: Around Chiang Mai

Head straight up the city's guardian mountain to **Wat Phra That Doi Suthep** ★★★ (p. 319), where you can listen to bells tinkling in the breeze and look down on the city sitting in the valley below. The classic image at this temple is of the gleaming stupa that stands in a marble courtyard at the heart of the complex.

At the base of the mountain, turn left onto the Superhighway, which sweeps around the north of the city, and look out for the turn to **Sankampaeng** (p. 317) along Route 1006. After breaking for lunch at **Fujian** ★★★ (p. 302), keep driving east, stopping at any showroom or workshop that catches your eye. These present good opportunities not only for interesting photographs, but for souvenir shopping too.

You can complete your shopping in the evening at the **Night Bazaar** ★ (p. 316), where you'll find everything from a 50¢ hill-tribe doll to a $50,000 antique. If you dine in the simple **Kalare Food & Shopping Center** (p. 306), you can also take in a performance of traditional dance as you eat.

Day 7: Chiang Mai to Bangkok

If you find that all your shopping won't fit into your bags, hurry to the post office and mail a box of goods back home. After that, head for the airport and wave goodbye to the friendly folks of northern Thailand.

ACTIVE TRIP PLANNER

4

For some, the ideal Thai holiday is spent lolling on a beach sipping smoothies or cocktails, while others want to push themselves to the limit, seeking thrills and adventure. Fortunately, Thailand's well-developed tourism industry offers lots of adventurous options for the more intrepid traveler. Whether your passion is trekking or rock climbing, Thai boxing or massage, cooking or diving, you'll find you can study or practice it in Thailand.

The activity you choose in some cases determines your destination, so divers will head to the islands of the south such as Ko Tao or Ko Similan, while trekkers will gravitate to the hills of the north that are home to colorful hill-tribes. Several activities, however, like biking, cooking, and golfing, are available countrywide, in which case you can choose where you'd prefer to be based. The great thing about all these activities is that they presume no previous training, and tour operators can offer exciting experiences that are well planned and safe for everyone, from beginners to experts. This chapter gives an overview of the many options available—along with some recommendations for tour operators—but refer to the specific destination chapters throughout this book for specific details.

ORGANIZED ADVENTURE TRIPS

Though people who enjoy challenging outdoor activities are often fiercely independent, there are lots of advantages to planning a trip through an adventure tour operator, whether it's one based in the country that has sound local knowledge, or an international operator that has a good reputation for organizing a particular activity and also has reliable in-country representatives.

The biggest advantage is time. If you only have a few weeks to spend in Thailand, you'll want to use this limited time to maximum effect, and that's where organized tours can help, by transporting you swiftly to the locations where the fun begins and planning everything else, including accommodation and eating. Equipment is another important consideration; why take a mountain bike or heavy diving gear halfway round the world when you can rent it locally at very reasonable rates?

One important consideration when booking an organized tour is group size. While there's every chance you'll meet like-minded people on the tour, and perhaps even begin some lifelong friendships, big groups can sometimes lead to conflicting interests and even arguments. So ask how many will be in your group before you sign on the dotted line, and try to find out something about their age and interests.

Some travelers prefer to sign up with international operators that have established a reputation for providing a smooth experience for their clients, though such tours usually come with a hefty price tag attached. These days, however, it's easy to browse the Web for details of tours offered by Thai-based tour operators, and their prices are significantly lower, in some cases up to half of what you might pay an international tour operator. Here I've listed the best operators based both in and outside Thailand.

Thai Adventure Tour Operators

Active Thailand ★★ (✆ 05385-0160 in Chiang Mai; www.activethailand.com) is based in North Thailand and can offer all types of multi-activity trip.

Green Earth Adventure (✆ 08199-28761 cell; www.greenearthadventure. com) specializes in off-road motorbike and 4x4 adventures, some of which include trekking or white-water rafting.

Wild Thailand (✆ 02901-0480 in Bangkok; www.wildthailand.com) is a small operator offering personalized service, mixing a host of activities like kayaking, elephant riding, and white-water rafting into their tours.

International Adventure Tour Operators

Audley Travel ★ (✆ 01993-838000 in the U.K.; www.audleytravel.com) is a well-established and excellent tailor-made travel operator reputed for its quality of personal service. It offers both independent and group travel in Thailand.

Geographic Expeditions ★★ (✆ 800/777-8183 in the U.S.; www.geoex.com) is an award-winning travel adventure operator offering several tours in Thailand, including trekking tours of the north.

Intrepid Travel ★★ (✆ 613/9473-2673 in Australia; www.intrepidtravel.com) features a range of tours for travelers with a yearning to get off the beaten track, lasting from 4 days to a month. Their 12-day Active Thailand tour combines trekking, cycling, rock climbing, and kayaking as well as the chance to soak in a mud bath.

Responsible Travel ★ (✆ 01273/600-030 in the U.K.; www.responsibletravel. com) is a leading ethical travel agent and a joint initiative with Conservation International. It works with local communities to create authentic experiences throughout Thailand.

ACTIVITIES A TO Z
Biking

Cycling is one of the most eco-friendly ways to experience any country, and given Thailand's tropical climate and well-developed road network, biking tours provide an ideal way to discover the country. Several companies offer tours throughout the kingdom, from beach destinations around Phuket to the lush paddies of the central plains and rugged highlands of the north.

Some cycling fanatics even take their own bikes with them, but this involves dealing with chaotic city traffic and speeding cars and buses on dangerous highways, which is not the best way for a newcomer to the country to learn about Thai culture. By contrast, organized cycling tours ensure that all your riding will be along country lanes where you can focus on the delightful surroundings rather than other vehicles on the road. Besides, if you get tired, you can just put the bike in the back of a pickup and be a passenger for a while. Tours are accompanied by knowledgeable guides and experienced mechanics, so you'll have no worries about getting lost or breakdowns in the middle of nowhere.

TOUR OPERATORS

Active Thailand ★★ (*©* **05385-0160** in Chiang Mai; www.activethailand.com) offers all types of adventure tours, but they specialize in cycling tours and have some of the most appealing itineraries, particularly for tours of the north.

Bike Tours Thailand ★ (*©* **07626-3575** in Phuket; www.biketoursthailand.com) is based in Phuket and offers some great 1-day tours of Phuket, Krabi, and Ko Yao Noi.

Spice Roads ★★★ (*©* **02712-5305** in Bangkok; www.spiceroads.com) offers cycling tours throughout Southeast Asia, but is based in Bangkok and probably offers the greatest range of tours in Thailand, covering the whole country and lasting between 1 day and 2 weeks.

Bird-Watching

With around 1,000 species of our feathered friends either living in or passing through the kingdom, Thailand is a rewarding destination for bird-watching. Babblers, woodpeckers, and kingfishers are just a few that you're likely to see, and if you're lucky you may spot a great hornbill or a green-tailed sunbird, which is endemic to the country.

As you might expect, Thailand's national parks are the best place to see a variety of species, with the most popular destinations being Khao Yai, Khao Sok, and Doi Inthanon. While any time of year is good for this activity, if you're planning to head for the mountains of the north the best time for good weather is from November to February.

TOUR OPERATORS

Thailand Bird Watching ★★ (*©* **08227-21127** cell; www.thailandbirdwatching.com) offers probably the widest range of bird-watching tours in Thailand. Choose from the north, south, or central region and check out their trip schedule online.

Wild Watch Thailand ★ (*©* **02615-4557** in Bangkok; www.wildwatch thailand.com) runs 3-day tours to Khao Yai National Park and 2-week countrywide tours for birders.

Cooking

Cookery courses have been hugely popular in Thailand for a long time now, with flexible courses that allow students to choose anything between half a day and a full week getting to grips with the subtleties of Thai cuisine. Try a 1-day course to start (a half-day is a bit short to learn anything), which usually involves taking a trip to the local fresh market to buy ingredients, then following the teacher's steps to produce a few Thai classics, such as *kaeng khiaw waan* (sweet green curry), *thawt man kung* (shrimp cakes), or *yam hua phli* (banana-flower salad). Then, if you enjoy the homework, which involves eating what you've cooked, sign up for another day. Bangkok (p. 58) and Chiang Mai (p. 288) have the widest choice of schools, but many guesthouses in small towns now also run cooking classes.

COOKERY SCHOOLS

Blue Elephant ★★ (© 02673-9353; www.blueelephant.com; see p. 93) is one of Bangkok's top restaurants, and also runs cookery classes for groups or one-on-one.

Chiang Mai Thai Cookery School ★ (© 05320-6388; www.thaicookery school.com; see p. 310) is Chiang Mai's longest-running cookery school, offering 1- to 5-day courses covering all the basics of Thai cuisine.

Time for Lime ★ (© 07568-4590; www.timeforlime.net; see p. 262) is based on Ko Lanta near Krabi, where you can learn to cook Thai and fusion food in between spells of lounging on the beach.

Diving & Snorkeling

Diving is probably the most popular type of active vacation in Thailand, and every year thousands of visitors get their PADI (recognized scuba diving qualification) certification here while thousands more experienced divers come for fun dives. Living coral reefs grace the waters of the Andaman Sea and the Gulf of Thailand. More than 80 species of coral have been discovered in the Gulf, while the deeper and more saline Andaman has more than 210. Marine life includes hundreds of species of fish, plus numerous varieties of crustaceans and sea turtles. With the aid of scuba gear, divers can get an up-close-and-personal view of this undersea universe. For those without certification, many reefs close to the surface are still vibrant for snorkelers, especially places like the Surin Islands in the Andaman Sea.

From Ko Tao or Phuket (see chapters 8 and 9), experienced divers can take a day trip that includes two or three dives. Long-term scuba trips on live-aboard boats run seasonally. For more information on diving, see chapter 8, "Southern Peninsula: The East Coast & Islands," and chapter 9, "Southern Peninsula: The West Coast & Islands," where many operators who schedule frequent trips are listed. Always check that an operator has PADI-certified dive masters, and that their boats are carrying the full bevy of certificates of approval issued by international marine safety organizations. Scuba training and certification packages are common and can have you ready to dive in 5 days. Pretty much every beach has independent operators or guesthouses that rent snorkels, masks, and fins for the day. A few boat operators take snorkelers to reefs off neighboring islands, especially from Ko Lanta, Ko Phi Phi, Krabi, Ko Samui, and Pattaya.

DIVE OPERATORS

See p. 242 for recommended outfits in Phuket, p. 195 for operators on Ko Samui, and p. 209 for dive schools on Ko Tao.

Elephant Handling

Though elephant shows and elephant rides have long been popular in Thailand, the owners of these gentle giants have discovered in recent years that visitors just can't get enough of being close to them and, as a result, several places now offer *mahout*, or elephant-handler, courses, in which students spend a day or more learning how to care for one elephant, which means washing it (expect to get wet yourself), feeding it (also a big job, they never seem to get full), and riding it bareback (getting up there is the hard part). You'll learn a bunch of elephant commands in a mix of Thai and Karen language (the Karen are traditionally elephant handlers) and probably a few other things you didn't know. Most set-ups offer this as a day course, but if that seems too short, you can sign up for a 3- to 10-day homestay at the Thai Elephant Conservation Center near Lampang.

ELEPHANT CAMPS

Thai Elephant Conservation Center ★★★ (© 05482-9333, near Lampang; www.thailandelephant.org; see p. 322) is operated by the Forestry Industry Organization, and features a daily show as well as elephant-handler courses lasting from 1 to 10 days.

Mae Sa Elephant Camp (© 05320-6247 in Chiang Mai; www.maesa elephantcamp.com) has a large number of elephants that perform two shows a day but they also run 1- to 3-day elephant-handler courses.

Patara Elephant Farm (© 08199-22551 cell, www.pataraelephantfarm.com; in Chiang Mai; see p. 312) runs a neat program called "Elephant owner for a day."

Golfing

Thailand is nothing short of a mecca for golfers, with hundreds, if not thousands, of courses scattered around the kingdom, many of them designed by top golfers. Add the warm climate and very reasonable fees, and you've got an activity that is appealing enough to attract golfers from all over the world. The combination of excellent courses and cheap fees is particularly attractive to Japanese and Koreans, who descend on the country in planeloads, hauling their golf bags through customs. However, it's not really necessary to cart your gear with you as all courses will rent you a bag of clubs for a reasonable fee. Caddies and buggies are also available just about everywhere at affordable prices.

See individual chapters under the heading "Golf" or "Hitting the Links" for the pick of the courses in that region.

Kayaking

Like cycling, kayaking is an eco-friendly activity that causes minimum impact to the environment while providing healthy exercise and some magical perspectives of Thailand's varied landscapes. The most popular area to practice this easy sport, which most beginners get the hang of very quickly, is around Phang Nga Bay near Phuket, where limestone outcrops seem to rear up out of the tranquil waters. If you sign up for a tour with an experienced outfitter, they will time the visit so that you can pass at low tide through shallow caves that lead into hidden lagoons (called *hong*, or "room" in Thai) that display a pristine beauty. Other popular areas for kayaking are Cheow Lan Lake in Khao Sok National Park, as well as the marine national parks of the Ang Thong Islands (near Ko Samui) and Ko Tarutao (in the Andaman Sea near the Malaysian border). Many organized adventure tours include kayaking on their itineraries, but for a specialist, contact one of the companies below.

TOUR OPERATORS

Paddle Asia (© 08189-36558 cell, in Phuket; www.paddleasia.com; see p. 175) is the best company to contact for a customized kayaking tour lasting several days. Their most popular destinations are Khao Sok National Park and the Tarutao Islands.

John Gray's Sea Canoe ★ (© 07625-4505 in Phuket; www.johngray-seacanoe. com; see p. 242) is a highly respected outfitter that specializes in tours of Phang Nga Bay that combine some fun kayaking with a seafood supper under the stars.

Kitesurfing & Windsurfing

Windsurfing has long been popular in Thailand, particularly at the popular beach destinations such as Pattaya, Phuket, and Ko Samui. It continues to be so, though these days it is being somewhat eclipsed by the more demanding, more exciting, and, it has to be said, more expensive, sport of kitesurfing, often referred to as kiteboarding. As well as at the main beach destinations, this sport can be studied and practiced at Ko Pha Ngan, Hua Hin, Chumphon, and Pranburi (south of Hua Hin). It takes a while to pick up the skills necessary to get airborne, but once you're up there, it all seems worth it. Of course, on windless days it's hopeless; check out Kiteboarding Asia's website for month-by-month wind conditions in each of their locations. A 3-day beginners' course costs in the region of 11,000B.

TOUR OPERATORS

Kiteboarding Asia (✆ **08159-14594** cell, in Phuket; www.kiteboardingasia.com; see p. 240) is currently the only operator in Thailand certified by the International Kiteboarding Association (IKO) and offers a variety of courses as well as equipment rental.

Massage

Thai massage courses are hugely popular among Westerners who appreciate the multiple benefits of a thorough, pressure-point massage and want to induce a deep relaxation in others. Courses are flexible, ranging from a few days to several weeks, with 10 days being the average. Though you can get a good traditional massage anywhere in Thailand, it's not so easy for foreigners to find somewhere to study the skill outside Bangkok and Chiang Mai. The school at Wat Po (see below) is the best known in the country, but for a more stylish and comfortable environment, check out the courses offered by Chiva Som (see below).

MASSAGE SCHOOLS

Chiva-Som Academy (✆ **02711-5270-3** in Bangkok; www.chivasomacademy. com; see p. 117), located off Sukhumvit Road, teaches a range of courses like hot stone massage and Oriental foot massage in a very comfortable setting.

International Training Massage (✆ **05321-8632** in Chiang Mai; www.itm thaimassage.com; see p. 310) is a long-established, highly reputed set-up that offers a basic, 5-day (30-hour) course leading to accreditation for 5,000B.

Wat Po Traditional Medical Practitioners Center (✆ **02622-3551** in Bangkok; www.watpomassage.com; see p. 114) offers a general, 30-hour course (5 days) for 9,500B.

Meditation

Meditation courses present perhaps the ultimate challenge to fast-living Westerners who couldn't get through a day without their smartphone or TV. The challenge also involves no reading, no idle gossip (in some monasteries, no talking at all), and, toughest of all, no thinking. Most temples teach the Theravada Buddhist tradition of meditation and developing insight, known as Vipassana. Don't consider attending such a course unless you intend to see it through; you'll need to dress in loose white clothes and take some basic vows such as no eating after midday—a tough challenge for most Western students.

MEDITATION TEMPLES

Suan Mokkhabalarama (© 07753-1552 in Chaiya, near Surat Thani; www. suanmokkh.org; see p. 174) runs 10-day courses beginning on the 1st of each month.

Wat Mahathat (© 02222-6011 in Bangkok; see p. 113) is a popular center for meditation study with instruction in English in downtown Bangkok. Call for details.

Wat Rampoeng (© 05327-8620 in Chiang Mai; www.watrampoeng.net; see p. 311) offers a 26-day course (starting any time) that should clear out any mental cobwebs, though expect some mood swings along the way.

Motorcycling

One of the best ways to explore Thailand, especially the mountainous north, is on a motorcycle, and the availability of inexpensive bike rental tempts many to hit the high road. However, there are several fatalities of foreigners on Thai roads every year, and many more who survive but hobble for months on crutches, so I'd advise you not to take the chance unless you are an experienced motorcycle rider. If you are, you can get lots of good advice for independent travel at www.gtrider.com. Even then, you might like to consider joining an organized biking tour with one of the companies below.

TOUR OPERATORS

Thai Bike Tours (© 08924-84123 cell, in Chiang Mai; www.thaibiketours.com) offers on-road and off-road tours, as well as 1-day off-road training courses.

Thai Motorcyle Tours (© 04232-5781 in Udon Thani; www.thai-motorcycle-tours.com) runs 5-day loop tours from Chiang Mai to Mae Hong Son, Nan, the Golden Triangle, and Sukhothai.

Rock Climbing

Rock climbing has exploded in popularity in Thailand during the last 2 decades and many choose to visit the country specifically to practice this thrilling sport. The cliffs around Krabi, particularly at Railay Beach, attract thousands of climbers, though there are also bolted routes on Ko Phi Phi and some around Chiang Mai. Though you need good stamina and balance for this activity (and, it goes without saying, a good head for heights) equipment rental and tuition is much cheaper than for many other extreme sports, and day-long introductory courses rarely cost more than 2,000B a day.

ROCK-CLIMBING SCHOOLS

King Climbers (© 07566-2096 in Krabi; www.railay.com; see p. 253) is one of the most popular schools based at Railay Beach, near Krabi.

The Peak Adventure (© 05380-0567 in Chiang Mai; www.thepeakadventure. com; see p. 313) has lots of bolted routes near Sankampaeng, about 35km (22 miles) from Chiang Mai.

Thai Boxing (muay thai)

If you ever wander empty, hushed streets in Thailand and suddenly hear a roar coming from inside bars and houses, you can be sure everyone's watching an important bout of *muay thai*, or Thai boxing, on the TV. This national obsession has now spread abroad and there's no shortage of travelers happy to spend an intensive week or two training at a Thai boxing camp. Most training camps charge 3,000B to 5,000B for a week's tuition, and many offer accommodation as well. The biggest camps are in Bangkok and Chiang Mai, but you'll also find them on Phuket and Ko Samui.

TRAINING CAMPS

Muaythai Institute (📞 **02992-0096** in Bangkok; www.muaythai-institute.net) offers training at all levels, including for instructors and judges.

Lanna Muay Thai (📞 **05389-2102** in Chiang Mai; www.lannamuaythai.com) has turned out many competent, foreign kick boxers over the years and can help with accommodation too.

Trekking

Thailand's mountainous jungle terrain in the north is a haven for trekkers, with a network of trails that vary in difficulty from easy to difficult. There are hundreds of agencies that offer trekking tours in Chiang Mai, and some of them claim to visit "untouristed areas," though this is highly unlikely, as the region has been overrun in the last 2 decades. Nevertheless, it should be possible to find a trek that takes you through several hill-tribe villages and some delightful countryside. Just keep in mind that human rights organizations have pointed out the damage that trekking does to sustainability in remote villages inhabited by poor hill-tribes, where the places visited have become little more than paying human zoos.

Choose your operator carefully (see p. 21) and look out for community-based projects, where the local people reap real benefits from your visit. Treks can last 1 to 5 nights but usually involve no more than 3 to 4 hours per day of walking on jungle

---

BEING A sensitive TREKKER

The face of rural life has changed in the far north—partly as a result of the tourist influx locally, and partly due to the steady development of Thailand's economy. Northern hill-tribe peoples have been exposed to the outside world and are being asked by Thai officials to stop slash-and-burn agricultural techniques and participate in the Thai economy by growing crops other than opium. Their children are educated in Thai and are discouraged from speaking their tribal language. Within the bounds of these influences, minorities struggle to maintain their cultural identities, livelihoods, and centuries-old ways of life.

Many travelers are drawn to the hill-tribe villages in search of a "primitive" culture, unspoiled by modernization—and tour and trekking operators in the region are quick to exploit this. Companies advertise treks as non-tourist, authentic, or eco-tours in an effort to set them apart from tacky tourist operations or staged cultural experiences. Do not

be misled: There are no villages here that are untouched by foreign curiosity. In the worst cases, as with the camps of "long-neck" (Padaung tribe) from Myanmar, they have become nothing more than human zoos, with fees paid to individuals for photographs and zero long-term sustainability.

This shouldn't discourage anyone from joining a trek or tour; just be aware and avoid any bogus claims. It is also advisable to leave any preconceptions of "primitive" people to 19th-century anthropological journals; rather, come to learn how these cultures on the margin of society grapple with complex economic and social pressures to maintain their unique identities. Awareness of the impact of tourists is also important: Practice cultural sensitivity. With this as a mission, visitors can have an experience that is quite authentic and, refreshingly, has little to do with preconceptions and expectations.

THAILAND'S top 10 NATIONAL PARKS

With well over one hundred national parks scattered around the kingdom, it can be difficult to choose which one to head for to appreciate the country's diverse plant and animal life. To help you decide, here is a list of my personal favorites that results from over 2 decades exploring Thailand's natural treasures.

Ang Thong   Most popular as a day trip from Ko Samui, this archipelago of limestone islands in the Gulf of Thailand features pristine beaches, hidden lagoons, and sweeping views.

Doi Inthanon   Home to Thailand's highest mountain, Doi Inthanon (2,565 m/ 8,415 ft.) is a favorite haunt of bird watchers because of the huge variety of birds that live or visit here. Nature trails near the summit pass through some dramatic terrain.

Erawan   If you visit Kanchanaburi, don't miss this park, which has the country's most beautiful waterfall, tumbling over seven tiers, and Prathat Cave with its impressive stalagmites and stalactites.

Kaeng Krachan   Occupying nearly 3,000 sq. km (1,158 sq. miles) of forest in Petchburi Province, this is Thailand's biggest national park and provides shelter for tigers, elephants, sambar deer, and gibbons, among other species.

Khao Sok   Easily reached from Phuket or Krabi, this park is very popular for kayaking trips on the lake and treks to look for sun bears, gaurs, hornbills, and pheasants.

Khao Yai   Located just a few hours' drive northeast of Bangkok, Khao Yai was Thailand's first national park (established 1962) and is still the best bet for seeing a variety of wildlife.

Ko Chang   Thailand's second-largest island, Ko Chang ("Elephant Island") is just one of 50 islands in the eastern Gulf under national park protection; it boasts some of the country's best beaches and dive sites.

Phu Kradung   Situated in Thailand's northeast, this pine-capped plateau is only accessible by a tough trek, though you can hire a porter to carry your gear up.

Sam Roi Yot   "Three hundred peaks" park is just south of Hua Hin; it's peppered with limestone hills (thus the name), and has some great viewpoints, a beautiful pavilion in Phraya Nakhon Cave, and lots of wading birds.

Similan   Whether you're a diver or snorkeler, you can't fail to be impressed by the countless varieties of corals and colorful fish surrounding these nine islands in the Andaman Sea.

paths. All tours provide local guides to accompany groups, and the guides will keep the pace steady but comfortable for all trekkers involved. Some trips break up the monotonous walking with treks on elephant-back, trips in four-wheel-drive jeeps, or light rafting on flat bamboo rafts. Chiang Mai (see chapter 11) has the most trekking firms, while Chiang Rai, Pai, and Mae Hong Son (see chapter 12, "Exploring the Northern Hills") also have their share of trekking companies.

TREKKING TOUR OPERATORS

Active Travel (✆ 05385-0160 in Chiang Mai; www.activethailand.com; see p. 50) offer 3-day treks with a maximum of 9 trekkers for 5,500B per person.

Trekking Collective (✆ 05320-8340 in Chiang Mai; www.trekkingcollective. com; see p. 311) specializes in customized trips planned around clients' interests.

White-Water Rafting

River rafting in rubber dinghies is very popular in North Thailand between July and December, after which river levels become too low. It's possible to take rafting trips of just a few hours, but it's much more fun to make a 2-day trip, and overnight in jungle camps. Rapids are rarely extreme but are big enough to be loads of fun, and safety measures are taken seriously.

Thai Adventure Rafting (✆ **05369-9111** in Pai; www.thairafting.com) started off the craze long ago and still run exciting 2-day trips along the Pai River.

Siam River Adventures (✆ **08951-51917** cell, in Chiang Mai; www.siam rivers.com) runs 1- and 2-day rafting trips on the Mae Taeng River, just north of Chiang Mai.

Watching Wildlife

Just a century ago, the jungles of Thailand were so thick with wildlife that people didn't dare travel alone for fear of attack by tigers, snakes, or some other unknown predator. These days it's just the opposite—naturalists sit in hides for days on end in the vain hope of glimpsing some of the country's few remaining exotic species. As the country's forests have been systematically stripped, the habitat of many animals has disappeared, so the animals have gone as well.

The country's first national parks were established in the 1960s in an attempt to offer some shelter for species in decline, and to date there are over a hundred parks scattered all over the country. These are inevitably the best places to go looking for wildlife, though in many parks visitors are unlikely to see much more than a few birds and butterflies, ants, and spiders. One notable exception is **Khao Yai National Park ★** (p. 130), where visitors accompanied by a guide are almost certain to see hornbills, gibbons, elephants, and deer in a single day. Other national parks, where you can enjoy the country's flora and fauna are **Doi Inthanon,** which contains Thailand's highest mountain, and **Kaeng Krachan,** the country's biggest park in Petchaburi Province.

TOUR OPERATORS

Wild Watch Thailand (✆ **02615-4557** in Bangkok; www.wildwatchthailand.com) runs several bird-watching tours, but also wildlife watching tours in Khao Yai and Kaeng Krachan national parks.

Tiger Trail Outdoor Adventures (✆ **05327-8517** in Chiang Mai; www.tiger trailthailand.com) operates 2- and 3-day tours in several national parks, including Khao Sok and Khao Yai.

SETTLING INTO BANGKOK

With a population of around 9 million in a country of only 66 million, Thailand's capital teems with humanity. As the cultural heart of the kingdom, the city keeps many traditions still visibly intact—yet Bangkok is also a rapidly changing city. If you go beyond the city's transport systems (the Bangkok Transit System [BTS] Skytrain and the Mass Rapid Transit [MRT] subway), it can be a challenge. Heavy traffic, excessive heat and humidity, and, at certain times of the year, smog can make Bangkok truly overwhelming. Nevertheless, to find the charm of the city, all you need to do is to be adventurous and explore areas outside the central business district packed full of skyscrapers and shopping malls.

5

Founded when King Rama I moved the city across the river from Thonburi in 1782, Bangkok is not a particularly ancient capital, but rather a cool mix of modernity and tradition. Saffron-robed monks mingle in the *sois* with Starbucks-drinking, cellphone-wielding business types or bouffant-wigged socialites known by the abbreviation *hi-so*. Luxurious, glass-clad condos brazenly penetrate the skyscape, juxtaposed by tin-roofed slums teetering along putrid canals. Among the concrete, glittering *wats* (temples) and ramshackle colonial edifices pepper this ancient and vibrant city.

What strikes many upon arrival in the Big Mango, as it's lovingly known, is the highly developed infrastructure, high-end shopping, world-class accommodation, and welcoming people; compared to Hong Kong and Singapore, though, the country is way behind in development, and locals aren't as fluent in English as in these wealthy former colonies. The modernity is often merely a beguiling façade—underneath there's grit and grime.

The culture here is so gloriously rich, though, that exploring Bangkok should be seen as a highlight of any trip to Thailand. And there are rooms to suit all budgets. Bangkok's luxury hotels offer unrivaled rates, and visitors can find anything from a basic 300B hostel to a ritzy high-rise suite. The cuisine is itself a worthy adventure; you can choose from fine dining in hip hangouts to simple street-side food stalls.

Rivaled only by Chiang Mai in the north, Bangkok is above all a great place to shop, for anything from brand name luxury items (and, of course, knock-offs that won't last a week) to fine local handicrafts, silk, and jewels. And when it comes to nightlife, the endless array of great-value night markets, bars, clubs, and eateries makes for a (potentially) sleepless night.

ORIENTATION

Arriving

BY PLANE

Bangkok's **Suvarnabhumi International Airport** (airport code BKK; ✆ **02132-1888**), which opened in 2006, is the main hub for all international travelers arriving in Thailand; it also handles domestic flights (with three-digit codes) in and out of the capital. It's 30km (over 18 miles) east of the city. Suvarnabhumi offers a wide range of services, including luggage storage, currency exchange, banks, a branch of the British pharmacy Boots, ATMs, a post office, medical centers (two are 24-hr. clinics), Internet service, and telephones. All of Suvarnabhumi's restaurant and shopping outlets are infamously overpriced (up to 10 times city prices), though; budget travelers would do well to stop by a downtown convenience store to stock up on snacks and drinks. Within the airport complex, just a couple of minutes from the terminal exit, is **Novotel Suvarnabhumi Airport** (www.novotel.com), a five-star hotel. For more detailed information on Suvarnabhumi, see **www.suvarnabhumiairport.com.**

Bangkok's former international airport, **Don Muang** (airport code DMK; ✆ **02535-1111**) is 24km (15 miles) north of the heart of the city and is currently serving nonconnecting domestic flights operated by One-Two-Go (Orient Thai) and Nok Air. It no longer offers the range of services it used to but still has cafes and diners as well as ATMs; with few flights arriving or leaving, it's a much less stressful place than Suvarnabhumi. **Amari Don Muang Airport Hotel** (www.amari.com/donmuang) is opposite the airport and is accessed via a sky bridge or a shuttle bus. For more details on Don Muang, see **www.donmuangairportonline.com.**

Note: There are no ATMs beyond Immigration (airside) at Suvarnabhumi, so all those leaving Thailand—or those in transit—must ensure they have enough cash for their onward destination before they enter passport control, especially those paying for visas on arrival in countries such as Myanmar and Indochina, where airside airport ATMs may not exist or may have run out of cash.

> ## The Real Bangkok
>
> Referred to as "Krung Thep" by Thais, meaning "The City of Angels," the official name of Bangkok is a proud description of Bangkok's royal legacy—and the world's longest: Krungthepmahanakhon Amonrattanakosin Mahintharayutthaya Mahadilokphop Noppharatratchathaniburirom Udomratchaniwetmahasathan Amonphimanawatansthit Sakkathattiyawitsanukamprasit.

GETTING TO & FROM THE AIRPORTS From both Suvarnabhumi and Don Muang, it takes about 40 to 60 minutes to drive to the city center, depending on traffic, and over 90 minutes in heavy rain or at rush hour (or both). The city's larger hotels offer **pickup services** for a fee, but both airports have public taxi, limousine, and bus services to Bangkok; Suvarnabhumi also has a high-speed rail link to the city center. The **Express Service** takes 17 minutes to **Phaya Thai** station on the skytrain line and costs 150B, while the **City Line** takes 30 minutes to cover the same journey, stopping at six stations along the way, with fares from 15B to 45B.

If you'd prefer to go by taxi, don't be tempted by the many touts who prowl around the exits. In both airports, simply follow signs to the public taxi stands. Get some small notes (20B or 50B) in the Arrivals Hall before you leave the airport, as you may need these for the tollbooths. Without tolls, expect to pay between 250B and 300B from either airport to reach most hotels downtown.

Private limousine services such as AOT offer air-conditioned sedans and drivers from both airports. Look for the booth in Arrivals. Trips from Suvarnabhumi start at 800B. Advanced booking is not necessary.

Airport Express buses have been terminated since the launch of the new rail link, and local bus services are really only for people who know their way around. For these, you will need to get on a free shuttle, located at Level 2 or 4, going to the **Public Transportation Center.** From there, buses costing around 35B cover 12 city routes, including major BTS stops and the Southern Bus Terminal. For intercity services, go to the relevant ticket counter (daily 6am–9pm) at the Public Transportation Center; three routes serve nearby Pattaya, Jomtien, and Chonburi.

BY TRAIN

While a few southern-bound locomotives still use **Thonburi's Bangkok Noi Station** (✆ 02411-3102), most intercity trains to and from the capital stop at **Hua Lampong Station** (✆ 02220-4334, or the hot line at 1690), east of Yaowarat (Chinatown). Lying at a major intersection of Rama IV and Krung Kasem roads, it's notoriously gridlocked at morning and evening rush hours, so allow 40 minutes extra for traffic delays. Inside the station, clear signs point the way to the public toilets, pay phones, food court, and baggage check area (one bag costs 30B per day).

Like all major train stations, Hua Lampong is rife with scammers, preying on foreigners and gullible out-of-towners just arrived in the metropolis. "Officials" may approach you in the station offering help. Be careful—not all may actually be officials; proceed to the ticketing counter or information booth directly.

Metered taxis from the station cost about 50B to 100B to nearby Sala Daeng BTS on Silom Road, depending on the time of day; there is an **MRT** (subway) station at **Hua Lampong** for connections to the BTS. For Sukhumvit Road, take the MRT to the Sukhumvit stop, and then transfer to the Asok BTS.

BY BUS

Bangkok has three major bus stations, each serving a different part of the country. All air-conditioned public buses to the West and the Southern Peninsula arrive and depart from the **Southern Bus Terminal** (✆ 02422-4444), on Putthamonthon Soi 1, west of the river, over the Phra Pinklao Bridge from the Democracy Monument. Service to the East Coast (including Pattaya) arrives and departs from the **Eastern Bus Terminal,** also known as **Ekkamai** (✆ 02391-2504), on Sukhumvit Road opposite Soi 63 (Ekkamai BTS). Buses to the north arrive and leave from the **Northern Bus Terminal,** aka **Mo Chit** (✆ 02936-2841), Kampaengphet 2 Road, near the **Chatuchak Weekend Market,** and a short taxi or bus ride from Mo Chit BTS or MRT stations.

Visitor Information

The **Bangkok Tourist Bureau** has offices at major junctions throughout the city. Call them with any questions at ✆ 02225-7612; or visit www.bangkoktourist.com. They provide basic information services, maps, brochures, and recommendations. Their main office is at 17/1 Phra Arthit Rd., just under the Phra Pinklao bridge, near Khao San, but they also operate out of the airports and in various kiosks around the city: opposite the Grand Palace, in front of MBK shopping mall, at River City mall, and along Sukhumvit. All offices are open Monday to Saturday from 9am to 4:30pm.

The **Tourism Authority of Thailand** (TAT; www.tourismthailand.org) offers general information regarding travel in Bangkok and upcountry, and has a useful hot line (✆ **1672**) reachable from anywhere in the kingdom; it's open daily 8am to 8pm. Ironically, TAT's offices are not always conveniently located for foreigners who don't read Thai. It has a kiosk at Suvarnabhumi International Airport's arrival floor, open daily 8am to 10pm, but their main office is off the beaten track, at 1600 New Phetchaburi Rd., Makkasan, Ratchathewi (✆ **02250-5500**).

USEFUL PUBLICATIONS   TAT produces an enormous number of glossy tourist brochures on destinations, including Bangkok; but beware, many may be outdated. Bangkok's free magazines, available in hotel lobbies, are more current. Look for *Where* or *Thaiways*, with maps, tips, and facts covering Pattaya, Chiang Mai, and Phuket. *BK Magazine* is a fun, free weekly with info on the capital's events (available at any Starbucks). English-language daily newspapers *Bangkok Post* and *The Nation* have sections devoted to Bangkok must-sees.

City Layout

Nineteenth-century photographs of Bangkok portray the busy life on the **Chao Phraya River,** where a ragtag range of vessels—from humble rowboats to sailing ships—crowded the busy port. This was the original gateway for early foreign visitors who traveled upriver from the Gulf of Siam. Rama I (r. 1782–1809), upon moving the capital city from Thonburi on the west bank to Bangkok on the east, dug a series of canals fanning out from the river. For strategic reasons, the canals replicated the moat system used at Ayutthaya, Siam's previous capital, in the hopes of protecting the city from invasion. The city waterways represented the primordial oceans that surrounded the Buddhist heavens. A small artificial island was cut into the land along the river-bank and became the site for the Grand Palace, Wat Phra Kaew (the Temple of the Emerald Buddha), and Wat Po. To this day, this quarter is referred to as **Ko** (island) **Rattanakosin.** This is the historical center of the city and the main tourist destination for day trips.

The canals, or *klongs*, continued eastward from Rattanakosin as the city's population grew. Chinese and Indian merchants formed settlements alongside the river to the southeast of the island. The mercantile district of **Yaowarat** (Chinatown) is a maze of busy back alleys. Its main thoroughfare, Charoen Krung Road (sometimes called by its former name, New Road), snakes southward, following the shape of the river. On the eastern edge of Chinatown, you'll find the arched **Hua Lampong railway station,** a marvelous example of fanciful Italian engineering that dates back to 1916.

Just beyond Yaowarat, along the river, lies **Bangrak** district, where foreign interests built European-style residences, trading houses, churches, and a crumbling colonial Customs House. **The Mandarin Oriental Hotel,** the Grande Dame of Bangkok (built in 1876), sits among them, one of the few great heritage properties left in town. Bangrak's main thoroughfares, Surawong Road, Silom Road, and Sathorn Road, originate at Charoen Krung, running parallel to Rama IV Road. Within Bangrak, you'll find many embassies, hotels and high-rises, restaurants, and pubs, as well as the sleazy nightlife at Patpong or glitzy gay clubs in Silom Soi 4.

Back to Rattanakosin, as you head upriver, you'll hit **Banglampoo,** home to Bangkok's National Museum, Wat Suthat, the Giant Swing, and Klong Phu Khao Thong (Golden Mount). Its central point is **Democracy Monument,** a traffic circle where the wide Ratchadamnoen Klong Road intersects Dinso Road. Around the corner is Khao San Road, which was once solely a backpacker hangout. It's still clinging onto its hippy past and has budget accommodation, inexpensive restaurants, lots of tour agents, and good nightlife—but is also heading into the mainstream. Starbucks and Burger King are all muscling in on the once funk-filled, alternative vibe here.

Farther north of Banglampoo is leafy **Dusit,** home to Wat Benchamabophit, Vimanmek Palace, the Dusit Zoo, and parks.

As Bangkok spread on the east shore of the river, **Thonburi,** the former site of the capital across the river, remained in relative isolation. While Bangkok was quick to fill in canals, ushering in the age of the automobile, residential Thonburi's canals remained, and a longtail boat ride through the area is a high point of any trip here. Thai riverside homes, both traditional and new, and neighborhood businesses (some housed in floating barges) reveal glimpses of life as it might have been 200 years ago. Access to Thonburi's **Bangkok's Southern Bus Terminal** is via the Phra Pinklao Bridge from Banglampoo.

Back on the other side of the river, Bangkok grew and fanned eastward. From Ko Rattanakosin, beyond Bangrak, lies **Pathumwan,** known for its huge market. American Thai silk connoisseur **Jim Thompson** lived in Thailand for over 20 years from the 1940s until the 1960s, and his stunning house, located opposite the National Stadium, is open to visitors daily. Nearby is busy **Siam Square,** with its myriad boutiques and huge shopping malls. This area's hotels, cafes, and nightclubs attract scores of local teenagers and students. Beyond Pathumwan, **Wireless (Witthayu) Road** runs north to south, between **Rama IV Road** (at the edge of Bangrak) and **Rama I Road** (at the edge of Pathumwan). Here, the huge U.S. Embassy complex stands just meters from a clutch of five-star hotels and chic shopping centers such as **All Seasons Place** and **Central Chidlom.**

From Siam Square, **Sukhumvit Road** extends due east, its length traced by the BTS. Many expatriates live along the small side streets, or *sois*, that branch out from Sukhumvit. This area is lined with tourist restaurants and entertainment spots, and big malls—you'll find luxury hotels alongside inexpensive accommodation, fine dining, and cheap local eats, as well as clothing stores and street-side bazaars. (Be aware that there are also lots of schemers in this area.) Easterly situated Sukhumvit is mostly a major commercial center and much of it is connected by the overhead BTS. **Bangkok's Eastern Bus Terminal** is at Ekkamai BTS, on Sukhumvit Soi 63.

FINDING AN ADDRESS   Note that even-numbered addresses are on one side of the street and odd-numbered ones the opposite, but they are not always close to each other. So 123 and 124 Silom Rd. will be on opposite sides of the street, but possibly 300m (nearly 1,000 ft.) or even farther apart. Most addresses are subdivided by a slash, as in 123/4 Silom Rd., which indicates that a particular plot has been subdivided into several sections. Some addresses also include a dash, which means that the building itself occupies several plots. You'll find the term *thanon* frequently in addresses; it means "street" in Thai. *Soi* is a lane off a major street and is either numbered or named. If you are looking for "45 Sukhumvit Soi 23," it means plot 45, on Soi 23, off Sukhumvit Road. On Sukhumvit Road, even-numbered *sois* will be on the south side (look for landmarks such as **JW Marriott, Sheraton Grande Sukhumvit,** or **Emporium Shopping Mall**) and odd-numbered *sois* on the north side (same as **Robinson's** and **Thong Lor**).

Neighborhoods in Brief

Hotels, restaurants, and attractions have been subdivided into smaller regions within the city.

On the River Bangkok's grandest riverside hotels are all clustered near Saphan Taksin. You'll find wholesale silver, jewelry, and antiques stores along Charoen Krung (New) Road and Soi Oriental. Farther upstream, colonial buildings and churches give these old rundown districts a certain charm. Across the river in Thonburi, you can discover Thai dance shows and theater, as well as low-cost riverside diners and luxury spas.

Yaowarat or Chinatown Also along the riverside and just south of the Grand Palace area and Banglampoo, Chinatown is a frenetic maze of stores, old trading warehouses, and great places to eat.

Banglampoo & Historic Bangkok Home to the Grand Palace, this area lies within the area known as Ko Rattanakosin. It contains the city's most important historical sites, including the Grand Palace, Wat Phra Kaew, and Wat Po, as well as the Dusit Zoo and Vimanmek Palace Museum. Within the area are numerous historic *wats* (temples), the National Museum, and the National Theater and Library. Khao San Road is the city's former backpacker district, and moderate accommodation are located among the many budget guesthouses. The only drawback here is that it's a real trek to get to the BTS or MRT.

Bangrak This area likes to think of itself as the Central Business District, though its "downtown" label is debatable. It is bound by Rama IV Road on the north, Yaowarat (Chinatown) on the northwest, and Charoen Krung (New) Road due west, while Silom and Surawong roads run through its center. Many banks, businesses, and embassies have offices in this area, but it is also a good choice for travelers, with malls—such as the Silom Complex—reasonably priced restaurants, tourist hotels, and the seamier Patpong red-light area.

Sukhumvit Road, Ploenchit Road, & Chit Lom Known as Rama I Road at its western end, this main east–west thoroughfare is straddled overhead by the BTS. After crossing Ratchadamri Road (at the Erawan Shrine), it then becomes Ploenchit Road and runs directly east, crossing Witthayu (Wireless) Road at Chit Lom BTS (for CentralWorld department store), until it finally becomes Sukhumvit Road at the mouth of the airport freeway. Hotels, shopping complexes, office buildings, and some smaller embassies serve a thriving expat community here. Though rather far from the historic sites, it's convenient for shopping and nightlife.

GETTING AROUND

The city has three bus stations (p. 60) and the main train station is Hua Lampong (p. 60), with another station called Bangkok Noi (p. 60), from where trains head south and west to Kanchanaburi. Within the city, taxis and tuk-tuks (three-wheeled motorized open vehicles) cruise the small streets. (**Note:** The latter often turn out to be more expensive than the former.) Motorcycle taxis cost little but are unsafe: They're useful only for short hops down *sois* and helpful only if you know your destination in Thai. The BTS (or Skytrain) is the city's efficient elevated rail line, while the subway is known as the MRT. Both connect with the main Hua Lamphong train station, but neither reaches the city's two airports.

Bangkok's taxis are quite affordable and the best choice for door-to-door transportation—depending on the traffic. It can take more than 2 hours by taxi to get from one side of town to the other during rush hour. The good news is that, with the convenient BTS and MRT lines (as well as the Chao Phraya River's many boats, which act as daytime river taxis), you can avoid the standstill in the city center. Access to the town's modern and effective public transport is often a key factor in visitors' choice of accommodation and dining, and such areas as Khao San Road, detached from the better modes of transport, are decreasing in popularity when compared to places such as Sukhumvit and Silom.

See the inside front cover of this book for a map of the Bangkok metro lines.

BY BTS   The **Bangkok Transit System (BTS)** is called "*rot fai fa*" by Thais, which translates as "skytrain"—an apt description. It opened in 1999 and is the best way to get around Bangkok. Sadly, its lack of elevators makes it unsuitable for the physically challenged or those who can't cope with lots of stairs. While coverage is still limited, several extensions will be added in coming years to follow the Silom Line extension to Wongwian Yai, which opened in 2009, and the Sukhumvit Line extension to Bearing, which opened in 2011. The efficient and air-conditioned (though often crowded) train system provides good access to Bangkok's commercial centers. The Silom Line runs from Wongwian Yai in Thonburi across the Chao Phraya River at Saphan Taksin (Taksin Bridge), then through the Silom area to Siam Square. The interchange point for the Sukhumvit Line is at Siam BTS, from where the Sukhumvit Line goes north to Chatuchak Weekend Market (at Mo Chit BTS), or east, along the length of Sukhumvit road to Bearing BTS.

Single-journey tickets cost from 15B to 40B. For single trips, it's fairly straightforward to buy tickets at the vending machines that have place names spelled phonetically in English; you can get small change at the information booth as needed. All ticket types let you through the turnstile and are required for exit, so be sure to hang on to them. You can also buy the **Sky Smart Pass** that can be topped up (you simply sweep them over sensors at the turnstile) for 100B plus a 30B nonrefundable deposit. It's used up as you travel and lasts 5 years. Alternatively there's a **1-day unlimited travel ticket** for 120B, as well as **30-day Smart Passes** (check student and adult fares), which, though they also require a deposit, save you from fumbling for change at the vending machines every trip. These multitrip cards give you discounted rates, thus counterbalancing the small deposit.

Hours of operation are daily between 6am and midnight. For route details, maps, and further ticket info, check **www.bts.co.th/en/index.asp.**

BY SUBWAY   Bangkok's **Mass Rapid Transit (MRT)** was completed in 2004. The 18-stop system will be extended in the future. Beginning at Hua Lampong Train Station, the MRT heads southeast past Lumphini Park before turning north, up to Lad Phrao, and then makes a wiggle westward to Bang Sue. It has a messy and confusing interchange outside the Dusit Thani Hotel, 100m (328 ft.) from Sala Daeng BTS (on Silom Rd.) and also at Asok BTS (on Sukhumvit Rd.) before its terminus near Mo Chit Bus Station in the north and the Chatuchak Weekend Market. Trains run from 5am to midnight and the system uses small plastic discs or stored-value Smart Passes, which, like the BTS Sky Smart Pass, are swept over sensors. A **1-day pass** costs 120B, while a **3-day pass** costs 230B. The official website, www.bangkok metro.co.th, is not half as useful as **www.bangkok.sawadee.com/mrta.htm.**

BY PUBLIC RIVERBOATS   Efficient and scenic, but not so comfortable, the public riverboats on the Chao Phraya are a great way to get around the sites in the city center and are a remarkable window into local life. Most sightseers will board at Central Pier, down the steps from Saphan Taksin (Taksin Bridge) BTS. The major stops going upstream from Saphan Taksin are Tha Ratchawong (for Chinatown), Tha Thien (near Wat Po), and Tha Chang (near the Temple of the Emerald Buddha).

The tourist boats operated by the **Chao Phraya Express Boat Co.** (✆ **02623-6001;** www.chaophrayaexpressboat.com) offer the most relaxed way to travel along

Surfing by Canal Boat

Canal boating is a fun if somewhat odorous way to beat rush-hour traffic, allowing you to cross Bangkok from a starting point close to the Grand Palace and trek across to Sukhumvit through the commercial heart of the city. A narrow, dirty canal, Klong Saen Saep, runs the length of New Phetchaburi Road, with stops in central Bangkok (and all the way to Thong Lor, after a change at Krung Kasem Rd.). These long, low boats are designed to fit under bridges and are fitted with tarps that are raised and lowered by pulleys to protect passengers from any toxic splashes. Rides start at just 14B. Board the boats just north of Wat Mahathat. These canal buses really zip along and churn up a stink, but they offer a unique perspective on the last vestiges of what was once called the "Venice of the East," and taking one gets you through central Bangkok without having to inhale noxious bus fumes in motionless traffic.

this busy river. These steady, wide-bodied vessels are huge and have plenty of seats and make regular stops along the river. Microphone-equipped guides explain in English about the sites you pass. The last boat leaving Taksin Bridge is at 4pm. **Short trips** start at 13B, but you can also buy an **all-day pass,** which includes a map showing all piers and nearby attractions, for 150B. This allows you to hop off and on at will. Boats take about 30 minutes to go from Taksin Bridge to Banglampoo.

Cross-river ferries are small ferries that run only from the east bank to the west, so they're useful for getting to such places as Wat Arun, Klong San Market, or Patravadi Theater. They cost about 3B each way.

BY CHARTERED LONGTAIL BOAT   Private boats are a great way to see the busy riverside area and to tour the narrow canals of neighboring Thonburi, though you might want to pack a pair of earplugs for the experience. Boat charters are available at any pier. You can wave one down and, within seconds, you'll be greeted by the shouts of operators. But it's more convenient and probably safer to arrange trips at the riverfront kiosk at **River City** or at the **Grand Palace** (✆ **02225-6179**). If you want a guide, check for one with a TAT license, as you're less likely to be overcharged. Trips of varying length cost up to 1,000B per hour, per boat (1–6 people)—though drivers will try to get more. Be specific about destinations and times before you agree to one.

BY PUBLIC BUS   Bangkok buses are very cheap, frequent, and fairly fast, but a little bit confusing and not user-friendly in terms of helpful ticket takers, or simply marked routes and stops. There are big blue buses with air-conditioned routes and also cheaper red or small green ones (non-air-conditioned). Anyone with asthma or respiratory conditions would do well to avoid these fume-filled tin cans. You'll need to be especially careful of pickpockets on buses, too.

The most practical air-conditioned routes are A1 (looping from the Grand Palace area to Rama IV Road, Siam Square, and then east down Ploenchit and Sukhumvit roads), A2 (running a loop through the Business District [Bangrak] area along Silom and Surawong roads), A3 (connecting the Dusit area near the zoo and Khao San Road before crossing the Chao Phraya), and A8 (running the length of Rama I, Ploenchit, and Sukhumvit roads). Fares are collected onboard, even for air-conditioned routes— try to have exact change. Fares are cheap, between 12B and 24B.

5

SETTLING INTO BANGKOK

Getting Around

BY TAXI   Taxis are everywhere in this city—except, of course, during a change of shift (3–4:30pm) and in heavy rain. But when they do appear, they are very affordable. Just flag them down (you can hail taxis along any road at any time, or join lines in front of hotels and shopping malls), and always insist that drivers use the meter. At night, especially around Patpong and the Oriental Hotel, stationary taxis will try to fleece passengers with demands for an extortionately high flat fare. Let these sharks be, and opt for flagging one down that's already traveling along the main road.

Taxis charge a 35B flag fare which covers the first minute; thereafter, it is about 5B per kilometer. Most Thai drivers do not speak English or read maps, so it's good to have your hotel concierge write out any destination in Thai.

Drivers rarely carry change. The best you will get is change from 100B notes, but drivers habitually claim that they have no change in the hope of getting a bit extra. Tipping is not necessary, but a small tip is appreciated.

BY CAR & DRIVER   You'd have to be a certified lunatic to drive yourself around Bangkok: Generally anarchic traffic, seas of cavalier motorbikes recklessly breaking every rule, and aggressive tactics by (sometimes amphetamine-fueled) cabbies and truck drivers are the norm. If you're in search of your own wheels, it is best to hire a car with a driver. Reputable companies provide sedans or minivans with drivers who know the city well, some of whom speak English. They also offer the option of an accompanying tour guide—professionals or students who can take you around each sight. The best hotels provide luxury vehicles with an English-speaking driver; otherwise, companies like **Sea Tour** (② 02216-5783) and **Avis** (2/12 Witthayu/Wireless Rd.; ② 02251-1131; www.avisthailand.com) offer chauffeured cars with an English-speaking driver or guide, but it will cost in the region of 8,000B per day (8 hr.).

BY TUK-TUK   As much a national symbol as the elephant, the tuk-tuk (named for the sound) is a small three-wheeled, open-sided vehicle powered by a motorcycle engine. It is noisy, smelly, and incredibly cramped for long legs but definitely provides an adventure, especially for first-time visitors to Thailand. They're not recommended for long hauls or during rush hour—if you get stuck behind a bus or truck you'll be dealing with unpleasant exhaust fumes and the resulting migraines. Tuk-tuks are also deathtraps in the event of an accident (and the drivers tend to be a bit kamikaze), so avoid using them on highways. For short trips off highways, during off-peak hours, though, they're convenient. All tuk-tuk fares are negotiated, usually beginning at 50B for foreigners on short trips. Bargain very hard, but know that you'll always pay 100% more than locals.

A warning: Tuk-tuk drivers are notorious for trying to talk travelers into shopping trips or stops at brothels masquerading as massage parlors. They will offer you a very low fare but then dump you at small, out-of-the-way gem and silk emporiums, and overpriced tourist restaurants or brothels. Insist on being taken to where you want to go directly or mention the word *poleet*; this is how Thais pronounce "police."

BY MOTORCYCLE TAXI   On every street corner, packs of drivers in colored, numbered vests stand by to shuttle passengers around the city. Though they get you around fast when you're in a hurry (weaving through traffic jams and speeding down one-way streets the wrong way), they're also incredibly unsafe. These guys don't bother with safety, or insurance, and they stay awake on long shifts with the help of energy drinks. Use them strictly for short distances (they're popular for short hops to the end of a long *soi*, or side street). They charge from 20B for a few blocks to 60B for greater distances. Hold on tight and keep your knees tucked in. Crash helmets are mandatory these days—so insist on one, but know the flimsy head wear on offer will be almost useless in the event of a crash.

ON FOOT In general, Bangkok is not a pedestrian-friendly city, though improvements have been made in the city center with the construction of skywalks. Bangkok sidewalks are a gauntlet of buckled tiles, loose manhole coverings, and tangled (live) wires. The city also suffers greatly from flooding; be on guard and don't wear open shoes in monsoon season. In addition, Bangkok's pedestrian traffic—particularly in the overcrowded BTS and at rush hour—moves at a painfully slow amble at best, infuriating folks in a hurry. It's best to go with the flow; otherwise, you'll only aggravate yourself. In commercial areas, street vendors take up precious sidewalk space (except on Mon). When crossing busier streets, look for pedestrian flyovers, or, if you have to cross at street level, find others who are crossing and follow them when they head out into traffic. Unlike in Western countries, crossing lights only serve as suggestions here—drivers rarely stop to allow pedestrians to cross.

[Fast FACTS] BANGKOK

ATMs See "Fast Facts: Thailand," in chapter 14.

Banks Many international banks also maintain offices in Bangkok, including **Bank of America,** 87/2 CRC Tower, Witthayu (Wireless) Road. (② 02305-2800); **JP Morgan Chase,** 20 Sathorn Nua Rd. (② 02684-2000); **Citibank,** 82 Sathorn Nua Rd. (② 02232-2000); **National Australia Bank,** 90 Sathorn Nua Rd. (② 02236-6116); and **Standard Chartered Bank,** 90 Sathorn Nua Rd., Silom (② 02724-6327). However, even if your bank has a branch in Thailand, your home account is considered foreign here; conducting personal banking will require special arrangements before leaving home.

Business Hours Government offices (including branch post offices) are open Monday to Friday 8:30am to 4:30pm, with a lunch break between noon and 1pm. Businesses are generally open 8am to 5pm.

Small shops often stay open from 8am until 7pm or later, all week. Department stores are generally open 10:30am to 9pm. **TOPS** and **Villa** supermarkets close at 10pm, but there is a 24-hour **Villa Supermarket** on Sukhumvit Road, almost opposite **The Emporium.**

Car Rentals See "By Car & Driver," under "Getting Around," above.

Climate See "When to Go," in chapter 2.

Embassies & Consulates Your embassy in Thailand can (to an extent) assist you with medical and legal matters. Contact them immediately if there is a medical emergency, if you've lost your travel documents, or if you need urgent legal advice. The following is a list of major foreign representatives in Bangkok: **Australian Embassy,** 37 S. Sathorn Rd. (② 02344-6300); **British Embassy,** 14 Witthayu (Wireless) Rd. (② 02305-8333); **Canadian Embassy,** 15th Floor, Abdulrahim

Place, 990 Rama IV Rd. (② 02636-0540); **New Zealand Embassy,** 14th Floor, M Thai Tower, All Seasons Place, 87 Witthayu (Wireless) Rd. (② 02254-2530); and the **Embassy of the United States of America,** 95 Witthayu (Wireless) Rd. (② 02205-4000). Listen carefully to the phone prompts for after-hours helplines.

Emergencies In any emergency, first call **Bangkok's Tourist Police,** who can be reached at a direct-dial four-digit number, ② 1155, or at ② 02678-6800. Someone at both numbers will speak English. In case of **fire,** call ② 199 or 191, both of which are direct-dial numbers. **Ambulance service** is handled by individual, private hospitals; see "Hospitals," below, or call your hotel's front desk. For operator-assisted **overseas calls,** dial ② 100.

Eyeglass Repair Charoen Optical shops are on Surawong and Silom roads, and in many shopping areas; most can provide replacement glasses at reasonable prices. Always travel with a copy of your prescription. For eye problems, try the **Rutnin Eye Hospital** at 80/1 Sukhumvit Soi 21 (Soi Asok; ☏ **02639-3399**) or private hospitals (see below).

Hospitals All hospitals listed here offer 24-hour emergency service. Be advised that you may need your passport and a deposit of up to 20,000B before you are admitted. Make sure you have adequate travel insurance before you leave home. Major credit cards are accepted. **Bumrungrad Hospital,** 33 Soi 3, Sukhumvit Rd. (☏ **02667-1000;** www.bumrungrad.com), has respected—but costly—health practitioners and is the destination of choice in Bangkok for cosmetic surgery and (comparatively) affordable procedures. **BNH Hospital** (Bangkok Nursing Home), at 9 Convent Rd., between Silom and Sathorn roads (☏ **02686-2700;** www.bnhhospital.com), is extremely central; **Samitivej Hospital,** at 133 Sukhumvit Soi 49 (☏ **02711-8000**), is recommended for dentistry for young children, and for its maternity and infant wards.

Hot Lines There are regular meetings of **Alcoholics Anonymous (AA)** in Bangkok and around Thailand. Check their regional website, www.aathailand.org; or call the AA hot line at ☏ **02231-8300.**

Internet & Wi-Fi Cafes such as Starbucks offering free Internet or Wi-Fi are everywhere, especially along Sukhumvit and Khao San roads. Many hotels offer a prepaid Wi-Fi access card to guests. On Silom, near Patpong, you'll find the city's most expensive connections.

At **Suvarnabhumi International Airport,** there are cash and credit card touch-screen phones (close to Concourse G), and **Internet facilities** on Levels 2 and 4.

Lost Property If you have lost anything or have had your valuables stolen, call the tourist police hot line at ☏ **1155.** If you lose something in a taxi, try to recall the color of the cab, the time and place where you picked it up, and the time and place it dropped you off. Even better, remember the cab registration number. Most hotel front desk staff will know which cab company to call to report the loss and make an appeal based on those details. You will need to make a police report at the closest station to the place of loss.

Luggage Storage Suvarnabhumi International Airport offers luggage storage for 100B a day, 24 hours a day, on both the Arrivals and Departures level. Most hotels will allow you to store luggage while away on short trips.

Mail & Postage See "Fast Facts: Thailand," chapter 14, for rates and info on the Thailand mail

system. Head to the **General Post Office** (opposite Soi 45) on Charoen Krung Road., for all mail, telegraph, and parcel services, including **Western Union** money transfers. It's open Monday to Friday 8am to 8pm, and weekends 8am to 1pm. If you want to send valuables home, use courier services such as **DHL** (☏ **02345-5000**). Or call **Federal Express** (☏ **1782;** press 2 for English). If this proves too costly, check rates with **Express Mail Service (EMS),** available at post offices throughout the kingdom.

Newspapers & Magazines *Bangkok Post* and *The Nation*, both English-language dailies, cover local, national, and international news as well as happenings around town, TV listings, and other useful information. Also check out *Where*, a free listings monthly, and *BK Magazine*, a free weekly publication, which publish lighthearted commentaries and event listings for Bangkok.

Pharmacies Bangkok has many local pharmacies. Drugs dispensed here differ widely in quality and authenticity; if in doubt, visit a doctor and get prescribed drugs at a hospital or pick them up at an international store such as Watson's or Boots. There's a 24-hour pharmacy at **Foodland** Supermarket on Sukhumvit Soi 5 (☏ **02254-2247**).

Police Call the **Tourist Police** at ☏ **1155** or 02678-6800, open 24 hours, for assistance. English is spoken.

Radio & TV   In Bangkok, **Smooth 105FM** and **Easy FM 105.5** play back-to-back easy-listening pop, with little English.

Most TV channels broadcast local Thai programs or English-language programs, either dubbed or with subtitles. Cable channels, such as CNN, Australia Network, NHK, BBC World, France's TV5, Star Movies, HBO, MTV, and Star Sports, are readily available in serviced apartments and hotels.

Safety   In general, Bangkok is a relatively safe city, but be aware, at night, of drug-spiked drinks and, in daytime—especially on transport—of pickpockets. Do not incite trouble; avoid public disagreements and hostility (especially with

locals), and steer clear of gambling-related activities. If traveling alone at night, be alert, as you would in any city, and rely on your gut instincts; if you get a bad feeling about a place or situation, remove yourself from the scene. A Thai temper is virtually unheard of, but on rare occasions, it erupts, seemingly out of nowhere, and makes for (potentially lethal) confrontations.

Telephone, Internet Telephone, & Fax   If you want to make international calls, the easiest option is Internet cafes, which offer extremely cheap international call rates via Internet or Skype. Another option is to head to the **Communications Authority of Thailand (CAT) building,** next to the **General Post**

Office, on Charoen Krung (New) Road. All post offices and 7-Elevens sell prepaid phone cards for use with domestic or international calls. Public phones can be found all over the city, but they are not enclosed so can be very noisy. These phones may also charge calls to credit cards and AT&T calling cards.

For information on a number within the Bangkok metropolitan area, dial ✆ **1133,** or ask your hotel concierge or operator.

These days, fax services are offered by most small Internet cafes and hotels. A single A4 page of typewritten English faxed to the United States costs around 100B.

See "Internet & Wi-Fi," on p. 379, for more information.

WHERE TO STAY

Bangkok offers fantastic value for money, but remember that the hotel prices listed here are, on the whole, the highest *published* rates. Wherever hotels don't have published rates, I've used those from the Internet and, when there are numerous room types and rates, only a selection may be given. Many hotels offer promotional packages that include extras such as breakfast or airport transfers; some airlines also offer great deals on hotels. Unless otherwise noted, hotel rates are subject to a 7% government value-added tax and a 10% service charge. In the high season (mid-Oct to mid-Feb), make reservations well in advance. Most hotel rooms are smoke free, so you'll need to specify when booking if you are a smoker.

Note: Hotel websites and Internet sites such as **www.asiahotels.com** often offer special rates for four- and five-star hotels in Bangkok.

At the Airports

Hotels at **Don Muang** and **Suvarnabhumi International** airports are useful if you have a very-early-morning flight and don't want to become a nervous wreck on the way to the airport. **Amari Don Muang Airport Hotel** (www.amari.com; ✆ **02566-1020**) is linked by a bridge to the terminal and comes with a pool. Expect standard rooms from 2,975B. **Novotel Suvarnabhumi Airport** has no set check-in time, meaning you can stay for 24 hours from whenever you arrive. It is just 5 minutes' away from the airport on a free shuttle and offers four restaurants, plus a

Bangkok Hotels

Where to Stay

SETTLING INTO BANGKOK

70

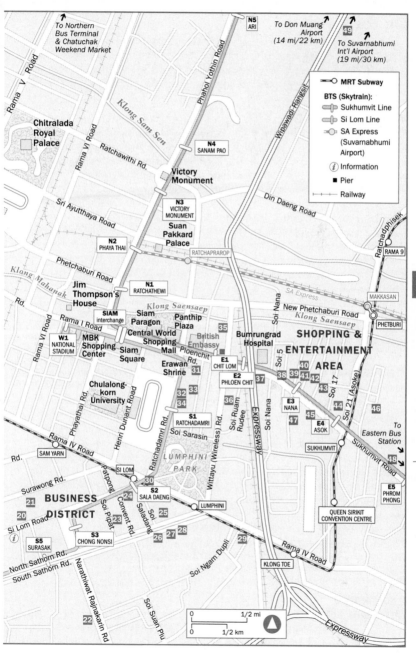

To Northern
Bus Terminal
& Chatuchak
Weekend Market

N5 ARI

To Don Muang
Airport
(14 mi/22 km)

49

To Suvarnabhumi
Int'l Airport
(19 mi/30 km)

Chitralada
Royal
Palace

Klong Sam Sen

Rama V Road

Rama VI Road

Ratchawithi Rd.

N4 SANAM PAO

Phahol Yothin Road

Wipawadi-Rangsit

MRT Subway

BTS (Skytrain):
Sukhumvit Line
Si Lom Line
SA Express
(Suvarnabhumi
Airport)

ⓘ Information
■ Pier
Railway

Sri Ayutthaya Road

Victory
Monument

N3 VICTORY MONUMENT

Din Daeng Road

Suan
Pakkard
Palace

Ratchadphisek

5

SETTLING INTO BANGKOK

Phetchaburi Road

N2 PHAYA THAI

RATCHAPRAROP

RAMA 9

Klong Mahanak

Rd.

Jim
Thompson's
House

N1 RATCHATHEWI

Klong Saensaep

SA Express

MAKKASAN

Soi Nana

New Phetchaburi Road

Klong Saensaep

PHETBURI

Rama VI Road

Rama I Road

SIAM interchange

Siam
Paragon

Panthip
Plaza

35

British
Embassy

Bumrungrad
Hospital

**SHOPPING &
ENTERTAINMENT
AREA**

Where to Stay

W1 NATIONAL STADIUM

MBK
Shopping
Center

Central World
Shopping
Mall

Soi 5

Phayathai Rd.

Siam
Square

Ploenchit
Rd.

E1 CHIT LOM

Soi Nana

38 39

40

41 42

Erawan
Shrine

31

E2 PHLOEN CHIT

37

43

Soi 17

Soi 21 (Asoke)

Chulalong-
korn
University

Henri Dunant Road

32 33

34

36

E3 NANA

44

46

Soi Ruam
Rudee

47

45

E4 ASOK

To
Eastern Bus
Station

S1 RATCHADAMRI

Soi Sarasin

Soi Nana

Rama IV Road

SAM YARN

Rd.

Ratchadamri Rd.

**LUMPHINI
PARK**

Wittayu (Wireless) Rd.

Expressway

SUKHUMVIT

Sukhumvit Road

48

E5 PHROM PHONG

SI LOM

21

**BUSINESS
DISTRICT**

20

ⓘ

Si Lom Road

Surawong Rd.

Patpong

Convent Rd.

Soi Pipat

30

S2 SALA DAENG

24

Soi
Saladang

23

25

S5 SURASAK

S3 CHONG NONSI

26

27 28

LUMPHINI

29

QUEEN SIRIKIT
CONVENTION CENTRE

Rama IV Road

North Sathorn Rd.

South Sathorn Rd.

Narathiwat Rajnakarin Rd.

Soi Ngam Dupli

Soi Suan Plu

KLONG TOE

22

0   1/2 mi
0   1/2 km

Expressway

business center, Wi-Fi, and fitness facilities. Rates run from around 5,000B per room (www.novotel.com; ✆ **02131-1111**).

On the River

A whole range of riverside hotels exists, all boast great views and most operate free shuttle boats along the teeming Chao Phraya River, which makes them handy for shoppers, diners, spa-goers, and anyone needing the BTS. The finest don't come cheap, but, in recent years, plenty of new and reasonable midrange choices have opened.

VERY EXPENSIVE

The Mandarin Oriental ★★★ ☺   Bangkok's oldest and best-known hotel has been frequented by Thai royalty and glitterati, as well as a long roster of sports and movie stars. Established in 1876, the hotel's original building has evolved into a modern, functional venue known for its exceptional service. But this grande dame does not rest easily on her laurels. Additions include two delightful pools, the revamped Sala Rim Nam restaurant (p. 100), a "Sanuk Sanuk" kids' club, and an Ayurvedic Penthouse at the Oriental Spa, proving the hotel is at pains to keep up with the times. Rooms and suites are furnished in Thai silks, using soft earthy tones or vivid hues; the older Garden Wing faces southwest onto the river, offering truly picturesque views. West-facing corner suites in the newer River Wing also have balconies overlooking the water. The hotel's restaurants, such as Le Normandie (p. 87), are all regarded as top-notch.

48 Oriental Ave., Bangkok 10500 (Soi 41, Charoen Krung Rd.). www.mandarin-oriental.com. ✆ **02659-9000.** Fax 02659-0000. 393 units. $410 superior; from $769 suite. AE, DC, MC, V. Saphan Taksin BTS. **Amenities:** 8 restaurants; lounge; bar; 2 outdoor pools; 2 lit outdoor tennis courts; squash court; health club & spa; children's club; room service; babysitting; ferry shuttle service. *In room:* A/C, TV, CD/DVD player, minibar, fridge, hair dryer, Wi-Fi (642B per day).

The Peninsula Bangkok ★★★   From its exclusive top-floor lounge bar, right down to its velveteen lawns at ground level, the Peninsula proves it is as classy as the rest. Located on the western banks of the river in Thonburi, it benefits from more dramatic views up and downstream than its nearby competitor The Mandarin Oriental. Its oversized rooms are luxurious, with all the amenities one expects of a five-star. Rooms reflect the perfect marriage of Thai tradition and high-tech luxury, with wooden paneling, silk wallpaper, and thick carpets. The large marble bathrooms have separate vanity counters and a large tub with a hands-free telephone and TV monitor built in. State-of-the-art business services and great shopping attract leisure and business guests alike, while the Peninsula Spa by ESPA, in a delightfully restored colonial-style house, is the perfect place to unwind. Guests can sign up to be part of the Peninsula Academy, which features guided walks of historic Bangkok.

333 Charoen Nakhorn Rd., Klongsan, Bangkok 10600. www.peninsula.com. ✆ **800/2828-3888** or 02861-2888. 370 units. 13,000B superior double; 14,000B deluxe; from 20,000B suite. AE, DC, MC, V. Saphan Taksin BTS. **Amenities:** 4 restaurants; 2 bars; pool; tennis court; health club; spa; room service; babysitting. *In room:* A/C, TV, minibar, hair dryer, CD player, Wi-Fi (free).

EXPENSIVE

Millennium Hilton ★★   Towering 32 stories over the west bank of the Chao Phraya River, the Millennium Hilton offers a stiff challenge to other riverside hotels with its fantastic views and comprehensive facilities. The Three Sixty Lounge on the top floor and infinity pool on a separate floor are particularly fine spots from which to admire the cityscape, and there are several restaurants to choose from. Rooms and suites are comfortably furnished and all have stylish work desks with high-speed Internet. When it's time for sightseeing, a shuttle boat is on hand to take guests across river to the Saphan Taksin BTS or to the River City shopping center.

123 Charoennakorn Rd., Bangkok 10600. www1.hilton.com. © **02442-2000.** Fax 02442-2020. 543 units. 4,800B–6,300B double; from 7,900B suite. AE, DC, MC, V. Shuttle boat from Saphan Taksin BTS. **Amenities:** 4 restaurants; 2 bars; outdoor pool; health club; spa; babysitting; cafe. *In-room:* A/C, TV, hair dryer, Internet (450B per day).

Praya Palazzo ★★★   This beautiful colonial mansion on the banks of the Chao Phraya River, originally constructed in 1923, has been lovingly restored to offer a very special experience to discerning guests who are looking for a hotel that offers a memorable stay. Its 17 rooms and suites are all individually designed and equipped with period furnishings that ooze character and the fact that the hotel is only accessible by boat helps to enhance the sense of privacy. Located on the west bank of the river opposite Phra Arthit Pier, it's ideally positioned for exploring the sights on Rattanakosin Island as well as indulging in the nightlife around Banglampoo. There's a swimming pool and lush gardens all around the two-story building, and the Praya Dining restaurant (p. 90) serves some of the best Thai cuisine in the city. A small library and a gallery are located beside the dining room, where informative boards tell the intriguing story of the mansion's history and painstaking renovation.

757/1 Somdej Prapinklao Soi 2, Bangyeekan, Bangkok 10700. www.prayapalazzo.com. © **02883-2998.** 17 units. 4,300B–7,700B double; 7,000B–14,700B suite. AE, DC, MC, V. Phra Arthit pier. **Amenities:** Restaurant; bar; outdoor pool; library. *In room:* A/C, TV, DVD player, minibar, hair dryer, Wi-Fi (free).

Shangri-La Hotel ★★★   The big, brassy Shangri-La, on the banks of the Chao Phraya, boasts acres of polished marble and a jungle of tropical plants and flowers surrounding the resort-style pool. Rooms are in two connecting wings, both with river views; the newer Krung Thep Wing has slightly smarter rooms and suites and offers a private pool and butler service. All rooms have elegant teak furniture and marble bathrooms. The views are better from the higher-floor deluxe rooms; some have either a balcony or a small sitting room, making them closer to junior suites—and a good value. The level of service and facilities is good and the stylishly contemporary Chi spa is superb. Underneath the Krung Thep Wing is the riverside swimming pool, and beyond, a large indoor-outdoor breakfast lounge. The hotel offers sunset river cruises on the Horizon II, a large motor cruiser equipped with live bands and broad outdoor decks.

89 Soi Wat Suan Plu, Charoen Krung Rd. (New Rd.), Bangkok 10500 (adjacent to Sathorn Bridge). www.shangri-la.com. © **866/565-5050** or 02236-7777. Fax 02236-8579. 802 units. From 6,100B double; from 9,500B executive suite. AE, DC, MC, V. Saphan Taksin BTS. **Amenities:** 4 restaurants; bar; lounge; 2 outdoor pools w/outdoor Jacuzzi; 2 outdoor lit tennis courts; 2 squash courts; health club w/aerobics classes; spa; room service; executive floors; dinner cruise; airport transfers. *In room:* A/C, satellite TV, minibar, fridge, hair dryer, high-speed Internet.

MODERATE

Anantara Riverside Resort & Spa ★★ ☺   Choose the Anantara Riverside (formerly the Bangkok Marriott) if you want to explore Bangkok and, at the same time, escape it. On the western banks of the Chao Phraya River and a few miles downstream from the heart of old Bangkok, this sprawling resort is accessed by shuttle boat or taxi. The three wings of the hotel surround a large landscaped pool area with lily ponds and fountains, and there is a Mandara Spa to soothe one's spirits. Children are well catered for with a kids' club and special activities programs. Recreation, dining, and drinking choices are many, including such familiar restaurants as Trader Vic's and Benihana, as well as the excellent Brio (Italian) and the indulgent Numero Uno bakery with its irresistible delicacies. There's also the popular Riverside Terrace restaurant, plus the Manohra cruises that offer the best dinner cruises in town (p. 133).

257/1-3 Charoen Nakhon Rd., Bangkok 10600. http://bangkok-riverside.anantara.com. (C) **02476-0022.** Fax 02476-1120. 413 units. 3,400B deluxe; 4,675B junior suite; 9,500B 1-bedroom suite premier. AE, DC, MC, V. Ferry to Central Pier. **Amenities:** 5 restaurants; bar and lounge; outdoor pool; 2 outdoor lit tennis courts; exercise room; spa; children's programs; room service; babysitting; airport transfers. *In room:* A/C, TV, minibar, fridge, Wi-Fi (1 hour free, then 425B per day).

Arun Residence ★★ ♦ This cool, arty hideaway comes with split-level suites, decorated in a colorful, unfussy, Thai-retro style, all with views across to its eponymous *wat* (temple). It's suited to those who want to feel at home in the thick of old Bangkok, as it's close to major sites. Though public transport isn't on your doorstep, the twinkling river is right there in front of you, and the property's lush plants and sun-filled lounge offer a uniquely Thai experience.

36–38 Soi Phratu Nokyung (Tha Maharaj), Maharaj Rd., Rattanakosin Island, Bangkok 10200. www.arunresidence.com. (C) **02221-9158.** Fax 02221-4493. 6 units. 3,500B deluxe; 5,500B suite with roof garden. AE, MC, V. Taxi from Hua Lamphong MRT. **Amenities:** Restaurant. *In room:* A/C, TV, DVD, minibar, fridge, Wi-Fi (free).

Ibrik Resort ★★ Pronounced "Eye-breek," this petite contemporary home, situated in Thonburi—a historic district where the first royal palace stood—is billed as a "resort by the river" but is more like a private home. Hidden in a narrow *soi*, its three bright, stylish rooms are all smoke free, with balconies overlooking the water. Its boutique size, small cafe, and location a few meters from the historic Wat Rakang make it popular with return visitors who want to explore more of the "real" Bangkok. Opposite is the Patravadi cafe and contemporary dance theater, and next door is Studio 9, a venue for weekend Thai dinner dances.

256 Soi Wat Rakang, Arunamarin Rd., Bangkoknoi, Bangkok 10700. www.ibrikresort.com. (C) **02848-9220.** Fax 02866-2978. 3 units. 4,000B. MC, V. Taxi from Hua Lamphong MRT. **Amenities:** Cafe. In room: A/C, TV, minibar, hair dryer, Wi-Fi (free).

Navalai River Resort ★ This newish riverside hotel has an excellent location (right next to Phra Arthit pier) and smartly furnished rooms with balconies. All rooms are bright with big windows, beige walls, and tiled floors, and those with river views are predictably more expensive, though they are worth going for as the rooms facing Phra Arthit Road can get noisy at night. There's a small rooftop pool and breezy restaurant beside the pier (Aquatini, see p. 99), both of which enjoy great riverside views, and staff are very helpful. There's also a 24-hour food store on site.

45/1-2 Phra Arthit Rd., Phra Nakorn, Bangkok 10200. www.navalai.com. (C) **02280-9955.** Fax 02280-9966. 74 units. 2,900B–4,300B double; 4,800B suite. AE, DC, MC, V. Taxi from Hua Lamphong MRT. **Amenities:** Restaurant; bar; rooftop pool. *In room:* A/C, cable TV, DVD player, Wi-Fi (free).

INEXPENSIVE

Bossotel Inn ♦ This cheap and cheerful option is not exactly on the river, but tucked away behind the Shangri-La, and offers reasonable accommodation at a fraction of the cost of its mammoth neighbor. A recent renovation has brought new life to its rooms, with bright, modern furnishings. Standard rooms are quite small so opt for "deluxe" if you want a more spacious stay—those at poolside present a good deal. You'll find the staff helpful; ask them about discount rates for longer stays. The quiet street in front has several homely cafes.

55/12–14 Soi Charoen Krung 42/1, Bangrak, Bangkok 10500 (on Soi 42, near Shangri-La Hotel). www.bossotelinn.com. ✆ **02630-6120.** Fax 02630-6129. 81 units. 1,800B–3,000B double; 4,500B suite. AE, MC, V. Saphan Taksin BTS. **Amenities:** 2 restaurants; small outdoor pool; exercise room; spa; room service. In room: A/C, TV, minibar, fridge, Wi-Fi (80B for 3hrs).

Sathorn, Silom, & Surawong

If Bangkok were to have one single business district (it actually has many), this would be it. The area between Surawong (also written Surawongse) and Silom roads contains the city's oldest shopping and tourist haunts—including the former G.I. haunt and today's red-light district, Patpong. Parallel to them is the busy eight-lane Sathorn Road, off which you'll find the city's bigger embassies, top hotels, police, and immigration HQs. Some hotels in *sois* off Sathorn (such as The Tivoli) even offer a shuttle to the Sala Daeng BTS. The one problem with this area is that it snarls up with static traffic every evening, but the Lumphini MRT stop at the top of Sathorn Road helps avoid the gridlock.

VERY EXPENSIVE

lebua at State Tower ★★★   Occupying the 64-story State Tower (easily spotted from afar by its gilded dome), this multi-award-winning stylish property is run by the same company responsible for the Dome's plethora of super-stylish dining joints, upstairs in the same building. The smallest suites here are a generous 66 sq. m (710 sq. ft.), but for an unforgettable experience, opt for a two- or three-bedroom suite in the Tower Club, which occupies floors 51–59 and offers dizzying views, though you'll need to sign a disclaimer if you want access to the balconies. Apart from offering some of Bangkok's most luxurious accommodation, lebua also hosts some of the city's top restaurants, such as Breeze (p. 92), on the 52nd floor, as well as Sirocco (p. 92) and the Sky Bar (p. 127), on the 63rd floor, which is ideal for a sundowner and has become something of an unmissable experience for all visitors to the Big Mango.

1055 Silom Rd., Bangrak, Bangkok 10500 (on the corner of Silom and Charoen Krung rds.). www. lebua.com/bangkok. ✆ **02624-9999.** Fax 02624-9998. 357 units. $389–$589 suite; from $709 2-bedroom suites. AE, DC, MC, V. Saphan Taksin BTS. **Amenities:** 6 restaurants; bar; lounge; outdoor pool; health club; sauna; room service. In room: A/C, TV/DVD, minibar, fridge, hair dryer, CD player, Wi-Fi (free).

The Sukhothai ★★★   This hip hotel is a maze of low pavilions, pools, and courtyards, deftly combining crisp, contemporary lines with Thai objets d'art, Thai silks, and rich tones. Colonnaded corridors surround lotus pools adorned with serried brick *chedis*; the terra-cotta friezes and the celadon ceramics are all motifs borrowed from its namesake city. Expansive guest rooms carry fine silk walls, mellow teak furniture, and rustic floor tiles; all have double bathrooms with oversize bathtubs, a separate shower, and toilet. The hotel's Thai restaurant, Celadon, is well established, while the modern La Scala is more relaxed (that is, until you see the check). The small gym is a popular appendage for its delightful dark-tile pool, meters away.

13/3 S. Sathorn Rd., Bangkok 10120. www.sukhothai.com. ✆ **02344-8888.** Fax 02344-8899. 210 units. 7,800B–10,500B double; 11,500B–14,500B suites. AE, DC, MC, V. Lumphini MRT. **Amenities:**

6 restaurants; bar; lounge; outdoor pool; outdoor lit tennis court; squash court; health club w/ aerobics classes; spa; room service; babysitting. *In room:* A/C, TV, fax (in some), minibar, hair dryer, Wi-Fi (free).

EXPENSIVE

The Banyan Tree ★★★   This immense all-suite skyscraper hidden behind Thai Wah Tower provides some exceptional panoramas, a plethora of trendy dining venues, and a chic spa with spacious suites (including segregated wet-rooms for thalasso-therapy treatments). While the brown, gold, and black lobby decor indicates its five-star status, The Banyan Tree has a relaxed, resort ambience throughout its public areas, highlighting its claim to provide a slick resort in the city. Pier 59 and Vertigo are just two of its popular, upscale dining options; both come with great views, and the latter offers alfresco dining on the vertiginous roof. Feast on Chinese dim sum galore at Bai Yun, or sip champagne under the stars at Moon Bar. Given its stellar reputation in Asia, the skyscraper hotel is popular with Asian families and tour groups. Mention the Thai Wah building right out in front to ensure your taxi doesn't miss the theatrical torch-lit entrance; it's on a busy one-way highway.

21/100 S. Sathorn Rd., Sathorn, Pathumwan, Bangkok 10120. www.banyantree.com. ℂ **02679-1200.** Fax 02679-1199. 327 units. From 5,800B deluxe suite; from 8,300B suite. AE, MC, V. Lumphini MRT. **Amenities:** 6 restaurants; 4 bars; lounge; outdoor pool; health club; spa; room service. *In room:* A/C, TVs, minibar, fridge, hair dryer, daily newspaper, daily fruit platter, Wi-Fi (642B per day).

The Dusit Thani ★★   Once upon a time this was Bangkok's grandest address (and tallest building). Now this old girl just across from Lumphini Park—close to the BTS and the Rama IV flyover—has undergone an extensive renovation to bring her in line with her flashy new neighbors. Despite the traffic jams in the area, the hotel still has one of the best locations in the city. The large outdoor pool is surrounded by foliage, providing a great escape after a day of sightseeing. Carpeted rooms come with solid furnishings, work desk, padded headboards and bedside control panels, plus views over the teeming intersection and park. The hotel chain's Devarana Spa wows spa aficionados with its superbly Thai-style double suites and stellar treatments.

946 Rama IV Rd., Bangkok 10500. www.dusit.com. ℂ **02200-9000.** Fax 02236-6400. 517 units. From 5,000B double; from 9,300B suite. AE, DC, MC, V. Sala Daeng BTS. **Amenities:** 8 restaurants; bar; lounge; pool; driving range and golf school; health club; spa; room service; babysitting. *In room:* A/C, TV, fridge, minibar, hair dryer, high-speed Internet (free).

The Metropolitan ★★   From the moment you step into the hushed lobby with its minimalist decor, this superhip residence engulfs you in a restful mood, despite being hemmed in by a cluster of towers on busy Sathorn Road. Staff are extremely friendly and helpful, and the rooms, while not huge, are well-equipped with the latest gadgets, and broadband Internet connections. If you feel frazzled after a hectic day's sightseeing, head for the spa and indulge in the signature COMO Shambala massage. This will leave you lightheaded and ready to partake of the wholesome food on offer at Glow restaurant. The hotel's other restaurant, Nahm, is also causing a stir in gas-tronomic circles in the city. At night, enjoy a cocktail in the Met Bar, exclusively for the use of hotel guests and members, where DJs spin eclectic lounge sounds.

27 S. Sathorn Rd., Bangkok 10120. www.metropolitan.bangkok.como.bz. ℂ **02625-3333.** Fax 02625-3300. 171 units. From 8,500B double; from 11,500B suite. AE, MC, V. Lumphini MRT. **Amenities:** 2 restaurants; bar/club; outdoor pool; spa; room service. *In room:* A/C, TV/DVD, hair dryer, Wi-Fi (428B per day).

MODERATE

Anantara Bangkok Sathorn ☺   While most Anantara hotels are luxurious five-star properties, this one caters to a wide variety of guests (including some tour groups), and this is reflected in the lower rates. Service is still top-class, though it lacks the panache of rural resorts such as that in the Golden Triangle. The twin 37-floor towers are located just a 10-minute walk (or shuttle ride) to the BTS station, and the views from the upper floors are breathtaking. Many of the rooms have a kitchen and dining area, and all are spacious with smart, modern furnishings. All rooms have a small balcony and floor-to-ceiling windows, plus a work station with high-speed Internet access. The two-bedroom suites are ideal for families, and the 32-m (105-ft.) swimming pool, pampering spa, and generous buffet breakfasts are other reasons to consider a stay here.

36 Narathiwat-Ratchanakarin Rd., Yannawa, Sathorn, Bangkok 10120. www.anantara.com. ⓒ **02210-9000.** Fax 02210-9040. 425 units. 2,635B–3,315B double; from 4,335B 2-bedroom suite. AE, DC, MC, V. Chong Nonsi BTS. **Amenities:** 2 restaurants; bar; outdoor pool; kids' plunge pool; health club; spa; room service; airport transfers. *In room:* A/C, TV, kitchens (in some), minibar, Wi-Fi (free).

Luxx ★★   Luxx is a tiny boutique property that has completely remodeled itself within a narrow, 1970s façade. This contemporary hideaway is the new face of Bangkok; its fashionably minimalist size and prime location appeal to the young and style conscious. Within walking distance of Silom's shops and night market, but off the busy main drag of Silom, Luxx provides large airy rooms, flatscreen TVs, wooden barrel tubs, rain showers, and pebble gardens in an eclectic mix of Thai-Zen minimalism. Such perks as Wi-Fi, iPod docks, and breakfast in bed confidently affirm its claims to evoke a "home away from home" feel. They have recently opened a newer, bigger location, aptly titled Luxx XL, just north of Lumphini Park (see website for details).

6/11 Soi Decho, off Silom Rd., Bangkok 10500 (30m/164 ft. from Silom). www.staywithluxx.com. ⓒ **02635-8800.** Fax 02635-8088. 13 units. From 3,400B double; 6,100B suite. AE, DC, MC, V. Chong Nonsi BTS. **Amenities:** Room service. *In room:* A/C, TV/DVD, minibar, fridge, iPod docking station, Wi-Fi (free).

Narai Hotel & 222 (Triple Two) ★   This hotel duo is found 15 minutes' walk from Chong Nonsi BTS. The larger, much older Narai Hotel is a clean, comfortable standard hotel, popular with tour groups. Rooms are perfectly adequate, everything works, and service is amenable. Downstairs is the swish Italian restaurant and just next door is their sister venture, the newer and much smaller Triple Two (referring to its Silom Rd. address), which shares its pool and fitness facilities. Rooms here come with a sleek, contemporary look, with silk furnishings and traditional Thai fixtures that provide a gentle contrast to the ultramodern lines. Triple Two's indoor-outdoor downstairs dining venue is sadly overshadowed by constant traffic noise and fumes, but Silom Road offers lots of alternative shopping and dining options.

Narai Hotel: 222 Silom Rd., Bangrak, Bangkok 10500. www.naraihotel.co.th. ⓒ **02237-0100.** Fax 02236-7161. 474 units. From 1,900B double; from 4,200B suite. AE, MC, V. Chong Nonsi BTS. **Amenities:** 3 restaurants; bar; lounge; outdoor pool; exercise room; room service. *In room:* A/C, TV, minibar, fridge, Wi-Fi (free). **222 (Triple Two):** 222 Silom Rd., Bangrak, Bangkok 10500. www. tripletwosilom.com. ⓒ **02627-2222.** Fax 02627-2300. 75 units. 2,560B–3,560B double; 4,200B suite. AE, MC, V. Chong Nonsi BTS. **Amenities:** Restaurant; bar; room service. *In room:* A/C, TV/DVD, minibar, fridge, Wi-Fi (free).

Siri Sathorn ★ 🏨   Officially, this gorgeously contemporary apartment hotel is for long-stay guests, but those in the know can get day rates. It boasts a spacious, pared-down designer chic that mimics New York loft-style living. All suites have fully equipped kitchens, smooth wood, and stone floors; some come with superb terraces and most have tubs. There's a very cool bar and small diner downstairs, next to a private dining room, and a few meeting rooms too, for busy executives. The pool is shady, and the gym and yoga room is bright and clean. Considering the quality and size of accommodation, rates are a bargain, and the location, in the quiet, tree-lined *soi* Sala Daeng 1 means you're just a short walk to Silom Road and the Sala Daeng BTS.

27 Soi Sala Daeng 1, Silom Rd., Bangrak, Bangkok 10500 (btw. Sathorn and Silom rds.). www.siri sathorn.com. ✆ **02266-2345.** Fax 02267-5555. 111 units. 3,300B junior suite; from 3,500B 1-bedroom suite; from 5,500B 2-bedroom suite. AE, DC, MC, V. Sala Daeng BTS. **Amenities:** Restaurant; bar; pool; exercise room; spa; room service; babysitting; children's play area. In room: A/C, TV, kitchen, minibar, fridge, hair dryer, CD player, Wi-Fi (free).

Swiss Lodge ★   Just a short skip down Convent Road (off Silom Rd.), near the Sala Daeng BTS, is this cozy, convenient hotel. Swiss Lodge started out as a small guesthouse and is now a popular choice for business folks (many Europeans on long-stay) and travelers. Though it's near the red-light district of Patpong, there's no sleazy vibe to the place, and the front desk staff is friendly. Rooms are large and quite plain, with simple furnishings; but everything is clean, and there are plenty of amenities (including a small library). They have a decent restaurant with daily buffet, and the swimming pool is but a postage stamp, but not a bad escape.

3 Convent Rd., Silom, Bangkok 10500. www.swisslodge.com. ✆ **02233-5345.** Fax 02236-9425. 55 units. 2,000B–2,690B double; 3,490B suite. AE, MC, V. Sala Daeng BTS. **Amenities:** Restaurant; bar; small outdoor pool; room service. In room: A/C, TV, minibar, fridge, Wi-Fi (450B per day; free if booking through website).

INEXPENSIVE

Lub.d 🏷   Meaning "sleep well" in Thai, Lub.d is designed as a comfortable and sociable hostel for backpackers who want a base in the center of the city. It offers a variety of accommodation, from eight-bed dorms with shared washing facilities to private rooms with en suite bathrooms. Furnishings are minimal but functional, and all dorm beds have a reading light, power point, and personal locker to store gear. All rooms are air-conditioned and there's a big communal room where travelers can get refreshments and surf the Web, as well as a small theater for watching movies. This original branch is well located on a side street off Silom Road, and there's also a newer branch in Siam Square (see website for details).

4 Decho Rd., Suriyawong, Bangkok 10500. www.lubd.com. ✆ **02634-7999.** Fax 02634-7510. 36 units. 550B dorm; 1400B–1800B double. MC, V. Chong Nonsi BTS. **Amenities:** Bar; cafe. In room: A/C, cable TV (in some), lockers (in dorms), Wi-Fi (free).

Silom Convent Garden ★★ 🏷   With an excellent central location, this apartment-cum-hotel is suited for longer stays or short stints (day, weekly, monthly, or yearly rates are offered accordingly), and all rates include breakfast. Rooms are clean, bright, and contemporary, and come with the added bonus of being equipped with kitchenettes and communal laundry facilities, while being just a few paces from Soi Convent and busy Sathorn Road. The petite building is decked out in bright colors and showcases good taste. Long stays warrant a bit of haggling, but prices remain incredibly affordable (as long as you ensure the electricity charges do not come with a hefty surcharge). Check the website for deals.

35/1 Soi Piphat 2, Convent Rd., Bangkok 10500. www.silomconventgarden.com. ⓒ **02667-0130.** Fax 02667-0144. 44 units. Daily rates 2,000B double, 4,800B suite. Rates include breakfast. AE, DC, MC, V. Sala Daeng BTS. **Amenities:** Restaurant. *In room:* A/C, TV, kitchenette, Wi-Fi (free).

The Tivoli ★★ 🎁 The tiny Tivoli outsmarts the competition. This wonderfully friendly, midsize hotel is set some way back from the fumes and traffic of Sathorn Road (and also accessible via Rama IV). Unusually, this hotel offers different rates for both single and double rooms, but all are superbly decorated in a contemporary Thai style and offer exceptional value. The hotel helpfully provides a free tuk-tuk to those guests heading to the shops, renewing a visa at immigration HQ, or seeing a doctor at nearby BNH hospital. It's a 5-minute ride to the Lumphini MRT station and an 8-minute ride to Silom in good traffic. Few Bangkok hotels of this range offer this luxury and service standard, plus the bonus of a rooftop swimming pool and spa.

71/2–3 Soi Sri Bumphen, Yen-Arkart Rd., Thungmahamek, Sathorn, Bangkok 10120. www.thetivoli hotelbangkok.com. ⓒ **02249-5858.** Fax 02249-2992. 133 units. 2,000B double, 6,000B suite. AE, DC, MC, V. Sala Daeng BTS. **Amenities:** Restaurant; bar; outdoor pool; spa. *In room:* A/C, TV/DVD, fridge, hair dryer, Wi-Fi (400B per day).

Sukhumvit Road Area

Accessed along its entire length by the convenient BTS, Sukhumvit Road is the heart of commercial Bangkok. Here you'll find many of the town's finest large shopping complexes and restaurants, as well as busy street-side shopping and dining stalls. Many businesses line this endless thoroughfare, and the small lanes, or *sois*, are crammed with bars and clubs—not all of them tacky hooker joints. Tourists as well as business travelers will find this the most convenient location to stay in town, with many comfortable hotel options. There are a few good budget choices (which are much better than busy and inconvenient Khao San Rd.), and direct access to the BTS means you can get anywhere you need to go in town at any time of day—which is a bonus when gridlock strikes.

Note: Siam (pronounced *See-yam*) BTS lies at the heart of the Rajadaprasong shopping area. Covered walkways link it to a number of Bangkok's larger and swankier malls, but sadly there are few elevators for wheelchairs or baby strollers.

VERY EXPENSIVE

Hansar Bangkok ★★★ This eye-catching, irregular-shaped tower tucked back off of Ratchadamri Road (just a few steps from the BTS station) with its superb all-suite accommodation has proved a huge success since opening in early 2011. These suites are huge, ranging from 59–125 sq. m (635–1,346 sq. ft.), and those on upper floors have sweeping city views. They are equipped with all kinds of luxuries, from huge TVs to free-standing bathtubs, plus king-sized beds that offer a sound sleep. As you might expect from a member of Small Luxury Hotels of the World, service is excellent, with daily newspapers delivered to the door, a turn-down service, and a bucket of ice provided each evening. Add the hotel's good-sized pool, the Luxsa Spa, and three classy dining options, and you've got a Bangkok base with comprehensive comforts.

3 Soi Mahadlekluang, 2 Ratchadamri Rd., Bangkok 10330. www.hansarbangkok.com. ℰ **02209-1234.** Fax 02209-1212. 94 units. 11,000B–40,000B suites. AE, DC, MC, V. Ratchadamri BTS. **Amenities:** 3 restaurants; bar; outdoor pool; spa; health club; room service. *In room:* A/C, TV/DVD, kitchenette with washing machine (some suites), minibar (complementary), hair dryer, Wi-Fi (free).

St. Regis ★★★ This is one of the city's newest luxury hotels with a fantastic location overlooking the Royal Bangkok Sports Club and right next to the BTS station, making it very easy to move around. All rooms are a good size, with floor-to-ceiling windows, and are sumptuously equipped with king-sized beds with upholstered headboards. A butler is on call 24 hours a day, ready to help with your unpacking, packing, ironing, and any other service you might require. Another neat feature of this stylish hotel is the media hub next to the desk where you can plug in a notepad or iPad and connect them to the TV. The 15th floor is given over to health and wellness, with a pool, fitness center, and gorgeous spa with 15 treatment rooms.

159 Ratchadamri Rd., Bangkok 10330. www.starwoodhotels.com/stregis. ℰ **02207-7777.** Fax 02207-7888. 227 units. 14,000B-15,000B deluxe; 16,000B-70,000B suites. AE, DC, MC, V. Ratchadamri BTS. **Amenities:** 2 restaurants; 3 bars; outdoor pool; health club; spa; concierge. *In room:* A/C, TV/DVD, minibar, hair dryer, movie library, Wi-Fi (400B per day).

EXPENSIVE

Amari Boulevard Hotel ★★ Set back from the heaving sidewalks of Sukhumvit, the Amari is an upscale option that caters well to businessmen and tourists alike. This well-known triangular-shaped landmark sits like a wedge of cheese right in the heart of the busy bar and red-light district known as Nana, off Sukhumvit Road. Wide-ranging shopping and dining options are on your doorstep here, but the late-night sleaze of the surrounding *sois* may put off families—in which case, check out the posher **Amari Watergate** (ℰ **02653-9000**), a 10-minute drive away. Inside, the Amari Boulevard is a world away from Sukhumvit Road's seedier side. Nicely decorated, its rooms—albeit average size—have sunny color schemes and pleasant touches such as elegant Thai handicrafts and teak wood detailing. Deluxe rooms afford a few more luxuries including a separate bathtub and shower. There's free Wi-Fi in the lobby and friendly staff.

2 Soi 5, Sukhumvit Rd., Bangkok 10110. www.amari.com/boulevard. ℰ **02255-2930.** Fax 02255-2950. 309 units. From 5,600B double; 11,900B suite. AE, DC, MC, V. Nana BTS. **Amenities:** 2 restaurants; bar; outdoor pool; health club; babysitting; room service. *In room:* A/C, TV, minibar, fridge, hair dryer, Wi-Fi (428B per day).

Conrad Bangkok ★★★ On Witthayu (Wireless) Road, just a few doors down from the U.S. Embassy's Consular section, this fashionable high-rise springs out of the smart All Seasons Place complex, cluttered with expensive shops and fast-food outlets. The Conrad boasts an elegant medley of contemporary styles and confidently chic decor, with rooms decked out in rich, earthy colors and furnished with pretty artwork and faux antiques. A spa and beautiful pool terrace give a sense of serenity and the restaurants are all top class. The hotel is also home to two of the city's trendiest nightspots—the Diplomat Bar, with live jazz, and Club 87 Plus. Service is sleek and professional.

87 Witthayu (Wireless) Rd., Bangkok 10330. http://conradhotels1.hilton.com. ℰ **02690-9999.** Fax 02690-9000. 391 units. From 6,100B double; 12,600B executive suite. AE, DC, MC, V. Ploen Chit BTS. **Amenities:** 3 restaurants; bar; outdoor pool; 2 outdoor lit tennis courts; health club; spa; room service; executive floor; club. *In room:* A/C, TV, minibar, fridge, hair dryer, Wi-Fi (free in executive rooms; 450B per day in others).

The Eugenia ★★   Nostalgia is the name of the game at the Eugenia, which has just a dozen suites that are full of character in a renovated colonial building. Rooms are equipped with period furnishings and many of them have four-poster beds. The sun loungers by the pool, the Jaguars sitting in the garage, the gourmet food served in the D.B. Bradley dining room (named after a 19th-century American missionary), and afternoon tea in the Zheng He lounge (named after a great Chinese seafarer) are effective in captivating guests and transporting them to a bygone era.

267 Sukhumvit Soi 31, Bangkok 10110. www.theeugenia.com. ✆ **02259-9011-9.** Fax 02259-9010. 12 units. 5,800B–7,200B suite. AE, MC, V. Phrom Phong BTS. **Amenities:** Restaurant; lounge; outdoor pool. In room: A/C, Wi-Fi (free).

The Four Seasons Bangkok ★★★   The Four Seasons, Bangkok (formerly The Regent) is a smart, well-appointed low-rise property. The entrance and lobby are overwhelming, with a sweeping staircase adorned with giant Thai murals and detailed gold paint work on the high ceilings. The impeccable service begins at the threshold, and an air of luxury pervades the urban resort. Rooms are spacious, featuring handsome color schemes, plush carpeted dressing areas, and large bathrooms. Cabana Rooms face the large pool and terrace area, which is filled with palms, lotus ponds, and tropical greenery. The Four Seasons' dining is exemplary, especially at Shintaro and Biscotti (see p. 97 and p. 96). The concierge service is second to none in Asia. Close to the center of town and the Ratchadamri BTS, it's a real hideaway.

155 Ratchadamri Rd., Bangkok 10330. www.fourseasons.com/bangkok. ✆ **02126-8866.** Fax 02253-9195. 353 units. From 6,830B superior; 9,350B deluxe; 10,150B deluxe view; 21,000B cabana; from 22,580B suite. AE, DC, MC, V. Ratchadamri BTS. **Amenities:** 4 restaurants; lounge w/live music; outdoor pool; health club; spa; room service; babysitting; executive floor. In room: A/C, TV/DVD, minibar, hair dryer, Wi-Fi (428B per day normal; 717B per day premium).

Grand Hyatt Erawan ★★★   Where, in the 1970s, the former Erawan Hotel famously stood, the hulking white Grand Hyatt now stands. It enjoys a great central (if smog-bound) location, though pool loungers and residents of the delightful spa cottages are regularly looked over by commuters on the BTS. The hotel's design epitomizes the glamour and exuberance of the 1980s, with giant columns and staircases reminiscent of the TV show *Dynasty*. Spacious rooms are decked out in delightful silks, celadon ceramics, pseudoantique furnishings, and parquet floors. The bathrooms are equally generous, and city views abound. The excellent spa occupies an entire floor, while next door is the opulent Erawan shopping center (p. 123) and the glittering Erawan Shrine (p. 109).

494 Ratchadamri Rd., Bangkok 10330 (corner of Rama I Rd.). www.bangkok.grand.hyatt.com. ✆ **800/492-8804** or 02254-1234. Fax 02254-6308. 380 units. 6,600B–9,300B double; from 13,100B suite. AE, DC, MC, V. Phloen Chit BTS. **Amenities:** 4 restaurants; lounge; outdoor pool; tennis court; health club; spa; room service; babysitting; executive floor; club. In room: A/C, TV, minibar, hair dryer, Wi-Fi (717B per day).

JW Marriott ★★   JW Marriott's downtown hotel is a huge, black marble hive of action, with great eats, a fine spa, and unparalleled convenience. Business travelers love it for its extensive executive services and efficient staff, but it tends to be emptier over the year-end holidays—giving vacationers an opportunity to enjoy its luxuries without paying a premium. Close as it is to shopping along Sukhumvit Road and to the Nana BTS, Marriott's drawback is that it's slap bang in the heart of the go-go club zone, which attracts drunk or unsavory characters late at night. The health club is popular, with a pleasant outdoor pool that lends an urban oasis feel. Rooms are tastefully upmarket, with famously soft beds, handy desk space, and large marble bathrooms with a separate shower and large bathtub. Suites are vast. A bonus is the fact that the tollway serving both Bangkok airports is right on the doorstep.

4 Sukhumvit Soi 2, Bangkok 10110. www.marriott.com. ☏ **02656-7700.** Fax 02656-7711. 402 units. Double from 5,900B; 60,000B royal suite. AE, DC, MC, V. Nana BTS. **Amenities:** 6 restaurants; 3 bars; outdoor pool; health club; spa; room service; babysitting; executive floor. In room: A/C, TV, minibar, fridge, hair dryer, Wi-Fi (free for Marriott members; 642B per day for others).

Sheraton Grande Sukhumvit ★★★   Be sure to get the name of this Sukhumvit Road behemoth exactly right (the Royal Orchid Sheraton is miles away, on the river); this one is located near both BTS and MRT stations. Each room has great amenities, and the height gives it superb views. There is a renowned spa downstairs with top-notch wraps and hydrotherapy. The beautiful 10th-floor lagoon pool looks as if it's set in a jungle. The Sheraton Grande's style places it firmly upmarket and comes with some high-end dining choices that suit businesspeople—but may not always fall within tourist budgets. Popular ground-floor BarSu has regular live acts, while the third-floor Living Room hums with jazz nightly.

250 Sukhumvit Rd. (btw. sois 12 and 14), Bangkok 10110. www.starwoodhotels.com. ☏ **02649-8888.** Fax 02649-8000. 420 units. From 6,400B double; from 14,600B grande suite. AE, DC, MC, V. Asok BTS or Sukhumvit MRT. **Amenities:** 4 restaurants; bar; outdoor pool; health club; spa; room service. In room: A/C, TV/DVD, minibar, fridge, Wi-Fi (free in most expensive rooms; 470B per day in others).

MODERATE

City Lodge ★ 🍴   Budget travelers will appreciate the two small, spiffy City Lodges that come under the OAM Hotels group. The newer lodge on Soi 9 and its nearby cousin, the older (but better equipped and slightly pricier) 34-room City Lodge on Soi 19 (☏ **02253-7710;** fax 02255-7340; www.oamhotels.com/citylodge19), provide pleasant, modern rooms. Each has its own pasta restaurant and Wi-Fi in rooms. Low-season discounts of up to 50% mean you can get great value for your money. Both hotels are very convenient for shopping, bars, and the Skytrain.

137/1–3 Sukhumvit Soi 9, Bangkok 10110 (corner of Sukhumvit and Soi 9). www.oamhotels.com. ☏ **02253-7759.** Fax 02255-4667. 70 units. 2,100B standard, 2,300B superior. MC, V. Nana or Asok BTS. **Amenities:** Room service; babysitting; cafe; access to nearby health club and pool. In room: A/C, TV, minibar, fridge, Wi-Fi (free).

Dream Bangkok ★   This addition to the burgeoning hotel scene along Sukhumvit Road is at the cutting edge of modern style—indigo lights in the corridor and under-bed lighting create a true dreamlike aura. Just in case you're not ready to sleep, rooms are also equipped with large plasma TVs and high-speed Internet connections. Dining and drinking choices follow the stylish theme, with innovative dishes on the menu at Flava Restaurant and unusual cocktails in the Flava Lounge.

10 Sukhumvit Soi 15, Bangkok 10110. www.dreambkk.com. ☏ **02254-8500.** Fax 02254-8534. 195 units. $100–$120 double; $150–$380 suite. AE, DC, MC, V. Asok BTS or Sukhumvit MRT. **Amenities:** Restaurant; bar; outdoor pool; health club; spa. In-room: A/C, TV, minibar, Wi-Fi (free).

SilQ 🍴   SilQ is one of a growing breed in Bangkok—hotels with a bit of character that provide all essential amenities with a stylish touch and rates that won't burn a hole in your pocket. This one is conveniently located near BTS and MRT stations, making it easy to get around the city, and some of Bangkok's best shopping venues, such as Emporium (p. 122), are close to hand. Rooms have laminated oakwood floors, and are equipped with flatscreen TVs, reading chairs, and work desks. A generous breakfast (a mix of buffet and a la carte) and unlimited Wi-Fi use are included in the rates, making this an excellent deal.

54 Sukhumvit Soi 19, Bangkok 10110. www.silqbkk.com. ✆ **02252-6800.** Fax 02252-6809. 50 units. 2,700B–3,500B double. AE, MC, V. Asok BTS or Sukhumvit MRT. **Amenities:** Restaurant; bar. *In room:* A/C, TV, minibar, hair dryer, Wi-Fi (free).

Swissôtel Nai Lert Park ★★ ☺   Sitting in the verdant Nai Lert Park, this hotel offers an inner-city oasis. There are four room types—including rooms decked out for those traveling with kids—and no less than six kinds of suites. The decor is plush, with either classic or contemporary furnishings, and all have city or garden views from their sunny balconies. Its gym, pool, and tennis courts all back onto leafy forest, and the Amrita Spa adds a touch of luxury. The cool Syn bar is the talk of the town, and provides an enjoyable ambience. The hotel is on a busy one-way road that makes access to Sukhumvit Road difficult and time-consuming in traffic, but it's only a short, 8-minute walk from Ploen Chit BTS and CentralWorld Department Store.

2 Witthayu (Wireless) Rd., Pathumwan, Bangkok 10330. www.swissotel.com. ✆ **02253-0123.** Fax 02253-6509. 338 units. From 3,500B double; from 5,400B suite. AE, DC, MC, V. Phloen Chit BTS. **Amenities:** 4 restaurants; 2 bars; outdoor pool; 2 tennis courts; squash court; health club; spa; room service; deli. *In room:* A/C, TV, minibar, fridge, hair dryer, Internet (free).

INEXPENSIVE

Federal Hotel ★   The Federal has been providing affordable lodgings with reasonable levels of comfort for about 50 years now, so the place runs very efficiently and staff are eager to help solve any problems. The lobby and restaurant on the first floor are classic 1960s design but thankfully rooms upstairs have been regularly renovated. Rooms are compact but well-equipped with comfy beds and cable TV, and are set well back from street noise. There's a small but inviting pool, and free Wi-Fi and breakfast is included in the price.

27 Sukhumvit Soi 11., Bangkok 10110 (a 5-min. walk from Nana BTS). www.federalbangkok.com. ✆ **02253-0175.** Fax 02253-5332. 24 units. 1,300B–1,500B double. MC, V. **Amenities:** Restaurant; small outdoor pool. *In room:* A/C, TV, minibar, Wi-Fi (free).

Grand Business Inn ★   Despite the name, there's nothing fancy about the facilities at this midrange hotel, but its convenient location (just round the corner from a BTS station), capable staff, and well-maintained rooms make it worth considering for an inexpensive stay in the Sukhumvit area. The carpeted rooms have comfortable beds, a couple of chairs, and a small table (some have writing desks), as well as a fridge and TV. Wi-Fi doesn't extend to the rooms, but is available in the lobby area.

2/11 Sukhumvit Soi 11, Bangkok 10110. www.grandbusinessinn.net. ✆ **02651-1871.** Fax 02651-1617. 127 units. From 1,600B double; from 2,500B suite. AE, MC, V. Nana BTS. **Amenities:** Restaurant (24-hr); computers in lobby (free for guests); Wi-Fi (free). *In room:* A/C, TV, fridge.

Refill Now ★ ▮▮   A fun and friendly budget choice, this little upmarket backpackers' joint is a cool place, way above the rest. It's a bright, breezy find, with bunk beds (each with a locker) and communal bathrooms, a cozy restaurant, and a lot more style than some of the comparable budget options elsewhere. Though it's situated at the eastern end of town, it's within a 60B ride to Phra Khanong BTS, on Sukhumvit Road (just one stop east of Ekamai Bus Station). Don't be put off that its location is off most maps. It's become a hip hangout, so book online, no matter what the season.

191 Soi Predi Bhanomyong 42, Yak 5, Sukhumvit Rd., Soi 71, Bangkok 10110. www.refillnow.co.th. ☏ **02713-2044-6.** 24 bunk beds, 8 private rooms. $15 bed in dormitory; $38 private twin. MC, V. Phra Khanong BTS. **Amenities:** Restaurant. *In room:* A/C, Wi-Fi (free).

Stable Lodge 🏨 This Scandinavian-run hotel (under Danish management) is tucked away down one of Sukhumvit's quieter lanes and offers tidy, wood-floored rooms with private balconies; those overlooking the pool are the most desirable. Staff are super-friendly and can help out with your sightseeing plans. There's a small but inviting pool set beside an equally inviting restaurant and bar, which features a Scandinavian buffet on weekend lunchtimes.

39 Sukhumvit Soi 8, Bangkok 10110. www.stablelodge.com. ☏ **02653-0017.** Fax 02253-5125. 41 units. 1,500B-1,700B double. MC, V. Nana BTS. **Amenities:** Restaurant; bar; outdoor pool. *In room:* A/C, TV, minibar, Wi-Fi (free).

Suk 11 Guesthouse The rusticated Suk 11 is modeled on a primitive wooden Thai house and provides convenient access to the Nana BTS. Rooms are basic, and many of them are rather shabby, so be sure to look first; they range from singles with shared bathrooms to family rooms with en suite bathrooms, but walls in all are thin. Single and double rooms with en suite bathroom are the best bets. Rates include a basic breakfast, but there are some strict rules, such as no guests, food, or alcohol in the rooms, and be warned that there are no elevators in this four-floor building. There are some quiet sitting areas and even a yoga room. If it's all a bit too basic for you, check out their smart serviced apartments, Suk11@13, on nearby Sukhumvit Soi 13 (same contact details), where there's a full-size pool, health club, and, predictably, higher prices (around 2,150B).

1/13 Soi Sukhumvit 11 (behind 7-Eleven), Bangkok 10110. www.suk11.com. ☏ **02253-5927.** Fax 02253-5929. 70 units. 535B single with shared facilities; 963B double with en suite bathroom; 1,284B triple. No credit cards except online. Nana BTS. **Amenities:** Restaurant; Wi-Fi in lobby (10B for 10 minutes); yoga room. *In room:* A/C.

Banglampoo & Khao San Road

This now-fast-gentrifying area still caters to a core clientele of budget backpackers, aging hippies, and young Thai tourists, which makes for noisy nighttimes in the cheaper guesthouses. It is slowly trying to court more mid-range customers, though. Cheap eats and funky fashions abound here; so do thieves: Secure your room and valuables well. It is handy for visiting sights such as the Grand Palace and National Museum, but it's a long way from the Skytrain and subway, so getting around is a bit of a problem; most tourists hop on a river taxi from Phra Arthit pier to Saphan Taksin BTS.

MODERATE

Buddy Lodge ★ This is one of the area's best-known, smaller-sized hotels providing upscale accommodation. Rates are higher than for the guesthouses for sure, but this brings a modicum of comfort, with facilities such as a spa, a rooftop pool, air-conditioning, TV, and, most of all, security. It can get pretty raucous in the echoing hallways, but all rooms are clean, with a pretty 1930s Thai rustic look, wicker furnishings, and comfy beds; some rooms have balconies. You can dine in their popular restaurant or feast in the many nearby eateries. There's also a mall right next door.

265 Khao San Rd., Bangkok 10200. www.buddylodge.com. ☏ **02629-4477.** Fax 02629-4744. 76 units. From 2,500B double. MC, V. Taxi from Hua Lamphong MRT. **Amenities:** Restaurant; bar; outdoor pool; health club; spa. *In room:* A/C, TV, minibar, fridge, Wi-Fi (free).

Hotel De' Moc ★ A great midsized budget option, this 1960s hotel provides 100 spick-and-span guest rooms with air-conditioning and small balconies overlooking a mostly residential area near Democracy Monument (from where the hotel takes its name). There are simple but good-quality room amenities, doubles and triples, marble bathrooms, and Wi-Fi, plus the added bonus of complementary use of a daytime tuk-tuk shuttle to Khao San Road, as well as bikes and the gym at Buddy Lodge. Out back, there's a big concrete pool surrounded by trees. It's a world away from the swanky five-stars, but old-world charm rides high here nonetheless.

78 Prachathipatai Rd., Pra-Nakorn, Bangkok 10200. www.hoteldemoc.com. ✆ **02282-2831.** Fax 02280-1299. 100 units. From 2,800B double. AE, MC, V. Taxi from Hua Lamphong MRT. **Amenities:** Restaurant; bar; outdoor pool; access to nearby exercise room. *In room:* A/C, TV, fridge, Wi-Fi (free).

Viengtai Hotel 🍴 This old standby is just a few steps away from Khao San Road, and caters to an odd mix of thrifty business people and budget tourists; you're bound to bump into folks of all nationalities here. The recently renovated rooms are a good deal, and rates include breakfast. Regular doubles are a bit cramped but the triples and family rooms are huge. The hotel also has a pool—unusual at these rates—and helpful staff. The 24-hour restaurant features classical dance performances on Saturday evenings.

42 Rambutri Rd., Banglampoo, Bangkok 10200. www.viengtaikhaosan.com. ✆ **02280-5434-45.** 144 units. From 2,200B double; 3,000B family room. MC, V. **Amenities:** Restaurant; outdoor pool; Internet. *In room:* A/C, TV, minibar, Wi-Fi (200B per day).

INEXPENSIVE

Ban Sabai Located on a quiet lane just a few steps from Khao San Road, Ban Sabai is perhaps better known for its popular bar and restaurant, but it also offers 100 very basic rooms as cheap as anywhere you'll find in the city. Single rooms are tiny and have no windows; doubles are bigger and have windows. Don't expect much more than a bed and a hook to hang your clothes on, and the cheaper, fan-cooled rooms share bathrooms, but everything is clean and there's little traffic noise.

12 Soi Rongmai, Chaofa Rd., Chanasongkram, Phranakorn, Bangkok 10200. ✆ **02629-1599.** Fax 02629-1595. 100 units. 170B (single fan w/shared bathroom); 550B deluxe (double w/air-con). No credit cards. Phra Arthit pier. **Amenities:** Restaurant; bar. *In room:* A/C (in some).

Royal Hotel ★ Located on the broad Ratchadamnoen Avenue, this three-story brick colossus is a 5-minute walk to the Grand Palace, but rather isolated from other sites. As a result, the Royal is a great choice for budget travelers who find the crazies on Khao San to be too much and who don't mind a smattering of shabbiness among the 1950s polished floors, chandeliers, and Corinthian columns. The clean, kitschy rooms are spacious and comfy. A small pool and buffet breakfast are added luxuries. Regular political rallies in nearby Sanam Luang can make it noisy, so choose a room at the back.

2 Ratchadamnoen Ave., Bangkok 10200 (2 blocks east of National Museum). ✆ **02222-9111.** Fax 02224-2083. 300 units. 1,300B single; 1,800B double. AE, MC, V. Taxi from Hua Lamphong MRT. **Amenities:** Restaurant; lobby bar; outdoor pool; coffee shop; Internet (350B per day). *In room:* A/C, TV, minibar.

Chinatown

Yaowarat (Chinatown) is a cramped, pungent trip back in time, riddled with traffic jams and chaotic at best. But it's also one of the most fascinating mercantile districts of Old Bangkok, with great eats, sights, and color.

Chinatown Hotel ★   From the rather ugly exterior, you can tell the Chinatown Hotel is hardly going to be an architectural stunner, but behind the blue glass façade there are some decent, if diminutive, rooms, decorated to an acceptable level and the public areas are well kept. Among the many different types of room, the China Rooms are the most spacious and comfortable. All rooms include free Wi-Fi but the general hotel facilities are limited.

526 Yaowarat Rd., Bangkok 10100. www.chinatownhotel.co.th. ✆ **02225-0204.** Fax 02226-1295. 75 units. From 1,500B double; 3,700B China room. MC, V. Hua Lamphong MRT. **Amenities:** Room service; cafe. *In room:* A/C, TV, minibar, fridge, hair dryer, Wi-Fi (free).

Grand China Princess Hotel ★   Affordable and close to many attractions, this towering edifice peers down from 10 stories above, overshadowing the bustling shops and businesses of colorful Chinatown. Guest rooms are typical of a Chinese-style hotel, with all the useful amenities usually found in more expensive hotels, but without sparing Thai-style touches and character. Suites are particularly spacious, with a separate living area and panoramic views. The 25th floor features Bangkok's first revolving diner, with spectacular views over the city and Chao Phraya River.

215 Yaowarat Rd., Bangkok 10100. www.grandchina.com. ✆ **02224-9777.** Fax 02224-7999. 155 units. From 4,200B double; from 8,400B suite. AE, MC, V. Hua Lamphong MRT. **Amenities:** 3 restaurants; outdoor pool; health club; spa; room service; Internet (500B per day). *In room:* A/C, TV, minibar, fridge.

Shanghai Mansion ★   This newish hotel is a small but superb example of some of Bangkok's more character-filled boutique hotels that are springing up. The average-sized rooms (and slightly larger suites) are all eclectically furnished in a 1930s style, with vivid pink, green, and red silks, and Chinese lattice-frame beds, all evoking Old Shanghai. While they tend to be on the small side, rooms make up for it in color and ambience. The hotel offers only a few facilities, such as delicious Chinese teas and free Wi-Fi, but its sumptuous atmosphere far outstrips its better-equipped neighbors.

479 Yaowarat Rd., Bangkok 10100. www.shanghaimansion.com. ✆ **02221-2121.** Fax 02221-2124. 55 units. From 2,500B double; from 4,000B suite. AE, MC, V. Hua Lamphong MRT. **Amenities:** Restaurant; spa; room service; library. *In room:* A/C, TV, minibar, fridge, hair dryer, Wi-Fi (free).

WHERE TO EAT

If you have tasted Thai food back home, it may not necessarily taste like the stuff you're about to try here. What you'll eat in Bangkok will (with any luck) be the real thing; however, be warned that many restaurants catering to foreigners in big resort towns tone down the spiciness of their Thai cuisine to cater to foreign palates. This is based on the belief, often quite justified, that foreigners do not crave great quantities of chilies in their food, as do the Thais. Happily, Bangkok offers many authentic choices, from simple noodle stands to sophisticated, upmarket joints, and not all Thai dishes are spicy. You don't have to limit your diet to Thai food either; the city is one of the best places in the world to dine out on international fare. Check the free listings magazines, such as *BK Magazine,* and you may even stumble across a visiting chef from an overseas Michelin-starred eatery making a quick visit to a five-star hotel or an annual food festival.

You will not go hungry in the Big Mango, and the truly adventurous will find interesting and more authentic fare off the beaten track in smaller roadside eateries.

Prices vary from really rock-bottom-priced street food to unashamedly wallet-melting, posh new restaurants. But on the whole, menu costs are comparatively reasonable. You'll be able to eat well for around 1,000B for two, even at some of the town's better restaurants. (If you order wine, Thai taxes on good vintages mean you may double that figure, though.)

On the River
VERY EXPENSIVE

Le Normandie ★★★ FRENCH   The Le Normandie is the apex of formal dining in Thailand, in price and quality. The ultra-elegant restaurant, atop the renowned Oriental Hotel, offers panoramic views of Thonburi and the Chao Phraya River. The dining room literally glistens, from place settings to chandeliers, and the warm tones of the butter-yellow silks impart a delicious glow. Some of the world's highest-ranked masterchefs have made guest appearances here, adding their own unique touches to the various menus, all of which change regularly. Main courses such as Dover sole, sea bass, and rack of lamb are good examples of the diversity. The service, as you might expect in such an establishment, is impeccable. If you want to indulge your sweet tooth, ask to look at the dessert trolley—you'll have a tough time choosing from the appealing options. Wines of every caliber pepper the extensive wine list, but be prepared to splash out for the best.

The Oriental, Bangkok, 48 Oriental Ave. © **02659-9000.** www.mandarinoriental.com/bangkok. Reservations required at least 1 day in advance. Jacket required for men, no jeans or sports shoes. Main courses 1,100B–7,500B. Set lunch 1,150B. AE, DC, MC, V. Daily noon–2:30pm and 7–10:30pm; closed Sun lunch. Ferry to Central Pier or Saphan Taksin BTS.

EXPENSIVE

Mei Jiang ★★★ CHINESE   In the plush lower level of the Peninsula lies a Chinese restaurant that serves fresh, unfussy Cantonese dim sum and superbly authentic regional specialties from the Chinese provinces of Guangzhou, Fujian, and Sichuan, not forgetting Northern classics, such as the succulent Beijing Duck, eaten with warm pancakes, sweet plum sauce, cucumber, and shallots. Elegantly simple Chinese decor that doesn't overwhelm and delightful private rooms give it an edge over the city's other—more showy—Chinese restaurants. As the dim sum selection attests, this place is all about quality. Reasonably priced set lunches (with dim sum) or set dinners make light work of a head-spinning broad menu that includes (more extravagantly priced) Chinese delicacies such as lobster, Australian abalone, and sharks' fin. Don't overlook desserts such as chilled sago pudding, black sesame ice cream, or the wonderfully warming sesame dumplings and ginkgo nuts in ginger tea.

The Peninsula, Bangkok, 333 Charoen Nakhorn Rd., Thonburi (overlooking the river). © **02861-2888,** ext. 691. www.peninsula.com/Bangkok. Reservations recommended. Main courses 380B–2,900B. Set lunches from 880B; set dinners from 1,800B. AE, DC, MC, V. Daily 11:30am–2:30pm and 6–10:30pm. Short ferry from Hotel Shuttle Boat Pier (next to Saphan Taksin BTS).

Thiptara ★★ 🛅 THAI   This alfresco venue next to the Chao Phraya River is set amid a pretty Thai garden with lotus ponds, goldfish pools, and individual, private wooden pavilions. The menu includes both spicy and milder Thai dishes, all of which carefully encapsulate the taste of simple home cooking. Try a refreshingly zesty appetizer of pomelo salad with grilled shrimp (mention it to the waitress, if you don't like it too spicy), or dip into a Thai-style duck curry or fresh seafood dishes. If you don't want to risk street eats and are dying to try some Thai classics, Thiptara offers the

Bangkok Restaurants

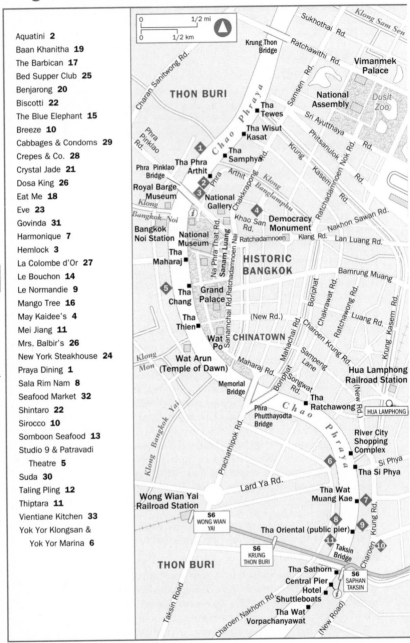

Aquatini **2**
Baan Khanitha **19**
The Barbican **17**
Bed Supper Club **25**
Benjarong **20**
Biscotti **22**
The Blue Elephant **15**
Breeze **10**
Cabbages & Condoms **29**
Crepes & Co. **28**
Crystal Jade **21**
Dosa King **26**
Eat Me **18**
Eve **23**
Govinda **31**
Harmonique **7**
Hemlock **3**
La Colombe d'Or **27**
Le Bouchon **14**
Le Normandie **9**
Mango Tree **16**
May Kaidee's **4**
Mei Jiang **11**
Mrs. Balbir's **26**
New York Steakhouse **24**
Praya Dining **1**
Sala Rim Nam **8**
Seafood Market **32**
Shintaro **22**
Sirocco **10**
Somboon Seafood **13**
Studio 9 & Patravadi
    Theatre **5**
Suda **30**
Taling Pling **12**
Thiptara **11**
Vientiane Kitchen **33**
Yok Yor Klongsan &
    Yok Yor Marina **6**

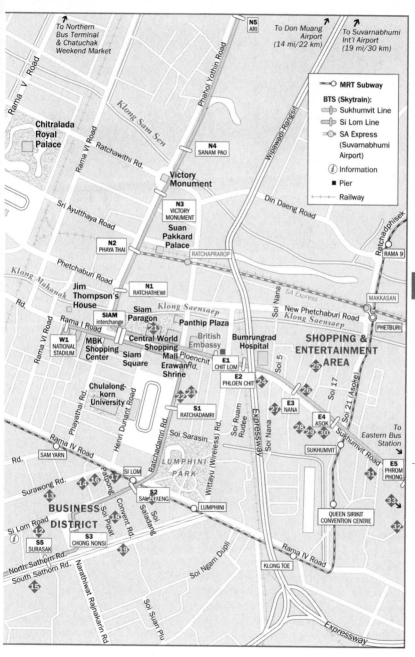

well-loved Thai-style noodle, *pad Thai goong sod*, or *tom yum goong* (spicy coconut and shrimp soup), as well as the addictive Thai dessert, mango and sticky rice. More adventurous diners can try the more unusual *pollamai nampheung*, a two-person dessert of Thai fruits roasted in honey with splashes of chili and vanilla, served with a refreshing lemon sorbet.

The Peninsula, Bangkok, 333 Charoen Nakhorn Rd., Thonburi. ℂ **02861-2888,** ext. 6930. www. peninsula.com/Bangkok. Reservations recommended. Main courses 480B–950B. AE, DC, MC, V. Daily 6–10:30pm. Short ferry from Hotel Shuttle Boat Pier (next to Saphan Taksin BTS).

MODERATE

Praya Dining ★★★ ▣ THAI/MEDITERRANEAN   A visit to the dining room of the Praya Palazzo, a riverside colonial-style hotel, promises a memorable experience, mostly for the superb cuisine, but also for the elegant decor, relaxing ambience, and super-attentive service. Though everything on the menu looks equally appealing, go for the Thai menu, which features some rare dishes you won't find anywhere else, such as *goong talai*, raw shrimps served in tiny cups with a tongue-tingling dip of pickled garlic, herbs, and peanuts, and *gaeng ranchuan*, a traditional spicy beef soup with shrimp paste. The setting matches the cuisine for class—wood floors, arched doorways with fine carvings, starched tablecloths, and candles on the tables. Smartly dressed staff hover in the wings, eager to help or recommend, and there's a healthy wine list too. If you'd like to see the lovely mansion in daylight, you could go for afternoon tea between 2 and 5:30pm.

757/1 Somdej Prapinklao Soi 2, Bangyeekan, Bangkok 10700. ℂ **02883-2998;** www.prayapalazzo. com. Main courses 350B–870B. AE, MC, V. Daily 6:30am–10pm (sometimes closed for private functions). Reservations required. Call from Phra Arthit pier for shuttle pickup.

INEXPENSIVE

Harmonique ★★ ✦ THAI   A popular tourist haunt, Harmonique is set in the courtyard of a century-old house that, despite the cramped space and unending clutter, oozes character. The entrance to this ramshackle eatery is via Wat Muang Kae. There is courtyard seating, as well as small open-air dining areas, stuffed with fun bric-a-brac and ephemera. The cuisine is Thai, tailored to Western tastes—the *tom yum* is delicious, served only as spicy as you like, and with enormous chunks of fish or shrimp. The sizzling grilled seafood platter is nice and garlicky (with chilies on the side). They also feature good Western desserts, such as brownies, which are great with a cool tea on a hot day. This is a convenient stop when you're touring the riverfront or visiting the antiques stores of nearby River City.

22 Charoen Krung (New) Rd., a few meters down Soi 34, on the right. ℂ **02237-8175.** Main courses 85B–220B. AE, MC, V. Mon–Sat 11am–10pm. Closed in summer. 20-min. walk from Saphan Taksin BTS.

Studio 9 ★★ THAI/INTERNATIONAL   Studio 9 provides the adjoining Patravadi Theater complex with a smart little eatery right on the water, with tables overlooking the Grand Palace on the opposite bank. Come on Friday or Saturday for the evening contemporary dance–dinner shows (p. 100), or just pop in after a performance at the theater, for a quick bite and glass of wine. The very reasonably priced menu leans toward Thai-fusion fare (chicken paprika is the specialty) but is aptly amended for foreign palates with a toned down spiciness. Because there's no charge for the weekend dance performances, it makes for a fantastic cultural evening without breaking the bank.

TIPS ON dining: BANGKOK CHEAP EATS

As in most areas of Thailand, the city's many night bazaars and hawker stalls are where you'll find the best eats, but those who are nervous of tummy bugs or who are not inclined toward culinary adventures would do well to stick to the many food courts usually located inside shopping malls. Here, young Thais enjoy cheap eats in the luxury of air-conditioning; they can get packed with office workers at lunchtime. In all food courts, you need to buy coupons first, exchange them for the dishes you order, and cash in any you don't use afterward. In addition to the ones reviewed below, other notable food courts include All Seasons Place, Emporium, MBK, and the CentralWorld's Loft concept. All are usually located on the top floor or basement of stores and resemble simple self-service cafeterias.

The city's small, open-air joints and markets are also popular for snacks and quick lunches; they open Tuesday to Sunday from dawn until late. Food vendors are now banned on Mondays in Bangkok, in an effort to free up the already cluttered pavements. Eating right next to smoke-belching buses may not be your idea of gastronomic heaven, but being surrounded by the pungent aromas of garlic, chili, and barbecued meats, as well as the cacophony of the traffic or glaring lights, makes it a totally Thai experience. On the other hand, if you are missing hearty home fare or a sugar fix from Western desserts, fear not; even budget-strapped travelers can enjoy a range of clean and hearty dining spots all over town, at all hours.

Khao San Road Area Starting from Phra Arthit Road, cutting through Soi Rambutri and heading toward Khao San Road, leads you past heaps of low-budget diners that serve Thai and Western food. Look out for great BBQ fish, served hot off the coals, or sizzling satays. These small-time diners extend to the busy Rambutri Road (parallel to Khao San Rd.), with many serving late into the night. Apart from Burger King and McDonald's, there are also plenty of stalls selling cheap pad Thai, Chinese congee (*johk*), or fried rice.

Siam Paragon Food Court Right at Siam BTS, this glitzy megamall doesn't just cater to big-brand boutique shoppers; downstairs, it has a host of low-cost diners, pastry shops, and ice-cream parlors, as well as upmarket restaurants. The cheaper food stalls have just about every type of fare, including Thai, Indian, Japanese, and Vietnamese, while the upscale restaurants such as Crystal Jade (p. 97) are as classy as they come.

Surawong & Silom Roads Every day except Mondays, the length of upper Surawong Road (the end closest to Rama IV Rd.) is a cluster of snack stalls and fruit vendors that spill into adjoining Thaniya Plaza. In places such as Soi Convent off Silom Road (close to California Gym), you'll find stalls selling crab and shrimp, noodles, fried vegetarian patties, and delicious boiled chicken on rice.

Note: For info on the safety of food stalls throughout Thailand, see p. 27.

69/1 Soi Wat Rakhang, Arunamarin Rd., Siriraj, Thonburi. ☏ **02866-2144.** Main courses 70B–250B. AE, MC, V. Sun–Thurs 11am–10pm; Fri–Sat 11am–midnight (performances start at 7:30pm). Tha Thien Pier and 5-min. shuttle-boat ride.

Yok Yor Klongsan & Yok Yor Marina THAI   These two riverside hangouts, which sit practically side by side, are both popular with Thais and Chinese tour groups, thanks to their seafood served outdoors or inside. Both restaurants offer no frills whatsoever, but the views, fresh air, and seafood make them good culinary escapes after sightseeing. In the evenings, expect painfully tuneless karaoke sessions to unfold on their stages. Lunch is certainly a more tranquil bet. Evening diners can catch the free Yok Yor ferry from River City shopping mall.

Soi Somdej Chaowpraya, 17 (at the Yok Yor Marina, Somdej Chao Phraya Soi 17). © **02863-0565.** www.yokyor.co.th. Main courses 80B–280B. AE, MC, V. Mon–Sun 11am–11pm. Saphan Taksin BTS and 5-min. shuttle-boat ride.

Silom & Surawong Roads

This is where you'll find Thailand's most expensive joints, nestled a few meters from busy street vendors and more familiar fare, ranging from McDonald's to Pizza Hut. Head to the basements of any large shopping mall (for example, **Silom Complex,** p. 121), great value Japanese sushi chains such as **Fuji,** or small cafes serving different noodles or Chinese hot pot to find excellent low-priced dinners. This area also has many independent restaurants; but beware, the majority serve up Thai food for tourists, so look out for places patronized by locals for more authentic eats.

VERY EXPENSIVE

Breeze ★★★ PAN-ASIAN/SEAFOOD   The lebua hotel has brought to Bangkok a unique Asian seafood experience that will amaze anyone who braves the giddy heights of this alfresco restaurant on the 51st and 52nd floors of State Tower. After crossing a long, illuminated "skybridge," descend into a cozy outdoor terrace overlooking the city. The fusion-inspired menu focuses on top-notch dim sum; fresh fish, such as steamed cod; and some contemporary pan-Asian seafood delicacies, including poached South Australian lobster and wasabi shrimp and soft-shell crab (some of which can cause major collateral damage to the holiday budget). The menu also includes a wide selection of barbecued meats, imported lamb rack, or prime rib-eye steak, and some decent desserts, such as the Breeze On Ice (a selection of mousses with cantaloupe served on crushed ice). The experience is guaranteed to blow you—and, if you're not careful, your wallet—away.

State Tower (corner of Silom Rd. and Charoen Krung [New] Rd.), 1055 Silom Rd. © **02624-9999.** www.breezebkk.com. Reservations required. Dress code smart-casual. Main courses 1,090B–3,490B. AE, DC, MC, V. Daily 6pm–1am. Saphan Taksin BTS.

Sirocco ★★★ ITALIAN   Like Breeze, Sirocco sits near the top of the State Tower with its distinctive gold dome. In fact it's even higher, sharing the 63rd floor with the iconic Sky Bar (p. 127). On a stunningly positioned, supper-only outdoor terrace, Sirocco serves top-class Mediterranean-inspired cuisine, with live jazz from 8pm–12.30am each night. There are plenty of tempting dishes on the menu, but I recommend the Chef's Tasting Menu (4,300B), which consists of a green and white asparagus veloute, Scottish salmon crudo and tartare, pan-seared soulard foie gras, roasted USDA prime beef tenderloin, and a yogurt mousse cake. If you're a movie-goer, you might recognize the location from the movie *Hangover Part 2*, a scene of which was filmed here. You can even indulge in a signature cocktail invented to commemorate the event—the Hangovertini. Just above Sirocco, on the 64th and 65th floors respectively, Distill features an oyster station plus sushi and sashimi, while Mezzaluna offers innovative set menus that change daily, at 4,900B–5,900B for three or six courses. Check the website for details.

State Tower (corner of Silom Rd. and Charoen Krung [New] Rd.), 1055 Silom Rd. © **02624-9999.** www.lebua.com. Reservations recommended. Dress code: Smart/casual. Main courses

1,470B–3,100B. AE, DC, MC, V. Daily 6pm–1am (last orders 11:30pm). See website for all details and individual outlet opening times. Saphan Taksin BTS.

EXPENSIVE

Benjarong ★★ THAI   Named for the exquisite five-color pottery once reserved exclusively for the royal family, Benjarong's fine Thai cuisine focuses on the five basic flavors of Thai cooking (salty, bitter, hot, sweet, and sour) in traditional "royal" dishes. While the menu is extensive, the most popular dishes are the sweet red curry crab claws and the exotic grilled fish with black beans in banana leaves. The illustrations will help you navigate your way through the choices. For after-dinner treats, the *khong-wan* is an ornate selection of typical Thai desserts—distinctive, light, and not too sweet.

The Dusit Thani, Rama IV Rd. (corner of Silom Rd. and Rama IV Rd.). *℘* **02200-9000,** ext. 2699. www.dusit.com/dusit-thani/dusit-thani-bangkok. Reservations recommended. Main courses 480B–1,550B. Set menu 900B–1,400B. AE, DC, MC, V. Daily 11:30am–2pm and 6–10pm. Sala Daeng BTS.

The Blue Elephant ★★ ROYAL THAI   Long-known and respected for its cooking school (p. 116), The Blue Elephant attracts diners looking for a taste of Royal Thai cuisine. Set in a gorgeously renovated colonial house, surrounded by futuristic towers, the restaurant boasts an ambience that's both elegant and unpretentious. Though the spiciness of some dishes has been tempered for foreign diners, the high standards and superb flavors of items, such as *mieng kham*—the classic betel leaf appetizer—sea bass, satay, and fish cakes, still make it extremely enjoyable. Dig into the signature dishes of salmon *larb*; foie gras accompanied by a tart, tamarind sauce; or the Thai green curry made with black-skinned chicken. There are also vegetarian dishes aplenty. The wine list contains Thai and international wines, some of which carry the restaurant's own label.

233 S. Sathorn Rd. *℘* **02673-9353.** www.blueelephant.com/bangkok. Reservations recommended. Dress code: smart/casual. Main courses 320B–780B. AE, DC, MC, V. Daily 11:30am–2:30pm and 6:30–10:30pm. 5-min. walk from Surasak BTS.

Eat Me ★ ASIAN FUSION   Eat Me is all about exposed industrial beams, dark wood, and indirect lighting on the walls of an ever-changing exhibition space. It tends to get billed as a supper-only art cafe, the art being provided by local painters and photographers. The menu features a smattering of great fusion dishes (the Tasmanian salmon tartare and spicy lemongrass chicken are delicious), a respectable wine list, as well as fantastic desserts, such as sticky date pudding or lemongrass crème brûlée, brilliant culinary inspirations from the Aussie-Thai owners. The main air-conditioned room is a better bet than the mosquito-infested balcony overlooking a small courtyard.

1/6 Soi Pipat 2, off Soi Convent (connecting Sathorn and Silom rds.). *℘* **02238-0931.** www.eat merestaurant.com. Reservations recommended. Main courses 350B–1,300B. AE, MC, V. Daily 3pm–1am. Chong Nonsi BTS.

MODERATE

Le Bouchon ★★ FRENCH   This hush-hush little French bistro is the kind of place that gets packed with French expats on lunch breaks and makes a great little candlelit venue in the evening. Because it's right in the thick of Patpong, you'll have to elbow your way past the hordes of sex show touts and cat-calling lady-boys to get there, but that is part of the fun. The food is delicious, though the rich sauces can make the main courses rather heavy going—go for the goat-cheese salad or poached salmon for lighter options. There are also classic French desserts such as pears poached in wine. Lunches and dinner here can linger on—the food's so good and the venue is so cozy you may not want to leave.

37/17 Patpong Soi 2 (btw. Surawong and Silom Rd.). ℂ **02234-9109.** Main courses from 300B. AE, DC, MC, V. Mon–Sat Noon–midnight; Sun 7pm–midnight. Sala Daeng BTS.

Mango Tree ★ THAI   In a lovely 80-year-old Siamese venue with its own tropical garden, the Mango Tree offers a quiet retreat from the hectic Patpong area. Live traditional music and classical Thai decorative touches fill the house with charm, and the attentive staff serves well-prepared dishes from all regions of the country. The mild green chicken curry and the crispy spring rolls are both excellent—but the menu is extensive, so feel free to experiment. Only trouble is, the food isn't exactly authentic—though it's still tasty.

37 Soi Tantawan, Bangrak (off west end of Surawong Rd.). ℂ **02236-2820.** Reservations recommended. Main courses 240B–580B. AE, DC, MC, V. Daily 11.30am–midnight. 10-min. walk from Sala Daeng BTS station.

Somboon Seafood ★ SEAFOOD   This place is good for anyone willing to sacrifice atmosphere for excellent food. Though it's packed nightly, you'll still be able to find a table because the place is so huge. The staff is extremely friendly—between them and the illustrated menu you'll have no problem picking out the best dishes. Peruse the large aquariums outside to see all the live seafood options such as shrimp, lobsters, and crabs (guaranteed freshness). The house specialty, chili crab curry, is especially good, as is the *tom yum goong* soup (spiced to individual taste).

169/7–11 Surawong Rd. (just across from the Peugeot building). ℂ **02233-3104.** www.somboon seafood.com. Main courses 190B–650B; seafood at market prices (about 800B for two diners). No credit cards. Daily 4–11.30pm. Chong Nonsi BTS.

INEXPENSIVE

The Barbican INTERNATIONAL   This old favorite is still packing in expatriate punters with its casual British-pub style and a menu featuring plenty of international staples, such as pasta, goulash, or "Guinness pie," while on Sundays it presents an all-you-can-eat Mexican buffet. It's hardly chic, but at the heart of the somewhat sleazy Thaniya Plaza, its casual atmosphere attracts foreign office workers and travelers hankering for some comfort food. It's most popular when the offices close and the happy hour starts, when it can be standing room only. Fight your way in—it's worth it.

9/4–5 Soi Thaniya, Silom Rd. (1 block east of Patpong, btw. Silom and Surawong rds.). ℂ **02234-3590.** www.greatbritishpub.com. Main courses from 140B. AE, DC, MC, V. Daily 11:30am–1am. Sala Daeng BTS.

Taling Pling 👘 THAI   I've just one word for this friendly low-end Thai diner: Go! It's packed with office workers at lunchtime, so try for a table after 1pm or in the evening. Rustic wooden decor and delightful old photographs adorn the walls. Menus come with pictures of the dishes to aid foreigners, but the taste is thoroughly Thai and the low prices reflect this. Try the dry, fluffy catfish salad or the spicy green curry with beef. For those who really want to taste local flavors, the roast duck *panaeng* is recommended. Chicken in *pandanus* leaf and Thai fish cakes appease those whose palates prefer it less spicy. It's a fabulous place to feast, and there are now branches on the third floor of CentralWorld department store (ℂ **02613-3160**) and the ground floor of Siam Paragon (ℂ **02129-4354**).

60 Pan Rd. (midway down the *soi*, connecting Silom and Sathorn rds.). ℭ **02236-4830.** Main courses 150B. AE, MC, V. Daily 11am–10pm. Surasak BTS.

Ratchadamri, Sathorn, & Sukhumvit Area

VERY EXPENSIVE

Bed Supper Club ★★ ASIAN FUSION   Billed as one of the coolest places in Bangkok since it opened in 2002, this place consists of an all-white, two-story eatery-cum-nightclub located in what can only be described as an industrially styled, white illuminated tube. The surreal atmosphere is accentuated by the trance music that's regularly spun by DJs. Instead of sitting at tables, diners take off their shoes and lounge on long white ottomans while the music pumps. (Great if you can eat lying down, not so fun if you can't.) A fixed, set menu is served nightly (including options for vegetarians), with three courses Sunday to Thursday and four courses on Friday and Saturday. Culinary combinations of dishes such as Australian beef tenderloin, truffle oil hollandaise, crispy potato fondant, and white asparagus, or Thai mushroom ragout, roasted shallots, oregano gremolata, and pappardelle pasta set the tone. For those who prefer, there is an a la carte menu from Monday to Thursday. If you like this style of contemporary Asian-meets-Mediterranean food and don't mind eating in bed, you'll think this supper club is fantastic.

26 Soi 11 (by Sukhumvit Rd.). ℭ **02651-3537.** www.bedsupperclub.com. Reservations required. No shorts for men. Set menu 1,550B–1,950B. AE, DC, MC, V. Mon–Fri 7:30pm–midnight and until 1am on weekends. 8-min. walk from Nana BTS.

New York Steakhouse ★★★ STEAK   One of the best steakhouses in the region, the JW Marriott's steakhouse offers plenty of dark wood and high, leather wing chairs, and is the best place for a juicy imported Angus steak served with a host of hearty sides (mushrooms, broccoli with cheese, mashed potatoes, and veggies). If money is no object, splash out on roast prime rib or grilled lamb chops. Seafood choices cover the whole gamut from oysters, to Alaskan crab, to tiger shrimp, to Phuket lobster. The long wine list is, not surprisingly, dominated by red wines. Dress code is casual (but no shorts or sandals). Expect professional service and a business-like atmosphere.

JW Marriott (2nd floor), 4 Sukhumvit Rd., Soi 2. ℭ **02656-7700.** www.marriott.com. Reservations recommended. Main courses 1,750B–6,500B. AE, DC, MC, V. Daily 6–11pm. Nana BTS.

EXPENSIVE

Eve ★★ MEDITERRANEAN   This laid-back restaurant on the ground floor of the Hansar Hotel, with a choice of indoor or outdoor eating (on a breezy terrace) has quickly become a favorite among locals who are always on the look-out for new gastronomic venues. Its elegant but unostentatious surroundings, along with impeccable service, make a great setting for an exploration of the menu, which is influenced by French Provencal cuisine. The foie gras is an excellent starter and prepares the palate for a succulent fish or meat main course; I recommend the Wagyu beef short rib, which almost melts in the mouth. Try to keep a little room for a dessert such as the vanilla and raspberry layered pannacotta crumble, then enjoy a post-dinner drink in the lobby bar while listening to the sweet-sounding trio who entertain.

Hansar Hotel, 3 Soi Mahadlekluang 2, Ratchadamri Road. ℭ **02209-1234.** www.hansarbangkok.com/eve. Reservations recommended. Main courses 390B–1,800B. AE, MC, V. Daily 6am–10.30pm. Ratchadamri BTS.

La Colombe d'Or ★★ FRENCH   Previously known as Le Banyan for the spreading banyan tree on the edge of the garden, this upscale venue serves suppers only, prepared by Michel Binaux and Bruno Bischoff. A disastrous fire in 2010 was followed by a refurbishment, but now it looks better than ever and presents a great opportunity for a lazy evening of indulgence in top-class French cuisine. The house special is a dish for two, a Rouennaise pressed duck with goose liver; other high-end choices include lobster bisque, chateaubriand with Armagnac, or Provençal-style rack of lamb. If you come on foot, you'll run the gauntlet of all the girly bars at the entrance of the *soi*, but ignore those until you arrive at this little upscale gem, and you'll enjoy an evening of fine dining and effusive service.

59 Sukhumvit Soi 8. ⓒ **02253-5556.** www.le-banyan.com. Reservations recommended. Dress code: Smart/casual (no jacket required). Main courses 900B. AE, DC, MC, V. Mon–Sat 6:30–midnight (last main order 10pm). 10-min. walk from Nana BTS.

MODERATE

Baan Khanitha ★★ 🍴 THAI   With one location on busy Sathorn Road and another (the original) on Sukhumvit Soi 23, Baan Khanitha offers authentic Thai in a comfortable, classy atmosphere. For starters, choose the *yam som o*, a tangy salad with pomelo, shrimps, and chicken. Then you can graduate to a curry, from spicy red to mellow yellow and green; light salads; and good seafood, prepared as you like it. An indication of the authentic nature of the food here is that most customers are Thai, a rarity for upscale Thai eateries in Bangkok, and both places are always packed: A couple of good signs.

69 S. Sathorn Rd. ⓒ **02675-4200** and 36/1 Sukhumvit Soi 23 (ⓒ **02258-4128**). www.baan-khanitha.com. Reservations highly recommended. Main courses 240B–580B. AE, MC, V. Daily 11am–11pm. Sala Daeng BTS or Lumphini MRT stations (for Sathorn); Asok BTS or Sukhumvit MRT stations (for Sukhumvit 23).

Biscotti ★★ ITALIAN   This must be Bangkok's most stylish and consistently praised Italian restaurant. Its open kitchen and slick, minimalist decor give it a modern sophistication that few Italian restaurants in Bangkok can match. The long tables and polished wood floors grant it a relaxed, welcoming air. Equally unmatched are its cuisine and top-class service, which don't come with too big a price tag, like so many others. Start with a green asparagus, fennel and orange salad, or a classic caprese (tomato, mozzarella, and basil). There's a great choice of fresh fish for mains, alternatively a range of wood-fired pizzas, and an unending list of antipasti, not to mention homemade pastas and risottos. Save space for one of the irresistible desserts, and accompany the meal with one of the first-rate wines. It's smart, it's elegant, and it's utterly timeless.

The Four Seasons, 155 Ratchadamri Rd. ⓒ **02126-8866.** www.fourseasons.com/bangkok. Reservations recommended. Dress code: Smart/casual. Main courses 290B–580B. AE, DC, MC, V. Daily 11:30am–2:30pm and 6–10:30pm. Ratchadamri BTS.

Crepes & Co. ★ ☺ MEDITERRANEAN/CAFE   Popular among Bangkok foreign residents (and their kids), this is a great place to satisfy your sweet tooth. Crepes here are light, fluffy, and filled with dozens of combinations, both savory and sweet—all of them scrumptious. They also serve Mediterranean main courses such as mezze or couscous. Everyone is friendly—even the cat, who sometimes likes to curl up and sleep next to diners. They have great coffee and a respectable selection of teas.

18/1 Sukhumvit Soi 12. ⓒ **02653-3990.** www.crepes.co.th. Reservations recommended. Main courses 150B–540B. AE, DC, MC, V. Daily 9am–midnight. 15-min. walk from Asok BTS.

Crystal Jade ★ CHINESE   Located in the heart of the shopping area, in the Siam Paragon Mall, this popular two-story Chinese restaurant has many branches across Asia. At Siam Paragon, the decor is elegant and enclosed—providing an escape from the seething food court. The Chinese fare is fast and fresh, with northern-style dumplings, noodles, and wonton soup. You'll also find Cantonese favorites such as suckling pig, deep-fried shrimp, and barbecue pork, plus extravagant dishes such as abalone. There's also a branch at Erawan mall, where the decor is more like a fast-food joint, and the food is cheaper and more casual.

Ground Floor, Siam Paragon Mall, 991 Rama I Rd. 🕐 **02129-4343.** Main courses from 160B. AE, MC, V. Daily 11am–2:30pm and 5:30–10pm. Siam BTS.

Mrs. Balbir's ★ INDIAN   There's a cheerful atmosphere at this restaurant, thanks to the affable and effervescent owner, Mrs. (Vinder) Balbir, whose jolly banter accompanies any lunch or supper when she's around. The menu covers all sorts of Punjabi goodies such as biryani, dahl, chicken tikka masala, and deliciously smooth cheese and spinach dishes. All of Mrs. Balbir's food comes with homemade pickled onions and chutneys. She now also offers several Indo-Chinese dishes. As famous for being a TV chef as much as a restaurateur, Mrs. Balbir runs highly enjoyable cooking classes at the restaurant (p. 116).

155/1–2 Sukhumvit Soi 11/1. 🕐 **02651-0498.** www.mrsbalbirs.com. Reservations recommended for dinner. Main courses 200B–380B. Set Thali 320B; 280B (vegetarian). MC, V. Daily 11:30am–10:45pm. Nana BTS.

Seafood Market ★ SEAFOOD   This place is fun but very touristy. Their motto is "If it swims, we have it," so if you're a seafood fan, you'll love it, though you may not have had a dining experience like this before. You'll enter the giant hangar of a fish market, and, before you sit down, you can wander around the seafood counters and choose your supper, either live or on ice, all priced by the kilo. Pay for it all at the cashier, and then cart it back to the table. At this point, choose how you'd like it cooked and what sauces you prefer. Waiters can help with suggestions for your catch, but what comes out of the kitchen is always good. Cooking and beverage charges are paid separately at the end of the meal. The seafood is market price, and the fish incredibly fresh.

89 Sukhumvit Soi 24 (Soi Kasami). 🕐 **02261-2071.** www.seafood.co.th. Reservations recommended for weekend dinner. Market prices. AE, MC, V. Daily 11:30am–midnight. Phrom Phong BTS.

Shintaro ★★ JAPANESE   A Japanese restaurant with a difference, as suggested by its name, which means "new vision." This small but snazzy diner is decked out in

---

Anyone for Cricket?

Look for the snack stands along Sukhumvit Road (also Khao San Rd.) that sell all sorts of fried insects. Grasshoppers, beetles that look like cockroaches, scorpions, ants, and grubs are all favorite snacks for folks from Isan, in the northeast, where bugs, in fact, are cultivated for the dining table and are an important source of protein in the region. How does it taste? Crickets are a bit like popcorn, and the beetles are something like—hate to say it—crispy chicken. Even if you don't indulge, it's a great photo opportunity.

contemporary decor—check out what look like noodle-clad walls, by designer Tony Chi. Packed as it is with young, well-heeled locals and businessmen, this is one of the city's most fashionable Japanese restaurants. Whether dining along a long bench, facing the busy chefs, or at the side tables, expect the unexpected; the finest quality slabs of sashimi, artfully hand-rolled sushi, succulent foie gras rolls, or tasty soba noodles. Hot dishes include grilled salmon, cooked to perfection. Don't pass up the desserts, such as sago with fresh melon; they're the perfect ending to a superb meal.

The Four Seasons, 155 Rachadamri Rd. *Ⓒ* **02126-8866.** www.fourseasons.com/bangkok. Reservations recommended. Main courses 340B–580B. AE, DC, MC, V. Daily 11:30am–2:30pm and 5–10:30pm. Ratchadamri BTS.

INEXPENSIVE

Cabbages & Condoms ★★ 🍴 THAI   Here's a restaurant with a purpose, and a humorous motto ("Our food is guaranteed not to cause pregnancy"). Opened by local senator Mechai Viravaidya, founder of the Population & Community Development Association, this restaurant helps fund population control, AIDS awareness, and a host of rural development programs. Set in a large compound, the two-story restaurant has air-conditioned indoor dining, but if you sit on the garden terrace, you're in a fairyland of twinkling lights that create quite a romantic atmosphere. Share a whole fish or try the *kai hor bai toey* (fried boneless chicken wrapped in pandanus leaves with a dark, sweet soy sauce for dipping). There's also a large selection of vegetable and bean curd entrees. Before you leave, be sure to check out the gift shop's whimsical condom-related merchandise. The restaurant hands out condoms instead of dinner mints.

10 Sukhumvit Soi 12. *Ⓒ* **02229-4610.** www.pda.or.th/restaurant. Reservations recommended. Main courses 130B–360B. AE, DC, MC, V. Daily 11am–10pm. 15-min. walk from Asok BTS.

Dosa King ★ INDIAN/VEGETARIAN   This restaurant serves the popular South Indian dish that is a large rice and lentil flour pancake, filled with savory goodies. It's folded and served with delicious sauces, and is 100% vegetarian. They now also serve Jain food, meaning with no onion or garlic. Dosa King does have other traditional Indian dishes, but stick with the house special of the thali combo (275B) and you'll enjoy a quick, healthy meal while escaping the masses along Sukhumvit.

153/7 Sukhumvit Soi 11/1. *Ⓒ* **02651-1700.** www.dosaking.net. Main courses 150B. AE, MC, V. Daily 11am–11pm. Nana BTS.

Govinda ★ ITALIAN/VEGETARIAN   No one can resist this home-style eatery that makes some of the best Italian food in the city and yet charges very reasonable prices. Plus, it's a wholly meat-free menu, featuring fabulous pastas, dozens of soya-meat dishes, and even vegetarian salamis and sausages. The Italian couple who runs this low-key, two-story diner is extremely welcoming and works hard to keep the food absolutely authentic. Dive into handmade gnocchi (made with pumpkin), excellent lasagna, or egg-based pasta. Though the desserts are not as impressive, the gelato is a great end to one of the best-value meals you can find in Bangkok.

6/5–6 Sukhumvit Soi 22. *Ⓒ* **02663-4970.** Reservations recommended for dinner. Main courses from 180B. AE, MC, V. Wed–Mon 11:30am–3pm and 6–11pm. 15-min. walk from Phrom Phong BTS.

Suda ★ 🍴 THAI   In a time when restaurants are often judged for the appearance of their food rather than its taste, it's reassuring to find somewhere as reliable as Suda for a delicious and inexpensive meal. Order up a shrimp tempura, fish cakes, and a spicy stir-fry, wash it down with a beer, and still get change from 500B. The decor wouldn't win any prizes but it's clean, comfortable, and congenial—the ideal solution when you're standing in front of Asok Station feeling hot, thirsty, and hungry.

6-6/1 Sukhumvit Soi 14. ℂ **02229–4664.** Main courses 70B–220B. No credit cards. Daily 11am–11pm. 3-min. walk from Asok BTS.

Vientiane Kitchen ★ LAOTIAN   The cuisine of Laos is the same as that of Isan, or northeastern Thailand, with sticky rice, grilled chicken, *som tam* (spicy green papaya salad), and *larb* (spicy ground pork salad) being a few of the most popular dishes. Isan food is generally very spicy, and adventurous eaters have ample opportunities to sample something out of the ordinary here, such as snails or red ants' eggs in a spicy salad. The place is large and barnlike, the decor is very simple—thatched roofs and bamboo chairs—and the clientele is an eclectic mix of Thais and foreigners. Most evenings, there is entertainment in the form of *mor lam* music (a very rhythmic style from Isan and Laos), with accompanying dancers, and they will arrange a special blessing ceremony for anyone celebrating their birthday.

8 Sukhumvit Soi 36. ℂ **02258-6171.** Main courses 150B–250B. AE, MC, V. Daily noon–midnight. Thong Lo Skytrain.

Banglampoo & Khao San Road

Khao San Road used to be Bangkok's busy backpacker quarter, but it's moved rapidly upmarket in recent years. It's still where you'll find every manner of food, from kosher and halal cuisine, to Italian, as well as tasty Thai food served street-side. Avoid the blander versions of Western food served at budget guesthouses, but do have a seat somewhere along the busy road, order up a fruit shake, and watch the nightly parade of young travelers. Below are a few well-known choices near Khao San.

Aquatini ★ THAI/INTERNATIONAL   The name combines the word for water, referring to the Chao Phraya River which flows constantly by, and martini, the international cocktail. With an ideal location right next to Phra Arthit pier, it tempts many travelers with tired legs to take a break and enjoy the riverside breeze with a refreshing drink, or to indulge in the comprehensive menu of Thai and international dishes. If you're in the mood for spicy, go for *larb ped*—a spicy duck dish—or settle for a sandwich or a big bowl of pasta. It's a great place to kick back, and watch the constant streams of people getting on and off the ferry.

45/1 Phra Arthit Rd., Banglampoo. ℂ **02280-9955.** Main courses 220B–350B. MC, V. Daily 6:30pm–1am. Ferry to Phra Arthit pier.

Hemlock 🍴 THAI   The extensive and wide-ranging menu, with expertly prepared dishes that include several vegetarian options, combined with a relaxing atmosphere and very reasonable prices, makes this a hot favorite for young Thais. It's also a good place to escape the hustle and bustle of nearby Khao San Road, though it's best to book a table on weekends. If you're feeling adventurous, try the *yam hua plii* (banana flower salad)—a marvelous blend of tastes and texture.

56 Phra Arthit Rd., Banglampoo. ℂ **02282-7507.** Reservations recommended. Main courses from 80B. MC, V. Mon–Sat 6pm–midnight. Ferry to Phra Arthit Pier.

May Kaidee's 🍴 VEGETARIAN/THAI   Over the years, May Kaidee's has become a bit of a pilgrimage spot for visiting foodies. This place has little more than a few modest tables tucked into a little alleyway, but nevertheless it's the home of some healthy and delicious Thai vegetarian dishes. Mrs. May (pronounced *My*) has developed a real following by cooking up dishes such as spicy massaman or Thai green curry, as well as soups and stir-fries. All dishes come with a choice of white or brown rice. For dessert, don't pass up the black sticky rice with mango. Her cookbook is for sale and she even offers cooking classes.

At the end of Khao San Rd., in a sub-*soi* off Soi Damnoen Klang. © **089-137-3173.** Main courses from 60B. No credit cards. Daily 8am–10pm. 10-min. walk from Phra Arthit Pier.

Dinner with Thai Dance

Patravadi Theatre ★ THAI   This cozy little theater on the Thonburi side of the river is a great spot to catch a performance of traditional Thai dance, or even a modern dance troupe or jazz band, while enjoying some delicious Thai dishes, though it's usually limited to Fridays and Saturdays only. Call or check the website for information about upcoming events. The theater restaurant is set in an attractive garden and serves Thai food, with some vegetarian and some pasta dishes, while the riverside Studio 9 specializes in Thai fusion dishes. The backdrop is particularly impressive at night, when the illuminated spires of the Grand Palace are visible across the river.

69/1 Soi Wat Rakhang, Arunamarin Rd., Siriraj, Thonburi. © **024-127-2878.** www.patravadi theatre.com. Main courses from 240B. AE, MC, V. Mon–Thurs 11am–10pm; Fri–Sun 11am–midnight. Tha Thien Pier and 5-min. shuttle-boat ride.

Sala Rim Nam ★★ THAI   The Oriental Hotel reopened this beautiful riverside Thai restaurant in late 2007 with a glittering new interior but the same impeccable standards of cuisine and commendable entertainment. The location is across the river from the main hotel, and the ferryboat ride is quite lovely. The set menu is more like an extensive degustation menu of Thai favorites. Nothing is too heavy, but do mention to the waiter before you dine if you can't take spicy food. Guests can choose between sitting Thai-style on floor pillows or using the plush Western-style seating, from where they watch classical Thai dancers, in full glittering regalia, perform ancient Thai legends and rousing drum-frenzied folk dances. Opt for the free shuttle boat that leaves the hotel's pier regularly, or take the BTS to Saphan Taksin and follow the signs to the Hotel Shuttle Boat Pier, just next to Central Pier. Guests now have the option of a buffet lunch as well as the set dinner, though there is no performance at that time.

The Oriental, Bangkok (on Charoen Nakhorn Rd., on the Thonburi side of the Chao Phraya River). © **02437-3080.** www.mandarinoriental.com/bangkok. Dress code: Smart/casual. Lunch 883B, dinner 2,650B. AE, DC, MC, V. Daily noon–3pm and 7–11pm, performance 8:15pm–9:30pm. Saphan Taksin BTS.

Dinner Cruises on the Chao Phraya River

There is a number of tour operators who offer dinner cruises along the Chao Phraya River. These vary from massive, floating discotheques with all-you-can-eat buffets to plush rice barges with delightful old-world decor and more intimate surrounds. All serve Thai set dinners or buffets, with the majority offering special rates for children; less pricey cruises may just offer cocktails at sunset. Some may come with traditional music, live rock bands, or Thai dance shows, depending on the operator; see individual websites for details. Based out of the **Anantara Riverside Resort & Spa,** the *Manohra, Manohra Moon,* and *Manohra Star* (© **02477-0770;** www.manohra cruises.com) are elegantly restored rice barges that offer dinner and cocktail cruises on the Chao Phraya River, from 1,400B. Numbers are limited and boats can be chartered for private functions. The **Shangri-La Hotel** (℃ 02236-7777; www.shangri-la.com) offers a totally different experience on the gargantuan *Horizon II*; this neon-drenched vessel heads upstream with Thai and Western pop music blasting out from 7:30 to 9:30pm and offers fun-packed nights of feasting and dancing. Cruises start at 2,200B. Similar in style to the *Horizon II* is the *Grand Pearl* cruise (℃ **02861-0255,** ext. 201; www.grandpearlcruise.com), with rates from 1,500B, while another rice barge option (though carrying more passengers than the *Manohra*) is offered by **Loy Nava** (℃ **02437-7329;** www.loynava.com), with two sailings daily at 6 to 8pm and 8 to 10pm; prices start from 1,530B.

Most cruises start from their respective hotels, or in the case of the two latter cruises, leave from River City Shopping Mall pier, next to the Royal Orchid Sheraton Hotel.

EXPLORING BANGKOK

A stroll down any of Bangkok's thousands of sprawling and labyrinthine alleyways can bring untold adventures for visitors who are keen to unearth the real Thailand. First-time visitors are often amazed by central Bangkok's glittering modernity (Siam Square), and at the same time, delighted by the treasures found amid the grunginess of ramshackle back streets; it's very easy to stumble across hidden markets or enjoy large ones such as Chatuchuk, museums, or spectacular temples (The Grand Palace). This chapter presents the main highlights of the city's sights.

THINGS TO DO The **Grand Palace** and **Wat Phra Kaew** (the **Emerald Buddha Temple**), a compound packed with striking architecture and dazzling decoration, is far and away the most important sight, not just in Bangkok, but in the entire country. A **longtail boat ride** along the Chao Phraya River and narrow canals of Thonburi opens a window on the lives of the city's inhabitants, and a visit to any of the city's mega-malls shows how its inhabitants have embraced the Western love of **shopping.**

SHOPPING Bangkok is a shopaholic's paradise, boasting some of Southeast Asia's biggest malls stocked with every type of designer product, as well as street markets that buzz with activity. Depending on your mood, you can stroll in air-conditioned comfort round one of the malls in **Siam Square,** or test out your bargaining skills at the mother of all markets—**Chatuchak Weekend Market.**

RESTAURANTS & EATING An exploration of Thai cuisine should begin on the street, by tasting the offerings at simple **food stalls** on the sidewalk that emit mouth-watering aromas; try Soi Convent off Silom Road. The next step should be a visit to a **food court** in a shopping mall to check out the bewildering range of soups, curries, and stir-fries that make up a Thai menu. Finally, splash out on a meal at one of the exclusive **rooftop restaurants** that pepper the city, such as Sirocco, serving not only top-class Thai dishes but some superb international cuisine too.

ENTERTAINMENT & NIGHTLIFE While the city is famed for its raunchy **go-go bars,** especially on **Patpong,** there are plenty of other ways to have a good time after dark. From graceful renditions of **traditional dances** to in-your-face **transsexual cabarets,** from thumping **dance clubs** like the **Bed Supper Club** to laid-back **jazz venues** such as the **Bamboo Bar,** the city has something to suit all tastes.

BANGKOK'S WATERWAYS

The key to Bangkok's rise lies in the Chao Phraya River, which courses stealthily through its center, feeding a complex network of canals and locks that, until relatively recently, were the focus of city life. Lying just a few miles from the Gulf of Thailand, the river was a major conduit for trade, and the main reason behind its rapid growth. Today, nothing much has changed: Great black barges filled with rice, coal, or sand are towed up and down the river by small yellow tugs; at any time of the day you might spot gray Royal Naval vessels, police on Port Authority jet skis, stout wooden sampans, and even blue barges stacked with Pepsi-Cola bottles, all plying these waters.

In the late 18th century, Thailand's first monarch of the Chakri dynasty, Rama I, moved the capital eastward from Thonburi (a suburb of today's Bangkok) across the river to the district that became known as Rattanakosin Island, so-called due to the man-made canals that surrounded this entire area. Like medieval moats, these canals (*klongs*) acted as a defensive barrier. Other canals were soon added, channeling the waters of the Chao Phraya into peripheral communities, feeding fish ponds or rice paddies, and nurturing the city's many tropical fruit orchards. These waterways fast became the aquatic boulevards and avenues of this low-lying, swampy city. Apart from structures built for royalty, ordinary Bangkok residents lived on water, in bamboo raft homes, or on boats. As foreign diplomats, missionaries, and writers traveled to Bangkok, they drew parallels with the Italian city of Venice and renamed it the "Venice of the East." Not until the early 1800s were nonroyal houses built on dry land.

Due to the health hazards posed by these open *klongs*, and the gradual need for more stable land with the advent of vehicular transport, many of the canals were paved over in the last century. By the late 1970s, most of the city's paddy fields had disappeared. In fact, much of today's Bangkok has been reclaimed from former marshland. Fears are growing as global warming raises sea levels and the effects of seasonal flooding on the city are becoming more drastic.

For a glimpse of traditional Thai life, schedule a few hours to explore the waterways. You'll see people using the river to bathe, wash their clothes, and even brush their teeth at the water's edge (not recommended). Floating kitchens occupy small motorized canoes from which the pilot-cum-chef serves rice and noodles to the occupants on other boats. Men, wrapped in nothing more than a loincloth, tiptoe across floating carpets of logs en route to the lumber mills; ramshackle huts on stilts adorned with 100-year-old fretwork tumble down into *klongs*; while at low tide, the rib cages of sunken boats appear out of the oozing mud.

Opportunities abound for exploring Bangkok's small *klong* networks and river arteries. The most frequently seen boat on the river is the **longtail,** a needle-shaped craft driven by a raucous outboard engine and covered in a striped awning. These act as river taxis for tourists and locals alike. Private longtails congregate at **Maharaj, Chang,** and **Si Phya** public piers and at **River City** (✆ 02225-6179). If you are confident of your haggling skills, you can try to charter a longtail yourself for about 1,000B an hour—be sure to agree on the charge before you get in the boat. *Note:* Beware of independent boat operators who offer to take you to souvenir or gem shops.

Otherwise, if you head to the riverside exit of Saphan Taksin BTS, there's also an official kiosk down on the riverfront, with tour information, including tickets for the hop-on, hop-off **Chao Phraya Express** (✆ 02623-6001). This runs every half-hour, daily from 9:30am to 4pm (tickets 150B), and is a more comfortable option than the (more cramped) longtails or tatty wooden express boats that act as the city's river taxis.

Bangkok Art &
   Culture Center **19**
Erawan Shrine **21**
The Grand Palace **12**
Jim Thompson's House **18**
Lumphini Stadium **23**
Museum of Siam **14**
The National Museum **6**
Patravadi Theatre **11**
Ratchadamnoen Stadium **3**
Red Cross Snake Farm **25**
Royal Barge Museum **4**
Siam Society **22**
Vimanmek Teak Mansion **1**
Wang Suan Pakkad **20**
Wat Arun **15**
Wat Benchamabophit **2**
Wat Mahathat **7**
Wat Phra Kaew **10**
Wat Po **13**
Wat Saket **8**
Wat Suthat & the
   Giant Swing **9**
Wat Traimit **17**

MARKETS
Khao San Road **5**
Pak Klong Talad
   Flower Market **16**
Patpong Night Market **24**

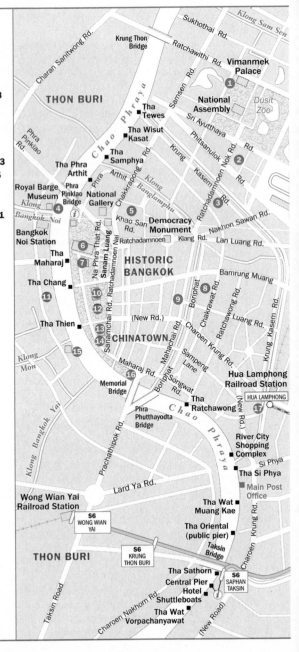

MRT Subway
BTS (Skytrain):
   Sukhumvit Line
   Si Lom Line
   SA Express
      (Suvarnabhumi
      Airport)
Information
Pier
Railway

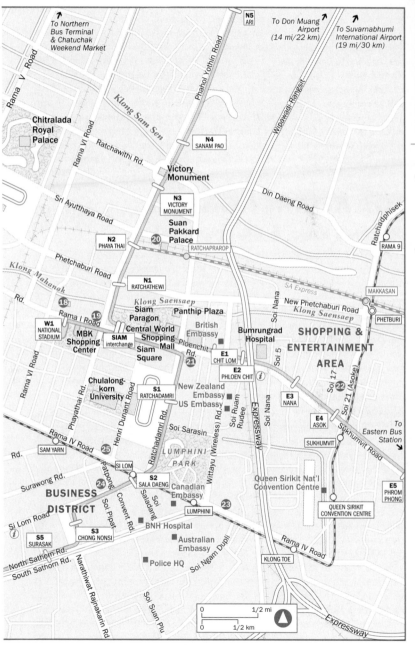

However you tour the *klongs*, take the time to explore **Klong Bangkok Noi** and **Klong Bangkok Yai.** Also stop at the **Royal Barge Museum** (see "Bangkok's Top Historical Treasures & Wats," below), a wonderful riverside hangar crammed with long, narrow vessels covered in gilt carvings, brought out only to commemorate rare events such as a milestone in the monarch's reign or the visit of a dignitary. Tour operators offer half-day tours that include a visit to the Royal Barges Museum and cost about 850B per person, including an English-speaking guide: contact **Thai River Cruise** (✆ **02476-5207**), or enquire at the front desk of your hotel.

Many visitors are disappointed by the touristy **floating market** at **Damnoen Saduak,** about 105km (65 miles) southwest of Bangkok, in Ratchaburi Province, though there's no denying it's a photogenic spectacle. A more authentic experience is to head either to the nearby **Amphawa Floating Market** or upstream along the Chao Phraya to picturesque **Ko Kret;** see "Side Trips from Bangkok," later in this chapter. Unlike Damnoen Saduak, which is at its best in the early morning so requires a pre-dawn start, the market at Amphawa buzzes between noon and 8pm, though it's only at weekends.

TOP ATTRACTIONS

Wat Phra Kaew & the Grand Palace

The number one destination in Bangkok is also one of the most imposing and visually fascinating. If you arrive at 8:30am, when the gates first open, you may have the place virtually to yourself; also remember that it closes at 3.30pm, so don't show up any later than 3pm. Though it's seen by thousands of tourists, who arrive at the gates in bus loads, its immensity still dwarfs the throngs. After passing muster with the fashion police at the main gate and lining up for your ticket (keep it safe for admission to other sites), you'll be directed to the entrance to Wat Phra Kaew (the Emerald Buddha temple). Note that strict dress codes apply to visiting these sites, so be sure to wear appropriate attire; remember, shoes must be removed in places of worship (so slip-ons are a good idea), and you won't be allowed into any royal or religious site if you're exposing your shoulders or dressed in skirts/shorts above the knee.

Wat Phra Kaew ★★★ TEMPLE   This is the most revered temple in the kingdom, and its name refers to the petite jadeite (not emerald) statue that sits atop a huge gold altar in the main hall, or *bot*. The Buddha image is clothed in seasonal robes, changed three times a year to correspond to the summer, winter, and rainy months. The changing of the robes is an important ritual, performed by the king, who also sprinkles water over the monks and well-wishers to bring good fortune during the upcoming season. The statue is the subject of much devotion among Thais; bizarrely, it is also the religious icon to which politicians (accused of corruption) swear innocence. The magically empowered statue was rumored to have been made in North Thailand in the 15th century, before being installed at a temple in Laos, only to be taken back by the Thais and brought to the capital around 1780—a sore subject between the nations.

As you enter the site, one of the first things you see is a stone statue of a hermit, considered a patron of medicine, before which relatives of the infirm pay homage and make offerings. The inside walls of the compound are decorated with murals depicting the entire *Ramakien*, a Thai epic, painted during the reign of Rama I in the 16th century and regularly restored. Its 178 scenes begin at the north gate and continue clockwise, and since it's an unfolding story, it's worth taking a separate tour of the cloisters after viewing the striking monuments housed in the complex.

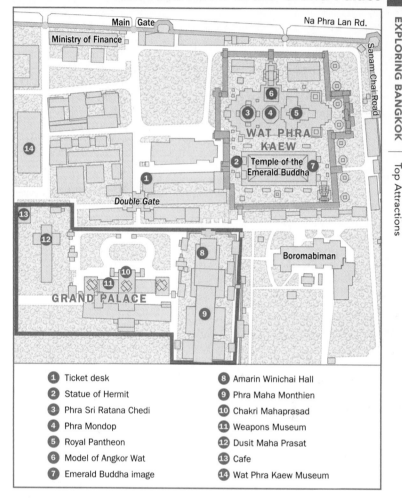

1. Ticket desk
2. Statue of Hermit
3. Phra Sri Ratana Chedi
4. Phra Mondop
5. Royal Pantheon
6. Model of Angkor Wat
7. Emerald Buddha image
8. Amarin Winichai Hall
9. Phra Maha Monthien
10. Chakri Mahaprasad
11. Weapons Museum
12. Dusit Maha Prasat
13. Cafe
14. Wat Phra Kaew Museum

Following around to the left, visitors are then faced with three much-photographed structures: The first, to the west, is **Phra Sri Rattana Chedi,** a dazzling gold, slender, Sri Lankan-style stupa in the shape of an inverted cone; second, in the middle, is the library, or **Phra Mondop,** built in Thai style by Rama I, famed for its mother-of-pearl doors, bookcases containing the *Tripitaka* (sacred Buddhist manuscripts), human and dragon-headed *nagas* (snakes), and statues of Chakri kings; and third, to the east, is the **Royal Pantheon,** built in Khmer style during the 19th century—it's open to the public in October for one day to commemorate the founding of the Chakri dynasty. To the immediate north of the library is a model of **Angkor Wat,** the most sacred of all Cambodian shrines. The model was constructed by King Mongkut (r. 1851–68) as a reminder that the neighboring state was once under the dominion of Thailand.

From here you can enter the central shrine, or *bot*, where the tiny **Emerald Buddha** is housed on a tall pedestal. There's always a crush of people around the entrance, but try to take note of the exquisite inlaid mother-of-pearl work on the door panels. The interior walls are decorated with late-Ayutthaya-style murals depicting the life of the Buddha; the images flow counterclockwise and end with the most important stage: Enlightenment. The surrounding portico of the *bot* is an example of masterful Thai craftsmanship.

As you leave the cloisters of Wat Phra Kaew and move into the grounds of **The Grand Palace ★★★**, it's easy to see that the buildings here were greatly influenced by Western architecture, including Italian, French, and British motifs. The royal family moved from this royal residence to the nearby Chitlada Palace after the death of King Ananda in 1946. Behind an intricately carved gate stands the **Phra Maha Monthien,** a complex of buildings, of which only the **Amarin Winichai Hall** is open to the public—it contains two elaborate thrones and is used officially only for coronations. Immediately west of this is the **Chakri Mahaprasad,** The Grand Palace Hall; built by British architects in 1888 as a royal residence for Rama IV to commemorate the centennial of the Chakri dynasty, it features an unusually florid mix of Italian and Thai influences. The Thai-temple-style roof rests physically (and symbolically) on top of an otherwise European building. The only part of this building open to the public is a **Weapons Museum,** with entrances on either side of the main entrance, which displays a collection of spears, swords, and guns.

To the west of the Chakri Mahaprasad is the **Dusit Maha Prasat,** an audience hall built by Rama I that is now used officially only for royal funerals. Inside is a splendid throne inlaid with mother-of-pearl. On each of the four corners of the roof is a *garuda* (the half-human, half-bird steed of the God Rama, an avatar of the Hindu god Vishnu). The *garuda* symbolizes the king, who is considered a reincarnation of King Rama. This is the most photographed building in the Grand Palace and has become something of an icon of Thai architecture.

Beyond the Dusit Maha Prasat is a small cafe where you can find some refreshment, and, finally, the **Wat Phra Kaew Museum** houses some unusual exhibits, including elephant bones and costumes once used to adorn the Emerald Buddha. Another interesting and new museum is the **Queen Sirikit Museum of Textiles,** which displays a huge variety of intricately woven textiles for which Thailand is justly famous.

East of the river, on Na Phra Lan Rd., near Sanam Luang. ℂ **02224-1833.** www.palaces.thai.net. Admission 400B. Price includes Wat Phra Kaew and the Grand Palace, as well as admission to the Vimanmek Palace (in Dusit Park). Daily 8:30am–3:30pm; most individual buildings are closed to the public except on special days proclaimed by the King. Take the Chao Phraya Express Boat to the pier called Tha Chang, and then walk due east, then south.

Bangkok Art & Culture Center ★ PERFORMING ARTS VENUE   This huge edifice, located opposite the Siam Discovery Center, recently opened its doors providing a showcase for Thai arts, music, theater, film, and design. There are always exhibitions or cultural and educational events taking place, so check out the website before visiting to see what's on. Besides promoting the arts in Thailand, the venue is intended as a platform for cultural exchange with emphasis on collaborations between students here and abroad. With over 3,000 sq. m (32,292 sq. ft.) of exhibition space, Bangkok finally has a major arts center for its inhabitants and visitors.

Corner of Rama I and Phaya Thai Rds. ℂ **02214-6630-8.** www.bacc.or.th. Free admission apart from special concerts and events. Tues–Sun 10am–9pm. National Stadium BTS.

Erawan Shrine ★★ RELIGIOUS SITE   The Erawan Shrine is not old, but it is an interesting testament to the belief in spirits in Thai society. Built in 1956, next to what is now the Grand Hyatt Erawan, it stands defiantly at the center of a busy corner plot, right next to fume-belching buses and overshadowed by the BTS. In a sumptuous spirit house at the center of this yard, a gilded statue of the four-faced Hindu god of creation, Brahma, named Phra Phrom in Thai, is enshrined. Construction of the shrine is believed to have put a stop to a spate of deaths of workers constructing the hotel site, and due to such mystic powers, it is today one of the most revered spots in the kingdom. The area is crowded with worshipers wafting bunches of incense and praying for success in business or love. Even taxi drivers raise their hands from the steering wheel to give a *wai* as they pass by. The shrine made news a while back, when a mentally deranged Thai man decided to take an axe to the statue. As painful testament to the depth of Thais' devotion to the spirits (and a pitiful lesson in human rights), the onlookers turned on him and beat him to death in broad daylight.

On the corner of Rama I and Ratchadamri Rd. (next to the Grand Hyatt Erawan). No entrance fee. Daily dawn–8pm. Phloen Chit BTS.

Jim Thompson's House ★ HISTORIC HOME   American architect Jim Thompson settled in Bangkok after World War II, where he worked for American Intelligence and became fascinated by Thai culture and artifacts. He dedicated himself to reviving Thailand's ebbing silk industry, bringing in new dyes to create the bright pinks, yellows, and turquoises we see sold today. It was Jim Thompson silks that were used by costumier Irene Sharaff for the Oscar-winning movie *The King & I*, starring Yul Brynner. Mr. Thompson mysteriously disappeared in 1967 while vacationing in the Cameron Highlands of Malaysia and, despite extensive investigations, his disappearance has never been resolved.

All visitors join a guided tour of the house, which contains a splendid collection of Khmer sculpture, Chinese porcelain, and Burmese carvings and scroll paintings. The walls lean slightly inward to help stabilize the structure; the original houses were built on stilts without foundations. The residence is composed of a cluster of six teak and *theng* (a wood harder than teak) houses from central Thailand, which were rebuilt—with a few Western facilities—in what must have been a lovely garden, next to what is today an oily, polluted *klong*. No doubt it would have been magnificent 50 years ago.

The attractions here include a relaxing cafe, a gallery space with a revolving collection of local artists' works, and a shop featuring silk garments, bags, and scarves.

6 Soi Kasemsan 2. ✆ **02216-7368.** www.jimthompsonhouse.com. Admission 100B. Daily 9am–5pm. On a small *soi* off Rama I Rd., near the National Stadium BTS.

Museum of Siam ★ ☺ MUSEUM   Bangkok's newest museum is conveniently located in a grand old colonial building just a short walk from the Grand Palace and Wat Po. It is worth considering while you're in this part of town, especially if you have kids with you, as there are so many hands-on exhibits. To begin, visitors are shown a short video contrasting the lives of traditional and modern Thais, and then over the three floors of displays, the museum attempts to answer the question "What is Thainess?" by looking at key aspects of the country's evolution. There are rooms dedicated to the importance of rice and bamboo in Thai culture, and there's also a chance to practice your cannon-firing skills and dress up in Edwardian clothes for a period snapshot.

4 Sanam Chai Rd. ✆ **02225-2777.** Admission 300B, free for children 14 and under and seniors 60 and over. Tues–Sun 10am–6pm. Express boat to Tha Thien, walk east to Sanamchai Rd, then 1 block south.

The National Museum ★★ MUSEUM   The National Museum, just a short (15-min.) walk north of the Grand Palace, is the country's central treasury of art and archaeology (32 branches are located throughout the provinces). Some of the buildings themselves can be considered works of art.

The current museum was built as part of the Grand Palace complex, when the capital of Siam was moved from Thonburi to Bangkok in 1782. Originally the palace of Rama I's brother, the deputy king and appointed successor, it was called the Wang Na ("Palace at the Front"). The position of princely successor was eventually abolished, and Rama V had the palace converted into a museum in 1884. Thammasat University, the College of Dramatic Arts, and the National Theater were also built on the royal grounds, along with additional museum buildings.

To see the entire collection, take a free map at the ticket office and give yourself a few hours; if you prefer not to wander, catch one of the Wednesday or Thursday guided tours, beginning at 9:30am. Start with the **Thai History and the Prehistoric Galleries** in the first building. If you're short of time, proceed to the **Red House** behind it, a traditional 18th-century Thai building that was originally the living quarters of Princess Sri Sudarak, sister of King Rama I. It contains many personal effects originally owned by the princess.

Another essential stop is the **Buddhaisawan Chapel,** built in 1795 to house one of Thailand's most revered Buddha images, brought here from its original home in Chiang Mai. The chapel is an exquisite example of Buddhist temple architecture.

From the chapel, work your way back through the main building of the royal palace to see the gold jewelry, some from the royal collections, and the Thai ceramics, including many pieces in the five-color *Bencharong* style. The **Old Transportation Room** contains ivory carvings, elephant chairs, and royal palanquins. There are also rooms full of all kinds of memorabilia: royal emblems and insignia, stone and wood carvings, costumes, textiles, musical instruments, and Buddhist religious artifacts. Fine art and sculpture are found in the newer galleries at the rear of the museum compound.

Na Phra That Rd. ✆ **02224-1333.** www.thailandmuseum.com. Admission 200B. Wed–Sun 9am–4pm. Free English-language tours Wed–Thurs 9:30am. Chao Phraya Express Boat to Tha Chang pier; about 1km/⅔ mile north of the Grand Palace.

Royal Barge Museum ★★ MUSEUM   If you've hired a longtail boat on the Chao Phraya, stop by this unique museum housing the sumptuous royal barges. These elaborately decorated sailing vessels—the largest measures over 46m (151 ft.)—are used by the royal family on state occasions or for religious ceremonies. The king's personal barge, the *Suphannahong*, has a swanlike neck and central chamber; the boat itself is decorated with scarlet and gold carvings of fearsome mythological beasts.

If you can't make it to the royal barges, there is a smaller display of vessels at the National Museum (see above).

On the west bank of the river, on Klong Bangkok Noi (canal), north of the Phra Pinklao Bridge. ✆ **02424-0004.** www.thailandmuseum.com. Admission 100B adults, 100B extra for cameras, 200B for video. Daily 9am–5pm. Taxi or cross-river ferry from Tha Phra Arthit.

Siam Society CULTURAL INSTITUTION   The 19th-century Kamthieng House, on the grounds of the Siam Society Headquarters, was a rice farmer's teak house, transplanted from the banks of Chiang Mai's Ping River. Its collection is oriented toward ethnographic objects illustrating the culture of everyday life. Many agricultural and domestic items, including woven fish baskets and terra-cotta pots, are on display, and there's an interesting exhibit on the Chao Vieng, or city dwellers, from the northern Lanna Thai kingdom.

Walking through the small but lush grounds, which are landscaped like a northern Thai garden, offers respite from the Asok intersection, just behind the hedge. The Siam Society also supports an excellent library and gallery, with information on nearly every aspect of Thai society, concentrating on regional culture. Check the website for music concerts, lectures in English, and study tours given by experts.

131 Soi Asok (north of Sukhumvit on Soi 21). © **02661-6470.** www.siam-society.org. Admission 100B adults, 50B children. Tues–Sat 9am–5pm. 10-min. walk from Asok BTS station.

Vimanmek Teak Mansion ★★ MUSEUM   Your ticket to the Grand Palace will also get you in to visit King Chulalongkorn's stunning golden teakwood mansion, often called Vimanmek Palace, situated in delightful Dusit Palace Park. Built in 1901, this mansion once stood on the small island of Ko Si Chang and was restored in 1982 for Bangkok's bicentennial. It's now a private museum with a collection of the royal family's memorabilia. Despite the (sometimes spotty) standard of English employed by the guides, the hour-long tour here does take you through several of the 80 exquisite apartments and rooms. Also in Dusit Park is the original **Abhisek Dusit Throne Hall,** housing a display of Thai handicrafts, and buildings displaying photographs, clocks, fabrics, royal carriages, and other regalia.

193/2 Ratchawithi Rd., Dusit Palace Park (opposite the Dusit Zoo). © **02628-6300** ext 5120. www.vimanmek.com. Admission 100B; free if you purchase a joint ticket for the Grand Palace. Daily 9:30am–4pm (last ticket 3:15pm). Taxi from Tha Thien pier.

Wang Suan Pakkad ⛪ PALACE   Wang Suan Pakkad ("Palace of the Lettuce Garden") is one of Bangkok's most delightful retreats. This peaceful oasis was the home of Princess Chumbhon of Nakhon Sawan, an avid art collector and one of the country's most dedicated archaeologists—credited with having partly financed the excavations at Ban Chiang I in 1967. In 1952, five 19th-century teak houses were moved from Chiang Mai and rebuilt in a beautifully landscaped garden on a private *klong*, separated by a high wall from the tumult of Bangkok's streets. The **Lacquer Pavilion** (moved here in 1958) came from a monastery grounds and was a birthday present from the prince to the princess.

Avoiding the Touts

Tourists are harangued going in and out of the major sites around the Grand Palace, and sadly this area is now famous for its scam artists. Avoid unnecessary frustration by not engaging with these characters just as you would at home. Visitors are frequently told that sites are "closed" by "helpful" types, who then suggest alternate destinations. This is the start of the famous **"Bangkok shopping tour scam."** If you are approached by a stranger, whether it's someone purporting to be a "guide," or a tuk-tuk driver in this area, just say "no thanks" and walk away. If you end up riding a tuk-tuk near these main sites, make sure you've agreed to a price with the driver and insist on "*No* shopping." If you have any problems, don't hesitate to use the word *poleet* (police in Thai), or call the **Tourist Police** at © **1155.**

The balance of the collection here is diverse, with Khmer sculpture, ivory boxes, and some marvelous prints by European artists depicting images of Siam before the country opened to the Western world. There is an entire room of objects from the Ban Chiang site, including pottery and jewelry. Look out for a superb Buddha head, from Ayutthaya, and an example of a royal barge, outside in a shed in the garden. Be sure to ask to see the pavilion housing the princess's collection of Thai and Chinese ceramics. The gift shop at Wang Suan Pakkad offers reasonably priced reproductions.

352 Sri Ayutthaya Rd. (btw. Phayathai and Ratchaprarop rds.). © **02245-4934.** www.suanpakkad. com. Admission 100B adults, 50B children, including material for a self-guided tour of grounds and collections. Daily 9am–4pm. 10-min. walk from Phaya Thai BTS.

TEMPLES (WATS)

Bangkok's many temples are each unique and inspiring. If you can see only a few, pay attention to the star ratings and hit the highlights (Wat Phra Kaew is listed earlier in the chapter due to its location within the Grand Palace compound and Wat Po is right next door). But while the big temples of Bangkok are highly recommended, don't pass up smaller neighborhood temples, where you have a good chance of learning about Buddhism in daily practice. Early morning is a good time to visit temples: the air is cool, monks busy themselves with morning activities, and the complexes are generally less crowded.

Thai people make regular offerings to temples and monasteries as an act of merit-making. Supporting the *sangha*, or monkhood, brings one closer to Buddhist ideals and increases the likelihood of a better life beyond this one. Many shops near temples sell saffron-colored pails filled with everyday supplies such as toothbrushes, soap, and other common necessities, and Thais bring these and other gifts as offerings to Buddhist mendicants as a way of gaining good graces. If you get up very early, you may even see a morning alms collection by (usually barefoot) monks carrying their bowls around the neighborhood.

Small monetary contributions (the amount is up to you) are welcome at any temple, though the better-known temples already charge an admission fee. Devotions at a temple involve bowing three times, placing the forehead on the ground at the foot of the Buddha, and lighting candles and incense and chanting. Tourists are welcome to participate, but they are asked to pay particular attention to proper dress—take off your shoes and avoid baring your shoulders, thighs, upper arms, or back. If you kneel or sit to pay your respects, take care not to point your feet toward the Buddha images.

Wat Arun (Temple of Dawn) ★★★ TEMPLE Formerly known as Wat Jaeng, the 79-m (260-ft.) high, Khmer-inspired tower was renamed the "Temple of Dawn," by King Thaksin, Bangkok's founder. He was keen to signal the rise of a new kingdom after Ayutthaya was decimated, and so borrowed the name—which means dawn—from the Hindu God, Aruna. Fittingly, it's at its most wondrous as the sun rises and sets.

The original tower was only 15m (49 ft.) high but was expanded during the rule of Rama III (1824–51) to its current height of 76m (250 ft.). The exterior is decorated with flower and decorative motifs made of ceramic shards donated to the monastery by local people, at the request of the King. At the base of the complex are Chinese stone statues, once used as ballast in trading ships, which were gifts from Chinese merchants.

You can climb the central *prang*, but be warned: The steps are treacherously narrow and steep—and even more precarious coming down—so cling to the rail at the side. If you go up, notice the Hindu gods atop the three-headed elephants. The view of the river, Wat Po, and Grand Palace is well worth the climb. Be sure to walk to the back of the tower to the monks' living quarters, a tranquil world far from the bustle of Bangkok's busy streets.

West bank of the Chao Phraya, opposite Tha Thien Pier. www.watarun.org. Admission 50B. Daily 9am–5:30pm. Take a water taxi from Tha Tien Pier (near Wat Po), or cross the Phra Pinklao Bridge and follow the river south on Arun Amarin Rd.

Wat Benchamabophit (the Marble Temple) ★ TEMPLE   Wat Benchamabophit, also known as the Marble Temple, was designed during the rule of Rama V and built in the early part of the 20th century. It is the most modern and one of the most beautiful of Bangkok's royal *wats*. Unlike the older complexes, there's no truly monumental *viharn* or *chedi* dominating the grounds. Many smaller buildings reflect a melding of European materials and designs with traditional Thai religious architecture. Even the courtyards are paved with polished white marble. Walk inside the compound, beyond the main *bot*, to view the many Buddha images that adopt a wide variety of postures. During early mornings, monks chant in the main chapel, sometimes so intensely that it seems as if the temple is going to lift off.

Sri Ayutthaya Rd. (south of the Assembly Building, near Chitralada Palace). Admission 20B. Daily 8am–5pm. Taxi from Phaya Thai BTS.

Wat Mahathat (Temple of the Great Relic) HISTORIC SITE   Built to house a relic of the Buddha, Wat Mahathat is one of Bangkok's oldest shrines and the headquarters for Thailand's largest monastic order. It's also the Center for Vipassana Meditation, at the city's Buddhist University, which offers some programs in English. (See "Cultural & Wellness Pursuits," below, for more information about courses.) The temple is not frequented by many tourists, and you'll probably find the young monks eager to engage you in conversation.

Adjacent to it, between Maharaj Road and the river, is the city's biggest **amulet market,** where a fantastic array of religious amulets, charms, talismans, and traditional medicine is sold. Each amulet brings a specific kind of luck—to get the girl, to pass your exams, to keep bugs out of your rice stock, or to ward off your mother-in-law—so if you buy one, choose carefully. (The newer amulet market is part of Wat Ratchanada, off the intersection of Mahachai and Ratchadamnoen Klang roads, across from Wat Saket.)

Na Phra That Rd. (near Sanam Luang Park, btw. the Grand Palace and the National Museum). ✆ **02222-6011** (meditation center). Donations welcome. Daily 9am–5pm. Water taxi to Maharaj pier.

Wat Po ★★★ TEMPLE   Wat Po is among the most photogenic of all the *wats* (temples) in Bangkok; it's also one of the most active. Also known as the Temple of the Reclining Buddha, Wat Po was built by Rama I in the 16th century and is the oldest and largest Buddhist temple in Bangkok. The compound is immediately south of the Grand Palace, but it takes 15 (often hot and sweaty) minutes to walk from one to the other. The huge compound contains many important monuments, and the block to the south of Chetuphon Road is where monks reside.

Most people go straight to the enormous **Reclining Buddha** in the northwestern corner of the compound section. It is more than 43m (141 ft.) long and 15m (49 ft.) high, and was built during the mid-19th-century reign of Rama III. The statue is brick, covered with layers of plaster and gold leaf; the feet are inlaid with mother-of-pearl illustrations of 108 auspicious *laksanas* (characteristics) of the Buddha.

Outside, the grounds contain 91 *chedis* (stupas or mounds), four *viharns* (halls), and a *bot* (the central shrine in a Buddhist temple). Most impressive, aside from the Reclining Buddha, are the four main *chedis* dedicated to the first four Chakri kings and, nearby, the library.

The temple is considered Thailand's first public university. Long before the advent of literacy or books, many of its murals and sculptures were used to illustrate and instruct scholars on the basic principles of religion, science, and literature. Visitors still drop 1-satang coins in 108 bronze bowls—corresponding to the 108 auspicious characteristics of the Buddha—for good fortune, and to help the monks keep up the *wat*.

Wat Po is also home to one of the earliest Thai massage schools and you can learn about the traditional methods and medicine at the **Traditional Medical Practitioners Association Center,** an open-air hall to the rear of the *wat*. True Thai massage, such as that taught here, involves chiropractic manipulation and acupressure, as well as stretching, stroking, and kneading. Massage courses are available (9,500B for 30 hours), but many students prefer schools with tutors who speak more proficient English. There are also a few astrologers and palm readers available for consultation, though foreign visitors are bound to encounter language difficulties.

Maharaj Rd., near the river (about 1km/⅔ mile south of the Grand Palace). ✆ **02226-0335.** Admission 50B. Daily 8am–5pm; Massage school ✆ **02622-3551;** massages offered until 6pm. A short walk or taxi from Tha Thien pier.

Wat Saket (The Golden Mount) ★ TEMPLE   Wat Saket is easily recognized by its golden *chedi*, atop a fortress-like hill near busy Ratchadamnoen Road and Banglampoo. King Rama I restored the *wat*, and 30,000 bodies were brought here during a plague in the reign of Rama II (r. 1809–24). The hill, which is almost 80m (262 ft.) high, is an artificial construction, begun during the reign of Rama III (r. 1824–51). R. Rama V built the golden *chedi* in the late 19th century to house a relic of Buddha, given to him by the British. The concrete walls were added during World War II to keep the structure from collapsing.

The Golden Mount is interesting for its vistas of Ratanakosin Island and the rooftops of Bangkok and is beautifully lit at night. Every late October to mid-November (for 9 days around the full moon), Wat Saket hosts Bangkok's most important temple fair, when the Golden Mount is wrapped with red cloth and a carnival erupts around it, with food, trinket stalls, and theatrical performances.

Ratchadamnoen Klang and Boripihat roads. Entrance to the *wat* is free; admission to the Golden Mount is 10B. Donations welcome. Daily 8am–5pm. Taxi from Hua Lamphong MRT.

Wat Suthat & the Giant Swing TEMPLE   This temple is among the oldest and largest in Bangkok, and Somerset Maugham declared its roofline the most beautiful. It was begun by Rama I and finished by Rama III; Rama II carved the panels for the *viharn* doors. It houses the beautiful 14th-century **Phra Buddha Shakyamuni,** a Buddha image that was brought from Sukhothai. The ashes of King Rama VIII, Ananda Mahidol, brother of the current king, are contained in its base. The wall paintings for which it is known were created during Rama III's reign.

Outside the *viharn* stand many Chinese pagodas, bronze horses, and figures of Chinese soldiers. The most important religious association, however, is with the Brahman priests who officiate at important state ceremonies, and there are two Hindu shrines nearby. The huge teak arch—also carved by Rama II—in front is all that remains of an original giant swing, which was used until 1932 to celebrate and thank Shiva for a bountiful rice harvest, and to ask for the god's blessing on the next. The Minister of Rice, accompanied by hundreds of Brahman holy men, would lead a parade around the city walls to the temple precinct. Teams of men would ride the swing on arcs as high as 25m (82 ft.) in the air, trying to grab a bag of silver coins with their teeth. Due to injuries and deaths, the dangerous swing ceremony has been discontinued, but the thanksgiving festival is still celebrated in mid-December, after the rice harvest.

Sao Chingcha Square (near the intersection of Bamrung Mueang and Thi Thong rds.). ✆ **02224-9845.** Admission 20B. Daily 9am–9pm. Taxi from Hua Lamphong MRT.

Wat Traimit (The Golden Buddha) TEMPLE Wat Traimit, thought to date from the 13th century, would hardly rate a second glance if not for its astonishing Buddha image, which is nearly 3m (9¾ ft.) high, weighs over 5 tons, and is believed to be cast of solid gold. It was discovered by accident in 1957 when, covered by a plaster image, it was dropped from a crane during a move. The impact shattered the outer shell, revealing the shining gold beneath. This powerful image is truly dazzling and is thought to have been cast during the Sukhothai period. It was perhaps covered with plaster to hide it from Burmese invaders. Pieces of the stucco are also on display at the site.

Traimit Rd. (west of Hua Lamphong Station, just west of the intersection of Krung Kasem and Rama IV rds.). Admission 20B. Donations welcome. Daily 9am–5pm. Walk southwest on Traimit Rd., look for a school on the right with a playground; the *wat* is up a flight of stairs overlooking the school. 2-min. walk from Hua Lamphong MRT.

CULTURAL & WELLNESS PURSUITS

Culture is all around you in Thailand—and there are ample opportunities to take part in the daily activities, festivals, ceremonies, events, and practices that weave the fabric of this society. Keep an eye on free magazines, such as *BK Magazine*, or local newspapers, *The Nation* and *Bangkok Post*, for major events during your stay (see also p. 29). You may want to check with the **TAT** (✆ **1672**) or the **Bangkok Tourism Bureau** (✆ **02225-7612**), though these organizations may not always be as well informed as the local press. The best part of Thai festivals is that, whether getting soaked by buckets of water at Songkran or watching candlelit floats drift downstream at Loy Krathong, foreign visitors are usually invited to join in. Thais are very proud of their cultural heritage, and opportunities abound to learn and participate.

Thai Cooking

Fancy a chance to make some of the delicious dishes you have been feasting on? Thai cooking is fun and easy, and there are a few good hands-on courses in Bangkok. Lectures on Thai regional cuisine, cooking techniques, and menu planning complement classroom exercises to prepare all your favorite dishes using unique local produce, herbs, and spices. Mention if you're a vegetarian and they'll tailor the class to your needs. The best part is afterward, when you get to eat what you've cooked.

○ **The Oriental Cooking School** ★★★ is located in a quaint colonial house across the river from the famed hotel (p. 72). Morning courses run daily (except Sun), and end with lunch. Their chefs are excellent, and you'll learn, through demonstration and practice, every aspect of Thai cooking. The course is open to anyone from beginner to expert. Different dishes are taught each day, so you can attend for a week and always learn something new. The cost is 4,000B person, per day. Call the hotel at ✆ **02659-9000.**

○ **The Blue Elephant** ★★ is part of a large, Belgian-owned Thai restaurant chain popular throughout Europe. The cookery school stands in the same locale as the restaurant, a yellow-painted mansion close to the Surasak BTS. Classes begin at 9am, with a visit to the market to pick up fresh ingredients for the day. Back in the classroom, you'll first watch demonstrations before stepping up to your own cooking station to practice what you've learned under the watchful eye of a teacher. Afterward, you can share your creations with the rest of the class, as part of a delicious lunch spread. Visit them at 233 S. Sathorn Rd., just below Surasak BTS, or call ✆ **02673-9353** (www.blueelephant.com). One-day (group) courses cost 2,943B per person; private classes are also available.

○ The woman behind **Mrs. Balbir's** ★★ is witty, dedicated, and an indefatigable charity worker, as well as a TV star. Vinder Balbir is fluent in several languages (including English and Thai), so these lessons are much more informative and interactive than most. She will carefully explain why a particular type of herb is required or what ingredients can be used as replacements in your home country. True to her ethnic roots, she can also teach fabulous Punjabi cuisine, as well as Thai. After a morning (10am–1pm) or afternoon (2–6pm) spent learning to cook a four-course meal with Mrs. B., you'll leave filled with good humor and great food. Courses start at 2,200B per person and take place above her restaurant (✆ **02651-0498**), in the first sub-*soi* at 155/1–2 Sukhumvit Soi 11, close to Nana BTS. For all course inquiries, call her restaurant Tuesday to Sunday from 11am to 2pm or 6 to 11pm. Or see the website www.mrsbalbirs.com.

Thai Massage

A traditional Thai massage involves manipulating your limbs to stretch each muscle and then applying acupressure techniques to loosen up tension and start energy flowing. Your body will be twisted, pulled, and sometimes pounded in the process.

For Thai massage to be beneficial, it should be fairly rigorous and at times it can be punishing: If the therapist is loath to use pressure from the start, you'll know you are wasting your time. If you chose a street-side spa, choose one away from tourist areas—such as Khao San, Sukhumvit, or Silom roads, where Thais are patrons. **Note:** Many massage parlors on Silom and Sukhumvit roads are fronts for brothels, where (male) tourists will be propositioned for a variety of sexual favors.

There are countless spas and massage parlors around Bangkok; many offer good services at very reasonable rates, such as the humongous **Healthland** (120 Sathorn Rd.; ✆ **02637-8883;** www.healthlandspa.com), which operates a bit like a neon-lit, spa production line, or the quieter **Ruen-Nuad** (✆ **02632-2662**), a small spa tucked in a small *soi* opposite the BNH Hospital on Soi Convent (between Silom and Sathorn rds.). It offers excellent foot massages as well as authentic Thai massage.

Wat Po (p. 113) has long been promoted as the only place to learn Thai massage, and though it's cheaper than some, it's still pretty overrated. These days, better options abound. Good courses are offered at the Sukhumvit Road location of the award-winning **Chiva-Som Academy** ★★ (© 02711-5270; www.chivasom academy.com). These cover therapies such as Reiki and other alternative treatments; but Bangkok's finest spas are almost always those in the most respected hotels, where time and money are invested in training and language skills. **The Elemis Spa** ★★★ (© 02207-7779; www.elemisspabangkok.com) at the **St Regis Hotel** (p. 80) and the **Oriental Spa & Ayurvedic Penthouse** ★★★ (© 02659-9000; www.mandarin-oriental.com/bangkok/spa) are two of the finest places going, but they come with a hefty price—you're paying for expertise that leaves your muscles soothed, gets your blood flowing, and gives you a feeling of unparalleled well-being.

Warning: Budget spas that use untrained staff with no English skills make for not just an unpleasant experience, but a potentially painful one. If your masseuse doesn't understand a word of English, or there is no one to help translate your needs or aspects of your current health, such as varicose veins or respiratory or skin conditions, you are taking a serious risk. Generally, places that offer "ancient" or "traditional" Thai massage have well-trained masseurs and masseuses who offer no extras, but if you are asked to pick a number from a group of dolled-up masseuses sitting behind a glass barrier, you can be sure the term "massage" is a euphemism for paid sex. Your chosen masseuse will then inform you of the "extras" available and the going rates.

Thai Boxing

Muaythai, or Thai boxing, is Thailand's national sport, and a visit to either of the two venues in Bangkok, or in towns all over Thailand, displays a very different side to the usually gentle Thai culture. The mystical prebout rituals, live musical performances, and, of course, the frenetic gambling, appeal to fans of this raw, and often bloody, spectacle. In Bangkok, catch up to 15 bouts nightly at either of two stadiums. The **Ratchadamnoen Stadium** (Ratchadamnoen Nok Ave.; © 02281-4205) hosts fights on Monday, Wednesday, Thursday, and Sunday, while the **Lumphini Stadium,** on Rama IV Road (© 02251-4303), has bouts on Tuesday, Friday, and Saturday. Tickets cost 1,000B to 2,000B at both venues; ringside seats are only bookable in advance. In the second-class seats, you may still have a good view of the action in the ring and will see close-ups of the gambling action. The guys with multiple cell-phones screaming and shouting often overshadow the action in the ring.

Keen to try some kicks and punches yourself? Check out the website **www.muay thai.com,** which details training camps for rookies.

Meditation

The House of Dhamma (© 02511-0439; www.houseofdhamma.com) and **Wat Mahathat** (see "Temples (Wats)" earlier in this chapter) serve as meditation centers for overseas students of Buddhism. The latter is one of Thailand's largest Buddhist Universities and has become a popular center for meditation lessons, with English-speaking monks overseeing students of *Vipassana,* also called Insight Meditation. Instruction is held daily; call ahead (© 02222-6011) to get the schedule and to make an appointment. Both offer good introductions to basic techniques.

Thai Language Study

So you've learned your "Sawadee-khrup" or "Sawadee-kha," but want to take it a little farther from there? Thais are very gracious and welcoming with foreigners butchering their language (the tones make you pronounce the most mundane phrases in laughable ways), but there are a few good schools in Bangkok to help you get the

Lovers of all things reptilian can witness a sight rarely encountered anywhere else. The **Red Cross Snake Farm,** at 1871 Rama IV Rd. (✆ **02252-0161**), is located in the heart of Bangkok. Don't expect a bucolic "farm" setting; in fact, this is nothing more than a cluster of pretty colonial buildings, in the heart of the city, that provide a research institute for the study of venomous snakes. Established in 1923, this was the second facility of its type in the world. For a fee of 200B, you can see slide shows and snake-handling demonstrations weekdays at 11am and 2:30pm, and on weekends and holidays at 11am. You can also watch the handlers work with deadly cobras and (equally poisonous) banded kraits, with demonstrations of venom milking. The venom is later injected into horses, which produce antivenin for the treatment of snakebites in humans. The Red Cross Snake Farm sells medical guides and will also inoculate you against such maladies as typhoid, cholera, and smallpox, in their clinic. The institute is open daily Monday to Friday 9:30am to 3:30pm, Saturday and Sunday 9:30am to 1pm. It's a short walk from Sala Daeng BTS station.

pronunciations right. Among the many offered, try the superlative **American University Alumni Language Center** (179 Ratchadamri Rd.; ✆ **02252-8170**) or the **Union Language School** (7th Floor, 328 CCT Office Building, Phayathai Rd.; ✆ **02214-6033**).

STAYING ACTIVE

Fitness

All the finest five-star properties in town boast quality health clubs complete with personal trainers and top equipment. In addition, **California WOW** (www.california wowx.com) has an enormous club just on the corner of Silom Road and Soi Convent, at Liberty Square (✆ **02631-1122**), and another at Siam Paragon mall (✆ **02627-5999**); expect to pay around 1,000B daily for access to both locations. Don't be intimidated into paying anything more than you can afford—the reps use famously hard-sell tactics. The upscale Ascott-serviced residences down on Sathorn Road benefit from the members-only **Cascade Club** (✆ **02676-6969;** www.cascadeclubandspa.com), a stunning state-of-the-art gym, which comes with two studios for Pilates and aerobics, a shady outdoor pool, and a spa. Day passes in 2011 cost 535B—good value if you love long workouts.

If these places listed are too expensive, check the three- to four-star hotels in your district; many offer day passes for as little as 350B.

Golf

Various golf courses lie close to the city, a number of which are championship quality. Due to their huge popularity, access is sometimes limited. Visitors can get around this by booking upscale packages offered by hotel concierges or agents, such as **Golf A La Cart** (www.golfalacart-thailand.com), who can arrange access during the busiest seasons. These fully inclusive deals include car transfer and all fees.

- **Thai Country Club** (𝄢 **03857-0234;** www.thaicountryclub.com), run by the Peninsula Hotel, is praised for its consistent greens and sumptuous clubhouse. This stunning 18-hole course lies just 45 minutes southeast of Bangkok. The following fees refer to low/high season rates: Greens fees are 3,600B–4,800B on weekdays, 4,800B–6,000B on weekends. Note that visitors' hours on weekends are restricted.
- **Pinehurst Golf & Country Club** (𝄢 **02516-8679;** www.pinehurst.co.th), located in Pathum Thani, is a popular 27-hole course that served as the venue for the 1992 Johnnie Walker Classic. Greens fees on weekdays are 1,800B, on weekends 2,400B.
- **Bangkok Golf Club** (𝄢 **02501-2828;** www.golf.th.com), a short 35-minute drive from the city center, is an 18-hole course that's always popular and regularly plays host to local and regional tournaments. Night golf is available. Greens fees are 1,950B on weekdays and 2,750B on weekends.

Horse Racing

The prestigious **Royal Bangkok Sports Club** (RBSC; 𝄢 **02652-5000;** www.rbsc.org) holds horse-racing events that are open to the paying public every second Sunday of the month, with occasional Saturday meetings; check the website for dates. The grounds occupy a prime spot on Henri Dunant Road, opposite Chulalongkorn University, north of Rama IV Road. Nominal admission fees and minimum bets apply.

Yoga

Apart from the many hotels in town that schedule regular yoga classes, some downtown studios may offer special packages for visitors on extended stays. Expect to pay up to 2,500B. One such studio is **Absolute Yoga** (𝄢 **02252-4400;** www.absoluteyoga bangkok.com), with many branches including one in Amarin Plaza, close to the Grand Hyatt Erawan, on Ploenchit Road. Hot yoga, sometimes called bikram yoga (where yoga is practiced in a room at sauna-like temperatures), is available at **Absolute Yoga's** Sathorn branch (𝄢 **02636-8342**). There are numerous daily classes and schedules are posted on the website. Wear loose workout gear, bring a big bottle of water, and be ready to sweat buckets. **Yoga Elements Studio** (𝄢 **02655-5671;** www.yoga elements.com), on the 23rd floor of the Vanissa Building, just behind Central Chidlom department store on Soi Chidlom (5 min. from Chit Lom BTS), is another locally run studio with a wide variety of yoga classes. The big commercial fitness clubs in town, such as **California WOW** (see above), also offer yoga and Pilates, though there's often an extra charge for this.

SHOPPING

Bangkok pulls in shoppers from all over the world, clamoring to find bargains at the endless street-side stalls or in the new ultrachic, brand-name boutiques. High-quality goods at very reasonable prices are available, if you look hard, but any discussion of shopping in Thailand must be prefaced with a warning about shopping scams; see p. 34. If you encounter problems with any merchants, take their business card and contact the **Tourist Police** (𝄢 **1155**), or report the incident to your hotel concierge.

Warning: If you wish to press charges for any reason, be prepared to waste a lot of time filling in a mountain of forms.

Where to Buy

Shopping is a real adventure in Bangkok. The big markets are a visual onslaught (don't miss the Weekend Market; see p. 125), and there are great upmarket gift and antiques dealers as well as small souvenir stalls scattered about town. Nancy Chandler's *Map of Bangkok* is available at bookstores throughout the city for 275B and has detailed insets of places such as Chinatown and the sprawling Weekend Market. Below is a breakdown according to the top shopping areas.

TOWARD THE RIVER

Charoen Krung (New) Road is full of goodies: antiques stores, jewelry wholesalers, and funky little galleries. Keep your eyes open, and you might stumble on a gem as you browse shop windows, especially at such places as **Lek Gallery,** at number 1124–1134 (✆ 02639-5871), near Soi 30, which has attractive decorative items such as table lamps and hatstands, as well as some fine antique furniture. The art and antiques shops at the low-rise mall known as **River City** (✆ 02237-0077; www.rivercity.co.th), on Charoen Krung Soi 38, have a great selection of porcelain, wood carvings, jewelry, and silk, but some outlets are overpriced (avoid the tailoring shops here, as the low standards of craftsmanship do not warrant the big bucks). If you're in the market for antiques, you need to know your stuff, as there are many fakes on sale. Close to the Oriental Hotel is **OP Place** (✆ 02266-0186), featuring a heap of high-end shopping venues, from stores selling expensive designer luggage to jet-setter jewelry stores and amazing antiques, carpets, and fine silver tableware (much of which is Tiffany-like quality). In the same *soi* as the Oriental Hotel are some of the city's better tailoring shops and, in the **Mandarin Oriental** (p. 72) itself, look out for exquisite one-off jewelry pieces at **Lotus Arts de Vivre,** or pop into the branch of **Jim Thompson's** for great silks (www.jimthompson.com).

SUKHUMVIT ROAD

This area is lined with shops from one end to the other, as well as some of Bangkok's biggest shopping malls (see "Department Stores & Shopping Plazas," below). For fine silk, stop in at **Almeta** (p. 125), a rival to the Jim Thompson brand. **Celadon House,** at 8/3–8/5 Ratchadaphisek Rd. (✆ 02229-5193), near the Asok BTS, carries attractive celadon ceramic.

For men's tailoring, there are many shops along Sukhumvit *sois* 11 and 19. Most ship your order off to have clothes made in a factory, and quality is iffy, so bargain like mad. **Ambassador Fashion** (28–28/1 Sukhumvit Soi 19; ✆ 02253-2993) has been in the business for years and is near the Asok BTS.

At night, the entire road fills up with **Night Market stalls.** Down at Soi 5, you will find endless supplies of wooden toys, crafts, suitcases, and pirate DVDs. After Soi 11, the pavements get packed with clothes, souvenirs, and surf wear. At Soi 15, there's the excellent **Asia Books** (✆ 02651-0429); it's close to **Robinson's Department Store** (✆ 02651-1533; www.robinson.co.th), which is the place to shop for quality brands. It has a fair range of midrange luggage, children's wear, ladies' fashions, T-shirts, and brand-name sunglasses, though clothing sizes will not normally extend to oversized European or American sizes.

SILOM & SURAWONG ROADS

This area is packed with shopping malls and vendors—you'll find any number of jewelry shops, silk retailers, and plenty of touristy tailors, but few places in this area are top-notch. Check out the main store of **Jim Thompson** (p. 125) or branches at

Siam Paragon and Emporium. **Silom Complex** (✆ 02632-1199), next to Sala Daeng BTS, contains the **Central** department store (www.central.co.th), which sells well-known brands of casual clothing such as Giordano and Esprit. On the second floor of Central, there's a Marks & Spencer store from the U.K., selling food and clothing—it's a great stop if you can't find any local fashions that fit or if you need things such as thermal underwear for your return trip. Right across the road from Silom Complex is the 24-hour British pharmacy **Boots** (✆ 02233-0571), which you should visit for such things as European prescription drugs and contact lens cleaner. **Watson's** (no phone), a similar Hong Kong-based pharmacy, is just at the entrance to Silom Complex.

The Patpong Night Market (p. 124), which runs between Silom and Surawong roads, sells mostly counterfeit goods.

What to Buy
ANTIQUES
Buying antiques to take out of Thailand is tricky. Authentic antiques are more than 200 years old (they must date from the beginning of the Chakri dynasty in Bangkok), but these days most items are good reproductions that have been professionally "distressed"—even the Certificate of Authenticity can be a forgery. If you do find something real, remember that the Thai government has an interest in keeping authentic antiquities and sacred items in the country, and will require special permission for export.

By law, Buddha images are prohibited from export, except for religious or educational purposes; even in these instances, you'll still have to obtain permission from the **Department of Fine Arts** to remove them from Thailand. This rule is little enforced, though, and the concern is more for antique Buddhas than the cheap replicas you'll find in tourist markets. (Details on how to contact the Department of Fine Arts and file for permission is provided on p. 378.)

Almost all the reputable antiques stores in Bangkok are along the endless **Charoen Krung (New) Road** (centered along the section on either side of the post office), but many of these are shamelessly priced for wealthier tourists, and most items are Chinese, not Thai. **River City** and **OP Place** are both convenient places to hunt for art and antiques, as you can hit several stores within an hour, but neither quality nor authenticity is guaranteed.

BOOKSTORES
You'll find a number of bookstores offering a wide variety of English-language books. The two chains with the best choice are **Asia Books** and **Kinokuniya.** Asia Books is a local chain that specializes in regional titles and some overseas publishers—depending on the outlet. Its main branch is at 221 Sukhumvit Rd., between *sois* 15 and 17 (✆ 02252-7277). Outlets with a large inventory are at the following locations: **The Emporium** on Sukhumvit at Soi 22, **Siam Paragon,** on level 2, and **CentralWorld,** sixth floor.

The eclectic **Kinokuniya** has three stores in Bangkok, at **The Emporium** on Sukhumvit Road Soi 22, at **Siam Paragon,** and on the sixth floor of the **Isetan department** store at **CentralWorld** (✆ 02255-9834). **Bookazine** has a good selection at its various locations: On the second floor of **Silom Complex** (✆ 02632-0130); on the second floor of **Gaysorn Plaza** at 999 Ploenchit Rd. (✆ 02656-1039); and at 62 Khaosan Rd. (✆ 02280-3785).

For secondhand books, try **Dasa Books,** 714/4 Sukhumvit (near **The Emporium,** between *sois* 26 and 28; ✆ 02661-2993; www.dasabookcafe.com), which is a great place to grab a coffee and browse for long-lost titles, or exchange old novels free of charge. Almost every international hotel has a newsstand with papers, magazines, and a few books.

DEPARTMENT STORES & SHOPPING PLAZAS

Bangkok's downtown looks more and more like urban Tokyo these days. The size and opulence of Bangkok's many malls and shopping areas are often a shock to those who imagine Bangkok to be an exotic, impoverished destination. Sipping cappuccino at a Starbucks overlooking a busy city street may not be what you've come to Asia to do, but to many it is a comfort (especially after long trips in more rugged parts of the kingdom). The truth is that malls are focused as much on today's consumer-obsessed Thai youth as anywhere else you'll visit; these hallowed halls of materialism are (sadly) much closer to the pulse of the nation than the many temples foreign visitors are keen to experience. Malls are where wealthy Thais hang out, meet friends, dine, and shop. I've listed some malls under "Where to Buy" above; below are some more highlights:

o **CentralWorld** (℡ 02635-1111; www.centralworld.co.th), on the corner of Rama I and Rachadamri roads, was gutted by arsonists during the political disturbances of May 2010, though reconstruction was almost complete at the time of this update. It contains Zen and Isetan stores and is crowned with a fab food hall and, of course, a bevy of cinemas. Open daily 10am to 9pm. The Chit Lom and Siam BTS stations are both nearby.

o **Emporium** (℡ 02269-1000; www.emporiumthailand.com), stands proudly on the corner of Sukhumvit Soi 24. Bangkok's first luxury shopping mall, this old-timer still offers the top designer outlets from Gucci to Prada and Sony to Walt Disney (there are cinemas on the top floor). The food court on the top floor covers just about any craving. Open daily 10am to 10pm. It's connected to Phrom Phong BTS.

o **Erawan** (next to Grand Hyatt Erawan, at the corner of Ratchadamri and Rama I rds.; ℡ 02250-7777; www.erawanbangkok.com) is a swanky, mercantile mecca that's truly glamorous but never crowded. Such brands as Coach rub shoulders with fashion stores such as Club 21 and the city's top watch shops. Drop in on Urban Kitchen, with a basement area that features a range of foodie shops and diners. The top floor is dedicated to an alternative health center, offering treatments such as colonic irrigation. Open daily 10am to 9pm. Take the Chit Lom BTS here.

o **Mah Boon Krong,** or **MBK** (℡ 02620-9000; www.mbk-center.co.th), lies at the intersection of Rama 1 and Phayathai. This massive megamall, in fact, is a mass of small shops, fast-food joints, and tiny vendors—try to imagine a cross between a street market and a shopping mall. The **Tokyu Department Store** is within the mall, and it attracts teenagers and tourists due to its bargain-priced local fashions, accessories, and gadgets, along with its huge array of tourist souvenirs on the lower floor. Cinemas are at the top. Open daily 10am to 10pm. Take the BTS to the National Stadium.

o **Panthip Plaza** (℡ 02793-7777), on Phetchaburi Road, is an older, rather scruffy mall that's dedicated to all things electronic. Among the shoddy bootleg software, there are stacks of innovative gadgets, as well as shops selling secondhand or new and affordable computers, cellphones, or components for either. Not much English is spoken, but it may not matter if you are into IT and can speak fluent Nerdish. Open daily 10am to 8pm. It's a 10-minute walk from Ratchathewi BTS.

- **Siam Paragon** ★★ (✆ **02690-1000;** www.siamparagon.co.th), on Rama I Road, is one of those glitzy malls that just goes on and on. Downstairs is **Siam Ocean World,** where kids can watch the sharks swim; above are floors of brand-name stores such as Hermès, MNG, Zara, and Shanghai Tang. The mall also has an entire floor of fun eateries, as well as a top-class food hall, a department store, and even a gymnasium. Open daily 10am to 10pm. There's direct access via Siam BTS.

FASHION & TAILORING

Bangkok has some small, independent designers of its own, who create Thai-influenced fashions that look good back home. **Nagara, Kloset, Fly Now, Grey by Greyhound,** and **Anurak** are all well-established local labels producing great ready-to-wear items for men and women. It's certainly not Parisian haute couture, but the designs are fresh and original, and prices will be a fraction of those in designer boutiques back home. If you want really unique clothes or accessories, have a trawl around **Siam Square** for the latest Thai styles—but don't expect European sizes!

If you want to check out the more cutting-edge, contemporary Thai design scene, **Thong Lor** (Sukhumvit Soi 55) has a great array of trendy boutiques catering to younger, well-heeled Thais. Another option is **J Avenue** (Thong Lor Soi 15), a small mall, with the yummy **Greyhound Café** (**www.greyhoundcafe.co.th**).

Tailors may be widespread in popular malls such as **River City** and in **Sukhumvit Road's Soi 11** and **19,** but remember, this is not Hong Kong and—as all the concierges of major hotels repeatedly attest—Thailand's back-street tailors aren't perfect. Men's shirts normally pose no serious problems, but ambitious ladies' wear can be a disaster when designs skills are limited and fabric quality is poor. Paying a knockdown price often leads to shoddy workmanship and cloth; don't risk it as you will still be expected to pay for the work. The rule of thumb is, expect to pay 60% of prices in Europe or the U.S. for something decent, and always schedule at least two fittings, with an English speaker present. Only very few places, such as **World Group** (✆ **02238-3344**), in Soi Oriental (off Charoen Krung Rd.), can cope with precise cutting or copying of garments. You will pay a high price for their expertise, though— around 15,000 to 30,000B.

GIFTS, CRAFTS, & SOUVENIRS

Street vendors throughout the city are a good source of affordable and fun souvenirs (though they are currently banned on Mon, for street cleaning). The best stalls are along **Sukhumvit Road,** beginning at Soi 4, and on **Khao San Road.** Little of the stuff sold there is unique, but the prices are great, and many people stock up on gifts such as mango wood bowls, chopsticks, candles, incense, or small decorative lamps made of mulberry paper or coconut shells. Impressive brass, bronze, and pewter items, as well as fine celadon (green ceramic ware), are all available in many outlets on **Sukhumvit** and **Charoen Krung (New) roads.**

Up on Sukhumvit Road, the **Emporium** (p. 122), boasts a dazzling range of beautiful crafts and textiles on its penultimate floor. **Mah Boon Krang** (MBK, p. 122) has a lower ground floor, stuffed with very reasonably priced gifts and handicrafts, carvings, and castings. The North Thailand-based charity **Mae Fah Luang** has duty-free boutiques located at Suvarnabhumi International Airport and a few of the larger provincial airports, such as Chiang Mai's.

JEWELRY

Sapphires, rubies, garnets, turquoise, and zircons are mined in Thailand, and nearly every other stone you can think of is imported and cut here. Thai artisans are among the most skillful in the world; work in gold and silver is generally of high quality at very good value. If you're interested in a custom setting, bring a photo or drawing of what you'd like and prepare to discuss your ideas at length.

You'll find gemstone, silver, and gold stores in every part of town. Head to the **Silom Galleria** (✆ 02630-0944) mall, on Silom Soi 19, for over 100 outlets specializing in jewelry, art, and antiques. Around **Charoen Krung (New) Road,** you'll find the wholesalers of gorgeous semiprecious stones. Gold is sold in **Chinatown;** try the lower end of **Silom and Khao San roads** for silver in bulk. **The Asian Institute of Gemological Sciences** (48th Floor, Jewelry Trade Center; 919/539 Silom Rd.; ✆ 02267-4315; www.aigsthailand.com) is useful for verifying the quality of cut stones (although it's not an appraiser) and also runs courses in gem identification and jewelry design. The TAT (p. 115) and the Thai Gem and Jewelry Traders Association have created an organization called the **Jewel Fest Club** (www.jewelfest.com). Check out their website to find which shops are members of this reputable organization.

MARKET GOODS

Visiting Bangkok's many markets is as much a cultural experience as it is a consumer experience; goods come in from all corners of the kingdom, and bargaining is a fast and furious experience. Smaller markets with fewer tourists are great for wandering. **Bangrak Wet Market,** behind the Shangri-La Hotel, is an early-morning gourmet's delight. **Pratunam Market,** at the intersection of Phetchaburi and Ratchaprarop roads, is a big wholesale center, with a vast array of inexpensive clothing. **Pak Klong Talad ★★**, near Saphan Phut (Memorial Bridge), on the fringes of Chinatown, is home to Bangkok's cut-flower market, with huge bouquets of cut flowers passing through here all day and all night. Most tourist markets are generally open daily from 6 to 11pm; exceptions are noted below.

A word of warning: Cheap goods flood many markets in Thailand, and Bangkok is no exception. Most market stalls, such as those in Patpong, are filled with stalls of brand-name purses, sneakers, and watches, all of which are fake. Though some tourists revel in getting cheap brand-name items for a few bucks, doing so can result in dire consequences (p. 111).

Khao San Road Area   The nighttime stalls on Khao San Road cater to young travelers and, as such, this is where you'll find the funkiest bits and bobs in town. From hip-hop fashions and cool T-shirts, to silver wares or original artworks, this is your place. It's worth the trip for the atmosphere alone—bass-thumping clubs, busy bars, and Internet cafes attract crowds of tattooed, pierced, and, yes, plain ordinary travelers, going or coming from all corners of Asia. The area just north of Khao San Road is a maze of small department stores, shops, and very affordable retail goods. Open daily from 11am to 11pm. In Banglampoo, just north of the Grand Palace area and Ratchadamnoen Rd.

Patpong Night Market   The Patpong area is famous for its bars, neon lights, girls, sex shows, and massage parlors, but it also hosts a bustling Night Market along the central streets (hemmed in on all sides by go-go bars and sex-show clubs) that sell mostly faux brands: Pirated CDs and DVDs, designer knock-offs, copy watches, leather goods stamped with desirable logos (sure to hold up better than cardboard)—not especially cheap, but lively and fun, especially if you enjoy crowds and the challenge of hard bargaining. Open daily after sundown. Patpong Soi 1, btw. Silom and Surawong rds.

Weekend Market (Chatuchak) ★★ This mother of all markets, which is open on Saturdays and Sundays from 9am to 5pm, is filled with head-spinning numbers of stalls selling everything: Souvenirs, art, antiques, fresh and dried seafood, vegetables and condiments, pottery, pets of every sort, orchids, and other exotic plants, clothing, and a host of strange exotic foods. A visit here is a great way to introduce yourself to the exotic sights, flavors, and colors of Thai life; and it is the best one-stop shop for all those souvenirs you haven't bought yet. In the hot season, try to get there early in the morning, before the heat, and leave by early afternoon, before the downpours. *Hint:* Hop off the BTS at Saphan Khwai and walk the one stop to the main market area, staying on the left (or west) side of the train. All along here you'll find some great antiques and jewelry stalls. Adjacent to the Mo Chit BTS, at the northern terminus of the BTS.

SILK

There are numerous silk outlets throughout the city, from shopping malls to the lobbies of international hotels. Synthetics are frequently sold as silk; if you're in doubt about a particular piece, select a thread and burn it—silk should smell like singed hair. Sometimes only the warp (lengthwise threads) is synthetic, because it is more uniform and easier to work with. For some of the city's priciest silk, try such outlets as **Jim Thompson** (9 Surawong Rd., near Silom; ✆ **02632-8100;** www.jimthompson.com), or the Thai silk specialists **Almeta** (20/3, Sukhumvit Soi 23; ✆ **02204-1413** or 02258-4227; www.almeta.com). They can even offer "silk a la carte," whereby silk is woven to the customer's desired weight and dyed to a particular shade. Products include silk wall coverings, silk fashions, bed linen, and casual wear.

One of the best outlets for cottons from all over the world, as well as chiffons and silks, is the **Cynosure,** on the ground floor of China World, 677–681 Chakraphet Rd. (✆ **02225-2001;** www.cynosurebangkok.com). Their products include ornate brocades, linens, and rainbow-hued satins, as well as top-class Chantilly laces, along with sequined and beaded fabrics. Expect to pay top price for what, in effect, is the cream of the crop.

BANGKOK ENTERTAINMENT & NIGHTLIFE

Bangkok's reputation for rowdy nightlife tends to precede it; however, it's not all raunchy sex shows and public debauchery. There are plenty of nighttime cultural events, such as music, theater, puppetry performances, and orchestral maneuvers. For the hippest nightlife updates, check out *BK Magazine* (free and available at bookstores and restaurants). Featuring weekly listings of events as well as up-to-date info about the club scene, it is the best entertainment source in Bangkok. Both the *Bangkok Post* and *The Nation* also offer daily listings of cultural events and performance schedules.

The Performing Arts

Most travelers experience the Thai performing arts at a commercially staged dance show in a hotel, sometimes accompanied by a Thai banquet; see "Dinner with Thai Dance," p. 100. Bangkok, however, does provide much more appetizing slices of theater, whether it is the avant-garde choreography seen at the **Patravadi Theatre,** traditional puppet shows at the new **Aksra Theater,** or international music recitals as part of annual festivals.

The National Theater, 1 Na Phra That Rd. (*☎ 02224-1342*), presents demonstrations of Thai classical dancing and music, by performers from the School of Music and Dance in Bangkok, which are generally superior to those at the tourist restaurants and hotels. There are also performances by visiting ballet and theatrical companies. Call the **TAT** (p. 115) or check with your hotel for the current schedule.

The **Thailand Cultural Center,** Thiem Ruammit Road, off Ratchadaphisek Road, Huai Khwang (*☎ 02247-0028*), is the largest performance center in town, offering a wide variety of programs. The Bangkok Symphony performs here during its short summer season. Other local and visiting companies also present theater and dance at the center.

Bangkok's unique contemporary dance theater, **Patravadi Theatre,** at Soi Wat Rakheng, off Anamarin Road (*☎ 02412-7287;* www.patravaditheatre.com), occupies a laid-back arty corner of the Thonburi district, and can be relied upon to challenge cultural conformity by putting on inspiring performances that combine all manner of Thai and international dance forms, including dazzling *likay* (similar to the style of Broadway musicals). Overseen since its founding by Patravadi Mejudhon, a former Thai classical dancer now in her 60s, the theater is well worth the trip for those fascinated by Thailand's performing arts.

Since the Suan Lum Night Market closed, and along with it the Joe Louis Puppet Theater, the only place to catch puppet shows is at the new **Aksra Theatre** on the third floor of the King Power Shopping Complex at 8/1 Rangnam Rd. (*☎ 02677-8888;* **www.aksratheatre.com;** Victory Monument BTS). Complex puppets are manipulated by up to three masters, and their movements are chillingly lifelike. Shows start at 7:30pm on Monday to Wednesday and 6:30pm on Thursday to Sunday, and tickets cost 800B.

Cinema

Bangkok cinemas are almost always located in malls and show a small selection of Hollywood films—with most leaning toward action films, though occasionally you may catch an art-house movie at **House RCA** or at two of the city's oldest cinemas, the **Lido** and the **Scala.** For general information on what's on and where, check out www.movieseer.com. A couple of **Film Festivals** are held annually; alas, poor publicity, movie-star no-shows, and haywire scheduling have been commonplace. Below are information hot lines for the city's major cinemas. The English-language newspapers also carry show times.

House RCA: *☎ 02641-5177-8* at UMG cinema, 3rd floor, 31/8 Royal City Avenue

Lido: *☎ 02252-6498,* at Siam Square.

Major Cineplex: *☎ 02381-4855,* at 1221/39 Sukhumvit Road

Paragon Cineplex: *☎ 02129-4635* at the Siam Paragon, Siam Square.

Scala: *☎ 02251-2861* at Siam Square.

SF Cinema City: *☎ 02611-6444,* at Mah Boon Krong (MBK) on Phayathai Road.

SFX Cinema: *☎ 02268-8888,* at Emporium, on Sukhumvit Road.

The Club & Bar Scene

From cool jazz lounges in top-end hotels to street-side dives in the backpacker district, Bangkok's got somewhere for everyone to feel good after dark. Many bars feature live music, and decor ranges from Wild West Saloon to English pub to futuristic dance club. The city is famed for its go-go bars, which are clustered in Patpong, Nana Plaza, and Soi Cowboy, so this aspect of the city is easy to avoid if it offends you (see "The Sex Scene," below). For a sundowner to remember, head for one of the city's rooftop bars, such as **Sky Bar,** and take in the panoramic view of this restless metropolis.

BY THE RIVERSIDE

If you'd prefer to unwind with an evening cocktail and avoid the sleaze, head to two of the coolest bars in town, both at the **Dome at State Tower ★★** (1055 Silom Rd.; ✆ **02624-9999**). The low-lit, indoor-outdoor lounge bar, **Distil,** sits on the 64th floor, just above the equally vertiginous, wholly outdoor **Sky Bar.** From both venues, the views of the city are amazing, and musicians perform every evening at Sky Bar. The Dome instigates strict (smart) dress codes at all its venues, but it's definitely worth dressing up for.

To take in the heavy aroma of cigars mixed with the sultry sounds of jazz, the **Bamboo Bar,** at the **Oriental Hotel** (Soi Oriental, Charoen Krung [New] Rd.; ✆ **02659-9000**) is the place to go see and be seen—it's popular with visiting celebs. Just across the river and upstream is the towering silhouette of the **Millennium Hilton,** Bangkok (123 Charoennakorn Rd.; ✆ **02442-2000**), whose rooftop lounge **360°** is where night owls congregate to watch the city lights.

SILOM ROAD & PATPONG

Patpong, which covers Soi Patpong 1 and 2, between Surawong and Silom roads, gets crammed with crowds, and is prime territory for pickpockets. Though the area is known for its go-go bars and sex shows, you don't need to visit for risqué entertainment—there's a night market area to check out, too (p. 124). The go-go bars are relatively modest, but if you venture into a sex show in an upstairs bar, be prepared to pay hugely inflated prices for your drinks. Web blogs recount vivid tales of how bars with sex shows sell overpriced drinks; when punters object, bouncers have been called in to "help." It can all end very nastily.

There are a number of non-sleazy bars just near Patpong. **The Barbican** (9/4–5 Soi Thaniya, off Silom Rd.; ✆ **02234-3590**) is a stylish hangout with good bar food and live music. **Molly Malone's** on Convent Road (at 1/5–6 Sivadon Building; ✆ **02266-7160;** www.mollymalonesbangkok.com) caters to foreign expatriates, with Irish pub style and live music after hours.

Head to Silom Soi 4 (between Patpong 2 and Soi Thaniya, off Silom Rd.) to find small homegrown clubs spinning great music, as well as the city's prominent gay clubs, **Telephone Bar** (114/11–13 Silom Soi 4; ✆ **02234-3279;** www.telephonepub.com) and the **Balcony** (86-8 Silom Soi 4; ✆ **02235-5891;** www.balconypub.com) foremost among them.

On Sathorn Nua Road, not quite as far as Surasak BTS, you'll find the supercool **Hu'u Bar ★★** (ground floor of Ascott-serviced residences; ✆ **02676-6677**), a hip bar with amazing cocktails as well as a classy art gallery-cum-diner upstairs.

KHAO SAN ROAD

Over on Rattanakosin Island, in Old Bangkok, the backpackers on Khao San Road still party on at **Gulliver's,** on the corner of Khao San and Chakrabongse roads (✆ **02629-1988;** www.gulliverbangkok.com). There are quite a few small dance clubs that come and go around here. You'll find lots of travelers in their 20s, and the atmosphere is always laid-back. In the middle of Khao San, look for **Silk Bar** (129–131 Khaosan Rd.; ✆ **02281-9981**), a dolled-up hideaway across from the Krung Thai Bank. Also don't miss **Lava** (249 Khao San Rd.; ☎ **02281-6565**), a popular basement dance club. For a more laid-back evening, head west of Khao San to **Phra Athit Road,** where there are any number of small cafes with live performances of folk, blues, and rock tunes. These small venues are full of Thai college students imitating a kind of beat poetry vibe, but some are well worth checking out, such as **Jazz Happens** (☎ **02282-9934**), a couple of doors north of Hemlock restaurant, where students from Silpakorn University play smooth versions of jazz classics and more. Down the small *sois* surrounding the Chana Songkhram temple compound (on the river end of Khao San), look for lots of little open-air bars—they're a good place to meet fellow travelers. One to try is **Ban Sabai** (12 Soi Rongmai; ☎ **02629-1596**).

SUKHUMVIT ROAD

As mentioned earlier, by sunset, the *sois* off Sukhumvit Road morph into a giant red-light zone, so don't venture off the main road here unless you are ready to be hassled by touts and hookers. Sukhumvit plays host to a wide range of pub-style bars as well as a couple of Bangkok's popular clubs.

Q Bar (34 Sukhumvit Soi 11; ☎ **02252-3274**) is a great venue with cool decor and sounds, but has more than its fair share of working girls. A few meters away, **Bed Supper Club** (26 Sukhumvit Soi 11; ☎ **02651-3537**; www.bedsupperclub.com) has a space-age dance club adjoining its sci-fi-inspired restaurant. Like Q Bar, it smacks of industrial chic, with polished concrete and unisex loos. The expat DJs are fantastic, and the clientele includes music and media stars.

The Robin Hood (Sukhumvit Soi 33/1; ☎ **02662-3390**; www.robinhoodbangkok. com), is a fun local pub that draws crowds with its imported Guinness and sports on TV, particularly rugby. The cavernous **Gulliver's** (6 Sukhumvit Soi 5; ☎ **02655-5340**; www.gulliverbangkok.com) is another branch of the popular Khao San bar featuring imported beers, international food, plus pool tables and sports on TV. For somewhere a bit classier, the **Huntsman** (at the Landmark Hotel, Sukhumvit Rd.; ☎ **02254-0404**; www.landmarkbangkok.com), is a popular place for cold draft beer and big-screen sports.

BarSu, at the Sheraton Grande Sukhumvit, 250 Sukhumvit Rd. (☎ **02649-8888**; www.barsubangkok.com), offers soul, funk, rock, and plenty of '70s and '80s sounds.

In a little alleyway off Soi 11 (near Suk 11 Guesthouse), there's a weird makeshift outdoor bar, known as **Cheap Charlie's,** where drinks are affordable and you'll encounter a mix of expats enjoying an after-work drink and tourists toting shopping bags.

The **Conrad Bangkok** ★ (87 Witthayu/Wireless Rd.; ☎ **02690-9999**) hosts two of Bangkok's hottest spots: **87 Plus** is a contemporary bar dance club patronized by wealthy locals, Indians, and expats, with theme nights and special events with guest DJs. Despite its name, the **Diplomat Bar** is not filled with diplomats, but young Thais or cigar-puffing corporate guests in smart suits, enjoying the regular jazz performances.

The Sex Scene

Since the 1960s—and particularly since the Vietnam War—Bangkok has had a reputation as the sin capital of Asia. Its hundreds of saunas, sex clubs, bars, and massage parlors act as fronts for organized prostitution, drug peddling, child-trafficking rackets, pedophile rings, and people smugglers. First-time tourists are sometimes staggered by the numbers of septuagenarian gentlemen trawling these areas looking for teenage Thais of either sex. Of course, the clientele is not just foreign; Thai men also frequently engage the services of hookers.

While prostitution is technically illegal in Thailand, this law is rarely enforced, making foreigners feel it is therefore "safe" to pay for sex in Thailand. But beware—it is not. Too often, the people working this industry are doing this because they have no choice; and some are underage, though they may purport to be older than they are. Reports about poor families selling their children into prostitution are true—many children are held in brothels against their will. Those adults seen making even the slightest sexual advances toward them, if caught, risk a heavy prison sentence and a subsequent, global media frenzy. The worst areas are concentrated around **Patpong** (off Silom Rd.), **Nana Plaza** (Sukhumvit Soi 4), and **Soi Cowboy** (between Sukhumvit Soi 21 and 23) districts.

A startling increase in HIV-positive cases in the past 20 years has encouraged the education of commercial sex workers about the use of condoms, but AIDS is still a major concern, as are other STDs. Occasional crackdowns in Patpong close some of the raunchier shows, but still, men and women in the clubs are all "for sale"—clients simply pay a "bar fine." If this is your scene, be aware of the risks and play it safe.

Note that the city's smarter hotels will all stop you if you bring a hooker into the lobby. Other hotels require guests to register night visitors, and the client will have to pay the hotel for this privilege. Also know that, every year in Bangkok, hundreds of cases are reported of prostitutes drugging their customers and robbing them in their hotel rooms. If you believe this cannot happen to you, think again. See p. 377 in "Planning Your Trip to Thailand" for more information.

SIDE TRIPS FROM BANGKOK

There are plenty of easy day trips from Bangkok. Favorites include visits to the floating market at Damnoen Saduak and to the ancient capital of Ayutthaya, north of Bangkok, with a stop at the Bang Pa-In Summer Palace. Kids will enjoy most of these listed below.

The Ancient City (Muang Boran) ★★ ENTERTAINMENT COMPLEX   This remarkable work-in-progress, now often referred to as Ancient Siam, is a giant scale model of Thailand spread over hundreds of acres, with more than a hundred models of the country's major landmarks either displayed as life-size or in reduced scale. For visitors short of time, it is an excellent way to get an overview of the country's most impressive buildings, such as the temples at Ayutthaya and Sukhothai and stilted houses from the north, in just 1 day. As you move from one section to another, keep your eyes open for deer who roam freely through the grounds. The project has been evolving over the past 30 years, financed by a local millionaire who has played out his obsession with Thai history on a grand scale. Because it is far from the heart of Bangkok, the Ancient City is best visited by organized tour, though you can certainly go on your own. All travel agents offer package tours that combine this with the nearby Crocodile Farm, though you could easily spend a day just in the Ancient City. You'll also need to arrange a method of getting around, as it's too far to walk everywhere; choices are a car and driver, rented bicycle, golf cart, or tram tour with guide.

Kilometer 33 on the old Sukhumvit Highway, in Samut Prakan Province. ✆ **02709-1644.** www.ancientcity.com. 400B adult, 200B children. Daily from 8am to 5pm.

Floating Market at Damnoen Saduak ★ MARKET   This, the best known of Thailand's floating markets is very photogenic, as the sampans on the canals are laden with colorful fruits and flowers, and the vendors dress in traditional costume, though it soon becomes clear that it's all staged for tourists. As it's over 100km (62 miles) from Bangkok, you'll need a very early start to catch the market at its best; if this is not convenient, consider a visit to nearby **Amphawa Floating Market,** which takes place in the afternoon, and is less staged. Some tours combine the Floating Market with a visit to the Rose Garden (see above for info). If you choose to go via organized tour, such as **World Travel Service** (© 02233-5900), expect to pay about 1,800B for the 1-day trip combo with the Rose Garden.

Damnoen Saduak, Ratchaburi, around 40 minutes south of Nakhon Pathom/ 100km (62 miles) from Bangkok.

Phra Pathom Chedi HISTORIC SITE   One of Thailand's oldest towns, Nakhon Pathom is thought to be where Buddhism first established a following in this region, over 2,000 years ago. Thus, it is fitting that it should be home to the tallest (120m/ 394 ft.) and most revered stupa in the kingdom. The site has been abandoned and rebuilt many times through the centuries, and the current structure was the work of Rama IV in 1853. Apart from its sheer enormity, the *chedi* impresses with its range of Buddha images in niches, all displaying different *mudras* (hand gestures). The *chedi* can be visited in combination with a trip to the **Floating Market** (see above) or en route to **Kanchanaburi** (see below).

56km/35 miles west of Bangkok, Nakhon Pathom. Admission 40B. Daily 6am–6pm.

Rose Garden Riverside THEME PARK   Besides its delightful rose garden, this attractive theme park and resort that sprawls over 28 hectares (69 acres) is known for its all-in-one show of Thai culture that includes classical and folk dancing, Thai box-ing, sword fighting, and cockfighting. It's hardly authentic, but it is a convenient way for visitors with limited time to digest some canned Thai culture. The resort's flagship restaurant, Inn Chan, offers an idyllic spot to take lunch and serves traditionally prepared Thai dishes.

32km (20 miles) west of Bangkok, on the way to Nakhon Pathom, on Highway 4. (© 03432-2544. www.rosegardenriverside.com. Admission to cultural show 500B adults, 250B children. Entry to gardens 50B. Daily 8am–6pm, shows start daily at 2:30pm.

Samphran Elephant Grounds & Zoo ZOO   This lush 24-hectare (59-acre) garden complex offers two entertaining elephant shows and crocodile wrestling shows daily. The elephants dance, play soccer, and re-create battle scenes from a bygone era, and elephant rides are available through the tropical garden for an extra 500B. Croco-dile wrestling shows are at 12:45 and 2:20pm; elephant show times are at 1:45 and 3:30pm, with additional shows on Saturday, Sunday, and holidays at 10:30am. There's also an international buffet restaurant and an extensive orchid nursery.

1km (⅔ mile) north of the Rose Garden, in Samphran (30km/19 miles from the city). © 02295-2938. www.elephantshow.com. 550B adult, 350B children (below 130cm/4.2 ft.). Daily 8:30am to 5:30pm.

Samutprakarn Crocodile Farm & Zoo ZOO   Only 3km (1¼ miles) from the Ancient City, you'll find the Samutprakarn Crocodile Farm and Zoo. Supposedly the world's largest, it has more than 60,000 crocs, both fresh and saltwater. During the hourly show (9am–5pm), handlers wrestle the crocs in murky ponds—enough to scare the living daylights out of junior.

Kilometer 30 on the Old Sukhumvit Highway. © 02703-4891. 300B adult, 200B children. Daily 7am–6pm; feeding times 4.30–5.30pm.

If the heat and the kids have gotten to you, splash out (literally) with a trip to **Siam Water Park** in Minburi (℃ **02919-7200;** www.siamparkcity.com), a large complex of water slides, enormous swimming pools with artificial surf, waterfalls, playgrounds, and a beer garden. It's a 30-minute drive east of town (or 1 hr. by bus no. 168 or 519, from Victory Monument). Admission is 300B (children 100B), including rides. Siam Water Park is open daily from 10am to 6pm. In the same direction from the city center, on the bus no. 26 route, is the **Safari World & Marine Park** (℃ **02914-4100;** www.safariworld.com; adults 530B, children 380B), an outdoor zoo tailor-made for restless kids, with restaurants and shows.

Sites Farther Afield

KANCHANABURI

139km (86 miles) NW of Bangkok

Kanchanaburi lies on the **River Kwae** (*Mae Nam Kwae*, in Thai), better known to the West as the **River Kwai.** The city became famous for a single-track rail bridge, built under the Japanese occupation in World War II by Allied prisoners of war (POWs), linking Myanmar and Thailand. Due to the thousands of servicemen and women who lost their lives in this project, and in the notoriously inhumane Japanese internment camps, it became known popularly as the Death Railway. The town, and the dark times associated with it, came to fame following the hugely successful British film *The Bridge on the River Kwai* (which was shot in Sri Lanka). The original wooden bridge no longer exists, so today's visitors, pilgrims, and former POWs head to a similar, but now heavily commercialized, iron bridge that was built around the same time. Every year, in the last days of November, the city hosts several evenings of light and sound shows to commemorate the bombing of the bridge in 1944. Many former Allied prisoners, as well as local Thai tourists, fill the city and hotels generally book up fast.

In addition to the bridge, lots of other worthwhile attractions are in the area, including golf courses, bike trails, caves, and waterfalls in the surrounding hills. The area's handful of nice hotels and riverside guesthouses also make this a popular escape from the heat of Bangkok.

Getting to Kanchanaburi

You can connect by railway from Bangkok's **Hua Lampong Station** (℃ **1690** or **02220-4334**) on regular weekend junkets that start in the early morning, or go by slow daily trains from **Thonburi Station** (formerly Bangkok Noi Station; ℃ **02411-3102**) to **Kanchanaburi Station** (℃ **03451-1285**); rail trips here are quite scenic and cost about 100B. They're a great experience—just be prepared for no air-conditioning for 3 long hours, unless you take the 10am train, a special tourist service for 300B (includes soft drink and certificate too). There are also frequent regular buses from the **Southern Bus Terminal** (℃ **02793-8111**).

Hotels & Resorts

There are a couple of new places, both located by the river some distance from town, that offer excellent amenities and efficient service. First, the colonial-style **Dheva**

Mantra (9/99 Moo 3, Tambon Tha Makam. ✆ **03452-7666;** www.dhevamantra. com) features a spa, pool, and fine dining with rates from 4,600B–39,000B. A cheaper and smaller alternative is the Oriental Kwai (194/5, Moo 1, Tambon Ladya. ✆ **03458-8168; www.orientalkwai.com**), which has just a dozen cottages and a pool in a lush tropical garden, and rates beginning at 2,900B.

If you'd rather be nearer the town, the pretty **U Inchantree Resort** (✆ **03452-1584;** www.ukanchanaburi.com), at 443 Mae Nam Kwai Rd., and the friendly **Ploy Guesthouse,** at number 79/2 on the same road (✆ **03451-5804;** www.ploygh.com), are atmospheric midrange choices near the bridge. See **www.kanchanburi-info.com** for more tips on accommodation.

Attractions

The town's sites focus on the World War II history of the area. Start any tour of Kanchanaburi at the so-called **Bridge over the River Kwai,** emulating its more famous predecessor, built by World War II prisoners, and the main backdrop to the suspenseful 1957 film *The Bridge on the River Kwai,* directed by David Lean, which won seven Oscars. The bridge is about 5km (3 miles) north of the Kanchanaburi city center.

The **Allied War Cemetery** is where many of the 16,000 POWs who died building the railway are laid to rest; graves are organized by country. It is a sobering thought to realize that over 100,000 people died in the construction of this project, mostly conscripted laborers and prisoners. It's a 10-minute walk from the train station on Saengchto Road. It's open daily 8:30am to 6pm, and charges no entry fee.

Adjacent to the cemetery is the **Thailand–Burma Railway Center** (✆ **03451-0067;** www.tbrconline.com; daily 9am–5pm; adults 100B, children 50B), which displays a well-organized collection of photos and memorabilia, with ample English descriptions, maps with detailed historical background, and good audiovisual presentations recounting the terrifying fate of the Allied POWs during World War II. Nearby (just south of the cemetery along the river), find the mustier but no less moving **JEATH War Museum** (Wat Chaichumpol, Bantai, Kanchanaburi; ✆ **03451-5203;** daily 8:30am–6pm; admission 30B). JEATH is an acronym for Japan, England, Australia/America, Thailand, and Holland. Here, you'll see haunting photos and artifacts in a rustic bamboo museum adjacent to Wat Chaichumpol. Most poignant are the letters and faded photos of the many GIs who've returned since the end of the war.

Some 45km (28 miles) north of Kanchanaburi, you'll find **Wat Pha Luangta Bua Yannasampanno Forest Monastery,** better known as the **Tiger Temple** (http://tiger temple.org). Featured in dozens of TV shows and magazines, this rural temple is home to various animals, including several tigers, most rescued from poachers as cubs. The monks here appear to have a remarkable understanding with these man-eating beasts, as the tigers are as tame as cats and pose placidly for photo ops. However, many criticize the monks for their attention-grabbing tactics and hefty admission fees (500B–5,000B depending whether you just look at them or go for the whole cuddling, bottle-feeding, souvenir photo experience), while others claim the animals are drugged. The temple is open daily from 8:30am to 5pm, but it is best to go in the afternoon, when the tigers are allowed to roam free.

Other sites farther afield from Kanchanaburi include the **Hellfire Pass,** on the route of the Death Railway, which can be visited by train, as well as the **Erawan National Park,** north of town, where you can see one of Thailand's most attractive waterfalls.

KHAO YAI NATIONAL PARK ★

120km (75 miles) NE of Bangkok

Located 3 hours from Bangkok, near Nakhon Ratchasima (known as Khorat), on the edge of Thailand's rural northeast, the park is home to some high peaks and therefore boasts cooler temperatures year-round. It's a good place to spot wildlife, such as lar gibbons, barking deer, hornbills, and any number of other bird species, as well as a good chance to see wild elephants congregated around roadside salt licks.

AYUTTHAYA & 1-DAY RIVERBOAT TRIPS ★★

76km (47 miles) NW of Bangkok

The temple town of Ayutthaya and the nearby Summer Palace compound of Bang Pa-In are both popular day trips from Bangkok. Ayutthaya was the capital of Thailand from 1350 until it was sacked in 1767 by the Burmese; thereafter, the capital moved briefly to Thonburi, and then to Bangkok. Ayutthaya's temples are magnificent—both Khmer and Thai-style ruins lie along the rivers here, in what was once Thailand's greatest city. It's also an excellent place to rent a bicycle (the terrain is flat) and worth an overnight, in conjunction with an enjoyable 1-day boat trip. Nearby Bang Pa-In is home to some wonderfully whimsical mid-19th-century royal palaces, set amid splendid gardens with topiary elephants.

Most people get to Ayutthaya and Bang Pa-In on a tour that goes by road and returns along the river. Travel agents or hotels can arrange this for you, including the early-morning transfer from your hotel to the boat pier or coach. It's an early rise and an all-day trip: Tour buses can leave as early as 6:30am in order to pick up tourists from a number of Bangkok hotels (which itself can take hours). Sometimes, there's an option to travel by bus both ways. Departure points are close to the River City pier, and tickets cost in the range of 2,000B per person (bus and boat) or less, if you choose to travel both ways by bus. Contact **River Sun Cruises** (✆ **02476-5207**) for more details, but check websites (such as www.thairivercruise.com) for the full range of cruise options.

For a superluxury cruise option, the Anantara Riverside Resort & Spa operates **Manohra Cruises** (✆ **02477-0770;** www.manohracruises.com), offering a variety of day and evening cruises, including overnight trips to Ayutthaya and Bang Pa-In. These trips use fully renovated, traditional rice barges. Though they usually cost hundreds of dollars, special packages are available online or through travel agents.

For more specific information on Ayutthaya, see the first section of chapter 10 "Central Thailand."

THE EASTERN SEABOARD

Tracing the coastline east of Bangkok along the Gulf of Thailand, there are three major tourist destinations, each with a distinct character. One important advantage of heading to places along the east coast is their proximity to the capital and Suvarnabhumi International Airport. The closest is **Pattaya,** one of the oldest resort developments in the country, which is working hard to shed its bad reputation as a center for sex tourism, not to mention the cagey underworld that goes with it. The town is repositioning itself as a family vacation spot, with an array of top-quality, self-contained resorts, a wide choice of restaurants, and numerous outdoor and water activities.

The main Pattaya beach is still overcoming the effects of unregulated construction, during which heavy industrial and human pollutants leaked into the bay, but there's now a sewage treatment plant nearby. The beach is a long, thin strip of coarse sand, and offshore motorboats buzz like hornets. Nearby **Jomtien,** just south of town, is quieter and more appealing but still suffers from pollution. For those who want to swim in the sea, it's best to rent a boat and go to the outlying islands, where the water is cleaner and a range of watersports is available.

Continuing east from Pattaya, **Ko Samet,** in Rayong Province, is a small island with lots of accommodation, both basic and luxurious, and beautiful beaches. It is a low-luxe, laid-back retreat reachable by a short ferry ride from the mainland in the town of **Ban Phe** (via Rayong). Though isolated, Samet is popular with foreigners on a budget and gets very crowded on weekends when well-heeled Thais from Bangkok visit.

Ko Chang, the last holiday stop before Cambodia, has grown rapidly during the past decade. It now boasts sprawling luxury resorts as well as a host of midrange and budget options. In terms of tourist numbers and accessibility, this—Thailand's second-largest island—is still behind both Phuket and Ko Samui, though it's catching up fast. By road, Ko Chang is 5 hours east of Bangkok; Bangkok Airways offers 1-hour flights from the capital or Ko Samui to nearby Trat, making it a much more manageable trip.

PATTAYA

147km (91 miles) SE of Bangkok

The slow evolution of Pattaya from a sleepy fishing town to a sprawling development of high-rise coastal resorts began in 1959 when U.S. Army GIs, stationed in the northeast, started coming here in their free time.

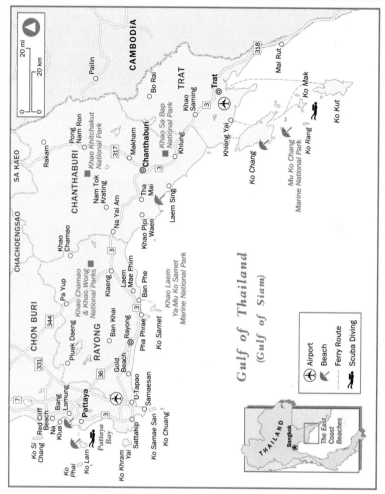

Word spread, and with more U.S. troops arriving to fight in the Vietnam War, the town became a hot destination for partying. The impression left by those early visitors accounts for its ill repute today, propagated by hundreds of go-go clubs, beer bars, and seedy massage parlors along the beachside.

Tourism boomed in the 1980s, and unchecked resort development was exacerbated by a lack of infrastructure upgrades—so much so that beaches became flooded with raw sewage. Recent years have seen a few civil projects to clean up the bay area with some success, but environmental work is still needed to improve water quality.

Despite this, Pattaya now supports several large, sophisticated international resorts. Smaller hotels set in sprawling, manicured seaside gardens and upscale

Pattaya

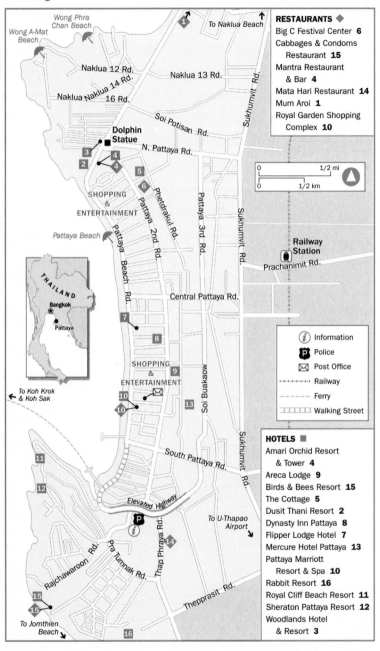

Wong Phra Chan Beach

Wong A-Mat Beach

Naklua 12 Rd.

Naklua 14 Rd.

Naklua 16 Rd.

Naklua 13 Rd.

To Naklua Beach

Soi Potisan Rd.

Sukhumvit Rd.

Dolphin Statue

N. Pattaya Rd.

3

2

4

4

5

6

SHOPPING & ENTERTAINMENT

Phetdrakul Rd.

Pattaya 2nd. Rd.

Pattaya 3rd. Rd.

Sukhumvit Rd.

Pattaya Beach

Pattaya Beach Rd.

THAILAND

Bangkok

Pattaya

Central Pattaya Rd.

Railway Station

Prachanimit Rd.

7

8

SHOPPING & ENTERTAINMENT

9

10

10

13

Soi Buakaow

To Koh Krok & Koh Sak

i Information

P Police

✉ Post Office

┼┼┼┼┼ Railway

- - - - Ferry

▯▯▯▯▯ Walking Street

11

12

South Pattaya Rd.

Sukhumvit Rd.

Elevated Highway

P

i

To U-Thapao Airport

Rajchawaroon Rd.

Pra Tumnak Rd.

Thap Phraya Rd.

14

Thepprasit Rd.

15

15

To Jomthien Beach

16

RESTAURANTS ◆

Big C Festival Center **6**

Cabbages & Condoms Restaurant **15**

Mantra Restaurant & Bar **4**

Mata Hari Restaurant **14**

Mum Aroi **1**

Royal Garden Shopping Complex **10**

| 0 | 1/2 mi |
| 0 | 1/2 km |

HOTELS ■

Amari Orchid Resort & Tower **4**

Areca Lodge **9**

Birds & Bees Resort **15**

The Cottage **5**

Dusit Thani Resort **2**

Dynasty Inn Pattaya **8**

Flipper Lodge Hotel **7**

Mercure Hotel Pattaya **13**

Pattaya Marriott Resort & Spa **10**

Rabbit Resort **16**

Royal Cliff Beach Resort **11**

Sheraton Pattaya Resort **12**

Woodlands Hotel & Resort **3**

restaurants dot the landscape. The town is also trying to create an image as a family destination, expat retirement magnet, and convention hub—and it now has the facilities to back this up. Pattaya's close-knit expatriate community not only is at the forefront in the effort to clean up the town's image, but also is very active in other local activities, particularly in charity-related events.

Neighboring Jomtien is a popular alternative to Pattaya. Less seedy surroundings complement the narrow beaches; however, government reports state that water quality is still under par. Jomtien's best accommodation is private condos, but it does have a few high-quality hotels.

Essentials

GETTING THERE

BY PLANE   The nearest airport is in U-Tapao, 45 minutes east of the city (℄ **03824-5595**). It is served by **Bangkok Airways,** which has flights daily to Phuket (3,900B one-way) and to Ko Samui (3,200B one-way). Trip time for both is approximately an hour. Make reservations through their offices in Bangkok (℄ **02270-6699;** www. bangkokair.com). They have an office in Pattaya at Fairtex Arcade, Building A, Room A5, 179/85–212 Moo 5, N. Pattaya Road (℄ **03841-2382**).

To get to and from the U-Tapao airport to Pattaya, you can arrange a private transfer through your resort. A limo can be as steep as 1,500B, though. If you are arriving at **Suvarnabhumi International Airport** and heading to Pattaya, your only option is by bus or taxi (see below).

BY TRAIN   An inconvenient and slow (weekdays only) local train chugs away from Bangkok's **Hua Lampong station** at 6:55am; the homebound train departs Pattaya at 2:20pm. The 4-hour trip costs only 31B. Call **Hua Lampong** in Bangkok (℄ **02220-4334** or 1690), or the train station in Pattaya (℄ **03842-9285**). The Pattaya train station is east of the resort strip, off Sukhumvit Road, and *songtaews* (communal pickup trucks) connect with all destinations on the main beach for around 40B.

BY PUBLIC BUS   The most common and practical form of transportation to Pattaya is the bus. Buses depart from **Bangkok's Eastern Bus Terminal,** on Sukhumvit Road (opposite Soi 63, at the Ekkamai BTS; ℄ **02391-2504**), every hour beginning at 5am until 11pm every day. For an air-conditioned bus, the fare is 113B. There are also regular buses from **Bangkok's Northern Bus Terminal,** on Kampaengphet 2 Road (near Mo Chit; ℄ **02936-2841**)—leaving from there is a good way to avoid the Bangkok rush hour.

The bus station in town is on North Pattaya Road (℄ **03842-9877**). From there, you can catch a shared ride on a *songtaew* to your hotel for about 40B, or a bit more for a taxi.

BY PRIVATE BUS   Major hotels or travel agencies in both Bangkok and Pattaya operate private shuttles, so be sure to inquire when booking. **Bell Travel Service** (℄ **03837-0055;** www.belltravelservice.com) has air-conditioned buses (fare 350B), departing regularly (trip time 2 hr.), to and from Bangkok's Suvarnabhumi International Airport.

BY TAXI   Taxis from the Suvarnabhumi taxi counter go for upward of 1,000B, and any hotel concierge in Bangkok can negotiate with a metered taxi driver to take you to or from your Pattaya resort, door to door, for about the same fare.

BY CAR Take Highway 3 east from Bangkok; tolls are payable on the toll roads. See "Getting Around," below, for info on car rentals.

VISITOR INFORMATION

The **Tourism Authority of Thailand (TAT) office** (609 Moo 10, Pratamnak Rd.; ℂ 03842-7667) is south of Pattaya City, up the hill on the road between Pattaya and neighboring Jomtien. Plenty of info is available in most hotel lobbies, along with free local maps and publications, such as *What's on Pattaya* and *Explore Pattaya and the East Coast. Pattaya Mail* is the local English-language paper, which costs 25B.

ORIENTATION

Pattaya Beach Road is the heart of the town; a long strip of hotels, bars, restaurants, and shops overlook Pattaya Bay. Pattaya 2nd and Pattaya 3rd roads run parallel to Beach Road and form a busy central grid of small, crowded *sois* bound by North Pattaya and South Pattaya roads, bisected by Central Pattaya Road. At both the far northern (The Dusit Resort) and the far southern (Sheraton Pattaya Resort) ends of the beach are two bluffs protecting the bay. Due south is condo-lined Jomtien Beach—a 15-minute ride from Pattaya.

GETTING AROUND

BY MINIBUS OR SONGTAEW *Songtaews* are red pickup trucks with wooden benches that follow regular routes up and down the main streets. Fares within Pattaya start at 10B, while getting to such far-flung beaches as Jomtien costs about 40B. However, agree on the fare before getting in, as drivers will charge you a taxi rate if the truck is empty. If you are on a shoestring budget, don't give in; bargain hard or wait for a full truck. Some hotels operate their own minibuses; check on this when you book.

BY CAR Car-rental agencies offering discounts in the off-season abound. Well-known car-rental companies, such as **Avis,** have counters at the **Dusit Resort** (ℂ 03836-1627); rates start at about 1,200B per day for a Toyota Vios. **Budget Car Rental,** at Thip Plaza, 219/1–3 Moo 10, Beach Road (ℂ 03871-0717), offers comparable rates. There are plenty of local agencies, but beware of the poor condition of the older-model jeeps; read the contract and check the vehicles before renting. One such agency is **Chalee Car Rental,** 340/20, Moo 9, Pattaya 3rd Rd. (ℂ 03872-0413; www.pattayacarrental.com), with cars from 700B per day (minimum 3 days).

BY MOTORCYCLE Let's be honest. Pattaya is a party town and its busy roads are full of drunk and reckless drivers. But the brave (or foolish) can rent 100cc motorcycles for around 200B a day, or less for a longer period. You just need your passport as collateral—nobody asks to see a license—but insurance is not included, so a big risk is involved as accidents are so common. Big choppers and Japanese speed bikes (500cc) start at around 1,000B per day. Helmets are mandatory by law—so wear one, even if the locals don't.

FAST FACTS

There are many independent **money-changing booths,** 24-hour bank exchanges (with better rates), and ATMs at every turn in town. The **post office** is on Soi Post Office, near the **Royal Garden Plaza** (ℂ 03842-9341). **Bangkok Pattaya Hospital** (ℂ 03825-9999) has full services and English-speaking staff. In Pattaya, the numbers for the **Tourist Police** are ℂ 03842-9371 or 1155. Internet services are easy to find. Rates are about 40B to 60B per hour. There are a number of **Internet cafes** along the waterfront (try Soi Yamato).

Exploring the Area

Wat Khao Phra Yai is a small temple complex high above town to the south (go by *songtaew* toward Jomtien, and then hop off and climb the steep hill). The temple has excellent vistas and a 10-m (33-ft.) gold Buddha serenely surveying the western sea.

Alangkarn is a high-tech entertainment complex, which includes the Thai Extravaganza Show. Featuring laser and lighting effects, the performance recreates scenes from famous historical events such as elephant battles between the Thais and Burmese, as well as Thai dancing. It also has a restaurant, which serves dinner at 5pm before the show, and a shopping area selling local goods. Alangkarn (© **03825-6000;** www.alangkarnthailand.com) is 10km (6¼ miles) from Pattaya at kilometer 155 on the Sukhumvit Highway. The entrance fee is 1,000B for adults, 700B for children, for the show only, or 1,200B for adults, 840B for kids, including dinner. It's open daily from 5 to 11pm (show time is 6–7pm).

For something a bit hokier, **Ripley's Believe It or Not,** Royal Garden Plaza, 218 Beach Rd. (© **03871-0294;** www.ripleysthailand.com), is open daily 11am to 11pm (admission 480B adults, 380B kids). It's crammed with unusual exhibits highlighting odd facts from around the globe, alongside an infinity maze, and a Motion Master simulation ride. Admission to all attractions is 1,100B (adults), 1,000B (children). It's great fun for kids of all ages.

The Pattaya Elephant Village (© **03824-9818;** www.elephant-village-pattaya. com) is a not-for-profit sanctuary dedicated to saving former working elephants. To help with funding, the village offers elephant treks and a 90-minute daily show, starting at 2:30pm, on elephant-training techniques. The treks range in price from 1,000B for a 1-hour ride to 2,000B for a full-day excursion, which also includes a guided walk in the forest and a 30-minute raft trip, while the show only costs 650B. The village is 7km (4⅓ miles) off Sukhumvit Road: Turn east at kilometer 144.5, follow the signs to Siam Country Club, and then turn right at the intersection and continue another 4km (2½ miles).

Another option outside Pattaya is **Nong Nooch Tropical Garden** (© **03870-9358;** www.nongnoochtropicalgarden.com), a 202-hectare (500-acre) botanical garden and elephant park 18km (11 miles) outside town, with elephants performing alongside dancers, musicians, and other acts. Cultural performances, music, Thai boxing, audience participation, and dozens of amusing photo ops make this a fun albeit touristy activity. Lovers of tropical gardens should allow plenty of time to look at the immaculate grounds. Book directly and take advantage of a shuttle from Pattaya at either 8:30am or 2:30pm at an all-inclusive fee of 600B. The shows run four times a day (9:45am, 10:45am, 3pm, and 4pm daily). Tickets for the garden and show cost 500B for adults and 250B for children.

Where to Stay

Busy central Pattaya features a range of accommodation, from downright seedy hotels to international upmarket resorts. Among the maze of bars, tailor shops, and eateries are some semi-isolated getaways. During the high season, reservations are recommended at least 2 weeks in advance, especially December through January.

EXPENSIVE

Amari Orchid Resort & Tower ★★★ ☺ On the northern end of busy Pattaya, just out of the fray but close enough to walk there, the Amari offers good amenities and a helpful staff. Rooms within the Garden Wing are large, with contemporary furnishings and parquet floors. The Ocean Tower offers a little more luxury, with open-plan bathrooms, ultramodern fixtures and fittings, and superb views of the bay. There's also a playground and lots of space in the grassy central area, including both a kids' and an enormous adults' pool. Amari also has good in-house dining (see Mantra Restaurant & Bar under "Where to Eat," below).

Pattaya Beach, Pattaya 20150 (on the northernmost end of the beachfront road). www.amari.com/orchid. ⓒ **03841-8418.** Fax 03841-8410. 525 units. 5,800B–7,500B double; from 14,500B suite. AE, DISC, MC, V. **Amenities:** 4 restaurants; 5 bars; 2 outdoor pools; health club; spa; Jacuzzi; kids' club and playground; room service; babysitting; Wi-Fi. *In room:* A/C, TV, minibar, fridge, Wi-Fi (in new building) and Internet (in old building)—both 471B per day.

Dusit Thani Resort ★★ This sprawling, manicured resort straddles the cliff on the north end of the main beach and is chock-full of top-notch amenities. Most of the balcony rooms overlook Pattaya Bay, but the garden-view rooms offer the best value. Tasteful, modern rooms are trimmed with stained wood, and each has fine furnishings and marble bathrooms. Larger rooms and suites have outdoor showers on breezy balconies. For those seeking extra amenities, the resort offers special Dusit Club and Dusit Grand rooms, a spa, and a health club. Overall, the accommodation is comfortable, with an old-world feel.

240/2 Pattaya Beach Rd., Pattaya 20150, Chonburi (north end of Pattaya Beach). www.dusit.com. ⓒ **03842-5611.** Fax 03842-8239. 457 units. From 4,000B double; from 13,500B suite. AE, DC, MC, V. **Amenities:** 3 restaurants; lobby bar w/live music; 2 pools; 3 outdoor tennis courts; health club; spa; watersports; room service; babysitting. *In room:* A/C, TV, minibar, fridge, hair dryer, Internet (free in most expensive rooms, 500B per day in others).

Pattaya Marriott Resort & Spa ★★ ☺ For those wanting to be right in the thick of it, the Marriott is the place to be. In the center of Pattaya, adjacent to the Royal Garden Plaza shopping complex, this five-star resort is abuzz with activities such as biking for adults and yoga for kids. Rooms have wooden floors and spacious balconies with views of gardens or the sea. Bonuses are the resort's beautiful pool area in the well-kept, spacious garden, large health club, and highly regarded spa. The resort contains several restaurants and bars, including the Elephant Bar, a popular meeting place overlooking the pool.

218 Beach Rd., Pattaya 20260, Chonburi. www.marriott.com. ⓒ **03841-2120.** Fax 03842-9926. 298 units. 5,500B–6,900B double; 8,900B–26,900B suite. AE, DC, MC, V. **Amenities:** 3 restaurants; 2 bars; outdoor pool; 2 lit tennis courts; health club; spa; room service; watersports; babysitting; executive floor. *In room:* A/C, TV, minibar, fridge, Wi-Fi (free for members, 321B per day for others).

Rabbit Resort ★★ 👣 The Rabbit Resort may be hard to find, but it's worth the search. This boutique hotel on Dongtan Beach, in Jomtien, lies just south of Pattaya and is an ideal place for those needing a quiet retreat and escape from name-brand luxury resorts. Set on 1.6 hectares (4 acres) of oceanfront land, it has superb gardens graced by two pools. The rooms are mostly two-story Thai-style villas, decorated with antiques thoughtfully selected by the owners. The friendly Thai staff members are always willing to please, and the proprietors are on hand to attend to special needs. The hotel serves complimentary buffet breakfasts and has a grill house overlooking the sea.

318/84 Moo 12, Soi Dongtan Police Station, Jomtien 20150. www.rabbitresort.com. © **03830-3303.** Fax 03825-1628. 49 units. From 5,500B double; 9,900B 2-bedroom villa. AE, DC, MC, V. **Amenities:** Restaurant; 2 outdoor pools; babysitting services; Internet (free). *In room:* A/C, TV, minibar, fridge, hair dryer, microwave.

Royal Cliff Beach Resort ★★★   Comprising the Royal Cliff Grand & Spa, the Royal Wing & Spa, the Royal Cliff Beach Hotel, and the Royal Cliff Terrace, this luxurious compound provides a variety of accommodation and the best range of facilities in Pattaya. High-end **Royal Cliff Grand** and all-suite **Royal Wing** are the best choices, catering to the well-heeled business traveler. Everything is luxe, from the columned public spaces, chandeliers, and fountains to the large and opulent guest rooms. The Grand's spacious rooms are set in a contemporary, scallop-shaped tower and have marble bathrooms with separate shower stalls. The **Royal Cliff Beach Hotel,** the most affordable choice, is Pattaya's top family resort. Rooms here are also spacious, with pastel decor and large terraces, most with bay views. The two-bedroom suites are perfect for families. The beachfront **Royal Cliff Terrace** was the resort's first property and is the most secluded. Rooms boast contemporary decor as well as ocean views.

353 Phra Tamnak Rd., Pattaya 20150 (on cliff, south end of Pattaya Bay). www.royalcliff.com. © **03825-0421.** Fax 03825-0511. 1,072 units. 6,400B–8,200B deluxe double; from 14,400B suite. AE, DC, MC, V. **Amenities:** All Royal Cliff Beach Resort properties share all facilities, including 10 restaurants; 5 bars (many w/live music); 5 outdoor landscaped pools; golf course; 7 outdoor tennis courts; 2 squash courts; health club; 2 spas; Jacuzzi; watersports equipment; children's playground; concierge; room service; babysitting. *In room:* A/C, TV, minibar, fridge, hair dryer, Internet (free).

Sheraton Pattaya Resort ★★   Perched in the hills south of Pattaya's main beach, the Sheraton is an excellent choice for a quiet and luxurious getaway. The guest rooms and pavilions descend the hillside, flanking a maze of gardens, waterfalls, and freeform swimming pools. Decorated in pleasing pastel peaches and sea greens, the generously sized guest quarters contain oversized king or queen beds. There's an attractive man-made white-sand beach by the water. While the rocky waterfront isn't the most inviting place for a dip, the adventurous will find the water much cleaner than that of Pattaya's main beach.

437 Phra Tamnak Rd., Pattaya 20150 (on cliff, south end of Pattaya Bay). www.sheraton.com/pattaya. © **03825-9888.** Fax 03825-9899. 156 units. 9,500B–12,700B double; from 32,000B villa. AE, DC, MC, V. **Amenities:** 3 restaurants; bar; 3 outdoor pools; health club; spa; room service; babysitting. *In room:* A/C, TV/DVD, minibar, hair dryer, Wi-Fi (450B per day).

MODERATE

Birds & Bees Resort ★★   This fun, inviting resort was originally known as Cabbages & Condoms. It was built by Senator Meechai Viravaidya, a Thai activist in the field of sex education and rural development projects throughout Thailand. Rooms have a rustic feel, but all the required amenities are there. Its attraction mainly lies in its two pools, a semiprivate beach, and its tucked-away location in a quiet part of Pattaya. The property is very family friendly and contains wishing wells, as well as an herb garden (with special exercise bikes designed to irrigate them). It is also home to the acclaimed Cabbages & Condoms Restaurant (see below), which has a branch in Bangkok (p. 98).

366/11 Moo 12, Phra Tamnak 4 Rd., Nongprue, Banglamung, Chonburi 20150 (south of town, on Hu Gwang Bay). www.cabbagesandcondoms.co.th. © **03825-0556.** Fax 03825-0034. 50 units.

2,500B–5,150B double; 6,000B–12,000B 1- and 2-bedroom suites. AE, MC, V. **Amenities:** Restaurant; 2 outdoor pools; room service. *In room:* A/C, TV, minibar, fridge, Wi-Fi (free).

Mercure Hotel Pattaya ☺   A friendly, well-run hotel, the Mercure is only a few minutes' walking distance from the city's best shopping area and the beach. The rooms are business-like in style, not so huge, but with bright contemporary artwork mixed with Thai touches and gorgeous, slick bathrooms. The trio of swimming pools that fill the gardens—including a large shaped pool—is among the best features of a stay here. Family-friendly amenities include TV video games—great if the weather turns wet!

484 Moo 10, Pattaya 2nd Rd., Soi 15, Pattaya 20150. www.mercure.com. ✆ **03842-5050.** Fax 03842-5080. 245 units. $85–$98 double, $118 suite. AE, MC, V. Private indoor parking included in rates. **Amenities:** 3 restaurants; bar; 3 outdoor pools. *In room:* A/C, TV, minibar, fridge, video games, Wi-Fi (200B per day).

Woodlands Hotel & Resort ⚑   This four-star hotel in Naklua, the quieter northern area of Pattaya, offers great seasonal deals, which tend to attract families, repeat visitors, and long-term guests, mainly from Europe. The rooms have benefitted from extensive renovations in 2011; though not luxurious, they are very comfortable, with views overlooking the pools and tropical gardens. It also has good spa facilities and a well-equipped health club, as well as an Italian restaurant and a French bakery.

164/1 Moo 5, Pattaya-Naklua Rd., Pattaya 20150. www.woodland-resort.com. ✆ **03842-1707.** Fax 03842-5663. 134 units. 2,700B–7,800B double. AE, MC, V. **Amenities:** 2 restaurants; bar; 2 outdoor pools; health club; spa. *In room:* A/C, TV, minibar, fridge, Wi-Fi (300B per day).

INEXPENSIVE

Budget lodgings in Pattaya attract a rough clientele and can be pretty unpleasant, but you're sure to find cheap deals starting as low as 500B. Many have counters for the mandatory registration of "new friends," meaning night visitors. Some of the more reputable establishments include the **Areca Lodge** (✆ **03841-0123;** www.arecalodge.com), on Soi Diana, not far from the beach and shops, with rooms starting at 1,650B. **The Cottage,** Pattaya 2nd Road, opposite Big C (✆ **03842-5650;** www.thecottage-pattaya.com), offers comfy brick bungalows set in a lush garden with two pools and rates from 850B. **Dynasty Inn Pattaya,** 596/16 Soi 13, Pattaya Beach Road (✆ **03841-5941;** www.dynastyinn.com), is centrally located and rooms start at 1,480B. **Flipper Lodge Hotel** (✆ **03842-6401;** www.flippergroup.com), at 520/1 Soi 8, Pattaya Beach Road, is in the thick of it, so it can get a bit noisy. Nevertheless, it's good value for the money. Rooms start at 1,300B.

Where to Eat

Pattaya is teeming with small storefront bars and eateries. You'll find the big fast-food chains well represented (mercifully for some, they include **Starbucks**) along the beachfront road, and **Subway Sandwich** at the **Royal Garden Shopping Complex** (south of town). The **Big C Festival Center** (on Pattaya 2 Rd., north end of town) supports a number of other familiar eateries, alongside some excellent high-end diners. Local dining is best at open-air joints down any *soi*. Various types of cuisine are available here and the prices range immensely. You'll get good-value meals at some of the fresh seafood establishments found in the beachfront areas, but check prices before you order.

EXPENSIVE

Mantra Restaurant & Bar ★★★ INTERNATIONAL   Offering a unique hotel dining experience, in the pleasant surrounds of the Amari (p. 140), the Mantra has an eclectic menu based on a mix of cuisines (including Japanese, Indian, Chinese, and Mediterranean), and it is by far the trendiest place in town. Everything is prepared in seven open kitchens, and the sleek glass building is decorated with artifacts from all over Asia. The Sunday brunch is particularly good value at 1,590B, for which you can eat as much as you like from all cooking stations (including some delicious desserts) between 11am and 3pm. Seating 260 over two levels, the restaurant also has an extensive walk-in wine cellar. The dress code is "chic, smart, and stylish," so that means no shorts, tank tops, or sandals.

Amari Orchid Resort & Tower, Beach Rd. ✆ **0384-29591.** www.mantra-pattaya.com. Reservations recommended. Main courses 440B–3,200B. AE, MC, V. Mon–Sat 5pm–1am; Sun 11am–3pm and 5pm–1am.

Mata Hari Restaurant ★★ CONTINENTAL/THAI   This highly acclaimed, dinner-only restaurant specializes in fine European cuisine and classic Thai favorites. The atmosphere is casual but elegant, and the innovative menu, featuring such tempting items as beef stew Dutch style, spicy mixed seafood soup with lime and lemongrass, and rock lobster tails in vermouth cream sauce with snow peas, is a favorite among the expatriate community. The convivial bar area, for pre-supper drinks, and the extensive wine list are big bonuses. It's often very busy (even in the low season), so reservations are recommended.

482/57 Moo 12, Thappraya Rd. ✆ **03825-9799.** www.mataharirestaurant.com. Reservations recommended. Main courses 390B–1,600B. AE, MC, V. Tues–Sun 6–10:30pm.

MODERATE

Mum Aroi ★ SEAFOOD   This upmarket restaurant is popular with both residents and Thai visitors. In addition to premium-quality seafood, it is known for its laid-back beach ambience. Go for a steamed fish with lemon and garlic, or the classic hot and sour shrimp soup *tom yam goong*. The restaurant is just 5 minutes north of Pattaya in Naklua, close to the luxurious Ananya, a block of condo flats. There's another branch on Pattaya 3rd Road, but it lacks the beachfront atmosphere.

Beachfront Condominium, 83/4 Moo 2 Naklua Banglamung. ✆ **03822-3252.** Main courses 220B–480B. No credit cards. Daily 11am–11pm.

INEXPENSIVE

Cabbages & Condoms Restaurant THAI   South of town on Hu Gwang Bay, in the Birds & Bees Resort (p. 141), this is Pattaya's version of the much-lauded restaurant in Bangkok. Both are known not only for their food, but also their efforts to educate Thais about HIV/AIDS. The mainly Thai cuisine is good, though, with a wide choice encompassing seafood and other regional specialties. (Tastes are only slightly adjusted for the foreign palate.) The open-concept restaurant is set in the resort's tropical gardens, affording coastal views.

Birds & Bees Resort, 366/11 Moo 12, Phra Tamnak 4 Rd., Nongprue, Banglamung, Chonburi. ✆ **03825-0056.** www.cabbagesandcondoms.co.th. Main courses 80B–250B. MC, V. Daily 11am–10pm.

Outdoor Activities in Pattaya

GOLF

The hills around Pattaya are known for their great courses, with many international-class greens in a short 40-km (25-mile) radius of the city. Caddy fees are reasonable, around 250B, and golf carts are usually compulsory but rationally priced. Among the recommended are:

- **Burapha Golf Club,** 281 Moo 4, Tambon Bung, Sri Racha (© 03837-2700; www.buraphagolfthailand.com), is the home of numerous tournaments. Greens fees are 2,000B on weekdays and 2,500B on weekends; it's 500B for a golf cart.
- **Laem Chabang International Country Club,** 106/8 Moo 4, Tambon Bung, Sri Racha (© 03837-2273, dial 0; www.laemchabanggolf.com), has three 18-hole courses (A, B, and C) designed by Jack Nicklaus and very dramatic scenery. Greens fees are 2,500B on weekdays, 3,000B on weekends.
- **Siam Country Club,** 50/6 Moo 9, Tambol Pong, Banglamung (© 03890-9600; fax 03890-9699; www.siamcountryclub.com), is a short hop from Pattaya and is one of the country's most challenging courses. Greens fees are 3,000B on weekdays and 3,600B on weekends.

WATERSPORTS

For those who come to Pattaya to do more than party, there is plenty on offer, particularly when it comes to watersports. Pattaya's less than pristine beaches are a good excuse to head to outlying areas, where the conditions are more inviting. Day trips to such nearby islands as **Ko Khrok, Ko Lan,** and **Ko Sok** start at around 1,000B per head on a full boat (more for a private charter). To go to far-out Bamboo Island, it will cost you a bit more—about 3,000B. **Paragliding** around the bay behind a motorboat is a popular beachfront activity, and a 5-minute flight costs from 800B.

Jomtien Beach hosts **windsurfing** and **sea kayaking;** boards and boats are rented along the beach for 800B per hour.

Pattaya is a good place to learn to **scuba dive.** It has a number of reputable dive companies with PADI- and NAUI-certified instructors. The underwater visibility is consistently good, so the sport can be done year-round. There are a few dive sites near the islands, just offshore in **Pattaya Bay,** as well as **Ko Si Chang** to the north—once famous as the summer playground of foreign ambassadors to Siam during the 19th century—and **Sattahip** to the south, with diving to a depth of 40m (131 ft.). **Adventure Divers,** 391/77–78 Moo 10, Tappraya Road. (© 03836-4453; www.pattaya divers.com), is one of many PADI-certified companies offering daily trips and courses for all levels.

Pattaya Entertainment & Nightlife

Central Pattaya is predominately a sea of flashing neon and blaring music, even in the smaller *sois*. **Walking Street** becomes a pedestrian zone in the evening in South Pattaya, on Beach Roach. Here you will see debauchery at its fullest, with an array of go-go bars, open-air drinking establishments, Thai boxing venues (before you place a bet, the fights are all fixed), and, of course, overpriced tourist restaurants. Regular bars and places with live music can also be found. The energy on the street, whether good or bad, is riotous by evening. In daylight, the passageway is bleak, with bleary-eyed revelers stumbling through seedy storefronts.

Sex for money in Pattaya is an unashamedly direct business. Dubious massage parlors are numerous in northern Pattaya. Hotels insist "visitors" (a euphemism for prostitutes) register their ID with security guards, whereupon the client pays a "joiner fee." Despite its prevalence, prostitution in Thailand is illegal, so be prepared to risk a police raid, or hefty bribe to the local police or mafia, not to mention a call to your embassy. It's *not* all innocent fun. Stories of laced drinks and aggravated theft (or worse) abound. AIDS and STDs are major concerns. To prove they are cracking down, authorities are particularly happy to splash photos of any foreigners caught with young girls or boys across the international media. (See "Sex for Sale," p. 377, for more info.)

Happily, Pattaya is not entirely sleazy these days, as indicated by some of its finer eateries and upscale resorts. There is a number of bars where you can go to enjoy a drink and maybe listen to live music without being propositioned. Topping the list is the **Hopf Brew House ★★★** (219 Beach Rd.; ☏ **03871-0650**). Designed like a German brewery, this spacious watering hole brews its own beer and has an in-house band that plays easy-listening tunes. **Shenanigan's** is a fun Irish-bar hangout at the Royal Garden Complex (near the Marriott; ☏ **03872-3939**), with the front entrance on Pattaya 2nd Road. It's a good place to watch major sporting events on the big screen. Then there's **Tavern by the Sea** (on the beach in front of the Amari Orchid Tower; ☏ **03841-8418**), a welcoming bar serving-up Tex-Mex food, cocktails, and a wide assortment of beers; they also show sports on TV.

The town's camped-up cabaret shows are always good, lighthearted fun. Pattaya's sensational *katoeys* (transsexuals) love to don sequined gowns and feather boas and strut their stuff to packed houses nightly. Both **Tiffany's** (464 Moo 9, 2nd Rd.; ☏ **03842-1700;** www.tiffany-show.co.th) and **Alcazar** (78/14 Pattaya 2nd Rd., opposite Soi 5; ☏ **03841-0227;** www.alcazarpattaya.com) have hilarious shows, much like those in other tourist towns in Thailand.

BAN PHE & KO SAMET ★

Ko Samet: 220km (137 miles) SE of Bangkok. Ban Phe: 25km (16 miles) southeast of Rayong City

Tiny Ko Samet, better known simply as Samet (or Samed), is well known to Thais through an epic poem by Sunthorn Phu, a venerated 18th-century author and Rayong native who set his famous work, *Phra Aphimani*, on Samet. Just 1km (⅔ mile) wide, the island is a long, triangular pennant shape, split by a rocky ridge, with some dazzling beaches on the east coast. It's deemed a national park, hence there's a 200B per-adult landing fee (children pay half that price). As with so many of Thailand's "protected" areas, though, developers have devoured so much of the long sandy coastline here that one has to wonder what is being protected with the admission fee.

Ferries from Ban Phe land at Na Dan, the island's main port on the northern coast, from where shared *songtaews* run passengers to the various beaches—**Had Sai Kaew** (Diamond Beach), a popular stretch with a serious party vibe, **Ao Wong Deuan,** or the more isolated **Ao Tubtim** (*Had* means "beach," and *Ao* means "bay"). Rates are posted by the ferry landing. Ao Phai's beaches just south of Had Sai Kaew can be treacherous for swimmers, so take care; in contrast, **Ao Thian** is popular with divers. Right down south are the chilled-out bays of **Ao Kiu Na Nok** (on the east coast) and **Ao Kiu Na Nai** (on the west coast), which are both the exclusive domain of the island's most expensive resort—*Paradee*. There are also a few upmarket resorts on the northwest side of the island at **Ao Prao** where speedboats take guests over to Ban Phe. Some ferries also run directly to Ao Wong Deuan, in the middle of the east coast.

Accommodation prices take a big hike here on weekends and in high season, and bookings may not always be honored. Stay cool and shop around. If you're looking for a relaxing break, avoid the busy weekend rush, when big groups of young Thai weekenders come over for some serious karaoke and drinking sessions. Peak season is similar to Pattaya's, with July through October bringing fewer travelers and lower rates, though it's also rainy season.

Essentials

GETTING THERE

BY BUS   Buses leave Bangkok every 30 minutes between 4am and 10pm for the 2½-hour journey, departing from **Ekkamai,** Bangkok's Eastern Bus Terminal, on Sukhumvit Road, opposite Soi 63 (✆ **02391-2504**). The one-way trip to Ban Phe costs 157B by air-conditioned bus. From Pattaya, either flag down a passing public bus from the corner of Sukhumvit and North Pattaya roads, or book a minibus at any agency. **Malibu-Garden Resort,** on Samet, owns **Samet Island Tour,** in Pattaya (✆ **03871-0676;** www.malibu-samet.com), from which they run regular minibus transfers (300B one-way, 600B round-trip including boat). Private cars can also be arranged. From Khao San, travel agencies offer minibus seats to Ban Phe for around 250B.

BY CAR   Take the Suvarnabhumi Airport tollway from Bangkok east to Pattaya, then Highway 36 to Rayong, and then the coastal Highway 3145 to Seree Ban Phe (for about 3 hr.). See p. 138, for car rentals.

GETTING TO KO SAMET

BY FERRY   From the Saphan Nuan Tip ferry pier at Ban Phe, ferries leave for Na Dan every half-hour (trip time: 40 min.; 50B one-way) or when full. Scheduled ferries also run at 9:30am, 1:30, and 5pm to Ao Wong Duean. Rates are one-way for 70B or 110B for a round-trip.

Speedboats to Ao Prao Resort can be booked at their dockside office in Ban Phe; prices vary. If you fancy whizzing over to Na Dan, it'll cost around 1,200B.

FAST FACTS

Ko Samet has a few ATMs. The easiest to find is at the 7-Eleven at the Na Dan pier. The **post office** is at the Naga Bungalows (✆/fax **03864-4035**), south of Had Sai Kaew; and there's a satellite phone for overseas calls at the visitor center in the National Parks office. There are plenty of Internet places, great nightlife, and seafood eateries by the beach. A clinic is just south of the Na Dan pier before Had Sai Kaew. (Though the island is no longer supposed to be malarial, it's plagued with mosquitoes; take plenty of repellent and an antihistamine-based cream to treat bites.)

GETTING AROUND

Island transport is limited to shared pickups or rented motorbikes, but many people simply choose to walk—it takes about 3 hours to walk the length of the entire east coast, which has most of the island's beaches. Motorbike rental prices are very high compared to the rest of the country (about 100B per hour, 300B per day), and staff at your resort can help arrange this. However, the roads are in poor condition, so drive carefully.

Where to Stay

It's always risky if you haven't booked a hotel ahead, especially on busy weekends, so it's worth arranging at least the first night to avoid the throng of touts who hover at the Ban Phe Pier hungry for commission. With few exceptions, budget accommodation is very basic here. There are now some gorgeous luxury resorts and midrange bungalows, though. **Samed Resorts** (www.samedresorts.com) represents six of the best.

VERY EXPENSIVE

Paradee ★★ Samet's most exclusive address is this fabulous villa-only resort, right on the island's southernmost tip and straddling two beaches (east and west coast). Expect elegant Thai decor and perks such as tranquil private pools, Jacuzzis, and personal DVD players. It's ideal for couples (in fact, families are actively discouraged from staying here). At this exclusive sanctuary for the chosen few, you even get a butler with each sumptuous villa just to ensure that your every need is met.

76 Moo 4, Tambon Phe, Rayong 21160. www.samedresorts.com. ✆ **03864-4283,** or 02438-9771 Bangkok office. Fax 03864-4290. 40 units. 17,300B garden villa; 19,900B garden pool villa; 77,300B suite villa. MC, V. **Amenities:** Restaurant; bar; individual pools in private villas; spa; room service; airport transfers; Internet. *In room:* A/C, TV/DVD, minibar, fridge, hair dryer.

EXPENSIVE

Ao Prao Resort ★★ One of the oldest upscale properties in the area, Ao Prao, located on the west-coast beach of the same name, is still one of the best. The pretty bungalows here make for quaint little vacation retreats. Rooms have delightful teak furnishings and decor, as well as four-poster beds, and some come with enormous double tubs overlooking the blissful scenery. There are plenty of watersports available and large meeting facilities, all set within a sprawling tropical garden.

60 Moo 4, Tambon Phe, Rayong 21160. www.samedresorts.com. ✆ **03864-4100.** Fax 0386-4099. 52 units. 7,100B deluxe; 14,100B 2-bed family suite. MC, V. **Amenities:** Restaurant/bar; outdoor pool; watersports rentals; room service; babysitting; Wi-Fi. *In room:* A/C, satellite TV, minibar, fridge, hair dryer.

Le Vimarn Cottages & Spa ★★★ Ao Prao's upmarket status is confirmed by this small, hillside hideaway for wannabe jet-setters; accommodation comes in three types: Deluxe cottages, spa villas, and one spa villa suite. All of the huge thatched villas come with four-poster beds and private balconies overlooking the beach and ocean, while the resort's pool villas have Jacuzzis sharing the same wondrous sea views. If you tire of looking at the view, indulge in a spa treatment at the Dhivarin Spa, or take a diving course and explore the vivid underwater world around the island.

40/11 Moo 4, Tambon Phe, Rayong 21160. www.samedresorts.com. ✆ **03864-4104,** or 02438-9771 Bangkok office. Fax 03864-4109. 31 units. 10,500B deluxe cottage; 13,000B spa villa; 21,000B spa villa suite. MC, V. **Amenities:** Restaurant; bar; outdoor pool; spa; Jacuzzi, room service. *In room:* A/C, TV, minibar, fridge, hair dryer, Wi-Fi (free).

Samed Club It's fun, it's young, and it's affordable. The Samed Club offers midrange luxury rooms and amenities; you get most of the frills of expensive resorts, but for far less. The decor is modern, walls are painted with bright colors, there are walk-in tiled showers, and rooms overlook the central pool, around which sun lovers can chill out under a parasol. The more active have a wide choice of beach sports, sailing, and windsurfing activities on hand. One of the highlights is the great location at Noi

Na Beach, a quiet spot on the northern coast but close enough to enjoy a good night out on Had Sai Kaew.

25 Moo 4, Tambon Phe, Rayong 21160. ✆ **03864-4341.** Fax 03864-4064. 30 units. 4,000B–5,700B double. MC, V. **Amenities:** Restaurant; bar; outdoor pool; Wi-Fi (free). *In room:* A/C, TV, minibar, fridge, hair dryer.

MODERATE

There are plenty of midrange options scattered along the east coast, most of them equipped with a good range of facilities. One is the **Samed Grand View** (✆ 03864-4220), which has well-spaced bungalows on busy Had Sai Kaew. Nearby, at Ao Phai, you'll find **Samed Villa's** (www.samedvilla.com; ✆ 03864-4094) bungalows, set in pretty gardens and with swish interiors. **Mooban Talay** (www.moobantalay.com; ✆ 08183-88682) offers an upscale feel to its 24 rustic bungalows on Noi Na Bay. Quiet **Samet Ville Resort** (www.sametvilleresort.com; ✆ 03865-1681), on Ao Wai, toward the southern end of the east coast, is a romantic midrange option away from the noise and popular with expats.

INEXPENSIVE

For cozy huts at good prices (and some great food in Jep's diner next door), head past Had Sai Khaew to Ao Hin Khok, where cool dudes hang at **Jep's Bungalows** (✆ 03864-4112); rooms with a fan start at 600B. Farther south, on the east coast at Ao Phai, the aptly named **Lost Resort** (✆ 03864-4041) has just 10 rooms (fan 500B, air-con 700B), and is the place for a bit of peace and quiet. Farther south still on Ao Tubtim, one of the island's longest-running resorts is **Tub Tim Resort** (www.tubtimresort.com; ✆ 03864-4025). It has a variety of smart rooms ranging from 1,000B to 3,300B on a protected bay that is good for swimming.

Where to Eat

The standard fish and rice dishes available at the island's resorts will keep you sated, but it'd be a shame to miss out on some of the upscale dining, as well as great local seafood restaurants, that are available around the island. Most bungalows on Samet have their own dining areas for inexpensive, fresh seafood (don't miss the locally caught squid and cuttlefish, which are barbecued on skewers). Every day around sunset on **Ao Hin Khok** and **Ao Phai beaches,** tables are set up under twinkling lights for big seafood barbecues brimming with the day's catch.

The **Baywatch Bar** (✆ 08182-67834, cell) on Ao Wong Deuan, serves-up great kebabs and Thai dishes, as well as reasonable Western fare. On Ao Phai, just south of Had Sai Khaew, **Naga Bar** (✆ 03864-4035) is a popular hangout and serves a fine menu of local eats and tasty baked items. If you fancy drinks by the bucket and dancing after dinner, head for the **Silver Sand Resort** (✆ 03864-4301), which is also on Ao Phai. Indeed, many restaurants on the island can turn into all-night party affairs depending on the crowd—and the amount of alcohol consumed.

CHANTHABURI PROVINCE

250km (155 miles) E of Bangkok

Travelers heading east to rugged Ko Chang (see "Trat & Ko Chang," below) will pass through (or over, if they're flying) Chanthaburi province and its capital, Chanthaburi (known as Muang Chan). This region is known for its tropical fruit and lucrative gem mines. Durian, pineapple, *lamyai* (longan), and rambutan thrive here. Don't be startled by the roadside 7.9-m (26-ft.) high durian "sculptures" you'll see piled at food stands along the way.

Essentials

Chanthaburi straddles the Chanthaburi River. The city's main avenue is Tha Chalab Road. The taxi stand and bus station (to Trat or Bangkok) are just west of the Chanthaburi Hotel on this street.

Exploring Chanthaburi

In **Taksin Park** (the center of Chanthaburi), there's a statue of King Taksin on horseback, commemorating the victory over the Burmese in 1767, and a few temples built over Khmer ruins, highlighting the city's Cambodian connections. A large Catholic church, built in 1909, stands in the center as well.

Gem Markets line the predictably named Gem Street, near the main market. If you are traveling in early December, take note—the annual Gem Fair packs the town with visitors. You may find a few choice rubies on offer, but no room at any inn.

The 17,000-hectare (42,000-acre) **Namtok Phlio National Park** (admission 200B adults, 100B children) is a popular day trip from Chanthaburi, as is **Laem Sadet,** a stunning beach and rocky cape located some 35km (22 miles) southwest of the city. Both sites can be visited by private car or taxi; arrange transport through your hotel.

Where to Stay

City lodging is spartan. **River Guest House** (3/5–8 Si Chan Rd.; ✆ 03932-8211) is not quite downtown but offers homey, air-conditioned rooms (starting at 350B), with quieter (fan only) rooms out back. **K. P. Grand** (35/200–201 Trirat Rd.; www.kpgrandhotel.com; ✆ 03932-3201) is a smart, modern facility with a pool, also a short way from the center, with rooms priced from 1,800B. If you're looking for a real country retreat, consider **Faasai Resort & Spa** (www.faasai.com; ✆ 03941-7404), a small, award-winning eco-resort on the coast at Khung Wiman, about 30km (18.6 miles) southwest of Chanthaburi. It's run by a Thai-New Zealand couple and rates are between 900B and 4,100B a night.

Where to Eat

Chanthaburi is famous for its noodles, which are called *sen chan*; you can taste them at any of the food stalls down by the river, along with Vietnamese spring rolls and *muu liang*, a spicy pork broth. For a wide-ranging menu of Thai and Chinese dishes, such as spicy salads and thick curries, head for **Chanthorn Pochana** (102/5–8 Benchama-Ratchutit Rd.; ✆ 03931-2339). They also serve wines made from local fruits, such as mangosteen, at very cheap prices.

If you're in the mood for Indian vegetarian food, make for the tiny **Sony Yadaw** (Si Chan Road; no phone), where you might also spot a few gem traders at work.

TRAT & KO CHANG

310km (193 miles) E of Bangkok

The capital of Trat Province is Trat, hitherto regarded as the gateway to the Ko Chang Marine National Park. Because of the region's direct transport links, though, visitors can now head straight to any of three piers to access the park's many islands, and Trat is becoming less of a gateway. On Ko Chang itself, a single, looping, cliff road runs along both coasts with the final, southern section still awaiting completion.

Despite having Marine National Park status, many of the islands here have been subjected to large-scale developments, particularly the largest, **Ko Chang** (Elephant Island), so called for its jumbo-like outline, with its highest point some 740m (2,428 ft.) above sea level. This development, which has transformed the character of the island, was instigated by former Prime Minister Thaksin Shinawatra—a clear case of putting financial gain before ecological interests. For years, it was purely a foreign-backpacker and Thai weekend getaway, but now, with a glut of fancy resorts having opened, a more upscale international clientele is visiting. A luxury marina and condo complex at Klong Son Bay, in the northwest, is almost finished, and several international hotel chains now operate here. These developments are bound to bring more visitors, but the environmental impact on the waste disposal system and dry-season water supply is a concern.

For now, adventurers will find plenty of activities, including elephant treks, water-falls, and kayak trips through the mangroves in Ko Chang. The island also has a top-notch vegetarian detox retreat at the **The Spa, Koh Chang** (p. 156). Plus, in dry season (late Oct–May), you can do scuba diving and snorkeling.

Essentials

GETTING THERE

BY PLANE   **Bangkok Airways** (✆ 02270-6699; www.bangkokair.com) has two to three flights daily, depending on the season, between Bangkok and Trat, each tak-ing 1 hour. Airport minivans meet each flight, pick up passengers, drive to and board the car ferry at Ao Thammarat pier, then drop passengers at their resort or guesthouse on the island for a return fee of 800B; get your ticket at the desk at the airport. Most resorts on Ko Chang can arrange airport transfers, but at higher rates.

There are now also four weekly flights to Trat from Phuket via Ko Samui (also on Bangkok Airways), making it possible to hop between the three top island destinations.

BY BUS   From Bangkok's two **Eastern Bus Terminals,** at **Ekkamai** (✆ 02391-2504) and **Khao San Road** (no phone), there are now dozens of buses direct to the three ferry piers; the trip time is around 5 to 6 hours. Fares range from 250B to 500B; the pricier tickets include the ferry. Buses usually stop at **Suvarnabhumi Inter-national Airport's Bus Terminal**.

Daily minivans operate from Pattaya, via Ban Phe (Ko Samet's ferry port). From Pattaya, allow 4 hours, and from Ban Phe, you'll need 2½ hours; costs are 400B and 300B, respectively.

BY CAR   There are two routes out of Bangkok: The faster Bagna-Trat tollway, past Suvarnabhumi International Airport, and a route via Highway 3 to Chonburi. From the latter route, take Highway 344 southeast to Klaeng (bypassing Pattaya and Ray-ong), and then pick up Highway 3 again through Chanthaburi, after which you can turn south to Trat. This route takes about 5 to 6 hours.

GETTING TO KO CHANG & BEYOND

From Trat, *songtaews* (shared pickups) journey between all three piers for around 50B. On the island, white *songtaews* charge from 40B to 100B to take visitors to their hotels. In low season, if you are alone, you may be obliged to charter the whole

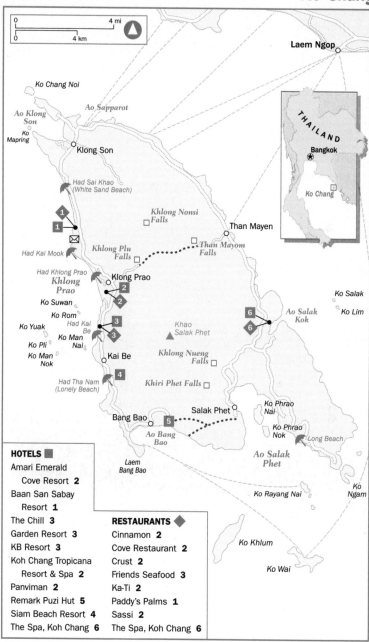

0   4 mi
0   4 km

Laem Ngop

Ko Chang Noi

Ao Sapparot

Ao Klong Son

Ko Mapring

Klong Son

Had Sai Khao
(White Sand Beach)

Khlong Nonsi Falls

Than Mayen

THAILAND

Bangkok

Ko Chang

Khlong Plu Falls

Than Mayom Falls

Had Kai Mook

Had Khlong Prao
Khlong Prao

Klong Prao

Ko Suwan

Ko Rom

Ko Yuak

Had Kai Be

Ko Man Nai

Ko Pli

Ko Man Nok

Kai Be

Khao Salak Phet

Khlong Nueng Falls

Ko Salak

Ko Lim

Ao Salak Kok

Had Tha Nam
(Lonely Beach)

Khiri Phet Falls

Bang Bao

Salak Phet

Ko Phrao Nai

Ko Phrao Nok

Long Beach

Ao Bang Bao

Laem Bang Bao

Ao Salak Phet

Ko Rayang Nai

Ko Ngam

Ko Khlum

Ko Wai

HOTELS

Amari Emerald
   Cove Resort **2**
Baan San Sabay
   Resort **1**
The Chill **3**
Garden Resort **3**
KB Resort **3**
Koh Chang Tropicana
   Resort & Spa **2**
Panviman **2**
Remark Puzi Hut **5**
Siam Beach Resort **4**
The Spa, Koh Chang **6**

RESTAURANTS

Cinnamon **2**
Cove Restaurant **2**
Crust **2**
Friends Seafood **3**
Ka-Ti **2**
Paddy's Palms **1**
Sassi **2**
The Spa, Koh Chang **6**

songtaew for 500B. If you have your own transport, it is possible to bypass Trat and go directly to or from Ko Chang from Bangkok. Take the right turning for Ao Thammachat Ferry on Highway 3 before you reach Trat.

The Ao Thammachat ferry is the shortest, fastest, and safest crossing, with an hourly service year-round (more frequent in high season and on public holidays), departing daily from 6:30am to 7pm (trip time is 30 min.) and landing at Ko Chang's Ao Sapparos on the north coast. One-way fares cost 60B, and a return trip is 120B. From the ramshackle **Center Point Pier,** it's 50 minutes and 80B one-way, 160B round-trip. Your slowest option is the cheap but infrequent fishing boat from **Laem Ngob,** costing 100B one-way, which takes an hour to reach Dan Mai Pier, on the east of Ko Chang, but it's often overcrowded. If you are prone to seasickness, be warned that during the monsoon season (July–Sept), the crossing can be rough.

VISITOR INFORMATION

The **TAT** has an office in Trat (Moo 1, Trat-Laem Ngop Rd.; ✆ **03959-7259**) providing information on the nearby islands. At the Bangkok Airways' counter at Trat Airport, you can pick up the latest *Ko Chang & Beyond*, with good maps and info. Other free magazines, *Koh Chang Guide and Koh Chang Guidebook*, are available in many restaurants and resorts on the island, and are packed with local information. Several of these publications, as well as a handy map, are published by Whitesands Publications (www.whitesandsthailand.com). Another useful website is **www.iamkohchang.com,** run by an expat resident on the island.

The island's narrow, mountainous cliff roads are steep and perilous; road fatalities are common, so think very carefully before renting a motorbike, which can be organized through most resorts, starting at 200B per day. For emergencies, call ✆ **1719.** For serious injuries, head for the **Ko Chang International Clinic** (✆ **03955-1555**), located near the southern end of White Sand Beach (Had Sai Khao).

ORIENTATION

Ko Chang, Thailand's second-largest island after Phuket, is the anchor of the 52-island **Mu Ko Chang Marine National Park.** Thickly forested hills rise from its many bays, which, due to the tides, are narrow and rocky in wet season (June–Oct) and sandier in dry season (Nov–May). Coconut palms (and now billboards) dominate the west coast. The island's only sealed road around its perimeter is hair-raisingly precipitous, and still doesn't make a complete circle due to a gap on the south end of the island. Ferry piers are all in the north; fishing villages, mangroves, and orchid farms exist on the flatter and more tranquil east coast. In high season, some dive and boat trips leave from **Bang Bao Bay,** on the southernmost tip. The island's west coast is chock-full with resorts of all types and prices. At the northern end is **Had Sai Khao (White Sand Beach),** the busiest place to hang out. Its kilometer-long (⅔-mile) sands are now so crowded that it's been divided into "north" and "south," like Samui's Chaweng. More upmarket and family options abound at **Had Klong Phrao;** farther south, at the ramshackle **Had Kai Be;** and last of all, at **Bang Bao,** a stilted fishing village that suffers badly from a terrifyingly roller coaster-like road and trash-strewn mud flats.

Where to Stay & Eat

For some of the best seafood on the island, head for **Friends Seafood** (✆ **08486-31221**), near the north end of the road behind Kae Be Beach, where you can feast on grilled platters, kebabs, and a tongue-tingling *tom yam goong* (hot and sour shrimp soup); it's open for dinner only. Another simple Thai restaurant worth tracking down is **Ka-Ti** (📞 03955-7252), which is almost opposite the entrance to the Tropicana Resort (p. 154) on Klong Phrao Beach. They specialize in coconut-based curries, but there are several other tasty options including spicy salads; there's also a cookery school here, with daily classes costing 1,200B.

As you might expect, all the five-star resorts provide gourmet dining options, though at considerably higher prices than local restaurants. Check out the modern Italian fare on offer at Amari's **Sassi** (📞 03955-2000; www.amari.com/emeraldcove; dinner only), in Klong Phrao, or choose from an eclectic menu of Thai and international dishes at the poolside **Cove Restaurant** (📞 03955-2000), which is open all day. On Had Sai Khao is **Paddy's Palms** (📞 03961-9083), an Irish pub serving homemade pies, Irish stew, Sunday roasts, and Guinness; they also have some inexpensive rooms. Farther south, on Had Klong Phrao, you'll find **Cinnamon,** at Aana resort (📞 03955-1359; www.aanaresort.com), which serves up Thai seafood favorites. For a picnic lunch, head to **Crust** (📞 03955-7157), a delightful bakery that serves fresh breads, sandwiches, and cakes in Klong Phrao (opposite the temple). Vegetarians should head to the **Spa** (📞 03955-2733), at Salak Kok; it's worth the hike.

TRAT

If you arrive after the last ferry and get stranded, head into Trat. The **Muang Trat Hotel,** at 40 Wijitjanya Rd. (📞 03951-1091), has 76 very basic rooms: A double with a fan costs 250B, or it's 650B for a double with air-conditioning.

KO CHANG

Accommodation-wise, Ko Chang has everything for everyone, from cheap jungle huts to full-on luxury resorts; keep in mind that smaller places will be very much DIY. If you fancy a week of serious detox, colonics, meditation, and yoga, head to the **The Spa, Ko Chang** (p. 156)—it's one of a handful of upscale resorts on the peaceful, less-developed east coast.

Nightlife and cheap eats are available all down the west coast from **Had Sai Khao** (White Sand Beach), through **Had Kai Mook** (Pearl Beach), **Laem Chaichet, Had Klong Phrao, Kai Bae, Had Tha Nam** (Lonely Beach), and **Bai Lan** down to **Bang Bao.** Some great seafood can also be found at no-name shacks on the east coast.

HAD SAI KHAO TO HAD KLONG PHRAO

The buzzing northern strip of Had Sai Khao and Had Kai Mook tends to pull in budget travelers, while Had Klong Phrao is more upscale. In between, Laem Chai Chet offers a relatively quieter option.

Expensive

Amari Emerald Cove Resort ★★★ ☺ Affordable luxury is the watchword at this glamorous resort. The Amari Emerald Cove is truly a study in contemporary comfort. Three-story guest-room wings skirt a delightful courtyard with wooden walkways over lily ponds. A 50-m (164-ft.) jade-green pool overlooks the ocean, while there's a smaller bathing pool for kids and a Jacuzzi too. Rooms are oversized, with slate tile and wood floors, marble bathrooms and thick, soft mattresses on the beds.

The resort's restaurants offer spicy Thai fare, modern Italian dishes, or international cuisine. Romantic seafood suppers can be arranged on the quiet, sandy beach, too. The Breezes bar rocks until 11pm (except Mon) with a sizzling Filipino band.

Children will be well entertained with free DVDs, and can splash about in the pool or enjoy the airy games room.

88/8 Moo 4, Had Klong Phrao, Ko Chang 23170. www.amari.com/emeraldcove. © **03955-2000.** Fax 03955-2001. 165 units. From 5,800B double; 16,000 suite. AE, MC, V. **Amenities:** 3 restaurants; 2 bars, 1 w/live music; 2 outdoor pools; health club; spa; room service; babysitting. *In room:* A/C, TV/DVD, minibar, fridge, hair dryer, CD player, Wi-Fi (428B per day).

Koh Chang Tropicana Resort & Spa ★ Palm-fringed bungalows scattered across gardens with ponds and tropical flora give this sprawling resort a Robinson Crusoe-like feel. A wide range of rustic one- and two-story bamboo and rattan rooms are on offer; the pricier ones are free-standing. For a small extra charge, opt for one with sea views. All come with tiled bathrooms, inside and outdoor showers, and petite sun decks. The huge beach restaurant sits on a vast wooden deck next to the crashing surf, which competes with the Filipino band. The nearby Sunset bar is a pleasant place for sundowners. A professional yoga tutor teaches classes near the beach and there are sea kayaks for rent. Room reservations should be made in advance through their website or Bangkok office.

26/3 Moo 4, Had Klong Phrao, Ko Chang 23170. www.kohchangtropicana.net. © **03955-7122,** or 02642-4420 (Bangkok). Fax 03955-7123. 157 units. 5,500B–9,000B superior, deluxe, and suites. MC, V. **Amenities:** Restaurant; 2 bars; outdoor pool; spa. *In room:* A/C, TV, minibar, fridge, Wi-Fi (350B per day).

Panviman ★★ The Panviman is another luxurious option on Klong Phrao Beach; its spacious grounds are meticulously manicured, and the main pool is a beautiful little meander flanked on one side by a casual bar, on the other by the resort's fine dining—all with views of the sea. Rooms are set in high-peaked, Thai-style buildings with arching roofs, each with a canopy bed, large sitting area, balcony, and huge stylish bathroom. It's not a private beach, but the resort is far south of central White Sand Beach, so even in high season you might have a vast stretch of sand to yourself. The excellent spa offers the chance of a memorable beachside treatment.

8/15 Moo 4, Had Klong Phrao, Ko Chang 23170. www.panviman.com. © **03955-1290,** or 02910-8660 in Bangkok. Fax 03955-1283. 50 units. From 10,500B double. MC, V. **Amenities:** Restaurant; bar; outdoor pool; health club; spa; Jacuzzi; watersports equipment; room service. *In room:* A/C, TV, minibar, fridge, Wi-Fi (500B per day).

Moderate

There are plenty of midrange places along busy Had Sai Khao, but a couple of the more popular larger hotels are the concrete behemoth **Cookies Hotel** (www.cookies kohchang.com; © **03955-1105**) and the more rustic **KC Grande Resort** (www. kckohchang.com; © **03955-2111**). Both have pools and a wide range of rooms beginning at around 2,000B.

Inexpensive

Baan San Sabay Resort ★ This pocket-sized bungalow resort is on the lower end of Had Sai Khao, opposite the Ko Chang Clinic, on the beach side (though it's a bit of a trek to get there). Rooms are clean, with rattan and wood decor, balconies, and small but adequate en suite shower rooms. All the basics are available, including air-conditioning, making it a good-value stopover in the busiest part of the island. It's a few minutes to the roadside restaurants. Because it's so small, you should book well ahead.

16/8 Had Sai Khao, Ko Chang 23120. ℂ **03955-1061.** Fax 03955-1063. 6 units 1,400B–1,800B detached bungalows. No credit cards. *In room:* A/C, TV, minibar, fridge.

KAI BAE TO BANG BAO
Expensive

The Chill ★★   Upmarket resorts are opening all the time on Ko Chang, but many lack the flair of the established resorts. The Chill is a notable exception. Bringing a touch of class to Kai Be Beach, it has a striking modernist design with clean white lines and furnishings in black and white. Rooms range from large deluxe rooms to splash rooms with big balconies and pool views, through to Jacuzzi suites and pool villas. Beds are set on platforms in the center of spacious bedrooms, whilst bright windows and sliding doors let plenty of light in, providing a fresh feeling about the place. It features a spa, a library, and chill-out cafe, as well as three pools, including one just for kids.

19/21 Moo 4, Kai Be Beach, Ko Chang 23170. www.thechillkohchang.com. ℂ **03955-2555.** Fax 03955-2599. 38 units. From 6,250B doubles; 10,000B Jacuzzi suite; 15,000B pool villa. AE, MC, V. **Amenities:** Restaurant; bar; 3 outdoor pools; spa; cafe. *In room:* A/C, TV/DVD, minibar, Wi-Fi (free).

Moderate

Garden Resort ★★   Like many resorts on Ko Chang, this place at Kai Be isn't right on the beach (though it's only about 200m/656 ft. away). However, it is a cozy and welcoming compound with good-sized thatched bungalows at reasonable rates. All the bungalows, which are well-spaced, have big balconies, sliding doors, and chunky bamboo furnishings, and they're a decent size too, especially the family rooms, which are basically two adjoining bungalows. It's under Western management and there are lots of nice touches like free Wi-Fi and computers for guests' use; there's also a small pool.

98/22 Moo 4, Kai Be, Ko Chang 23170. www.gardenresortkohchang.com. ℂ **03955-7260.** 20 units. 2,500B–2,750B double; 5,000B family room. MC, V. **Amenities:** Restaurant; bar; small outdoor pool; diving courses. *In room:* A/C, TV, fridge, Wi-Fi (free).

KB Resort ★   Off the busy main drag but still only a short walk to shops, this sprawling bungalow property perches amid well-kept gardens, a few steps from the beach. Free-standing bungalows (of varying size and quality) sleep up to four—making this good value for families. Resort accommodation runs from basic to top-end beach-front villas—the latter have extra amenities such as DVD players. All rooms are decorated with simple wood furnishings and bright yellow walls. The beach here is not as crowded as farther north, and there's a decent pool and Thai massage services.

10/16 Moo 4, Had Kai Bae, Ko Chang 23170. www.kbresort.com. ℂ **03955-7125.** 49 units. 1,250B–3,500B. MC, V. **Amenities:** Restaurant; outdoor pool; Jacuzzi; Wi-Fi (free). *In room:* A/C (in some), TV, DVD (in some), fridge.

Siam Beach Resort ★ 🍴   This popular resort is a good-value hideaway with direct beach access (though take care if swimming here as the current can be treacherous). Older rooms come in two-story (upper or lower) units, built amid gardens, while newer, more expensive beachfront accommodation comes complete with extra luxuries such as a DVD player, flatscreen TV, and MP3 player. The best rooms are those called "Deluxe C," located right on the beach where the soothing hiss of the surf creates a calming background. All rooms are airy with excellent amenities, bathtubs, and showers, and there's in-house dining near the sea, plus a helpful reception staff that can advise on tours.

100/1 Moo 4, Had Tha Nam (Lonely Beach), Ko Chang 23170. www.siambeachkohchang.com. ✆ **03955-8082.** Fax 03955-8082. 92 units. From 2,500B deluxe; 5,900B pool villa. MC, V. **Amenities:** Restaurant; beach bar; outdoor pool. *In room:* A/C (in some), TV, DVD (in some), minibar, fridge, hair dryer, Wi-Fi (free).

Inexpensive

Remark Puzi Hut ★   About as far off the track as you can get in Ko Chang, and quite difficult to reach in wet weather, this quaint little collection of thatched huts sits on the southern tip of the island, near Bang Bao pier. Choose from sea or garden-view thatched huts with fans. Each one is raised on stilts, with a basic bathroom and lots of rattan decor, and is positioned in a shady coconut grove. The same owners have another appealing rustic resort, **Remark Cottage** (✆ **03955-1261;** www.remark cottage.com), with higher prices (2000B–3000B) and better facilities, on Had Kai Mook (between Had Sai Khao and Had Klong Phrao).

11/1 Moo 1, Bang Bao Bay, Ko Chang 23170. www.remarkpuzi.com. ✆ **03955-8116.** Fax 03955-8117. 20 units. 600B–900B double. No credit cards. **Amenities:** Restaurant. *In room:* A/C (in some).

EAST COAST

The Spa, Koh Chang ★★ 🏠   Far away from the busy west-coast strip, this delightful health retreat offers very reasonably priced 4 to 7-day fasting retreats and colonic cleansing. However, you don't have to detox to stay here as a guest (slightly different rates apply for nonfasters). Rooms are set in stilted one- and two-story houses built of rustic recycled wood, which stand almost hidden from view by a lush hillside garden. The resort's rooms are best described as a mix of modern Thai–European, with sleek bathrooms of polished terrazzo, and good-sized balconies. The restaurant is open to anyone and serves superb vegetarian food, smoothies, and powerfully cleansing shots of home-grown wheat grass or the green herb *gotakula,* but there's plenty of choices for carnivores, all made using wholesome organic produce. A pool sits among sculpted rocks and tropical flora next to a vast pond, yoga and massage pavilion, and delightful sauna.

15/4 Moo 4, Salak Kok, Ko Chang 23170. www.thespakohchang.com. ✆ **03955-2733.** Fax 03955-2722. www.thespakohchang.com. 26 units. 1,500B–2,900B. AE, MC, V. **Amenities:** Restaurant; outdoor pool; sauna; Jacuzzi. *In room:* A/C, TV/DVD, fridge, hair dryer, Wi-Fi (free).

Outdoor Activities

DIVING & SNORKELING

Dive and snorkeling trips operate here only in the dry season, from mid-October until May; most trips head to the islands of Ko Khlum and Ko Wai (a particularly beautiful island), or to Ko Phrao (for wreck dives). **BB Divers** (✆ **08615-56212;** www.bb divers.com) is probably the best of the island's many diving outfits.

KO CHANG ADVENTURE: HIKING, KAYAKING, & ELEPHANT SAFARIS

Several well-marked hiking trails crisscross the island's peaks, but possibly the most enjoyable leads up from Had Klong Phrao to **Klong Plu Waterfall,** which is most spectacular July through August.

Four operators run elephant treks on Ko Chang, but the best regarded is **Ban Kwan Chang,** in the north at Ban Klong Son village (✆ **08191-93995**). You can book tours of varying durations (starting at 8am) at most hotels, which can involve an elephant safari and then a chance to feed the animals before a splashy bath.

During the dry season, you can glide through the east coast's mangrove forests on sunset dinner **gondola cruises** for around 1,400B per person (minimum of four persons), which can be booked through **Salak Khok Village Tour** (📞 08774-89497), or paddle yourself in a **kayak** to nearby offshore islands; many hotels have kayaks for guests' use.

More outdoor fun can be had at the **Treetop Adventure Park** (www.treetop adventurepark.com; 📞 **08431-07600**), in Bai Lan, where you can teeter along walkways and whiz along ziplines suspended over the jungle. A half-day swinging through the canopy, including hotel pickup, costs 1,100B.

SOUTHERN PENINSULA: THE EAST COAST & ISLANDS

8

Thailand's slim peninsula extends 1,250km (777 miles) south from Bangkok to the Malaysian border at Sungai Kolok. The towns of Cha-Am and the royal retreat of Hua Hin are just a short hop south of Bangkok, and the ancient temples of **Phetchaburi**—the last outpost of the Khmer Empire—are a good day trip from there. Passing through such coastal towns as Prachuap Kiri Khan and Chumphon and heading farther south, you come to Surat Thani, the jumping-off point for islands in the east: **Ko Samui, Ko Pha Ngan,** and **Ko Tao.** If the beach resorts of Phuket dominate the tourist landscape on the west coast, Ko Samui, a heavily developed resort island in the Gulf of Siam, dominates the east. Nearby Ko Pha Ngan, famed for its wild full-moon parties, continues to gain prominence as a rustic resort destination, as does Ko Tao for its access to some of Thailand's best dive sites.

With its fine islands and beaches, the Gulf of Siam is truly Thai paradise. Whether you come armed with little money and lots of time, or lots of money and little time, there's an adventure and a little bit of heaven for everyone among its palm-draped beaches, lacy coral reefs, small mainland towns and fishing villages, and Buddhist retreats.

HUA HIN/CHA-AM ★

Hua Hin: 265km (165 miles) S of Bangkok; 223km (139 miles) N of Chumphon. Cha-Am: 240km (149 miles) S of Bangkok; 248km (154 miles) N of Chumphon

Hua Hin and Cha-Am, neighboring towns on the Gulf of Thailand, form the country's oldest resort area. Developed in the 1920s as getaways for Bangkok's elite, the beautiful "Thai Riviera" was a mere 3 or 4 hours' journey from the capital by train, thanks to the southern railway's completion in 1916. The Thai royal family was the first to embrace these two small fishing villages as the perfect location for summer vacations and for health retreats. In 1924, King Vajiravudh (Rama VI) built the royal Maruekatayawan Palace amid the tall evergreens that lined these

The Southern Peninsula: East Coast

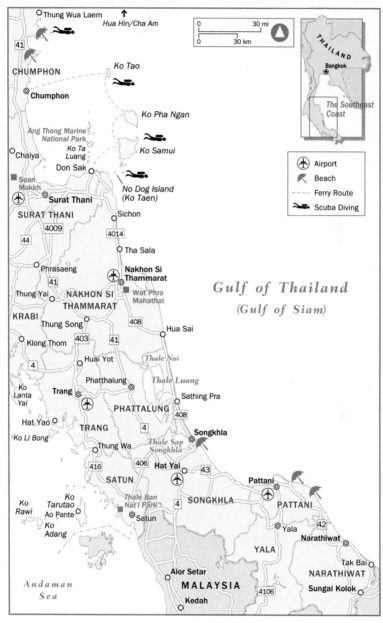

Thung Wua Laem

Hua Hin/Cha Am

41

CHUMPHON

Chumphon

Ko Tao

Ko Pha Ngan

Ang Thong Marine National Park

Ko Ta Luang

Ko Samui

Chaiya

Don Sak

No Dog Island (Ko Taen)

Suan Mokkh

Surat Thani

SURAT THANI

Sichon

4009

4014

44

Tha Sala

Phrasaeng

Nakhon Si Thammarat

NAKHON SI THAMMARAT

Thung Yai

Wat Phra Mahathat

41

KRABI

Thung Song

408

Hua Sai

403

41

Klong Thom

Huai Yot

Thale Noi

4

Thale Luang

Ko Lanta Yai

Phatthalung

Trang

Sathing Pra

Hat Yao

TRANG

PHATTALUNG

408

Ko Li Bong

Thung Wa

Thale Sap Songkhla

Songkhla

4

416

406

Hat Yai

43

SATUN

Pattani

Ko Rawi

Ko Tarutao

Ao Pante

Thale Ban Nat'l Park

SONGKHLA

4

PATTANI

Ko Adang

Satun

Yala

Narathiwat

42

YALA

Tak Bai

Andaman Sea

Alor Setar

MALAYSIA

NARATHIWAT

Sungai Kolok

Kedah

4106

Gulf of Thailand
(Gulf of Siam)

THAILAND

Bangkok

The Southeast Coast

0   30 mi
0   30 km

Airport
Beach
Ferry Route
Scuba Diving

stretches of golden sand. Around the same time, the Royal Hua Hin golf course opened, the first of its kind in Thailand. As Bangkok's upper classes began building summer bungalows along the shore, the State Railway opened the Hua Hin Railway Hotel for tourists, which stands today as the Centara Grand Resort and Villas. King Bhumibol (Rama IX) spends much of his time at his regal residence called *Klai Klangwon* (meaning "Far from Worries") just north of town (note the constant presence of Royal Thai Naval frigates offshore). Yet despite the town's venerable connections, the beaches here cannot compare with those on the offshore islands, and the sea is often murky.

When Pattaya, on Thailand's eastern coast, hit the scene in the 1960s, it lured vacationers away from Hua Hin and Cha-Am with promises of a spicier nightlife. Since then, Pattaya's tourism has grown to a riotous, red-light din, and Hua Hin and Cha-Am are a discerning alternative, though several hostess bars have now opened in downtown Hua Hin. These days, the younger generation of Thais are driving 45 minutes farther south to Pranburi, where a clutch of Thai-run resorts on isolated beaches are drawing well-heeled families away from Hua Hin.

Plan your trip for the months between November and May for the most sunshine and least rain, but note that from about mid-December to mid-January, Hua Hin and Cha-Am reach peak levels, and bookings should be made well in advance. Low season means more rain, but rarely all day long.

Essentials

GETTING THERE

BY PLANE   Solar Air (℡ 02535-2448; www.solarair.co.th) operates daily flights from Bangkok (time 45 min.) costing 2,500B.

BY TRAIN   Both Hua Hin and Cha-Am are reached via the train station in Hua Hin, which has been well-preserved and is an attraction in itself. Eleven trains make the daily trek from Bangkok's **Hua Lampong Railway Station** (℡ 02220-4334 or 1690). A second-class seat in an air-conditioned compartment from Bangkok to Hua Hin generally costs 382B, and the trip takes nearly 4 hours.

The **Hua Hin Railway Station** (℡ 03251-1073) is at the tip of Damnoenkasem Road, which slices through the center of town straight to the beach. Pickup trucks acting as taxis (*songtaews*) and tuk-tuks wait outside to take you to your hotel; fares start at 50B.

BY BUS/MINIBUS   Going by road is the best choice from Bangkok to Hua Hin and the best means of transport are the minibuses that connect with central Cha-Am and Hua Hin. You can arrange **minivan connections** from your hotel in the city, or go to the busy traffic circle at the base of the **Victory Monument** (a stop on the BTS) and look for the minivans that depart when full throughout the day, costing just 180B to Hua Hin.

Buses depart from **Bangkok's Southern Bus Terminal** (℡ 02422-4444) every 40 minutes from 5am to 10pm (160B). There are also hourly buses to Cha-Am between 5am and 8pm (140B). They pull up in Hua Hin on the Phetkasem Road to the south of the town center. From here it is easy to find a *songtaew* or tuk-tuk to take you to your destination. Buses to **Cha-Am** pull up in the middle of town, at the junction of Phetkasem and Narathip Roads.

BY CAR   From Bangkok, take Route 35, the Thonburi-Paktho Highway, southwest, then follow Route 4 via Petchburi; allow 2 to 4 hours, depending on traffic.

SPECIAL EVENTS

A free **jazz festival** is held annually some weekends between June and August. It lasts for 2 or 3 days and features local and international bands. The event attracts thousands of visitors to a unique beach setting, with a stage usually set up in front of the Sofitel hotel. Spectators sit on the sand or can hire chairs. Extra jazz events take place around town at the same time. For this year's dates, see www.huahinafterdark.com/events, or contact the Hua Hin Tourist Information Center at *©* **03261-1491.**

The **King's Cup Elephant Polo** 🖼 takes place in Hua Hin for a week or so in September, and makes for a memorable spectacle. Teams come from around the world to vie for the prestigious trophy, and the event is accompanied by activities such as charity dinners. Find out more at www.anantaraelephantpolo.com.

ORIENTATION

Despite all the tourist traffic, Hua Hin is easy to navigate. The main artery, Phetkasem Road, runs parallel to the waterfront about four blocks inland. The wide Damnoenkasem Road cuts through Phetkasem and runs straight to the beach. On the north side of Damnoenkasem, toward the waterfront, you'll find a cluster of guesthouses, restaurants, shopping, and nightspots lining the narrow lanes. Across Phetkasem to the west are the railway station and Night Market.

Smaller Cha-Am is a 25-minute drive north of Hua Hin along Phetkasem Road. Ruamchit Road, also known as Beach Road, hugs the shore and is lined with shops, restaurants, and hotels. Cha-Am's resorts line the 8-km (5-mile) stretch of beach that runs south from the village toward Hua Hin.

GETTING AROUND

BY SONGTAEW   Pickup trucks (*songtaew*) follow regular routes in Hua Hin, passing the railway station and bus terminals at regular intervals. Flag one down that's going in your direction. Fares are 20B within town, while stops at outlying resorts cost up to 50B. If the truck is empty, the driver will likely demand an extortionate fee to hire the whole vehicle; just wait till a shared truck comes along.

BY TUK-TUK   Tuk-tuk rides are negotiable; always agree on a price before you start, but expect to pay at least 50B for a ride within town.

BY MOTORCYCLE TAXI   Within each town, motorcycle taxi fares begin at 30B. These taxis, whose drivers are identifiable by colorful numbered vests, are a good way to get to your resort or hotel.

BY SAMLOR   Trishaws, or *samlors* (bicycle taxis), can be hired for short distances in town, from 40B. You can also negotiate an hourly rate.

BY CAR OR MOTORCYCLE   **Avis** has an office at 15/112 Phetkasem Soi 29, in Hua Hin (*©* **03254-7523**). **Budget** has an office at the Grand Hotel (*©* **03251-4220**). Self-drive rates start at around 1,200B. Call ahead to reserve at least a day in advance. A cheaper alternative is to rent from one of the small-time agents near the beach on Damnoenkasem Road. Motorbikes (100cc) are available for about 200B per day.

ON FOOT   Hua Hin is a labyrinth of busy streets and narrow alleys, with little guesthouses, colorful local bars, and a wide assortment of casual eating venues. Almost everything in town is accessible on foot.

VISITOR INFORMATION

The **Hua Hin Tourist Information Center** (☏ 03261-1491) is at the junction of Phetkasem and Damnoenkasem Roads. Opening hours are from 8:30am to 4:30pm daily. The website www.tourismhuahin.com is also quite useful. There's a branch of **TAT** in Cha-Am at 500/51 Phetkasem Rd. (☏ **03247-1005**).

FAST FACTS

IN HUA HIN   All major banks are along Phetkasem Road, to the north of Damnoen-kasem, and there are many money-changers throughout the town. The main **post office** (☏ 03251-1567) is on Damnoenkasem Road, near the Phetkasem intersection. Both Hua Hin and Cha-Am have Internet cafes along the more-traveled shopping streets. The **Hua Hin Hospital** (☏ 03252-0401) is in the north of town, along Phetkasem Road. Call the **Tourist Police** for either town at ☏ **03251-5995**.

IN CHA-AM   Banks are dotted along Phetkasem Road, and the post office is on Beach Road. The **Cha-Am Hospital** (☏ 03247-1007) is at 8/1 Khlong Thian Road to the north of the town center. Internet access is available in a few places along Beach Road.

Exploring the Area

The stunning Khmer-style temples of **Phetchaburi** (see "Side Trips from Hua Hin & Cha-Am," at the end of this section) are the most significant cultural sites near Hua Hin and Cha-Am, but really what attracts so many to this area is what first attracted the Thai royal family: Proximity to the capital; sandy beaches; watersports; and activities such as golf, scuba diving, and horseback riding. Hua Hin also supports fine resorts, which come with great facilities, extensive dining, and top-notch spas.

One of the oldest resorts here is the **Centara Grand Resort and Villas,** originally built as the Railway Hotel for Thai royalty and their guests in the 1920s. Visitors are welcome to wander around its pretty colonial buildings and gardens (don't miss the giant topiary elephant). High Tea at the Centara (daily 3–6pm) costs 690B per person; it not only offers a chance to sip tea and nibble on sandwiches, cakes, and scones in a lovely original wing of the hotel, but transports guests back in time to the era when Hua Hin was a getaway purely for the Thai upper crust.

Don't miss the town's **Night Market** (on Decha Nuchit Rd., at the northern end of the town center), which is busy from dusk to late with small food stalls and vendors. There are also lots of shops in and around the central beachfront, and Hua Hin is a good place to pick up some souvenirs such as a Buddha ornament.

The **Maruekhathaiyawan Palace ★★**, often romantically referred to as "the palace of peace and hope" (no phone; Thurs–Tues 8am–4pm; 50B), consists of three connected teakwood mansions and is located on the coast halfway between Hua Hin and Cha-Am; it is one of Thailand's most attractive colonial buildings and a must-see for anyone interested in architecture. Built and designed in 1924 by King Rama VI, it served for many years as the royal summer residence and is now open to the public. A stroll through the preserved rooms with their polished teak floors, period furnishings, and shuttered windows is enough to be transported back to another era. Wander along the raised, covered walkway to the pavilions over the beach (formerly the royal changing rooms) and feel the fresh sea breeze on your face.

The big standing Buddha and viewpoint from spiky **Khao Takiap (Chopstick Hill)**—a small cape 7km (4⅓ miles) south of Hua Hin (hop on a green *songtaew* for

20B)—is a scenic area worth a visit; if you climb the hill (272m/892 ft.) to enjoy the panoramic view, hang on to your bags and camera, as the local macaques will snatch anything unattended.

Pony riding is popular along the busy beaches at Hua Hin and Cha-Am. Frisky young fillies can be rented by the hour from 600B, but you'll need to bargain hard. At 100B for 10-minute kids' rides, you can ride with a Thai escort leading the pony (which is the safest way), or on your own if you're confident. If you're interested, take a walk down to the beach, and you'll be besieged by young men eager to rent out their ponies.

In recent years, Hua Hin has become popular for kiteboarding (see **Activities,** below).

See "Side Trips from Hua Hin & Cha-Am," at the end of this section, for trips to nature sites.

Where to Stay in Hua Hin

Developers have been busy in Hua Hin in recent years, and beside the recommendations below, you can also find top hotels run by **Hyatt, Intercontinental,** and **Six Senses.**

VERY EXPENSIVE

Anantara Resort & Spa ★★   A series of elegantly designed Thai-style pavilions are set in 5.6 hectares (14 acres) of possibly the most exotic gardens you'll see in Thailand, just north of Hua Hin. The open-air *sala*-style lobby is tastefully decorated with ornately carved teak wooden lanterns, warm wood floors, and oversized furniture with Thai cushions. The Lagoon is an area of teak pavilions surrounded by lily ponds; and from the hotel's most luxurious rooms, you can hear chirping frogs and watch buzzing dragonflies from wide balconies. Other rooms cluster around a manicured courtyard. Superior rooms have a garden view, and deluxe rooms overlook the sand and sea. Lagoon rooms have large patios perfect for private barbecues. Suites have enormous aggregate bathtubs that open to guest rooms by a sliding door. Fine dining includes an Italian restaurant, and the resort's spa is large and luxurious.

43/1 Phetkasem Beach Rd., Hua Hin 77110. http://huahin.anantara.com. ℭ **03252-0250.** Fax 03252-0259. 187 units. 10,600B–12,000B double; 16,000B suite. AE, DC, MC, V. **Amenities:** 4 restaurants; lounge; outdoor pool w/children's pool; outdoor lit tennis courts; health club; spa; watersports equipment and instruction; bike and motorcycle rental; children's playground; room service; babysitting. *In room:* A/C, TV, minibar, fridge, hair dryer, Wi-Fi (free in most expensive rooms, 475B per day in others).

Centara Grand Resort ★★★   The Centara (formerly the Sofitel) offers the classiest accommodation in the area. Renovations over the years have expanded the hotel into a large and luxurious hotel without sacrificing a bit of its former '20s charm. The whitewashed buildings, shaded verandas and walkways, fine wooden details, red-tile roofs, and immaculate gardens with topiaries create a cool, calm, colonial effect. There is a small museum of photography and memorabilia, and the original 14 bedrooms are preserved for posterity. These rooms have a unique appeal, but the newer rooms are larger, brighter, and more comfortable. Though they boast furnishings that reflect the hotel's old beach resort feel, they are still modern and cozy.

1 Damnoenkasem Rd., Hua Hin 77110 (in the center of town, by the beach). www.centarahotels resorts.com. ℭ **800/221-4542** in the U.S., or 03251-2021. Fax 03251-1014. 249 units (including 42 villas). 16,500B–88,000B suite; from 25,000B villa. DC, MC, V. **Amenities:** 5 restaurants; lounge; bar;

outdoor pool; golf course nearby; outdoor lit tennis courts; health club; spa; watersports equipment; mountain bikes (400B per day); children's club; room service; babysitting; executive floor. *In room:* A/C, TV, minibar, fridge, hair dryer, Wi-Fi (free for club guests, 250B per day for others).

Chiva-Som International Health Resort ★★★
One of the finest high-end health resorts in the region, this ultra peaceful campus is a sublime collection of handsome pavilions and bungalows dressed in fine teak and sea-colored tiles nestled in 2.8 hectares (7 acres) of exotic tropical gardens beside the beach. Fine accommodation aside, what brings so many to Chiva-Som are the extensive fitness, spa, and holistic health facilities. There are more than 120 treatments and fitness programs, including tai chi, Pilates, yoga, and personal training.

Upon check-in, you'll have a brief medical check and meet with an advisor who can tailor a program to fit your needs, goals, budget, or package you have booked (there is a wide range). From there, guests might focus on early-morning yoga, stretching, and tough workouts, or go for gentle massages, aromatherapy, or even isolation chambers and past-life regression workshops. No children under 16 or cellphones are allowed, and a 3-day minimum booking is required. Day-spa visitors are welcome. It all comes with a high price tag, but it is worth it.

73/4 Phetkasem Rd., Hua Hin 77110 (5-min. drive south of Hua Hin). www.chivasom.com. © **03253-6536.** Fax 03251-1154. 57 units. Contact the resort directly about spa and health packages. 49,995B oceanview double; 62,865B pavilion; from 99,000B suite (all prices for minimum 3-night stay). Rate includes 3 spa cuisine meals per day, health and beauty consultations, daily massage, and participation in fitness and leisure activities. AE, DC, MC, V. **Amenities:** Restaurant; indoor and outdoor pools; golf course nearby; health club w/personal trainer and exercise classes; his-and-hers spas w/steam and hydrotherapy treatments; watersports equipment; bike rental; room service. *In room:* A/C, TV, minibar, fridge, Wi-Fi (free).

EXPENSIVE

Hilton Hua Hin Resort & Spa ★★ ☺
Right in the heart of downtown Hua Hin, this 17-story tower block overlooks the main beach. The staff is courteous and professional and the hotel is geared for families, with many activities for kids, such as making animals from balloons, sand painting, and fun diving. The property displays a top international standard and its environs are ideal for strolling the main beach area, in-town shopping, and nightlife. One of the restaurants here, the Hua Hin Brewing Company, sells imported beers like Guinness and features a live guitarist in the evening.

33 Naresdamri Rd., Hua Hin 77110. www.huahin.hilton.com. © **03253-8999.** Fax 03253-8990. 296 units. 7,100B–10,700B double; from 10,700B suite. AE, DC, MC, V. **Amenities:** 4 restaurants; 2 bars; outdoor pool; 2 tennis courts; health club; spa; children's center; room service; babysitting. *In room:* A/C, TV/movie library, minibar, fridge, hair dryer, Wi-Fi (400B per day).

Hua Hin Marriott Resort & Spa ★★★ ☺
From the giant swinging couches in the main lobby to the large central pavilions, this hotel is decked-out in a grand, if exaggerated, Thai style. The Marriott often attracts large groups but is a good choice for families too, though it's situated quite a way from the town center. Ponds, pools, boats, golf, tennis, and other sports venues dot the jungle-like grounds leading to their open beach area, and there is even a zoo. Deluxe rooms are the top choice—large, amenity-filled, and facing out to sea. Terrace rooms at beachside are worth the bump up.

107/1 Phetkasem Beach Rd., Hua Hin 77110. www.marriot.com. © **800/228-9290** in the U.S., or 03251-1881. Fax 03251-2422. 216 units. 5,200B–7,300B double; 7,800B beach terrace; from 18,000B suite. AE, DC, MC, V. **Amenities:** 3 restaurants; 2 bars; golf course nearby; outdoor pool; outdoor lit tennis courts; health club; spa; watersports equipment bikes; children's center; room service; babysitting. *In room:* A/C, TV, minibar, hair dryer, Internet (free for members, 624B a day for others).

MODERATE

There are lots of mid- and low-range choices in and around central Hua Hin. **City Beach Resort** (16 Damnoenkasem Rd.; www.citybeachhuahin.com; ✆ 03251-2870) is fairly central, with a pool and nightclub (rooms from 2,500B), and nearby **Sirin Hotel** (6/3 Damnoenkasem Rd.; www.sirinhuahin.com; ✆ 03251-1150) has smallish but smart rooms (from 1,900B), and also has an outdoor pool.

INEXPENSIVE

Chomsin Hua Hin   The rooms in this place are a bit cramped but very comfortably equipped, and some have small balconies looking out over a street of well-preserved buildings. It is well located between the beach and the Night Market. The friendly staff can help arrange outings to nearby attractions.

130/4 Chomsin Rd., Hua Hin 77110. www.chomsinhuahin.com. ✆ **03251-5348.** Fax 03251-5336; 18 units. 1,200B–1,500B double. MC, V. **Amenities:** Internet (in lobby, free). *In room:* A/C, TV, fridge.

Jed Pee Nong Hotel   This hotel is a clean and comfy budget choice less than 100m (328 ft.) from the Centara Grand. There is a small pool, and the simple balconied rooms are carpeted and have air-conditioning. The higher-priced rooms have better decor and hug the pool, cabana style. Its friendly staff and decent rates make it popular with Thai weekenders as well as tourists, so book well ahead.

17 Damnoenkasem Rd., Hua Hin 77110 (on the main street, near the town beach). www.jedpee nonghotel-huahin.com. ✆ **03251-2381.** Fax 03253-2063. 25 units. 1,700B–2,000B double. No credit cards. **Amenities:** Restaurant; outdoor pool. *In room:* A/C, minibar, Wi-Fi (free).

Where to Stay in Cha-Am

Along the quiet stretch between Hua Hin and Cha-Am, there are a number of fine resorts (and a growing number of condos). Cha-Am village itself is a bit raucous (the Ocean City, New Jersey, to Hua Hin's The Hamptons) and most stay outside of town; for in-town lodging, try the Cha-Am Methavalai, reviewed below.

EXPENSIVE

Dusit Thani ★   The Dusit has all the amenities of a fine resort. The elegant marble lobby features bronze horses and hunting tableaux; hall doors have polo mallet handles and other equine-themed decor. Guest rooms carry the same theme and are spacious, with big marble bathrooms. Room rates vary with the view, although every room's balcony faces the pool, and those on the ground floor have private verandas. Suites are enormous, with elegant living rooms, and a full pantry and dressing area. For all its air of formality, the resort is ideal for those who prefer swimsuits and T-shirts to riding jodhpurs, and a relaxed holiday air pervades. It is a bit far from both Hua Hin and Cha-Am, but the resort is completely self-contained.

1349 Phetkasem Rd., Cha-Am 76120. www.dusit.com. ✆ **03252-0009.** Fax 03252-0296. 296 units. 5,400B–13,900B double; from 21,900B suite. AE, DC, MC, V. **Amenities:** 4 restaurants; lounge; outdoor pool; golf course nearby; minigolf; outdoor lit tennis courts; squash courts; health club; watersports equipment; bikes and motorbikes; room service; babysitting; executive floor. *In room:* A/C, satellite TV, minibar, fridge, hair dryer, Wi-Fi (free).

MODERATE

The Cha-Am Methavalai Hotel ★★   The Methavalai is the best of the ragtag collection in busy Cha-Am town, providing clean accommodation on the main Beach Road, closeby restaurants, shopping, and nightlife. Guest rooms are painted from a pastel palette and are peaceful, all with balconies and sun decks and tidy, but not luxurious, bathrooms. Rooms look out over the good-sized central pool (front-facing rooms can be a bit noisy, though). If you want to stay in downtown Cha-Am, this is the best choice of the lot.

220 Ruamchit Rd., Cha-Am 76120. www.methavalai.com. ✆ **03243-3250.** Fax 03247-1590. 215 units. From 2,690B double; from 5,670B pavilion and suite. AE, DC, MC, V. **Amenities:** 2 restaurants; lounge; outdoor pool; golf course nearby; room service; babysitting. *In room:* A/C, TV, minibar, fridge, Wi-Fi (2 hr. 150B).

Holiday Inn Regent Beach Cha-Am ★★   This sprawling beachside property consists of 560 rooms, suites, and villas and offers a wide range of leisure and recreational facilities, including large pools, squash, and a small fitness area. The main resort is set around a massive courtyard, while the Regency Wing and Anavana Villas provide more secluded options. Standard rooms are comfortable and affordable, as you would expect from an average chain hotel. The resort is on the road between Hua Hin and Cha-Am and a long ride to either; there's a shuttle bus to Hua Hin and private taxis outside. This place is always busy on the weekends with Bangkok visitors.

849/21 Phetkasem Rd., Cha-Am 76120. www.chaam.holidayinn.com. ✆ **03245-1240.** Fax 03247-1491. 560 units. 2,800B–3,700B double; from 6,300B suites and villas. AE, MC, V. **Amenities:** 2 restaurants; lounge; 2 outdoor pools; kids' pool; outdoor lit tennis courts; squash courts; health club; spa; room service; babysitting. *In room:* A/C, TV, minibar, fridge, Internet (428B per day).

Where to Eat in Hua Hin

If you wake up at about 7am and walk to the piers in either Hua Hin or Cha-Am, you can watch the fishing boats return with their loads. Workers sort fish, crabs, and squid, packing them on ice for distribution around the country. In both Hua Hin and Cha-Am, look for the docks at the very north end of the beach; to sample the catch, head for the string of open-air restaurants on stilts, along Naresdamri Road in Hua Hin, where prices are very competitive.

The Night Market on Dechanuchit Road, west of Phetkasem Road, in the north end of town, is a great place for authentic local eats for very little money. The resorts have more restaurants than there is room to list, and no matter where you stay, you'll have great dining options in-house. In town, there are lots of small storefront eateries and tourist cafes as well.

Itsara ★ THAI   In a two-story seaside home built in the 1920s, this restaurant has real laid-back charm, from the noisy, open kitchen to the terrace seating with views of the beach—it's quite atmospheric and a good place to get together with friends and enjoy the good life. Specialties include a sizzling hot plate of glass noodles with shrimp, squid, pork, and vegetables. A variety of fresh seafood and meats are prepared steamed or deep-fried, and can be served with salt, chili, or red curry paste.

7 Napkehard St. (seaside, a 150B tuk-tuk ride north from the town center). ✆ **03253-0574.** Reservations recommended for Sat dinner. Main courses 100B–470B. MC, V. Daily 10:30am–10pm.

Meekaruna Seafood SEAFOOD   This small family-run restaurant, on a wooden deck overlooking the main fishing pier in Hua Hin, serves fresh fish prepared however you like it—grilled, steamed, and fried. Though it's surrounded by other seafood restaurants, there's no carnival barker out front to drag you in, and such a lack of hype alone is refreshing. They have great *tom yum goong*—also try the fried crab cakes, and baby clams fried in chili sauce.

26/1 Naresdamri Rd. (near the fishing pier). ✆ **03251-1932.** Main courses 80B–1,300B. AE, DC, MC, V. Daily 10am–10pm.

Sawasdee ★ THAI/SEAFOOD   Located just across from the Hilton in the middle of Hua Hin, this place dishes up Thai flavors with a particular emphasis on seafood. Try the shrimp cakes and the stir-fried crab, made with freshly caught ingredients. If you're not in the mood for seafood, they have a few Italian dishes as well, such as pizza. It's a family-run place with attentive and helpful staff—topped off with very reasonable prices.

122/1–2 Naresdamri Rd. ✆ **03251-1935.** Main courses 100B–440B. MC, V. Daily 11am–10pm.

Activities

GOLF

Probably the most popular activity in Hua Hin and Cha-Am is **golf,** and the town boasts some fine courses. Reservations are suggested and necessary most weekends. Many of the hotels run FOC (free of charge) shuttles, and most clubs can arrange pickup and drop-off to any hotel.

○ **Palm Hills Golf Resort and Country Club,** 1444 Phetkasem Rd., Cha-Am (✆ **03252-0800**), just north of Hua Hin, is a picturesque course set among rolling hills and jagged escarpments (greens fees: 2,500B; daily 6am–7pm).

○ **Royal Hua Hin Golf Course,** Damnoenkasem Road, near the Hua Hin Railway Station (✆ **03251-2475**), is Thailand's first championship golf course, opened in 1924. Don't miss the many topiary figures along its fairways (greens fees: 2,000B; daily 6am–6:30pm).

○ **Springfield Royal Country Club,** 208 Moo 2, Tambon Sam Paya, Cha-Am (✆ **03270-9222;** www.springfieldresort.com/golf), designed by Jack Nicklaus in 1993, is in a beautiful valley setting—the best by far (greens fees: 3,500B; daily 6am–dusk).

WATERSPORTS

While most of the larger resorts will plan watersports activities for you upon request, you can make arrangements with small operators on the beach (for significant savings). Most resorts forbid noisy **jet skis,** but the beaches are lined with young entrepreneurs renting them out for around 2,000B per hour. **Kiteboarding** is also becoming popular on the beach to the south of town; the season runs from November to April and a 3-day beginner's course costs 11,000B. Contact **Kiteboarding Asia** (Soi 71/1 Baan Ratchadamnoen Hotel, opposite Market Village; ✆ **08159-14593;** www.kiteboardingasia.com) for more details.

   Western Tours (✆ **03253-3303;** www.westerntourshuahin.com) can arrange **snorkeling trips** to nearby islands for about 2,700B per person. Their office is at 11 Damnoenkasem Rd., in the city center.

SPAS

Hua Hin is famous for its fine spas, and each of the top resorts features excellent services (see the Marriott, Anantara, and Hilton, in "Where to Stay in Hua Hin," above). There are lots of small massage storefronts in Hua Hin, but this is a great place to go upscale and get the royal treatment.

The best choice for a day of pampering is at **Chiva-Som ★★★** (73/4 Phetkasem Rd., Hua Hin; 5-min. drive south of town; ✆ **03253-6536**), where the expense feels totally justified. There's nothing like it.

Far south of town, luxurious **Six Senses Hua Hin ★★** (9/22 Moo 5, Paknampran Beach, Pranburi 77220; 30km/19 miles south of Hua Hin; ✆ **03261-8200**), in and of itself, is a destination spa worth visiting, but also a fine stop for high-end day treatments. It's comparable in quality with Chiva-Som.

Shopping

Hua Hin is a popular tourist town and close to the country's largest city, and, as a result, it has all the good shopping services you would find in Bangkok—from fine tailors and jewelers to souvenir shops. The **Day Market** along Damnoenkasem Road, near the beach, features local crafts made from seashells, batik clothing, and other handicrafts. The two-block-long **Night Market** on Dechanuchit Road, west of Phetkasem Road, is a great stop for tasty treats and fun trinkets. Steer away from buying fake brands (p. 34).

Hua Hin Entertainment & Nightlife

A 15-minute stroll through the labyrinth of *sois* between Damnoenkasem and Dechanuchit roads near the beach reveals all sorts of small places to stop for a refreshing drink and some fun. **O'Neill's Irish Pub,** on Phunsuk Road, shows sports on TV and serves draught beer, while **Takaeng Bar,** on Soi Bintaban, offers live country and pop music in a rustic setting. Most of Soi Bintaban is lined with Pattaya-style girlie bars, while Naresdamri Road, which runs north–south parallel to the beach, is home to several stylish restaurants and bars such as **Mai Tai** (✆ **03253-3344**), and **Monsoon** (✆ **03253-1062**).

Side Trips from Hua Hin & Cha-Am

PHETCHABURI ★★

Phetchaburi, one of Thailand's oldest towns, possibly dates from the same period as Ayutthaya and Kanchanaburi, though it is believed to have been first settled during the Dvaravati period. After the rise of the Thai nation, it served as an important royal military city and was home to several princes who were groomed for ascendance to the throne. Phetchaburi's palace and historically significant temples make it an excellent day trip. It is just 1 hour north of Hua Hin.

The main attraction is **Phra Nakhon Khiri** (also called Khao Wang), a summer palace in the hills overlooking the city. Built in 1858 by King Mongkut (Rama IV), it was intended not only as a summer retreat for the royal family, but for foreign dignitaries as well. Combining Thai, European, and Chinese architectural styles, the palace buildings include guesthouses and a royal Khmer-style *chedi*, or temple. The Phra Thinang Phetphum Phairot Hall is open for viewing and contains period art and antiques from the household. Though it was once accessible only via a 4-km (2½-mile) hike uphill, you'll be happy to hear there's a funicular railway (it's called a "cable car," but that's not an accurate description) to bring you to the top for 70B, which includes admission to the palace. It's open daily 8:30am to 4pm.

Another fascinating sight at Phetchaburi, the **Khao Luang Cave,** houses more than 170 Buddha images underground. Outside the cave, hundreds of noisy monkeys descend upon the parking lot and food stalls looking for handouts. Sometimes you'll find a guide outside who'll escort you through the caves for a small fee.

Wat Yai Suwannaram is a stunning royal temple built during the Ayutthaya period. The teak ordination hall was moved from Ayutthaya after the second Burmese invasion of the city (don't miss the axe-chop battle scar on the building's carved doors). Inside there are large religious murals featuring Brahmans, hermits, giants, and deities.

Another *wat* (temple) with impressive paintings is **Wat Ko Keo Suttharam,** also built in the 17th century. These representational murals, painted in the 1730s, even depict some Westerners: There are several panels portraying the arrival in the Ayutthaya court of European courtesans and diplomats (including a Jesuit dressed in Buddhist garb).

Another fabulous temple is **Wat Kamphaeng Laeng,** originally constructed during the reign of Khmer ruler King Jayavarman VII (r. 1157–1207) as a Hindu shrine. Made of laterite, it was once covered in decorative stucco, some of which still remains. Each of the five *prangs* (towers) was devoted to a deity—the center *prang* to Shiva is done in a classical Khmer style. During the Ayutthaya period, it was converted to a Buddhist temple.

Lastly, the **Phra Ratchawang Ban Peun,** or Ban Peun Palace (✆ 03242-8506; daily 8am–4pm; admission 20B adults, 10B children), was a royal residence built by Rama V. The German-designed grand summer home comes alive with colorful tile work, neoclassical marble columns, and floor motifs. Today it sits on military grounds and is a popular venue for ceremonies and large occasions.

Western Tours, 11 Damnoenkasem Rd. (✆ 03253-3303; www.westerntours huahin.com), has day excursions for 1,500B per person that includes most of these sights, or they can be seen on a day trip by rented car.

KHAO SAM ROI YOT NATIONAL PARK★

Just a 40-minute drive south of Hua Hin, Khao Sam Roi Yot, or the "Mountain of Three Hundred Peaks," is comparatively small in relation to the nation's other parks, but offers great short (and steep) hikes to panoramic views of the sea. There is abundant wildlife here (seen only if you're lucky). Of the park's several caves, **Phraya Nakhon Cave** is the most interesting, housing a *sala* pavilion that was built in 1890 for King Chulalongkorn. For more information, call the national parks office at ✆ 02562-0760, or check out their website at www.dnp.go.th. A guided visit can be organized with **Western Tours** (✆ 03253-3303; 1,700B per person). The tour stops at a pineapple plantation and fishing village before the short but steep walk up to Phraya Nakhon Cave.

A half-day trip to the Pala-U waterfall close to the Burmese border (63km/39 miles west of Hua Hin) is another nature trekking option. Nature trails take you through hills and valleys until you end up at the falls. The excursion costs 1,700B per person with Western Tours.

PRACHUAP KHIRI KHAN

If you've had enough of Thailand's many overdeveloped beach areas, the small town and coastline near Prachuap Khiri Khan (just a 1-hr. drive south of Hua Hin) might just be the answer. Some of the kindest people in Thailand live here, the beaches are lovely and little-used, and the town begs a wander. There is little in the way of fine dining and accommodation, but it is a good stop on the way south to Chumphon.

CHUMPHON

463km (288 miles) S of Bangkok; 193km (120 miles) N of Surat Thani

Chumphon was once known for simply being a stop on the way south, but it's now become a popular jumping off point for trips to offshore islands. Boats leave from here to **Ko Tao** to the southeast and **Ang Thong Marine National Park** due south, both of which are popular diving areas, and ferries continue to **Ko Pha Ngan** and **Ko Samui,** though for these islands the ferry trip is shorter from Donsak Pier near Surat Thani. Surrounded by fruit orchards inland, and a couple of great beaches, such as **Sairi Beach,** 22km (14 miles) east of town, and **Thung Wua Laem Beach,** 12km (7½ miles) northeast, it's a good place to slow down and take time out.

Essentials

GETTING THERE

BY PLANE Solar Air (✆ 08190-29466; www.solarair.co.th) operates a daily flight from Bangkok (time 1hr. 15min.) costing 2,700B.

BY TRAIN Eleven daily trains stop in Chumphon from Bangkok. Call Bangkok **Hua Lampong Railway Station** (✆ 02220-4334 or 1690) for info; the second-class air-conditioned sleeper fare to Bangkok is 770B. **Chumphon Railway Station** (✆ 07751-1103) is on Krom Luang Chumphon Road, where there are oodles of restaurants and guesthouses.

BY BUS Standard air-conditioned buses depart from Bangkok's **Southern Bus Terminal** (✆ 02422-4444). The trip lasts 8 to 9 hours and costs around 400B. The main Chumphon bus terminal is 16km (10 miles) north of the town center (a tuk-tuk will cost around 150B–200B).

BY FERRY Songserm (✆ 07750-6205; www.songserm-expressboat.com) and **Lomprayah** (✆ 07755-8212; www.lomprayah.com) run daily express boat services connecting Chumphon with Ko Tao, Ko Pha Ngan, and Ko Samui. Lomprayah also links up with flights from Bangkok. Expensive (and totally un-eco-friendly) speedboats run in dry season.

BY CAR From Bangkok, use Highway 4 or Highway 35 (Thonburi-Pak Tho) and join Highway 4; continue past Phetchaburi, Prachuap Khiri Khan to Chumphon junction, and then turn left along Highway 4001 to reach town.

VISITOR INFORMATION

A **tourist information office** (✆ 07750-4833) is on the corner of Sala Daeng and Krom Luang Chumphon Roads. Local tour operator **New Infinity Travel** (✆ 07750-1937) is located at 68 Tha Taphao Rd., a 10-minute walk southeast of the train station, or there's **Suwannatee Tour** (✆ 07750-4901), on Rotfai Road.

GETTING AROUND

BY SONGTAEW *Songtaews,* or covered pickups, cruise the main roads and charge about 20B to 40B per trip.

BY MOTORCYCLE TAXI Look for the colored vests designating motorcycle taxi drivers, and bargain hard. Trips start from 20B.

BY TAXI Taxis stop behind the old market, opposite Chumphon Bus Terminal. Vehicles can be hired to Lang Suan, Ranong, and Surat Thani; inquire at your hotel for details.

ORIENTATION

Chumphon's center is small enough to negotiate on foot: Krom Luang Chumphon Road, near the railway station, is the place for dining and accommodation options, and Tha Taphao Road houses a variety of tour operators.

FAST FACTS

Numerous **banks** sit on Sala Daeng Road, which runs parallel to Tha Taphao Road. The main **post office,** on Poramin Mankha Road, is out of the town center; mail can generally be sent from your hotel. For **Internet service,** the guesthouses and travel agencies along Tha Taphao Road can all assist. For **police** assistance, call ✆ **07751-1300.**

Exploring Chumphon

Most guesthouses and tourist offices can arrange rafting trips and tours to local waterfalls in the nearby rainforest. The best beaches are **Sairi Beach,** for island excursions, and **Thung Wua Laen** beach, to the northeast of town, where kiteboarding is proving popular. Diving over Chumphon's offshore pinnacles reveals pristine reefs and abundant marine life—including whale sharks (in season), turtles, and tropical fish.

The **Chumphon National Museum** (Office of Archeology, Sam Kaew Hill, Na Cha Ang subdistrict; ✆ **07750-4105;** admission 100B) is open 9am to 4pm from Wednesday to Sunday and covers historic events such as the Japanese invasion in 1941 and the devastation caused by Typhoon Gay in 1989.

Where to Stay

EXPENSIVE

Away Tusita Chumphon ★★ This swish resort of petite red-tiled villas is virtually unknown to tourists and provides a laidback hideaway. Sitting on the unspoiled Arunothai beach, Thai exteriors shield homey interiors that fuse flamboyant colors. Elegant bathrooms and an abundance of light are the main advantages, and the beach villas couldn't get closer to the sea if they tried. Service is good (though it should be exceptional, given the prices). A big plus is the elegant, high-standard restaurant Murraya, serving Thai and international cuisine.

259/9 Moo 1, Arunothai Beach, Paktako, Chumphon 86220. www.tusitaresort.com. ✆ **07757-9073.** Fax 07757-9050. 22 units. From 5,700B double; 17,300B beachside villas. AE, MC, V. **Amenities:** Restaurant; bar; outdoor pool; health club; spa; watersports equipment. *In room:* A/C, TV, minibar, hair dryer, Wi-Fi (free).

MODERATE

Chumphon Cabana Resort & Diving Center ★★ ☺ 🔥 Located 30 minutes from town on the fabulously tranquil Thung Wua Laen Beach, this low-rise, family-friendly resort of staggered concrete rooms and pretty bungalows has great views, a 30-m (98-ft.) pool, and, most important, an outstanding reputation for its ecological work. Part of the pull is the long list of activities and the organic rice and vegetable gardens. Produce from the latter gets served up in the superb seafood restaurant that's on-site. A regular shuttle bus runs guests to and from Chumphon.

69 Moo 8, Thung Wua Laen Beach, Chumphon 86230. http://cabana.co.th. ✆ **07756-0245.** Fax 07756-0159. 118 units. 1,500B double; 2,050B bungalow. AE, MC, V. **Amenities:** Restaurant; lounge; outdoor pool and children's pool; watersports equipment and dive center; Wi-Fi (free). *In room:* A/C, TV, minibar.

INEXPENSIVE

Budget hotels with basic amenities such as air-conditioning and en suite bathrooms include the **Sri Chumphon Hotel** (✆ 07751-1280) on Sala Daeng Road; On Thai Taphao Road, there's **Chumphon Gardens Hotel** (✆ 07750-6888) and the perennially popular **Suda Guest House** (Soi Bangkok Bank; ✆ 07750-4366). Expect to pay between 250B and 500B at any of these properties.

Where to Eat

The best bites can be had at the diners scattered around Tha Tapao and Krom Luang Chumphon roads, or the seafood eateries at the beach hotels. Try **PaPa** (Kromluang Rd.; ✆ 07750-4504), a popular and affordable seafood restaurant, or **Fame,** on Sala Daeng Road (✆ 07757-1077), which serves up tasty Western breakfasts, filling sandwiches, and Italian dishes such as pizza and pasta.

SURAT THANI

644km (400 miles) S of Bangkok

Surat Thani, or "Surat," was an important center of the Sumatra-based Srivijaya Empire during the 9th and 10th centuries. Today, it is a rich agricultural province yielding rubber and coconuts. Before the opening of the airport on Ko Samui, Surat was constantly busy with travelers heading for the island, but now there's little reason to go there unless you plan to take a ferry to the islands. Apart from the town's night market, its seedy massage parlors and pushy touts give it little appeal. From Surat, you can access ferries to **Ko Samui, Ko Pha Ngan,** and **Ko Tao.** It's not impossibly far to the jungles of **Khao Sok National Park,** or to go west from here to **Phuket, Krabi,** and the **Andaman coast.** Popular local produce includes the Surat oyster and the rambutan (*ngor* in Thai). Near Surat is **Suan Mokkh,** an international meditation center (see "Day Trips from Surat Thani," at the end of this section).

Essentials

GETTING THERE

BY PLANE From Bangkok, there are two choices. **Thai Airways** (✆ 02356-1111; www.thaiairways.com) has daily flights (trip time: 70 min.). Thai Airways' office is at 3/27–28 Karunrat Rd. (✆ 07727-2610), just south of town. Budget airline **Air Asia** (✆ 02515-9999; www.airasia.com) also has daily flights from Bangkok. **Buses** connecting the airport and town cost around 100B per person.

BY TRAIN Eleven trains leave daily from **Bangkok's Hua Lampong station** (✆ 1690; www.railway.co.th) to Surat Thani (trip time: 13 hr.). Second-class sleepers cost 848B, and second-class seats 578B. Surat Thani station is some 12km (7½ miles) from town.

If you are connecting with the ferry, avoid the aggressive touts and look for representatives from the boat companies **Songserm** (**☎ 07728-9894**) or **Panthip** (**☎ 07727-2230**), who provide buses to meet trains. Otherwise, you can grab a shared minivan to town for around 80B, or a taxi for around 200B.

BY BUS   VIP 24-seater buses leave daily from **Bangkok's Southern Bus Terminal** (**☎ 02422-4444;** trip time: 12 hr.; 843B). *Note:* These buses are safer than the cheaper private buses from Khao San Road, on which organized theft is endemic. Air-conditioned buses leave daily from **Phuket's bus terminal** off Phang Nga Road, opposite the Royal Phuket City Hotel (**☎ 07621-1977;** trip time: 4 hr.; 170B). The Surat Thani Bus Terminal is on Kaset II Road, a block east of the main road.

BY MINIVAN   Privately operated air-conditioned minivans offer affordable and regular services from Surat Thani to/from Chumphon, Ranong, Nakhon Si Thammarat, Had Yai, Phuket, and beyond. The best way to arrange these trips is via your hotel's front desk.

BY CAR   Take Highway 4 south from Bangkok to Chumphon, and then Highway 41 directly south to Surat Thani (trip time: 12 hr.).

VISITOR INFORMATION

For information about Surat Thani, Ko Samui, and Ko Pha Ngan, contact the **TAT** office, 5 Talad Mai Rd., Surat Thani (**☎ 07728-8818**), near the Wang Tai Hotel.

ORIENTATION

Surat Thani is built up along the south shore of the Tapi River. Talad Mai (meaning new market) Road, two blocks south of the river, is the city's main street. The TAT office is on this same road but to the far west of town, en route to the bus and train stations. Ferry piers are on Ban Don, Na Meuang; out of town to the east is the Tha Thong pier. (Depending on your arrival hour, you can get transfers directly to the piers from the bus and train stations without going through town.)

FAST FACTS

Major **banks, exchange kiosks,** and a branch of the **post office** lie along Na Meuang Road, close to Witeetad Road, in the center of town. The **Taksin Hospital** (**☎ 07727-3239**) is at the north end of Talad Mai Road. The **tourist police** (**☎ 07728-8818**) are on Talad Mai Road.

Exploring Surat Thani

Surat is a typical small Thai city, with few sites worth mentioning, though the Day and Night Markets are worth a look if you have time to kill. Those with some extra time may want to head to **Khao Sok** and the beautiful **Ratchaprapha Dam,** or visit the small town of **Chaiya** and its Suan Mokkh monastery, a renowned Buddhist retreat with meditation study programs in English (see "Day Trips from Surat Thani," below). If you are in town at the end of Buddhist Lent (around mid-Oct), it's worth seeing the **Chak Phra festival,** where Buddhist images are towed up the river and boat races take place.

Where to Stay

For most, Surat Thani is just a stopping-off point for trips to the islands. If you have a layover, the best choice in town is the **100 Islands Resort & Spa** (19/6 Moo 3,

Bypass Rd.; www.roikoh.com; 📞 **07720-1150**), a fancy boutique hotel just south of the town center, with attractive doubles beginning at 770B. Nearby, with doubles at 850B and a swimming pool too, is the **Wang Tai Hotel** (1 Talad Mai Rd.; www. wangthaisurat.com; 📞 **07728-3020**). More convenient to the market and town transport is the **Tapee Hotel** (100 Chonkasem Rd.; www.tapeehotel.com; 📞 **07727-2575**), with basic but clean rooms from 440B.

Where to Eat

When in season, Surat Thani's famous oysters are on the menu at any street-side cafe; there is a small cluster of open-air eateries along Talad Mai (New Market).

Day Trips from Surat Thani

CHAIYA TOWN & SUAN MOKKHABALARAMA

The town of **Chaiya** itself is a little-visited stop on the southern railroad line, a kind of "Main Street, Thailand." There's an active central market and small stores by the dozen. Most people here are visitors to **Suan Mokkh Forest temple,** and the people of Chaiya are used to lots of wide-eyed foreigners wandering the town before and after retreats. There are a few Internet cafes along the main drag and food stalls selling low-priced Thai meals.

Suan Mokkhabalarama (the Grove of the Power of Liberation; better known as Suan Mokkh), just south of Chaiya, was founded in 1932 by the late Bhikkhu Buddhadasa, a widely published monk who is highly respected in Thailand. His back-to-basics approach attracts Buddhist monks and students of meditation from many countries, and his knowledge of English (among other languages) brought him many Western students in the 1970s and 1980s.

After his death in 1993, Bhikkhu bequeathed a large forest monastery to Dhamma study; foreign visitors are invited to join retreats from the 1st to the 10th of each month. Retreats are open to beginners, and applicants are accepted on a first-come basis from the end of each month (it's a good idea to pitch up a few days early, on the 29th or 30th, in high season). The meditation schedules are rigorous but short. Despite the rule of silence, there are opportunities to pose questions to monks, nuns, and lay volunteers.

Check in at the main monastery (follow signs to "information"), and then walk or ride the 1km (⅔ mile) to the retreat center. For 10 days of dorm lodging and meals, the registration fee is 2,000B. See www.suanmokkh.org, or call the retreat manager at 📞 **07753-1552.**

Day visitors are welcome at the forest monastery, where you can wander the many jungle paths and visit the **"Spiritual Theatre,"** which Buddhadasa described as a pictorial interpretation of Dhamma featuring an eclectic mixture of Thai, Egyptian, Chinese, Indian, Japanese, Tibetan, and European-style murals and sculptures. The monastery is just south of the town of **Chaiya,** 50km (31 miles) north of Surat Thani on Highway 41. Long-distance buses and public pickup trucks pass the entrance throughout the day and can drop you off as requested. *Songtaews* (pickups) costing 20B also connect to and from Chaiya; you have to wave them down.

KHAO SOK NATIONAL PARK

One of the largest unspoiled areas of rainforest in the south, Khao Sok is known for its stunning scenery, caves, and exotic wildlife. The park is a convenient stop between

Surat Thani and Phuket, and the main east–west road (Rte. 401) passes the park headquarters.

The park is some 646 sq. km (249 sq. miles) in area and is traced by jungle waterways; steep trails climb through underbrush, and thick vines hang from craggy limestone cliffs—imagine the jutting formations of Krabi, only inland. Rising some 1,000m (3,280 ft.), the dense jungle habitat is literally crawling with wildlife, tigers, leopards, and even elephants, but you may be hard-pressed to actually spot any. More commonly seen are gaur, Malaysian sun bears, gibbons, macaques, civets, and squirrels, along with more than 200 species of such birds as hornbills, woodpeckers, and kingfishers. The flora is equally varied. This is one of the rare places where you may come across the stinking "rotting flesh" odor that typifies the Rafflesia, the largest flower in the world. (The largest blooms are up to 1m/3¼ ft. wide.)

One of the best ways to see the varied fauna of the park is by kayak, along the nether reaches of a large reservoir, about an hour from Surat Thani on Route 415. At **Rajaprarabha Dam,** you can go boating, rafting, and fishing among the limestone cliffs that appear as islands, or stay in beautiful floating bungalows and explore this pristine jungle on elephant back.

Farther west, the **park area** (off Highway 401, at kilometer 109) has several resorts in the jungle off the 1.5km-long (1-mile) entrance road, some with treehouses. There are several Internet cafes, too. From here, well-marked trails lead you through the park. The park office can provide camping equipment, and guides will offer their services and help plan your itinerary.

Caution: It's important to know that waterfalls and caves pose real risks during rainy season. In 2006 and 2007, a number of Thai and foreign tourists lost their lives when flash floods inundated caves in this very park. Whether visiting the caverns and waterfalls, or considering a jungle hike or tubing down the River Sok, always book through a reputable travel agent so that help is at hand if you run into trouble.

Contact the **Department of National Parks, Wildlife and Plant Conservation Office** (61 Pahonyothin Rd., Chatuchak, Bangkok 10900; ✆ **02561-0777;** www.dnp.go.th), or the TAT offices in Phuket Town (p. 215) or Surat Thani (p. 173), for maps and info. Alternatively, contact **Paddle Asia,** in Phuket (18/58 Rasdanusorn Rd., Tambon Rasada, Phuket 83000; ✆/fax **07624-1519;** www.paddleasia.com), for details on their soft adventure trips.

KO SAMUI ★★★

644km (400 miles) S of Bangkok to Surat Thani; 84km (52 miles) NE from Surat Thani to Ko Samui

The island of Ko Samui lies 84km (52 miles) off the east coast in the Gulf of Thailand, near the mainland town of Surat Thani. Since the 1850s, Ko Samui was visited by Chinese merchants from Hainan Island in the South China Sea. The island is said to have more coconut species than any other place in the world. The harvesting of coconuts (and rubber) still takes place in the hills of the island's hinterland, but alas, many plantations have given way to wide-scale tourist development, which is now the island's main income.

Once a hippie haven of pristine beaches, idyllic thatched bungalows, and eateries along dusty red-dirt roads, Samui is now packed with upscale resorts, low-end bars, and posh spa retreats. Up to 20 flights a day land at Samui International Airport, and

Ko Samui

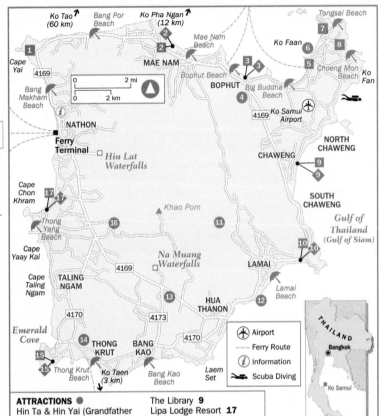

Ko Tao ↗ (60 km)
Bang Por Beach
Ko Pha Ngan ↗ (12 km)
Mae Nam Beach
Tongsai Beach
Ko Faan
Cape Yai
4169
MAE NAM
Bophut Beach
BOPHUT
Big Buddha Beach
Choeng Mon Beach
Ko Fan
Bang Makham Beach
4169
Ko Samui Airport
NATHON
Ferry Terminal
Hin Lat Waterfalls
NORTH CHAWENG
CHAWENG
Cape Chon Khram
Thong Yang Beach
Khao Pom
SOUTH CHAWENG
Gulf of Thailand (Gulf of Siam)
Cape Yaay Kai
Cape Taling Ngam
TALING NGAM
4169
Na Muang Waterfalls
LAMAI
Lamai Beach
Emerald Cove
THONG KRUT
BANG KAO
HUA THANON
4170
4173
4170
Laem Set
Thong Krut Beach
Ko Taen (3 km)
Bang Kao Beach

0   2 mi
0   2 km

✈ Airport
--- Ferry Route
ⓘ Information
≈ Scuba Diving

THAILAND
Bangkok ✶
Ko Samui

ATTRACTIONS ●
Hin Ta & Hin Yai (Grandfather
  & Grandmother Stones) **12**
Magic Statue Garden **11**
Paradise Park Farm **16**
Samui Monkey Theater **4**
Snake Farm **14**
Wat Khunaram **13**
Wat Phra Yai & Big Buddha **6**
HOTELS ■
Amari Palm Reef Koh Samui **9**
Anantara Bophut **3**
Ark Bar Beach Resort **9**
Baan Chaweng **9**
Bandara Resort **3**
The Briza Beach Resort & Spa **9**
Centara Grand Beach Resort **9**
Conrad Samui **15**
Coral Bay Resort **9**
Four Seasons Samui **1**
Hansar Samui **3**
Ibis Samui Bophut **3**
Jungle Club **9**
Lamai Wanta **10**

The Library **9**
Lipa Lodge Resort **17**
Maenamburi **2**
Mae Nam Resort **2**
Mercure Samui Fenix **10**
Napasai **2**
Orchid Suites **10**
Outrigger Samui **5**
Pavilion Samui
  Boutique Resort **10**
Peace Resort **3**
Poppies Samui Resort **9**
Rocky's Boutique Resort **10**
The Saboey **5**
Sala Samui **8**
Sandalwood Luxury Villas **9**
Santiburi Resort **2**
Six Senses Hideaway **7**
The Spa Resort **10**
The Tongsai Bay **7**
Weekender Resort & Spa **10**
White House Beach
  Resort & Spa **8**
W Retreat **3**

RESTAURANTS ◆
Art Café **3**
Bayview Restaurant **9**
Big John Seafood **17**
Dr Frog's **9**
The Farmer **2**
Happy Elephant **3**
H Bistro **3**
Jahn **15**
Jun Hom **2**
Krua Bophut **3**
Noori India **9**
The Pier **3**
Poppies **9**
Prego **9**
Radiance **10**
Red Snapper **9**
Sabeingle **10**
The Shack **3**
Zico's **9**

this voracious tourist onslaught has brought severe water shortages and environmental problems such as wastewater and refuse disposal.

If you leave the main tourist hubs (Chaweng and Bophut), Ko Samui still has a few idyllic sand beaches and simple villages, but it is certainly not the sleepy island it was 20—or even 10—years ago, and prices reflect this.

Peak season is from mid-December to mid-January, but January to April has the best weather—before its gets very hot—with the occasional tropical storm bringing relief; this is high season for most resorts. October through mid-December are the wettest months, with November bringing some heavy rain and winds that make the east side of the island rough for swimming. July and August see a brief increase in visitors, but during those months, the island's west side is often buffeted by summer monsoons from the mainland.

Essentials
GETTING THERE
BY PLANE Thai Airways (℡ 02356-1111; www.thaiairways.com) now has at least a couple of flights each day from Bangkok to Samui, though **Bangkok Airways** (℡ 02270-6699 in Bangkok, or 07742-8500 in Samui; www.bangkokair.com) is the main server, with up to 20 flights daily (depending on demand). Bangkok Airways also has two daily flights that connect with Phuket (Bangkok Airways' Phuket office is at ℡ 07622-5033) and another daily flight that connects with U-Tapao airport near Pattaya (Pattaya office ℡ 03841-2382). They also have convenient direct flights connecting Ko Samui with Hong Kong and Singapore.

Ko Samui Airport (℡ 07724-5600) boasts open-air pavilions with thatched roofs surrounded by gardens and palms. Most resorts can arrange an airport transfer when you book your room, but some add a hefty price tag for this convenience; if it's over 500B, you'd be better off taking a cab. There's also a convenient minivan service from the airport that will cost you less than haggling with taxi drivers. Book your ticket at the transportation counter upon arrival, and you'll get door-to-door service for around 100B–200B, depending on how far it is to your resort. A trip to the farthest corner of the island (Taling Ngam) will take around 45 minutes and costs 600B.

BY FERRY Songserm Travel (℡ 07728-9894 in Surat Thani) runs a loop from Surat Thani pier to Chumphon, stopping at Ko Samui, Ko Pha Ngan, and Ko Tao, and taking around 11 hours for the complete journey. Rates are 250B for Surat–Samui, 200B for Samui–Ko Pha Ngan, 300B for Ko Pha Ngan–Ko Tao, and 450B for Ko Tao–Chumphon. **Lomprayah** (℡ 07742-7765) links the islands by high-speed catamaran and runs some specialized trips, with slightly higher rates. **Seatran Discovery** (℡ 07747-1174 in Surat Thani) offers a popular choice with hourly ferries costing 150B from Surat to Samui. Car ferries run from Donsak pier, which is 60km (37 miles) northeast of Surat Thani. **Raja Ferries** (℡ 07747-1206; www.rajaferryport.com) offers a car and passenger service from Donsak to either Ko Samui (cost 140B per person, or 450B with car) or Ko Pha Ngan (cost 210B per person, or 550B with car).

You can buy ferry tickets at the port, although many book a bus or train ticket with the ferry ride included from Bangkok or other points in Thailand. Not only does this work out a bit cheaper, but it also means you don't have to be troubled by touts along the way.

If you book ahead at a resort, most will arrange transport from the Samui ferry pier at Nathon to your hotel, though check their fees as some places overcharge. Otherwise, songtaews make the trip to most beaches on the east coast for as little as 70B, if they can get a packed truckload from the boat landing (and it can be very packed). *Songtaews* make stops along the way as required, so you can jump on or off. There are also private taxis at the pier; expect to pay around 500B from Nathon pier to Chaweng.

ORIENTATION

Though Ko Samui is Thailand's third-largest island, with a total area of 247 sq. km (95 sq. miles), its entire coastline can be toured by car or motorcycle in about 2½ hours, though if you stop to look at the sights it can take a full day. The island's main road (Hwy 4169), also called the "ring road," circles hilly, densely forested terrain. Ko Samui airport is in the northeast corner near Bophut. The ferries and express boats arrive on the west coast, in or near Nathon (depending on the boat).

Samui's best beaches are on the north and east coasts. The long, sandy east coast is home to Chaweng and Lamai beaches, both frenetic in high season. It's here you'll find the heaviest concentration of hotels and bungalows. The south coast has a few little hideaways, and the west coast reveals a handful of sandy strips, but few amenities.

Nathon is where the ferries dock on the west coast, and being the island's main town and community, this is where you'll find banks, the TAT office, and the post office.

The Beaches

Clockwise from Nathon, **Mae Nam Beach,** on Samui's north shore, is 12km (7½ miles) from the ferry pier, facing nearby Ko Pha Ngan. The coarse sand is shaded by palm trees, and its peaceful calm bay has water deep enough for swimming; it is often spared the fierce winds that whip up during the stormy months. Although bigger, upmarket resorts have moved in here, there are still some affordable resorts and a number of simple, charming bungalows—it's fast becoming the budget choice on Samui. Ban Mae Nam, a small commercial hub, is just east of the Santiburi Resort and has a variety of restaurants and shops.

Bophut Beach, the next village along the north coast, is one of the island's fastest-developing areas. Bophut's long coarse-sand beach narrows considerably in the monsoon season, but the water remains fairly calm year-round. Turning off at "Big Buddha," there's a sign marking the entrance to **Fisherman's Village,** a pleasant street where you'll find restaurants, bars, and guesthouses among a beachside clutch of houses and shops. It's definitely worth a wander, especially in the evening.

Big Buddha Beach (Bangrak) is just east of Bophut and has a fairly clean, coarse-sand beach and a calm bay for swimmers (shallow in the low season, May–Oct). Many small restaurants, businesses, shops, and an increasing number of new resorts create a busier pace than is evident at other, more removed beaches. However, it is becoming a popular choice, with several new resorts that look out over Ko Faan, the island home of Ko Samui's huge seated Buddha. The Queen Ferry leaves from Big Buddha pier, taking Full-Moon partygoers to Had Rin on Ko Pha Ngan four times a day. Speedboats also leave from a nearby pier, departing hourly during **Full-Moon Party** time (see "Ko Pha Ngan," later in this chapter).

Ko Samui's northeastern tip features the beautiful headland of **Choeng Mon,** with stunning views all around from west to east; this is home to some of the island's most exclusive resorts. Bold rock formations create private coves and protected swimming areas—though from mid-October to mid-December, the monsoon can stir up the wind and waves, creating a steep drop-off from the coarse-sand beach, and a strong undertow. **Tongsai Bay** is a beautiful cove dominated by one resort called the **Tongsai Bay** (p. 186); its privacy is a plus or a minus, depending on what you are looking for.

Southeast of Tongsai, as the road descends from the headland down toward Chaweng, is the fine sandy stretch called **Choeng Mon Beach,** a gracefully shaped crescent about 1km (⅔ mile) long, and lined with shady palm trees (and an increasing number of shops). Swimming here is excellent, with few rocks near the central shore, although the water level can become very low from May to October (low season). Across the way is **Ko Fan Fa,** a deserted island with an excellent beach. You can swim or, if the tides are right, walk there—but be careful of the rocks at low tide.

Although Chaweng is the busiest destination on Ko Samui, if you don't mind the hustle and bustle (or Starbucks or McDonald's), it can be great fun. Money-changing, high-speed Internet cafes, laundry facilities, travel and rental agencies, medical facilities, shopping, restaurants, and nightlife are all on your doorstep. The two Chaweng beaches (**North Chaweng** and south **Chaweng Noi**) are the longest on the island, but, in the north, an offshore reef limits the water to wading depth only—an advantage if you have young children. The swimming is better to the south (though a bit shallow near the shore in low season).

The long sandy beach of **Lamai Bay,** in the southeast, is comparable to Chaweng's, and although many top-range resorts have moved in, there are a few budget options offering bungalows at the north end of the beach. The town area is less developed but does have a wide range of services, cafes, and restaurants, although nightlife tends to center on the small bars on the main street. Samui's waterfalls lie inland of Lamai, toward Ban Thurian at Na Muang.

Laem Set Bay is a small rocky cape on Samui's southeast coast, with dramatic scenery and a few isolated resorts, as well as **The Samui Butterfly Garden** (✆ **07742-4020**), opposite Centara Villas.

On the west coast, you'll find one of Samui's better beaches at Ao Phang Kha (Emerald Cove), south of **Ban Taling Ngam,** on Route 4170. Generally, the west coast beaches are the most isolated on the island, offering few facilities and rocky waters, making the beaches barely swimmable. Many Thai families stop for picnics at **Hin Lat Falls,** a rather uninteresting inland site 2km (1¼ miles) southeast of Nathon. Samui used to supply enough freshwater for the whole town, but now high-season droughts blight the island.

VISITOR INFORMATION

The **TAT Information Center** is at 370 Thawi Ratchaphakti Rd. just north of the main ferry terminal in Nathon (✆ **07742-0504**). This office has TAT accommodation lists and information pamphlets, published annually, but such websites as www.kohsamui.org and www.samuiguide.com are often more up-to-date. Pick up free magazines, such as the *Samui Explorer*, *Samui Guide*, and *What's On Samui*, in restaurants, bars, and shops. The *Samui Dining Guide* (www.samuidiningguide.com) lists the best restaurants on the island. You can also pick up any number of free maps with lots of adverts and info on spas, events, or fun local happenings.

GETTING AROUND

BY SONGTAEW OR TAXI   Pickup trucks are the cheapest way to get around the island and advertise their destinations with colorful signs. They follow Route 4169, the "ring road," around the island. Hail one anywhere along the highway and beach roads. Most stop after sundown, after which they tour Chaweng. Daytime fares are fixed at around 40B to 60B, but after dark they charge like taxis; night owls face steep fares (500B and up). Taxis are not metered and tend to ask extortionate rates, though a short trip from, say, Chaweng to Bo Phut should cost no more than 100B; ask hotel staff to help you negotiate a reasonable fare. If you plan to do much exploring on Ko Samui, consider renting a car, with or without a driver.

BY RENTAL CAR   Renting a car is far safer than a motorcycle, though you should employ defensive driving skills; you will be required to deal with obstacles such as motorcycles coming at you in your lane, a wandering dog, or an intoxicated truck driver with a death wish.

Budget Car Rental (© 07796-1502) has an office at Samui Airport and another at Chaweng Beach (© 07743-0022). Avis (© 084700-8161, cell) and Hertz (© 07742-5011) also have offices at the airport. All offer a range of vehicles, starting as low as 1,200B, and do pickup and delivery.

Local rental companies and travel agents have good deals for car rentals and they're generally sound. Bargains can come as low as 900B per day, but don't expect comprehensive insurance coverage. Read all the fine print, particularly how much you must pay in case of an accident.

BY MOTORCYCLE   The roads on Samui are busy, narrow, and poorly maintained, with plenty of novice drivers (usually gung-ho foreigners) and (unusual for Thailand) huge billboards reminding foreigners to drive on the left. Road accidents injure or kill an inordinate number of tourists and locals each year, mostly motorcycle riders, but two wheels and a motor is still the most popular way to get around the island. A 500B fine is imposed on anyone not wearing a helmet, so keep it on despite the temptation to feel the wind in your hair. Technically, you should have an international license, but small operators rarely ask to see it; they prefer to keep your passport in case of problems. Travel agencies and small operators rent motorcycles, and most resorts can make arrangements. A 100cc Honda scooter goes for around 150B per day, while a 250cc chopper or trail bike starts at around 500B. For the best big bikes, look for **Ohm Cycles,** on the far southern end of Chaweng (on the road heading to Lamai; © 08595-04109; www.ohmcyclessamui.com).

FAST FACTS

All the major **banks** now have branches in every town, with their main branches in Nathon along the waterfront Thawi Ratchaphakti Road. You will find numerous money-changers and ATMs across every part of the island, many with Western Union **money transfer services;** the latter has an office in Chaweng at the Centara Grand Beach Resort. There are post offices in Chaweng, Mae Nam, and Lamai—all on the main Samui ring road. The **main post office** is on Chonwithi Road in Nathon, but you probably won't hike all the way back to the main pier just for posting. Most resorts will also handle post for you, and stamps can be purchased in small shops in beach areas; be warned that any postcards you send will probably arrive long after you have returned home. For Internet service, there are numerous places scattered throughout the island, though these days there are few hotels that do not offer this service to their guests.

There are excellent private hospitals and 24-hour rescue and evacuation services if required. They are expensive but will deal directly with medical insurance companies. **Bangkok Samui Hospital** (✆ **07742-9500;** www.samuihospital.com) and **Samui International Hospital** (✆ **07723-0781-2;** www.sih.co.th) provide top-class medical care. **Bandon International Hospital** (✆ **07724-5236;** www.bandon hospitalsamui.com) is also a fine facility, with English-speaking physicians who make house calls. All are located around Chaweng.

For emergencies, dial ✆ **1155** or 07742-1281 for **Tourist Police.**

Exploring Ko Samui

Busy Samui has a host of entertainment apart from the usual beach outings. Have a look at the end of this section, for more outdoor activities and happenings.

Many of the sites below can be seen on day trips or combined with **jungle tours** in jeeps, such as **Mr Ung's Magical Safari Tour** (✆ **07723-0114;** www.ungsafari. com), starting at a reasonable 1,700B (children 1,100B). Join in and enjoy the adventure—even lunch is taken care of. There are also several companies offering trips with multichoice activities, including **quad biking, jungle coaster cable rides,** and even **mountain biking**—so look around to find the best travel agent for you. You can find a list of available tours and operators at http://samui.sawadee.com/tour.

Samui has a number of important temples and Buddhist sites to visit. **Wat Phra Yai** is home to Samui's primary landmark, the **Big Buddha,** more than 12m (39 ft.) tall and the most important temple for the local islanders. It is set on **Ko Faan,** a small islet connected to the shore on the northeast coast by a causeway, with shops and restaurants at the base. Admission is free, but donations are accepted.

Two temples in Samui hold bodies of **mummified monks,** which some may find ghoulishly interesting. The most popular is **Wat Khunaram,** along the main road (Rte 4169) as it shoots inland far south of Lamai. Here the **mummified body** of monk Loung Pordaeng is in the same meditation position, or *mudra,* as when he died over 20 years ago.

Four engraved imprints of the **Lord Buddha's Footprint** are held in a shrine near the turnoff to the **Butterfly Farm** off the 4170 Road near Laem Din. At the southernmost end of Lamai Beach lie Ko Samui's two famous rocks, **Hin Ta** and **Hin Yai,** Grandfather and Grandmother Stone, respectively. They have always caused a stir due to their likeness to male and female genitalia (you can guess which is which), and are seen as strong fertility symbols.

Just across Route 4169 from Wat Khunaram is the dirt track leading up to the **Na Muang Falls,** to which there is a lower and upper level. The lower reveals a large bathing pool (be careful of sharp rocks), though the upper is more photogenic. You can walk the steamy 5-km (3-mile) trek from the coast road to the upper falls (sometimes called Na Muang Falls 2) or take the easier route on the back of an elephant (any travel agency in town can arrange this). You could also visit the **Wang Saotong Waterfall** a little farther east along Route 4169. *Caution:* Due to a fatal accident at a waterfall in 2007, visitors are warned to be aware of the likelihood of sudden landslides here during heavy rain.

You can escape the heat with the family at **Paradise Park Farm** (*℗ 08606-33318*; http://paradiseparkfarm.net; daily 9am–6pm; adults 800B, children 600B, including hotel pickup). The cool mountain air of the island's interior will be a welcome relief as you walk through towering natural rocks surrounded by waterfalls, small rivers, canyons, wildlife animals, and exotic birds. You can then dine in the restaurant, relax in the infinity pool with spectacular views down the valley, or unwind in the spa.

Also well worth a visit is the **Magic Statue Garden,** if only for the trek deep into the jungle-clad mountains. Built by local farmer Nim Thongsuk in 1976, when he was 77, it is now proudly maintained by his son. The road is challenging, so book with a tour company such as **Mr Ung's Magical Safari Tour** (*℗ 07723-0114*; www.ungsafari.com).

The more adventurous can swing through the jungle with **Canopy Adventures** (*℗ 07741-4150-1*; www.canopyadventuresthailand.com; 1,900B adults, 1,450B children). Or, if you prefer a quicker adrenaline rush, **Samui Bungy** (*℗ 07741-4252*; http://samuibungy.com), on Soi Reggae behind Central Chaweng Beach.

If you don't intend to snorkel, but would like to see some underwater life, **Samui Aquarium and Tiger Zoo** (*℗ 07742-4017-8*; www.samuiaquariumandtigerzoo.com) is open daily from 9am to 5pm at Samui Orchid Resort, Laem Set Beach, and costs 650B (400B for children).

Most Thai tourist spots have a **snake show,** and Samui's **snake farm** is at the far southwest corner of the island, on 4170 Road (*℗ 07742-3247*; http://samuisnakefarm.com), with daily shows at 11am and 2pm. The handlers love to give the audience a scare as they kiss cobras and swallow scorpions. Tickets cost 300B (children 200B). **Samui Crocodile Farm** (*℗ 07723-9002*) also has **reptiles and monkeys.** It's open from midday to 5:30pm daily and the hourly show costs 500B for adults, 250B for children. At the **Samui Monkey Theater** (*℗ 07796-0128-9*), just south of Bophut village, on 4169 Road, you can see "working" demonstrations of monkeys collecting coconuts. Show times are at 10:30am, 2, and 4pm daily; entrance is 300B for adults, 150B for children.

Watch out also for notices about seasonal **buffalo fights,** which vary according to Thai holidays. Rather than being bloody affairs, the animals in these competitions don't actually gore each other—the losing steer simply runs off to fight another day. These rituals are steeped in animist traditions and superstition, with special offerings and prayers made to the buffalo before the matches, and of course a huge amount of betting and boozing accompanying the fights.

Where to Stay on Ko Samui

Thirty years ago there were but a few makeshift beachside bungalows along the nearly deserted coast of Samui. Today, luxury resorts stand shoulder to shoulder with upscale beach bungalows, all vying for supremacy. But whatever your budget, all enjoy virtually the same sand and views.

For more detailed information on each beach, check out "The Beaches," on p. 178. Below is a small accommodation selection from each area, including some of the best of the many new options. Listings follow a clockwise order around the island, beginning in the northwest corner.

LAEM YAI
Four Seasons Samui ★★★   Located on a steep hillside in the extreme northwest of the island, this is not the place to go if you want to be in the thick of nightlife,

but for anyone looking for a relaxing break, it is an ideal choice. All villas and suites enjoy expansive views out to sea, and guests have a choice of swimming at the beach (for resort guests only), in the communal pool, or in their private infinity pool attached to each villa. Rooms are furnished in typically sumptuous Four Seasons style and are equipped with large, flatscreen TVs, Wi-Fi, and wine coolers. Buggies are on hand to run guests up and down the steep hill, and service is both personal and extremely efficient.

219 Moo 5, Angthong, Ko Samui 84140. www.fourseasons.com/kohsamui. © **07724-3000.** Fax 07724-3002. 74 units. From 28,000B villa; from 32,500 1-bedroom villa. AE, MC, V. **Amenities:** 2 restaurants; bar; outdoor pool; 2 tennis courts; health club; spa; room service. *In room:* A/C, TV, DVD, minibar, Wi-Fi (450B per day normal; 700B per day premium).

MAE NAM BAY
Very Expensive

Napasai ★★★   Orient-Express Hotels run this prize resort that nestles on a rocky headland leading to the white-sand Baan Tai beach at the western end of Mae Nam. A selection of eight different types of rustic-themed teak cottages with high ceilings come with private pools, sumptuous decor, and large bathtubs, all with balconies. The largest is a four-bedroom, oceanfront pool residence that offers total privacy, yet easy access to the resort's services. Though isolated, this top-end resort is gorgeously self-contained. Superb spa facilities and in-house dining make it a plum choice for well-heeled romantics.

65/10 Baan Tai, Maenam, Ko Samui 84330. www.napasai.com. © **07742-9200.** Fax 07742-9201. 69 units. 10,200B–12,700B seaview/beachfront cottages; 14,900B–40,200B suites and 2 to 4-bed villas. AE, MC, V. **Amenities:** Restaurant; bar; outdoor pool; tennis courts; health club; spa; watersports rentals; room service. *In room:* A/C, TV, minibar, fridge, Wi-Fi (free).

Santiburi Resort ★★   Just a few steps east of the Napasai, the Santiburi Resort was the first high-end property in the area and has recently been subject to a thorough make-over. Modern state-of-the-art amenities are discreetly infused into the contemporary Thai architecture. The resort's top villas—with outside Jacuzzis—front the beach, while the others are set among lush greenery around a central pool and spa. Each bungalow comes with a large sunken tub. Guests can take advantage of windsurfing and sailing (free), and there is a sailing junk to tour surrounding islands (it's also used for supper cruises). Santiburi also hosts the island's top golf course, **Santiburi Golf,** near the resort.

Santiburi has a slightly more affordable companion in nearby Bophut, called the **Bophut Resort and Spa** (© **07724-5777;** www.bophutresort.com), at a similar high standard, with 61 luxury seaside villas.

12/12 Moo 1, Tambol Mae Nam, Ko Samui 84330. www.santiburi.com. © **07742-5031.** Fax 07742-5040. 71 units. 9,250B–18,800B suites and villas; from 22,000B plunge-pool villas. AE, DC, MC, V. **Amenities:** 2 restaurants; 2 bars; lounge; outdoor pool; golf course (nearby, connected by free shuttle); outdoor lit tennis courts; health club; spa; watersports equipment room service; babysitting. *In room:* A/C, TV/DVD, minibar, fridge, hair dryer, stereo system, movie library, Wi-Fi (free).

W Retreat ★★★   Perched on the promontory that separates Mae Nam and Bophut beaches on Samui's north coast, this resort sets a benchmark for sleek, cutting-edge design and a contemporary philosophy that is summed up in their "Whatever, whenever" policy to fulfill their guests' every wish. The W factor is in all the facilities–the fitness room is SWEAT, the pool is WET, the bar is the WOOBA, and the spa is AWAY. The design of the pool villas is hip and modern, with light-wood paneled walls, cool, clean lines and bright red throw rugs and lampshades. Even the minibar menu contains innovative snacks and drinks, and the two dining options, The Kitchen Table and Namu, the signature Japanese restaurant serving "Asia tomorrow" cuisine, promise exciting culinary adventures.

4/1 Moo 1, Tambon Mae Nam, Ko Samui 84330. www.whotels.com/kohsamui. ⓒ **07791-5999.** Fax 07791-5998. 75 units. 27,000B–157,000B pool villas. AE, DC, MC, V. **Amenities:** 2 restaurants; 3 bars; outdoor pool; health club; spa. *In room:* A/C, TV/DVD, minibar, Wi-Fi (free).

Moderate/Inexpensive

Maenamburi ★★ Under the swaying palms of peaceful Mae Nam beach, this bargain bungalow resort provides the fast-disappearing beach ambience that Samui was once famous for. The accommodation ranges from spacious garden rooms surrounded by greenery to pool villas and on-the-beach bungalows for those who like to hear the sea lapping outside their door. Staff can help you arrange sightseeing tours or rent vehicles, and there are massage and spa services on site. However, you probably won't want to go too far as the beach right in front is ideal for swimming and wiggling your toes in the sand.

82/2 Moo 1, Mae Nam Beach, Ko Samui 84330. www.maenamburi.com. ⓒ **07742-7036.** Fax 07742-7037. 15 units. From 2,500B double; from 6,000B pool villas. MC, V. **Amenities:** Restaurant; room service; Wi-Fi (in lobby, free). *In room:* A/C, TV, minibar.

Mae Nam Resort ★ 🍴 These spacious bungalows form a secluded little village in overgrown jungle gardens. Each has teak paneling and floors, rattan furnishings, a small bathroom with polished stone walls, and a deck. Beachfront bungalows (2,000B) will have you stepping off your balcony right into the silky, palm-shaded sand for very little, considering the neighboring Santiburi Resort's beachfront villas run about 30,000B. Okay, so Mae Nam Resort can't compare to five-star luxury, but it's still the same sand and view.

1/3 Moo 4, Mae Nam Beach, Ko Samui 84330 (next to the Santiburi Resort). www.maenamresort.com. ⓒ **07724-7286-7.** Fax 07742-5116. 41 units. From 1,800B bungalow; 3,000B family bungalow. AE, MC, V. **Amenities:** Restaurant; room service. *In room:* A/C, TV, minibar, Wi-Fi (50B per hour), no phone.

BOPHUT BEACH
Expensive

Anantara Bophut ★★★ This has to be one of Samui's most atmospheric resorts, starting from its grand entrance and high-ceilinged lobby, where there's a cozy library with computer terminals for guests' use. Generous-sized rooms have a modern feel and plenty of wood, and make use of exquisite local textiles; each room has a private balcony with loungers overlooking the garden or beach. Some of the most attractive features of the resort are the free-form infinity pool that has a couple of tiny islands set in it, and the Italian restaurant (Full Moon) that enjoys lovely views across to the bay. The Anantara provides yoga sessions, Thai cooking classes, wine appreciation instruction, and superb spa therapies—while maintaining a low-key, unpretentious approach. It's also just a short walk from Fisherman's Village where there are plenty of shops, bars, and restaurants.

99/9 Moo 1, Bophut, Ko Samui 84320. www.anantara.com. ⓒ **07742-8300.** Fax 07742-8310. 106 units. 7,680B–9,480B deluxe double; 10,580B–13,180B suite. AE, MC, V. **Amenities:** 2 restaurants; bar; outdoor pool; tennis court; health club; spa; watersports rental; room service. *In room:* A/C, TV, minibar, fridge, Wi-Fi (475B per day).

Bandara Resort Bandara has a range of villas, standard, and deluxe rooms that flank a main courtyard area, and a good-sized, raised pool. Seaside villas are luxurious, and many of them have private gardens and pools. A free-form pool is set at the beachside next to the restaurant. Water babies have complementary use of water-sports facilities such as the fleet of Hobie Cats (small catamarans). The vibe is slick and contemporary, with some nice Thai touches.

178/2 Moo 1, Bophut, Ko Samui 84320. www.bandarasamui.com. © **07742-5795.** Fax 07742-7340. 150 units. 7,400B–9,000B double superior/deluxe; from 14,000B pool villa. AE, DC, MC, V. **Amenities:** 2 restaurants; bar; outdoor pool; health club; watersports equipment; room service. *In room:* A/C, TV, minibar, fridge, Wi-Fi (free).

Hansar Samui ★★ This three-story, rust-colored building is set around an enormous infinity pool, and the generous balconies of all rooms enjoy views of the palm-fringed beach in front. Like the Hansar Bangkok, this property oozes style; its spacious, elegant rooms have wooden floors, canopy beds, free-standing stone bathtubs, and rocking chairs on the balcony. There's free Wi-Fi in the rooms, and the luxurious spa and H Bistro restaurant with divine Mediterranean cuisine are other big attractions here (even the buffet breakfast is a gourmet experience). The resort is right next to Fisherman's Village, which is lined with shops, restaurants, and bars and makes a good place for a stroll in the evening.

101/28 Moo 1, Bophut, Ko Samui 84320. www.hansarsamui.com. © **07724-5511.** Fax 07724-5995. 74 units. 11,000B-18,000B double. AE, DC, MC, V. **Amenities:** Restaurant; 2 bars; outdoor pool; health club; spa; babysitting. *In room:* A/C, TV, minibar, Wi-Fi (free).

Peace Resort ☺ Living up to its name, this family-run resort offers five types of free-standing bungalows set in lush, peaceful gardens, the largest being 49 sq. m (527 sq. ft.). All villas come with terraces and feature sunny yellow interiors and modern furnishings that have a rustic quality. Great for families, the large central pool has a separate kids' pool and a playground, but, when the place is busy, you'll have to rise early if you want to bag a sun bed.

178 Moo 1, Bophut, Ko Samui 84320 (central Bophut). www.peaceresort.com. © **07742-5357.** Fax 07742-5343. 122 units. 5,500B–11,500B double. AE, DC, MC, V. **Amenities:** Restaurant; bar; outdoor pool w/kids' pool; spa; children's club; room service; babysitting. *In room:* A/C, TV/DVD, minibar, fridge, Wi-Fi (200B per day), no phone.

Moderate
Ibis Samui Bophut ✦ Ibis hotels have a reputation for providing clean and comfortable lodgings at affordable prices, and this is no exception. Now that most of Samui's hotels have gone upmarket, this place goes some way to filling the void of simple, cheap accommodation without all the buzzers and bells. Rooms are smartly furnished, with safety boxes and tea- and coffee-making facilities, and the resort faces an attractive stretch of Bophut Beach. There's a swimming pool and an all-you-can-eat buffet breakfast. About the only extra you'll need to pay for is Internet use.

Bophut Beach, Ko Samui 84320. www.ibishotel.com. © **02659-2888** (in Bangkok). Fax 02659-2889. 250 units. From $75 double; $95 family room. MC, V. **Amenities:** Restaurant; bar; outdoor pool; children's playground. *In room:* A/C, TV, minibar, Wi-Fi (500B per day).

BIG BUDDHA BEACH
Expensive
Outrigger Samui ★★ Tucked away near the Big Buddha temple, this resort features three attractive pools to which most rooms have direct access. Superior rooms are a bit small, but the deluxe and studio rooms are spacious and all have private balconies. Furnishings are very stylish, all made of light wood and decorated

with seashell motifs—the lampshades, beds, and even waste baskets, giving the place a genuine seaside feel. The excellent spa—Navasana—offers competitively priced spa treatment packages. There are cooking courses available at 1,950B per person, and daily activities such as a temple tour, muay thai lesson and beach soccer; some of these are free and others carry a small charge. There are great sunset views from the pool, restaurant, and artificial beach, and a shuttle runs guests to Chaweng or Fisherman's Village for shopping or dining.

69/34 Moo 5, Tambon Bophut, Ko Samui 84320. www.outrigger.com. © **07741-7300.** Fax 07741-7360. 79 units. 5,746B–12,768B double, from 15,680B villa. AE, DC, MC, V. **Amenities:** Restaurant; 2 bars; 3 outdoor pools; health club; spa; children's club. *In room:* A/C, TV, minibar, hair dryer, Wi-Fi (free).

Moderate

The Saboey ★★ 🏠   This gorgeous boutique resort oozes style with its sumptuous-hued interiors and Morocco-meets-Asia style. Rooms offer top-quality furnishings and useful added extras such as a writing desk, Wi-Fi, and other mod-cons, mark it out from the fray. The long, glassy infinity pool has ocean views and a Jacuzzi cascading down to the beach. Dine surrounded by candles and the sounds of waves at the beachside Breeze restaurant or try the **Quo Vadis** restaurant.

51/4 Moo 4, Tambon Bophut, Ko Samui 84320. www.saboey.com. © **07743-0450.** 18 units. 3,200B suites; 4,300B garden villas; 4,800B ocean villas; 5,800B beach villas. **Amenities:** 2 restaurants; bar; outdoor pool; Jacuzzi. *In room:* A/C, TV/DVD, minibar, CD player, Wi-Fi (free).

LAEM SAMRONG

Six Senses Hideaway ★★★   Set on a gently sloping headland among 8 hect-ares (20 acres) of lush vegetation, this resort was proclaimed "Best in the World" by the prestigious Readers' Travel Awards doled out by *Condé Nast Traveler* in 2008. Those who voted for it were impressed by not only its lovely location and environmen-tal friendliness, but also its sophisticated ambience and extensive leisure facilities. These facilities include private pools beside most villas and suites, a spa with a com-prehensive range of treatments, and activities such as aquarobics, island tours, diving trips, and cooking classes. All the villas are equipped with every imaginable comfort and are attended by personal butlers, while the views are simply fabulous. The resort is in Laem Samrong, on the northeastern tip of Samui (just around the promontory that shelters Tongsai Bay).

9/10 Moo 5, Baan Plai Laem, Boput, Ko Samui 84320 (northeast tip of island). www.sixsenses.com. © **07724-5678.** Fax 07724-5671. 66 units. 12,426B–27,906B villas; 73,715B 2-bedroom villa. AE, DC, MC, V. **Amenities:** 2 restaurants; 2 bars; outdoor pools; health club; spa; watersports equip-ment. *In room:* A/C, TV/DVD, Wi-Fi (free).

TONGSAI BAY

The Tongsai Bay ★★★   Built like an amphitheater, and tripping down a hillside to its own beach, this all-suite complex has some very unique touches—such as its "Bath-with-a-View"—that set it apart. You'll get plenty of outdoor terrace space to enjoy the sea views, and the Grand Tongsai Villas have gazebos for guests who like open-air sleeping. Tongsai Pool Villas have private plunge pools. There is a beautiful half-moon-shaped pool set in the gardens halfway down, and a large pool at the beach with a sepa-rate children's pool. The end result is casual outdoors ambience. The only drawback is the many steps between the hilltop reception area, bungalows, and beach.

84 Moo 5, Ban Plailaem, Bophut, Ko Samui 84320 (northeast tip of island). www.tongsaibay.co.th. © **07724-5480,** or 02381-8774 in Bangkok. Fax 07742-5462. 83 units. 13,000B–16,500B beachfront

or cottage suite; 18,250B seafront cottage; from 25,900B grand villa; from 29,500B pool villa. AE, DC, MC, V. **Amenities:** 3 restaurants; 2 bars; 2 outdoor pools; tennis court; health club; spa; watersports equipment; room service. *In room:* A/C, TV/DVD, minibar, fridge, hair dryer, Wi-Fi (free).

CHOENG MON BAY
Very Expensive

Sala Samui ★★★   Hip, slick, and cool; that's the vibe at Sala Samui. Stylish rooms, most with their own private pools, have views onto private courtyards or the sea. The place has a boutique feel, blending traditional Thai architecture with modern facilities. Polished concrete is accented in Thai silk hangings and canopy beds. Rooms are equipped with every imaginable comfort, including DVD players. With its in-house Sala spa waiting to pamper guests, this is a real honeymooners' haven.

10/9 Moo 5, Baan Plai Lam Bophut, Ko Samui 84320. www.salaresorts.com/samui. ©**07724-5888.** Fax 07724-5889. 69 units. 13,400B deluxe; 20,200B–38,900B pool villa; 50,500B presidential villa. AE, MC, V. **Amenities:** 2 restaurants; 2 bars; 2 outdoor pools; health club; spa; room service. *In room:* A/C, TV/DVD, minibar, fridge, Wi-Fi (free).

Moderate

White House Beach Resort & Spa ★★   This resort in the graceful Khmer style, built around a central garden with a lotus pond and swimming pool, is a good choice in Choeng Mon for comfort at a reasonable cost. The spacious and elegant rooms flank a central walkway that's lined with orchids. Each house accommodates four spacious rooms, which have separate sitting areas, huge beds, fine furnishings, and bathrooms. By the beach, there's a pool with a bar and an especially graceful teak *sala*. The resort's quality Swiss management team is very efficient and assures a pleasant stay. This is top comfort spilling onto a beautiful stretch of white-sand beach.

59/3 Moo 5, Choeng Mon Beach, Ko Samui 84320. www.samuithewhitehouse.com. © **07724-7921.** Fax 07724-5318. 43 units. From 3,650B double; from 4,600B suite. AE, MC, V. **Amenities:** Restaurant; bar; outdoor pool; spa; Jacuzzi; Internet. *In room:* A/C, TV, minibar, fridge, Wi-Fi (free).

CHAWENG & CHAWENG NOI BAYS
Very Expensive

The Briza Beach Resort & Spa ★★   The Briza offers a pure lifestyle experience, aiming to recapture the spirit and serenity of the Srivijaya Empire, a historic Buddhism-inspired period. You'll almost feel the tranquillity as you mount the majestic entrance steps. Just steps away from north Chaweng beach, the accommodation ranges from pool-access to beachfront villas with large private pools. All are supersize, with a bathtub and a separate shower; fine furnishings reflect the grandeur and serenity of the resort's theme. Guests are treated to exclusive perks, such as a private butler, who endeavors to satisfy guests' every whim, and lessons on Thai culture are on offer.

173/22 Moo 2, Chaweng Beach, Tambon Bophut, Ko Samui 84320. www.thebriza.com. ©**07723-1997.** Fax 07723-1990. 57 units. 11,000B–17,000B pool villas; 19,000B beachfront villas. AE, DC, MC, V. **Amenities:** Restaurant; bar; outdoor pool; health club. *In room:* A/C, TV/DVD, minibar, fridge, hair dryer, Wi-Fi (free).

Centara Grand Beach Resort ★★   Renovations in late 2011 to several parts of this hotel, including the suites, restaurant, and kids' club, have breathed new life into this grand edifice located right in the heart of Chaweng. All rooms are a generous size, particularly the deluxe pool suites, and are furnished with relaxing sofas. There's a club lounge that is open to pool villa guests, and the whole place sports a whole spanking-new luxury feel. Happily, though, for its many returning guests, Centara hasn't lost any of its well-loved village ambience; and its plethora of dining options still include Brazilian fare at **Zico's,** across the road (p. 194), and **Hagi,** for Japanese food. Centara offers peace and seclusion from the rampant development around this busy strip, and off-season discounts make the resort a very reasonable choice considering the quality.

38/2 Moo 3, Chaweng Beach, Ko Samui 84320. www.centarahotelsresorts.com. ☎ **07723-0500.** Fax 07742-2385. 203 units. From 10,000B double; from 19,000B suite. AE, MC, V. **Amenities:** 5 restaurants; 2 bars; outdoor pool and children's pool; tennis courts; health club; spa; watersports rentals; children's club; room service; dive center. *In room:* A/C, TV, minibar, fridge, hair dryer, Wi-Fi (249B per day, free in suites only).

The Library ★★★   This ravishingly minimalist resort offers a startlingly different contemporary slant. Designed by a Bangkok architect, its rooms are divided into studios and suites, and in keeping with the hotel's name, the resort's main feature is a library with an array of books and films. State-of-the-art rooms (with Jacuzzis and rain showers) provide an extraordinary range of luxuries, from huge plasma TVs, iMacs, and iPods, to light boxes and self-controlled colored lighting. It's cool, it's original, and it appeals to those with a leaning toward techno-Zen.

14/1 Moo 2, Bophut, Ko Samui 84320. www.thelibrary.co.th. ☎ **07742-2767.** Fax 07742-2344. 13 units. 14,000B studio; 16,000B suites. AE, MC, V. **Amenities:** Restaurant; bar; outdoor pool; health club. *In room:* A/C, TV/DVD, iMac, iPod (suites), Jacuzzi (suites), Wi-Fi (free).

Expensive

Amari Palm Reef Koh Samui ★★★ ☺   This fine-looking Amari hotel is both a fun family choice and a honeymooners' delight, with sea-facing suite rooms that merge slick-contemporary with traditional decor. A block of midrange units lies in a "Thai village" location across the road from the beach and with a separate pool and Jacuzzi. The central beachside pool area is appealing, as is the dining terrace overlooking it. The resort is far enough from Chaweng strip to be quiet and comfortable (but close enough to party), and their tour desk can fix you up with a rented car or motorbike. The place is often busy, yet the staff handle everything effortlessly and efficiently, making it a pleasure to stay.

Chaweng Beach, Ko Samui 84320 (north end of the main strip). www.amari.com/palmreef. ☎ **07742-2015.** Fax 07742-2394. 188 units. 6,500B superior; 7,500B deluxe; 15,000B suite. AE, MC, V. **Amenities:** 2 restaurants; 2 outdoor pools; health club; spa; Jacuzzi; children's club; babysitting. *In room:* A/C, TV/ DVD, minibar, fridge, hair dryer, Wi-Fi (390B per day).

Coral Bay Resort ★★   North of giddy Chaweng, but close enough to commute, these upscale thatched bungalows sit atop a picturesque hill and present a marked contrast to the super-hip vibe of ultra-modern resorts such as The Library. Here the decor blends with the natural environment, and laudable efforts are made to recycle wastewater and decrease the resort's negative impact on Samui's fragile ecosystem. The 56 rooms are scattered across the hillside (you have to trudge a bit to get to some), and each has a large balcony (some are shared with adjoining rooms). Bathrooms are set in gardens with waterfall showers. At the side of the resort is a private villa with two master bedrooms and its own pool. The central pool area is high above the rock and coral beach below, which is not good for swimming, though farther out the bay offers good snorkeling and fishing. Guests can dine at the Pakarang restaurant, and a small spa provides affordable treatments.

9 Moo 2, Bophut, Chaweng Beach, Ko Samui 84320 (on a hill crest, at the north end of Chaweng). www.coralbay.net. ☎ **07723-4555.** Fax 07723-4558. 56 units. 6,850B–8,500B double bungalow; 8,750B–16,200B family units/suites; 20,000B–32,000B Baan Chomjan villa. MC, V. **Amenities:** Restaurant; bar; outdoor pool; spa; children's club; babysitting. *In room:* A/C, TV/DVD, minibar, fridge, Wi-Fi (free).

Poppies Samui Resort At the southern end of busy Chaweng, this popular old-timer, unlike the concrete behemoths around this part of town, features just two dozen luxury cottages nestled among lush foliage, with paths and wooden bridges crossing over streams and cascading waterfalls. The Balinese-style cottages have unique open-air bathrooms with sunken bathtubs and marble floors, set in private gardens. Unwind at the Body Care Spa, in a *sala* by the central free-form pool, which is surrounded by natural boulders. The Ayutthaya-style wooden pavilion is home to the resort's well-loved restaurant Poppies, known for years as one of Samui's finest (p. 194). Given its top service and amenities, this place books up quickly—reserve in advance.

P.O. Box 1, Chaweng, Ko Samui 84320 (on the south end of the Chaweng strip). www.poppiessamui. com. ✆**07742-2419.** Fax 07742-2420. 24 units. 9,750B double. AE, MC, V. **Amenities:** Restaurant; outdoor pool; spa; room service. *In room:* A/C, TV, minibar, fridge, Wi-Fi (free).

Sandalwood Luxury Villas ★★ Set back from the coast on a hill with sweeping views over the gentle curve of Chaweng Beach, this complex of just 10 individually decorated villas that sleep between two and six people offers the ultimate in personalized service to its guests. Some villas have a private pool, others share one, and some feature Jacuzzis on the terrace. Bathrooms are all marble and granite, and furnishings are a pleasing fusion of traditional and up-to-date styles. There are two infinity pools on site, as well as an inviting restaurant and boutique spa. They also offer cookery classes and can help plan your island sightseeing.

211 Moo 4, Tambon Maret, Ko Samui 84320 (behind Chaweng Beach). www.sandalwoodsamui. com. ✆**07741-4016.** Fax 07741-4017. 10 units. 6,516B–13,673B villa. AE, DC, MC, V. **Amenities:** Restaurant; bar; 2 outdoor pools; spa; room service; babysitting. *In room:* A/C, TV/DVD, minibar, fridge, hair dryer, movie library, Wi-Fi (free).

Moderate

Ark Bar Beach Resort Ark Bar is a good choice for party people. Its two-story hotel rooms may have been squeezed into a narrow strip of gardens leading to the beach right in the heart of Chaweng, but they're all equipped with air-con, satellite TV, minibar, and balcony, and the resort even has a small pool. In fact it's so popular that two further branches have now opened nearby. The restaurant, serving Western and Thai cusine as well as fresh seafood, is popular, with both indoor and beachside seating. As the sun goes down, Ark Bar becomes one of the main focal areas on Chaweng beach to gather at nighttime. On Wednesdays and Fridays, from 2pm until 2am, bikini-clad tourists and locals join in the fun, when some of the island's best funk and house music DJs perform.

159/75 Moo 2, Chaweng Beach, Ko Samui 84320. www.ark-bar.com. ✆**07796-1333.** Fax 07796-1334. 186 units. 2,800B–3,400B double; 4,000B junior suite. MC, V. **Amenities:** Restaurant; outdoor pool. *In room:* A/C, TV, minibar, fridge, Wi-Fi (free).

Baan Chaweng ★ This place offers a comfortable stay at prices that won't burn a hole in your pocket. You're right in the heart of Chaweng here, but far enough removed from the thumping bass to get a peaceful night's sleep. Quiet paths lead past rooms and bungalows, through the attractive gardens and palms of the main courtyard, to a cozy beachfront pool and restaurant. Guest rooms are comfortable and sparsely decorated, though not displeasingly so. The cheapest rooms (superior) are in modern two-story blocks farthest removed from the beach, while free-standing deluxe bungalows and villas take the prime spots and are not a bad upgrade. The hotel's restaurant, Leelawadee, has terrace seating right on the beach and serves excellent seafood.

90/1 Moo 2, Chaweng Beach, Ko Samui 84320 (middle of Chaweng Beach). www.baanchaweng. com. ⓒ **07742-2403.** Fax 07742-2404. 94 units. 2,800B superior; 4,000B–6,750B villa; 13,000B beachfront suite. Rates include breakfast. AE, MC, V. **Amenities:** Restaurant; outdoor pool; spa; babysitting. *In room:* A/C, TV, minibar, hair dryer, Wi-Fi (500B for 7½ hr).

Inexpensive

Jungle Club ★   Set high on a hill behind Chaweng Noi Beach, this attractive resort offers something for all budgets, from a very basic jungle hut with just a fan, mattress, and mosquito net, to a sturdier jungle bungalow, a spacious jungle house, and luxurious lodges and villas. The setting is truly idyllic, but it is so isolated (only 4WD vehicles and motorbikes can get up the hill), that you'll need to take a shuttle down to the beach or town (free at 10.30am and 6pm; other times 50B/100B). The resort is under French/Thai management and its popular restaurant attracts many visitors to enjoy the view, the romantic, candle-lit setting and the range of Thai and French dishes.

Chaweng Noi Beach, Soi Panyadee School, Ko Samui 84320 (call for pickup). www.jungleclub samui.com. ⓒ **08189-42327.** 11 units. 800B jungle hut; 1,800B–5,000B bungalow/house; 3,500B–4,500B lodge/villa. AE, DC, MC, V. **Amenities:** Restaurant; outdoor pool. *In room:* A/C, TV/DVD (lodge and villa), minibar, fridge, Wi-Fi (free).

LAMAI BAY
Very Expensive

Pavilion Samui Boutique Resort ★★★   Lots of hotels on Samui describe themselves as "boutique," but the term is apt in this instance. Boasting grand-scale style with top service, the Pavilion offers everything from Mediterranean-themed bungalows to luxurious honeymoon suites. Most feature private pools or huge, opu-lent bathrooms, plus a courtyard area where guests can enjoy a Jacuzzi and shower under the stars. They have a dining pavilion on the beach, and the proximity to Lamai's nightlife is a plus for night owls.

124/24 Moo 3, Lamai Beach, Ko Samui 84310 (north end of Lamai Beach). www.pavilionsamui.com. ⓒ **07742-4030.** Fax 07742-4029. 70 units. 12,000B deluxe Jacuzzi room; 14,000B plunge pool suite; 20,000B hydro villa; 30,000B grand pool villa; 35,000B beachfront grand pool villa. AE, DC, MC, V. **Amenities:** Restaurant; bar; outdoor pool; health club; spa; Jacuzzi; room service. *In room:* A/C, TV/DVD, minibar, hair dryer, CD player, Wi-Fi (free).

Expensive

Rocky's Boutique Resort ★★★   Rocky's pushes the boundaries of luxury with two beautiful pools and individually designed one- to four-bedroom villas, which cas-cade down a rocky hillside to a private sandy beach. Just 5 minutes south of Lamai, it's easily accessible—but a hard slog up steep hills for villa residents. The resort boasts a one-to-one staff/guest ratio and enviable views from the private villa terraces. The hotel longtail boat can whisk you to the Marine Park or secluded beaches (for a price).

438/1 Moo 1, Lamai, Tambon Maret, Ko Samui 84310. www.rockyresort.com. ⓒ **07741-8367.** Fax 07741-8366. 34 units. 5,500B gardenview suite; 7,500B oceanview suite; 9,500B beachfront suite; 15,000B deluxe villa. AE, MC, V. **Amenities:** restaurant; bar; 2 outdoor pools; bikes; watersports equipment; babysitting. *In room:* A/C, TV, CD player, Wi-Fi (free).

Moderate

Lamai Wanta   Located in the center of Lamai Beach, this little complex of clean and contemporary cottages complements a cluster of rooms in a two-story hotel block. There is little in the way of service here, but the small seaside pool is an oasis, and you are close to town for services. Tidy rooms have balconies, terra-cotta tiles, and high ceilings. Rooms in the two-story block are good value, but are also within earshot of local bars, which can get noisy so pack your earplugs.

124/264 Moo 3, Lamai, Ko Samui 84310 (north end of Lamai Beach). http://lamaiwanta.com. © **07742-4550.** Fax 07742-4218. 74 units. 2,650B basic room; 3,550B deluxe; 4,100B–6,000B villas. MC, V. **Amenities:** Restaurant; bar; outdoor pool. *In room:* A/C, TV/DVD, minibar, fridge, Wi-Fi (free).

Mercure Samui Fenix ★   Located at the south end of Lamai beach, the Mercure Fenix offers a good midrange alternative that is a 5-minute ride from the restaurants and bars of Lamai, accessible by shuttle. Rooms are not huge but all are equipped with the essentials—modern furnishings, satellite TV, work desk, and safety boxes; Wi-Fi is available in rooms, though you'll need to pay for the privilege. There's a good-sized pool, exercise room, and smart restaurant, and it's located right next to one of Samui's unmissable sights—the "Grandfather and Grandmother Stones." (p. 181). It's also just a few steps from one of Samui's best seafood restaurants—**Sabeingle** (p. 192).

26/1 Moo 3, Lamai, Tambon Maret, Ko Samui 84310. www.mercure.com. © **07742-4008.** Fax 07742-4009. 60 units. From 3,861B double; 4,469B villa. MC, V. **Amenities:** Restaurant; bar; outdoor pool; exercise room. *In room:* A/C, TV, minibar, fridge, Wi-Fi (300B per day).

The Spa Resort ★★ ✔   This family-operated wellness retreat has been around for years and is known for its fasting and cleansing programs as well as vegetarian/raw food and yoga and meditation courses. There are two resorts on Samui: The original **Samui Beach Resort,** comprising a laid-back cluster of rustic bungalows and a pool just north of Lamai, and the newer **Samui Village,** a hillside retreat studded with rock formations. Rooms at both locations range from simple bungalows to large private suites with large balconies. Spa Village has a pool, herbal steam bath in a large stone grotto, massage, body wraps, and facial treatments—and is open to day visitors.

Samui Village: Lamai Beach, Ko Samui 84320 (just south, in the hills over Lamai Beach). www. thesparesorts.com. © **07723-0855.** Fax 07742-4545. 34 units. 800B–2,000B double; 2,800B suite. MC, V. Spa Beach: Lamai Beach (on the north end of the main strip in Lamai). 24 units. 900B–1,000B room; from 5,000B villa. MC, V. **Amenities:** Restaurant; outdoor pool; spa; sauna; juice bar. *In room:* A/C, minibar, fridge, Wi-Fi (400B for 6 hours).

Weekender Resort & Spa ★ ✔   This resort offers many accommodation options at a very reasonable price, from superior, and deluxe rooms spread across three separate buildings to Thai-style houses. Plus, there are lower rates for singles, appealing to solo travelers who don't want to pay for twin occupancy. The teak-floored rooms are spread over a large area of beautiful landscaped tropical gardens. It's right on the soft white-sand beach of southern Lamai (with great swimming), but—just as important—it's also near enough to town.

124/19 Moo 3, Lamai, Ko Samui 84310. www.weekender-samui.com. © **07742-4429.** Fax 07742-4011. 133 units. 1,950B bungalows; 2,300B standard room; 3,100B Thai house; 3,500B superior; 4,900B deluxe; 14,800B sunrise suite. MC, V. **Amenities:** Restaurant; bar; outdoor pool; spa. *In room:* A/C, TV, minibar, fridge, Wi-Fi (500B unlimited use).

Inexpensive

Orchid Suites ✔   This wonderful and informal family resort is made up of very simple thatched cottages with wooden floors. These are hidden in beautiful tropical gardens in the middle of Lamai Beach; a free shuttle bus runs here from Chaweng and Samui Yacht Club. Simple rattan furnishings are quite adequate, and the balconies are large and airy, with sea or pool views. The flat rate is excellent value, though a high-season surcharge applies as in many places. The large pool with a poolside bar looks out over Lamai Bay.

129/11 Moo 3, Lamai Beach, Ko Samui 84310. www.orchidsuite.com. © **07723-2304.** Fax 07723-2305. 20 units. 500B garden/seaview. MC, V. **Amenities:** Restaurant; bar; outdoor pool. *In room:* A/C, TV, Wi-Fi (free).

WEST COAST
Very Expensive

Conrad Samui ★★★ 🔲 As soon as you reach the arrivals desk of this new resort in the extreme southwest corner of the island, you know you're somewhere special. The sweeping views out to sea and the relaxed and assured manner of the staff are just the beginning of a truly unforgettable experience; in fact, if we authors were permitted to award four stars, I'd give them to this place. The super-modern one- and two-bedroom pool villas have huge TVs, stylish marble bathrooms with over-sized free-standing bathtubs, and the sunset views across the infinity pool, looking over islands toward the mainland, are to die for. The beach in front of the resort is not great for swimming as there are some rocks in the bay, but few will worry about this as all villas have their own pool.

49/8-9 Moo 4, Hillcrest Rd., Tambon Taling Ngam, Ko Samui 84140. http://conradhotels1.hilton.com. © **07791-5888.** Fax 07791-5889. 80 units. From 32,000B pool villas. AE, DC, MC, V. **Amenities:** 3 restaurants; 2 bars; outdoor pool; health club; spa; children's club; concierge; diving and sailing center. *In room:* A/C, TV, minibar, hair dryer, Wi-Fi (free).

Moderate

Lipa Lodge Resort Situated on the quiet west coast, this small resort is hard to beat if you're looking for an affordable and tranquil escape. In business for 40 years, the owners have learned the art of giving personal attention; and with just 11 bungalows, there's no chance of it getting crowded. As the resort was founded by an award-winning chef, you can look forward to great tastes in the restaurant, and the infinity pool is just the spot to watch a spectacular sunset. Bungalows are comfortable and well equipped, and each has a private balcony.

75/4 Moo 3, Tambon Lipa Noi, Ko Samui 81410. www.lipalodgeresort.com. © **07748-5616.** 11 units. 3,600B–5,300B double; 6,200B family bungalow. MC, V. **Amenities:** Restaurant; outdoor pool; Internet (free). *In room:* A/C, minibar, TV/DVD.

Where to Eat on Ko Samui

Since most people while away their days on Samui lounging by the pool or being pampered in a spa, there's plenty of time to make the day's most important decision—where to dine. There are so many options out there that you could spend a year eating somewhere different every day and still not exhaust Samui's culinary possibilities. Here I present some personal favorites, but to ponder a wider range of dining venues, pick up a free copy of *Eating on Samui* or log on to www.samuirestaurantguide.com.

It comes as no surprise that **seafood** is the number one choice for visitors to Samui, and you'll find simple shacks on every beach serving up fresh fish, shrimp, and squid in a huge variety of preparations. A couple of local seafood restaurants that are worth tracking down are **Jun Hom** (© 07760-2008) on Bangpor beach, just west of Mae Nam beach, and **Sabeingle** (© 07723-3082), which is perched above the south end of Lamai beach.

MAE NAM BEACH

The Farmer ★ THAI/INTERNATIONAL   It may not be on the beach, but there's a wonderful ambience at this classy joint located in the middle of rice paddies, where you can sit on the terrace soaking up the view or settle in to the smart, air-conditioned interior. Take your pick from classic Thai dishes such as *yam hua plee* (a spicy banana-flower salad), or international favorites like grilled sirloin steak and marinated rack of lamb. The menu is rounded out with a wide choice of cocktails and a healthy selection of wines. A definite plus is that service, which can often be sloppy (read inattentive) on Samui, is spot-on here.

1/26 Moo 1, Ban Tai, Mae Nam (look for the lane opposite Samui Lapidary on the ring road). © **07744-7222.** www.thefarmerrestaurantsamui.com. Main courses 210B–1,150B. MC, V. Daily 10am–10:30pm.

BOPHUT & FISHERMAN'S VILLAGE

You should take time out to wander through the Fisherman's Village area, located more or less in the middle of Bophut beach. Now transformed into a foodie paradise, it is lined with several atmospheric pubs and small upmarket restaurants along the water's edge. You can savor good seafood at either the perennially popular **Happy Elephant** (© 07724-5347) or the elegant, antique-laden **Krua Bophut** ★ (© 07743-0030), toward the western end of the village, which serves delicious shrimp in tamarind sauce, and features traditional musicians some evenings. Vegetarians can head to the friendly, laid-back **Art Café** (© 089724-9673, cell), while carnivores will grunt with pleasure at the grilled steaks turned out at **The Shack** (© 08726-46994, cell), which describes itself as a "jazz and blues barbecue grill."

H Bistro ★★ MEDITERRANEAN/THAI   The signature restaurant at Hansar Samui, H Bistro is located right next to the beach with a breezy terrace and cozy interior. The decor is minimalist and so is the menu, though there are plenty of tempting options. I recommend the Manila clam and potato soup starter—it's a great combination of tastiness and texture. Follow with poached snowfish and chickpeas purée, or the pork loin wrapped in Parma ham, but try to save space for the deadly chocolate rosemary cake.

Hansar Samui, 101/28 Moo 1, Bophut. © **07724-5511.** www.hansarsamui.com/hbistro. Main courses 260B–1,650B. MC, V. Daily 11:30am–3pm and 6–11pm.

The Pier ★★ 🍴 FRENCH/INTERNATIONAL/THAI   This well-known, fine French restaurant sits in Fisherman's Village overlooking the sea. Famous not only for its food but also for its romantic atmosphere, the place is run by an experienced Franco-Belgian couple who go to great lengths to please all palates; the menu offers monthly specials to cater to the oft-returning expatriate clientele. For a starter, try the king shrimp *a la plancha*, followed by salmon with balsamic ginger sauce. Don't scrimp on dessert: Try the rich chocolate mousse or crème brûlée.

50 Moo 1, Tambon Bophut. © **07743-0681.** www.thepier-samui.com. Main courses 280B–1,950B. MC, V. Daily 11am–midnight.

CHAWENG

Chaweng is lined with eateries, with everything from McDonald's to the finest dining (the best of which are below). Increasingly, larger resorts in the area are setting up free-standing restaurants for both in-house and outside guests. **Poppies** (✆ **07742-2419**; www.poppiessamui.com), on South Chaweng, is famous for its beachside dining, Balinese fare, and romantic atmosphere, and brings in guest chefs from around the world. Reservations are recommended. Look out also for the highly recommended **Red Snapper** (at the Chaweng Regent; www.redsnapperbarandgrill.com), which serves up not only great Mediterranean fusion food, but also live jazz nightly.

In addition to the places reviewed below, it's worth dropping by for lunch or a sundowner at either **Dr Frog's** (✆ **07741-3797**; www.drfrogssamui.com) or **Bayview Restaurant** (✆ **07741-3540**), which sit on the hill between Chaweng and Lamai (Bayview is part of Best Western's Samui Bayview Resort). Both these restaurants are popular for their tasty Thai and Western food, but the real attraction is spectacular views over the bay.

Bear in mind that if you use any credit cards on Samui, your payments are often surcharged up to 5%.

Noori India ★ INDIAN This long-running family business is based right in the heart of Chaweng. Noori serves a variety of true Indian dishes, offering an alternative to those for whom Thai spices may be a little bit too piquant. The music and decor of traditional Indian artworks makes for a truly authentic experience. Go for the classic chicken tikka masala to play it safe, or for something different, try the Goan seafood curry.

17/1 Moo 2, Chaweng Beach Rd. ✆ **08674-07873** (cell) for reservations. www.nooriindiasamui.com. Main courses from 150B–350B. No credit cards. Daily 11am–11:30pm.

Prego ★★★ ITALIAN If you can't make up your mind where to dine, you could do much worse than just turn up at Prego (though I'd recommend reserving a table as it can get very busy) and trust that you'll leave contented. The large dining area is well laid-out so it never seems crowded. The extensive menu was created by the resident chef from Milan and includes wood-fired pizzas, a wide range of pastas and risottos, and several appealing main courses. If you're in the mood for seafood, try the egg fettuccine with Phuket lobster followed by the pan-fried snow fish medallion. If you can possibly manage it, finish off with the tiramisu *al caffe*, which is made with the chef's special recipe. The staff is accomplished at recommending wines to accompany dishes; in fact, the attentive and efficient service is one of the restaurant's main features.

Chaweng Beach (opposite the Amari Palm Reef). ✆ **07742-2015.** www.prego-samui.com. Main courses 200B–780B. MC, V. Daily 11am–11pm.

Zico's ★★ BRAZILIAN For a wild night out, this unique Brazilian-themed restaurant (part of the Centara Resort) is a riot of music, drink, and dance, with Brazilian performers shaking their tail feathers from table to table. Roving waiters, called *passadors*, come around with massive skewers of meat and trays of delicacies (you can also choose from the extensive salad bar). For a set price, you pick what you like, and as much as you like, by laying a small coin on the table with the green side up for "More please," and the red side up for "Enough for now." It's quite an experience.

38/2 Moo 3, Chaweng Beach (on the south end of Chaweng across from the Centara Resort). ✆ **07723-1560.** www.zicossamui.com. 790B for an unlimited buffet. MC, V. Daily 6–10:30pm. Dance shows at 8, 9, and 10pm.

LAMAI

Radiance ★★ VEGETARIAN   This restaurant at the Spa Resort (p. 191) is not just for veggies (they serve a few seafood and chicken dishes as well), but for anyone who'd like to get away from Big Macs and enjoy a healthy, tasty dish made almost entirely from organic fare. Open from breakfast time for its house guests, it serves up yummy smoothies, Mexican snacks, an amazing variety of great tofu dishes (the tofu burgers are huge), and delicious curries—along with excellent Thai fare. If you can, plan to arrive a few hours in advance to take advantage of the herbal steam and massage facilities at the Health Center here.

Rte. 4169, at the north end of Lamai beach. ✆ **07723-0855.** www.thesparesorts.net. Reservations recommended in peak season. Main courses 70B–280B. MC, V. Daily 7am–10pm.

WEST COAST

Big John Seafood ★ SEAFOOD   This is worth the ride across the island—to Lipa Noi—especially if you like fresh seafood. Although the atmosphere is a mix of raucous revelry and Thai families out to graze, this has become a longtime popular spot, with great sunset views. Order the day's catch as you like, and accompany it with a delicate Thai curry or stir-fry. Big John overlooks a pretty stretch of palm-lined beach.

The Lipa Lovely Resort, 95/4 Moo 2, Lipa Noi Beach. ✆ **07748-5676.** www.thelipa.com. Seafood priced by kg. No credit cards. Daily 7am–11pm.

Jahn ★★★ THAI/INTERNATIONAL   Unless you're lucky enough to be staying at the Conrad Samui, getting to this restaurant is quite an adventure and requires some preparation (as well as a reservation), but boy is it worth it! Executive Sous Chef Joe Diaz has worked in some of the world's top restaurants, including *El Bulli* in Spain, and he puts his talents to great use here, creating a menu that reflects his flair and imagination. The Wagyu beef with massaman curry sauce is a culinary masterpiece, and is perfectly accompanied by a glass of Kanonkop Pinotage 2007 from South Africa, as recommended by the restaurant's wine sommelier. Desserts are to die for too–I recommend the coconut crème brûlée, which just melts in the mouth. There are also superb sunset views if you arrive around opening time.

Conrad Samui, 49/8–9 Moo 4, Hillcrest Rd., Tambon Taling Ngam, Ko Samui 84140. ✆ **07791-5888.** http://conradhotels1.hilton.com. Main courses 1,100B–1,800B. AE, DC, MC, V. Daily 6–11pm (last orders 10pm).

Exploring Ko Samui

SCUBA & SNORKELING

Local dive shops can offer advice on sites around Samui, and, more importantly, know local prevailing conditions (the open water around Samui can be notoriously wild). Many shops are attached to PADI dive schools offering trips ranging farther afield to some of the 80 or so islands scattered across this archipelago. **Ang Thong Marine National Park** (with 40 islands) makes a great destination from Samui, for either diving or a day's sightseeing. The few shops listed below are good options among the many on the island. *Note:* There is a **decompression chamber** on Samui; call ✆ **07742-7427** for info; if there's no response, try their 24-hour hot line at **08108-19555** (cell).

   Planet Scuba (opposite Coyote Bar, Chaweng Beach; ✆ **07741-3050;** www. planetscuba.net) is a good bet for full services. **Easy Divers,** open since 1987, has locations in Chaweng (© **07741-3373;** www.easydivers-thailand.com) and at other beaches, and offers good deals for beginners. Both outfits offer all sorts of PADI courses and daily dive tours, and have international safety standard boats, good equipment, and complete insurance packages. Daily dives (two dives per day) start from about 4,000B per person including land transportation, breakfast, equipment, lunch, and drinks.

Big Blue (© **07745-6415;** www.bigbluediving.com), based on Ko Tao, provides trips for divers of any skill level and is a good choice for small groups or those seeking private attention.

Some of the better **snorkeling** off Ko Samui is found along the rocky coast between Chaweng Noi and Lamai bays. Several shops along Chaweng Beach rent snorkeling gear for about 200B per day.

GOLF

Samui boasts the picturesque hilltop Santiburi Golf Course, part of the Santiburi Samui Country Club (12/15 Moo 4, Baan Dansai, Mae Nam; © **07742-1700;** www.santiburi.com). It sits high in the hills on the north end of the island. Greens fees start from 3,350B for 18 holes. Opposite the turnoff to Fisherman's Village, the **Bophut Hills Golf Club** (© **07743-0811**) offers a more affordable option for golfers on a par-27, 9-hole course and costs 875B (greens fee only), 1,475B (including club rental and caddy), or 1,700B including hotel transfer. If you feel that you haven't gotten the swing just yet, the game of **football golf** needs no special skills, or even clubs; it's as it sounds, a matter of kicking a soccer ball into the holes. Just north of Chaweng, in Choeng Mon, the course at **Samui Football Golf** (© **07724-8084;** www.samuifootballgolf.com) is set under swaying palms.

KAYAKING

Blue Stars Sea Kayaking at 83/23 Moo 2, Chaweng Lake Road. (© **07741-3231;** www.bluestars.info) takes people kayaking and snorkeling to the Marine National Park at 2,200B for adults, 1,400B for children. The rubber canoes are perfect for exploring the caverns underneath limestone cliffs. If you can't get to Phang Nga Bay near Phuket (which has the most fantastic sea cave scenery), this trip is another fun option. Alternatively, try **Samui Island Tour** (© **07742-1382;** www.samui-islandtour.com).

CRUISING, SAILING, & KITEBOARDING

Short cruises can be taken on a stunning **Chinese junk,** *Chantara* (© **08706-43126** cell; www.jonque-fortune.com), which operates from Fisherman's Village, on Boput Beach, accommodates up to 10 people (or wedding parties), and offers trips from a day to a week. Onboard activities include diving, snorkeling, fishing, and island trekking. **Easy Charter** (© **08726-32323** cell; www.easy-charters.com) has a traditional Indonesian **wooden ketch,** *Kaisso Kaia,* for sunset and day (or longer) luxury cruising.

For **catamaran** or **yacht sailing,** check out **Sailing Samui,** in Chaweng (© **08363-30365** cell; www.sailingkohsamui.com). There's now a growing bunch of **kiteboarders** descending on Samui in the peak season (Nov–Mar); more information can be found on such sites as **www.kiteboardingasia.com.** Their main center is based at the Samui Orchid Resort & Aquarium, on Laem Set Beach (www.samui orchid.com), in the island's southeast.

Cultural Activities

COOKING COURSES

For daily Thai cooking and fruit-carving lessons, try **Samui Institute of Thai Culinary Arts** (**SITCA; ✆ 07741-3172;** www.sitca.net), which is a professional operation with a friendly cooking school; it's a great way to have fun and meet others—especially if your beach plans get rained out. After the course, you can invite a guest to dine with you at a group meal. Classes meet daily at 11am and 4pm and cost 1,950B; they accept all major credit cards. Call for more details, or pop into the Institute on the Chaweng Beach strip, across from the Centara Grand Beach Resort (p. 187).

SPAS

Like many places in Thailand, the spa scene has really taken off on Samui. All the big, international five-star resorts, such as **Anantara** (p. 163), offer top-range (and top-priced) treatments by well-trained staff. But there are also some reasonably priced haunts too, including a number of good day spas for those wanting a serious and dedicated wellness retreat that won't leave them financially destitute. Whether as an escape from the kids on a rainy day or as part of a larger health-focused mission, Samui has all the services you'll need.

   Ban Sabai, on Big Buddha Beach (✆ **07724-5175;** www.ban-sabai.com), has a wide range of therapies that take place in one of two teak Thai houses or in a *sala* at the beach side. Personal attention is the hallmark in this little Garden of Eden. Two houses are available for booking as part of a package or simply as a relaxing accommodation. Treatments start around 1,200B for an hour's facial massage.

   Also on Big Buddha Beach, in the beautiful grounds of the Outrigger Resort, is the **Navasana Spa ★** (✆ **07741-7300**), one of Samui's newest spas with nine treatment rooms as well as a Jacuzzi and steam room. The therapists here really know their stuff and can confidently recommend treatments that are suitable for each guest. Perhaps the best news is that rates here are generally cheaper than at other top hotels, with a 90-minute Flow Massage costing just 2,200B.

   The highly respected day spa **Tamarind Springs ★★** (✆ **07723-0571;** www.tamarindsprings.com) is set on a palm-clad hillside just above the beach at Lamai and is a rare place that truly takes you back to nature. The natural herbal steam room sandwiched between huge, smooth boulders is awesome; after a few minutes, you'll savor slipping into the outdoor plunge pool. Make sure you book well in advance.

   Traditional massage is available at any number of storefronts in Chaweng and along the beach. Expect to pay between 200B and 400B per hour for services; it's much the same as the average spa, but without the pomp, ceremony, or incense.

Shopping

There is very little in terms of local craft production on the island—almost everything is imported from the mainland—so save the big purchases for Bangkok or Chiang Mai. New shopping areas are growing in number by the day, however, around Chaweng. **Pearls** are cultivated locally, and you'll see some good examples in the shops. Ask local tour operators about trips to **Naga Pearl Farm,** on **Ko Matsum.**

Ko Samui Entertainment & Nightlife

At any given time, the Chaweng strip is certain to be disrupted occasionally by roaming pickup trucks with crackling PA systems blaring out advertisements in Thai and English for local **Thai boxing bouts.** Grab a flyer for times and locations, which vary.

Many of Samui's hotels and resorts have cultural shows featuring Thai dance that can be magical. If you like sequins and glamour, Samui puts on some entertaining *katoey* (drag queen) shows as well. **Christy's Cabaret** (✆ 08194-0356) in Central Chaweng near Soi Green Mango puts on a gala extravaganza of high camp that's free of charge. Come well before the show starts at 11pm to get a good seat, and be prepared to make up for the free admission with a purchase of a cocktail.

For bars and discos, Chaweng is the place to be. There are classy clubs, such as the fashionable **Q Bar** (✆ 07796-2420) up on the hill, a little remote from the main center, which features international DJs. **Bar Solo** (✆ 07741-4012; www.barsolosamui.com), on the beachfront road in the center of Chaweng (next to Starbucks), is another popular hang-out; people tend to gather at Solo early for the happy hour before going on a walkabout to the bigger clubs like Green Mango (see below). If you need to chill out, the obvious place to head for is the **Ice Bar** (✆ 07748-4933; www.baricesamui.com), where the ambient temperature is a cool –7°C (19.4°F); don't worry—they'll hand you a cape, gloves, and hat to wear while you sip a cocktail from an ice glass and admire the ice sculptures of Buddha and tuk-tuks.

A somewhat dubious legend among a certain crowd in Chaweng is the nearby **Green Mango** (✆ 07742-2661; www.thegreenmangoclub.com), which bangs out cheesy house music while commercial sex workers cruise for foreign business. Irish-owned/managed **Tropical Murphy's,** across from McDonald's in south Chaweng (✆ 07741-3614; www.tropicalmurphys.com), is a slice of Ireland, with an authentic pub atmosphere, a full range of beers, and good tasty British grub. Live music on the upper floor boosts the ambience but doesn't hinder conversation.

Over at Lamai Beach, there's everything from beer bars of the sleazier variety to mud wrestling, lady Thai boxing, and a few decent music venues. **Fusion** (✆ 08137-07386 cell; www.fusionclubsamui.com), breaks the mold with acid jazz, funk, soul, and drum 'n' bass nights; and just behind Fusion at **Super Club,** decent DJs, a good drink selection, and professional dancers (not go-go girls) whip the crowd up into a frenzy till the small hours. Sports fans may be impressed by the gigantic screen that looms over the beer garden here. **Bauhaus** (✆ 07741-8387) has cheap drinks and holds foam parties and attracts soccer fans to its screens in high season.

If you'd like to steer clear of the seedy side of Samui, meaning the go-go bars, hostess bars and dodgy massage parlors, the solution is simple—take a stroll through **Fisherman's Village** on Bophut Beach, where you'll find any number of inviting restaurants and bars. Settle on to a bar stool in the **Frog & Gecko** (✆ 07742-5248), the **Crow's Nest** (✆ 08179-71193 cell), or the **Billabong Surf Club** (✆ 07743-0144) and sink a few cool ones while exchanging travel tales with total strangers.

Side Trips from Ko Samui

ANG THONG NATIONAL MARINE PARK ★★

Ang Thong National Marine Park comprises over 40 more islands northwest of Samui and is well known for its scenic beauty and coral reefs. Many of these islands are limestone rock towers of up to 40m (131 ft.), fringed by beaches and tropical rainforest.

Ko Wua Talab (Sleeping Cow Island) is the largest of the 40 and is home to the **National Park Headquarters,** where there is some very basic four- to eight-person accommodation (book through the park headquarters at ✆ **07728-6025,** or online at www.dnp.go.th), but most just visit for the day. The island has freshwater springs and a park-run restaurant. *Note:* Pack a pair of strong walking shoes for the steep hills; flip-flops won't be able to take the gradient.

Ko Mae Ko (Mother Island) is known for both its beach and Talay Noi, an **inland saltwater lake** with a hidden outlet to the sea (the inspiration behind the film *The Beach*). Known to the Thais as **Ang Thong,** or "Golden Bowl," this turquoise-green lagoon gave its name to the entire archipelago. Endless companies offer day trips by speedboat. Some include snorkeling and kayaking trips with a range of prices; **Blue Stars** (✆ **07741-3231;** www.bluestars.info), in Chaweng, is a good operator to try.

KO PHA NGAN ★

644km (400 miles) S of Bangkok to Surat Thani; 75km (47 miles) NE from Surat Thani to Ko Pha Ngan

Ko Pha Ngan is a more rustic alternative to busy and developed Ko Samui, attracting many backpackers in search of that well-used cliché, "island paradise." However, although Ko Pha Ngan still attracts an adventurous young crowd, it is following the same model of development as Samui and Phuket—once-basic bungalow resorts are turning into upmarket villas with air-conditioning and swimming pools. This, in turn, is forcing prices to increase.

Easily visible from Ko Samui but about two-thirds its size, with similar terrain and flora, Ko Pha Ngan boasts beautiful beaches and some secluded upmarket resorts on the farther reaches of the island—the rugged north and west coast areas are accessible only by bumpy road, or chartered boat. The southeastern peninsula of **Had Rin** (also written Haad Rin) is home to the now-infamous monthly **Full Moon Party,** a night-long beach rave that attracts thousands of revelers who pack the island to groove to every kind of dance music—and consume (and usually later regurgitate) buckets of alcohol. For those who can't make it for Full Moon, there are also (smaller)

Just Say "Mai!"

When it comes to doing drugs in Thailand, remember that "mai" means "no." Thai authorities issue harsh penalties to anyone dealing, in possession of, or using drugs. Numerous undercover drug busts are staged, not just at Full Moon parties, but at bungalow hotels, and at pre- and post-party roadblocks. Many of these stings are setups that you'll never be able to disprove. Dealers and police often work in cahoots, and the lackadaisical Thai legal system offers you no protection or parole. Even scarier, recent reports have highlighted not just the selling of dodgy pharmaceuticals but the lethal herbal hallucinogen *ton lamphong,* a poisonous weed. Taking this is nothing short of suicide. Every month, local hospitals repeatedly find themselves treating tourists suffering severe psychological damage after taking recreational drugs or hallucinogens—they are the lucky ones; some revelers simply go home in a body bag.

Half Moon and Black Moon parties—check out http://fullmoonparty-thailand.com for dates. These parties are not like the hippy, trippy, lovefests of the '70s, but blatantly commercial gigs geared to squeeze as much cash out of revved-up partygoers as possible. As evidence of this, there is now a 100B entrance fee to the Full Moon Party. At Full Moon, even the basic bungalows are going for double the normal rates. As a result, **Leela Beach,** on the northern spur, now pulls more punters than the noisier beach at Had Rin Nok (known as Sunrise Beach).

A word of warning: Party time is also a petty thief's paradise. Do yourself a favor and lock all your valuables in the hotel safe before you party—as experienced thieves take the opportunity to swoop on insecure accommodation while you're having fun.

Boats from Ko Samui leave at regular intervals all day and night on full moon nights from either Big Buddha Beach or Bophut (running from 5pm; returning between 3 and 8am). Many revelers just make a night of it, crash on the beach, and come back to Samui in the morning. At other times, the small area of Had Rin is busy with young travelers. You'll find New Age crystal, trinket, and T-shirt shops, vegetarian restaurants, bars playing DVDs, masseurs, cheap beer, and bungalows just a frisbee's throw away from perfect white-sand beaches. Be careful of the riptides here in monsoon months, and pay attention to the attendant lifeguards now present on the beach.

Don't be too put off by Ko Pha Ngan's party reputation. Had Rin can be avoided altogether and, even during the full moon, you can find peace and quiet in any of a number of tranquil hideaways on the island, such as **Thong Nai Pan,** to the north, and **Had Salad** or **Had Yao,** to the west. **Ko Ma** is a small island connected to Ko Pha Ngan by a sandbar on **Had Mae Had** beach. It's a paradise surrounded by an amazingly colorful, living reef—making it an ideal location for snorkeling or learning to dive.

Essentials

GETTING THERE

Frequent boats link the mainland towns of Chumphon or Surat Thani with the islands of Ko Samui, Ko Pha Ngan, or Ko Tao. From Samui's Nathon Pier, the trip to Thong Sala, in Ko Pha Ngan, takes 45 minutes with the **Songserm Express Boat** and costs 200B. Contact them at their local office (℡ 07742-0157). The **Seatran** ferry service (℡ 07723-8129) is twice daily, leaves from Big Buddha Beach, takes 30 minutes, and is slightly cheaper.

The fastest way to Ko Pha Ngan from Samui is by the twice-daily **Lomprayah Catamaran** (on Samui, ℡ 07742-7765; on Ko Pha Ngan, ℡ 07723-8412; www.lomprayah.com), which leaves from **Wat Na Phra Larn** on Maenam Beach. The crossing takes about 20 minutes and costs 300B. Lomprayah also makes daily connections on to Ko Tao and back to the mainland at Chumphon (but not to Surat Thani). The **Haad Rin Queen** also runs a service four times daily from Big Buddha beach directly to Had Rin Pier that takes 50 minutes for 200B. Boats can also be chartered from **Petcharat Marina** at Samui's Big Buddha Beach (℡ 07742-5262) or Bophut Beach (rates are greatly inflated during Full Moon parties). You'll also find getting back to the mainland much cheaper than getting to Pha Ngan, but beware bad weather between June and December, as freak storms have been known to put lives at risk.

FAST FACTS

The **tourist police** operate a small information kiosk on the north end of the ferry offices at Thong Sala pier; contact them at © **07737-7114** for info or 1155 in an emergency. There are branches of all the high street banks with **ATMs** both along the main street of Thong Sala and in Had Rin. **Internet** service is chock-full around the island, though prices are inflated—about 120B per hour. For more information about the island, visit www.phangan.info.

GETTING AROUND

Jeep and **motorbike rental** on Ko Pha Ngan is available at most tour companies and resorts across the island (basic jeeps run from 1,000B; regular motorbikes run from 200B per day). However, the island roads are steep and treacherous—especially over the hills near Had Rin—so this is really only an option if you are a very experienced driver/rider, and even then you should drive with extreme caution. Many interior roads, including the trek to secluded Thong Nai Pan in the north, are hilly, muddy tracks, requiring off-road skills. (It's not just the state of the roads, but also the inexperienced riders on the road, that are problematic.) Jazzed-up **scooters** are rented out for about 300B per day, but if you are not experienced in off-road biking, it's much safer to stick to **songtaews** (communal pickups), which follow the main routes and cost from 50B to 100B, more at night or during party season.

Exploring Ko Pha Ngan

The rugged roads of Ko Pha Ngan beg to be explored, and interior routes connect bays and small towns across unspoiled countryside—a window into a laid-back island lifestyle that's now slowly disappearing. **Wat Khao Tham** is a well-known international meditation center and temple compound just north of Ban Tai; see www.watkowtahm.org for info. Since 1988, Steve and Rosemary Weissmann (from the U.S. and Australia, respectively) have been offering intensive Theravada Buddhism-based meditation retreats. Introductory 10 to 20-day courses, as well as 3-month work retreats, are open to anyone over 20 years of age, and prices start at 5,000B. As with any retreat, rules governing behavior apply, such as "No talking, reading, writing, or body sign language with others"; if this sounds a bit tough, best give it a miss. The temple is also open for day visitors and overlooks one of the most impressive views on the island. For more details, check the Web or write to Wat Kow Tahm, P.O. Box 18, Ko Pha Ngan, Surat Thani 84280.

Where to Stay

Visitors to Pha Ngan basically fall into two groups—those coming for the Full Moon Party and those trying to avoid it. Those in the former group inevitably look for somewhere around Had Rin, where the party takes place, and those in the latter group look for somewhere as far from Had Rin as possible. Note that at the time of the Full Moon Party, prices quoted below tend to increase by 50% or 100%, and many places have a minimum 4- or 5-night stay during this period.

BAN TAI BEACH

Many visitors head east from Thong Sala to nearby Ban Tai Beach—here they find a quiet stretch of sand away from the hubbub of Had Rin but close enough to visit the party zone and readily accessible by communal taxi (*songtaew*). The water, unfortunately, is not really deep enough for swimming, but the fine-sand beach is wide, and most resorts now have pools set on the beachfront. There is a range of accommodation on hand, from a few original fan bungalows to newly built complexes offering every amenity.

Coco Gardens ★   This place offers a choice of fan and air-con wooden bungalows with balconies, hammocks, and lots of character, and you won't find cheaper prices, which begin at 500B. If you really want to splash out, go for the recently renovated double beachfront bungalow at 1,250B. Most are set in a garden just a few steps from the beach, and there's a restaurant and bar as well. The helpful and friendly staff, combined with the attractive beachside location, lull many into extending their stay.

100/7, Moo 1, Ban Tai Beach, Ko Pha Ngan 84280. ✆ **07737-7721.** 20 units. 500B double with fan; 1,250B double with A/C. MC, V. **Amenities:** Restaurant; bar; Wi-Fi (free). *In room:* A/C in some.

Milky Bay Resort ★★   Friendly service and midrange luxury are on tap at this beautifully presented resort set in lush gardens with meandering paths to individual villas. Choose from five room types, each of which is different in style and creature comforts; rates vary according to low, high, and peak seasons (the rates below just give an idea of the huge range). Most rooms are bright and spacious, apart from standard rooms, which are little more than a shoebox. Next to the stunning oceanfront pool, the restaurant serves delicious BBQ, Thai, and Italian food (you'll even find a proper pizza oven) and overlooks a white-sand beach lapped by the sea. A couple of pool tables will keep some guests happy, while others can indulge in a wonderful Thai massage. The fitness room and steam room come at no extra charge. You can request a pickup from the ferry pier.

103/4 Moo 1, Ban Tai Beach, Ko Pha Ngan 84280 (6½km/4 miles east of Thong Sala). www.milkybay thailand.com. ✆ **07723-8566.** Fax 07737-7726. 34 units. 2,700B standard; 3,900B superior; 8,900B beachfront studio. MC, V. **Amenities:** Restaurant; bar; outdoor pool; exercise room; steam room. *In room:* A/C, TV/DVD, minibar, Wi-Fi (free).

HAD RIN & THE EAST COAST

Had Rin (aka Haad Rin), is a narrow peninsula on the island's southeastern tip filled with bungalows, busy shopping streets, funky clothes shops, and an array of restaurants between east-facing Had Rin Nok (Sunrise Beach, where the Full Moon Party is held) and Had Rin Nai (Sunset Beach) on the west side. Check out the popular **Rin Bay View Bungalow** (✆ 07737-5188), with smart, clean bungalows from 500B to 1,000B.

If you wish to transcend it all, tucked away on the soft white-sand beach of **Leela** (or Had Seekantang) Beach, just 5 minutes over the hilltop, is **Cocohut Village** (www. cocohut.com; ✆ 07737-5368). Spacious bungalows of all sizes start at 2,600B. Next door, the stylish **Sarikantang** ★★ (www.sarikantang.com; ✆ 07737-5055-7) has beautifully designed and well-equipped rooms that range from 1,700B to 5,400B. Both places have beachside restaurants and pools, and are just far enough from town for a bit of peace and quiet, but are close enough to walk down and join the festivities. The original **Leela Bungalows** (✆ 07737-5094), in front of a lovely stretch of white-sand beach, offers rustic bungalows, some with fan and cold water and others with air-con and hot water. **Lighthouse** (http://lighthousebungalows.com; ✆ 07737-5075) has secluded bungalows set around the rocky cape hillside, accessible by a wooden bridge. Rates for both Leela and the Lighthouse start at around 350B.

Sea Breeze Resort (94/11 Moo 6, Had Rin; ℂ **07737-5162**) also offers a quiet, lofty perch high enough above town, yet it is close enough to walk down and join the fun. Rooms are all air-conditioned and vary from simple standard (1,800B) to imperial Jacuzzi suites (8,000B), though prepare to pay more at party time. There's a hilltop pool with a bar, a wooden boardwalk, and a rickety stairway that provides access to Seekantang Beach.

Drop Inn Club Resort and Spa (154/1–10 Had Rin; www.dropinclubresortand spa.com; ℂ **07737-5444**) is a resort made up of elegant Thai-style houses clustered around a pool. Prices range from 1,715B for a standard economy room to 4,515B for a Jacuzzi villa.

Centara Pariya Resort & Villas ★ This place claims to be the island's first boutique resort, and there's no denying it's an exclusive little hideaway, with a clutch of smart rooms and villas that cater to the better-heeled traveler. The resort lies on the increasingly popular and totally gorgeous Had Yuan (Yuan Beach) in the east. Being accessible only by boat has guarded it against the crowds, but it won't be long before it becomes a well-known spot. The style is modern-rustic and comes with the kind of modern amenities that would have been unheard of in this neck of the woods 10 years ago.

152/2 Moo 6, Ban Tai, Had Yuan, Ko Pha Ngan. www.centarahotelsresorts.com. ℂ **08173-73883** (cell). 39 units. 6,000B–7,000B double. AE, MC, V. **Amenities:** Restaurant; bar; outdoor pool and kids' pool; spa; watersports center. In room: A/C, TV, minibar, hair dryer, Wi-Fi (1,200B per day).

The Sanctuary Resort & Spa ★★ Hidden behind trees on Had Thien, just a short boat ride to the north of Had Rin, the Sanctuary bills itself as alternative—and it certainly is, with a dazzling range of wellness, dance, and meditative activities and courses, as well as colonic treatments at its adjacent **Wellness & Detox Center.** As much as its yoga, massage, and cleansing programs, the main draw is its tranquillity, and there are plenty of beach activities, too. Choose from simple low-cost dorms and yogi rooms to houses tucked away in the jungle. It's a stark (and perhaps much needed) contrast to the endless nights of overindulgence at Had Rin.

Note: Not all rooms can be booked in advance; dorms and bungalows are on a first-come, first-served basis. If coming from Ko Samui, the Thong Nai Pan ferry departs from Mae Nam pier every day at noon (Jan–Oct) and brings you directly to Had Thien on its way.

Had Thien, Ko Pha Ngan. www.thesanctuarythailand.com. ℂ **08127-13614** (cell). 48 units. From 200B dorm; 450B–1,600B bungalows (some with en suite bathroom); 3,350B–4,050 suites; 1,500B–5,400B houses. No credit cards. **Amenities:** Restaurant; bar; spa; watersports rentals; Wi-Fi (free). In room: A/C (in some), TV, fridge, no phone.

WEST & NORTH COAST

Both the west and north coast have white-sand beaches and are far from the monthly hippy hoedown at Had Rin, which might be a relief for many. Resorts here are quiet and affordable, and growing in number and quality of attractions. The beautifully tranquil Laem Son freshwater lake lies close to Ao Chao Phao, but it's on the site of a former tin mine and is thought to be toxic, so don't try swimming there. The resorts below follow a clockwise route starting at Had Chaophao on the west.

Had Chaophao

Seaflower Bungalows ★ 🍴 Located just 10 minutes west of Thong Sala, Seaflower has a wide range of rooms, from very simple, fan-cooled bungalows to air-conditioned, beachfront suites. All rooms have a generous balcony on which to enjoy the sea breezes. There's a decent restaurant and bar, plus a scuba diving office and kayak rentals.

Had Chaophao, Ko Pha Ngan. www.seaflowerbungalows.com. ℂ **07734-9090.** 20 units. 500B fan-cooled bungalow; 1,000B A/C bungalow; 2,600B beachfront suite. No credit cards. **Amenities:** Restaurant; bar; kayak rentals; motorbike/jeep rental; scuba diving office. *In room:* A/C (in some), Wi-Fi (free).

Had Son

Haad Son Resort ★   This place is a great find, on its own secluded sandy beach over from Had Yao, with good hilltop views of the sea. Some of the rooms are in two-story villas and the others are thatched, lakeside villas; all rooms are comfortably equipped and well-spaced. It's a family friendly place with a big pool as well as a children's pool; kayaks and mountain bikes can be rented.

Had Son Beach, Ko Pha Ngan. www.haadson.net. ℂ **07734-9103-4.** 57 units. 1,700B–2,550B villa; 6,500B penthouse suite. MC, V. **Amenities:** Restaurant; bar; 2 outdoor pools; kayak rentals. *In room:* A/C, TV, minibar, Wi-Fi in some (free).

Had Yao ★★

Had Yao, or Long Beach, is considered by many to be a perfect beach, a quiet but huge stretch of white sand, good for swimming, with the same beautiful sunset views and a laid-back vibe that drew the first travelers here. Supermarkets and Internet cafes up on the main road provide the bulk of services you'll need; good eats can also be found along the beach—it's big enough to play soccer on.

There are several bungalow resorts ranging from very basic choices, such as the rough-and-ready **Ibiza** (www.ibizabungalow.resort.com; ℂ **07734-9121**), starting at 150B for fan rooms with a shared bathroom, to classier places like **Sandy Bay Bungalows** (www.sandybaybungalows.com; ℂ **07734-9119**), with everything from fan-cooled, gardenview bungalows at 700B to beachfront villas for 5,000B. However, for its combination of great service, good-value rooms and excellent restaurant, **Shiralea Backpackers Resort ★** (www.shiralea.com; ℂ **07734-9217**) is the pick of the bunch. Choose from fan-cooled rooms at 600B or air-con rooms at 1,200B; all have thatched roofs, are raised on stilts, and have balconies with hammocks.

Had Salad

This beautiful and secluded sandy beach used to be a pirates' hideout and is good for swimming (Nov–Apr), with a reef about 150m (492 ft.) offshore that is a well-known dive site.

Salad Beach Resort ★   Like Salad Hut, this place is also good value though it's more of a hotel style with half the rooms in one big block. Bungalow rooms feature stylish sleeping areas and designer bathrooms. There's a huge sun deck facing out to sea where you can relax on sun loungers or indulge in a massage treatment. Thankfully, the sometimes less-than-helpful staff does not detract from the otherwise beautiful setting.

Had Salad, Ko Pha Ngan 84280 (on the far northwest of the island, about 16km/10 miles north of the ferry). www.saladbeachphangan.com. ℂ **07734-9274.** 50 units. 1,870B superior; from 2,543B bungalow. MC, V. **Amenities:** Restaurant; bar; outdoor pool; watersports equipment. *In room:* A/C, TV, minibar, fridge, Wi-Fi (free).

Salad Hut ★★ 🍃 ☺   There are just a dozen "huts" here, all within a few steps of the beach. They're not exactly luxurious but all have touches of style and at the going rates they are excellent value. All but the cheapest cottages have air-con and all have large verandas, while the two modern, beachfront family villas have two bedrooms and a huge deck overlooking the beach. There's also an infinity pool, a welcoming beachfront restaurant and bar, a library, pool table, Wi-Fi corner, and shop renting snorkeling gear and kayaks. With a good-natured and helpful staff, what more could you ask?

61/3 Moo 3, Had Salad, Ko Pha Ngan 84280 (on the far northwest of the island, about 16km/10 miles north of the ferry). www.saladhut.com. ✆ **07734-9246.** 12 units. 1,900B–3,500B cottage; 4,500B 2-bed family villa. MC, V. **Amenities:** Restaurant; bar; outdoor pool; watersports equipment rental. *In room:* A/C (in most), TV, minibar, Wi-Fi (1B per minute).

NORTHEAST/AO THONG NAI PAN

Two adjoining crescent-shaped beaches, 17km (11 miles) north of Had Rin, are differentiated by the suffix *yai* (big) and *noi* (small). This secluded paradise is home to the island's most upmarket resorts and is easily reached by rented boat, or less easily by bumpy dirt track. **Thong Nai Pan Yai** is quieter, while **Thong Nai Pan Noi** has a more bohemian vibe and a small village with some cool bars and restaurants.

Anantara Rasananda ★★★ The most recent luxury resort to open on this secluded bay, the Anantara is trying to outdo the opposition with its enormous pool suites, which vary in size, and like most Anantara resorts, successfully fuse traditional Thai design with modern architecture. Privacy is paramount here and all guests can feel completely away from it all in their cozy cocoons. Fancy touches like iPod docking stations and espresso machines assure guests will not lack for anything, and the in-room bar with complementary spirits in local decanters is a spark of genius. As you'd expect from Anantara, spa facilities are top-notch and the restaurant offers a warm ambience and great cuisine.

5/5 Moo 5, Ao Thong Nai Pan Noi, Ko Pha Ngan 84280. www.phangan-rasananda.anantara.com. ✆ **07723-9555.** Fax 07723-9559. 44 units. From 16,400B pool suites; from 21,100B pool villas. AE, MC, V. **Amenities:** Restaurant; bar; outdoor pool; water sports facilities. *In room:* A/C, TV/DVD, bar with complementary spirits, MP3 docking station, Wi-Fi (free).

Panviman ★★★ The Panviman has got everything you need for a good hideaway vacation. Designed for sophisticated travelers craving tranquillity and natural beauty, this sprawling resort's luxury cottages are scattered over the hillside above Thong Nai Pan Beach. Rooms are set on a hill with stunning views across the bay, surrounded by tropical plants and shaded by swaying coconut palms. Service is of a high standard with most staff members speaking good English. The pool is a multi-tiered affair, with views of the bay below. You're a long hike from the hilltop to the beach, but they have convenient shuttles, and their upscale dining options mean you never have to leave home to find great food.

22/1 Moo 5, Ao Thong Nai Pan Noi, Ko Pha Ngan 84280. www.panviman.com. ✆ **07744-5101.** Fax 07744-5100. 72 units. 10,500B–12,500B superior and deluxe hotel rooms; 11,500B–14,500B cottages; 24,000B spa villas; 30,000B presidential suite. MC, V. **Amenities:** 3 restaurants; 2 bars; outdoor pool; Jacuzzi; watersports rental; room service. *In room:* A/C, TV, minibar, fridge, hair dryer, Jacuzzi (in some), Wi-Fi (300B per day).

Santhiya Resort & Spa ★★★ The teakwood villas that sprawl across 7.2 hectares (18 acres) of prime beachside property offer every luxury to its pampered guests, and along with near-neighbors Panviman and Anantara Rasananda, this resort provides the top accommodation option on Ko Pha Ngan. All rooms are huge and enjoy fabulous views of the bay, while the top-end villas feature private pools. The

Ayurvana Spa is the perfect place to while away an afternoon after an exhausting swim in the 1,200-sq.-m. (12,917-sq.-ft.) pool; and the terrace of the Chantara Restaurant is ideal for a delicious Thai dinner. As a member of the Small Luxury Hotels of the World, you can depend on impeccable service, too.

22/7 Banthai, Ko Pha Ngan 84280. www.santhiya.com. © **07742-8999.** Fax 07742-8900. 99 units. 12,000B deluxe room; 16,000B seaview villa suite; 50,000B royal pool villa suite. MC, V. **Amenities:** Restaurant; 2 bars; huge outdoor pool; health club; spa; watersports equipment; room service. *In room:* A/C, TV/DVD, minibar, hair dryer, CD player, Wi-Fi (free).

Where to Eat

There are no outstanding dining venues on Ko Pha Ngan, though as most people come here to chill out, they end up settling for whatever their resort offers. Cheap eats of every type abound in busy Had Rin and, increasingly, even in the smaller villages here. Note that most restaurants here use cell numbers, not landlines.

Serving up all kinds of tasty seafood treats, **Fisherman's** (© 08445-47240) is located by the pier on Ban Thai Beach. They also mix a mean fruit shake. Near the pier on Had Rin Nai, **Om Ganesh** (© 07737-5123) serves up authentic curries and all-you-can-eat Indian *thali* meals, but it's very popular—so do book ahead. The Italian restaurant **Kimera** (no phone), on the beach road, serves delicious pizzas. Also on the beach road in Had Rin, don't miss **Emotion of Sushi** for fresh sushi and **Bamboozle** for Mexican delights.

For a special occasion, try **Me'n'u,** over near Ao Hin Kong, on the coastal road north of Thong Sala (© 089289-7133, cell). It's open for dinner only and closed on Mondays. In Had Yao, check out the two-story **Eagle Pub** (no phone), built into the rocks at the southern end of the beach; it's a cool nightspot, with a steakhouse and DJs playing tunes to suit every mood.

KO TAO ★

55km (34 miles) N of Ko Samui; 80km (50 miles) SE of Chumphon

Some 75 years ago, tiny **Ko Tao,** or **Turtle Island**—so-named for its outline and resident marine life—was a penitentiary for insurgents, though few visitors these days would find any punishment in being marooned on its idyllic shores. Until lately, it has been known almost exclusively as a destination for divers. With the arrival of some chic new resorts recently, the island's appeal is far wider and, in turn, the island is rapidly moving upmarket. Though dive resorts (and a social scene based around the local diving expats) do dominate, there are still lots of rustic budget choices, as well as the sort of secluded high-end hideaways that won't oblige you to book a dive.

As its popularity grows, power outages become more frequent and, each high season, the island suffers from a scarcity of water. Nonetheless, it is blessed with pretty offshore isles, clear turquoise waters, and pristine coral reefs. Nestled in secluded bays are numerous stunning resorts, reached by boat, or by a roller coaster ride in a jeep or four-wheel drive. Just off the northwest corner lies a trio of islets known as **Ko Nang Yuan** or **Ko Hang Tao** (Turtle's Tail). **Had Sai Ree** and **Ban Mae Had,** both on the west coast, form the main centers, where you'll find most of the budget accommodation and dive resorts. There are excellent restaurants, some fun bars, and Internet cafes along this long shore, and there are plenty of funky boutiques and trendy shops over at the **Sairee Shopping Center.**

As many properties here don't have landlines, you should instead head to the useful website www.kohtaoonline.com. It offers an Internet booking service as well as lots of up-to-date info on island life, boat timetables, dive packages, and environmental concerns.

Essentials

GETTING THERE

Songserm Express (in Ko Tao; ✆ 07745-6274) boats leave from Surat Thani and connect nearby islands; fares from Ko Samui are 500B, fares from Ko Pha Ngan are 300B, plus there's a daily morning boat from Chumphon leaving at 7am for 450B. Boats run subject to weather conditions in monsoon season.

Lomprayah High Speed Catamarans (✆ 07745-6176 local office; www.lomprayah.com) also makes the connection from Samui, via Ko Pha Ngan, and onto Chumphon twice daily: From Chumphon the fare is 600B; from Ko Samui, 600B; and from Ko Pha Ngan, 450B. There are also night boats from Surat Thani and Chumphon with basic sleeping accommodation.

Caution: The south and western beaches can get blasted by the monsoon winds June through October, when the normally transparent seas get churned up; but even during November to January (high season), there can be squalls. If you have an onward flight to catch, reserve an extra day or two, in case of delays.

ORIENTATION & GETTING AROUND

All boats arrive in **Ban Mae Had** on the west of the island. Touts from resorts and scuba operators alike line the quay. (As long as it's not high season, and you can be flexible, you can find good deals by bargaining here.) A single concrete road connects the northwestern tip of the island to **Ban Had Sai Ree** and heads south (with the island's longest beach running parallel) through **Ban Mae Had** to **Ao Chalok Ban Kao,** but elsewhere the roads are steep, loose dirt tracks, most of which are very challenging. It's possible to walk over the headlands (just be mindful of the occasional dropping coconut). Pickups and motorbike taxis (prices vary from 20B–300B) are easy to find in Mae Had or by the pier, but difficult to find elsewhere. Taxi prices are not fixed, and fares tend to double after dark. Make sure you negotiate an acceptable fare before setting out.

Scooters can be rented for upward of 200B per day from most resorts; it's a good idea not to hire bikes from the cowboys around the pier. If you are looking at car hire, beware that some companies charge outrageously for damages.

More remote bays, such as the eastern bays of **Ao Leuk, Ao Ta Note,** and **Ao Hin Wong,** are reachable by four-wheel-drive or boat, but most high-end resorts there can simply arrange pickup.

Where to Stay

EXPENSIVE/MODERATE

Charm Churee Villa ★★ These rustic lodgings sit on a forested hill atop a secluded cove, just a 10-minute walk from Ban Mae Had. The resort covers an enormous 120 acres (48 hectares) of hillside and beachside jungle, with some massive, smooth boulders giving the place a distinctive character. Every room is uniquely designed, with magnificent sea views; and the private cove is a great spot to explore the surrounding blue waters with a snorkel and mask. Chaba Seafood restaurant here is known as one of the best in the area.

30/1 Moo 2, Jansom Bay (just south of the ferry landings at Ban Mae Had), Ko Tao 84360. www. charmchureevilla.com. ☏ **08134-65657** (cell). 30 units. 5,700B–10,400B double; from 8,700B cottage or suite. MC, V. **Amenities:** 3 restaurants; bar; spa; cafe. *In room:* A/C, TV, minibar, fridge, Wi-Fi (100B per hour).

Jamahkiri Spa & Resort ★★★   Perhaps the island's most upmarket resort, the awesomely designed Jamahkiri is accessible by precipitous mountain track that might make you reconsider the return trip. The good news is that you might not mind being stranded at this unique boutique gem. Overlooking the bay are a clutch of gray-tile and glass pavilions and suites; some are duplex, but all have oceanview balconies. There is a top-notch spa area and fine dining outlet; public areas are grand, with pleasant nooks but lots of steep steps. Though it's far from the action, this is undoubtedly the most extravagant option on the island.

Ao Thian Ok, on the southern end of the island. www.jamahkiri.com. ☏ **07745-6400.** 20 units. 3,900B deluxe room; 6,900B–8,900B deluxe and pavilion; 10,900B–25,000B suite. MC, V. **Amenities:** Restaurant; bar; outdoor pool; exercise room; spa; babysitting. *In room:* A/C, TV/DVD, minibar, fridge, hair dryer, Wi-Fi (free).

Thipwimarn Resort ★★   Tiny, but utterly charming, this vertiginous cliffside boutique resort may not have that many bells and whistles, but is one of the most inviting places in the north. Thatched cottages with lots of steps and wood walkways teeter above the azure ocean. Superbly designed rooms are furnished with canopy beds, stunning Thai silks, and teak wood. The four suite types all offer glorious views of the Nang Yuan islets, while the sunset can be seen from either the huge balconies or the picture-perfect infinity pool. A spa with a Jacuzzi tops off this elegantly rustic, but nonetheless refined, gem. Book well in advance to secure a room; note that it closes during November.

16/7 Had Sai Ree (northern tip of Had Sai Ree), Ko Tao 84360. www.thipwimarnresort.com. ☏/fax **07745-6409** or 07745-6512. 11 units. 2,850B–5,400B double; 7,850B–11,600B suite; 14,250B pool villa. MC, V. **Amenities:** Restaurant; spa. *In room:* A/C, TV/DVD, minibar, fridge, Jacuzzi (in suite), Wi-Fi in some (free).

INEXPENSIVE

Had Sai Ree and **Mae Had Beach** both have a huge range of budget options available to walk-in guests, but many are booked through budget scuba packages—popular with long-stay guests who want to get more extensive scuba certification. On Mae Had Beach, one popular all-inclusive scuba resort is **Crystal Dive Resort** (☏ 07745-6106; www.crystaldive.com); rooms range from 600B to 1,500B.

   Sairee Cottages (☏ **07745-6126;** www.saireecottagediving.com) on Had Sai Ree is another popular dive resort, with rooms from 350B and a good restaurant, while **Simple Life** (☏ **07745-6142;** www.kohtaosimpleliferesort.com) is probably the most stylish of these cheap dive resorts; comfy bungalows with fans or air-conditioning run from 500B, and it has a popular bar.

Where to Eat

The choices for where to dine here are endless, as most resorts have their own inhouse dining facilities or fun bars. On Sai Ree Beach, **Chopper's Bar and Grill** (☏ 07745-6641) has a multilevel diner with big screen sports. On the same beach, look out for **Blue Wind Bakery,** a popular sandwich and breakfast stop, though they serve some Thai dishes too.

In Mae Had, there's **La Matta** (✆ **07745-6517**), for delicious Italian pizzas and a shot of good Italian espresso; **Café Del Sol** (✆ **07745-6578**), for great bruschetta and steaks (among many other goodies); and **Dirty Nelly's** (✆ **07745-6569**), down near the pier, a great place for pub grub and a pint of Irish beer.

Ko Tao Entertainment & Nightlife

Most of the action is right on Mae Had beach, where you'll find stacks of stylish retro bars, dance spots where international DJs spin their best sounds, and fire jugglers performing amid stunning sand sculptures. **Whitening** (✆ **07745-6199**) is a popular beachside bar perfect for cocktails and soothing sounds. Another fashionable drinking venue is **Dragon Bar** (✆ **07745-6423**), which has an unusually upscale vibe for Ban Mae Had.

Most big bars here also have dance floors; one of the best is at **Pure Beach Lounge** (www.project-32.com/pure), which is a great place to sprawl on beanbags while watching the sunset, before partying into the night.

Outdoor Activities

Known as one of the best diving areas in Thailand, Ko Tao is a great place to get a very affordable start with the sport or to advance on your levels. Responsible divers should check out the **Ko Tao Dive Operators' Club (DOC)**, which imposes a uniform code of conduct and safety standards on its members. Some to consider are:

o **Planet Scuba,** in Ban Mae Had (✆ **07745-6110;** www.planetscuba.net).
o **Easy Divers,** in Ban Mae Had (at the catamaran jetty; ✆ **07745-6010;** www.thaidive.com).
o **Scuba Junction,** on Sai Ree Beach (✆ **07745-6164;** www.scuba-junction.com).

Side Trips from Ko Tao

Local aquanauts agree that the best **scuba diving** in the region is off nearby **Ko Nang Yuan** (just off the northwest tip of Ko Tao), which benefits from deep water just offshore and great visibility. Ko Nang Yuan consists of three small islands joined by a spectacular sandbar. Because it's famed for its wonderful snorkeling, numerous companies offer day trips here. Look into unique dive-and-stay packages at **Nang Yuan Resort** (✆ **07745-6088-93;** www.nangyuan.com), uniquely set over the three islands, with rooms starting as low as 1,500B to plush family suites at around 14,000B.

THE FAR SOUTH & ON TO MALAYSIA

From Surat Thani south, Thailand slowly gives way to Malay culture, and Buddhism—predominant in the central and northern parts of the country—is replaced by Islam. Nakhon Si Thammarat is an ancient Buddhist city of note but often ignored by visitors from overseas. In the far south, Had Yai is a major transport hub and a destination popular with Malay and Singaporean sex tourists, where HIV rates are known to be extremely high; in 2000, a *Time* magazine report called it a boomtown "built on the sex trade." It's mostly a stopover for onward travel to or from Malaysia.

Note: The far south of Thailand has seen years of violence by separatist insurgents. Their attacks are becoming increasingly widespread but are aimed at any institution with government or Buddhist links. Few travelers pass Nakhon Si Thammarat, except those going on to Malaysia or to Singapore via Had Yai. Get abreast of events before traveling here.

Nakhon Si Thammarat

Nakhon Si Thammarat is one of the south's oldest cities, though it has a rather unappealing "new" town in addition to its more charming older quarters. It has long been a religious capital and stages some dazzling festivals. **Wat Phra Mahathat,** the town's 1,000-year-old main temple, houses some of the Buddha's relics in its large *chedi* brought from Sri Lanka, from where it is believed Theravada Buddhism came to Thailand; it's therefore an important place of pilgrimage for Thai Buddhists. This region is also the locus for traditional Thai shadow plays. **Ban Nang Thalung Suchart Subsin** (Mr. Subsin's House of Shadow Plays), at 6 Sri Thammasok, Soi 3 (✆ 07534-6394), makes for an interesting introduction to this art form. It's open from 9am to 5pm and admission is 50B.

Budget carrier **Nok Air** (✆ 1318; www.nokair.com) connects Nakhon Si Thammarat with Bangkok. All north–south trains make a stop at the main train station (✆ 07535-6364), and affordable minivans (which are the best way to travel in the south) can be arranged from any tour company. Southeast of the city, the **Twin Lotus Hotel,** 97/8 Phattanakan Rd. (✆ 07532-3777), is a high-rise block, providing comfortable rooms at 1,400B.

Had Yai

Known to travelers as the gateway to Malaysia and one of the bigger cities in Thailand, Had Yai is today a hotbed of political unrest. For some time now, it has been plagued with bouts of violence, regular pipe bombings, fatal attacks, and frequent murders of Buddhist monks, rubber workers, and schoolchildren. The situation is now extremely unstable. Its busy **Night Market** was once a highlight, but, these days, I recommend asking around if it's safe to visit. Still, the unspoiled beaches at nearby **Songkhla** (45 min. away) are a great escape from the urban sprawl of Had Yai. Famous for its seafood and the attractive island of Ko Yo, floating in the inland sea, this little isle is a cotton-weaving center, with a folklore museum and hiking paths. Had Yai is also the gateway to **Tarutao National Park,** a chain of 51 islands originally settled by sea gypsies, later used as prison colonies, and now a far-flung tropical island getaway. The jumping-off point for Tarutao is Ban Pak Bara, a port city reached by bus from Hat Yai. Check out the Department of National Parks' website (www.dnp.go.th) for information about staying there.

GETTING AROUND

Had Yai International Airport (airport code HDY), 9km (5⅔ miles) from downtown Had Yai, welcomes flights from Malaysia and Singapore frequently throughout the week via Silk Air, Malaysia Airlines, and some budget airlines, and there are domestic connections to Bangkok and Phuket. Check p. 369 for airline info.

Minibuses still make trips to the border at Pedang Besar and connect from other parts of the region, and long-distance buses connect with the **Bangkok Southern Bus Terminal** (✆ 02422-4444). Five trains depart daily from **Bangkok's Hua**

Lampong Station (℡ **02220-4334** or 1690) to Had Yai Junction, with connections on to Malaysia. The once-daily Singapore–Bangkok Express also stops at Had Yai.

Where to Stay

There are dozens of low- and midpriced hotels located near the railway station, most with air-conditioned rooms, and several tourist-class hotels with the usual amenities. The best on offer is the **Novotel Centara,** (3 Sanehanusom Rd.; www.novotel.com; ℡ **07435-2222**), with rooms from $65 a night. A slightly cheaper alternative is the **Hansa JB Hotel,** 99 Jootee-Ausom Rd., Had Yai (www.jbhotelhatyai.com; ℡ **07423-4301**), with rooms from 1,600B. Finally, the popular backpacker haunt, **Cathay Guest House,** 93/1 Niphat Uthit 2 Rd. (℡ **07424-3815**) has reasonable fan-cooled doubles from 200B.

SOUTHERN PENINSULA: THE WEST COAST & ISLANDS

9

The island of Phuket, linked by a causeway to peninsular Thailand, was one of Thailand's first tourist developments. Today, it's a perennially popular mass-tourism magnet. In the dry season (Nov–Mar), this coast is a great place to kick back on a soft-sand beach or to island-hop by ferry.

With its increasing wealth and popularity come less savory influences, however: Mafia activity and unscrupulous developers keen to earn a fast buck from the once-pristine environment are common, and there's now hardly a stretch of beach that isn't backed by a glut of resorts.

The province of **Krabi** has been a bit more eco-savvy than bolder, brassier Phuket and has long banned such beach activities as jet skis and parasailing, making it popular with crowds looking for nature, not nightlife. The province encompasses all the land east of **Phang Nga Bay,** including **Ko Phi Phi** and **Ko Lanta.** Close to Krabi town, **Ao Nang Beach** and **Railay** offer backdrops of dramatic limestone cliffs, powder-soft beaches, and high-end resorts. **Ko Phi Phi** is a popular venue for snorkeling and dive trips; however, the island's National Park designation (theoretically, meant to preserve its outstanding beauty) has been shamefully ignored. **Ko Lanta Yai,** better known as **Ko Lanta,** lies southeast of Krabi Town. Once home solely to Muslim fishing villages, it now boasts the whole gamut of resorts from budget to superluxe.

Right at the southernmost tip of Phuket is the idyllic isle of **Ko Racha** (sometimes called Ko Raja or Raya), with its jade-green seas. Northward is **Phang Nga Bay** with its glorious vistas of karst outcrops and, on the west coast, **Khao Lak,** the gateway to the **Similan** and **Surin Islands,** rated by many among the top 10 dive sites in the world. This coastline was worst hit by the tsunami in 2004, but reconstruction has been rapid and there are now few reminders of that tragic day. To the south, **Trang Province's** white-sand beaches, caves, and waterfalls make it one of Thailand's best-kept secrets.

During high season (Nov–Apr), bookings for all west coast resorts should be made well in advance; expect hefty surcharges across the Christmas and New Year weeks. This season is great for all watersports.

The Southern Peninsula: West Coast

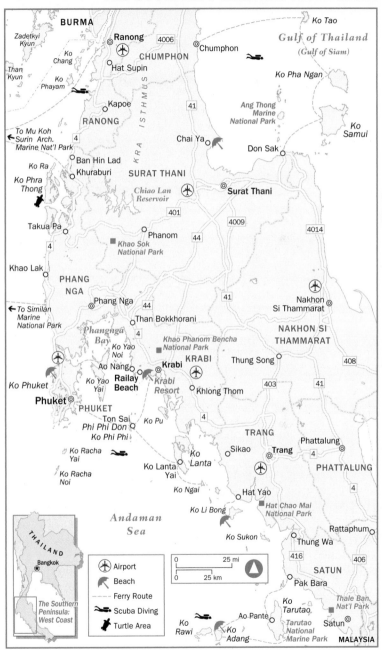

BURMA

Zadetkyi Kyun

Than Kyun

Ko Chang

Ko Phayam

Ranong

4006

CHUMPHON

Chumphon

Hat Supin

Ko Tao

Gulf of Thailand
(Gulf of Siam)

Ko Pha Ngan

Kapoe

RANONG

41

Ang Thong
Marine
National Park

Ko
Samui

To Mu Koh
Surin Arch.
Marine Nat'l Park

4

Chai Ya

Don Sak

Ko Ra

Ban Hin Lad

Khuraburi

SURAT THANI

Ko Phra
Thong

Chiao Lan
Reservoir

Surat Thani

Takua Pa

401

4

Phanom

44

4009

4014

Khao Sok
National Park

Khao Lak

PHANG
NGA

To Similan
Marine
National Park

Phang Nga

44

41

Nakhon
Si Thammarat

Than Bokkhorani

NAKHON SI
THAMMARAT

*Phangnga
Bay*

4

Khao Phanom Bencha
National Park

Ko Yao
Noi

Ao Nang

Krabi

Thung Song

408

Ko Phuket

Ko Yao
Yai

**Railay
Beach**

*Krabi
Resort*

KRABI

403

41

Phuket

PHUKET

Khlong Thom

Ton Sai
Phi Phi Don

Ko Pu

4

Ko Phi Phi

TRANG

Phattalung

Ko Racha
Yai

Sikao

Trang

4

Ko Racha
Noi

Ko Lanta
Yai

Ko
Lanta

PHATTALUNG

Ko Ngai

Hat Yao

Hat Chao Mai
National Park

*Andaman
Sea*

Ko Li Bong

Rattaphum

Ko Sukon

Thung Wa

416

406

SATUN

Pak Bara

Thale Ban
Nat'l Park

THAILAND

Bangkok

Ko
Tarutao

Ao Pante

*Tarutao
National
Marine Park*

Satun

The Southern
Peninsula:
West Coast

Ko
Rawi

Ko
Adang

MALAYSIA

Airport

Beach

Ferry Route

Scuba Diving

Turtle Area

0 ___ 25 mi
0 ___ 25 km

Many hotels offer discounts in the off-season, when heavy rains bring very strong winds and rough seas. Swimming becomes dangerous then, with heavy surf and a strong undertow, so pay attention to flags flown on beaches that indicate current safety levels. Islands in the eastern Gulf of Thailand (**Ko Samui, Ko Pha Ngan,** and **Ko Tao**) are more sheltered, and off-season discounts and fewer crowds make this region most appealing then.

GETTING TO KNOW PHUKET ★★

867km (539 miles) SW of Bangkok

The name "Phuket" is derived from the Malay word "Bukit" (meaning hill); true to the name, lush, green hills dominate much of the island's interior. There are still some rubber plantations and relics of the island's tin mining operations remaining. Most folks head west to the beaches; Phuket's are some of the best in Thailand. The ideal way to explore the island is by hiring a car (with or without driver) and taking a hair-raising drive along the cliff roads and through the island's interior. Activities on offer include a totally touristy "elephant safari" into the jungle, and an unforgettable sea kayak tour with John Gray, whose guided trips visit incredible offshore caves and limestone *hong* (literally "rooms"—hidden lagoons with sheer walls that become accessible at low tide).

In dry season, Phuket is at its optimum: You'll find long sandy beaches, warm water, snorkeling, and scuba diving. It also boasts some of the most delectable seafood in Thailand, not to mention some of the best international gourmet food available anywhere on the planet. Sure, its prices are more than a tad overblown, but for well-heeled fun-seekers who want to be at the heart of the action, Phuket is a fabulous choice.

Phuket does, however, have a downside: Tracts of hideous overdevelopment have spawned unsightly concrete bunkers patronized by budget tour groups from Asia, Russia, and Europe. Areas such as Patong, with its seedy commercial strip and sleazy nightlife, can be a bit much for families or single women travelers in search of tranquillity, but the presence of a swish shopping mall, JungCeylon, and a clutch of upmarket diners such as Baan Rim Pa and La Gritta, give this bustling beach resort a classy edge.

If escape at any cost is what you need, Phuket has heaps of elegant resorts designed for tropical solitude; an increasing number, such as Paresa and Anantara Villas, offer private villas and pools. Evason Phuket even offers a honeymoon villa on its own island, Ko Bon. Expect superlative facilities with levels of service beyond those in Europe. But with prices here way above those even in Bangkok, it's not suited to travelers on a tight budget. If you need to keep costs down, consider staying in Phuket Town, from where you could visit a different beach each day, or head south to more reasonable Trang.

Arriving

BY PLANE **Thai Airways** (✆ **02545-3691** domestic reservations in Bangkok; www.thaiair.com) flies daily from **Suvarnabhumi International Airport** (trip time: 1 hr. 20 min.). Thai Airways' office in Phuket is at 78 Ranong Rd. (✆ **07636-0444**).

Bangkok Airways (✆ **02270-6699** in Bangkok, or 07742-8500 on Ko Samui; www.bangkokair.com) connects Phuket with Ko Samui at least two times daily. The Bangkok Airways office in Phuket is at 158/2–3 Yaowarat Rd., Phuket Town (✆ **07622-5033,** or 07620-5401 at Phuket Airport).

Budget airlines flying here include **Air Asia** (✆ 02515-9999; www.airasia.com) and **Nok Air** (✆ 1318; www.nokair.com). Connecting with Singapore is **Silk Air** (✆ 07630-4020 in Phuket; www.silkair.com). Budget carriers **Tiger Airways** (✆ 80060-15637; www.tigerairways.com) and Qantas subsidiary **Jetstar** (✆ 02267-5125; www.jetstar.com) also have regular connections from Phuket to Singapore; Jetstar flies directly to Australia, too.

GETTING FROM THE AIRPORT TO TOWN The modern **Phuket International Airport** (✆ 07632-7230-7; www.phuketairportonline.com) is in the north of the island, about a 45-minute drive from Patong Beach in off-peak hours, or an hour in rush hour (8–9am and 4–7pm). There are banks, money-changing facilities, car-rental agents (see "Getting Around," below), and a post office at the airport. The **Phuket Tourist Business Association** booth there can help you make hotel arrangements if you need accommodation.

For a fee, most resorts will pick you up at the airport; check if this is included in your booking. An **airport bus** runs (approximately hourly until 6:30pm) to Phuket Town bus terminal and costs 85B, while a **minibus** service charges 150B to Phuket Town, 150B to Patong Beach, or 150B to Kata Beach. Just outside the terminal to the right is a **meter taxi** stand. You'll need to check the estimated price with the driver—based on how far you are going, plan on spending 600B to 800B. There is a ready supply on exiting the terminal. To book a meter taxi, call ✆ 08242-11644.

The airport **limousine** counter (✆ 07635-1347) offers many options for getting to your hotel from the airport. A prepaid **car** from the airport can also be arranged at the limousine counter; you'll pay around 500B to Phuket Town and 750B to Kata Beach.

BY BUS Three supercooled air-conditioned VIP buses leave daily from **Bangkok's Southern Bus Terminal** (✆ 02422-4444) and cost 927B. These buses feature fewer seats, more room, Arctic temperatures, a usually deafening all-night action movie, hostesses, and snacks. Numerous regular air-conditioned buses go each day and cost around 600B. Standard buses make frequent connections to Surat Thani and nearby towns on the mainland (to Surat is 5 hr. and about 160B).

The intercity bus terminal is at the **City Park Complex** on Phang Nga Road (✆ 07621-1977), east of Phuket Town, just opposite the Royal Phuket City Hotel. For information on how to get from here to the beaches, see "Getting Around," below.

BY MINIVAN Minivans to and from Surat Thani, Krabi, Nakhon Si Thammarat, Ranong, and other southern cities leave on regular schedules throughout the day. In each city, minivan operators work with the hotels and arrange free pickup, so it is best to book through your hotel front desk or a travel agent. Tickets to destinations in the south, to such places as Surat Thani or Had Yai, go for between 200B and 500B. *Note:* Operators of minivan companies rarely speak English.

Visitor Information

The **Tourism Authority of Thailand (TAT)** has an office in Phuket Town at 191 Thalang Rd. (✆ 07621-2213), but, in general, hotel concierge or independent tour desks offer more up-to-date information. There are lots of free maps on offer (financed by advertisements); for driving around the island, pick up the detailed *Map of Phuket* (Periplus Editions) at bookstores. Restaurants and hotel lobbies are good places to pick up any of a number of free local publications: *Phuket Food-Shopping-Entertainment* is packed with dining suggestions and ads for many of the island's

Phuket

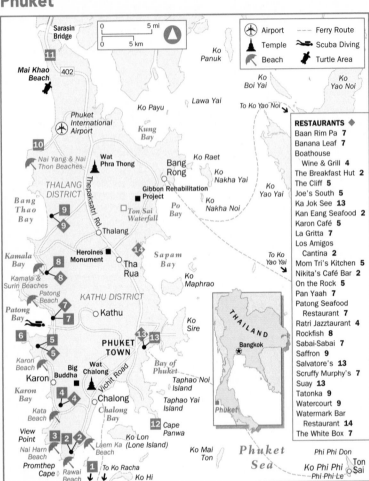

RESTAURANTS ◆
Baan Rim Pa **7**
Banana Leaf **7**
Boathouse
   Wine & Grill **4**
The Breakfast Hut **2**
The Cliff **5**
Joe's South **5**
Ka Jok See **13**
Kan Eang Seafood **2**
Karon Café **5**
La Gritta **7**
Los Amigos
   Cantina **2**
Mom Tri's Kitchen **5**
Nikita's Café Bar **2**
On the Rock **5**
Pan Yaah **7**
Patong Seafood
   Restaurant **7**
Ratri Jazztaurant **4**
Rockfish **8**
Sabai-Sabai **7**
Saffron **9**
Salvatore's **13**
Scruffy Murphy's **7**
Suay **13**
Tatonka **9**
Watercourt **9**
Watermark Bar
   Restaurant **14**
The White Box **7**

HOTELS ■
Amari Coral Beach Resort **7**
Anantara Phuket Villas **11**
Andaman Seaview Hotel **5**
Ayara Hilltops **8**
Baan Krating Phuket Resort **3**
Baan Oui Guest House **3**
Baan Suwantawe **13**
Banyan Tree Phuket **9**
Boathouse **4**
Burasari Resort **7**
Cape Panwa Hotel **12**
Centara Villas Phuket **5**
Dusit Thani Laguna Resort **9**
Evason Phuket & Bon Island **2**
Golden Sand Inn **5**

Golden Tulip Mangosteen Resort **2**
Hilton Phuket Arcadia Resort & Spa **5**
Holiday Inn Resort Phuket **7**
Indigo Pearl Resort **10**
JW Marriott Phuket Resort & Spa **11**
Karona Resort & Spa **5**
Karon Beach Resort **5**
Kata Country House **4**
Katanoi Resort **4**
Katathani Phuket Beach Resort **4**
Kelly's Hotel **7**
Le Meridien Phuket **6**
Marina Phuket **5**
Millennium Resort Patong, Phuket **7**
Mövenpick Resort & Spa **5**
Novotel Phuket **7**

Old Town Guesthouse **13**
Outrigger Resort & Villas **9**
Palmview Resort **7**
Paresa **8**
Phuket Pavilions **9**
The Racha **1**
Royal Phuket City Hotel **13**
The Royal Phuket Yacht Club **3**
Sawasdee Village **4**
The Shore **4**
Sino House **13**
The Surin Phuket **8**
Thalang Guesthouse **13**
Trisara **10**
Twin Palms, Phuket **8**
Villa Royale **4**

activities; *What's On South* has some useful information on Phuket, Ko Phi Phi, and Krabi; and there are a few fun local magazines for sale. Also look out for the useful *Art & Culture South* and *Old Phuket Treasure Map.*

Island Layout

If you arrive by car or coach, you'll cross into Phuket from the mainland at the northern tip of the island via the **Sarasin Bridge,** along Route 402. Phuket Town, the island's historic and commercial center, is in the southeast of the island at the terminus of Route 402; local buses connect at **Phuket Town Bus Station,** on Ranong Road, west of the town center. Phuket's picturesque stretches of sand dot the western coast from Nai Harn, on the southern tip, to Mai Khao, about 48km (30 miles) north, via Kata Noi, Kata, Karon, Patong, Kamala, Surin, Bang Tao, and a number of smaller beaches north along this corridor. A busy coastal road links the popular tour towns in the south, but stops north of Patong, requiring a short detour from the main highway. The four corners of Phuket are linked with just a few busy main arterial roads. Renting a vehicle is the best way to tour the island's smaller byways or make the trip to jungle parks, such as **Khao Phra Thaew National Park,** in the northeast of the isle, famed for diverse flora and fauna. The western beaches have all the services visitors might need, but everything comes with resort prices—and don't expect to find any real Thai feel here. For a taste of Thai life, affordable services, and authentic restaurants, explore Phuket Town (especially if this is your only urban destination down south).

THE BEACHES   There's a beach for everyone in Phuket, from private stretches artfully cordoned off by exclusive hideaways to public bays lined with beach chairs and buzzing with jet skis. Each beach is distinct, and selecting the appropriate area makes all the difference.

Nai Harn, the southernmost bay on the west coast, is home to several upmarket beachfront resorts, but also has a host of smaller family-friendly resorts set back from the coast. Laid-back and quiet in the monsoon season, with fine sand and deep water, Nai Harn attracts surfers and other watersports enthusiasts. As a public beach, with a few local eateries, it makes for a great day trip, if you're staying in Phuket Town or at a more populated beach and want to run away for the day (a long motorbike/car ride south of Kata/Karon).

Rawai Beach and **Chalong Beach** are two well-known, eastern-facing beaches, both hosting a few resorts, such as the luxurious Evason Phuket, and some outdoor seafood or barbecue restaurants. **Cape Panwa,** between Chalong and Phuket Town, also has scenic hidden beaches with a range of hotels and restaurants.

North of Nai Harn on the west coast are the more popular developed beaches: **Kata, Kata Noi,** and **Karon beaches.** Though they are quite developed, they've not reached the levels of over-the-top Patong. Along this section of sandy, picturesque coastline, you'll find resorts large and small. In general this area is all upmarket, though there are a few budget places that haven't been bulldozed and made high-end yet. This area (Kata is the quieter of the two) has more restaurants than the remote bays and some shopping, nightlife, and travel agents as well. But you won't find rowdy crowds here and, even with all the development, the area manages to maintain a laid-back character.

Heading north of the Kata and Karon bays, you'll pass **Relax Bay,** a small cove with a few resorts, before rolling down the mountain to **Patong Beach,** the most famous (perhaps infamous) strip on the island. Patong's draw is its seamy Patpong-styled nightlife, bustling shops and restaurants, and brash in-your-face beat. Not surprisingly, commercial sex workers flock here. Accommodation runs the gamut from five-star resorts to budget motels. Love it or hate it, the town has the most diverse selection of dining and highest concentration of tour and dive operators, watersports, and entertainment. Most visitors end up spending a few nights on this strip. The drawbacks are all too visible—endless parades of pushy touts and hawkers pounce on you at every step. While some adults may find the nightlife titillating, families with kids may want to avoid some of the lurid displays of obscenity on offer around **Bang La Road.** If you love to be in the center of it all, stay in Patong; if you want some peace, stay away.

North of Patong, **Kamala Bay, Surin Beach,** and **Bang Tao Beach** have more secluded resorts on lovely beaches for those who want the convenience of nearby Patong but cherish the serenity of a quiet resort. Be prepared to dig deep for the privilege, though; this stretch is sometimes referred to as "the millionaire's mile."

About two-thirds of the way to the northern tip of the island, **Bang Tao Beach** is home to the **Laguna Resort Complex,** a partnership of seven world-class resorts sharing excellent facilities and a fabulous beach. While this area is rather far from both Patong Beach and Phuket Town, the many dining and activity options make it quite self-sufficient for those with the means.

Far north of the main resort areas, **Nai Thon** and **Nai Yang Beaches** have limited facilities and may not appeal to most, but for real beach lovers they are a dream come true. Nai Thon is possibly the most beautiful beach on the entire island, while at Nai Yang there is a coral reef 1,000m (3,280 ft.) offshore, just a short ride in a longtail boat. If you are looking to get back to nature, these two beaches or Mai Khao, a little farther north, are your best bet.

Mai Khao, about 17km (10½ miles) long, is the northernmost beach in Phuket and is famed as being prime habitat for sea turtles. It is designated National Parkland, but with all the development in the area, few sea turtles are returning here to lay eggs. This steep and wide beach is well-shaded by casuarinas trees and sections of it are still deserted, though it now hosts several luxury resorts, all of which claim to respect the local ecology.

Getting Around

Public transportation on Phuket is a problem that has still to be improved. If you've spent any time in other parts of the country, you'll know that the covered pickup trucks that cruise the streets picking up and dropping off passengers are called *song-taews*, while the noisy motorized three-wheel vehicular demons are known as tuk-tuks. Not on Phuket: Here, locals call communal pickup trucks tuk-tuks, while *songtaews* are the giant colorful buses that ply the main roads (also called baht buses).

Here's the problem: *Songtaews* are only permitted to travel from a beach to Phuket Town (not from beach to beach). Tuk-tuk drivers have exclusive rights to transport people between beaches, so the "service" is run as a racket—pay the fare they demand, or walk. At night, tuk-tuk drivers are known to charge solo passengers up to 1,000B to go from Karon to Patong Beach, but they are the only game in town. Budget travelers on limited funds must bear this in mind to avoid getting stranded late at night. If you plan to stay several days and want to explore the island, renting a car is the obvious answer.

BY SONGTAEW The local bus terminal is in front of the Central Market, on Ranong Road, in Phuket Town. Fares to the most popular beaches range from 20B to 30B. *Songtaews* leave when full, usually every 30 minutes, and they run from 7am to 6pm between Phuket Town and the main beaches on the west coast.

BY TUK-TUK Within Phuket Town, tuk-tuks charge 100B to 200B even for the shortest trips, but they can get away with it because there's no alternative for short hops. They provide the most convenient way to get to the bus station or to Phuket Town's restaurants.

In the busy west-coast beaches, tuk-tuks and small Daihatsu minitrucks roll around town honking at any tourist on foot, especially in Patong. It is the only way to travel between beaches. Bargain hard and beware that these guys will try to eke every baht out of you. Expect to pay about 600B from town to the airport, 500B from town to Patong Beach, and 200B from Patong Beach to Karon Beach. At night, you'll have to pay through the nose, usually double the normal day rates. In places like Patong, the one-way traffic means a tuk-tuk will take you round several blocks to reach your hotel a block away, so it's worth giving thought to how you'll get around before going out.

BY MOTORCYCLE TAXI Motorcycle taxi drivers, identifiable by colored vests, make short trips within Phuket Town or along Patong Beach for fees as steep as 100B. Don't let them talk you into anything but short in-town rides, unless you're looking for a death-defying F1-style race along the switchback highways between beaches.

BY CAR You should be extremely cautious when driving yourself around Phuket. Roads between the main beaches in the west and connecting with Phuket Town across the center of the island are dangerously steep and winding, with more than a few hairpin turns and lots of unpredictable traffic. Having said that, renting a vehicle here offers maximum freedom to explore the island, and road surfaces are generally in good condition. You could always get a car and driver for around 2,000B a day. As in other parts of the kingdom, drivers pass aggressively, even on blind curves, and self-driving visitors should be defensive and alert at all times.

Avis (© **07635-1244**) and **Hertz** (© **07632-8545**) have counters at the Phuket airport. Plan on spending around 1,200B per day for the cheapest four-door sedan. **Budget** (© **07632-7744** at the airport, 07629-2389 in Patong) charges similar rates. All international renters have sound insurance coverage available, which is highly recommended. Check the vehicle carefully for minor scratches before signing any agreement to avoid issues later.

Inexpensive Suzuki Caribbeans can be rented from almost all travel agents and from hotels at the beach areas, though they're not great on hairpin bends; prices start at 800B per day. Independent agents hang around under umbrellas along Patong Beach and offer great bargains on open-topped jeeps, if you negotiate, but don't count on them having an insurance policy.

BY MOTORCYCLE Also along the Patong strip, the same car-rental guys will offer cheap bike rental. A 100cc Honda scooter goes for 150B to 200B per day, while a 400cc Honda Shadow chopper will set you back at least 600B per day. Significant discounts can be negotiated if you plan to rent for a longer time. Wear your helmet, as police enforce fines of 500B for going without, and practice extreme caution while driving.

[Fast FACTS] PHUKET

Banks Banks are located in Phuket Town, with many larger branches on Ranong and Rasada roads. There are bank branches of major Thai banks at Chalong, Nai Harn, Kata, Karon, and Patong beaches. **Money-changers** are located at the airport, in major shopping areas on each beach, and at most resorts. Banks offer the best rates. **ATMs** are now found all over Phuket.

Bookstores   There are lots of bookstores to be found at the megamalls of Central Festival Phuket Town, and JungCeylon shopping mall, Patong. Also look for **The Books** at 53–55 Phuket Rd., Phuket Town (✆ **07622-4362**).

Hospitals   There are three major private hospitals, all with English-speaking staff: **Bangkok Phuket Hospital,** at 2/1 Hongyok-Uthit Rd. (off Yaowarat Rd., in Phuket Town; ✆ **07625-4425**), has high-quality facilities. **Phuket International** (✆ **07624-9400**) is at 44 Chalermprakiat Ror 9 Rd., next to Big C Shopping Mall, outside Phuket Town. **Mission Hospital** also offers decent medical services and is at 4/1 Thepkasattri Rd., Phuket Town (✆ **07623-7220**).

Internet   Internet service is fairly easy to find on the island. Most hotels offer in-room ADSL cable connections or Wi-Fi, either free or for an hourly/daily fee. Good connections can be found at small cafes and tour agencies at most beaches. In Patong, the best Internet cafes are farther away from the beach. Along Rat-U-Thit Road, in the center of Patong (a 5-min. walk east, away from the beach), you'll find 1B-per-minute service.

Police   The emergency number for the **Tourist Police** is ✆ **1155** or 1699; for **Emergency Police,** dial ✆ **191;** for **Marine Police,** dial ✆ **07621-1883.**

Post Office   The **General Post Office,** in Phuket Town (✆ **07644-3081**), is at 158 Montri Rd.

Special Events

If you are on Phuket around October/November, don't miss the **Vegetarian Festival.** The name is misleading—it is not about Animal Rights or being health conscious, but a Thai-Chinese tradition on Phuket (and now celebrated widely throughout southern Thailand) that corresponds with the Buddhist Lent. For 9 days, not only do devotees refrain from meat consumption, but many also submit to violent public acts of self-mutilation through piercing their bodies with long skewers or swords, and often walking over hot coals. The festival began as an act of penance to the spirits to help early inhabitants ward off malaria, but these days, the rituals are more for young men to prove themselves and for gaining merit and good luck. Early-morning processions follow through the streets of Phuket Town and major temples around the island, with onlookers clad in white for the occasion. During this time you can also feast on terrific vegetarian buffets at many restaurants on the island. See **www.phuketvegetarian. com** for exact dates and more info.

Exploring Phuket

If Phuket is your only destination in Thailand, you'll certainly want to get a sense of local culture, which you can do at the Muslim fishing villages, small rural temples, and in the backstreets of Phuket Town. Outdoor activities top the list of things to do, and there's something for everyone.

More or less in the center of the island, the **Heroines' Monument** is a good place to get a taste of local history. It was erected in honor of two women who rallied the troops and saved the town from an attack by the Burmese in 1785. Locals frequently arrive to make offerings and prostrate themselves before the monument, making it more than a simple statue.

Thalang National Museum, just off Highway 402 beside the Heroines' Monument (✆ **07631-1426;** daily 8:30am–4pm; 100B), exhibits Phuket's indigenous cultures, the history of Thai settlements on Phuket, and crafts from the southern Thai regions as well as a 9th-century statue of the Hindu deity Vishnu—evidence of early Indian merchants visiting the burgeoning kingdom.

There are a few Buddhist temples on the island that are notable: The most unique is **Wat Phra Thong** (daily 6am–6pm), along Highway 402, in Thalang, just south of the airport. Years ago, a boy fell ill and dropped dead after tying his buffalo to a post sticking out of the ground. It was later discovered that the post was actually the top of a huge Buddha image that was buried under the earth. Numerous attempts to dig out the post failed—during one attempt in 1785, workers were chased off by hornets. Everyone took all this failure to mean that the Buddha image wanted to just stay put, so they covered the "post" with a plaster image of The Buddha's head and shoulders and built a temple around it.

The most famous temple among Thai visitors here is **Wat Chalong** (daily 6am–6pm). Chalong was the first resort on Phuket, back when the Thais first started coming to the island for vacations. Nowadays, the discovery of better beaches on the west side of the island has driven most tourists away from this area, but the temple still remains the center of Buddhist worship. The temple is on the Chaofa West Road, about 8km (5 miles) south of Phuket Town. On a hilltop to the west of Wat Chalong, sits an enormous (45-m/148-ft. high) **Big Buddha** (daily 6am–6pm), which has quickly become one of the island's main attractions both to pay homage and to admire the peerless views, which include Kata and Karon beaches to the west.

Sea Gypsies, or Chao Ley, are considered the indigenous people of Phuket. This minority group used to shift around the region, living off subsistence fishing, but commercial fishing interests and shoreline encroachment have virtually put paid to their lifestyle and livelihood. Related to the Malaysian Orang Laut people and the southern Thai Sakai tribes, Phuket and Phang Nga's Sea Gypsies form a few tiny settlements on Phuket island: One on Ko Siray (aka Ko Sire), east of Phuket Town, and another at Rawai Beach, just south of Chalong Bay. The villages are simple seashore shacks, with vendors selling souvenir shells. Though it should be educational to visit these people and their disappearing culture, sadly the experience on tours is tantamount to visiting a human zoo, with tourists taking photos of unkempt, unwashed kids who pester them for hand-outs.

WHERE TO STAY IN PHUKET

The hotels and resorts below are divided by beach area to simplify your choices on the island. Phuket is thick with development, so the list below is but a small selection, according to each beach. Nowadays, hotels do not always publish rack rates—instead the rates are governed by occupancy. In Phuket, the peak season runs from December 15 to January 15, when rates are at their most expensive; rates quoted here are for high season (Nov 1–Dec 15 and Jan 15–Apr 30). If the rate here is marked "from," it means no rack rate is available, and the price has been based on Internet rates for high season. In low season (May 1–Oct 31), rates can drop 30% to 50%.

Nai Harn Beach

There are several resorts on **Rawai** and **Chalong** beaches in the southeast corner of the island, including the **Evason Phuket & Bon Island** (100 Vised Rd., Moo 2, Tambon Rawai; ✆ **07638-1010;** fax 07638-1018; www.sixsenses.com), a luxury, family-friendly enclave and popular day-spa destination, with room rates starting at around 5,000B; and the **Golden Tulip Mangosteen Resort** (99/4 Moo 7, Soi Mangosteen; ✆ **07628-9399;** fax 07628-9389; www.goldentulipmangosteen.com) a newer high-end choice, where rooms start at around 7,000B.

The remainder of our recommendations are all on the west coast and are presented from south to north. In the extreme southwest, Nai Harn Beach is a choice escape, with a range of accommodation on offer.

VERY EXPENSIVE

The Royal Phuket Yacht Club ★★★   Perched above the northern edge of Nai Harn Beach, the Royal Yacht Club is one of the earliest forms of luxury accommodation in Phuket (established by Mandarin Oriental in 1987), yet it still rivals nearly anything on the island for setting and comfort. The pagoda-style foyer overlooks terraced gardens overflowing with pink and white bougainvillea. Common areas have terra-cotta tiles and open views. Interiors are spacious and decorated with cheerful fabrics and tasteful furniture; bathrooms are huge, many with sunken tubs. All rooms have large balconies for viewing the beach and Promthep Cape.

23/3 Viset Rd., Nai Harn Beach, Phuket 83130 (above Nai Harn Beach, 18km/11 miles south of Phuket). www.puravana.com. ✆ **07638-0200.** Fax 07638-0280. 110 units. 6,000B–7,500B double (varies with view); 10,500B–19,440B suite. AE, DC, MC, V. **Amenities:** 3 restaurants; lounge; outdoor pool; 2 outdoor lit tennis courts; health club; spa; extensive watersports equipment; room service; babysitting. In room: A/C, TV, minibar, fridge, hair dryer, Wi-Fi (free).

MODERATE

Just up the coastal road from the Royal Yacht Club are quaint seaside, forest bungalows at **Baan Krating Phuket Resort** (11/3 Moo 1, Viset Rd.; ✆/fax **07628-8264;** www.baankrating.com/phuket). Boasting a pool, Internet corner, a clubhouse, and watersports equipment, this is a good value getaway with rooms starting at 2,850B.

INEXPENSIVE

Baan Oui Guest House (14/95-96 Moo 1, Saiyuan Rd., Rawai; www.baanoui. com; ✆ **07638-8538**) is in a secluded spot just a short walk from the beach. It's run by a friendly, helpful family and has just eight clean, bright rooms from 1,200B, including breakfast.

Kata Beach

One of Phuket's best tourist beaches, Kata is a wide strip of soft sand and rolling surf, with Kata Noi located beyond a headland to the south. Rent an umbrella, get a massage, or grab a kayak or surfboard and hit the waves (there's good surf May–Oct). Unfortunately, the best beachfront real estate on Kata Beach itself is taken up by the sprawling **Phuket Club Med** (www.clubmed.com; ✆ **07633-0455**), an all-inclusive, club-style resort, but the beach is open to all. In the evening, Kata comes alive in the bars and music cafes along the beach roads.

VERY EXPENSIVE

The Shore ★★★   This sister hotel to the Katathani is located on a steep hill just south of the main resort, and aims directly at the romantic getaway market with its secluded, luxurious pool villas; in fact, no children are allowed to stay here. With a size of 130 sq. meter (1,399 sq. ft.), the pool and oceanview villas are wonderfully spacious, and apart from a private infinity pool, each contains a living/dining area, a bedroom, and an ample bathroom with a deep bathtub. The two-bedroom pool villas are twice as big again, with an upstairs bedroom and huge living area downstairs. Facilities include a top-class restaurant, The Harbor, a relaxing bar, and, of course, a spa.

14 Kata Noi Rd., Kata Noi Beach, Phuket. www.theshore.katathani.com. ✆ **07633-0124.** Fax 07733-0426. 48 units. 25,200B pool and seaview villas; 37,800B 2-bedroom pool villas. AE, DC, MC, V. **Amenities:** Restaurant; bar; health club; spa; wine cellar. In room: A/C, TV, minibar, hair dryer, Wi-Fi (free).

Villa Royale ★★★ For a very special stay, the Villa Royale offers 10 extravagant suites, all housed in traditional Thai buildings. These huge rooms are perched over a steep cliff with stunning views of the sea and are sumptuously decorated in a unique mix of local materials: Dark teak, mosaics of bamboo and coconut, black tile with stone inlay in the bathrooms, and elegant textiles. With one freshwater pool and two saltwater pools, you'll never be short of somewhere to cool off. There's also an excellent spa and one of Phuket's top dining venues—Mom Tri's Kitchen (p. 235).

12 Kata Noi Rd., Kata Noi Beach, Phuket 83100. www.villaroyalephuket.com. ℂ **07633-3569.** 35 units. 12,900B–25,500B suite. AE, DC, MC, V. **Amenities:** Restaurant; bar; lounge; 3 outdoor pools; health club; spa; Internet. In room: A/C, TV/DVD, minibar, hair dryer, Wi-Fi (free).

EXPENSIVE

Boathouse ★★★ At the quieter south end of Kata Beach, the Boathouse is a small inn that has been a longtime favorite with many returning visitors. In 2011, under new ownership, it received a major renovation that has provided the inn with a contemporary new look. Comfortable, attractive rooms all face the sea, each with a terrace overlooking a courtyard pool and beach beyond; they're all equipped with writing desks, flatscreen TVs, and most have wooden floors. The Boathouse Wine & Grill (p. 235) is also one of the most highly regarded dining options on Phuket, and its chef teaches cooking classes each Saturday and Sunday from 10am to 2pm for 2,200B per guest.

182 Koktanod Rd., Kata Beach, Phuket 83100 (north end of Kata Noi Beach). www.boathouse phuket.com. ℂ **07633-0015-7.** Fax 07633-561. 38 units. 9,600B–10,700B double; 14,000B–19,000B suite; 35,000B 2-bedroom villa. AE, DC, MC, V. **Amenities:** Restaurant; lounge; outdoor pool; golf course nearby; spa; room service; babysitting. In room: A/C, TV, minibar, fridge, hair dryer, Wi-Fi (free).

Katathani Phuket Beach Resort ★★★ ☺ The Katathani is on the quiet cul-de-sac of lovely Kata Noi Beach, a haven of luxury. Rooms are contemporary, but cozy—all with large balconies and indoor sitting areas; top-end rooms are beachfront while cheaper rooms are set back from the beach in the Bhuri Wing. Wide, well-groomed lawns surround sizable pools and lead to the graceful curve of the pristine cove. There is a nightly poolside buffet in high season. Service is excellent, and kids have their own pool and a great club supervised by specially trained activity and arts instructors. The place is usually quite crowded and very popular with families, so this is not the resort for a quiet, romantic getaway; if that's what you're after, check out their sister hotel **The Shore** (see above), where kids are not allowed.

14 Kata Noi Rd., Kata Noi Beach, Phuket 83100. www.katathani.com. ℂ **07633-0124-6.** Fax 07633-0426. 479 units. 7,800B–8,550B double; 10,050B–25,500B suite. AE, DC, MC, V. **Amenities:** 6 restaurants; 6 bars; lounge; 6 outdoor pools; putting green; 2 outdoor lit tennis courts; health club; spa; room service; babysitting; scuba diving; Internet. In room: A/C, TV/DVD, fridge, hair dryer, Wi-Fi (500B/day).

Sawasdee Village ★★ 🛍 A short walk from Kata Beach, you'll pass a small portico of stone with some Khmer statuary; walk in and you'll discover a little Eden. An attractive garden surrounds a small pool with ornate fountains bordered with fine masonry and overflowing with greenery. The garden rooms here are fairly compact but stylish, with canopy beds and shower-only bathrooms. The stunning new triple pool access **Baray Villas** are enormous, featuring a delightful blend of Arabic and Thai design and private butlers. There are elegant Thai touches throughout the compound, such as *salas* (pavilions) for relaxing and sliding doors that connect each room to the courtyard.

38 Katekwan Rd., Kata Beach, Phuket 83100 (down a small road north of the sprawling Club Med). www.phuketsawasdee.com. ⓒ **07633-0979.** Fax 07633-0905. 54 units. 6,200B garden room; 13,000B Baray Villas. **Amenities:** 2 restaurants; bar; small outdoor pool; spa. *In room:* A/C, TV, minibar, fridge, hair dryer, Wi-Fi (free), no phone.

INEXPENSIVE

Kata Country House Set in an attractive garden, this smart place offers decent-sized rooms with rustic furnishings at budget prices. The wood or concrete bungalows are the best bet, though standard and superior rooms in two-story blocks are also good value. The only downside is that it's tucked away behind Club Med and about a 10-minute walk from the beach, but there are two pools on-site, including one for kids.

82 Kata Rd., Kata Beach, Phuket 83100. www.katacountryhouse.com. ⓒ **07633-3210.** Fax 07628-4221. 88 units. 1,800B standard room; 2,850B bungalow. MC, V. **Amenities:** Restaurant; 2 outdoor pools; Internet (Wi-Fi in public areas 200B per stay). *In room:* A/C, TV, fridge.

Katanoi Resort ★ 🗡 This tiny resort is dwarfed by the enormous Katathani, which stands right across the road, but with smart rooms that cost a fraction of the price and are located just a couple of minutes' walk from Kata Noi beach, it's excellent value. The apartments are small but well-equipped with cable TV, small balconies, and decent-sized bathrooms, while the villas have two bedrooms and fully fitted kitchens.

37 Kata Noi Rd., Kata Noi Beach, Phuket 83100 (Kata Noi is south of Kata Beach). www.katanoi resort.com. ⓒ **07633-3078.** Fax 07628-4665. 15 units. 1,900B apartment; 3,000B villa. MC, V. **Amenities:** Restaurant; bar; outdoor pool. *In room:* A/C, TV, fridge, Wi-Fi (free), no phone.

Karon Beach

Karon Beach is a long stretch of beach lined with upper and midrange hotels and resorts, which is particularly popular with Scandinavians. You'll find heaps of tailors, gift shops, bars, small restaurants and cafes, Internet services, local markets, and minimarts on the north end of the beach.

VERY EXPENSIVE

Hilton Phuket Arcadia Resort & Spa ★★★ Set in 30 hectares (74 acres) of lawns and lush tropical gardens, this is a modern, full-facility resort. Many of the stylish guest rooms overlook Karon Beach. Upgraded rooms are luxurious, with cool Thai touches and contemporary furnishings throughout. The hotel sports a large spa village with 15 purpose-built villas connected by raised wooden platforms in a mellow, wooded glen at the heart of the resort. The in-house dining choices are top-notch (do try the Thai restaurant), and everything about the place is classy, with snappy service. There are no rack rates, but the rates below are a good overall guide.

333 Patak Rd., Karon Beach, Phuket 83100 (middle of Karon Beach Rd.). www.hilton.com. ⓒ **07639-6433.** Fax 07639-6136. 676 units. From 10,000B double; from 11,500B suite. AE, DC, MC, V. **Amenities:** 4 restaurants; lounge bar w/live band; 5 pools; golf course nearby and putting green on-site; outdoor lit tennis courts; health club; spa; watersports equipment; room service; babysitting. *In room:* A/C, TV, minibar, Wi-Fi (650B per day).

Karon Beach Resort ★★ This is the only Karon Beach property with direct beach access (from all others you'll have to walk across the road). Rooms are midsize, with dark wood entrances, clean tile floors, and some Thai elements in the decor, but are most noteworthy for their orientation to the sea: Balconies are stacked in receding, semicircular tiers and all look onto the pool below (first floor with direct pool access) or to the beach and sea beyond.

51 Karon Rd., Tambon Daron, Phuket 83100 (the south end of Karon Beach, just as the road bends up to cross to Kata). www.katagroup.com. ✆ **07633-0006.** Fax 07633-0529. 81 units. From 10,573B double; 19,988B suite. AE, MC, V. **Amenities:** 2 restaurants; babysitting; 2 outdoor pools; golf course nearby. In room: A/C, TV, fridge, minibar, hair dryer, Wi-Fi (450B per day).

EXPENSIVE

Andaman Seaview Hotel ★★ 🏨   A real Karon Beach gem, Andaman Seaview's bright and airy public spaces are decorated in hues of pale blue and white, flanked by ponds and a large central courtyard with a garden and meandering pool. Rooms overlook the pool area and are large and nicely appointed—they're better than most in this category. The hotel is charming in a way that is less about luxury than it is about the warm welcome and tidy appearance of the place. The restaurant is a typical hotel coffee shop, but the poolside seats make for a great dining experience. In fact, I recommend taking as much advantage of the nearby beach as possible, and indulging yourself in the hotel's small spa.

1 Karon Rd., Soi 4, Phuket 83100 (along the main strip at Karon Beach). www.andamanphuket.com. ✆ **07639-8111.** Fax 07639-8177. 161 units. 6,700B superior double; 9,900B deluxe double. AE, MC, V. **Amenities:** Restaurant; bar; 2 outdoor pools; 1 kids' pool; exercise room; spa; room service; babysitting. In room: A/C, TV, minibar, fridge, Wi-Fi (300B per day).

Centara Villas Phuket ★★ ☺   Set on a hillside perch on the north end of Karon Beach—along the crest of a hill between Karon and Relax Bay—this hideaway consists of free-standing, luxury bungalows in tropical garden surrounds, overlooking the majestic crashing surf. The room decor is tasteful with slick, modern bathrooms with skylights. The Cliff restaurant is first-rate (see p. 236), and this self-contained gem has a friendly staff who can handle any eventuality. The outdoor waterfall pool overlooks the sea; and their outdoor spa *salas* are a great place to chill out. Thai cooking classes are on offer as well.

701 Patak Rd., Tambon Karon, Phuket 83100. ✆ **07628-6300.** Fax 07628-6316. 72 units. 6,700B–16,500B villas. AE, MC, V. **Amenities:** 2 restaurants; bar; 2 outdoor pools; room service; babysitting. In room: A/C, TV, fridge, minibar, hair dryer, Wi-Fi (249B per day).

Marina Phuket ★★   These simple cottages tucked in the jungle above a scenic promontory between Kata and Karon beaches provide an adequate level of comfort, and offer four room types. Rates vary according to the view, but all have a jungle bungalow charm, connected by hilly walkways and boardwalks past the lush hillside greenery (keep your eyes peeled for wildlife). It is a hike down to the rocky shore and the swimming isn't great, but they have a good seaside restaurant, On the Rock (see p. 236), and their in-house **Marina Divers** (✆ **07633-0272**) is a PADI International Diving School, which conducts classes, rents equipment, and leads good multiday expeditions. Heavy discounts apply during low season.

47 Karon Rd., Karon Beach, Phuket 83100 (on bluff at south end of Karon Beach Rd.). www.marinaphuket.com. ✆ **07633-0625.** Fax 07633-0516. 92 units. $220–$300 double; $690 grand villa. MC, V. **Amenities:** 2 restaurants; outdoor pool; watersports equipment; room service. In room: A/C, TV, minibar, Wi-Fi (free).

Mövenpick Resort & Spa ★★ ☺   Occupying a huge area right opposite the center of Karon Beach, this Swiss-run, luxury hotel is ideal for those who want everything on-site. Rooms range from gardenview doubles in the main building to plunge pool villas decorated in Balinese-style, with thatched roofs, and massive, two-bedroom family suites. Guests have a choice of four pools, as well as several restaurants and bars scattered around the site. There's a play zone for kids and a spa, fitness room, and PADI diving courses, run by the reliable Euro Divers, for adults.

509 Patak Rd., Karon Beach, Phuket 83100. www.moevenpick-hotels.com. 📞 **07639-6139.** Fax 07639-6144. 364 units. From 6,700B double; 10,500B plunge pool villa; 16,800B family suite. AE, MC, V. **Amenities:** 4 restaurants; 3 bars; 4 outdoor pools; 2 tennis courts; health club; fitness room; spa. *In room:* A/C, TV, minibar, Internet (642B per day).

MODERATE

Karona Resort & Spa ★ Tucked in a little side street where Karon and Kata beaches meet, the Karona Resort is a low-luxe find, with simple rooms surrounding a tiered central pool, all just a short walk from Karon Beach and the busy Kata strip. Deluxe rooms, in a block overlooking the pool, are worth the upgrade—you'll get a few more amenities, including a safe. They also provide affordable spa treatments, and the place feels stylish and offers good service for the price. Long-stay discounts apply.

6 Karon Soi 2, Karon Beach, Phuket 83100. www.karonaresort.com. 📞 **07628-6406.** Fax 07628-6411. 96 units. 3,500B–4,500B double; 6,000B–10,000B suite. MC, V. **Amenities:** Restaurant; bar; outdoor pool; spa; room service. *In room:* A/C, TV, minibar, fridge, Wi-Fi (free).

INEXPENSIVE

Golden Sand Inn One of only a few acceptable budget accommodation offers on this part of the island, this inn is clean, reasonably quiet, and well maintained. The location isn't bad, on the northernmost end of Karon and not far from all the town services and the beach. Rooms are a reasonable size and sparsely but smartly furnished. There's a nice coffee shop and a small pool. Off-season rates are very reasonable.

556 Moo 1, Karon Beach, Phuket 83100 (across highway from north end of beach above traffic circle). www.phuketgoldensand.com. 📞 **07639-6493.** Fax 07639-6117. 89 units. 1,600B–2,300B double; 3,500B family room. AE, DC, MC, V. **Amenities:** Restaurant; outdoor pool; babysitting; Internet (free). *In room:* A/C, TV, minibar.

Relax Bay

Le Meridien Phuket ★★★ ☺ Tucked away on secluded Relax Bay, the Le Meridien features a 549-m (1,800-ft.) beach—with trained lifeguards—and 16 hectares (40 acres) of tropical greenery, making it one of the largest resorts on the island. It has numerous facilities and its popularity makes it very busy. The resort caters to families, and there are plenty of activities and a day-care center that kids seem to love. The large building complex combines Western and traditional Thai architecture, and one of the advantages to its U-shape layout is that it ensures that 80% of the rooms face the ocean, with the lowest category getting a garden view. The modern furnishings in cheerful rooms are of rattan and teak, each with a balcony and wooden deck chairs. The seven restaurants on hand mean you'll have all kinds of dining choices.

29 Soi Karon Noi, Relax Bay, Phuket 83100. www.lemeridien.com. 📞 **800/543-4300** or 07637-0100. Fax 07634-0479. 470 units. 6,840B–22,750B garden deluxe–royal suite. AE, DC, MC, V. **Amenities:** 7 restaurants; 3 bars w/games and live shows; 2 large outdoor pools; golf driving range and on-site pro; outdoor lit tennis courts; squash courts; health club; spa; watersports equipment; bikes; kids' club; room service; babysitting. *In room:* A/C, TV, minibar, fridge, hair dryer, Wi-Fi (400B per day).

Patong

Once the popular haunt of the U.S. Navy's 9th Fleet, Patong built its nightlife on cheap sex and even cheaper beer. Today, it's Phuket's main tourist center, with plenty of cheap shopping, dining, clubbing—and prostitution. The main strip can be unpleasant for those not used to catcalling touts, who incessantly hassle passersby, accompanied by the constant beeping of tuk-tuks attempting to take tourists for a ride (in both senses). Though one of the hardest hit of Phuket's towns in the 2004 tsunami, the damage here was fairly limited (in international media reports, Patong was often confused with Khao Lak—3 hours' drive farther north—which was almost completely wiped out). With a few exceptions, mid- and high-range hotels on this busy strip were up and running soon after the tsunami, and prices are still rocketing. The town did lose some of its pleasant budget options, however.

These days, sprawling Patong is a heap of what appears to be hastily built—or where the tsunami hit, hastily rebuilt—three-story concrete bunkers. Though some new landscaping has greatly improved a few parts of town—especially along the beach—once you move into the backstreets, many are disappointed to find a tawdry mess of touts and tatty beer halls, interspersed with the odd smart resort or posh diner. It's not all bad: Patong has many great eateries and some good accommodation. Since the opening of the swish JungCeylon shopping mall and the glamorous five-star Millennium Resort next door, Patong has started to move away from its sad and sordid past. With more upscale bars and restaurants opening all the time, this trend seems set to continue.

EXPENSIVE

Amari Coral Beach Resort ★★★ The Amari Coral Beach stands on the rocks high above the southern end of busy Patong, well away from the congested beach strip, but close enough to dip into the mayhem. This seafront resort, from the very grand terraced lobby, guest rooms, and fine pool, is oriented to the incredible views of the majestic bay below. The rooms have ocean tones, balconies, and all the comforts of home. There is live music nightly and the hotel's Italian restaurant, La Gritta (p. 237), is a great lazy option. Don't miss The Jetty for sunset cocktails.

2 Meun Ngern Rd., Phuket 83150 (south and uphill of Patong Beach). www.amari.com/coralbeach. ✆ **07634-0106.** Fax 07634-0115. 197 units. 5,687B–7,372B double; from 9,500B suite. AE, DC, MC, V. **Amenities:** 3 restaurants; bar; 2 outdoor pools; outdoor lit tennis court; health club; spa; watersports equipment; room service; babysitting. *In room:* A/C, TV, minibar, Wi-Fi (471B per day).

Burasari Resort ★★ ✦ Welcoming staff make the Burasari a great choice if you prefer it chic and petite; just don't expect a sea view. This tiny resort-styled hotel has been squeezed into the middle of a *soi*, just off the main drag, and styled as a contemporary hanging-garden resort. The stylish rooms, set amid a narrow courtyard of waterfalls, pools, and greenery, fuse a blend of contemporary and rustic Thai design. The basic rooms are rather compact, so if size matters to you, opt for one of the more spacious Mood Collection rooms. For this convenient location, just a stroll from the beach and madness of the main street, it represents good value.

18/110 Ruamjai Rd., Patong, Phuket 83150. www.burasari.com. ✆ **07629-2929.** Fax 07629-2930. 186 units. 5,500B–7,900B double; 7,900B–9,400B elite; from 9,400B Mood Collection. AE, DC, MC, V. **Amenities:** 2 restaurants; 3 bars; 2 outdoor pools; spa; room service; babysitting. *In room:* A/C, TV/DVD, minibar, fridge, hair dryer, Wi-Fi (free).

Holiday Inn Resort Phuket ★★ ☺ What distinguishes this place from the others on the busy front is that it's well equipped for families and has some creative cost-saving services. The central pool areas have elaborate fountains and a fun meandering pool suited to all ages, and there are family activities and excursions. Family Suites, with separate "kids' rooms," come with pirate-themed decor, a TV with a video player and PlayStation, and toy boxes; some have bunk beds. The hotel also has a self-service launderette, so you don't have to pay hotel laundry prices. The hotel's minibar scheme is quite unusual—rooms have just a bare fridge, but guests can pick out supplies from a small convenience store in the lobby and have them delivered for not much more than standard minibar prices.

52 Thaweewong Rd., Patong Beach, Phuket 83150 (Patong Beach strip). www.phuket.holiday-inn. com. ℂ **800/HOLIDAY** (465-4329) or 07637-0200. Fax 07634-9999. 369 units. 6,300B–7,600B double; 13,600B–24,600B suite/villa. AE, DC, MC, V. **Amenities:** 3 restaurants; lounge; 2 outdoor pools; health club; children's club; room service; babysitting. *In room:* A/C, TV/VCR, fridge, hair dryer, movie library, gaming station, toys, Wi-Fi (free).

Millennium Resort Patong ★★★   This low-rise, ultra-contemporary hotel is the first truly international five-star chain to set up a resort on the Patong strip. Two completely separate wings (named "Beachside" or "Lakeside") fan out from a beautiful atrium, linked by a grand staircase to a ballroom. Upstairs on the rooftop area is the pool and spa level, facing the mountains. Clean, modern lines and slick designer touches can be found in the rooms, and the tropical landscaping reminds guests that they're just a short walk to the sea. Catering to more upscale leisure and business travelers, the Millennium sets a new benchmark for Patong. Because it's annexed to the JungCeylon mall, there are dozens of eating options close by, in addition to those within the resort.

199, Rat-U-Thit, 200 Pee Rd., Patong, Phuket 83150 (within JungCeylon shopping mall). www. millenniumhotels.com. ℂ **07660-1999.** Fax 07660-1986. 418 units. 6,800B–8,800B double; 10,800B–22,300B suite. AE, DC, MC, V. **Amenities:** 2 Restaurants; 2 bars; outdoor pool; health club; spa. *In room:* A/C, TV, minibar, Internet (400B per day).

MODERATE

Novotel Phuket ★   Located on a hillside toward the northern end of Patong beach (the quieter end), this resort offers most of the facilities of a top-end hotel at midrange prices. Bright, tiled rooms all have balconies, most with views of the bay, and stylish furnishings are complemented by Thai flourishes throughout. Facilities include several restaurants and bars, a three-tiered swimming pool, and a customized tour desk where you can plan a tailor-made tour. Service is smooth and efficient, as you would expect of this international chain.

Kalim Beach, Patong, Phuket 83150. ℂ **07634-2777.** Fax 07634-2168. www.novotelphuket.com. 215 units. 4,500B–7,000B double. From 9,000B suites. MC, V. **Amenities:** 2 restaurants; 2 bars; 2 outdoor pools; room service; babysitting. *In room:* A/C, TV, minibar, fridge, Wi-Fi (free).

INEXPENSIVE

Budget lodgings are difficult to find on Patong beach, and what there is tends to be located in the backstreets where it's a bit of a trek to the beach. If you need to find a really cheap place to stay, you'll fare better in Phuket Town or on the beaches farther south at Kata and Karon. Of the budget accommodation at Patong, the following offers reasonable value:

Palmview Resort (135 Nanai Rd.; ℂ **07634-4837;** www.palmview-resort.com) is a recently renovated place with just 20 rooms set around a pool, though it's a few blocks back from the beach; rates start at 1,650B in high season. **Kelly's Hotel** (47/1 Nanai Rd.; ℂ **086630-11196,** cell; www.kellyshotelphuket.com) is also a bit of a trek from the beach but is very popular for its helpful management, small pool, and free Wi-Fi.

The Northwest Coast

KAMALA & SURIN BEACHES

These two attractive beaches, both flanked by cliffs and steep hillsides, are home to some of Phuket's most exclusive hideaways, so the area is worth considering if your main objective is peace and quiet at any price.

Very Expensive/Expensive

Ayara Hilltops ★★★   Fancy hillside suites give guests at this ultra-contemporary resort the impression of being suspended high above the cliffs, but there are snappy buggies to take you to your rooms, and, once you've arrived, you won't want to leave. Rooms have an organic feel to them, with wooden floors, earth-toned decor, and floor-to-ceiling windows that take maximum advantage of the views. Choose from either villas or suites, many with private plunge pools. The Spice Terrace restaurant offers romantic dining either outside under the stars, or in the air-conditioned interior. It all makes for a good honeymoon hideaway.

125 Moo 3, Srisoonthorn Rd., Cherng Talay, Thalang, Phuket 83110. www.ayarahilltops.com. © **07627-1271.** Fax 07627-1270. 48 units. 8,100B–35,000B suite/villa. AE, MC, V. **Amenities:** Restaurant; bar; outdoor pool; health club; spa; room service; babysitting. *In room:* A/C, TV, fridge, minibar, hair dryer, Wi-Fi (free).

The Surin Phuket ★★★   The Surin commands an excellent view of Pansea Bay and has its own private stretch of sand, with shady wooden walkways under the trees. From the exotic lobby, with columns and a lily pond, to sleek private bungalows, it is one of the most handsome properties on the island. True, the quality comes with a big price tag, but this romantic getaway has all the details down pat. Each room is a thatched minisuite with a private sun deck and top amenities. The black-tile swimming pool is large and luxurious. The fine service here caters to the likes of honeymooners and celebrities, and everyone is treated like a VIP. The Surin is chic, quiet, comfortably informal, and unpretentious, with fine-dining options.

118, Moo 3, Surin Beach Rd., Cherng Talay, Thalang, Phuket 83110 (next to the Amanpuri). www.thesurinphuket.com. © **07662-1580.** Fax 07662-1590. 108 units. From 10,900B superior cottage; from 20,500B beach suite. AE, DC, MC, V. **Amenities:** 3 restaurants; bar; outdoor pool; 2 outdoor lit tennis courts; spa; watersports equipment & dive center; room service; babysitting. *In room:* A/C, TV, minibar, Wi-Fi (free).

Paresa ★★★   "Paresa" is a Sanskrit word meaning "heaven of all heavens," and while this may seem an extravagant claim to make, this award-winning resort does instill a feeling of peace and contentment in its guests. Paresa offers an idyllic location (on a steep hillside with private infinity pools that seem to merge with the Andaman Sea beyond) and stylish luxury (spacious brick villas with wood floors and solid wood furnishings). The resort sprawls over such a wide area that a fleet of buggies and SUVs is needed to transport guests to and from their villas, which come in five categories of ascending magnificence. Facilities are all top class, including the Diavolo restaurant, and the luxurious spa, from which I emerged after a 90-minute Aroma Relax treatment as if I was walking on air. Cooking classes at Recipe use state-of-the-art cooking stations, and the Master Chef shares his secrets in helping guests throw a dinner party to remember.

49 Moo 6, Layi-Nakalay Rd., Kamala, Phuket 83150 (to the south of Kamala Beach). www.paresaresorts.com. © **07630-2000.** Fax 07630-2049. 49 units. 25,410B–61,690B suites and villas. AE, DC, MC, V. **Amenities:** 2 restaurants; bar; outdoor pool; health club; spa; butler (in selected villas). *In room:* A/C, TV/DVD, minibar, Wi-Fi (free).

Twin Palms, Phuket ★★★   The brainchild of a Swedish entrepreneur, this gorgeous Thai contemporary resort is not as flashy as its neighbors, but nonetheless has sublime charm and a timeless, yet cutting-edge style. A stunning, open-rafter lobby with glassy stone floors makes way to a vast tropical water garden, the centerpiece of the property. Guests have use of an excellent spa and highly acclaimed restaurant, Oriental Spoon, as well as an extensive wine room. The airy Lagoon rooms and suites are a good choice, some of which have terraces that go straight into the water. The room decor uses numerous Thai references, such as sleek dark wood floors and local art and crafts (including rugs made by the Mae Fah Luang crafts charity). Twin Palms is the place to be after dark too, as its Catch Beach Club is currently one of the hottest spots for Phuket scene-makers to be seen.

106/46 Moo 3, Surin Beach Rd., Cherng Talay, Thalang, Phuket 83110 (opposite the golf course). http://twinpalms-phuket.com. ✆ **07631-6500.** Fax 07631-6599. 97 units. From 10,500B deluxe palm room; from 11,750B deluxe lagoon room; from 19,400B 1-bedroom deluxe pool suite; 33,400B 2-bedroom penthouse residence. AE, DC, MC, V. **Amenities:** 2 restaurants; bar; outdoor pool; watersports equipment; room service; babysitting; Internet. *In room:* A/C, TV, minibar, Wi-Fi (free).

Bang Thao Bay (The Laguna Resort Complex)

Twenty minutes south of the airport and just as far north of Patong Beach on the western shore of Phuket, this isolated area is Phuket's high-end, "integrated resort" of several properties that share some of the island's most top-rated facilities. Among them you'll find world-class health spas, countless restaurants, and the island's best golf course. The grounds are impressively landscaped, and the hotel properties are scattered among the winding lagoons, all navigable by boat. The best thing about staying here is that you can dine at any of the fine hotel restaurants, connecting by boat or free shuttle, and be charged on one simple bill at whatever resort you choose to stay at. Those below are the pick of the bunch, but if you'd like to hob-nob with the jet-set without paying top dollar, consider the **Best Western Allamanda Laguna** (✆ **07636-2700;** www.allamanda phuket.com), which enjoys all the same facilities at much lower rates; a spacious junior suite here will set you back around 5,000B.

VERY EXPENSIVE

Banyan Tree Phuket ★★★   This is possibly Phuket's most famous hideaway for honeymooners, sports stars, and high society. Private villas with walled courtyards, many with private pools or Jacuzzis, are spacious and grand, and lavishly styled in teakwood with outdoor bathtubs. The main pool is truly impressive—a free-form lagoon, landscaped with greenery and rock formations—with a flowing water canal. A small village in itself, the spa provides a wide range of beauty and health treatments in luxurious rooms—you can request a private massage in your room or in outdoor pavilions. The resort can arrange barbecues at your villa, or you can dine at the Tamarind Restaurant, which serves delicious, light, and authentic health food. The Banyan Tree garners many international awards, especially for its Green Initiative and eco-friendly stance. In high season, peak surcharges apply.

33/27 Moo 4, Srisoonthorn Rd., Cherng Talay District, Amphur Talang, Phuket 83110 (north end of beach). www.banyantree.com. ✆ **800/591-0439** or 07632-4374. Fax 07632-4375. 150 units. 20,000B–80,000B villas. AE, DC, MC, V. **Amenities:** 5 restaurants; lounge; outdoor pool; golf course; 3 outdoor lit tennis courts; health club; spa; watersports equipment; room service; babysitting. *In room:* A/C, TV, minibar, fridge, Wi-Fi (free).

Dusit Thani Laguna Resort ★★★ ☺   The Dusit hotel group has some fine properties in Thailand, and the Dusit Laguna is no exception. Opt for a deluxe room with a balcony and oceanview and you'll find rates are reasonable. Suites are large and luxurious, while the oceanfront pool villas are veritable palaces, occupying almost 300 sq. m (3,229 sq. ft.). The hotel offers four excellent restaurants; of note is their quaint Italian restaurant, La Trattoria, serving authentic Italian cuisine in a chic but laid-back pavilion. The well-landscaped gardens open onto a wide white-sand beach flanked by two lagoons. Facilities for families are excellent, with a whole gamut of entertainment, including computer games.

390 Srisoonthorn Rd., Cherng Talay District, Phuket 83110 (south end of beach). www.dusit.com. ℂ **07636-2999.** Fax 07636-2900. 254 units. 8,200B–13,700B double; from 19,700B suite; from 46,000B villa. AE, DC, MC, V. **Amenities:** 4 restaurants; lounge; outdoor pool; pitch and putt on premises and golf course nearby; outdoor lit tennis courts; health club; spa; watersports equipment; bikes; room service; babysitting; Internet. *In room:* A/C, TV, minibar, fridge, Wi-Fi (535B per day).

Outrigger Resort & Villas ★★ ☺ Situated on the northern fringe of the Laguna complex, Outrigger consists of two sections: The older part consisting of detached, spacious villas of two to four bedrooms, some with a private pool, and a newer section that contains the lobby, an inviting angular pool, health club, and a seven-story block of one- to three-bedroom suites. The latter occupy the top floor and boast rooftop private pools with impressive views across the Laguna complex. All suites have huge open-plan living, dining, and cooking areas with floor-to-ceiling windows and big balconies, plus cozy bedrooms and sparkling-clean bathrooms. There's free bicycle use for all guests for one day, and a cheery kids' club right next to the pool and lobby. The resort's main restaurant, Panache, serves a tempting range of Thai and Mediterranean dishes, and each morning it receives a visit from a young elephant that gives rides to kids and hopes to receive a few bananas.

Laguna Village, 142/3 Moo 6, Cherngtalay District, Phuket 83110. www.outrigger thailand.com. ℂ **07633-6900.** Fax 07633-6970. 87 units. 12,700B–19,400B 1- to 3-bedroom suites; 14,400B–37,900B 2- to 4-bedroom villas. AE, MC, V. **Amenities:** 2 restaurants; bar; 2 outdoor pools and outdoor kids' pool; health club; bikes; children's club. *In room:* A/C, TV/DVD, kitchen, Wi-Fi (free).

Layan Beach

Phuket Pavilions ★★ "No tan lines" is the catchphrase at this intimate escape, by which guests should understand that they can enjoy total privacy within the grounds of their spacious pool villa. The resort is situated on a hill just north of the Laguna complex, and while it's a bit of a trek from the beach, most guests will settle for lounging around the luxurious pavilions. Furnishings are supermodern and comfortable, and each pavilion has its private pool within stepping distance of the bedroom, as well as fantastic views out to sea. Buggies are on hand to run guests to the Plantation Club restaurant or 360° Lookout bar, and spa treatments are offered in specially constructed rooms beside each private pool. No children under 16 are allowed to guarantee a quiet atmosphere for guests.

31/1 Moo 6, Cherng Talay, Phuket 83110. www.thepavilionsresorts.com/phuket. ℂ **07631-7600.** Fax 07631-7601. 49 units. From 17,000B pool villa; 35,000B 3-bedroom pool villa. AE, MC, V. **Amenities:** Restaurant; bar; spa; shuttle to beach. *In room:* A/C, TV/DVD, hair dryer, Wi-Fi (free).

Nai Thon & Nai Yang Beaches

Nai Thon and **Nai Yang Beaches** form part of the **Sirinath National Marine Park,** which was established to protect offshore coral reefs and turtles that nest in this region. These casuarina-fringed stretches of sand are good for leaving the crowds behind, but be warned that the region is isolated, and, apart from a few upmarket resorts, there are limited facilities in this remote corner of the island.

Nai Yang is known for its annual release of hatchling sea turtles into the Andaman Sea. Mature sea turtles weigh from 45 to 680kg (100 to 1,500 lb) and swim the waters around Phuket, and though the law is supposed to protect them from fishermen and poachers, who collect their eggs from beaches, their numbers are dwindling. If not for the efforts of international volunteer groups such as **Naucrates** (www. naucrates.org), which has spent years working out of a small conservation center at Ko Phra Thong near Khuraburi, about 100km (62 miles) north of Phuket, these creatures would probably have become extinct already. As it is, the number of Olive Ridley turtle nests has plummeted in recent years, and Thai scientists predict that they will soon be extinct in Thailand. Leatherback turtles fare even worse, and are rarely seen in this part of the world these days.

Nai Thon is just south of Nai Yang (closer to Laguna) and is home to a handful of resorts. It is one of the quietest beaches, yet is also possibly the most picturesque, on the entire west coast of Phuket.

NAI THON
Very Expensive

Trisara ★★ Well away from the fray, Trisara is a small boutique property some 15 minutes from the airport. The resort affords a high level of comfort in a clutch of private, contemporary pool villas right at the seaside. There's a high price tag attached to its luxury villas, which are priced according to proximity to the sea. It's definitely not as classy as The Surin, nor as celebrity-friendly as The Banyan Tree, but it would like to think it outdoes both; at times, you'll rub up against a distinct attitude here. Still, its private spaces are picturesquely flamboyant, with pools overlooking the blue water below—it should appeal to those who enjoy the isolation.

60/1 Moo 6, Srisoonthorn Rd., Cherng Talay, Thalang, Phuket 83110. www.trisara.com. ©**07631-0100.** Fax 07631-0300. 39 units. 26,794B–38,651B room/suite; from 85,617B 2-bedroom villa. AE, MC, V. **Amenities:** 2 restaurants; bar; private outdoor pool; seaside public pool; tennis courts; health club; spa; watersports equipment/rentals; bikes; children's center; room service; babysitting; free airport transfers. In room: A/C, TV, fax, minibar, fridge, hair dryer, Wi-Fi (free).

NAI YANG
Expensive

Indigo Pearl Resort ★★★ ☺ One of the earliest resorts on Phuket, the Pearl Village was destroyed in the 2004 tsunami and, after extensive restoration, was reborn as Indigo Pearl Resort. Its reincarnation was the work of landscape designer and Bangkok resident Bill Bensley and a team of local artisans. The revamped resort is a creative masterpiece. On the periphery of the national park, the hotel is isolated from the ravages of overdevelopment characterizing the rest of touristy Phuket. The facilities are excellent, especially for families—with rooms ranging from pavilions and villas to exquisitely furnished suites. The one drawback is that you're out in the sticks here, but, for rest and recreation, the resort is perfectly self-contained and close to nature. The resort was voted "Asia's leading design hotel" at the World Travel Awards in 2010.

Nai Yang Beach and National Park, Phuket 83104 (5 min. south of the airport). www.indigo-pearl. com. ©**07632-7006.** Fax 07632-7338. 277 units. 8,598B–50,000B suites and villas. AE, DC, MC, V. **Amenities:** 6 restaurants; bar; outdoor pool; golf course nearby; outdoor lit tennis courts; health club; watersports equipment; bikes; children's club; room service; babysitting. In room: A/C, TV, minibar, fridge, hair dryer, Wi-Fi (free).

Mai Khao Beach & the Far North of Phuket

Mai Khao is a wide sweep of beach on the northeastern shore close to the airport. It is Phuket's longest beach and is the site where sea turtles lay their eggs during December and January. The eggs are coveted by Thai and Chinese people, who eat them for their supposed life-sustaining power. Efforts are being made to assist these glorious animals and protect their potential hatchlings, but unfortunately it seems a case of too little, too late. Though the habitat is becoming less attractive to turtles, it is certainly more appealing to humans since several international hotel chains have opened new properties here in recent years.

VERY EXPENSIVE

Anantara Phuket Villas ★★★   Behind the tall laterite wall that separates the Anantara from the outside world lies a wonderland of tropical gardens and lagoons with secluded pool villas and a stretch of beach shaded by casuarina trees. The villas are artfully designed, with lots of traditional Thai ornamentation and the utmost in creature comforts. Beside the generous pool, the private gardens include sun loungers, a sala, and a huge outdoor bath, and there's a choice of indoor or outdoor showers. The large rooms are equipped with canopy beds and flatscreen TVs. The two restaurants are both extremely stylish—La Sala serving Thai and Sicilian cuisine all day and Sea Fire Salt specializing in seafood, with a resident salt sommelier sharing his secrets with diners. The beautiful grounds are a delight to stroll around, and there's even a thatched villa on a tiny island for the resident population of ducks.

888 Moo 3, Mai Khao, Talang, Phuket 83110. www.anantara.com. ✆ **07633-6100-9.** Fax 07633-6177. 83 units. 20,500B–27,000B 1-bedroom villa; 60,000B 2-bedroom villa. AE, DC, MC, V. **Amenities:** 2 restaurants; bar; outdoor pool; health club; spa. *In room:* A/C, TV/DVD, minibar, hair dryer, wine cabinet; Wi-Fi (free).

JW Marriott Phuket Resort & Spa ★★★   From the moment you set foot in this beachside paradise, you are encouraged to let the troubles of the outside world slip away. Set on a desolate and windswept stretch of Mai Khao Beach, the relaxing sounds of birds and flowing water follow you wherever you step. Comfortable spots to curl up and read are around every corner, from daybeds on stairwell landings to reading nooks in each beautifully appointed room. It is a 30-minute drive to Phuket Town, but the resort facilities are complete and few guests will need to leave, unless it's to take a bike ride to the next village or a kayak trip with nearby eco-outfit John Gray. Service at the JW Marriott is impeccable and the dining exemplary.

231 Moo 3, Mai Khao, Talang, Phuket 83110. www.marriott.com. ✆ **07633-8000.** Fax 07634-8348. 265 units. 6,960B–10,300B room; from 12,200B suite. AE, DC, MC, V. **Amenities:** 7 restaurants; 3 bars; 2 outdoor pools; 2 tennis courts; health club; spa; watersports equipment; children's club; room service; babysitting; executive level rooms w/private check-in; Internet. *In room:* A/C, TV, fridge, minibar, hair dryer, Wi-Fi (free in most expensive rooms, 1,000B per day in others).

Phuket Town

Most just pass through the island's commercial hub, but Old Phuket culture abounds in the many Sino-Portuguese homes and unusual architecture (much of which has recently been restored to its former splendor), and it's the best place to base yourself if you want to explore all the island's beaches. Even if you stay on the beach, it's well worth a visit, especially if Phuket Island is your only destination in Thailand (see "Where to Eat in Phuket," below, for dining options here).

EXPENSIVE

Cape Panwa Hotel ★★   Just 10 minutes outside Phuket Town, set on a former beachfront coconut plantation, Cape Panwa Hotel is one of Phuket's best-kept secrets and a haven of tranquillity. European-run, but with local staff, the hotel is popular with families and honeymooners who come for the relaxed charm and island ambience. All suites face the Andaman Sea and are set in tropical gardens. Dinner, or sunset cocktails at Panwa House—a grand Sino-Portuguese mansion—is a highlight after a day spent combing Old Town streets or relaxing on the beach.

27 Moo 8, Sakdidej Rd., Cape Panwa, Phuket 83000. www.capepanwa.com. © **07639-1123.** Fax 07639-1177. 246 units. From 6,100B–10,000B suite; 25,000B lodge. AE, DC, MC, V. **Amenities:** 4 restaurants; bar; 2 outdoor pools; tennis court; health club; watersports equipment; room service; babysitting. *In room:* A/C, TV/ DVD, minibar, fridge, hair dryer, Wi-Fi (500B per day).

MODERATE

Royal Phuket City Hotel ★★   For such a small town as Phuket, this hotel is surprisingly cosmopolitan. A true city hotel, Royal Phuket's facilities include one of the finest health clubs going, a full-service spa with massage, a large outdoor swimming pool, and a very professional executive business center. Above the cavernous marble lobby, guest rooms are smart with simple, contemporary furnishings. Views of the busy town below pale in comparison to the beachfront just a short ride away. The Atrium Lounge cocktail bar is one of the smartest in town.

154 Phang Nga Rd., Amphur Muang, Phuket 83000 (located to the east of Phuket Town, across from the intercity bus terminal). www.royalphuketcity.com. © **07623-3333.** Fax 07623-3335. 251 units. 2,600B–2,900B double; from 5,000B suite (discounts available). AE, DC, MC, V. **Amenities:** 3 restaurants; bar; outdoor pool; health club; spa; room service; cafe; Wi-Fi. *In room:* A/C, TV, minibar, fridge, hair dryer, Wi-Fi (200B per day).

Sino House   This place offers an economic alternative while providing all the essentials and a touch of style as well. Rooms are divided into two types—Beijing and Shanghai—and all feature period furnishings and classy decorative touches. There are floor to ceiling windows, a microwave and kitchen equipment, and free Wi-Fi too. Those rooms overlooking the road can be a bit noisy, so opt for a room out back.

1 Montri Rd., Phuket Town, Phuket 83000. www.sinohousephuket.com. © **07623-2494-5.** Fax 07622-1498. 57 units. 2,000B deluxe; 2,500B suite. MC, V. **Amenities:** Restaurant; spa; cafe. *In room:* A/C, TV/DVD, minibar, hair dryer, Wi-Fi (free).

INEXPENSIVE

Besides the recommendation below, there are a couple of other basic places worth considering. The **Thalang Guesthouse** (37 Talang Rd.; © **07621-4225;** www.talangguesthouse.com) is an old standby at the town center with fan rooms starting at 350B. Rooms are basic, but this Sino-Portuguese shophouse has lots of character and makes a convenient base to explore the town. The **Old Town Guesthouse** (42 Krabi Rd.; © **07625-8272;** www.phuketoldtownhostel.com) is under the same management and has slightly higher rates.

Baan Suwantawe ★ 📖   With just 20 well-equipped rooms, this place is a great base for budget travelers. It's located just north of the town center, within easy walking distance of the sights, yet has a strong rural feel to it as it's next to the Queen Sirikit public park. Rooms have comfortable beds, cable TV, a desk, and balcony, and there's even a small pool too. There's no restaurant but plenty of eateries nearby and staff are very helpful.

1/9-10 Dibuk Rd., Phuket Town, Phuket 83000. www.baansuwantawe.com. © **07621-2879.** Fax 07621-5541. 20 units. 1,400B studio; 2,200B–3,000B suite. MC, V. **Amenities:** Outdoor pool. *In room:* A/C, TV, minibar, Internet (100B per day).

WHERE TO EAT IN PHUKET

From tip-to-toe, north to south, it takes about an hour to drive all of Phuket, but the availability of hired tuk-tuks, hotel transport, or even self-drive vehicles means that for dining and nightlife, you can choose from any of the many options on the island. The beach areas in the west are chock-full with small eateries or smart hotel restaurants. In the throbbing Patong strip, culinary options stretch from fast-food outlets clustered around the beach to snazzy designer diners and Asian chains.

Kata & Karon

The busy road between Kata and Karon (as well as the many side streets) is crammed with small cafes and restaurants serving affordable Thai and Western food. There are also lots of outdoor beer bars and travelers cafes on the far southern end of Kata Beach, just behind Club Med; these places rock till late and are handy for grabbing a quick bite, local style. On the north end of Karon, stop by **Karon Café** (526/17 Soi Islandia Park Resort, off Patak Rd.; © **07639-6217;** www.karoncafe.com) for casual Western dining, including Aussie steaks. For a more expensive treat, **Joe's South** (Kata Gardens on Kata Noi Rd.; © **07628-5285;** www.baanrimpa.com/joessouth/ index.html) is a fine-dining spot set amid tropical gardens, with the same management as Baan Rim Pa at Patong.

EXPENSIVE

Boathouse Wine & Grill ★★★ THAI/INTERNATIONAL   So legendary is the Thai and Western cuisine at the Boathouse that the management arranges cooking lessons from its chef, Jean-Noel Lumineau, Thailand's only Maitre Cuisinier de France. A large bar and separate dining area sport nautical touches, and through huge picture windows, or from the terrace, diners can watch the sun set over the watery horizon. The cuisine combines the best of East and West and utilizes only the finest ingredients. Go for the French or Thai degustation menu (1,500B or just over 3,000B with paired wines)—a four-course feast of delectable dishes. However, if you're tempted by items on the a la carte menu, the Boathouse also has an excellent selection of international wines to accompany your choice—over 800 labels.

The Boathouse, 182 Koktanode Rd., Kata Beach. © **07633-0015.** www.boathousephuket.com. Reservations recommended during peak season. Main courses 560B–1,600B; seafood is sold at market price. AE, DC, MC, V. Daily 6:30am–11pm.

Mom Tri's Kitchen ★★★ INTERNATIONAL/THAI   Located at the Villa Royale Resort, Mom Tri's Kitchen serves fine cuisine from its luxury perch above the ocean, and is regularly honored with awards such as the Wine Spectator's Award of Excellence. It stocks over 700 wine labels including several organic wines, so you shouldn't have difficulty finding something to accompany your choice of Thai or international cuisine. The international menu includes lots of favorites such as chicken prosciutto and veal parmigiana, but I'd suggest being adventurous and opting for one of the Thai mains like the jumbo shrimp with pineapple in red curry. If you've still room for more, there are plenty of appealing desserts such as passion fruit crepe soufflé.

Villa Royale, 12 Kata Noi Rd., Kata Noi. ☎ **07633-3569.** www.momtriphuket.com. Reservations recommended. Main courses 460B–1,980B. AE, MC, V. Daily 6:30am–11:30pm.

On the Rock ★★ THAI/SEAFOOD   Part of the Marina Phuket (see p. 225), this little unassuming restaurant serves Thai cuisine on a scenic deck high above the south end of Karon Beach. Unlike so many of Phuket's trendy restaurants, the menu here is refreshingly unpretentious, featuring a range of classic dishes and every kind of seafood. Try the Seafood Basket featuring the local catch, grilled or fried. The staff is friendly and the restaurant is a great choice for a candlelit evening.

47 Karon Rd., Karon Beach (on bluff at south end of Karon Beach Rd.). ☎ **07633-0625.** www.marinaphuket.com. Main courses 350B–1,200B. AE, MC, V. Daily 11am–10:30pm.

MODERATE

The Cliff ★ INTERNATIONAL/ASIAN   High above Karon on the rise heading toward Patong, The Cliff is located in Centara Villas (see p. 225). Serving contemporary Thai and Mediterranean dishes (which they describe as "Mediter-Asian") from atop their hilltop perch, the restaurant offers an escape from town. Try the thinly sliced tuna for an appetizer. They also have worthy grilled items, from Aussie tenderloin to roast lamb, and a long list of excellent Thai curries, all artfully presented.

701 Patak Rd., Tambon Karon. ☎ **07628-6300.** www.centarahotelsresorts.com. Main courses 250B–750B. AE, MC, V. Daily 6:30–10:30pm.

Ratri Jazztaurant ★★ THAI   Perched high at the top of a precipitous hill slope, Ratri is worth the hideously steep 1-km (⅔-mile) climb for their classic local dishes, most of which pack an explosively spicy punch. An enthusiastic live jazz band plays late into the night. The music is great, but if you are looking forward to some dinnertime conversation, it makes that hard (you should go before sunset, in that case). There's a full wine cellar and cigar bar (so nonsmokers beware). The somewhat surly service is the only drawback.

Patak Rd., Kata Hill (behind Big One convenience store). ☎ **07633-3538.** www.ratrijazztaurant.com. Main courses 220B–850B. MC, V. Daily 3pm–late; live band 8:30pm–late.

Patong

Most of the small seafront *sois* offer pricey Thai and Italian food—often in expat-run places. If you have a hankering for seafood (and who doesn't at the seaside?), head to the southern end of the beach drag (Thaweewong Rd.). What was once just a collection of wooden shacks 10 years ago is now a long strip of chic diners. Though this road is plagued with touts, armed with menus and imploring tourists to choose their restaurant, this end of it is slightly less intense, so stand your ground. Pick a menu that you like the look of, and order from a wide selection of fresh seafood that is often displayed on ice at the front.

One popular little breakfast place is **Sabai-Sabai** (100/3 Thaweewong Rd.; ☎ **07634-0222**); the name means "relaxed," and indeed it is so, just a laid-back storefront in a small *soi* off busy Patong Beach Road. **Scruffy Murphy's** (Soi Bangla; ☎ **07629-2590;** http://scruffymurphysphuket.com) is a popular Irish pub that also serves good pub grub and fry-ups (great hangover chow).

EXPENSIVE

Baan Rim Pa ★★ ROYAL THAI   In a beautiful Thai-style teak house, Baan Rim Pa has dining in a romantic indoor setting or with gorgeous views of the bay from outdoor terraces, though the experience comes with a high price tag, and the wine list, if you go for it, even higher. Among high-end travelers, this restaurant serving Royal Thai cuisine is one of the most popular stops on the island, so be sure to reserve your table early. The piano bar features live music every evening. The owner of Baan Rim Pa has opened up a few other restaurants next door on the cliffside, including **Joe's Downstairs,** for cool cocktails and tapas (🕿 **07661-8245**), and the Italian restaurant **Da Maurizio** (🕿 **07634-4079**). He also runs **Joe's South** at Kata Noi.

223 Kalim Beach Rd. (on the cliffs just north of Patong Beach). 🕿 **07634-0789.** www.baanrimpa. com. Reservations required. Main courses 425B–1,350B. AE, DC, MC, V. Daily 1pm–midnight.

La Gritta ★★ ITALIAN   La Gritta is notable not just for its food but also for its stunning views of Patong Beach, which unfurls in a long silver strip off into the distance. It's well away from the fray, yet only a 15-minute walk northward to the end of the main beachfront road up on the headland. The walk will let you work up an appetite for the restaurant's extensive menu and superb wine list. The clam chowder makes a satisfying appetizer, while main dishes include plenty of seafood, such as sea bass, shrimp, or scallops—though there are imported steaks and lamb, too. For dessert, don't miss the chocolate Amaretti cake.

At the Amari Coral Beach Resort & Spa, 2 Meun-ngern Rd. (on the headland south of Patong Beach). 🕿 **07634-0106.** Main courses 480B–1,320B. AE, MC, V. Daily 10am–11:30pm.

The White Box ★ MEDITERRANEAN/THAI   As its name suggests, this restaurant is housed in a striking white cube with floor-to-ceiling windows near the north end of Patong Bay, and you could be forgiven for forgetting the reason for coming here (which, of course, is to eat) as you take in the chic furnishings and ultra-modern decor. You can tell from the look of the place that the food won't be cheap, and most main courses are over 500B, but fortunately the care that goes into the preparation makes them worth the high price tag. The menu is divided between The Sea (seafood), The Land (meat dishes), and Land & Sea—the first two being Mediterranean style and the last covering Thai.

245/7 Prabaramee Rd., Patong. 🕿 **07634-6271.** Reservations recommended. Main courses 480B–2,200B. AE, DC, MC, V. Daily 11am–11:30pm.

MODERATE

Pan Yaah THAI   This good escape from busy Patong dishes up some real Thai home cooking. The restaurant is a wooden deck overlooking the bay some 2km (1¼ miles) north of central Patong, with perhaps the best view in town. The menu is classic Thai, with some one-dish meals, such as fried rice or noodles, but is best enjoyed with friends sharing a number of courses, such as spicy *tom yum* soup with shrimp, stir-fried dishes, and whole fish cooked to order. Prices are reasonable and service is friendly and laid-back.

249 Prabaramee Rd., Patong (2km/1¾ miles north of Patong along the coast). 🕿 **07634-4473.** Main courses 180B–350B. MC, V. Daily 11am–11pm.

Patong Seafood Restaurant SEAFOOD   Take an evening stroll along the lively strip next to the beach and you'll find dozens of open-air seafood restaurants displaying their catch of the day on ice out front, accompanied by a pushy tout. This one is pretty typical of the lot, but has a long-established reputation. Like all the neighbors along here, it offers a selection of local fish such as grouper (*garoupa*), lobster, squid, shrimp, shellfish, and sometimes crab. Service is on the ball, and it's always busy—so head here early to avoid the crowds.

98/2 Thaweewong Rd., Patong Beach. ☏ **07634-1244.** Reservations not accepted. Main courses 180B–950B; seafood at market prices. AE, DC, MC, V. Daily 7am–11:30pm.

INEXPENSIVE

Banana Leaf THAI/SEAFOOD   Located in the heart of Patong, on the corner just north of the Holiday Inn Resort, this is a good choice for classic Thai dishes and every type of seafood at reasonable prices. The setting is an open-sided pavilion and the helpful staff is on hand to help with recommendations. Popular options are the whole steamed fish with sour plum, ginger, and spring onion, and the chicken aroha salad, served in a pineapple shell. There's a wide range of drinks as well, including some delicious shakes.

212 Soi Kepsup, Rat Uthit 200 Pee Rd., Patong (one block south of Jung Ceylon). ☏ **07629-4032.** Main courses 80B–250B. MC, V. Daily 7am–11:30pm.

Kamala Bay

Rockfish THAI/INTERNATIONAL   It's worth making the short journey from Patong Beach (or indeed from any other beach on Phuket) to sample this stylish oceanfront restaurant, which features different menus for daytime and evening. Try the Thai marinated chicken breast with Caesar salad for lunch, or crispy white snapper filet, cauliflower risotto, asparagus, and yellow curry sauce for dinner. Finish it off with a slice of white chocolate cheesecake and a sip of a cleverly named cocktail while admiring the sweeping view of the bay.

33/6 Kamala Beach Rd. (opposite the temple at the south end of the bay). ☏ **07627-9732.** Reservations recommended. Main courses 250B–900B. AE, MC, V. Daily 8am–1am.

Bang Tao Bay (the Laguna Resort Complex)

The many hotel restaurants of the five-star properties in the Laguna Complex could fill a small guidebook of their own. You can't go too wrong in any of the hotels, with **The Banyan Tree Phuket** (p. 230) topping the lot for sheer style and enormous variety (try the pan-Asian delicacies at **Saffron,** or delicious Mediterranean fare at **Watercourt**). One restaurant just outside the complex is worth mentioning; it's where all the hotel managers eat when they get out of work:

Tatonka ★★ INTERNATIONAL   Billed as "Globetrotter Cuisine," dining at Tatonka is indeed a foray into the realm of nomadic gastronomy. The owner is himself a well-traveled chef (check out his résumé written on the bathroom wall). Dishes here reflect those travels, a creative fusion of Mediterranean and Pacific-Rim cuisine, such as Peking Duck Pizza and Thai Bouillabaisse. Ask the waiter for a recommendation and enjoy.

382/19 Moo 1, Srisoonthorn Rd., Cherng Talay (at the entrance of the Laguna Resort, in Bang Tao Bay). ☏/fax **07632-4349.** www.phuket.com/tatonka. Main courses 275B–560B. MC, V. Thurs–Tues 6–10:30pm.

Chalong Bay & Rawai

A good bet for fresh seafood is in the far south of the island at Chalong Bay's **Kan Eang Seafood** (9/3 Chaofa Rd., Chalong Bay; ☏ **07638-1323**). You'll find whole fish or Phuket lobster (a giant clawless langoustine) just fresh from the ocean. If you've rented a car, a ride down this way makes for a fun day out. **Nikita's Café Bar** (☏ **07628-8703**) on the Rawai seafront is a cool seaside hangout for coffee and sundowners. Down Nai Harn Beach way, look out for **Los Amigos Cantina**

(© **08947-29128,** cell), next to Nai Harn Lake, for Mexican. The **Breakfast Hut** (© **07628-9823**), on the same road, serves tasty Western food.

Phuket Town

Though quite a long ride from the West coast beach areas, a night out in Phuket Town is worth it for some fine meals and a taste of local culture, and the range of dining options is yet another reason to base yourself in town. Besides the places listed below, one place worth checking out is the slickly styled **Siam Indigo ★** (8 Phang Nga Rd.; © **07625-6697;** www.siamindigo.com), which serves up Thai cuisine alongside steaks, cocktails, and a good range of wines.

Ka Jok See ★★ THAI   A truly special find, Ka Jok See is a smart and intimate European-styled venue set in an old Sino-Portuguese house, but what really sets it apart is its dancing, led by the friendly and fun-loving staff. The place has been here for years hiding mysteriously behind a façade dripping with ivy, and is patronized by well-heeled local professionals; it's so well known, there is no sign (look for the small Kanasutra Indian restaurant next door). Though its name means "stained glass," the decor opts for ceilings of huge wooden beams, giant plants, and candlelight instead. A great selection of music sets the stage for a romantic evening, one that's well worth a venture from the beach.

26 Takua Pa Rd., Phuket Town (a short walk from central Rasada Rd.). © **07621-7903.** Reservations recommended. Main courses 380B–620B. MC, V. Tues–Sat 6:30–11:30pm.

Salvatore's ★ ITALIAN   This is the real thing: Huge salads, pasta, and great pizza in a large air-conditioned dining room in the town center. The wine list is first-class, and, if you're lucky, the owner Salvatore may drop by your table. Commendable pasta, lasagna, steaks, and a range of daily specials are all made with loving care, plus many of the wines are imported. Don't miss the meringue lemon pie, which melts in your mouth and goes very well with a black coffee.

15 Rasada Rd., Tambol Taladyai (central Phuket Town). ©/fax **07622-5958.** Main courses 340B–850B. AE, MC, V. Tues–Sun Noon–2:30pm and 6:30–11pm.

Suay ★★★ 🍴 THAI/FUSION   A truly delightful find, this small place with a tiny attractive garden stands out for its superb preparation and presentation of classic Thai and fusion dishes at very reasonable prices. Choose between the cozy interior or the appealing patio and order up a spicy salad or curry from the main menu, or go for one of their daily specials such as lamb chop with tomato salsa. They also have some yummy desserts, a good range of shakes and juices, and a reasonable choice of wines and cocktails. Chances are that once you've finished your meal, you'll want to go back the next day.

50/2 Takua Pa Rd., Phuket Town (just west of the town center). © **08174-72424.** Reservations recommended. Main courses 85B–650B. MC, V. Tues–Sun 11am–3pm and 6–10pm.

Watermark Bar Restaurant ★ THAI/INTERNATIONAL   The Watermark is an expat hangout serving a choice of mostly fusion seafood dishes, and overlooking the marina, just north of Phuket Town; patrons can choose to dine either on the alfresco dining deck or in the glass-walled, air-conditioned interior. Try the delicious crab cakes for an appetizer, followed by the grilled white snapper in pistachio crust, or if you'd like to sample several dishes, opt for one of the set dinners, which are priced at around 1,000B per person. It's best to call first to reserve a table, as the place is occasionally booked for corporate events.

Phuket Boat Lagoon, 22/1 Moo 2, Thepkasattri Rd., Amphur Muang (10 min. north of Phuket Town; 30 min. from the west coast beaches). ℃ **07623-9730.** www.watermarkphuket.com. Reservations recommended. Main courses 320B–1,050B. MC, V. Daily 11am–11pm.

EXPLORING PHUKET

You can spend a lot of time on Phuket and still not do everything. Thanks to years of resort growth, a host of activities are on hand, appealing mostly to those who like a bit of action. The beachfront areas are full of tour operators, each vying for your business and offering similar trips (or copycat tours). Listed below are the most reputable firms, but ask lots of questions before signing up for anything, so there are no surprises.

Beachfront Watersports

A 10-minute **parasailing ride** is about 800B–1,000B at most beaches. You'll also find **Hobie Cats** for around 600B per hour, as well as **windsurf boards** for 200B per hour. On Patong, there are no specific offices to organize these activities, just small operators with hand-painted signs usually hanging around under umbrellas—bargain furiously.

Jet skis are technically illegal, but alas, as you'll hear them all along the length of Patong, it seems plenty of people are willing to spend their money on screaming up and down the beach on a gasoline-belching scooter. (Most of the noisier watersports activities are concentrated along Patong Beach.) Accidents are now so common between swimmers or divers and jet skis (some resulting in amputations or death) that areas are now being cordoned off from these (wholly unecological) aquatic toys.

You'll find small **sailboats and kayaks** for rent along all of the beaches. Kata is a good place to rent a kayak and play in the waves for 200B per hour, but ask about the strong riptides along this dangerous coast.

The hottest new beach activity is **kiteboarding** or **kitesurfing,** and a few companies, such as **Kiteboarding Asia** (℃ **08159-14594;** www.kiteboardingasia.com), offer 3-day introductory courses for around 11,000B. The best beaches for kiteboarding on Phuket are Rawai and Chalong in the south, and the best months for wind are January/February and July/August.

Day Cruising & Yachting

The turquoise waters of the Andaman Sea near Phuket are every city dweller's dream. Every December, Phuket hosts the increasingly popular **King's Cup Regatta,** in which almost 100 international racing yachts compete. For more information, check out www.kingscup.com.

For a different view of gorgeous Phang Nga Bay, book a trip aboard one of Asian Oasis's three luxury Chinese junks, the *June Bahtra 1, 2,* and *3.* Full-day trips include lunch and hotel transfers. Passage on an all-day cruise in stunning Phang Nga Bay, to the likes of James Bond Island, starts from 3,700B per person in high season, depending on the number in a group (alcoholic beverages are not included). Book through their website, www.asian-oasis.com.

There are more and more options for chartering yachts in Phuket. Contact **Asia Marine** for details (c/o Phuket Boat Lagoon, 20/8 Thepkasattri Rd., Tambon Koh-kaew, Phuket 83200; ℃ **07623-9111;** http://asia-marine.net) or **Sunsail** (Ao Po Grand Marina, 113/1 Moo 6, Tambon Paklok, Thalang,, Phuket 83110; ℃ **07633-6212;** www.sunsail.com).

Fishing

Blue Water Anglers are deep-sea fishing experts with well-equipped boats. They'll take you out for marlin, sailfish, swordfish, and tuna, and also have special night-fishing programs; but be warned that if you're new to the sport, it isn't cheap—boat charter alone begins at 53,000B, and on top of that you'll pay 3,000B per person. For more information, look up www.bluewater-anglers.com or call ☎ **08189-33650.**

Golfing

There are some superb golf courses on Phuket attracting enthusiasts from around the globe. Golf package tour companies offer some great discounts on greens fees; try **Phuket Golf** (www.phuket-golf.com) or, alternatively, give **Phuket Golf Holidays** (www.phuketgolfholidays.com) a go. Below is a selection of some of the best courses on the island.

○ **The Blue Canyon Country Club,** 165 Moo 1, Thepkasattri Rd., near the airport (☎ **07632-8088;** fax 07632-8068; www.bluecanyonclub.com), has two courses, the Canyon Course, a par-72 championship course with natural hazards, trees, and guarded greens, and the Lakes Course, which features water hazards on 17 holes (greens fees: 4,800B Lakes Course; 5,600B Canyon Course).

○ **Laguna Phuket Golf Club,** 34 Moo 4, Srisoonthorn Rd., at the Laguna Resort Complex on Bang Tao Bay (☎ **07627-0991;** fax 07632-4351; www.lagunaphuket golf.com), is a par-71 championship course with many water features (greens fees: 4,000B; guests of Laguna resorts receive a discount).

○ **Mission Hills Golf Resort & Spa,** 195 Moo 4, Phla Khlok (☎ **07631-0888;** fax 07631-0899; www.missionhillsphuket.com), was designed by Jack Nicklaus and offers oceanviews over 18 holes and a 9-hole bayview, night course (greens fees: 4,500B).

○ An older course, the **Phuket Country Club,** 97/4 Vichitsongkram Rd., west of Phuket Town (☎ **07631-9365;** fax 07631-9372; www.phuketcountryclub.com), has beautiful greens and fairways, plus a giant lake (greens fees: 3,500B).

Horseback Riding

A romantic and charming way to see Phuket's jungles and beaches is on horseback. The **Phuket International Horse Club,** 394 Moo 1, Bangtao Beach (☎ **07632-4199**), welcomes riders of all ages and experience levels, and can provide instruction for beginners and children. Prices start at 800B per hour, and a 90-minute trot along Bang Tao beach at sunset costs 1,180B.

Sea Kayaking

Phang Nga Bay National Park, a half-hour drive north of Phuket, hosts great trips by sea kayak. The scenery is stunning, with limestone karst towers rising from the bay of more than 120 islands. These craggy rock formations were the backdrop for the James Bond classic *The Man with the Golden Gun.* Sadly, due to unfettered commercialism, the most frequently visited islands are completely overrun with teeming tour groups dropping litter and packing the narrow paths. Sea kayaks are a perfect way to avoid these crowds and explore the many breathtaking caves and chambers that hide beneath the jagged cliffs. All tours include the hour-plus ride to and from Phang Nga, the cruise to the island area, paddle-guide, kayak, and lunch.

John Gray Sea Canoe ★ (124 Soi 1, Yaowarat Rd., Phuket Town 83000; ✆ **07625-4505;** www.johngray-seacanoe.com) is the most respected, low-impact, eco-tour operator and a pioneer of sea kayaking in the region. Their main trip is a "*hong* by starlight" tour (3,950B adults, 1,975B children), which runs from midday to 10pm and includes kayaking in the *hongs* and a seafood buffet in Phang Nga Bay. Their day trip is now only available for private charter (29,500B for a group of four). A guide will paddle you dexterously in and out of the caves—which is frustrating if you actually like paddling—but the caves are stunning, and there's free time for paddling on your own later. Multiday and more adventurous "self-guided" tours are also offered.

The folks at **Paddle-Asia** (18/58 Rasdanusorn Rd., Tambon Rasada, Phuket 83000; ✆ **08189-36558;** www.paddleasia.com) make Phuket their home and do trips throughout the region, with a focus more on custom adventure travel, not day junkets. They have options for anyone from beginner to expert, and on any trip you'll paddle real decked kayaks, not inflatables. A highlight is their trip to **Khao Sok National Park** (p. 174), a 3-day adventure in which you may even spot amazing jungle wildlife. Due to tragedies in this park in rainy season, Thai authorities often close it during storms, so stay abreast of the weather, especially in monsoon season. In Phuket, Paddle Asia can arrange offshore trips to outlying islands, kayak surfing on Kata Beach, or custom-made adventures ranging as far as Laos.

Scuba Diving

Because it's world renowned for its access to nearby **Surin** and **Similan Islands** (rated by many among the world's best dive sites), scuba diving is a huge draw to the island of Phuket. Thailand is one of the most affordable places to get into this hugely rewarding sport, yet it is not without its risks—safety is paramount when choosing your operator. When you are selecting a company, always check that it is PADI certified. Many of the storefront operations are just consolidators for other companies (meaning you get less quality care and pay a fee to a middle man), so ask if they have their own boats and make sure you'll be diving with the folks you meet behind the counter. Also check about the ratio of divers to instructor or dive master; anything more than five-to-one is not acceptable, and it should be more like two-to-one for beginner courses.

Below are a few of the best choices in Phuket. All these companies can arrange day trips to the nearby coral wall and wrecks, as well as overnight or long-term excursions to the Similan Islands (also PADI courses, Dive Master courses, or 1-day introductory lessons and Open Water certification). Multiday "Open Water" courses begin at around 14,000B.

- **Dive Asia** is a highly reputable firm on Phuket that appeals to serious divers. Their main office is at 24 Karon Rd., Kata Beach (✆ **07633-0598;** fax 07628-4033; www.diveasia.com). Dive packages include 4-day PADI certification courses, while full-day trips around Phuket run around 3,900B (for experienced divers only), including two or three dives.
- The folks at **Scuba Cat** ★ (94 Thaweewong Rd., Patong; ✆ **07629-3121;** www.scubacat.com) have one of the best things going in Patong. With some 10 years of experience, a large, friendly expatriate staff, and their own fleet of boats, Scuba Cat is very much a professional outfit, offering the full range of trips for anyone from beginner to expert (and at competitive prices). You can't miss the small practice pool in front of their beachside Patong office.

- **Sea Bees Diving** (1/3 Moo 9, Viset Rd., Chalong Bay; ©/fax **07638-1765;** www.sea-bees.com) is another good outfit offering day trips.
- **Thailand Divers** (198/12 Rat-U-Thit Rd., Patong; © **07629-2052;** www.thailand-divers.com) provides competitive services; they also have their own boats.

Snorkeling

In the smaller bays around the island, such as Nai Harn Beach or Relax Bay, you'll come across some lovely **snorkeling** right along the shore. For the best coral just off the shoreline, trek up to **Nai Yang Beach** for its long reef in clear, shallow waters. Nearby Raya Island is popular, and many venture farther to the **Similan Islands** or **Ko Phi Phi.** The best times to snorkel are from November to April before the monsoon comes and makes the sea too choppy. Almost every tour operator and hotel can book day trips by boat that include hotel transfers, lunch, and gear for about 1,000B per person.

Trekking & Other Activities

To experience the wild side of Phuket's interior, try a **rainforest trek** through the **Khao Phra Thaew National Park** in northeast Phuket; it's still relatively rich with tropical trees and wildlife. The park trails were recently upgraded and the reserve also houses the **Gibbon Rehabilitation Project** (see "Back to Nature," below, for info).

Then there's **elephant trekking,** a perennial favorite for children and adults. Elephants are not indigenous to Phuket, so what you get here is more-or-less a pony ride, but arguments over captive elephant-tour programs aside, the animals are reasonably well cared for here, and the tour cost goes toward their enormous feed bill. **Siam Safari Nature Tours** (45 Chaofa Rd., Chalong; © **07628-0116;** www.siam safari.com) offers a variety of tours. Their "four-in-one safari" lasts about 6 hours and includes an elephant trek through jungles to rubber estates, watching monkeys pick coconuts, a ride on a buffalo cart, and then a cruise on a junk in Chalong Bay. Prices are 2,350B for adults and 1,600B for children.

River Rovers (© **07628-0420;** www.riverrovers.com) is one way to see old Phuket and nature at its finest; this cruise takes in mangrove swamps with monkeys clambering in the branches, fish and mussel farms, and the chance to do a bit of exploring by kayak, with a fabulous fresh seafood lunch at a floating restaurant.

Back to Nature

Sirinath National Marine Park, 90 sq. km (35 sq. miles) of protected land and sea (mostly the latter) in the northwest corner of the island, offers a peaceful retreat from the rest of the island's tourism madness. There are two fantastic reasons to make the journey out to the park. The first is for Phuket's largest coral reef in shallow water, only 1,000m (3,280 ft.) from the shore. The second is for the rare chance of spotting the endangered Olive Ridley turtles that once came to nest every year between November and February. The Park headquarters (© **07632-8226;** www.dnp.go.th) is a very short hop from Phuket Airport off Highway 402.

At bars, restaurants, and guesthouses around Thailand, but particularly on Phuket, caged or drugged **lar gibbons** provide a dubious form of entertainment for tourists, many of whom are completely ignorant of the abuse these endangered creatures endure. These fragile primates are poached as pets when young, and caged until they are mature—and become aggressive. At this point they are sold to a bar, dressed in children's clothes, and fed amphetamines to stay awake at night (when they are normally asleep). Imprisoned by their owners by day, by night they are fed a diet of cigarettes and whisky—all in the name of "entertaining" the tourists. Some visitors unwittingly exacerbate the problem by paying to have their photo taken with a captive gibbon; some simple advice is—don't do it.

Many gibbons develop psychological problems and become extremely menacing, which is when the owners want to get rid of them. **The Gibbon Rehabilitation Project,** off Highway 4027, at the Bang Pae waterfall, in the northeastern corner of the island (✆ **07626-0492;** www.gibbonproject.org), is operated by the Wild Animal Rescue Foundation (WARF); it cares for mistreated gibbons, and volunteers are always welcome. Guides offer tours of the facility, open daily from 9am to 4:30pm. Admission is free, but donations are expected.

The **Phuket Aquarium** (✆ **07639-1126;** www.phuketaquarium.org), at the **Phuket Marine Biological Center** (51 Moo 8, Sakdidet Rd.), seeks to educate the public about local marine life and nature preservation. There's also a science and nature trail along the adjoining coast. Most of the signs throughout are in Thai but it is still worth a trip. It's open daily 8:30am to 4:30pm, and admission is 100B for adults, 50B for children.

Phuket Butterfly Garden & Insect World, Soi Phaneung, Yaowarat Road, Tambon Rasada, Phuket Town (✆ **07621-0861;** www.phuketbutterfly.com), breeds hundreds of gorgeous butterflies in a large enclosed garden. There are plenty of photo opportunities. It's open daily from 9am to 5pm; adult admission is 300B, and children aged 4 to 10 pay 150B.

You'd never think seashells were fascinating until you visit the **Phuket Shell Museum** (12/2 Moo 2, Viset Rd., Rawai Beach, just south of Chalong Bay; ✆ **07661-3666;** www.phuketseashell.com; admission 200B adults, 100B for kids). Billed as "the largest shell museum in the world," it's actually not the quantity that amazes (over 2,000 species), but the quality; don't miss the world's biggest golden pearl. As always, the gift shop sells a range of tempting high-quality shell products; however, these days, any eco-savvy traveler will be well aware that the retail shell industry is depriving a sea creature of a home, and that such countries as Australia actively prohibit their import. The museum is open daily from 8am to 6pm.

Spas

If you've come to Phuket to escape and relax, there's no better way to accomplish your goal than to visit one of the island's many spas. Even the smallest resort now offers full spa services (of varying quality), and you can find good, affordable massages along any beach and in storefronts in the main tourist areas.

For luxury treatments, the most famous and exclusive facility here is **The Spa at The Banyan Tree, Phuket ★★★**. In its secluded garden pavilions, you'll be treated regally; you may choose from many types of massage, body and facial treatments, or health and beauty programs. To make reservations, call ✆ **07632-4374** or visit www.banyantreespa.com. Expect to pay for the luxury, in the region of 4,000B for a 90-minute facial, or from 8,500B for a 2½-hour package, which combines several treatments.

Another high-end resort, in the farthest southeast part of the island, **Evason Phuket** makes for a great day-spa experience. Its **Six Senses Spa** is at 100 Vised Rd., Moo 2, Rawai Beach, Phuket 83130 (✆ **07638-1010;** fax 07638-1018; www.sixsenses.com), and it's as renowned, in both standards and price, as any other top spa on the island. A 90-minute Thai herbal massage costs 4,100B.

Hilton Phuket Arcadia Resort & Spa (Karon Beach; ✆ **07639-6433;** www. hilton.com) is home to one of the finest spas on the island, a village complex of individual spa suites connected by a meandering boardwalk; it's a great choice for luxury treatments.

Mom Tri's Spa Royale, at the Villa Royale, Kata Noi Beach (12 Kata Noi Rd.; ✆ **07633-3568;** www.villaroyalephuket.com), is home to a chic spa area at their luxury hilltop resort, with well-trained staff. Treat yourself to The Royale Treatment, a 3-hour indulgence that combines an organic body mask, a gentle scrub and a soak in an aromatic milk bath followed by a penetrating massage with coconut oil, all for 5,500B.

Patong Medical Spa (behind Patong Hospital, 57 Sainamyen Rd.; ✆ **07634-4855;** http://phuketthaispa.com/patongmedicalspa) is a more affordable day spa with trained Thai practitioners offering unique treatments such as herbal steam, reflexology, or the soothing, hot herbal poultice, called *prakob*. A 1-hour Thai massage begins at 700B.

Shopping

Patong Beach is the center of handicraft and souvenir shopping in Phuket, and its main streets and small *sois* are teeming with storefront tailors, leather shops, jewelers, and ready-to-wear clothing boutiques. Vendors line the sidewalks, selling everything from bras to batik clothing, arts and crafts, northern hill-tribe silver, and of course the usual fake brands and dodgy CDs—their importation is now illegal in many countries. Vendors everywhere in Patong have the nasty habit of hassling passersby; just ignore any greeting, and you may get away tout-free. Most prices are inflated compared to Bangkok or other tourist markets in Thailand, but some hard bargaining can get you the right price. Many items, such as northern handicrafts, are best if purchased closer to the source, but if this is your only stop in Thailand, everything is cheap compared to the West—you might as well stock up.

To avoid rip-off merchants, take a stroll to **JungCeylon** ★ (181 Rat-U-Thit Rd.; ✆ **07660-0111;** www.jungceylon.com), a megamall devoted to shopping, dining, and entertainment. Check out the section called "That's Siam," which is filled with a great range of local handicrafts from all over Thailand. JungCeylon also hosts some of the popular teenager label boutiques, sport shops, fast-food outlets, and fashions, as well as popular Asian brands. It's a much more relaxed and hassle-free shopping experience than most here.

The island's other malls consist of the humongous **Central Festival** (✆ **07629-1111**), about 10km (6¼ miles) inland from Patong and 3km (1¾ miles) inland from Phuket Town on Chalermprakiet Road. **Big C** (✆ **07624-9444**), a midrange mall, is next door. Nearby **Tesco Lotus** (✆ **07625-4888**) is unlike the British supermarket in that it sells mostly Thai-oriented consumer and food items, but it's also a good source of cheap clothing that won't fall apart in a week.

Visit **Phuket Town** for local arts, a few whacky boutiques, and some reputable antiques stores; don't miss a walk down Thalang Road, both for the shopping and the old architecture. For good-quality shopping suggestions and a great walking map of the Old Town, see www.artandcultureasia.com. The same company publishes the *Art & Culture South* guide, available around town, which offers pointers on where to buy antiques and original art, from boutiques in town to the galleries of Surin Beach and beyond.

One of the best tailors in the area is **Instyle,** in Patong (92/7-8 Thaweewong Rd.; ✆ **08966-56195;** www.phukettailor-instyle.com).

Phuket Entertainment & Nightlife

Patong is the center of nightlife on the island, though it serves up the same old sordid stuff as Patpong, in Bangkok; you'll find plenty of bars, nightclubs, karaoke lounges, snooker halls, and dance shows with pretty sleazy entertainment. While some wide-eyed teenagers or washed-up barflies may find it titillating to trawl the hundreds of hostess bars, many people, especially couples with families, may find these venues a complete turnoff. Lit up like a seedy Las Vegas in miniature, the Patong bar areas are filled with (often underage) working girls and boys in pursuit of wealthy foreign men. Since the Vietnam War, prostitutes (some of which are transsexuals) have plied Patong's girlie bars. See p. 377 for info on the risks associated with going with any commercial sex worker (CSW) during your visit.

Some hotels realize their guests may want to experience a more sophisticated side of Thai culture, so they stage occasional **Thai dance shows,** which, if done well, can be mesmerizing; check with the resorts listed earlier for info.

For those who don't head for the bars (which are open pretty much all night), Patong's endless markets and restaurants usually stay open till 11pm around the main beach towns, especially Patong.

BARS & CLUBS

Scruffy Murphy's (✆ **07629-2590;** http://scruffymurphysphuket.com), 50m (164 ft.) from the beach, down Bangla Road in Patong, is a typical Irish pub with mostly young Aussie or Brit tourists revving up to make a night of it. There's often live music or sports on TV. **Paradise** complex, in Soi Paradise (off Rat-U-Thit Rd.; no phone), is a gay-friendly zone of funky bars, clubs, and cafes. The classy **Seduction Disco** (off Soi Bangla; no phone; www.seductiondisco.com) usually has fabulous DJs and dancing, whatever your persuasion, while the **Banana Disco** (124 Thaweewong Rd.; ✆ **07634-0306**) is right on the beach road and has an outside bar where you can down a few while building up the courage to hit the dance floor upstairs. Admission is 200B, which includes a free drink.

Joe Kool's, at Ramada Resort, Karon Beach (568 Patak Rd.; ✆ **07639-6666**), is a family-friendly diner and entertainment venue with live music most nights. Near the center of the island, on the road between Kata Beach and Phuket Town, is the **Green Man** (82/15 Moo 4, Patak Rd., Chalong; ✆ **07628-1445;** www.the-green-man.net), a half-timbered English pub, filled with local expats and tourists. There are salsa classes on Tuesdays and a quiz night on Thursdays, and it's open until 1am.

Phuket Town also offers a few worthy music clubs; check out **Timber Rock** for local live bands that get the audience going after 10pm (118/1 Yaowarat Rd; ✆ **07621-1839**). For a more low-key evening, take a stroll down **Soi Rommanee** (which runs between Dibuk and Thalang Roads), admire the Sino-Portuguese architecture and drop into any street-side cafe that catches your fancy.

Jazz fans should make the trip down to Kata Beach to visit **Ratri Jazztaurant** (p. 236), the only real jazz venue on the island.

LIVE ENTERTAINMENT

It's kitschy, it's exhilarating, and, heck, it's *so* lifelike: **Dino Park Mini Golf ★** (✆ **07633-0625;** www.dinopark.com) is a great night out for bored teenagers or unruly whippersnappers who will love the Jurassic Park background of giant, roaring mechanical dinosaurs and (very lifelike) erupting volcanoes. Not only is it a good place to let them loose, but adults can even enjoy some grown-up time in the outdoor Flintstone-inspired bar and restaurant while the kids hit the links. Find the course in the heart of Kata Beach, adjoining the popular Marina Phuket Resort (p. 225).

The island's premiere theme attraction, **Phuket Fantasea** (© **07638-5111** for reservations; www.phuket-fantasea.com), is as touristy and kitschy as the huge billboards and glossy brochures around town make it seem. The show—set in a theme park filled with glitzy shops—is at Kamala Beach, north of Patong, on the coastal road. After a huge buffet in the palatial Golden Kinaree Restaurant, visitors proceed to the Palace of the Elephants for the show. As one might expect, the prices are inflated; the souvenirs, an exercise in haute tackiness; and the suppers, so-so (you can at least save your stomach by buying a show-only ticket). That said, the 75-minute spectacle itself is enormously entertaining. You can buy a ticket (including transport) in most any hotel lobby or travel agency, so check for deals. The park opens at 5:30pm, the buffet begins at 6pm, and the show starts at 9pm (in high season, Dec–Jan, there are occasionally extra performances at 5 and 7pm). Tickets for the show are 1,500B for adults and children alike, while dinner adds another 400B for adults and 200B for children (4–12 years old), and transportation another 300B per person.

On the south end of Patong, crowds of tourists pack the long-established transsexual extravaganza **Simon Cabaret,** 8 Sirirach Rd., Patong Beach (© **07634-2011;** www.phuket-simoncabaret.com). There are two evening shows nightly, at 7:45 and 9:30pm. This glitzy entertainment features scantily clad beauties (yes, they really are all male, or male transsexuals), who lip-sync their way through popular Asian and Western pop songs. If you enjoy theatrical high camp, it can be a lot of fun and its burlesque humor draws busloads (especially Asian grannies). The dance numbers have pretty impressive sets and costumes and the numbers are interspersed with light comic acts. The cost is 700B for adults and 500B for kids.

SIDE TRIPS FROM PHUKET: KHAO LAK & OFFSHORE ISLANDS

Khao Lak

Just over an hour from the northernmost tip of Phuket, in the province of **Phang Nga,** the coastal town of **Khao Lak** was the area hardest hit by the 2004 tsunami. Now almost entirely rebuilt, today it's a burgeoning eco-tourism destination with some magnificent resorts, some new, and some wholly rebuilt. Popular with the Euro and Scandinavian crowds, today it attracts nature lovers who come to go bird-watching and soak in its waterfalls. However, the town's main attraction is as a jumping-off point for visits to some superb dive sites around **Ko Similan National Marine Park ★★★** (the best months to visit are Dec–May; the park is closed May–Oct). Admission to the park is 400B for adults, 200B for children.

Comprising nine islands, the **Similan Islands** are rated in the top-10 best dive sites in the world for the stunning arrays of unspoiled corals, sea fans, and sponges, as well as angelfish, parrotfish, manta rays, and sometimes white-tipped sharks. Numerous local dive operators offer short (approx. 3 hr. by speedboat) or long trips to these regions from Thap Lamu Pier, 8km (5 miles) south of Khao Lak. For information about bungalows or camping on the islands, contact **Similan National Park** (local office ✆ **07645-3272**). An air-con bungalow costs 2,000B a night, while a fan room is 1,000B.

To the north of the Similan Islands lies **Ko Surin National Park ★★★** (✆ **07647-2145**), which comprises five islands with some of the best shallow water corals you could wish to see (great for snorkeling!). Whale sharks are known to frequent these waters, which, in the past, were once the exclusive domain of Phuket's indigenous people, the Sea Gypsies—known in Thai as "*chao ley*," or "sea people." You might even spot a few of them on the islands, easily identifiable with their dark skin and light hair, with their simple thatched-roof boats bobbing on the limpid waters offshore. At park headquarters, a fan-cooled bungalow costs 2,000B and an air-conditioned bungalow with two bedrooms costs 3,000B.

Boats to Ko Surin leave from Khuraburi Pier, north of Khao Lak, with a journey time of 4 hours to the islands, though the islands are closed to visitors from mid-May to mid-November. From Khuraburi, fans of marine life can take a day trip to isolated **Ko Phra Thong** to visit the island's conservation center. Manned (only in dry season) by an international team of experts and volunteers, it surveys and protects rare turtles and the region's disappearing, yet ecologically vital, mangroves. See www.naucrates.org for info.

Another stellar outfit, the **Ecotourism Training Center (ETC)**, is a nonprofit organization set up by a dynamic American, Reid Ridgway, to provide long-term career training to tsunami-affected youth. Established in 2005, the Khao Lak program trains local Thais in sustainable community tourism and diving skills to PADI Dive Master and Instructor level. For more information, see www.etcth.org.

Other local attractions include miles of peaceful white-sand beaches, elephant trekking, temple tours, white-water rafting, and jungle treks. Visit **Khao Lak Land Discovery** (21/5 Moo 7, Petchkasem Rd., Khao Lak; ✆ **07648-5411;** www.khao laklanddiscovery.com) for information about such activities.

WHERE TO STAY

Many visitors who are tired of Phuket's full-on party vibe head up here for a more tranquil break, and the range of accommodation is constantly growing, with properties ranging from dream resorts to simple shacks.

Very Expensive

The Sarojin ★★★   This multiple-award-winning property set on 4 hectares (10 acres) of beachside land offers the opportunity for either complete relaxation or adventures in the forest or out at sea with the aid of its "imagineers"—personal concierges intent on satisfying guests' every whim. The suites and residences are surrounded by lush gardens and feature wooden floors, floor-to-ceiling windows, intimate baths for two, complementary Wi-Fi, and daily fruit baskets. The Pathways Spa blends ancient massage techniques with modern comforts, while the two dining options, Ficus and The Edge are truly top class.

60 Moo 2, Kukkak, Takuapa, Phang Nga 82190. www.sarojin.com. ✆ **07642-7900-4.** Fax 07642-7906. 56 units. AE, MC, V. 11,375B garden residence; 14,785B pool residence; 16,850B suite. **Amenities:** 2 restaurants; bar; outdoor pool; nearby golf course; nearby tennis courts; health club; spa; watersports equipment; bikes. *In room:* A/C, TV/DVD, hair dryer, Wi-Fi (free).

Expensive

Le Meridien Khao Lak Beach & Spa Resort ★ ☺   Occupying an enormous stretch of beach to the north of town, this large resort offers plenty in the way of activities and dining. It is especially fun for kids, as there is a designated beach for them, located beside the award-winning spa, and a Penguin Club, where supervisors organize treasure hunts, dancing classes, and face painting, among other activities. The villas are particularly appealing, with spacious lounges, private pools, and personal butlers.

9/9 Moo 1, Kukkak, Takuapa, Phang Nga 82190. www.starwoodhotels.com. ✆ **800-543-4300** or 07642-7500. Fax 07642-7575. 243 units. AE, MC, V. From 7,500B deluxe; from 10,000B suite; from 14,000B villa. **Amenities:** 6 restaurants; bar; 3 outdoor pools; 2 tennis courts; health club; spa; watersports equipment; children's club. *In room:* A/C, TV, hair dryer, Wi-Fi (free in most expensive rooms, 470B per day in others).

La Flora Resort & Spa ★   This stylish resort is the ideal place for a romantic getaway, with an attractive garden, a good swimming beach, and excellent service. Rooms are fitted out in contemporary Asian style, and most have balconies with daybeds. The two-bedroom villas right on the beach feature Jacuzzis and outdoor rain showers. Check their website for current offers for packages of a few days, and for information on available Thai cooking and boxing classes.

59/1 Moo 5, Kukkak, Takuapa, Phang Nga 82190. www.lafloraresort.com. ✆ **07642-8000.** Fax 07642-8029. 138 units. AE, MC, V. From 6,345B deluxe room; from 11,745B villa. **Amenities:** Restaurant; bar; 2 outdoor pools; tennis court; health club; spa; watersports equipment; bikes. *In-room:* A/C, TV, hair dryer, Wi-Fi (free).

Moderate

There are plenty of midrange options in Khao Lak. Apart from the recommendation below, it's worth considering **Palm Galleria Resort** (27/102 Moo 2, Kukkak, Khao Lak, Phang Nga 82190; ✆ **07642-7000;** www.khaolakpalmgalleria.com) on scenic Pakarang Beach, about 15km (9⅓ miles) north of Khao Lak.

Baan Krating Phuket Resort 🌶   Like its property at the southern tip of Phuket, this small resort of thatched bungalows is wonderfully secluded among dense vegetation at the edge of Khao Lak–Lam Ru National Park. As it is set on a cliff above a rocky beach, it was one of the few places that did not have to completely rebuild after the tsunami. Rooms don't have all the bells and whistles of the top-end resorts, but all are comfortably furnished and service is of a high standard, making this resort good value.

28 Moo 7, Kukkak, Takua Pa, Phang Nga 82190. www.baankrating.com/khaolak. ✆ **07648-5188-9.** Fax 07648-5187. 32 units. MC, V. From 3,200B deluxe room. **Amenities:** 2 restaurants; bar; outdoor pool; Internet; Wi-Fi (free in lobby). *In room:* A/C, TV, minibar, hair dryer.

Inexpensive

On the budget end, there are bungalows in a coconut grove near the beach at **Phu Khao Lak** (Moo 7, Kukkak, Khao Lak, Phang Nga 82190; ✆ **07648-5141;** www. phukhaolak.com), with fan rooms starting at 600B, and air-con rooms from 1,800B. **Khao Lak Banana** (Soi Bang La On; ✆ **07648-5889;** www.khaolak.phang-nga. org) is another good deal, with fan rooms at 700B and rooms with air-conditoning 1,000B; a pool and Wi-Fi are bonus features at both places.

WHERE TO EAT

In addition to the many hotel restaurants on hand, there are countless dining venues in town, though several places close during the low season (May–Oct). Among the best, try **Joe's Steak House** (56 Moo 5, Bang Niang, Khao Lak; ✆ **08789-36833**), which is open for dinner only (except Mon)—reservations are highly recommended. For Thai food, **Jai Restaurant** (Main Rd.; ✆ **07648-5390**) is excellent and just two doors down from Khao Lak's most happening late-night live music bar, **Happy Snapper**

(Main Rd., 5/2 Moo 7, Khao Lak; ℂ **07648-5500;** www.happysnapperbar.com).
O'Connor's Irish Pub (5/52 Moo 7, Kukkak; no phone) is a few steps away, offering
Thai cooking classes and serving draft Guinness with home-cooked European meals.

Yao Islands ★

In the middle of Phang Nga Bay, about halfway between Krabi and Phuket (an hour's
boat ride from Phuket's Bang Rong Pier—north of Boat Lagoon, turn east at the
Heroines' Monument), the twin islands of **Ko Yao Yai** and **Ko Yao Noi** ("Big Long
Island" and "Little Long Island") are where nature lovers head to enjoy some scenery
and relax. A world apart from the clamor of Ko Phi Phi, Phang Nga Bay's two largest
islands are not as yet very touristy and are great for cruising by motorbike or mountain
bike (available for rent on both islands at around 200B/100B per day).

A couple of reasons these islands never became as popular as Ko Phi Phi is that
most beaches are rather stony and the sea is not as clear as around nearby islands, so
they are not great for swimming. The nearest things to civilization on Ko Yao Noi are
the 7-Eleven store and ATM, and there's still not a traffic light to be seen. Yet this is
the more developed of the two islands, with a road running all the way around it and
a rapidly growing choice of resorts (mostly on the east coast). Ko Yao Yai, by contrast,
has just a few roads and a handful of places to stay.

More active travelers can go kayaking, bird-watching, or head off to snorkel and
explore nearby uninhabited islands by longtail; any resort can make arrangements. In
addition, there's fishing, jungle walks, or the exhaustive sport of hammock swinging:
It all makes for a perfect island escape.

Ferries to both islands leave Bang Rong Pier approximately hourly throughout the day,
and cost 120B. Call ahead to your accommodation to arrange transport from the pier.

WHERE TO STAY

Some resorts on Ko Yao Noi open all year, while others close during the rainy season
(May–Sept). There's such a range of choice that you might pay anywhere between
1,000B and 50,000B for a night's stay. For a laid-back budget bungalow resort, try
Sabai Corner (ℂ **07659-7497;** www.sabaicornerbungalows.com), which has a
handful of bungalows from 1,000B; each has a different design but all have spacious
balconies and hammocks. The restaurant here serves up tasty Thai and Italian dishes.
A good midrange choice is **Lom'Lae Resort** (ℂ **07659-7486;** www.lomlae.com),
situated on a tranquil beach at the south end of the island, with rooms from 2,500B
(closed May–Sept); it also has a dive shop. Right next door (though vegetation is so
dense that guests probably never know) is the tiny, upmarket **Koyao Bay Pavilions**
(ℂ **07659-7441;** www.koyaobay.com), where the gorgeous suites, cottages, and villas go for around 10,000B. You'll find similar prices and facilities at **Ko Yao Island
Resort** (ℂ **07659-7474;** www.koyao.com), about halfway down the east coast in a
former coconut plantation. This place has 15 thatched and well-spaced villas with
indoor and outdoor bathrooms.

If you need a break from your chosen resort on Ko Yao Noi, head on down to **Pyramid Bar & Restaurant** (ℂ **08141-55274**) at the south end of the east coast,
where they serve decent Thai food and good burgers. They also have a pool table and
live music on Friday nights.

On **Ko Yao Yai,** the **Yao Yai Island Resort** (ℂ **081968-4641;** www.yaoyai
resort.com) has bungalows from 1,350B, while the **Heimat Gardens Guesthouse**

(© **085794-7428;** www.heimatgardens.com) has rooms starting at 800B. It is equally close to the beach and offers friendly service.

Six Senses Yao Noi ★★★ If there's one person whose job I envy, it's whoever gets to choose the locations for Six Senses resorts. They are always in spectacular places with breathtaking views, and this resort on Ko Yao Noi is no exception—the surrounding seascape is studded with karst outcrops. There's no need for guests to rough it on the regular longtail ferry either; they get whisked to and from the island by swanky speedboat, or helicopter if they prefer. The private pool villas here are set on a hillside that faces a dramatic cluster of limestone peaks rising from the sea. Rooms are equipped with every conceivable luxury, including chilled wine cabinets, and each villa is assigned a personal butler. The simple but stylish teak architecture is a treat for the eyes, and true to its name, Six Senses leaves no sense unfulfilled, with superb cuisine in the Dining Room and Living Room, a host of watersports including sailing classes, and the usual range of heavenly spa treatments.

56 Moo 5, Ko Yao Noi, Phang Nga 82160. www.sixsenses.com. © **07641-8500.** Fax 07641-8518. 54 units. AE, MC, V. 18,500B–51,500B pool villa. **Amenities:** 2 restaurants; bar; tennis court; health club; spa; watersports equipment; bikes (free). *In room:* A/C, TV/DVD, minibar, private pool, Wi-Fi (free).

Racha Islands & Phang Nga Bay ★★

From Chalong Bay at the south end of Phuket, there's a daily ferry service to the idyllic islet of **Ko Racha** (aka Ko Raya or Ko Raja), a delightful island getaway with a perfect white-sand beach. It's hugely popular with day-trippers in the dry season. Sybarites in search of seclusion can also splash out on a pool villa at **The Racha** (© **07635-5455;** www.theracha.com), a magnificent contemporary-styled luxury hotel that cascades down the hill to the cerulean sea. (The hotel offers speedboat transfers to its guests, subject to the weather.) You'll need deep pockets for their premium Lighthouse suite, which costs 52,000B, but if that seems a bit steep, you can get deluxe villa rates online for 9,600B.

Phang Nga Bay, with its towering karst limestone spires, is a very popular day trip by boat. Some might say it's *too* popular, with hordes of tour groups descending on its tiny beaches, but it depends where you go—some of the smaller islands are still not overrun. A more peaceful trip around the bay by sea kayak is possibly a better bet. **Ko Phi Phi** is another oversold day trip for snorkeling, or more commonly an overnight stay from Phuket (p. 260).

KRABI ★★ (AO NANG, RAILAY, & KHLONG MUANG BEACHES)

814km (506 miles) S of Bangkok; 165km (103 miles) E of Phuket; 42km (26 miles) E of Ko Phi Phi; 276km (171 miles) N of Satun; 211km (131 miles) SW of Surat Thani

For many tourists, Krabi has become an eco-friendly alternative to the heavily commercialized Phuket and resort boomtown of Ko Phi Phi. For others, it's an easy stop along the way. Flights connecting with Krabi's international airport mean visitors can bypass Bangkok and arrive directly from Singapore, Kuala Lumpur, Ko Samui, or arrange a road transfer from Phuket International airport. Ferries and minivans from other destinations connect via *songtaew* and boats to the nearby tourist strip of Ao Nang and farther-flung beaches. Railay, with its famed soft sands, and limestone cliffs with ample abseiling opportunities, is accessed by boat (from either Krabi Town to the northeast, or more commonly from Ao Nang Beach to the west). Khlong Muang Beach, more recently developed, lies just north of Ao Nang by road.

The best time to visit the Krabi area is November through April, with January and February the ideal months. The rainy season runs May through October when the crowds disperse and the wet weather and choppy seas drive away all but the hardiest.

Essentials
GETTING THERE
BY PLANE   **Tiger Airways** (✆ 80060-15637; www.tigerairways.com) has direct flights from Singapore. **Thai Airways** (✆ 02356-1111; www.thaiair.com), **Bangkok Airways** (✆ 02270-6699; www.bangkokair.com), and **AirAsia** (✆ 02515-9999; www.airasia.com) all fly from Suvarnabhumi International Airport in Bangkok. Air Asia also flies from Kuala Lumpur in Malaysia and Bangkok Air has direct flights from Ko Samui

From **Krabi airport** (✆ 07563-6541), you can catch a minivan to town for 90B, while taxis charge around 350B. To go directly to Ao Nang beach, a minivan costs 150B, while a taxi is about 600B.

BY BOAT   Twice-daily trips leave from Ko Phi Phi to Krabi (9am and 2pm; trip time: 2 hr.; cost 350B). There are two daily boats from Ko Lanta to Krabi in the high season (8am and 1pm; trip time: 2½ hr.; cost 350B).

BY BUS   Two air-conditioned VIP 24-seater buses leave daily from **Bangkok's Southern Bus Terminal** (✆ 02422-4444; trip time: 12 hr.; fare 970B) to Krabi Town. Frequently scheduled air-conditioned minibuses leave daily from Surat Thani to Krabi (trip time: 2¾ hr.; 250B). Three air-conditioned minibuses leave daily from Phuket Town to Krabi (trip time: 3½ hr.; fare 300B).

VISITOR INFORMATION
Most services in Krabi town are on Utarakit Road, paralleling the waterfront (to the right as you alight the ferry). Here you'll find the **TAT Office** (✆ 07562-2163) and a number of **banks** with ATM service. The **post office** and **police station** (✆ 07561-1222) are located south on Utarakit Road, to the left as you leave the pier. There are also banks in Ao Nang, near the Phra Nang Inn, but at Railay there are only ATM machines.

Check the small shops around town for a copy of the local free map of the resort area, town, and surrounding islands.

GETTING AROUND
Krabi Town is the commercial hub in the area, but few bother to stay. There is frequent *songtaew* (pickup truck) service between Krabi Town and Ao Nang Beach; just flag down a white pickup (the trip takes 30 min. and costs 50B).

Railay Beach and the resorts on the surrounding beaches are cut off by a ridge of cliffs from the mainland and, therefore, are accessible only by boat. From the pier in Krabi Town, you'll pay anything from 150B; trip time 45 min.). From the beach at **Ao Nang** (at the small pavilion across from the Phra Nang Inn), the trip takes just 20 minutes and costs 80B.

Khlong Muang beach is some 25km (16 miles) northwest of Krabi Town. Expect to pay at least 500B for a taxi.

The limestone formations around the coastline here not only are gorgeous visually, but also are great spots to explore by small boat. Some, such as the famous **Ko Hong ★**, to the northwest of Ao Nang, are almost entirely enclosed—with brilliant blue lagoons at their heart. Boats slip inside them at low tide via almost invisible, narrow chasms; ask at your resort for information about boat tours.

If you're checking in at any resort, ask about transportation arrangements (which are often included) and prevailing weather conditions.

Exploring Krabi

Krabi has a number of sites, but most visitors head straight for the beaches to relax. Popular activities are day boat trips, snorkeling, and rock climbing at Railay East.

Just north and east of Krabi Town, though, you will find **Wat Tham Sua** (The Tiger Temple), a stunning hilltop pilgrimage point. A punishing 30 to 40-minute climb up 1,272 steep steps brings you to the rocky pinnacle where a collection of Buddhist statuary overlooks the surrounding area stretching from Krabi Town to the cliffs near Railay. There is a large monastery and temple compound built into the rock at the bottom of the mountain, where you may chance upon a monk in silent meditation or chat with one of the friendly temple stewards (most are eager to practice English). The abbot speaks English and welcomes foreign students of vipassana meditation. If you decide to climb the steep temple mountain, go in either the early morning or the late afternoon to beat the heat. The view from above is worth it. *Note:* Be careful of the many monkeys here. Ignore them at all cost, and don't hold anything tempting in your hands or it will be taken.

The beaches and stunning cliffs of **Railay Beach** are certainly worth a day trip, even if you don't stay there. Divided into Railay East and West, the former offers the best rock-climbing cliffs, situated next to mud flats. The West has the sort of soft powdery sands that attract beach bunnies, though longtails dock right here and the resulting noise of the motors can ruin the peacefulness of the gorgeous cerulean sea. At **Ao Nang,** longtail boat drivers try to drum up groups of passengers at a small pavilion just across from the Phra Nang Inn for the 80B ride (20 min.). From the docks in Krabi Town, it costs 200B and takes 40 minutes. (The trip is offered dawn till dusk only.)

The craggy limestone cliffs of Railay make it one of the best-known **rock-climbing** spots in the region. It is certainly not for the fainthearted; nevertheless, the whole cliff area is well organized (with mapped routes) and safety bolts drilled into the rock. There are a number of companies offering full- and half-day courses, as well as equipment rental. There are also many routes suitable for beginners. Climbing schools set up "top rope" climbing for safety, whereby climbers are attached by a rope through a fixed pulley at the top, and to a guide on the other end, holding you fast. The schools all offer similar rates and have offices scattered around Railay Beach, with posters and pamphlets everywhere. Try **King Climbers** (✆ 07566-2096; www.railay.com) or **Hot Rock** (✆ 07566-2245; www.railayadventure.com). Half-day courses start at about 1,000B, full-day courses are from 1,800B, and 3-day courses run from 6,000B.

Near Railay Beach is **Phra Nang Beach ★**, a secluded section of sand that is either a short 50B boat trip from Railay proper, or a cliffside walk east, past Rayavadee Resort and south along a shaded cliffside path (again, watch out for monkeys). From here, you can swim or kayak around the craggy hunk of rock just a few meters away offshore, or explore the **Tham Phra Nang,** or Princess Cave, a small cavern at the base of a tall cliff, filled with huge phallic sculptures where, legend has it, donors attain fertility. The cliffs are stunning and the sunsets spectacular.

Along the path to **Phra Nang Beach,** you'll find signs pointing up to a small cleft in the rocks. After a short hike up a steep escarpment and then an often treacherously muddy downward climb (use the ropes to avoid slipping), you'll arrive at a shallow saltwater lagoon. How it got up here is anyone's guess.

Full-day boat trips and **snorkeling** to **Ko Poda ★** can be arranged from any beachfront tour agent or hotel near Krabi, which will take you to a few small coral sites as well as any number of secluded coves and islets (or *hongs*); **Sea Kayak Krabi** (40 Ruenrudee Rd., Krabi; ✆ **07563-0270;** www.seakayak-krabi.com) run a half-day, four-island trip costing 1,200B per person (700B for kids). During the monsoon season, boats leave from Nam Mao Beach (near Krabi Town) only and are subject to cancellation in rough weather. Or you can rent snorkel gear from any of the tour operators along Ao Nang or Railay for about 150B per day.

Day **kayak tours** to the mangroves near **Ao Luk** are becoming popular for visitors to Ao Nang. Contact **Sea, Land and Trek Co.** (34/12 Moo 5, Ao Nang; ✆ **07563-7364;** www.krabisealand.com) to set up a trip. Rates for a day out begin at 2,100B.

There are some dive operators in Krabi, but you'll have to travel farther to reach the better sites. Most people prefer to book from Ko Phi Phi (p. 260) or Phuket (p. 242).

Where to Stay

KRABI TOWN

Few travelers stay in Krabi Town as there's no beach there, but if you're stuck or are too tired to leave, the best hotel in town is **Maritime Park & Spa** (1 Tungfah Rd.; ✆ **07562-0028;** www.maritimeparkandspa.com), with superior rooms starting at 3,200B.

RAILAY BEACH
Very Expensive

Rayavadee ★★★   Rayavadee offers unique two-story rondavels (circular pavilions), most of which are large and luxurious. These come with every modern convenience and some, set in enclosed gardens, can be very private. Ground-floor sitting rooms have a central, double-sized hanging lounger with cushions. Upper-story bedrooms are all silk and teak, and private bathrooms have big Jacuzzi tubs and luxury products. Some gardens feature hammocks or (unheated) whirlpools. The resort grounds lie at the base of towering cliffs on the island's most choice piece of property, with direct access onto the beautiful Phra Nang beach. The resort feels very much like a peaceful village, with paths meandering among private lotus ponds and meticulous landscaping. The price is high, but the location, luxury, and exclusivity warrant it.

214 Moo 2, Tambol Ao Nang, Amphur Muang, Krabi 81000 (30 min. west of Krabi Town by longtail boat, or 70 min. from Phuket on the resort's own launch). www.rayavadee.com. ✆ **07562-0740.** Fax 07562-0630. 102 units. 22,300B deluxe pavilion; from 28,300B hydro-pool pavilion; from 36,800B family pavilion; from 72,000B specialty villas. AE, DC, MC, V. **Amenities:** 2 restaurants; lounge; outdoor pool w/children's pool; outdoor lit tennis courts; air-conditioned squash court; health club; spa; watersports equipment; room service; Wi-Fi. *In room:* A/C, satellite TV, minibar, fridge.

Moderate

Railay Bay Resort ✦   Stretching right through from West Railay to East Railay, this resort offers seven different types of lodgings, scattered around a shady coconut grove. All rooms, including the well-priced deluxe rooms, look sparkling, and the spa, beachside patio, and pool are great places to laze the days away. The beachfront suites enjoy superb oceanviews from the private terrace; they are very spacious and include marble bathrooms with separate showers and a Jacuzzi tub, king-sized bed with padded headboard and a small library corner. The restaurant, which serves up seafood and pizzas, is yet another reason to rest up here.

145 Moo 2, Railay Beach, Ao Nang, Krabi 81000 (on Railay Beach, longtails from Ao Nang pull up onshore). www.railaybayresort.com. ✆ **07581-9407.** 130 units. 4,100B–8,700B cottages; from 10,500B suites and villa. MC, V. **Amenities:** Restaurant; outdoor pool; spa; watersports equipment. *In room:* A/C, TV, fridge, hair dryer, Wi-Fi (free).

Inexpensive

Diamond Cave Bungalows & Resort   Located on the eastern side of the peninsula, Diamond Cave is a clean, cozy bungalow resort set in shady gardens with a choice of fan or air-con rooms—it's a pleasant escape from the vagaries of life and an ideal base to enjoy the nearby climbing spots. Since Diamond Cave is at the far end of Railay Beach East, it's far from the better sandy beaches, but close to lots of budget dining and bars.

36 Moo 1, Ao Nang Krabi 81000 (north end of Railay East Beach). www.diamondcave-railay.com. ✆ **07562-2589.** Fax 07562-2590. 32 units. From 2,000B double. MC, V. **Amenities:** Restaurant; bar; outdoor pool; Internet (free in lobby). *In room:* A/C, TV, no phone.

AO NANG BEACH
Moderate

Golden Beach Resort   Comparable in service to the nearby Phra Nang Inn (see below), the Golden Beach's deluxe rooms are more traditional in design. The free-standing pavilion suites make masterful use of curved lines inside and out, and feature luxurious canopy beds and indoor/outdoor bathrooms. The pool is large and inviting, and the resort is just a short hop down a cul-de-sac and away from busy, central Ao Nang.

254 Moo 2, Ao Nan, Krabi 81000 (the eastern end of Ao Nang, behind the boat pavilion for trips to Railay). www.goldenbeach-resort.com. ✆ **07563-7870.** Fax 07563-7875. 70 units. From 4,080B double; from 5,340B suite. AE, MC, V. **Amenities:** Restaurant; bar; outdoor pool; room service. *In room:* A/C, TV, minibar, fridge, Wi-Fi (300B for 2 hours).

Krabi Resort   The popular Krabi Resort is the only property in Ao Nang with direct beach access. It is a compound of two hotel blocks and an array of free-standing beachside bungalows and tidy grounds that surround a swimming pool. More private seaview bungalows are the best choice: They're generously sized and clean, with parquet floors, high ceilings, rattan furnishings, and lots of Thai touches. The resort is just north of the main shopping and restaurant area at Ao Nang, but a lovely beach walk.

232 Moo 2, Ao Nang Beach, Krabi 81000 (overlooking beach at Ao Nang). www.krabiresort.net. ✆ **07563-7030.** 170 units. 3,200B–7,400B bungalow priced according to view; from 10,000B suite; 20,000B beach house. MC, V. **Amenities:** Restaurant; lounge; outdoor pool; outdoor lit tennis courts; health club; watersports equipment; bikes; room service. *In room:* A/C, TV, minibar, fridge, Wi-Fi (300B for 2 hours).

Phra Nang Inn   The Phra Nang Inn, famed for its eccentric decor, has undergone a complete renovation and toning down of its wild side, though you'll still probably find funky local artwork somewhere in your room. Rooms are bright and breezy, beds are big and comfy, and the wood-paneled floors are a pleasure to walk on. The hotel's two wings are on either side of the busiest intersection in Ao Nang, and the helpful staff can help arrange tours and onward boat travel (from right across the street).

119 Moo 2, Ao Nang Beach (P.O. Box 25), Krabi 81000 (overlooking beach at Ao Nang-Railay boat dock). www.phrananginnkrabi.com. ☎ **07563-7130.** Fax 07563-7134. 88 units. From 3,700B double; from 6,200B suite. MC, V. **Amenities:** 2 restaurants; 2 bars; small outdoor pool; spa; sauna; room service; Wi-Fi in lobby (free). *In room:* A/C, TV/movie library, minibar, fridge.

Inexpensive

Ao Nang has lots of budget guesthouses to choose from. The friendly folks at **J Mansion** (302 Moo 2, Ao Nang; ☎ **07569-5128;** www.jmansionaonang.com) have clean, simple rooms with a fan or air-conditioning starting at 1,000B, just 100m (328 ft.) from the beach. If you're looking for a few more comforts, try **Ao Nang Village Resort** (49/3 Moo 2, Ao Nang Village; ☎ **07563-7544**), with gardenview rooms from 1,800B.

KLONG MUANG BEACH

Following the coast north of the busy Ao Nang strip, you'll come to quiet Khlong Muang with a long stretch of quiet beach and a few excellent resorts from which to choose.

Expensive

Nakamanda ★★★ This slickly designed resort sits on the far northern end of Krabi (just past the Sheraton; see below), and consists of a collection of luxurious private villas sprinkled among indigo pools and pavilions and surrounded by high stone walls. The name means the "sacred sea dragon," and this stylish outcrop does look otherworldly. Public spaces are delightfully spartan; the eclectic decor tends to mix Angkorian antiquities with a cool contemporary style; and everything is set amid meticulously kept gardens. Villas are aligned for optimal privacy, and inside everything is sumptuous bleached wood and granite. Rooms range from a basic villa to a couple of over-the-top private-pool villas with huge terraces and sea views. The spa is inviting; the seaside pool, an oasis; and the resort restaurant, excellent.

126 Moo 3, Klong Muang Beach, Tambon Nongtalay, Krabi 81000. www.nakamanda.com. ☎ **07562-8200.** Fax 07564-4390. 39 units. From 7,800B *sala* villa; 11,500B Jacuzzi villa; from 17,000B pool villa. AE, MC, V. **Amenities:** Restaurant; 2 bars; outdoor pool; health club; spa; watersports rentals; room service. *In room:* A/C, TV, fridge, minibar, hair dryer, Wi-Fi (free).

Sheraton Krabi Beach Resort ★★★ A large circular drive and luxurious modern lobby pavilion usher you into this expansive resort. Rooms are set in large blocks, a U-shaped configuration connected by boardwalks above mangrove flats that flood with the daily tide. Moderate-sized rooms come with fine tile and dark wood furnishings, a fusion of simple lines, and more flamboyant Art Deco details. Services range from fine-dining choices in the main building to more laid-back fare taken by the large, luxurious beachside pool. Also on hand are plenty of fitness facilities, which offer a great variety of programs (from kickboxing to meditation), after which a treatment at the spa will dispel all aches or stress.

155 Moo 2, Klong Muang Beach, Nong Talay, Krabi 81000 (15km/9⅓ miles north of Ao Nang; 26km/16 miles from Krabi Town). www.sheraton.com. ☎ **07562-8000.** Fax 07562-8028. 246 units. From 8,700B double; 18,500B suite. AE, DC, MC, V. **Amenities:** 4 restaurants; 3 bars; outdoor pool; tennis court; health club; spa; watersports equipment; bikes; children's club; room service; babysitting. *In room:* A/C, TV, minibar, fridge, hair dryer, Wi-Fi (470B per day).

Sofitel Phokeethra Krabi ★★★ ☺ The latest luxury resort to grace this pretty coastline has the full complement of extensively manicured lawns, and a gigantic sculpted pool, surrounded by coconut groves. Boasting an opulent mix of Thai and colonial architecture, this awesome property features a palatial lobby and magnificent views. The vast rooms are classically furnished, with polished teak floors, broad balconies, and a warm butterscotch-and-cream decor. Because it caters not only for upscale tourists but also to large conference groups and wedding parties, expect high standards of service and dining—including a Lancôme spa, a wide range of business facilities, and a children's playground for the hotel's junior guests.

Klong Muang Beach, Tambon Nongtalay, Krabi 81000. www.sofitel.com. © **07562-7800.** Fax 07562-7899. 276 units. From $180 superior oceanview; from $280 suite. AE, MC, V. **Amenities:** 3 restaurants; 5 bars; outdoor pool; health club; spa; watersports rentals; room service. *In room:* A/C, TV, fridge, minibar, hair dryer, Internet (702B per day).

The Tubkaak ★★★ 🏨 On Tubkaak Beach, just 4km (2½ miles) beyond Klong Muang Beach, this boutique resort enjoys superb views across a surreal horizon of limestone outcrops rising from the sea. The solid, wooden buildings are very pleasing to the eye, and, with only 42 rooms, the place is small enough for staff to provide the kind of personal attention that makes every guest feel special. Interiors are very tastefully designed, with lavish use of trademark Thai materials such as teak and silk. Such facilities as a huge free-form swimming pool, an elegant spa, and a health club guarantee that guests don't get bored, and the resort has already won several awards for its outstanding quality.

123 Moo 3, Tubkaak Beach, Tambon Nongtalay, Amphur Muang, Krabi 81000. www.tubkaak.com. © **07562-8400.** Fax 07562-8499. 42 units. 15,000B–19,000B double; from 30,000B suite. AE, MC, V. **Amenities:** Restaurant; bar; outdoor pool; health club; spa; watersports equipment. *In room:* A/C, TV/ DVD, minibar, hair dryer, Wi-Fi (free).

Moderate

In addition to the hotels reviewed above, also try the family-run, eco-friendly **Krabi Sands Resort** (118 Moo 3, Nong Talay; © **07560-0027;** www.krabisands.com), with bungalows from 3,500B.

Where to Eat

Apart from the good dining choices at the many resorts listed above, here are a few more recommendations around the region: In the north end of Krabi Town, the **Night Market** (no phone), just off Utarakit riverside road, on Maharaj Soi 10, has good local specials such as deep-fried oysters and noodles. For good Western food, try **Café Europa** (© 07562-0407), at 9 Ruamjit Soi 1, Maharat Road, a popular spot with local expats. In Ao Nang, the beachside tourist street is already turning into a mini-Patong, with heaps of neon-lit shops and storefront eateries: Try **Ao Nang Cuisine** (© 07569-5260) for good Thai fare, or **Irish Rover** (© 08986-64592) for continental cuisine. On Railay, all the beachside bars and bungalows serve good Thai and continental nosh.

KO PHI PHI ★

814km (506 miles) S of Bangkok, then 42km (26 miles) W of Krabi; 160km (99 miles) SW of Phuket

Phi Phi is in fact two islands: **Phi Phi Leh** and **Phi Phi Don.** The latter is the main barbell-shaped island whose central isthmus (the barbell handle) was hit badly by the 2004 tsunami. Ko Phi Phi is a popular choice for day trips, snorkeling, and scuba junkets from Krabi and Phuket. Crowds of noisy tourists also descend upon **Maya**

Bay, on Phi Phi Ley, where filmmakers shot the Hollywood film *The Beach*, with Leonardo DiCaprio. Thai students and environmentalists have long protested about the amounts of rubbish left by these tour groups. (**Note:** Day-trippers should dispose of trash after arriving back onto the mainland, not while they are there.)

All visitors arrive at the busy ferry port in south-facing **Tonsai Bay.** The beach is quite attractive but the constant coming and going of boats makes it inadvisable for swimming. Most people just walk the 300m (984 ft.) across the barbell handle to north-facing **Loh Dalam Bay,** a spectacular, horseshoe-shaped crescent of blinding-white sand. Small beachfront outfits rent snorkel gear and conduct longtail boat tours to quiet coves with great views of coral reefs and sea life for as little as 1,000B for an all-day trip (packing your own lunch). You can rent kayaks and do a little exploring on your own, or hike to one of the island viewpoints and soak up the memorable view of back-to-back bays and rugged limestone cliffs.

Phi Phi Ley is famed for its coveted **swallow nests** and the courageous pole-climbing daredevils who collect them (the saliva-coated nests fetch a hefty price as the main ingredient in a much-favored bird's-nest soup). Though nobody lives on Phi Phi Ley, it is frequently visited on day trips as there are some good snorkeling areas nearby.

Before the 2004 tsunami, many of the settlements and hotels on Phi Phi Don had been built illegally by squatters on land belonging to the once-pristine National Marine Park. These facilities were—almost literally—wiped off the map by the tragic disaster. With the help of many international volunteers who cleared the land of refuse, the crowds have returned to the island, but unfortunately so has the unplanned chaos of pre-tsunami days. Beaches are once again crammed with hotels, low-end guesthouses, and backpackers.

In the aftermath of the tsunami, the government had hinted at earmarking Phi Phi Don as a luxury destination (indeed Phi Phi already supported a number of high-end resorts on more remote beaches), but amid the unregulated rush to make as much money as possible from this once-sublime location, the plan failed. In terms of wholesale environmental degradation, we are, sadly, right back to square one.

Getting There

Boats from Krabi Town run at least twice daily (9am and 1:30pm; more in high season) and cost from 550B. From Phuket, ferry services leave at around the same time and charge the same fee, but some include hotel pickup as well. The journey from either place takes 1½ hours. Be sure to check out where the life jackets are stashed, as several Phi Phi ferries have sunk in the past, fortunately with no serious injuries.

Where to Stay

Because Ko Phi Phi is very crowded these days, it's difficult to find worthy, budget accommodation at a reasonable price. It's best to book in advance, especially in high season when everywhere fills up quickly. In addition to the hotels below, which are all on remote beaches, good options on the main beaches include **Phi Phi Hotel** and **Phi Phi Banyan Villa** (near the ferry dock; © **07560-1023;** www.phiphi-island-hotel.com), on Tonsai Beach, under the same management with rooms from 3,000B. On Loh Dalam Bay, the luxury resort **Phi Phi Island Cabana** (© **07560-1170;** www.phiphi-cabana.com) has rooms that start from 8,000B for a double.

EXPENSIVE

Holiday Inn Resort Phi Phi   The Holiday Inn has a lot of things going for it—a great location on beautiful Laem Tong beach, manicured lawns, hammocks gently swaying under beachfront palm trees. The bungalows are comfortable enough, with spacious balconies, though the rooms lack local touches to give them character. A step-up are the studios in the new Coral Wing, featuring big balconies, flatscreen TVs, and DVD players. There are plenty of activities to keep guests busy, such as a dive center, game fishing, and cookery classes, and the restaurants offer decent fare.

Laem Thong Beach, Ko Phi Phi, Krabi. Phuket Office: 100/435 Moo 5, Chalermprakiet Rama 9 Rd., T. Rassada, Phuket 83000. www.phiphi.holidayinn.com. ✆ **07562-7300.** 97 units. From 4,770B bungalow; from 6,030B studio. AE, DC, MC, V. **Amenities:** 2 restaurants; bar; 2 outdoor pools; health club; spa; Jacuzzi; watersports rentals & dive center; room service; babysitting. *In room:* A/C, TV/DVD, minibar, fridge, CD player, Wi-Fi (450B per day).

Phi Phi Island Village ★★★   Accessible only by a 30-minute boat ride (regular shuttles are available from the ferry pier), this is a top choice among the islands' more far-flung resorts. Deluxe bungalows offer private balconies and unusual open-plan bathrooms (shower only); with such unrivaled oceanviews, it's not surprising this place proves a popular choice for families, couples, and honeymooners. A luxury spa, two large pools, fine-dining options, and an in-house tour program service and scuba school complete the picture. There's obviously a need to be self-contained with this location; apart from a few nearby jungle walks, it's all about relaxing. The beachfront at high tide is lovely and sunset is inspiring.

Phuket Office: 89 Satoon Rd., Phuket 83000. (Hotel located on Loh Ba Kao Bay, at the northeast end of the island, 30 min. by longtail boat). www.ppisland.com. ✆ **07636-3700.** Fax 07636-3789. 112 units. 7,800B–9,800B double; from 21,000B villa. AE, MC, V. **Amenities:** 3 restaurants; 3 bars; 2 outdoor pools; spa; watersports equipment; babysitting; Internet (200B per hour). *In room:* A/C, TV, minibar, fridge, no phone.

Zeavola ★★   Many Thais long for a return to their rural village roots, a time when life was simple. That is what Zeavola, tucked away in the northeast corner of the island, is all about—a return to traditional Thai living. Sand walkways cut through palm trees, leading to free-standing thatch-roofed teak suites. Each is luxuriously appointed with polished teakwood floors, oversized daybeds, and both indoor and outdoor rain showers. The living areas extend past glass doors to covered teakwood patios, where privacy is supplied by electronically controlled bamboo blinds. What makes the suites truly unique, however, are the rustic flourishes: Old-fashioned copper piping, wooden taps, pottery sink basins, and *mon khwan* cushions (the traditional triangular Thai pillows) for the patios. The resort also has a PADI dive center and private dive boat. **Hint:** The beachfront suite trades privacy for the sea view; some garden suites have partial ocean views without the loss of privacy.

11 Moo 8, Laem Tong Beach, Ko Phi Phi, Krabi 81000. www.zeavola.com. ✆ **07562-7000.** Fax 07562-7023. 52 units. 9,900B village suite; 10,900B garden suite; 16,400B beachfront suite. AE, MC, V. **Amenities:** 2 restaurants; saltwater pool; spa; watersports equipment. *In room:* A/C, TV/DVD, minibar, hair dryer, CD player, Wi-Fi (free).

Where to Eat & Drink

Phi Phi Don is packed with eateries. In downtown central Tonsai, look out for **Mama's Restaurant, Pee Pee Bakery, Le Grand Bleu, Ton Sai Seafood, Jasmine, Sawasdee,** and **Papaya**—the last three for Thai food. You'll also find a few little halal food stands and vendors with wheeled carts making Southern-style sweet *roti* (pancake) with banana. Over on Loh Dalum, check out **Ciao Bella** for tasty Italian fare.

Once a Muslim village, Phi Phi now parties into the night at such places as the **Reggae Bar** (with a Thai boxing ring), **Hippies Bar, Apache,** and **Carlito's;** there's even an Irish pub and a sports bar. Don't miss the laid-back, beachfront **Sunflower Bar** on Loh Dalam Bay.

Ko Phi Phi Activities

Kayaks can be rented on the beach for leisurely paddling for around 200B per hour. **Snorkeling** trips around the island are popular and you can sign up for a group tour with any hotel or with any of the many beachfront travel agencies for around 800B–1,200B per day. To hire a longtail boat with pilot for a half-day private trip, expect to pay around 1,200B.

Scuba diving is quite popular here, too, and **Phi Phi Scuba** (✆ **07560-1148;** www.ppscuba.com), among other full-service, professional outfits, offers anything from day trips to multiday adventures, as well as all the requisite PADI course instruction. Alternatively, try **Visa Diving** (✆ **07560-1157;** www.visadiving.com) on the main strip just east of the ferry pier. Check the websites for prices.

Spider Monkey, in Tonsai Village (✆ **07581-9384;** www.spidermonkeyclimbing. com), runs rock-climbing trips around the gnarled cliffs of the two Phi Phi islands; prices run around 1,000B for a half day, 1,600B for a full day.

If you feel like a real adrenaline rush, you can sign up with a tour operator to go **cliff jumping** (jumping off a cliff into the sea), Phi Phi's latest craze, but be prepared to end up with a dislocated shoulder, broken back, or worse, and don't expect the operator's insurance to cover the damages.

KO LANTA ★

70km (43 miles) SE of Krabi

The two islands of Ko Lanta Yai (Big Lanta Island) and Ko Lanta Noi (Small Lanta Island) are a few hours' road and boat trip from Krabi airport. Ko Lanta Yai has already become a bohemian alternative to heady Samui, or pricey Phuket. However, the island is big enough that, during the high season (Nov–Mar), small pockets of seclusion can be found—especially in the far south and over on the east coast, where Muslim fishing villagers carry on with their traditional economy, ignoring the rolling cement trucks and noise of construction on the upper west coast, where most resorts are located. Despite the island's growing popularity, the endless white-sand beaches are far from crowded. A great mix of international visitors ensures excellent nightlife, with an array of funky bars and small dance clubs. During March, when the crowds have left, regional locals head to historic Lanta Old Town for the annual Laanta Lanta Festival—a celebration of street art, performance, cultural shows, music, dance, fun, and games.

Getting There

Minivans from Krabi Town, Trang, and Phuket make connections to Ko Lanta Yai via two vehicular ferries: One from the mainland to Ko Lanta Noi and across the island by car before another ferry to Ko Lanta Yai. Most transport stops in the small town of Saladan near the ferry pier on the northern tip of Lanta Yai. From Saladan, catch a pickup truck ride to the resort of your choice. Contact **Kanokwan Tour** (Lanta office: © **07568-4419**) or **Lanta Transport Co.** (© **07568-4080**), if you need to make transportation arrangements.

Where to Stay

VERY EXPENSIVE

Layana ★★ A small boutique resort located near the northern end of the west coast, Layana has an excellent spa and offers stylish, contemporary thatched bungalows close to the ocean, many of them snuggled around a grand pool. Each room has an open, airy feel with a lush decor of hard woods, silks, and local art. It carries a high price tag, but the resort's high-quality facilities and service make it worth considering. This resort is for over-18s only.

272 Moo 3, Saladan, Phra-Ae Beach, Ko Lanta Yai, Krabi 81150. www.layanaresort.com. © **07560-7100.** Fax 07560-7199. 50 units. From 11,900B double; from 17,700B suite. AE, MC, V. **Amenities:** Restaurant; bar; outdoor pool; health club; spa; watersports rentals; bikes; room service. *In room:* A/C, TV, minibar, fridge, Wi-Fi (free).

Pimalai Resort & Spa ★★★ Located in the far southwest of the island, close to the National Park headquarters, Pimalai was the first luxury resort on the island. Designed by a young, eco-sensitive Thai architect, it continues to win awards in hospitality excellence, and environmental awareness. A fine marriage of comfort and proximity to nature, these stylish villas sprawl down rolling hills and gardens right onto the pristine beach; some have pools and small luxuries such as CD and DVD players. Shady walkways have been built around the trees and the infinity pool is beautiful; there's first-rate dining in a large open-air *sala*, or down on the beach in a funky thatched bar and eatery hewn from logs. The design throughout—from the simple thatched treatment *salas* and trickling waterfall in the spa, to the many small touches of Thai arts—reminds you that you are indeed in Thailand.

99 Moo 5, Ba Kan Tiang Beach, Ko Lanta Yai, Krabi 81150 (on the far SW coast of Lanta Yai). www.pimalai.com. © **07560-7999.** Fax 07560-7998. 118 units. From 14,000B double; from 27,000B suite; from 29,000B beach villa; from 36,000B pool villa. AE, DC, MC, V. **Amenities:** 5 restaurants; 3 bars; outdoor pool; tennis courts; health club; spa; watersports equipment; bikes; room service. *In room:* A/C, TV, fridge, minibar, Internet (free).

EXPENSIVE

Costa Lanta ★★ Lauded for its unique architectural design, the Costa Lanta boasts sleek rooms, which beautifully balance Western minimalism and Thai rustic decor, oceanside decks, and long pools. The resort has also garnered positive reviews for its innovative back-to-nature approach, and for its reputation for offering some of the island's best cuisine and cocktails. In the interest of environmental preservation, the resort is built back from the beach under the natural tree line and caters to well-to-do Thai visitors as much as to foreign tourists.

212 Moo 1, Saladan, Ko Lanta Yai, Krabi 81150. www.costalanta.com. © **07566-8186** in Bangkok. Fax 07566-8185. 22 units. 6,200B–9,700B double. MC, V. **Amenities:** Restaurant; bar; outdoor pool; watersports rentals; Wi-Fi (free). *In room:* A/C, TV, minibar, fridge, CD player.

MODERATE/INEXPENSIVE

Mango House ★ This unique guesthouse is on the east coast, in an area that was once a hub of Chinese mercantile trade. The studio rooms and two- and three-bedroom villas here are historic Thai fishermen's homes built on stilts over the sea, adjacent to a sea gypsy village, though not all rooms have air-con. The solid post and beam structures feature modern touches of Chinese decor, with spectacular views from private seafront patios. Downstairs, there's the Mango Bistro for eats, and occasional parties with international DJs. This is Old Town living at its finest.

45 Sriraya Rd., Moo 2, Lanta Old Town, Ko Lanta Yai, Krabi 81150. www.mangohouses.com. ℭ **08694-86836** (cell). 2,000B–6,000B double (varies with location and size). MC, V. **Amenities:** Bistro; bar. *In room:* TV/DVD, minibar, fridge, Wi-Fi (free).

Moonlight Bay Resort ★★　Long popular in the far south of Lanta, Moonlight Bay is situated by a small river facing the sea. The cottages are more contemporary chic than rustic, but the vibe is laid-back and, for many, the isolation blissful. Don't miss the excellent treatments at the Na Lanta spa. All rooms include private balcony, free drinking water, and hot beverage-making facilities.

69 Moo 8, Khlongtob, Ko Lanta Yai, Krabi 81150. www.moonlight-resort.com. ℭ **07566-2590.** Fax 07566-2594. 30 units. 2,500B–4,500B double (varies with location and size); 6,500B–8,900B suite. AE, MC, V. **Amenities:** Restaurant; bar; outdoor pool; spa; Jacuzzi; Internet (free in lobby). *In room:* A/C, TV, minibar, fridge.

Where to Eat & Drink

Cool places to chill on Ko Lanta include **Red Snapper** (176 Moo 2, Phra Ae Beach; ℭ **07885-6965;** www.redsnapper-lanta.com), which specializes in fusion food; **Mango Bistro** (see above) at Lanta Old Town, and **Time for Lime Cooking School,** at Khlong Dao Beach (ℭ **07568-4590;** www.timeforlime.net). Ko Lanta can't compare with Ko Phi Phi for nightlife, but there are a few beachfront bars on Ao Phra-Ae (aka Long Beach), including **Ozone** (no phone), which hosts a party every Thursday night.

TRANG ★

129km (80 miles) SE of Krabi

Trang Province, south of Krabi, is where it's at if you're looking for a real Thai-style beach holiday in the south. Popular with Thai tourists, the large province is spectacularly placed, with plenty of unspoiled national parks and 46 islands. The jumping-off point for the islands is at **Pak Meng Beach,** about 40km (25 miles) west of the small town of Trang. Day tours for snorkelers are affordable and the scenery is much like nearby Krabi, but cheaper and without as many tourists. Bear in mind that during the monsoon season (May–Oct), there are no day tours and many resorts close down.

Trang Province is also great for light adventure activities such as sea kayaking and diving. **Had Chao Mai National Park,** which consists of several islands—**Ko Kradan,** one of the Andaman's real gems, with healthy coral reefs, azure seas, and powder-soft sands; **Ko Mook** (Muk), famous for the Emerald Cave, a hidden lagoon, which is accessible only at low tide; **Ko Waen** and **Ko Chueak,** which offer excellent deep-sea diving and also a chance to spot the rare dugong. The most convenient island for a base is **Ko Ngai,** a short boat ride from Pak Meng Beach.

For mainland nature visits, visit wildlife sanctuaries such as **Namtok Khao Chong** and **Khlong Lamchan Park,** which boast waterfalls, trails, and caves. The **Southern Thailand Botanical Garden** (Thung Khai), on the Trang-Palian Road (Hwy. 404), offers stunning nature trails through lowland jungle and tropical gardens. For keen adventurers, there are some remote islands—one such island is **Tarutao Marine National Park,** which lies close to the Malaysian border, in Satun province. This region is great for kayaking and pristine diving. For more adventure tour info, see **www.paddleasia.com.**

Getting There

BY PLANE Daily flights from Don Muang airport in Bangkok are serviced by **Nok Air** (✆ 1318; www.nokair.com) and **Orient Thai** (✆ 1126; www.flyorientthai.com).

BY TRAIN Trang city is connected by train with Bangkok on the main north–south line. Two daily departures make the 16-hour trek. Ask for details at **Bangkok's Hua Lampong Station** (✆ 1690).

BY BUS There are frequent buses from Bangkok's **Southern Bus Terminal** (✆ 02422-4444) and minibus connections from Krabi and Surat Thani. When you arrive in Trang, connect by minibus with Pak Meng Beach for around 50B per person, or 500B to hire the entire vehicle; it's about a 1-hour ride.

Ferryboats to the outlying islands leave regularly all day from the pier on the north end of the beach. It costs around 1,000B to 1,500B for an all-day tour by boat (including lunch), and they can drop you off at any number of islands (Ko Ngai, Ko Mook, or Ko Kradan); though, if you are staying at one of the island resorts, your hosts will usually arrange transfers for you. Try **Chao Mai Tour** (✆ 07521-4742), just one among many tour operators at the port, or contact any of the hotels below and they can help with arrangements.

Where to Stay

Near the Anantara is **Pakmeng Resort** (60/1 Moo 4, Tambol Maifad, Trang; ✆ 07527-4112; www.pakmengresort.com), rustic but cozy and quiet in a mangrove plantation near the sea wall. Rooms range from 900B to 1,600B.

Anantara Si Kao Resort ★★ Trang's foremost luxury beach resort enjoys an ideal location in a quiet spot on the west-facing coast, with dramatic views of sunsets behind karst outcrops in the Andaman Sea. With fine dining, a spa and wellness center, plus neat contemporary Thai room design, this is the kind of place that is now attracting escapees from busy Phuket and Phi Phi. The suites, with 90 sq. m (969 sq. ft.) of space, are particularly attractive, and include neat extras like iPod docking stations and espresso machines.

Changlang Beach, Trang 92150. www.sikao.anantara.com. ✆ **07520-5888.** Fax 07520-5899. 138 units. From 5,400B double; from 15,400 pool suite. AE, MC, V. **Amenities:** 2 restaurants; 2 bars; outdoor pool; health club; spa; watersports equipment; bikes; room service. *In room:* A/C, TV/DVD, minibar, fridge, Wi-Fi (750B per day).

WHERE TO STAY ON THE ISLANDS

If you prebook a stay on the nearby islands, the resorts will help with transfers; otherwise, head for the ferries that leave frequently from Pak Meng Pier. **Ko Ngai** (aka Ko Hai) is the most developed island, with half a dozen smart places, including the quaint **CoCo Cottages** (✆ 07522-4387; www.coco-cottage.com), an environmentally friendly cluster run by a cheerful Thai family; beach cottages range from 2,800B to 4,800B. Another good bet is right next door, where the **Thapwarin Resort** (✆ 081894-3585, cell; http://thapwarin.com) has big, comfy bamboo and rattan cottages for similar rates. On **Ko Mook,** go for **Sivalai Resort** (✆ 08972-33355, cell; www.komooksivalai.com), which stands on a dramatic spur of land with a beach on both sides; rooms start at 4,000B. Finally, on gorgeous **Ko Kradan,** the best place to stay is the **Seven Seas Resort** (✆ 07520-3389; www.sevenseasresorts.com), where rooms and villas go for 6,500B to 13,000B.

CENTRAL THAILAND

G oing north from Bangkok, travelers who trace the route of the Chao Phraya River will feel as if they are traveling back in time. Starting with the ruins of Ayutthaya, as you go north, you will discover a series of former capitals: After Ayutthaya comes **Lopburi.** Farther north, the nation's most famous architectural wonder, **Sukhothai,** is traditionally considered the seat of the first Thai kingdom, from 1238. Beyond Sukhothai, to the north of the Central Plains, is the mountainous land once called Lanna, or the "Land of a Million Rice Fields." This distinct ancient kingdom meandered between Chiang Mai and Chiang Rai (chapters 11–12, and brought totally different customs and architecture.

10

Central Thailand is also the country's "Great Rice Bowl," known for its agricultural abundance. Winding rivers cut through a mosaic of rice fields, and smaller villages and towns provide a window into the heart of Thailand's rural culture. If you have the time, the most atmospheric way to travel from Bangkok to Ayutthaya is by boat. It's also a short ride by train, and many make the hop to Lopburi before going on to **Phitsanulok,** the commercial and transportation hub of the Central Plains. Farther west, bordering Myanmar (Burma), the town of **Mae Sot** is surrounded by refugee camps, which, for years, have been offering humanitarian aid to the Burmese. Travelers can also choose to continue north to Chiang Mai by road or rail from Phitsanulok.

AYUTTHAYA ★★

76km (47 miles) N of Bangkok

Ayutthaya can be one of the highlights of any trip to Thailand. Many travelers take the day tour from Bangkok, which allows about 3 hours at the sites (the majority of these lie inside the Historical Park), but for anyone with a strong interest in archaeological ruins, Ayutthaya justifies an overnight or more.

From its establishment in 1350 by King U Thong (Ramathibodi I) until its fall to the Burmese in 1767, Ayutthaya was the capital of Siam, home to 33 kings and numerous dynasties. At its zenith and until the mid-18th century, Ayutthaya was a majestic city with three palaces and 400 temples on an island threaded by canals. The former capital rivaled European cities in splendor and was a source of marvel to foreigners.

The Central Plains

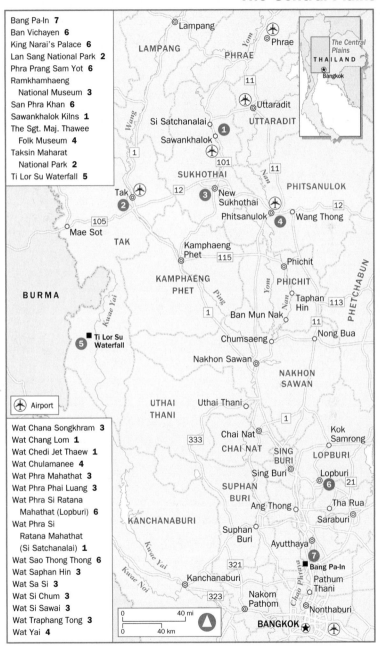

Bang Pa-In **7**
Ban Vichayen **6**
King Narai's Palace **6**
Lan Sang National Park **2**
Phra Prang Sam Yot **6**
Ramkhamhaeng
   National Museum **3**
San Phra Khan **6**
Sawankhalok Kilns **1**
The Sgt. Maj. Thawee
   Folk Museum **4**
Taksin Maharat
   National Park **2**
Ti Lor Su Waterfall **5**

⊕ Airport

Wat Chana Songkhram **3**
Wat Chang Lom **1**
Wat Chedi Jet Thaew **1**
Wat Chulamanee **4**
Wat Phra Mahathat **3**
Wat Phra Phai Luang **3**
Wat Phra Si Ratana
   Mahathat (Lopburi) **6**
Wat Phra Si
   Ratana Mahathat
   (Si Satchanalai) **1**
Wat Sao Thong Thong **6**
Wat Saphan Hin **3**
Wat Sa Si **3**
Wat Si Chum **3**
Wat Si Sawai **3**
Wat Traphang Tong **3**
Wat Yai **4**

The Central Plains
THAILAND
⊕ Bangkok

Lampang
Phrae
LAMPANG
PHRAE
11
⊕ Uttaradit
Si Satchanalai ○
UTTARADIT
1
Sawankhalok
Wang
101
SUKHOTHAI
Tak ⊕
2
12
3 ○ New
   Sukhothai ⊕
11
PHITSANULOK
12
Phitsanulok
4 ○ Wang Thong
105
Mae Sot
TAK
Kamphaeng
Phet
115
○ Phichit
KAMPHAENG
PHET
Ping
PHICHIT
Yom
Nan
Taphan
Hin
113
PHETCHABUN
1
Ban Mun Nak ○
11
○ Nong Bua
BURMA
Kwae Yai
5 ■ Ti Lor Su
   Waterfall
Chumsaeng ○
Nakhon Sawan ○
NAKHON
SAWAN
UTHAI
THANI
Uthai Thani ○
1
Chai Nat ○
Kok
Samrong
333
CHAI NAT
SING
BURI
LOPBURI
Sing Buri ○
Lopburi ○
6
21
SUPHAN
BURI
Ang Thong ○
Tha Rua ○
KANCHANABURI
Suphan ○
Buri
Saraburi ○
Ayutthaya ○
Kwae Yai
7
Bang Pa-In
Chao Phraya
Pathum
Thani
321
Kwae Noi
Kanchanaburi ○
323
Nakorn
Pathom
○ Nonthaburi
0 ——— 40 mi
0 ——— 40 km
BANGKOK ★ ⊕

10

CENTRAL THAILAND | Ayutthaya

Ayutthaya

THAILAND
Ayutthaya
* Bangkok

0 — 1/2 mi
0 — 1/2 km
+++ Railway

ATTRACTIONS ●
Ayutthaya Historical
    Study Center **6**
Chan Kasem Palace **9**
Chao Sam Phraya
    National Museum **7**
Grand Palace **2**
Viharn Phra Mongkhon Bophit **5**
Wat Chai Wattanaram **1**
Wat Na Phra Meru **3**
Wat Phra Mahathat **21**
Wat Phra Si Sanphet **4**
Wat Ratburana **10**
Wat Yai Chai Mongkhon **18**

HOTELS ■
Ayothaya Riverside Hotel **14**
Baan Lotus **11**
Bann KunPra **20**
Kantary Hotel **16**
Krungsri River Hotel **15**
P.U. Inn Guest House **13**
Tony's Place **12**
Woraburi Ayothaya
    Convention Resort **17**

RESTAURANTS ◆
Chao Phrom Night Market **22**
Hua Raw Night Market **8**
Pae Krung Kao/
    The Floating Restaurant **19**

Railway Station

To Bangkok →
Pridi Damrong Bridge
Pasak River
Uthong Rd.
Bus Station
Ferry Pier
Pa Maphrao Rd.
Naresuan Rd.
Dechawat Rd.
Uthong Rd.
Chao Phraya River
Lopburi River
Ayutthaya Historical Park
Phra-Ram Lake
PA-RAM PARK
Rotchana Rd. (Tambon Rojana Rd.)
Pathon Rd.
Chao Phraya R.
Uthong Rd.
St. Joseph's Cathedral
DUTCH SETTLEMENT
ENGLISH SETTLEMENT
PORTUGUESE SETTLEMENT
FRENCH SETTLEMENT

Then, in 1767, after a 15-month siege, the town was destroyed by the Burmese. Today there is little left but ruins and rows of headless Buddhas where once an empire thrived. The temple compounds are still awe-inspiring even in disrepair, and a visit here is memorable and a good starting point for those drawn to the relics of history.

The architecture of Ayutthaya is a fascinating mix of styles. Tall, corncob-shaped spires, called *prangs*, point to ancient Khmer (Cambodian) influence (best seen in Bangkok at Wat Arun, p. 112). These bear a resemblance to the architecture of Angkor Wat, in Cambodia. The pointed stupas are ascribed to the Sukhothai style.

Essentials

GETTING THERE

BY TRAIN   Trains depart at 7, 8:30, and 9:25am daily from Bangkok's **Hua Lampong Railway Station** (© **1690;** trip time 1½ hr.; 66B first class, 35B second class; 15B third class).

BY BUS   Buses leave every 15 minutes from Bangkok's **Northern Bus Terminal** on Kampaengphet 2 Rd., Mo Chit (© **02936-2841**), from 4:30am to 7:30pm (trip time 1½ hr.). Rates run from 50B for second class.

BY MINIBUS   Minibuses leave every 20–30 minutes from Victory Monument (on the BTS). They cost around 70B and take just an hour to arrive.

BY BOAT   All-day river cruises are a popular option to and from Ayutthaya, and there are a number of companies making the connection. **Grand Pearl Cruises** (© **02861-0255;** www.grandpearlcruise.com) runs a huge floating diner-cum-dance club; it can be booked through most hotels. Departure points are at River City pier, off Charoen Krung (New) Road, daily at approximately 7:30am. Day trips involve a morning air-conditioned bus ride to the ancient city and then a return by boat, where a buffet lunch is served; the cost is 1,900B.

The most luxurious way to travel upriver is aboard the *Anantara Song*, a renovated teak rice barge, or its newer and even more exclusive sister, the *Manohra Dream*. For reservations, contact **Anantara Cruises** (**02477-0770;** www.manohracruises. com). Three-day, two-night trips on the *Song* leave the hotel pier every Monday and Thursday, while private trips on the *Dream* can be arranged at your convenience. The *Song* has four staterooms with en suite bathrooms, while the *Dream* has two large rooms with A/C, full showers, and king-sized beds. Each ship's crew serves cocktails, snacks, and Thai meals in its covered lounge. The trip includes a stop and elephant ride at Wat Nivet, in Ayutthaya. Inclusive of meals, tours, and transfers (but not alcohol), the *Song* runs at a steep 69,000B for a double stateroom, while the *Dream* costs a hefty 200,000B for the entire boat (maximum four people). Reservations should be made well in advance.

ORIENTATION

Ayutthaya's old city is surrounded by a canal fed by three rivers—Chao Phraya, Lopburi, and Pasak—and thus is often referred to as the "island." The main ferry pier is located on the east side of the island, just opposite the train station. The Bangkok bus makes its last stop at the station opposite the Siam Commercial Bank Building, off Chao Prom Road in downtown.

VISITOR INFORMATION

There is a **Tourism Authority of Thailand (TAT)** office at Si Sanphet Road (✆ **03524-6076**), opposite the Chao Sam Phraya National Museum. Stop by for maps and other information.

GETTING AROUND

A tuk-tuk from the train station into town will cost about 50B. The best way to visit the ruins is by renting a bicycle (about 50B per day) from any guesthouse or hotel. If you're feeling lazy, negotiate a fee with the rider of a *samlor* (bicycle taxi); enlist the help of hotel staff to negotiate, or this unique and environmentally friendly way of getting around will cost an arm and a leg. A much noisier but faster longtail boat can take you on a 2-hour trip to the main sights for about 800B for up to eight people (arrange this through your hotel, or look for the boat operators by the pier at the northeast end of the island, near the night market). You can also hire a tuk-tuk, with a fixed fee of 200B per hour for temple tours. There is also regular minibus service between Ayutthaya and the pretty 19th-century palaces at Bang Pa-In, departing from Chao Prom Market on the road of the same name; the trip takes 50 minutes and costs 30B.

FAST FACTS

Bank of Ayudhya (which uses a different spelling of the city's name) has a branch on U Thong Road next to the ferry pier, across the river from the train station, and there are plenty of ATMs in the city. The main **post office** is also on U Thong Road in the northeast corner of town (but any hotel or guesthouse can help with posting mail). A number of shops on Naresuan Road Soi 1 offer **Internet** service for around 30B per hour.

Exploring Ayutthaya

The bulk of the historical sites here are concentrated on the "island," with ancient ruins interspersed with the modern buildings that have risen around them. The Ayutthaya Historical Park lies in the center of the island, but the sites below are just a few of many, and a guide can be helpful (contact any hotel front desk to arrange one).

Most temples sell tickets until 4:30pm and close at 5pm. If you plan to visit several temples, there is a package ticket that costs 220B available at all temples; it is valid for 30 days and permits entrance to all temples mentioned below except Wat Na Phra Meru and Wat Chai Mongkol. Though you can't go inside the temples after dark, several of the exteriors are dramatically lit at night, and worth seeing on their own. Some hotels even arrange night tours to look at these illuminations. Brightly caparisoned elephants are on hand for short rides around the center of the ancient city, and cost 500B for 30 minutes.

MUSEUMS

Ayutthaya Historical Study Center MUSEUM   As a resource for students, scholars, and the public, this center presents displays of the ancient city, including models of the palace and the port area and reconstructions of ships and architectural elements, giving a strong sense of how the city looked in its heyday. There's also a library on the premises, which will probably only appeal to historians. If you're interested in seeing historical artifacts from the Ayutthaya era, you'd be better off visiting the nearby Chao Sam Phraya National Museum (p. 269).

Rotchana Rd. ✆ **03524-5124.** Admission 100B, students 50B. Mon–Fri 9am–4:30pm; Sat–Sun 9am–5pm.

Chan Kasem Palace ★ PALACE/MUSEUM   Housing the **Chantharakasem National Museum,** the impressive Chan Kasem Palace was built in 1577 by King Maha Thamaraja (the 17th Ayutthaya monarch) for his son, who became King Naresuan. It was destroyed, but was later restored by King Mongkut (Rama IV), who stayed there whenever he visited Ayutthaya. On display are gold artifacts, jewelry, carvings, Buddha images, and domestic and religious objects from the 13th to the 17th century.

Northeast part of the island. ☏ **03525-1586.** Admission 100B. Wed–Sun 9am–4pm.

Chao Sam Phraya National Museum ★★ MUSEUM   This museum, one of Thailand's largest, boasts a comprehensive collection of antique bronze Buddha images, carved panels, religious objects, and other local artifacts. Though most of the city's treasures were plundered by the Burmese in the 18th century or have been moved to the National Museum in Bangkok, it's still worth taking a look at the collection of gold objects that includes a relic casket from Wat Mahathat and a kneeling elephant studded with gems that was found in the crypt at Wat Ratburana. It's close to the Ayutthaya Historical Study Center (see above) and across from the TAT office.

Rotchana Rd. (1½ blocks west of the center near the junction of Si Sanphet Rd.). ☏ **03524-1587.** Admission 150B. Wed–Sun 9am–4pm.

THE TEMPLES & RUINS

Viharn Phra Mongkon Bophit ★ RELIGIOUS SITE   Home to one of Thailand's largest seated bronze Buddhas, this sanctuary was reconstructed in the 1950s with the help of funding from the Burmese who destroyed the original a couple of centuries ago. The area was originally designated for royal cremation ceremonies, and the *viharn* (assembly hall) was later constructed to house the Buddha image. It is the only newish building in the ancient city and is generally the first port of call for Thai visitors, who come to pay their respects to the huge Buddha image.

West of Wat Phra Mahathat and near Wat Si Sanphet. Free admission. Daily 8am–5pm.

Wat Chai Wattanaram HISTORIC SITE   A long bike ride from the other main temple sites, in the southwest of the city, this *wat* (temple) is an excellently preserved example of Khmer architecture in the Ayutthaya period. You can climb to the steep steps of the central *prang* for beautiful views of the surrounding countryside. Its intact structure offers visitors a good sense of what a working temple might have looked like some 300 years ago.

Opposite bank of the Chao Phraya River, southwest of town. Admission 50B. Daily 8am–5pm.

Wat Na Phra Meru HISTORIC SITE   Located on the Lopburi side of the river, Wat Na Phra Meru survived Ayutthaya's destruction in 1767 because it was used as a base for the invading Burmese army. It's worth visiting to see the black-stone Buddha dating from the Mon (Dvaravati) period, as well as the central sanctuary, with the principal 1.8m-tall (6-ft.) Buddha and stunning vaulted ceilings supported by ornate columns. A Burmese king died here when his cannon backfired during an attack.

Across the Lopburi River, north of the Grand Palace area. Admission 20B. Daily 8am–5pm.

Wat Phra Mahathat ★★★ HISTORIC SITE   The most striking of all of the temples in Ayutthaya, Wat Phra Mahathat was built in the heart of the city in 1384 during the reign of King Rachatirat. It is typical of Ayutthaya ruins, with large crumbling stupas surrounded by low laterite walls and rows of headless Buddhas. One

Buddha head remains a draw for merit-makers and photographers, however—it's embedded in the gnarled roots of a bodhi tree. Opposite Wat Phra Mahathat stands **Wat Ratburana ★★**, built in 1424 and splendidly restored—the towering monuments (both rounded Khmer-style *prangs* and Sukhothai-style pointed *chedis*) have even retained some of their original stucco. In the two crypts, excavators found bronze Buddha images and votive tablets, as well as golden objects and jewelry, many of which are displayed in the Chao Sam Phraya National Museum (p. 269). There are also murals, as well as a frieze of heavenly beings and some Chinese scenes. Both *wats* remain damaged despite restoration.

Along Chee Kun Rd., near the intersection with Naresuan. Admission for each 50B. Daily 8am–5pm.

Wat Phra Si Sanphet ★★ HISTORIC SITE   Built in the 14th century for private royal use, Si Sanphet lies right next to the Viharn Phra Mongkul Bophit, so is the first of the ancient ruins that most visitors see. During the heyday of Ayutthaya, this was the city's largest temple, but little now remains apart from brick foundations and three 15th-century, Sri Lankan-style *chedis*, enshrining the ashes of three Ayutthayan kings, which are probably the most photographed sight in the historical park. Nothing remains of the **Grand Palace,** just to the north, which is included in the same ticket, apart from the foundations of three buildings and a wall around the compound.

Next to Viharn Phra Mongkul Bophit in the northwest end of the island. Admission 50B. Daily 9am–5pm.

Wat Yai Chai Mongkhon ★ HISTORIC SITE   Visible for miles around, the huge, brick *chedi* of Wat Yai is a long walk (or a short bicycle or tuk-tuk ride) southeast of ancient Ayutthaya (across the river and out of town). King U Thong founded the temple in 1357, and the white reclining Buddha near the entrance was built by King Naresuan. The massive pagoda celebrates the defeat of the Burmese at Suphanburi in 1592, and King Naresuan's defeat of the crown prince of Burma in an elephant joust. The receding rows of Buddha images draped in saffron robes make for interesting photos.

East of the city, across the Pridi Damrong Bridge and south on Dusit Rd. Admission 20B. Daily 8am–5pm.

Where to Stay

As most people visit Ayutthaya on a day trip, there is no luxury accommodation available, though there are plenty of acceptable and affordable choices. All along Naresuan Road, which is like a smaller version of Khao San Road in Bangkok, you'll find good budget accommodation; the street gets busy in the high season (Nov–Feb). Try the lively **Tony's Place** (12/18 Naresuan Soi 1; http://tonyplace-ayutthaya.com; ✆ **03525-2578**), with wireless Internet access, or **P.U. Inn Guest House** (20/1 Moo 4, off Naresuan; www.puguesthouse.com; ✆ **03525-1213**), which has some rooms with air-conditioning, TV, and minibar.

MODERATE

Kantary Hotel ★   Located to the west of the Chao Phraya River on Rojana Road, the Kantary is both Ayutthaya's newest and best hotel. Facilities such as the inviting pool and well-equipped health club make it worth the rates. Choose between a studio or a one- or two-bedroom apartment complete with separate living room, dining area, and balcony. The modern decor is simple but stylish and all rooms are fitted with satellite TV, music system, and Internet.

168 Moo 1, Rojana Rd., Tambol Tanu, Ayutthaya. www.kantarygroup.com. ☏ **03533-7177.** Fax 03533-7178. 193 units. 2,400B studio; 3,000B–4,800B apartment. AE, DC, MC, V. **Amenities:** Restaurant; bar; outdoor pool; health club; sauna/steam room; children's playground. *In room:* A/C, TV/DVD, kitchenette inc. washing machine (in apartments), Wi-Fi (321B per day).

Ayothaya Riverside Hotel Just across from the train station, this is a Thai business-class hotel worth the upgrade from the town's small guesthouses for its bright, clean rooms—though there's nothing particularly special about the decor. Furnishings are sparse but bathrooms are a good size and have separate bathtub and shower. Their riverside restaurant is a pleasant spot for a drink, and many of their large, clean rooms overlook the river. The five executive suites are particularly good value for the extra space that they offer along with a comfortable three-piece suite.

91 Moo 10, Wat Pako Rd., Ayutthaya 13000 (across from the train station). www.ayothayariverside. com. ☏ **03523-8737.** Fax 03524-4139. 117 units. From 850B double; 1,600B suite. **Amenities:** 2 restaurants (one floating at riverside); bikes. *In room:* A/C, TV, fridge, Wi-Fi (150B per day).

Krungsri River Hotel ★ This four-star hotel is within walking distance of the train station and provides probably the best standard of comfort in town after the Kantary. Rooms have large bathrooms with comfortable furnishings and views over the river as well as satellite TV and complementary Wi-Fi. The hotel also offers several leisure facilities, including a six-lane bowling center, a snooker club, massage services, and a pub that has live music from 9pm; there's also a coffee shop and a small indoor pool.

27/2 Rotchana Rd., Ayutthaya 13000 (northeast side of Pridi Damrong Bridge). www.krungsririver. com. ☏ **03524-4333.** Fax 03524-3777. 202 units. From 1,700B double; from 4,200B suite. AE, DC, MC, V. **Amenities:** 3 restaurants; pub with beer garden; outdoor pool; health club w/sauna; room service; babysitting. *In room:* A/C, satellite TV, minibar, fridge, Wi-Fi (free).

Woraburi Ayothaya Convention Resort Overlooking the Pasak River, this newish hotel offers some of the best facilities in town. As its title of "convention center" suggests, it's especially well-suited for large groups, and breakfast is included in the room rates. Rooms are not large, but are well-equipped. Riverboat dining cruises, complete with floating karaoke fun, are available for up to 100 guests.

89 Watkluay Rd., Ayutthaya 13000. www.woraburi.com. ☏ **03524-9600.** Fax 03524-9625. 170 units. 1,500B–1,950B double; from 2,600B suite. MC, V. **Amenities:** Restaurant; exercise room; cafe. *In room:* A/C, TV, minibar, fridge, Wi-Fi (150B per day).

INEXPENSIVE

Baan Lotus This charming restored teak house lies just outside the town's main cluster of budget options, but you'll be glad you took the short walk to get there. The welcoming staff makes it a nice place to unwind, as does the large garden and pond. Rooms are simply furnished, and the wooden walls are thin—a problem if you have noisy neighbors. Staff offer tours at night, when the ruins are romantically lit.

20 Pa Maphrao Rd., Ayutthaya 13000. ☏ **03525-1988.** 20 units. 400B double fan with private bathroom; 600B double A/C with private bathroom. No credit cards. **Amenities:** Restaurant; bikes. *In room:* A/C (in some), Wi-Fi (free) no phone.

Bann KunPra Bann KunPra is a beautiful riverside teak house converted into comfortable, if very basic, guest quarters which include a couple of dormitories. A recent renovation of the small house ("Ruen Lek") has transformed it into three very attractive rooms that are great value at 1,100B, though the river view rooms in the

"Ruen Rim Nam" (house next to water) are appealing too. There are three buildings in the compound, all set around a small common area that exudes a rustic charm. Their open-air candlelit restaurant overlooks the river.

48 Moo 3, U Thong Rd., Ayutthaya 13000. www.bannkunpra.com. ©**03524-1978.** 12 units. 250B dorm with shared bathroom; 500B–600B river view double with shared bathroom; 1,100B double with private bathroom. No credit cards. **Amenities:** Restaurant; bikes; Internet. *In room:* Wi-Fi (free), no phone.

Where to Eat

Particularly if this is your first stop outside of Bangkok, don't miss the **Hua Raw Night Market,** along the river in the northeast of town, with fresh produce and a wide selection of Thai/Muslim dishes. More central is the **Chao Phrom Night Market** near the pier. Many of the guesthouses along **Naresuan Road** serve decent Thai fare geared to foreigners, and this area also hosts a few **open-air restaurants** right on the street, a great place to meet, greet, eat, and party late.

Pae Krung Kao/The Floating Restaurant THAI/CHINESE   On low floating pallets at the riverside, this restaurant allows diners to have great views of passing boats and river life while bobbing up and down with the water's movement. The satisfying Thai/Chinese stir-fry and curries are further complemented by a tranquil Chinese garden, a strumming balladeer, and candlelight at the water's edge. Giant river shrimp is the restaurant's specialty, though they turn out a tasty pork knuckle as well.

4 Moo 2, U Thong Rd. (west bank of Pasak River, north of Pridi Damrong Bridge). ©**03525-1807.** Main courses 60B–350B. MC, V. Daily 5–10pm.

Side Trips from Ayutthaya
BANG PA-IN

Only 61km (38 miles) north of Bangkok, this delightful **royal palace** (admission 100B; 8am–5pm, last admission 3.30pm) is usually combined with Ayutthaya in most 1-day tours and is accessible by minivan. Not all the buildings are open to the public, but the elegant colonial architecture makes a fascinating contrast with Ayutthaya's crumbling temples.

The 17th-century temple and palace at **Bang Pa-In** were originally built by Ayutthaya's King Prasat Thong, later abandoned when the capital moved in the late 1700s, and then rebuilt by King Chulalongkorn in the late 1800s. In the center of the small lake, **Phra Thinang Aisawan Thippa-At** is an excellent example of classic Thai style. Behind it, in Versailles style, are the former **king's apartments,** which today serve as a hall for state ceremonies. The **Phra Thinang Wehat Chamrun,** also noteworthy, is a Chinese-style building (open to the public), where court members generally lived during the rainy and cool seasons. Also worth looking into is the **Phra Thinang Withun Thatsuna,** an observatory on a small island that affords a fine view of the countryside.

LOPBURI

77km (48 miles) N of Ayutthaya; 153km (95 miles) N of Bangkok; 224km (139 miles) S of Phitsanulok

Lopburi is famous for its 14th- to 17th-century temple ruins, as much as for its sometimes very aggressive troupes of monkeys that call them home. The town hosted kings and emissaries from around the world some 400 years ago, and archaeological evidence suggests a highly developed Buddhist society was here as early as the 11th century. These days, Lopburi is a popular day trip from Ayutthaya or a good stopover on the way north.

Essentials

GETTING THERE

Lopburi is along Highway 1 just past Saraburi (connect with Lopburi via Hwy. 3196 to Rte. 311). The fastest way to go straight there from Bangkok is by minivan from Victory Monument (accessible by BTS) for 100B. Vans leave when full from in front of Rachavithee Hospital. Regular buses connect to Lopburi via Ayutthaya from Bangkok's **Northern Bus Terminal** (℡ 02936-2841) for the same price. Numerous trains make a daily connection with Lopburi via Ayutthaya from Bangkok's **Hua Lampong Railway Station** (℡ 1690), from 28B upward.

INFORMATION & ORIENTATION

The **TAT Office** is located in a teak house built in the 1930s just a short walk from the train station (follow the signs) on Ropwat Phrathat Road (℡ 03642-2768). They have a useful map and can point you to sights within walking distance.

Exploring Lopburi

You should visit Lopburi by approaching its attractions in a clockwise circle pattern. From the train station, stop in to **Wat Phra Si Ratana Mahathat** just out front. Built in 1257, Mahathat is a stunning ruin, much like the temples of Ayutthaya (admission 50B; daily 7am–5pm).

Directly west of the TAT, the large complex of **King Narai's Palace** was built in 1666 and combines a large museum of Lopburi antiquities with the *wats* and palace of the king. When nearby Ayutthaya was little more than a marsh, King Narai hosted emissaries from around the world (note the many Islamic-style doorways). The museum now houses displays of Thai rural life and traditions from weaving and agriculture to shadow puppetry (admission 150B; Wed–Sun 8:30am–4:30pm). After leaving the museum, take some time to saunter around the atmospheric grounds around the palace.

From Narai's palace, head north through the town's small streets and market areas to **Wat Sao Thong Thong,** which houses a large golden Buddha and fine Khmer and Ayutthaya period statues. Heading farther north brings you to **Ban Vichayen,** the manicured ruins of the fine housing built for visiting dignitaries (admission 50B; Wed–Sun 9am–4pm).

Going east along Vichayen Road, toward the town center, the three connected towers at **Phra Prang Sam Yot** are stunning examples of the Khmer influence in what is known as "Lopburi style." This is the site where you'll find the town's famous *macaques* (monkeys) most hours of the day (admission 50B; daily 7am–5pm). Be careful around these mischievous apes: They have been known to get aggressive and can be very dangerous. You can take pictures, but keep a tight grip on your camera, and don't carry any food.

Reaching Prang Sam Yot brings you full circle back to the train tracks just north of the station. If you're in Lopburi in late spring, ask about the occasional *macaque* **banquets,** where a formal table is set for the little beasts, who tear it to bits—they've no manners at all. Most days they are fed at a temple just east of Sam Yot, called **San**

Phra Khan (across the train tracks). Groups of the mischievous animals trapeze along the high wires and swoop down on shop owners armed with sticks, who keep a close eye on outdoor merchandise. It's a different kind of rush hour altogether.

Where to Stay & Eat

Few stay in little Lopburi, instead visiting the town on a day trip from Ayutthaya or as a brief stopover on the way to points north. If you do choose to stay here, try the **Lopburi Inn Resort** (144 Phaholyothin Rd.; www.lopburiinnresort.com; ✆ 03642-0777), with rooms from 1,800B, with A/C, TV, and breakfast included.

There are lots of small open-air restaurants in and around town. One of the best options is the friendly, air-conditioned **Thai Sawang** (11/8 Surasak Rd.; ✆ 03641-1881), just southeast of the main entrance to King Narai's Palace. They do decent Western breakfasts as well as Thai and Vietnamese dishes such as *bun hoi* (noodles and pork) at very reasonable prices.

PHITSANULOK

377km (234 miles) N of Bangkok; 93km (58 miles) SE of Sukhothai

Phitsanulok is a bustling agricultural, transportation, and military center, with a population of over 100,000, nestled on the banks of the Nan River. It is the crossroads of Thailand, located in the center of the country and roughly equidistant from Chiang Mai and Bangkok. Like most transportation hubs, it's hectic, noisy, and just a stopover for most people on their way to the more charming Sukhothai.

Outside of town, the terrain is flat and the rice paddies are endless—they turn a vivid green in July to August. In winter, white-flowering tobacco and pink-flowering soybeans are planted in rotation. Rice barges, houseboats, and longtail boats ply the Nan and Song Kwai rivers, which eventually connect to the Chao Phraya River and feed into the Gulf of Thailand.

For 25 years, Phitsanulok served as the capital, and it is the birthplace of King Naresuan (the Great), the Ayutthayan king who, on elephant-back, defended Thailand from the Burmese army during the 16th century.

When a tragic fire burned most of the city in 1959, one of the only buildings to survive was Wat Yai, famed for its unique statue of Buddha; the temple is now a holy pilgrimage site. For travelers, Wat Yai is worth a visit on the way west to Sukhothai or farther to the Burmese border. Phitsanulok is also famous for the Bangkaew dog, a notoriously fierce and faithful breed that's prized globally, and is thought to have originated from the Bang Rakham District.

Essentials

GETTING THERE

BY PLANE Nok Air (✆ 1318; www.nokair.com) has two flights daily to Phitsanulok from Bangkok, one leaving in the morning and the other in the evening (flying time: about 1 hr.). The Nok Air office in Phitsanulok is at the airport (✆ 02627-2667). **Kan Air** (✆ 05530-1522; www.kanairlines.com) operates a daily flight to Chiang Mai, and has an office at the airport too. Taxis cost about 200B into town from the airport.

BY TRAIN About 10 trains per day travel between Phitsanulok and Bangkok. The trip time is about 7 hours and costs 449B for an air-conditioned second-class seat.

"Rapid" trains can take up to 9 hours, so it is worth the expense to go "sprinter" or "express" class—the difference being that express has sleeping berths. There are five daily connections between Phitsanulok and Chiang Mai (7 hr.; fare 440B). For information and reservations, call Bangkok's **Hua Lampong Railway Station** (☏ 1690), **Chiang Mai Railway Station** (☏ 05324-5363), or the **Phitsanulok Railway Station** (☏ 05525-8005).

In front of the station in Phitsanulok, throngs of *samlors* (pedicabs) and motorcycle taxis wait to take you to your hotel. The station is right in town, so expect to pay just 50B to get where you need to go. The bidding will start at around 100B; smile and get ready to haggle.

BY BUS   Standard air-conditioned buses leave daily every hour for the trip to Phitsanulok from Bangkok from 7am to midnight (trip time 6 hr.; about 490B). The VIP bus leaves at midnight and is about the same price; the wide seats recline enough to get a decent sleep, and the overnight trip is a timesaver. Buses depart from Chiang Mai in similar numbers. Frequent non-air-conditioned buses connect with Sukhothai. The intercity bus terminal in Phitsanulok is 2km (1¼ miles) east of town on Highway 12 (about 50B by tuk-tuk or taxi). Contact **Bangkok's Northern Bus Terminal** (☏ 02936-2841), the **Arcade Bus Station** in **Chiang Mai** (☏ 05324-2664), or the **Phitsanulok Bus Terminal** (☏ 05521-2090).

VISITOR INFORMATION

The **TAT office** (☏ 05525-2742) has maps and basic information, but is inconveniently located on Boromtrailokanart Road, two blocks south of the central clock tower, down a small side street. Most hotels also offer free city maps.

ORIENTATION

The town is fairly compact, with the majority of services and sights for tourists concentrated along or near the east bank of the Nan River. Naresuan Road extends from the railway station and crosses the river from the east over the town's main bridge. Wat Yai is north of the bridge and just a hitch north of busy Highway 12. The main market, featuring souvenirs during the day and food stalls at night, is just south of the bridge on riverside Phutta Bucha Road. One landmark is the clock tower at the southern end of the commercial district, Boromtrailokanart Road.

GETTING AROUND

BY TUK-TUK & SONGTAEW   Tuk-tuks (called taxis here) stop near the bus and train stations. Negotiate for an in-town fare, usually about 50B. *Songtaews* (covered pickup trucks) follow regular routes outside of town.

BY BUS   There's a well-organized city bus system with a main terminal south of the train station on A-Kathotsarot Road. Trips are about 10B, but you would do just as well to hire tuk-tuks or taxis.

There are frequent (every half-hour 6am–6pm) buses from the intercity bus terminal east of town to **New Sukhothai** (trip time 1 hr.; fare 42B).

BY HIRED MINIVAN   Any hotel in Phitsanulok can arrange minivan tours in the area and to Sukhothai. Expect to pay around 2,000B with a driver, plus fuel.

BY TRAM   The **Phitsanulok Tour Tramway** offers a 45-minute sightseeing tour (adults 30B, kids 20B), departing from Wat Yai from 9am to 3pm and returning to the temple.

BY RENTAL CAR **Budget** (℗ 05530-1020) and **Avis** (℗ 08996-8672) have offices at the airport.

SPECIAL EVENTS

The **Buddha Chinarat Festival** is held annually on the 6th day of the waxing moon in the 3rd lunar month (usually late Jan or early Feb). Then, Phitsanulok's Wat Yai is packed with well-wishers, dancers, monks and abbots, children, and tourists, all converging on the temple grounds for a 6-day celebration.

FAST FACTS

Bangkok Bank has an after-hours (until 8pm) exchange service at 35 Naresuan Rd. The **General Post Office** is on Phuttha Bucha Road, along the river two blocks north of Naresuan Road. The **Overseas Call Office** is on the second floor of the post office and offers **Internet** service at about 30B per hour.

Where to Stay

In addition to the hotels listed below, the bright, clean rooms at **Lithai Guest House** (73 Phayalithai Rd.; ℗ 05521-9626) are a welcome addition to the city's accommodation options; the price (250B–350B single; 460B double) includes breakfast, except for the cheapest fan rooms. South of town, near the airport, the **Phitsanulok Youth Hostel** (38 Sanambin Rd.; ℗ 05524-2060) has basic rooms starting from 120B for a dorm room and 300B for a double.

MODERATE

Amarin Lagoon Hotel ★   This is certainly one of the most attractive resort hotels in the area, and due to its location just a few kilometers east of the town center the hotel operates a shuttle service into town. Rooms are spacious, attractive, and quiet, with white-washed walls and local art adding a touch of color. If you plan to spend much time in the room, go for a deluxe, which has a separate sitting area. There is a huge pool and spa and the hotel offers Wi-Fi; plus, it's only 40 minutes from a golf course.

52/299 Moo 6, Praongkhao Rd., Phitsanulok 65000. www.amarinlagoonhotel.com. ℗ **05522-0999.** Fax 05522-0944. 301 units. 2,000B–3,500B double; from 8,000B suite. AE, MC, V. **Amenities:** Restaurant; lounge; pool; health club; room service. *In room:* A/C, satellite TV, minibar, fridge, Wi-Fi (500B per day).

Grand Riverside ★★   In a perfect location on the west bank of the Nan River and just a short walk from the night market, the Grand Riverside certainly justifies its name with its palatial lobby and lavishly furnished rooms. Fixtures and fittings follow a traditional design but in this smart new place there are no loose faucets or broken switches. Most rooms have great views across the river, and the suites are the city's most luxurious lodgings. There are also private karaoke rooms, served by waitresses.

59 Praroung Rd., Phitsanulok 65000. www.tgrhotel.com. ℗ **05524-8333.** Fax 05521-6420. 79 units. From 2,000B double; from 4,000B suite. AE, MC, V. **Amenities:** Restaurant; bar. *In room:* A/C, TV, minibar, Wi-Fi (free).

Topland Hotel & Convention Center ★★   Adjoining the town's largest shopping center and just a short distance from Wat Yai, this is one of the most conveniently located hotels in the area, and is particularly popular among Thai business people. Service is snappy, though the lobby can be a pretty busy place at checkout time. It's a good idea to take a look at a room before booking it, as some are getting a bit tatty and in need of renovation. However, the restaurant turns out reasonable food, there's a big, relaxing pool, and a disco on the 7th floor (which stays open till 2am and could be a problem for light sleepers).

68/33 Akathodsarod St., Phitsanulok 65000. www.toplandhotel.com. ⓒ **05524-7800.** Fax 05524-7815. 253 units. From 2,000B double; from 5,000B suite. AE, MC, V. **Amenities:** Restaurant; 2 bars; outdoor pool; exercise room; spa; room service. *In room:* A/C, TV, minibar, fridge, hair dryer, Wi-Fi (free).

INEXPENSIVE

Pailyn Hotel This 12-story business hotel is a reasonable budget choice for down-town lodging, with sweeping views of the surrounding countryside from the top floors, though the building is beginning to show its age. The bright marble lobby gives the place some panache, and rooms are clean, fairly quiet for the location, and styl-ishly decked out with rattan furnishings. Rooms are priced according to size; upper standards are slightly smarter. Bathrooms are standard, with no frills. The bar and disco attract more locals than hotel guests.

38 Borom Trailokanart Rd., Phitsanulok 65000. ⓒ **05525-2411.** Fax 05522-5237. 247 units. From 1,000B double; from 3,000B suite. AE, MC, V. **Amenities:** 2 restaurants; bar and disco; sauna room service; babysitting; Internet (free in lobby). *In room:* A/C, TV, minibar, fridge.

Where to Eat

No fine-dining options exist in Phitsanulok but there are lots of small eateries in and around the train station. Be sure to try the local specialty, *khaew tak*, sun-dried banana baked with honey; packages are sold everywhere and cost just 30B. At the **Night Bazaar** you can enjoy "flying vegetables"—morning-glory greens sautéed, tossed high in the air, and adeptly caught in the chef's pan.

Pae Fa Thai Floating Restaurant THAI   The best of many similar places along the riverbank, just in front of the main tourist attraction, Wat Yai, Pae Pha Thai is a friendly, casual eatery with no pretense. Indulge in the kind of spread you might find in a Thai home—*tod man plaa* (deep-fried fish cakes), *kai phad kaprow* (chicken with basil and chili), *tom yum* soup, and a whole fish encrusted with garlic and lemon. Dishes seem to be made all the better by being served at the water's edge.

Phutta Bucha Rd. (on Nan River in front of Wat Yai). ⓒ **05524-2743.** Main courses 100B–200B. MC, V. Daily 11am–11pm.

Phitsanulok Entertainment & Nightlife

You won't find much in the way of nightlife in Phitsanulok, but for a beverage or a late snack set to noisy Thai pop music, stop by the **Tree House** (ⓒ **05521-2587**), a small bar with an adjoining garden at 48 Sanambin Rd., across from the Phitsanulok Thani Hotel.

Exploring Phitsanulok

Most use Phitsanulok as a jumping-off point for Sukhothai, but there are a few sights in the town proper—with Wat Yai being the foremost among them (see below).

The Sgt. Maj. Thawee Folk Museum ★ MUSEUM   This small campus of low-slung pavilions houses a private collection of antique items from the country's rural life. Farming and trapping equipment, household items, and old photographs of the city are lovingly displayed by the sergeant major, with descriptions in English. Just across the road is the **Buranathai Buddha Casting Foundry** (admission free), where you can see the carving and casting of large Buddhas, most of which are copies of the Chinarat Buddha image from Wat Yai. The foundry is also operated by Dr Thawee, as is the adjacent **Thai Bird Garden** (daily 8:30am–5pm; admission 50B), which contains examples of some of the country's most colorful species, including a hornbill and a silver pheasant.

26/43 Wisut Kasat Rd. 🕐 **05521-2749.** Admission 50B adults, 20B students. Tues–Sun 8:30am–4:30pm.

Wat Chulamanee TEMPLE   The oldest temple in the area and the site of the original city, about 7km (4 miles) south of the modern city, Wat Chulamanee is still an active monastery. The temple was restored in the 1950s and is admired for the fine, laterite, Khmer-style *prang* that dates back to the Sukhothai era and its elaborate stucco work; also look out for the finely carved lintels above the doorways. It's best to have your own transport if you want to visit, or you may find yourself stranded due to limited public transportation.

7km (4⅓ miles) south of the Nakon Sawan Hwy., on Boromtrailokanart Rd. Suggested donation 20B. Daily 6am–7pm.

Wat Yai ★★ TEMPLE   This temple's full name is **Wat Phra Si Ratana Maha-that,** and it's one of the most important temples in the country. The Phra Buddha Chinarat statue is a bronze image cast in 1357 under the Sukhothai king Mahatm-maracha; its most distinctive feature is its flamelike halo (*mandorla*), which symbol-izes spiritual radiance. Only the Emerald Buddha in Bangkok (p. 106) is more highly revered by the Thai people.

The *viharn* housing the Buddha is a prized example of traditional Thai architec-ture, with three eaves, overlapping one another to emphasize the nave, and graceful black and gold columns. The mother-of-pearl inlaid doors leading into the chapel were added in 1576 as a gift from King Borommakot of Ayutthaya. Inside, you'll discover an Italian marble floor, two painted *thammas* (pulpits), and murals illustrat-ing the life of Buddha. Other than the *viharn* and *bot* (ordination hall), the *wat's* most distinctive architectural feature is the Khmer-style *prang*, rebuilt by King Boromtrailokanart. It houses the relic from which the *wat* takes its name; *mahathat* means "great relic." The small museum houses a collection of Sukhothai- and Ayutthaya-era Buddhas.

The *wat* is always packed with worshipers paying their respects and making offer-ings. Conservative dress is obligatory—this means clothing that covers the shoulders, elbows, and knees; you'll also need to remove your shoes before entering the *wat*.

1 block north of the Hwy. 12 bridge and just a short walk east of the river. Admission 50B. Wat daily 6am–6pm (during the Buddha Chinarat Festival 6am–midnight); museum daily Wed–Sun 9am–4pm.

SUKHOTHAI ★★★ &
SI SATCHANALAI
HISTORICAL PARKS

Sukhothai: 58km (36 miles) E of Phitsanulok; Si Satchanalai: 56km (35 miles) N of Sukhothai

The emergence of Sukhothai ("Dawn of Happiness" in Pali) in 1238 is considered the birth of the first Thai kingdom. Under King Ramkhamhaeng the Great, Sukhothai's influence covered a larger area than that of present-day Thailand. The ruins here are more intact and less encroached upon than those in Ayutthaya, making this the country's most gratifying historical site.

The **Sukhothai Historical Park,** the main attraction, is a World Heritage Site situated 12km (7½ miles) west of the town of Sukhothai, also known as **New Sukhothai.** Not surprisingly, the new town lacks any of Old Sukhothai's historic grandeur.

Si Satchanalai, north of New Sukhothai, is another legacy of the Sukhothai kingdom. Visitors often enjoy these ruins the most as they are less frequented and therefore quieter, so they are certainly worth the 1-day detour.

Essentials

GETTING THERE

BY PLANE   From Bangkok, **Bangkok Airways** (© 02270-6699; www.bangkok air.com) operates at least one daily flight connecting Bangkok with Sukhothai through their private airport 27km (17 miles) from Sukhothai. Contact them at the Sukhothai airport (© 05564-7224). Bangkok Airways can arrange transfers to New Sukhothai by minivan for 120B.

BY TRAIN   The nearest rail station is in Phitsanulok (p. 274). From there, you can connect by local air-conditioned bus, leaving hourly for New Sukhothai (trip time 1 hr.; fare 42B) from the intercity terminal on Highway 12.

BY BUS   Three daily first-class, nonstop, air-conditioned buses leave from Bangkok (10am–10:30pm; trip time 7 hr.; fare 435B for VIP bus), departing from the **Northern Bus Terminal** (© 02936-2841). There are also more arduous second-class buses, but avoid them unless you're desperate. Several air-conditioned buses leave daily from Chiang Mai's **Arcade Bus Terminal** (© 05324-2664) for the 5½-hour trip (fare 249B for second class with A/C).

VISITOR INFORMATION

The **TAT** office in Sukhothai is at 130 Charot Withi Thong Rd. (© 05561-6228). There's a **tourist police point** (© 1155) opposite the Ramkhamhaeng National Museum. The main police station is at the junction of Singhawat and Si Intharathit roads. The **Sukhothai Hospital** (© 05561-1720) is at 2/1 Jarot Withithong Rd. The **post office** is down near the river on Nikhon Kasem Road.

ORIENTATION

Sukhothai Historical Park (or *muang kao,* "old city") lies 12km (7½ miles) west of **New Sukhothai.** Built along the banks of the Yom River, New Sukhothai has lots of accommodation options, though there are now several fancy places near the Historical Park and in the surrounding countryside. The selection is growing—whether you're looking for laid-back cool or decked-out comfort, you're likely to find your desired niche. **Si Satchanalai Historic Park,** also along the Yom River, is 56km (35 miles) north of New Sukhothai.

SPECIAL EVENTS

The **Loy Krathong ★★** festival here is an exceptional spectacle. This 3-day festival is held on the full moon of the 12th lunar month (usually Nov). Crowds gather at rivers, *klongs* (canals), lakes, and temple fountains to drop small banana-leaf floats or *krathong,* bearing candles, incense, a flower, and a coin. As the *krathong* glides downstream, it symbolizes a letting go of the previous year's sins and unhappiness.

Sukhothai celebrates with fireworks, traditional dancing, and a music and light show in the Historical Park; book early for VIP seats with the best view.

Where to Stay

EXPENSIVE

Ananda Museum Gallery Hotel ★   Located to the east of New Sukhothai town (on the opposite side from the temples), Ananda is a bit remote for some, but it is well designed, with relaxing earth tones and lots of Thai elements, giving it plenty of character. Standard rooms are a bit dingy, so go for the superior or deluxe if you can, as they have a separate living area. Artisan handicrafts (reproductions of Sukhothai-style Buddha images) and antique furnishings are on display in the gallery, while classic Thai cuisine such as *tom yam goong* and *phad thai* is served in the smart restaurant.

10 Moo 4, Bantum Muang, Sukhothai 64000. www.anandasukhothai.com. ✆ **05562-2428.** Fax 05562-1885. 33 units. 3,750B–4,650B double; 9,600 suite. MC, V. **Amenities:** Restaurant; bar and cafe (in the gallery); spa; room service; Internet. *In room:* A/C, TV, minibar, fridge.

Sukhothai Heritage Resort ★★   Set in an organic farm right next to Sukhothai Airport, this place offers a quiet, rural retreat (aircraft land here rarely) and the chance to learn more about rice culture at the neighboring research center. Superior rooms in this two-story hotel are not huge but are comfortably furnished, and they all look out over a pool. Bicycles are on hand for exploring the area (free for guests) and staff can arrange transport to the Historical Park.

999 Moo 2, Tambon Klongkrajong, Sukhothai 64100. www.sukhothaiheritage.com. ✆ **05564-7567.** 68 units. 2,500B–3,500B double; 6,500B suite. MC, V. **Amenities:** Restaurant; bar; 2 pools; bikes. *In room:* A/C, TV, minibar, Wi-Fi.

Tharaburi Resort ★★   After being remodeled from a simple backpacker pad to a high-class haven, this is now one of Sukhothai's most stylish resorts, with rooms covering a huge range of prices. Luxurious double rooms and suites are fitted with Jacuzzis, flatscreen TVs, and spacious balconies. The original guesthouse, Baan Thai, can accommodate a large family with its seven rooms and four bathrooms. Individual rooms in the house are also available.

11/3 Srisomboon Rd., Sukhothai 64000. www.tharaburiresort.com. ✆ **05569-7132.** Fax 05569-7131. 20 units. 1,200B–1,450B double with A/C and shared bathroom; 4,200B double with Jacuzzi and DVD; 5,000B family suite with 2 bedrooms, 1 bathroom; 6,500B suite; 7,800B house (incl. 7 bedrooms, 4 bathrooms). MC, V. **Amenities:** Restaurant; outdoor pool; room service. *In room:* A/C, TV, minibar, fridge, Jacuzzi (in some), Wi-Fi (free).

MODERATE

Lotus Village ★ 🌿   This place has a spa, a boutique, and an abundance of style, yet the prices are surprisingly affordable. Garden paths connect the raised Thai-style bungalows, housing large, sturdy air-conditioned rooms with polished teak. The helpful owners, a Franco-Thai couple, can arrange a tour with a certified guide; plus, it's only a short walk from New Sukhothai's market and town center. An added bonus is that the complementary breakfast includes great coffee and home-made jam.

170 Ratchathanee Rd., Sukhothai 64000. www.lotus-village.com. ✆ **05562-1484.** Fax 05562-1463. 28 units. 920B double with fan; 1,150B–1,540B double with A/C; 2,750B family house. MC, V. **Amenities:** Restaurant; lounge; spa; Wi-Fi (free). *In room:* A/C (in some), minibar, fridge, (both in deluxe rooms), no phone.

Pailyn Sukhothai Hotel ★ Pailyn's biggest advantage is its location, about halfway between the town and temples. The four-story structure is bright, modern, and comfortable, with a granite lobby, carpeted rooms, and a small pool and sun deck. Higher rates bring minibars, fridges, and TVs. All rooms are air-conditioned, and deluxe rooms, while not luxurious, are a decent size. The suites are enormous, with comfy carpets and floor-to-ceiling drapes, but their bathrooms are rather compact in comparison.

10/2 Moo 1, Jarot Withithong Rd., Sukhothai 64210. www.pailynhotel.com. ✆ **05561-3310.** Fax 05561-3317. 238 units. 1,200B double; from 2,500B suite. MC, V. **Amenities:** Restaurant; outdoor pool; room service; Internet (free). *In room:* A/C, TV, minibar (in some), fridge, no phone.

Ruean Thai Hotel ★ Stay once at this charming establishment and it's likely you'll keep coming back. The rooms surround a pool, and the Thai-style design employs lots of wood and pretty antiques. Bathrooms are very spacious and there's a garden in which to wander and relax in (watch out for the resident rabbits). They also offer useful extras such as complementary Thai or Western style breakfast and transfer to the bus station (free) or airport (350B).

181/20 Soi Pracharuammit, Jarot Withithong Rd., Sukhothai 64000. www.rueanthaihotel.com. ✆/ fax **05561-2444.** 28 units. 1,200B–3,200B double. MC, V. Rates include breakfast. **Amenities:** Restaurant; outdoor pool; sports-equipment rentals. *In room:* A/C, TV, minibar, fridge, Wi-Fi (free).

INEXPENSIVE

Ban Thai Guesthouse ★ Ban Thai is the best budget choice in New Sukhothai, and even if you don't stay in this small guesthouse, you'll want to drop by their excellent restaurant and peruse maps and the helpful advice book. They also run popular cooking classes in the restaurant; prices depend on how many dishes you prepare. If you have the cash, splash out on the newer bungalows with air-conditioning and private bathrooms.

38 Pravet Nakhon Rd., Sukhothai 64000. ✆ **05561-0163.** 15 units. 200B with fan and shared bathroom; 300B bungalow with fan; 500B bungalow with A/C. No credit cards. **Amenities:** Restaurant, Wi-Fi (free). *In room:* A/C (in some), no phone.

Where to Eat

Eating in Sukhothai is all about sampling the city's famous dish, *kwaytiaw sukhothai,* or **Sukhothai noodles**—a mouth-watering plate of rice noodles with crispy pork, garlic, green beans, cilantro, chili, and peanuts in a broth seasoned with soy sauce. For the best, try **Baan Kru Iew** on Vichien Chamnong Road; another good spot for the same dish is **Kwaytiaw Thai Sukhothai,** on Jarot Withithong Road, close to the Ruean Thai Hotel (see above). New Sukhothai's **night food stalls** (close to the bus stop for the Historical Park) are also good for casual grazing.

Dream Café ★ THAI/INTERNATIONAL This is a cozy place bathed in warm, soft light. With its oddball collection of ceramics, memorabilia, and old jewelry, it looks more like an antiques store than a restaurant. In addition to Thai dishes, including many family recipes, you can try some excellent European and Chinese cuisine. Opt for the Sukhothai Fondue, a "cook it yourself" hot pot of meat, veggies, and noodles. Save room for an ice-cream sundae for dessert, and if you're feeling adventurous, order one of their stamina-enhancing drinks made from local herbs.

86/1 Singhawat Rd. (center of new city). ✆ **05561-2081.** Main courses 80B–250B. V. Daily 10am–10pm.

Exploring Sukhothai ★★★

In 1978, UNESCO named Sukhothai a World Heritage Site, and the Thai government, with international assistance, completed the preservation of these magnificent monuments and consolidated them with an excellent museum into one large park.

Every Saturday night from 8pm, a **"Walking Street"** outside the historical park comes alive with food, handicrafts, and cultural shows.

GETTING TO THE SITE   The easiest way to get to the Sukhothai Historical Park from New Sukhothai is by *songtaew* (cost 30B), which leave around every 15 minutes from Jarot Withithong Road just west of the bridge over the Yom River.

TOURING THE SITE   The tuk-tuks that cruise around New Sukhothai can be hired to whiz you out to the monuments on a 4-hour tour around the park for about 500B, but if you have the energy it's much more rewarding to rent a bike from shops outside the park entrance; prices start at 30B. At peak times, there is a tram service that runs visitors around the central zone for 30B, starting near the national museum. Maps are available at the museum or at the nearby bicycle-rental shops. The park is open daily 8am to 6pm; admission is 100B to the central area within the park walls, with additional charges of 100B for each of the four zones outside the walls of the park. Alternatively, you can buy an all-inclusive ticket for 350B that also grants entry to the Ramkhamhaeng Museum and the ruins at Si Satchanalai. Be sure to bring water and go early in the morning to beat the tour buses. Or consider coming back in the evening with picnic provisions, when it's cooler and the sun is going down.

SEEING THE HIGHLIGHTS

RAMKHAMHAENG NATIONAL MUSEUM   This museum, located in the center of the old city near the park entrance, houses a detailed model of the area, and an admirable display of Sukhothai and Si Satchanalai archaeological finds. Before exploring the temple sites, stop here for maps and information. It's open every day from 9am to 4pm; admission is 150B. Call ✆ **05561-2617** for info.

WAT PHRA MAHATHAT ★★   The most extraordinary monument in the park, this temple is dominated by a 14th-century lotus-bud tower and encircled by a moat. Surrounding its unique Sukhothai-style *chedi* are several smaller towers of Sri Lankan and Khmer influence, and a grouping of Buddhist disciples in the adoration pose. An imposing cast-bronze seated Buddha used to be placed in front of the reliquary (this image, Phra Si Sakaya Muni, was removed in the 18th century to Bangkok's Wat Suthat). Be sure to examine the lowest platform (south side of Wat Phra Mahathat) and its excellent stucco sculpture, the crypt murals, and two elegant Sri Lankan-style stupas at the southeast corner of the site. Some of the best architectural ornamentation in Sukhothai is found on the upper, eastern-facing levels of the pediments in the main reliquary tower. Dancing figures, Queen Maya giving birth to Prince Siddhartha, and scenes from Buddha's life are among the best-preserved details.

OTHER MONUMENTS IN THE PARK   Southwest of Wat Phra Mahathat, you'll come to the 12th-century Hindu shrine **Wat Si Sawai,** later converted to a Buddhist temple. The architecture is distinctly Khmer, with three Lopburi-style *prangs* commanding center stage. Just west of the palace, is **Wat Traphang Tong,** set on its own pond. Though little remains other than an attractive *chedi*, the vistas of the surrounding monuments are among the most superb in the park. North of Wat Phra Mahathat is **Wat Chana Songkhram,** where there's a Sri Lankan-style stupa of note. Nearby is **Wat Sa Si,** also on a small island.

Outside the Old City walls, **Wat Phra Phai Luang** lies 150m (492 ft.) beyond the northern gate. Originally a Hindu shrine, it housed a *lingam*, a phallic sculpture representing Shiva. To the northwest, **Wat Si Chum** holds one of the more astonishing and beautiful monuments in Sukhothai: a majestic seated Buddha 15-m (49-ft.) tall, in the Subduing Mara pose. The fingers of this Buddha, draped over the right knee and frequently smothered with gold leaf, provide one of the country's most iconic images.

A few kilometers west of the old city walls, the ruins of **Wat Saphan Hin** sit atop a hill that's visible for miles. It is worth the steep, 5-minute climb to visit the Phra Attaros Buddha, his right hand raised in the Dispelling Fear pose, and towering above the *wat*'s laterite remains.

LUNCH AT THE HISTORICAL PARK　There are a number of small store-front eateries in and among the bike-rental shops and souvenir stands at the gate of the park (just across from Ramkhamhaeng Museum).

Exploring Si Satchanalai ★

Many people enjoy the secluded ruins at Si Satchanalai even more than those at Sukhothai, so try to make this day trip if you have the time. Si Satchanalai's riverside site was crucial to the development of its famous ceramics industry. More than 1,000 kilns operated along the river, producing highly prized pots that carried a greenish-gray glaze known as celadon. These were eventually exported throughout Asia. Academics believe that ceramic manufacture began more than 1,000 years ago at Ban Ko Noi (there's a small site museum 6km/3¾ miles north of Satchanalai), and ceramic shards today are sold as souvenirs.

GETTING TO THE SITE　Si Satchanalai is north of New Sukhothai on Route 101. Buses from Sukhothai depart every half-hour from the bus stop on Jarot Withithong Road for 38B. Just ask the driver to let you off at *"muang kao"* (Old City). There are two stops; the second is closer to the park entrance, across the river. The last bus returns at 4:30pm. A taxi, private car, or guided tour can also be arranged through your hotel or guesthouse.

An adventurous alternative, if you are starting in Bangkok, is to go by train. A daily "Sprinter" express (train 3) runs daily at 10:50am (fare 482B) from Bangkok to Sawankhalok, 20km (12 miles) south of Si Satchanalai park, stopping at Phitsanulok on the way, and arriving at 6pm. The line to Sawankhalok is a spur that King Rama VI had built so that he could visit the ruins at Si Satchanalai, and the well-preserved station seems trapped in a time bubble. The train returns to Bangkok at 7:40pm. It is second class, with air-conditioning but no sleepers, and fare includes dinner and breakfast. For information, call Bangkok's **Hua Lampong Railway Station** (© **1690**) or the **Phitsanulok Railway Station** (© **05525-8005**). From the station, you would need to charter a *songtaew* for the remaining 20km (12 miles).

TOURING THE SITE　There is an **information center** at the park, and bicycles (30B) for rent. Open daily from 8am to 6pm, admission to the historical park is 100B, or 220B including entrance to Chaliang (for Wat Phra Si Ratana Mahathat) and the ancient pottery kilns of Sawankhalok.

SEEING THE HIGHLIGHTS
WAT CHANG LOM & WAT CHEDI JET THAEW　The discovery of presumed relics of Lord Buddha at this site during the reign of King Ramkhamhaeng prompted the construction of the temple, an event described in stone inscriptions found at

Sukhothai. Thirty-nine elephant buttresses surround a central stupa—it's unusual to find so many elephant forms intact. If you climb the steps to the stupa's terrace, you can admire the 19 Buddhas installed in niches there. Opposite Wat Chang Lom to the south, within sandstone walls, Wat Chedi Jet Thaew is distinguished by a series of lotus-bud towers and rows of *chedis* resembling those at Sukhothai's Wat Phra Mahathat and thought to contain the remains of the royal family.

OTHER MONUMENTS IN THE PARK You can see most of the monuments within the ancient city walls in an hour's drive. Nothing compares to **Wat Phra Si Ratana Mahathat ★**, located 1km (⅔ mile) southeast of the big bridge and directly adjacent to the footbridge connecting to the main road. The exterior carving and sculpture are superb, particularly the walking Buddha done in relief.

SAWANKHALOK KILNS During the 14th and 15th centuries, there were hundreds of kilns operating in this area, producing some of the best ceramics in all of Asia from local clay. You can take a look at some of these excavated kilns at the **Sawankhalok Kiln Preservation Centre** (daily 9am–4.30pm; admission 100B or included in 220B ticket for the historical park), which is located a few kilometers along the Yom River from the historical park.

TAK PROVINCE: MAE SOT & THE MYANMAR (BURMA) BORDER

Tak: 138km (86 miles) W of Phitsanulok. Mae Sot: 80km (50 miles) W of Tak

Tak Province doesn't get a lot of tourists, possibly because there are no major attractions in the provincial capital, but the region is certainly not lacking in natural beauty, situated as it is at the beginning of the mountainous north. It is home to the **Bhumibol Dam,** the country's largest, and the area is covered in lush forests that offer a quiet retreat at **Taksin Maharat** and **Lan Sang** national parks, both about 25km (16 miles) west of Tak. Just a few kilometers from the border with Myanmar (Burma), **Mae Sot** displays all the hallmarks of a small border town. For decades it has played host to camps that take in an endless stream of refugees fleeing from Myanmar, many of whom are from the persecuted Karen tribe. As a result of these border tensions, the province is likely to stay relatively undeveloped in terms of tourism for the foreseeable future. Most visitors in Mae Sot are on their way to **Umphang,** some 150km (93 miles) south along one of the country's most hair-raising roads. Umphang boasts **Ti Lor Su ★★**, Thailand's most spectacular waterfall, and some of the best trekking and white-water rafting in the kingdom, making the arduous journey there worthwhile.

Essentials

GETTING THERE

BY PLANE Kan Air (✆ 08158-54489; www.kanairlines.com) has a daily flight to and from Chiang Mai leaving around midday; the office is at the airport, about 2km (1.2 miles) west of the town center.

BY BUS From Bangkok's **Northern Bus Terminal** (✆ 02936-2841), VIP and first-class, air-conditioned buses leave for **Tak's bus terminal** (✆ 05551-1057) daily in the early morning and late evening. The trip takes around 7 hours and rates are 487B (VIP) and 313B (first class). There are also three second-class trips per day, but travel on those buses can be slow and uncomfortable.

From Bangkok to **Mae Sot's bus terminal** (✆ 05556-3435), a VIP bus runs three times daily, departing in the evening (8 hr.; 612B). First-class buses leave twice daily, also in the evening (8 hr.; 392B).

There are also second-class connections from **Phitsanulok's Bus Terminal** (✆ 05521-2090) to Tak (hourly departures from 5am–5pm; trip time: 3 hr.; 90B) and a minibus service to Mae Sot approximately every 2 hours from 7am to 2.30pm (5 hr.; 163B).

Privately operated minivans connect Tak and Mae Sot, leaving when they're full (about every half-hour), for about 60B per person. The trip time is 1½ hours. There are good buses operated by the **Green Bus Line** (✆ 05553-6433) from Mae Sot to Tak and on to Lampang and Chiang Mai (first-class buses depart daily at 8am from Mae Sot; 6 hr. to Chiang Mai; 304B).

From the bus terminals in Tak and Mae Sot, motorcycle taxis, *samlors*, and *songtaews* wait to take you to any hotel for about 50B. *Songtaews* also make the dizzying 5-hour drive between Mae Sot and Umphang several times daily and charge about 120B.

VISITOR INFORMATION

Tak has a **TAT** office near the bus terminal, at 193 Taksin Rd. (✆ 05551-4341).

SPECIAL EVENTS

Every year from December 28 to January 3, the **Taksin Maharachanuson Fair** is held in Tak to honor King Taksin the Great. The streets around his shrine (on Taksin Rd., at the north side of town) fill with food vendors, dancers, musicians, and monks. The shrine is decorated with floral wreaths and gold fabric to welcome pilgrims.

FAST FACTS

In Tak, there is a handful of **ATMs** along Mahat Thai Bamrung Road, and where it meets Thetsaban 1 Road, there's a **police station.** In Mae Sot, banks with ATMs are located on the main thoroughfare, on Prasat Withee Road. The **post office** in Mae Sot is on Intharakiri Road diagonally opposite the main police station. There are a number of **Internet** cafes along Intharakiri Road in the center of Mae Sot.

Where to Stay

TAK

Suansin Lanna Garden Resort This property offers excellent value in a city that previously had very few accommodation options. The pleasingly clean and tidy rooms, offered as doubles or triples, are decorated simply in yellows and creams, with attractive, dark wood furniture, and all have TVs and air-conditioning.

8 Moo 8, Paholyothin Rd., Tak 63000. www.suansin.com. ✆ **05589-1333.** 76 units. 250B double with fan; 370B double with A/C. No credit cards. **Amenities:** *In room:* A/C, TV, fridge, Wi-Fi (free).

Viang Tak 2 This unremarkable low-rise offers good service and a surprisingly wide range of amenities, including a pool and an Internet cafe. The location isn't bad at all, just a 5-minute tuk-tuk ride from the bus terminal. Many rooms have great views across the broad Ping River to fields and mountains in the west, and in the evening the riverside promenade by the hotel buzzes with snack vendors and locals exercising.

236 Chumpon Rd., Tak 63000. www.viangtakriverside.com. © **05551-2507.** 143 units. 700B double; 2,500B suite. AE, MC, V. **Amenities:** Restaurant; 2 lounges; outdoor pool. *In room:* A/C, TV, fridge, Wi-Fi (free).

MAE SOT

In addition to the places listed below, Mae Sot has quite a number of small, affordable guesthouses lining the main street, perhaps due in part to the number of itinerant NGO workers passing through town. **DK Hotel** (298 Intharakiri Rd., near the police station; © **05553-1699**) is a local hotel popular with NGO workers; rooms with fans go for 250B and rooms with air-conditioning 450B-550B. **Ban Thai** (740 Intharakiri Rd.; © **05553-1590**) also offers rooms from 300B.

Centara Mae Sot Hill Resort ★   This contemporary four-story hotel is built in two long wings fanning out from a classy open atrium lobby and is the highest standard hotel in town. Providing a comfortable base from which to explore the area, the hotel can still feel like a bit of a hike to the town center. The staff is helpful and can arrange tours and onward travel. All rooms have modern facilities and views of the mist-shrouded, wooded hills.

100 Asia Rd., Mae Sot, Tak 63110. www.centarahotelsresorts.com. © **05553-2601.** Fax 05553-2600. 120 units. From 2,800B double; from 4,000B suite. MC, V. **Amenities:** 2 restaurants; lounge; 2 outdoor pools; 2 outdoor tennis courts; room service; dance club. *In room:* A/C, TV, minibar, fridge, Wi-Fi (free).

First Hotel ★ 🏠   This hotel's dull concrete exterior belies an interior that appears like a wood-carved wedding cake, with intricate bas relief representations of flora and fauna on the walls and ceiling. Standard rooms have large carved headboards and furnishings, as well as tidy marble bathrooms. It all adds up to a memorable place to stay, well situated in the town center.

444 Intharakiri Rd., Mae Sot, Tak 63110. © **05553-1233.** Fax 05553-1340. 33 units. 270B double with fan; 450B double with A/C. No credit cards. **Amenities:** Internet. *In room:* A/C (in some), TV, Wi-Fi (free), no phone.

Where to Eat in Mae Sot

INEXPENSIVE

Khaomao-Khaofang Restaurant ★ THAI   This little oasis along the Burmese border verges on the surreal, but the food is delicious. Ponds overgrown with lush vegetation surround an enormous central thatched pavilion. Be sure to go to the bathroom, even if you don't have to; these water closets are large grottos with flushable fixtures at odd heights and stalactites hanging from the ceiling. The menu surveys the whole country, with an emphasis on curries and authentic spice. Portions are small, so you may want more than one dish if you're alone or several dishes if you're with a group, and don't forget to ask about the daily specials.

382 Moo 9, Maepa, Maesod (head for the Myanmar border, turn north just before the checkpoint, and follow the highway 2km/1¼ miles). © **05553-2483.** Main courses 80B–260B. AE, MC, V. Daily 11am–10pm.

Krua Canadian INTERNATIONAL   This restaurant's name is Thai for "Canadian kitchen," and that's just how it feels—as if you've been invited into the home of Canadian Dave and his wife, Chulee, the owners and chefs. From this simple, central storefront, they serve hearty Western-style breakfasts, local coffee, and a unique tofu burger that is both messy and delectable. You can also just drop in for a drink and for some advice on local happenings.

3 Sri Phanit Rd., Mae Sot. ℭ **05553-4659.** Main courses 50B–150B. No credit cards. Daily 7am–10pm.

Exploring the Area

Along Highway 105, 20km (12 miles) west of Tak, a left turn leads to **Lan Sang National Park** (ℭ **05557-7207**), where there are hiking trails and waterfalls, and on weekdays usually no visitors, so you might have the place to yourself. About 5km (3 miles) farther along H105, a right turn leads to **Taksin Maharat National Park** (ℭ **05551-1429**), known as the home of *Krabak Yai*, Thailand's largest tree. A hike brings you to this colossal tree beside a stream—it takes 16 people's stretched arms to wrap around the conifer. Accommodation is available at both parks and admission to each is 200B for adults and 100B for children. For more information, check out the Thai national parks website, www.dnp.go.th.

Mae Sot is perched on the Myanmar border, and the area is always buzzing with trade. The town has a surplus of Burmese woven cotton blankets, lacquerware, jewelry, bronze statues, cotton sarongs, and wicker ware. Business is conducted in Thai baht, U.S. dollars, or Myanmar kyat.

There is a dark side to the border, though: Trade means the movement of not just produce and crafts, but also drugs, precious stones, and women (or children) for prostitution. There's something disquieting about the many European luxury cars parked in front of two-story brick homes lining this village's main street—they hint at the substantial illegal profiteering. Be careful about buying gems unless you know what you're doing; you can find yourself walking away with a handful of plastic and a dent in your wallet. The border also sees a heavy flow of refugees, and there are a number of camps in the surrounding hills.

The border between Mae Sot (at the town of Rim Moei) and Myawaddy, Myanmar, is open daily from 8am to 4:30pm, and—when relations are good—you can cross the bridge on foot or by car for a day for 500B. You'll need to leave your passport at the Myanmar immigration booth, and pick it up by 4:30pm. Many visitors cross just for a walk around Myawaddy and a glimpse of Burmese culture. Remember that any official fees you pay to the Myanmar government only add to the coffers of the junta, though.

Trekking and rafting in the area around Umphang is very popular, especially to visit the fabulous **Ti Lor Su waterfall,** which cascades down a cliff in several plumes, and is at its best around October and November. **Umphang Hill Resort** (ℭ **05556-1063;** www.umphanghill.com) provides basic lodging (rooms 500B–2,000B) in the tiny town of Umphang, and organizes a variety of trekking and rafting tours in the region, lasting between a day and a week. Prices work out to around 1,500B per person per day, depending on the size of the group.

CHIANG MAI

From 1296, under King Mengrai, Chiang Mai (meaning New City) was the cultural and religious center of the northern Tai. The city was overtaken and occupied by the Burmese in 1558 until Chao (Lord) Kavila retook the city in 1775, driving the Burmese forces back to near the present border. Burmese influence on religion, architecture, language, cuisine, and culture, however, remained strong. Local feudal lords (sometimes referred to as princes) carrying the title *chao*, remained in nominal control of the city in the late 18th and early 19th centuries, but under continued pressure from King Chulalongkorn (Rama V), the Lanna kingdom was brought under the control of the central government in Bangkok. In 1932, the city was formally and fully integrated into the kingdom of Thailand, becoming the administrative center of the north.

These days, Chiang Mai is booming, with an estimated population of 250,000 (in a province of some 1.6 million) and growing; with those numbers come the attendant "big city" problems of suburban sprawl, noxious pollution, rush-hour traffic, and water shortages, as well as serious flooding (Aug–Oct).

It would be difficult to find a city that reflects more of the country's diverse cultural heritage and modern aspirations than Chiang Mai. Its heart is its Old City, an area surrounded by vestiges of walls, bastions, and a moat originally constructed for defense. It lies in the shadow of an increasingly expanding city, encircled by gargantuan concrete highways, lined by giant hoardings and superstores. Modern tour buses crowd Burmese-style *wats* (temples) ablaze with monks in saffron robes chanting ancient mantras. Increasingly, old shophouses are giving way to 7-Elevens, multistory shopping malls, boutiques, and big-name resorts, while towering apartment blocks fill the skyline. Vendors dressed in hill-tribe costume sell souvenirs in tourist areas. Narrow streets lined with ornately carved teak houses lie in the shadow of contemporary skyscrapers.

From March to October, the north's climate follows the pattern of the rest of the country—hot and dry followed by hot and wet. Yet, from November to February, it's almost like another country, with cool breezes blowing down from China, bright sunny days, and rarely a cloud in the sky. During these cooler months, Chiang Mai is an excellent base for exploring the north.

ORIENTATION

Getting There

Before the 1920s, when the railway's Northern Line to Chiang Mai was completed, one traveled throughout this area by either boat or elephant. So when your train ride gets boring or the flight is crowded, remember that not so long ago the trip here from Bangkok took 4 to 6 weeks.

BY PLANE When planning your trip, keep in mind that Chiang Mai has international links with major cities throughout the region. **Air Asia** (© 05392-2170; www.airasia.com) flies to Singapore and Kuala Lumpur (Malaysia). **Lao Airlines** (© 05322-3401; www.laoairlines.com) connects Chiang Mai to Luang Prabang in Laos four times each week. **Air Mandalay** (© 05381-8049; www.airmandalay. com) has limited flights to Yangon, in Myanmar (Burma). **Silk Air** (© 05390-4985; www.silkair.com), the regional arm of Singapore Airlines, connects Singapore with direct service at least twice a week. **Korean Air** (© 05392-2556; www.koreanair. com) operates two flights a week to Seoul.

Domestically, **Thai Airways** (240 Phra Pokklao Rd.; © 05392-0999; www. thaiair.com) flies from Bangkok to Chiang Mai at least a dozen times daily (trip time 70 min.). There's a direct flight from Chiang Mai to Phuket daily (note the return sector is *not* direct). The daily 35-minute hop on **Nok Air** (© 05392-2183; www. nokair.com) is the fastest way to get out to Mae Hong Son. **Bangkok Airways** (© 05328-1519, or 02270-6699 in Bangkok; www.bangkokair.com) flies at least six times daily from Bangkok, and they also operate a direct daily flight to Ko Samui. **Kan Air** (© 05328-3311; www.kanairlines.com) is a budget carrier which operates flights to Chiang Mai from small towns like Mae Sariang and Pai.

Chiang Mai International Airport (airport code CNX; © 05327-0222; about 3km/1¾ miles and a 10-min. ride from the Old City) has several banks for changing money, a post and overseas call office, and an information booth. Taxis from the airport are a flat 120B to town, a bit more for places outside of Chiang Mai proper. Buy a ticket from the taxi booth in the arrival hall, and then proceed to the taxi line with your ticket.

BY TRAIN Of the six daily trains from Bangkok to Chiang Mai, the 8:30am *sprinter* (trip time 12 hr.; fare 611B for a second-class air-conditioned seat) is the quickest, but you sacrifice a whole day to travel and spend the entire trip in a seat. The other trains take between 13 and 15 hours; but for overnight trips, second-class sleeper berths are a good choice (881B lower berth, air-conditioned; 791B upper berth, air-conditioned). Private sleeper cabins are also available, which cost 1,353B.

Purchase tickets at Bangkok's **Hua Lampong Railway Station** (© 02220-4334 or 1690) up to 90 days in advance. For local train information in Chiang Mai, call © 05324-5363; for advance booking, call © 05324-4795. Reservations cannot be made over the phone, but you can call and check to see if space is available.

BY BUS Buses from Bangkok to Chiang Mai are many and varied: From rattletrap, non-air-conditioned numbers to fully reclining VIP buses. The trip takes about 8 to 10 hours. From **Bangkok's Northern Bus Terminal,** close to the Mo Chit BTS

(© **02936-2841**), six daily 24-seater VIP buses provide the most comfort, with larger seats that recline (fare 806B). There is also a frequent service between Chiang Mai and Mae Hong Son, Phitsanulok, and Chiang Rai.

Most buses arrive at the **Arcade Bus Station** (© **05324-2664**) on Kaeo Nawarat Road, 3km (1¾ miles) northeast of the Thapae Gate; a few arrive at the Chang Puak station (© **05321-1586**), north of the Chang Puak Gate on Chotana Road. Expect to pay 80B to 150B for a tuk-tuk (motorized three-wheeler) into town, and around 30B for a red pickup, *songtaew*, to the town center and your hotel.

Visitor Information

The **TAT** office is at 105/1 Chiang Mai–Lamphun Rd., 400m (1,312 ft.) south of the Nawarat Bridge, on the east side of the Ping River (© **05324-8604**). Keep your eyes open for a few free magazines available in hotels and restaurants, such as *Guidelines Chiang Mai* and *Citylife Chiang Mai*, which contain maps, features on local culture, and useful information. You can also find any of a number of detailed maps distributed free, chock-full of adverts for local shopping, dining, and events.

City Layout

The heart of Chiang Mai is the **Old City,** completely surrounded by a moat (restored in the 19th century) and remains of the massive wall at the four corners and five gates, laid out in a square. Several of the original gates have been restored and serve as handy reference points, particularly **Thapae Gate** to the east. The most important temples are within the walls of the Old City.

All major streets radiate from the Old City. The main business and shopping area is the 1-km (⅔-mile) stretch between the east side of the Old City and the **Ping River.** Here you will find the **Night Bazaar,** many shops, trekking agents, hotels, guesthouses, and restaurants—plus some of the most picturesque backstreets.

To the west of town and visible from anywhere in the city is the imposing wall of Doi Suthep Mountain (1,685m/5,528 ft.), where, near its crest, you'll find the most regal of all Chiang Mai Buddhist compounds, Wat Phra That Doi Suthep, standing stalwart as if to give its blessing to the city below. The road leading to the temple takes you past a big mall, a strip of modern hotels, the zoo, and the university.

The Superhighway circles the outskirts of the city and is connected by traffic-choked arteries emanating from the city center. If you're driving or riding a motorbike in Chiang Mai, the many one-way streets in and around town are confounding. The moat that surrounds the city has concentric circles of traffic: The outer ring runs clockwise, and the inner ring counterclockwise, with U-turn bridges between. The streets in and around the Night Bazaar are all one-way as well. This means that even if you know where you're going, you'll have to pull your share of U-turns.

Getting Around

BY BUS   Chiang Mai has a few irregular bus routes that are more useful for locals than visitors. Your best bet is to look out for the ubiquitous *songtaews* and flag one down.

BY SONGTAEW   *Songtaews* (red pickup trucks) cover all routes. Fitted with two long bench seats, they are also known locally as *seelor* (four-wheels). They follow no specific route and have no fixed stopping points. Hail one going in your general direction and tell the driver your destination. If it fits in with the destinations of other passengers, you'll get a ride to your door for around 20B to 40B. Some drivers will ask for exorbitant fees to hire the complete vehicle when they're empty; let these guys just drive on. If you can deal with a bit of uncertainty along the confusing twist of roads, a *songtaew* is a great way to explore the city.

Songtaews can also take you up to the temple on Doi Suthep Mountain for 50B and only 40B for the easier downhill return trip. You can find them waiting outside the zoo at the western end of Huay Kaeo Road.

BY TUK TUK   The ubiquitous tuk-tuk is the next best option to the *songtaew* for getting around Chiang Mai. Fares are negotiable—and you will have to bargain hard to get a good rate—but expect to pay at least 40B for any ride. When talking price, it is good to write it down on a scrap of paper, so there is no argument when you get there and the driver asks for 200B instead of the 20B you thought you'd agreed on.

BY TAXI   In late 2004, metered taxis finally arrived in Chiang Mai, but taxi drivers are generally unwilling to use the meter, so rates are rather expensive. Taxis mostly operate from the airport into town, but they are difficult to flag down on the street. If you phone for a pickup (✆ 05327-9291), they usually quote a fixed (and expensive) rate; get a staff member in your hotel to help negotiate a fare for you.

BY CAR   **Avis** has an office conveniently located at the airport (✆ 05320-1798; www.avisthailand.com). Avis self-drive rental rates for Chiang Mai are the same as they are elsewhere in Thailand, from 1,400B and up for a compact sedan. **Budget** (✆ 05320-2871-2; www.budget.co.th) has an office near the airport and offers comparable rates and services. Both companies offer comprehensive insurance and provide good maps—even a mini-guidebook.

There are dozens of **local car-rental companies** with sedans for 1,200B to 1,800B per day. Most travel agents will arrange a car or minivan and driver for about 2,000B. **North Wheels,** 70/4–8 Chaiyaphum Rd. (✆ 05387-4478; www.north wheels.com), has a wide range of vehicles and does pickup or drop-off service to the airport or your hotel.

BY MOTORCYCLE   Motorcycle touring in northern Thailand is another option and best considered in the cool season (Nov–Feb). For up-to-date info on the best routes to follow, check out the **Golden Triangle Rider** website (www.gt-rider.com); you can pick up their map of the Samoeng Loop or Mae Hong Son Loop at many outlets in Chiang Mai (listed on the website).

Many guesthouses along the Ping River and shops around Chaiyaphum Road (north of Thapae Gate, in the Old City) rent 100cc to 150cc motorcycles for about 150B to 200B per day (discounts for longer durations). Larger 250cc Hondas (as well as others) with good suspension are commonly available and are the best choice for any trips upcountry because of their added power and large fuel tanks; they rent for about 700B. Try **Mr. Mechanic** (4 Soi 5, Moon Muang Rd.; ✆ 05321-4708), one of many mechanic shops near Thapae. Helmets are mandatory—even if locals tend to ignore this law, they may be able to wriggle out of arrest, but as a foreigner, you won't be let off lightly. Expect to leave your passport as security (don't leave any credit cards). Traffic congestion and confusing one-way streets make riding within the city dangerous, so if you are tempted, employ defensive driving techniques and take it slow.

BY BICYCLE   Cycling in the city is fun and practical, especially for getting around to the temples within the Old City. Avoid rush hour and take great care on the busy roads outside of the ancient walls. Bikes are available at any of the many guesthouses in or around the Old City and go for about 50B per day.

[FastFACTS] CHIANG MAI

ATMs For ATMs and money-changers, go to Chang Klan and Charoen Prathet roads. For the most convenient major bank branches look around the Night Bazaar. You can also find them outside most convenience stores, such as 7-Elevens.

Embassies & Consulates There are many representative offices in Chiang Mai. Contacts are as follows: **American Consulate General,** 387 Wichayanon Rd. (✆ **05310-7700); Canadian Honorary Consul,** 151 Super Highway Rd. (✆ **05385-0147); Australian Honorary Consul,** 165 Sirimungklajarn Rd. (✆ **05349-2480);** and **British Consul,** 198 Bumrungraj Rd. (✆ **05326-3015).**

Doctors & Dentists The Consulates detailed above will supply you with a list of English-speaking dentists and doctors. There are also several medical clinics,

and standards are very high; but for serious illness, you should seek professional and advanced care in Bangkok.

Emergencies Dial ✆ **1155** to reach the Tourist Police in case of emergency.

Hospitals Try the private **McCormick** hospital, on Kaeo Nawarat Road (✆ **05392-1777),** out toward the Arcade Bus Terminal. The Ram and Lanna hospitals are also popular choices for expats.

Internet Access Most hotels and guesthouses provide Internet access, often free of charge. All around the city, there are numerous small, inexpensive cafes with service sometimes costing only 30B per hour. **Starbucks** offers Wi-Fi access at half a dozen locations, including Chaiyaphum Road opposite Tha Pae Gate and at the Suriwong Hotel on Chang Klan, in the Night Bazaar area.

Mail & Postage The most convenient branch is at 186/1 Chang Klan Rd. (✆ **05327-3657).** The General Post Office is on Charoen Muang (✆ **05324-1070),** near the train station. The Overseas Call Office, open 24 hours, is upstairs from the GPO and offers phone, fax, and telex services. There is a 24-hour branch at the airport (✆ **05327-7382). UPS** has an office at 77 Sri Phum Rd. (✆ **05341-8767-9;** Mon–Sat 9am–5:30pm), making it easy to send your finds back home.

Pharmacies There are dozens of pharmacies throughout the city; most are open daily 7am to midnight. Bring along any prescriptions that you need filled.

Police For police assistance, call the **Tourist Police** at ✆ **1155,** or see them at the TAT office.

WHERE TO STAY

City accommodation listed below is separated as follows: Outside of town; east of town near the Ping River/Night Bazaar area; within the Old City walls; or west of town, on the road to Doi Suthep (near the university).

Outside Chiang Mai

VERY EXPENSIVE

Four Seasons Chiang Mai ★★★ About 30 minutes north of Chiang Mai in the Mae Sa Valley, the Four Seasons was Chiang Mai's first five-star hotel and still sets the standard for luxuriously equipped rooms, the range of facilities and activities on offer and, perhaps most important, efficient and personalized service. The spacious pavilions, each with its own covered outdoor veranda, are set among rice paddies with gorgeous mountain views, and the cookery school and spa are just a couple of guest options. Enormous pool villas with private garden and dining pavilion are the

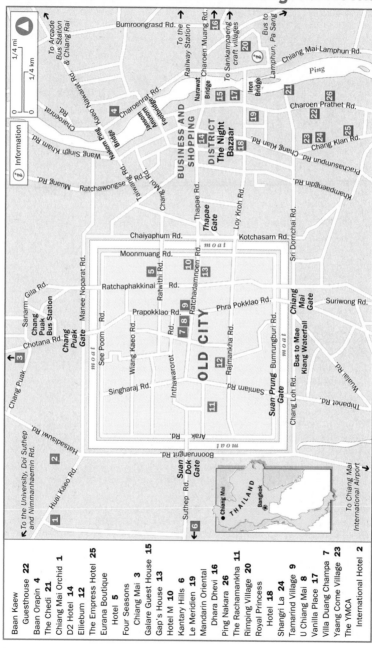

To Arcade Bus Station & Chiang Rai

To the Railway Station

Bumroongrasd Rd.

Charoen Muang Rd.

To Sankampaeng craft villages

Bus to Lamphun, Pa Sang

Chiang Mai-Lamphun Rd.

Ping

Charoen Prathet Rd.

Chang Klan Rd.

Kaeo Nawarat Rd.

To Arcade Bus Station Rd.

Charoenrat Rd.

Charoenrat Rd.

Faham Rd.

Charoenrat Rd.

Jansom

Footbridge

Nakhon Ping Bridge

Narawat Bridge

Iron Bridge

Chang Moi Rd.

Prachasumpun Rd.

Khampaengdin Rd.

BUSINESS AND SHOPPING DISTRICT

The Night Bazaar

Wang Singh Kham Rd.

Muang Rd.

Ratchawongse Rd.

Taiwang Rd.

Chang Moi Rd.

Thapae Rd.

Thapae Gate

Loy Kroh Rd.

Kotchasarn Rd.

Sri Domchai Rd.

Chaiyaphum Rd.

moat

Moonmuang Rd.

Manee Noparat Rd.

Ratchaphakkinai Rd.

Ratwithi Rd.

Ratchadamnoen Rd.

Phra Pokklao Rd.

Suriwong Rd.

Chiang Mai Gate

Gila Rd.

Sanarm Rd.

Chang Puak Bus Station

Chotana Rd.

Prapokklao Rd.

Wiang Kaeo Rd.

See Poom Rd.

Inthawarorot Rd.

Rajmankha Rd.

Rajpakinai Rd.

OLD CITY

Chang Puak Gate

moat

Singharaj Rd.

Samlarn Rd.

Suan Prung Gate

Bumrungburi Rd.

Chang Loh Rd.

Bus to Mae Klang Waterfall

Thipanet Rd.

Wualai Rd.

To the University, Doi Suthep and Nimmanhaemin Rd.

Huai Kaeo Rd.

Hatsadisuwi Rd.

Arak Rd.

moat

Boonruangrit Rd.

Suan Dok Gate

Suthep Rd.

THAILAND

Chiang Mai

Bangkok

To Chiang Mai International Airport

latest additions. A shuttle bus runs to the city regularly. The traditional Lanna design of the complex and its rural setting creates a memorable experience.

Mae Rim–Samoeng Old Rd., Mae Rim, Chiang Mai 50180. www.fourseasons.com/chiangmai. ℂ **05329-8181.** Fax 05329-8190. 93 units. From 23,000B pavilion; from 33,000B pool villa; from 43,000B resort residence. AE, DC, MC, V. **Amenities:** Restaurant; 2 bars; outdoor pool; golf course nearby; 2 floodlit tennis courts; health club; spa; mountain bikes. *In-room:* A/C, satellite TV, DVD, minibar, hair dryer, Wi-Fi (600B per day).

Mandarin Oriental Dhara Dhevi ★★★ ☺ About 20 minutes east of central Chiang Mai, this superluxe resort is designed like an enclosed Lanna city, complete with a small moat, grand city gate, delightfully lush gardens, and flowering trees. Horse-drawn carts or modern golf carts bring guests to a palatial lobby. The resort comprises immaculate suites and rustic, free-standing villas, all sumptuously decorated. Standard perks in the villas include a sauna, piano, sun deck, and Jacuzzi. Around a working rice paddy lie well-placed pool villas with outdoor pavilions, and even hill-tribe-style stilt cottages next to a working vegetable patch. All units have large balconies, but the rice barns offer two stories of teak-lined luxury. Colonial suites have Persian rugs, pretty fretwork, high ceilings, and pleasant pastel hues. At times the more over-the-top suites may teeter on kitsch, but it somehow seems to work well with the contrasting rustic ambience.

51/4 Chiang Mai–Sankampaeng Rd., Moo 1, Tambon Tasala, Chiang Mai 50000. www.mandarin oriental.com/chiangmai. ℂ **05388-8929.** Fax 05388-8928. 123 units. 17,500B villa; 19,500B colonial suite; 50,500B grand deluxe 2-bedroom villa; 280,000B royal residence. AE, DC, MC, V. **Amenities:** 3 restaurants; 3 bars; babysitting; 2 pools; tennis courts; health club; spa; bikes; kids' club; room service. *In room:* A/C, satellite TV, kitchenette, minibar, hair dryer, butler service, whirlpool tub, Wi-Fi (642B per day).

Near the Ping River

VERY EXPENSIVE

The Chedi ★★ On what was once the site of the venerable British Consulate, The Chedi is a luxurious oasis facing some beautiful river scenery along the Ping River. Mixing eclectic styles of architecture by the inimitable Kerry Hill, along with pretty lawns and a central riverside location, the hotel has finally brought luxury downtown. The Chedi's rather daunting exterior of minimalist wooden slats gives way to a crisp interior of large reflecting pools and polished concrete paths leading to a gem of a colonial mansion: In sum, it's a pleasing mix of modern and colonial. Rooms are up to crisp business hotel standards, and all offer a private courtyard entrance. Chedi Club Suites are enormous and come with lots of extras. The glassy pool pops right out, and spa treatments are on tap.

123 Charoen Prathet Rd., Chang Klan Rd., Chiang Mai 50100. www.ghmhotels.com. ℂ **05325-3333.** Fax 05325-3352. 84 units. 13,700B deluxe double; 20,600B suite. AE, MC, V. **Amenities:** Restaurant; 3 bars; outdoor pool; health club; spa; room service; babysitting. *In room:* A/C, satellite TV, fax, minibar, fridge, hair dryer, Wi-Fi (free).

EXPENSIVE

D2 Hotel ★★ Every corner of this hotel is bathed in a postmodern minimalist cool. Oranges and browns are the dominant colors, and the furniture and decor seamlessly blend sharp lines with rounded edges—everything flows. Rooms are very livable and have all the finer creature comforts: Daybeds, flatscreen TVs with DVD players, and well-stocked bathrooms. An upgrade to the club deluxe level allows access to the chic club lounge, with free cocktails and Internet service. Dusit's famous Devarana Spa is the one part of the hotel that sits slightly apart—it retains its traditional Thai elegance. The hotel's staff exudes a laid-back cool, but is very attentive and helpful. Its location in the heart of the shopping district couldn't be better. Overall, this is an enjoyable and unique choice.

100 Chang Klan Rd., Chiang Mai 50100 (2 blocks south of Tha Pae Rd., 2 blocks west of river, just north of Night Bazaar). www.dusit.com ✆ **05399-9999.** Fax 05399-9900. 131 units. 8,000B deluxe; 9,500B club deluxe; from 12,500B suite. AE, DC, MC, V. **Amenities:** Restaurant; bar; outdoor pool; health club; spa room service; babysitting; concierge. *In room:* A/C, satellite TV, DVD, minibar, hair dryer, Wi-Fi (free).

Le Meridien ★★   With an ideal location on Changklan Road, right next to the Night Bazaar, this hotel is an imposing presence in central Chiang Mai. The design both outside and inside is very pleasing on the eye, and the spacious and well-lit rooms are packed with state-of-the-art furnishings and fittings, including high-definition TVs and high-speed Internet access. This is a rare example of an area hotel with wheelchair access, too. The muted earth tones of the decor are very restful, and some upper-floor rooms have wonderful views of the nearby mountain, Doi Suthep. The hotel's restaurants and bars offer an appetizing array of culinary delights, exotic cocktails, and fruit infusions.

108 Changklan Rd., Chiang Mai 50100. www.starwoodhotels.com. ✆ **05325-3666.** 384 units. From 7,800B double; from 12,600B suite. AE, DC, MC, V. **Amenities:** 2 restaurants; 2 bars; pool; fitness facility; spa; sauna; babysitting. *In room.* A/C, satellite TV, minibar, hair dryer, Wi-Fi (470B per day).

Ping Nakara ★★   Taking its inspiration from the teak boom in Chiang Mai in the late 19th century, this award-winning new boutique property has an elegant colonial design, with delicately carved woodwork around the eaves and balconies. The theme continues in the rooms, where old-style telephones, fans, and carpets hark back to another era. Other fixtures and fittings are thoroughly modern, however, from the flatscreen TV and minibar to hushed but efficient air-conditioning units and Jacuzzis in top-end rooms. All of the 19 rooms are named after different Thai flowers and are individually decorated, giving each a separate identity. Hotel facilities include an infinity pool, an Ayurvedic spa, a small but smart restaurant, and a cozy library, while the high staff to guest ratio guarantees prompt and attentive service.

135/9 Charoen Prathet Rd., Chiang Mai 50100. www.pingnakara.com. ✆ **05325-2999.** Fax 05325 2111. 19 units. 7,500B–9,500B double. AE, MC, V. **Amenities:** Restaurant; bar; infinity pool; spa; library. *In room:* A/C, satellite TV, DVD player (and in-house movies on request), minibar, Wi-Fi (free).

Shangri La ★★   Located in a lush garden setting in the heart of the city's business district, the Shangri La is a city resort designed to facilitate both business and leisure travelers. It is just a few steps away from the Night Bazaar, a 10-minute ride from the city's airport, and within easy reach of all major sights, and combines a broad range of facilities such as the CHI Spa with Shangri La's inimitable service. They offer special packages for honeymooners and golfers, as well as excellent dining and drinking options. Ask for a room with a mountain view.

89/8 Changklan Rd., Chiang Mai 50100. www.shangri-la.com. ✆ **05325-3888.** Fax 05325-3800. 281 units. From 4,500B double; from 9,350B suite. AE, DC, MC, V. **Amenities:** Restaurant; 3 bars; pool; putting green; tennis court; spa; kids' corner; babysitting. *In room:* A/C, satellite TV, minibar, Wi-Fi (free).

Yaang Come Village ★   Named after the massive 40-year-old yaang tree that provides shade for the reception area, the Yaang Come is a small oasis in developing Chiang Mai. The resort aims to re-create the feel of a traditional Thai Lue village (the Thai Lue migrated from Yunnan Province to northern Thailand a couple centuries ago). While Jacuzzis and wireless Internet access are not regular features of Thai Lue villages, the resort does have a laid-back charm. The lavishly decorated open-air reception leads to an inner courtyard dominated by a swimming pool and Jacuzzi. Flanking the pool area are the guest rooms, housed in brick buildings with Lanna-style roofs, red-tile floors, balconies, glossy tile bathrooms, and unique wall murals painted by local artisans. The hotel is tucked away from the bustle of the Night Bazaar, yet still within striking distance.

90/3 Sri Dornchai Rd., Chiang Mai 50100 (btw. Chang Klan and Charoen Prathet roads, just off Sri Dornchai Rd.). www.yaangcome.com. © **05323-7222.** Fax 05323-7230. 42 units. From 5,800B double; 8,500B family room; 9,000B suite. AE, MC, V. **Amenities:** Restaurant; bar; outdoor pool; Jacuzzi. In room: A/C, satellite TV/DVD, minibar, hair dryer, high-speed Internet, Wi-Fi (free).

MODERATE

Baan Orapin ★★ 🏠   For those looking for a more intimate and personal stay in Chiang Mai, Baan Orapin is a real gem. Owned and operated by Khun Opas Chao, who spent over a decade studying and working in the U.S. and U.K., the hotel is set on land that has been in his family for over 100 years. Two-story Lanna-style buildings surround the 90-year-old mansion and attached gardens. While the rooms and suites are rustic in comparison with the larger resorts and hotels, they are stylish and extremely clean, with sturdy teak-wood furniture, mosquito netting for the beds, and handicrafts to add some local flavor. Large bathrooms are outfitted in beautifully polished, locally made green-and-blue tiling. Khun Opas knows a wealth of information about the town and its history; he and his staff will bend over backward to attend to your every need.

150 Charoenraj Rd., Chiang Mai 50100 (east side of river, north of Narawat Bridge). www.baanorapin.com. © **05324-3677.** Fax 05324-7142. 15 units. 2,400B superior; from 2,800B suite. AE, MC, V. **Amenities:** Restaurant; small pool. In room: A/C, satellite TV, fridge, Wi-Fi (free).

The Empress Hotel ★   This 17-story tower, opened in 1990, is south of the main business and tourist area, though it's within walking distance. The hotel has all the standard amenities, and, even when swarming with tourist groups, doesn't seem overrun. The impressive public spaces are filled with glass, granite, and chrome, with integrated northern Thai touches. Large rooms with picture windows are carpeted and the color scheme makes good use of pastel hues. Bathrooms are small but decked out in marble and offer good complementary amenities. Ask to be on the mountain side, as there are panoramic views from upper floors there.

199/42 Chang Klan Rd., Chiang Mai 50100 (a 10-min. walk south of Night Bazaar, 2 blocks from river). www.empresshotels.com. © **05327-0240.** Fax 05327-2467. 375 units. 2,200B–2,850B double; from 3,200B suite. AE, DC, MC, V. **Amenities:** 3 restaurants; lounge; outdoor pool; health club w/sauna; room service; babysitting; executive floor. In room: A/C, satellite TV, fridge, minibar, hair dryer, Wi-Fi (500B for 12 hours).

Rimping Village ★ 🍴   Nestled in a peaceful compound just to the east of the Ping River, this two-story place offers great value with its well-equipped rooms, thoughtful extras such as free bicycle use for guests, and rates much lower than you'd expect. Rooms are simply but smartly furnished and there is free Wi-Fi in all rooms. The family suite is huge and particularly good value. A saltwater pool and dining terrace stand in the shade of a huge banyan tree, and the staff is so friendly you'll feel like family from the first day.

13/1 Soi 2, Chiangmai-Lamphun Rd., Chiang Mai 50000. www.rimpingvillage.com. © **05324-3915.** Fax 05324-7944. 34 units. 2,700B–3,600B double; 5,000B family suite. AE, MC, V. **Amenities:** Restaurant; bar; outdoor pool; free bicycle use; room service. *In room:* A/C, satellite TV/DVD player, minibar, hair dryer, Wi-Fi (free).

Royal Princess Hotel ★   This northern cousin of Bangkok's Dusit Thani is one of Chiang Mai's longest-running hotels, but it has managed to maintain its standards to compete with newer choices. Guest rooms are finished in a mix of cool pastels with matching carpets and subdued lighting. The downtown location means easy access to shopping and nightlife; all guest rooms have a good vantage on the glittering lights of the city. You're right in the heart of it here, so be warned that stepping out of the hotel means that touts and tuk-tuk drivers will be waiting to pounce.

112 Chang Klan Rd., Chiang Mai 50100 (located just south of the Night Bazaar). www.dusit.com. © **05325-3900.** Fax 05328-1044. 198 units. From 2,208B double; from 5,300B suite. AE, DC, MC, V. **Amenities:** 2 restaurants; lobby bar; small outdoor pool; mini gym; room service; babysitting. *In room:* A/C, satellite TV, minibar, fridge, hair dryer, Wi-Fi (300B per day).

INEXPENSIVE

Baan Kaew Guesthouse ★   This motel-style guesthouse—an enclosed compound in a quiet neighborhood—just a short walk south of the Night Bazaar, has a well-tended garden and a manicured lawn. Rooms are very simple but spotless, with new floor coverings (guests are asked to remove shoes before entering) and tiled bathrooms with hot-water showers. Breakfast is served in a shaded pavilion. You're close to the market, but the place is quiet.

142 Charoen Prathet Rd., Chiang Mai 50100 (south of Sri Dornchai Rd., opposite Wat Chaimongkol; enter gate, turn left, and find guesthouse well back from street). www.baankaew-guesthouse. com. © **05327-1606.** Fax 05327-3436. 20 units. 800B double. No credit cards. **Amenities:** Restaurant (breakfast only). *In room:* A/C, Wi-Fi (free).

Galare Guest House   This Thai-style, two-story, brick-and-wood guesthouse has broad covered verandas overlooking a pleasant garden and courtyard. Rooms are small but have air-conditioning and king-sized beds. Even with linoleum floors, the rooms are very comfortable. The restaurant serves breakfast, lunch, and dinner on a covered deck overlooking the river. An in-house trekking agency organizes trips to hill-tribe villages, as well as local tours of Chiang Mai; ask about discounts in the off-season. It's popular with expats, so is often full.

7 Charoen Prathet Rd., Soi 2, Chiang Mai 50100 (on river south of Thapae Rd.). www.galare.com. © **05381-8887.** Fax 05327-9088. 35 units. 990B–1,150B double. MC, V. **Amenities:** Restaurant; computer w/Internet access. *In room:* A/C, TV, fridge, Wi-Fi (free), no phone.

Vanilla Place   There are just 15 rooms in this small guesthouse situated near the river and the Night Bazaar, all quite cozy, though standard rooms lack a window. Some rooms have balconies, but you'd be better out the back than the front as the road can be very busy and noisy. There's free Wi-Fi throughout the building and a computer for guests' use in a large communal area on the second floor. What makes the difference between places at this price is not facilities, which are largely similar, but service, and the owners here have earned much praise from guests for their friendly approach.

73/2-3 Charoen Prathet Rd., Chiang Mai 50100. www.vanillaplace-chiangmai.com. © **05323-3925.** Fax 05323-3926. 15 units. 900B–1,100B double. MC, V. **Amenities:** Communal room; computer use. *In room:* A/C, satellite TV, Wi-Fi (free).

In the Old City

EXPENSIVE

The Rachamankha ★★★ 📷 This immaculate hotel is a great escape from the city gridlock and pollution. Just south of Wat Phra Singh, the unique, boutique property is designed in a courtyard style, much like a Thai temple, and the rooms are a bit like luxurious lodgings for monks. Service is professional, and rooms are well-appointed, with terra-cotta tile floors, high ceilings, traditional Chinese furnishings, and stylish contemporary features; plenty of stunning Lanna antiques are scattered around the long, cool verandas. Deluxe rooms are just larger versions of superior ones and bathrooms are bright and large. An indigo pool lies in the peaceful courtyard. Hotel dining is in either a gravel courtyard or the long, peaceful antiques-filled hall. Upstairs is a spectacular boutique.

6 Rachamankha 9 (on the western edge of the Old City), Phra Singh Rd., Chiang Mai 50200. www.rachamankha.com. ✆ **05390-4111.** Fax 05390-4114. 25 units. 8,040B superior double; 9,100B deluxe double; 19,400B suite. AE, MC, V. **Amenities:** Restaurant; bar; outdoor pool; room service. *In room:* A/C, satellite TV, fridge, minibar, hair dryer, Wi-Fi (free).

Tamarind Village ★★ After passing down a long, shaded lane lined with new-growth bamboo, and following meandering walkways among the gobo buildings of this stylish little hideaway in the heart of the Old City, it'll be hard to believe that you're in Chiang Mai (though you can still hear the traffic). Rooms at the Tamarind are marvels of polished concrete burnished to an almost shining glow, complemented by straw mats and chic contemporary Thai furnishings, all making for a pleasing minimalist feel. Bathrooms are spacious, with large double doors connecting with the guest rooms, topped off with vaulted ceilings. There's an almost Mediterranean feel to the whole complex—with all of the arched, covered terra-cotta walks joining buildings in a village-style layout. There's a fine pool and an excellent restaurant, Ruen Tamarind, serving delicious Thai fare (see "Where to Eat," below), plus the staff members are helpful and the atmosphere is quite unique.

50/1 Ratchadamnoen Rd., Sri Phum, Chiang Mai 50200 (a short walk to the center of the Old City from Thapae Gate). www.tamarindvillage.com. ✆ **05341-8896.** Fax 05341-8900. 45 units. 4,200B double; 5,600B deluxe; from 9,800B suite. MC, V. **Amenities:** Restaurant; bar; outdoor pool. *In room:* A/C, satellite TV, minibar, fridge, hair dryer, Wi-Fi (200B per day).

U Chiang Mai ★ With an ideal location right in the center of the Old City, this place makes it easy to walk to the city's main temples, and the Sunday Walking Street (p. 316) sets up right in front. Rooms are tastefully equipped in Lanna style, and guests have use of the gym, infinity pool, and spa facilities. Added touches, such as the ability to check in any time (most hotels insist you check in after 2pm on the day reserved), breakfast whenever and wherever you like it, plus the on-site restaurant and free Wi-Fi, make this an attractive option.

70 Ratchadamnoen Rd., Sri Phum, Chiang Mai 50200. www.uhotelsresorts.com. ✆ **05332-7000.** Fax 05332-7096. 41 units. From 4,399B double. MC, V. **Amenities:** Restaurant; bar; outdoor pool; health club; spa. *In-room:* A/C, satellite TV, minibar, Wi-Fi (free).

MODERATE

Eurana Boutique Hotel This cozy little courtyard hotel in the heart of the busy backpacker area in the northeast corner of the Old City (just inside the moat) offers a serious degree of luxury. Though the cheapest rooms are on the small size, splurge and you'll enjoy delightful contemporary digs with fun, colorful decor and even a glimpse of the (tiny) gardens. It's also convenient for many services (restaurants, cooking schools, and massage parlors) in the Old City.

7/1 Moon Muang Rd. Soi 7, Chiang Mai 50200. www.euranaboutiquehotel.com. © **05321-9402.** Fax 05322-3042. 72 units. 2,100B–2,700B double; 5,000B suite. MC, V. **Amenities:** Restaurant; outdoor pool; spa. In room: A/C, TV, fridge, Wi-Fi (free).

Villa Duang Champa ★   This cute, refurbished colonial house is full of character and superbly located for sightseeing in the heart of the Old City. There are just 10 rooms in the main building, each individually furnished, and a restful spa in the wooden villa out back. Some of the well-equipped rooms have small balconies and others have views of the nearby mountain, Doi Suthep. The place lacks amenities such as a restaurant and bar, but there are plenty of places just a few steps away and the friendly staff members are happy to give advice.

82 Ratchadamnoen Rd., Sri Phum, Chiang Mai 50200. www.villaduangchampa.com. © **05332-7198-9.** Fax 05332-7197. 10 units. 2,400B–3,200B double. Breakfast included in rates. MC, V. **Amenities:** Breakfast room; spa. In-room: A/C, satellite TV, fridge, Wi-Fi (free).

INEXPENSIVE

Elliebum   There are just two large and comfortable rooms in this homely place that is well worth considering. Both rooms have a sofa and desk and the room rate includes a tasty breakfast. The location couldn't be better, in the heart of the Old City, and there's a cafe and gift shop downstairs. When the guesthouse is full, they can put visitors up at another comfy place round the corner, the Rachamankha Flora House, which has the same rates. The owner of Elliebum, Gade, is a mine of information and also offers guided food walks that take in local markets, restaurants, and dessert stalls—a great way to explore the city.

114/3-4 Ratchamankha Rd., Chiang Mai 50200. http://elliebum.com. © **05381-4723.** 2 units. 1,400B double. Breakfast included in rates. MC, V. **Amenities:** Guest lounge. In room: A/C, satellite TV, DVD player, Wi-Fi (free).

Gap's House   Gap's House is tucked down a quiet lane just inside the city wall near Thapae Gate, a great location. Long popular among budget travelers, the hotel does not accept bookings, but operates on a "first come, first served" basis. It boasts a calm atmosphere, with a leafy central garden area surrounding a large, teak Lanna pavilion. Rooms are in free-standing teak houses and feature woven rattan beds, chunky furniture, and small tiled bathrooms. It's a cheap, atmospheric choice in the town center, and its vegetarian restaurant and cooking classes are particularly popular.

3 Ratchadamnoen Rd. Soi 4, Chiang Mai 50000 (1 block west of Thapae Gate on left). www.gaps-house.com. ©/fax **05327-8140.** 20 units. 470B–700B double. Rates include breakfast. MC, V. **Amenities:** Vegetarian restaurant. In room: A/C, Wi-Fi (free), no phone.

Hotel M ★   Formerly the Montri Hotel, this was the earliest address of note for foreigners in Chiang Mai, and it is still a convenient, inexpensive choice just inside the Old City—and across from Thapae Gate. Newly renovated rooms are comfortable, with a soft sofa, wide-screen TV, and free Wi-Fi. Bathrooms are small but functional, with a walk-in shower. Their main advantage is that they are good value. *Note:* Ask for a room at the rear; you'll get more peace and quiet, and from the higher floors you can see the outline of Doi Suthep.

2–6 Ratchadamnoen Rd., Chiang Mai 50100 (just northwest across from Thapae Gate). www.hotelmchiangmai.com. © **05321-1069.** Fax 05321-7416. 75 units. From 1,300B double. MC, V. **Amenities:** Restaurant. In room: A/C, satellite TV, minibar, fridge, Wi-Fi (free).

West Side/University Area

MODERATE

Chiang Mai Orchid ★   The Orchid has attractive facilities and friendly service, and is next to one of Chiang Mai's most popular hangouts, Gad Suan Kaew Shopping Complex. Spacious, quiet rooms are large, familiar, and pleasantly decorated with local woodcarvings. The lobby and other public spaces are furnished with clusters of chic, low-slung rattan couches and chairs and are decorated with flowers. They cover all the bases in amenities, from dining to car rental—plus there's a knowledgeable tour desk.

23 Huai Kaeo Rd., Chiang Mai 50200 (northwest of Old City, next door to Gad San Kaew/Central Shopping Complex). www.chiangmaiorchid.com. © **05322-2099.** Fax 05322-1625. 266 units. 2,186B-2,748B double; from 7,027B suite. AE, DC, MC, V. **Amenities:** 3 restaurants; lounge and pub; outdoor pool; health club; sauna; children's playground; room service; babysitting. *In room:* A/C, satellite TV, minibar, fridge, Wi-Fi (free).

Kantary Hills ★★   This stylish hotel and serviced apartments serve as a great base near the fashionable Nimmanheimin Road, which is lined with boutiques, restaurants and cafes, to the west of the city center. Studios and one- and two-bedroom apartments are all bright and spacious, some with private balconies and views of Doi Suthep mountain. All have a living room, bedroom, and dining area, modern furnishings, and wood floors. There's a reading room, pool, and health club, and the staff take great pleasure in assisting guests in any way possible.

44, 44/1-2 Nimmanheimin Rd., Chiang Mai 50200. www.kantarycollection.com. © **05340-0877.** Fax 05322-3244. 174 units. 3,400B studio; 4,300B 1-bedroom apartment; 6,300B 2-bedroom apartment. AE, MC, V. **Amenities:** Restaurant; pool; health club; sauna & steam room; concierge; coffee shop; reading room. *In room:* A/C, Satellite TV/DVD player, pantry with cooking utensils, Wi-Fi (321B per day).

INEXPENSIVE

Yes, the Village People are here in Chiang Mai: The rooms at **The YMCA International Hotel** (11 Sermsuk Rd., Chang Puak; www.ymcachiangmai.org; © 05322-1819) have attracted missionaries and budget travelers for years. Rooms start at just 400B for a standard fan-cooled room. They also have air-conditioned dorms, though rates are a bit higher (720B–800B).

WHERE TO EAT

Northern-style Thai cooking is influenced by the nearby Burmese, Yunnanese, and Lao cuisines. Many northern Thai dishes are not served with steamed rice, but *khao niaow* (glutinous or sticky rice), which can be cooked as an accompaniment to a savory dish or used in a dessert. Sticky rice is sometimes served simply in a knotted banana leaf or in a small cylindrical basket with a lid, and it is eaten with the hands, by squeezing it into a small ball then pressing it into dips or sauces. Chiang Mai specialties include *sai ua* (Chiang Mai sausage), *khao soi* (a spicy, yellow, Burmese-style curry with pickles and both fried and boiled noodles), and many other slightly sweet meat and fish curries. You may be relieved to know that chili peppers are used less than in other Thai regional cuisines.

The formal northern meal is called *khan toke* and refers to the practice of sharing a variety of main courses, with guests seated around *khan toke* (low, lacquered teak tables); eating is done using the hands. Most of the restaurants that serve *khan toke*

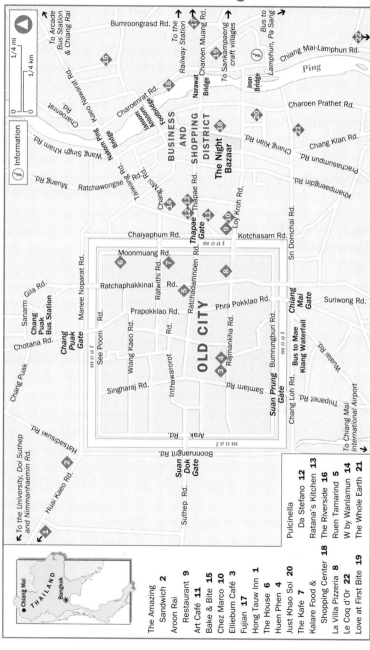

The Amazing
Sandwich **2**
Aroon Rai
Restaurant **9**
Art Café **11**
Bake & Bite **15**
Chez Marco **10**
Elliebum Café **3**
Fujian **17**
Hong Tauw Inn **1**
The House **6**
Huen Phen **4**
Just Khao Soi **20**
The Kafe **7**
Kalare Food &
Shopping Center **18**
La Villa Pizzeria **8**
Le Coq d'Or **22**
Love at First Bite **19**

Pulcinella
Da Stefano **12**
Ratana's Kitchen **13**
The Riverside **16**
Ruen Tamarind **5**
W by Wanlamun **14**
The Whole Earth **21**

combine a dance performance with the meal. The best such places are covered in "Chiang Mai Entertainment & Nightlife," later in this chapter.

Chiang Mai is also blessed with good street food and markets. **Anusarn Market** on the corner of Sri Dornchai and Chang Klan roads near the Night Bazaar is a good place for authentic local food, though the seafood tends to be a bit pricey. Also try **Somphet Market** on the northeast corner of the old city; it's a good place to pick up snacks like fried bananas or sticky-rice desserts in the daytime or have a good cheap meal in the evening, at which point the area bustles with locals and young backpackers.

Chiang Mai folks take their *khao soi*—Burmese curry and noodles—pretty seriously; it's a favorite lunchtime dish. The best is to be had in **Faharm,** an area about 1km (⅔ mile) north of central Nawarat Bridge, on Charoenrat Road, along the east bank of the Ping River. A number of open-air places serve the delicacy for just 30B to 40B, along with tasty skewers of chicken and pork satay. One of the best is **Khao Soi Samoe Jai ★★**; there's no English sign but it's immediately north of Wat Faharm, and open lunchtimes only. Count on this place always being packed, as it's well known to locals.

Near the Ping River

EXPENSIVE

Fujian ★★★ CHINESE Set in an elegant 1930s Shanghai mansion, at the entrance to the traditional Lanna village that contains the Mandarin Oriental Dhara Dhevi hotel (p. 294), this restaurant turns out some of the tastiest Chinese cuisine to be found in Thailand. Choices range from delicious dim sum lunches (around 800B) to indulgent dinners featuring Cantonese and Sichuan specialties. While eating, diners are invited to taste the black tea from Fujian Province after which the restaurant is named.

51/4 Chiang Mai–Sankampaeng Rd. (4km/2½ miles east on Charoen Muang). ☏ **05388-8888.** www.mandarinoriental.com/chiangmai/dining. Main courses 520B–950B; set dinners 800B–1,500B. AE, MC, V. Daily 11:30am–2:30pm and 6:30–10:30pm.

Le Coq d'Or ★★★ FRENCH In a colonial house setting, Le Coq d'Or has been around for years and is known for its nice atmosphere and good service. The menu offers imported beef, lamb, and local fish prepared in French and Continental styles. Try the chateaubriand, or the poached Norwegian salmon as a lighter choice. For starters, the foie gras is popular, as is the unique salmon tartare served with toast and a sour-cream-and-horseradish sauce. There's a long wine list and live music (gentle jazz) performed from Monday to Saturday evenings.

11 Soi 2, Koh Klang Rd. (5-min. drive south of the Mengrai Bridge, following the river). ☏ **05314-1555.** www.lecoqdorchiangmai.com. Reservations recommended for dinner Sat–Sun. Main courses 580B–1,850B; set dinner around 2,000B. AE, DC, MC, V. Daily noon–2pm and 6–10pm.

MODERATE

Chez Marco ★★ MEDITERRANEAN The western end of Loy Kroh Road is shoulder-to-shoulder girlie bars—an odd place to find one of the city's best gourmet restaurants, but that doesn't prevent its patrons from packing the place most evenings. Following the simple principles of using fresh ingredients that are sensibly combined and subtly flavored, Marco manages to impress most diners. Choose between indoor and outdoor tables, and from a mouth-watering range of dishes, including daily specials on a chalkboard. I went for a flavorful home-made broccoli soup followed by pork tournedos with mashed potatoes and a light sauce—all delicious. There's a long drinks list and tempting desserts as well.

15/7 Loy Kroh Rd. ℂ **05320-7032.** Main Courses 200B–800B. MC, V. Daily 5–11pm.

W by Wanlamun ★★ THAI   This stylish restaurant is tucked away down a side street off Chang Moi Road, so still remains a secret to most local residents, but probably not for long. Choose between a table in the air-conditioned, colonial-style house or in the garden, and indulge in a few classic Thai dishes such as *tom yam kung*—hot and sour shrimp soup. The menu is not extensive, but everything is prepared to perfection and beautifully presented. Try to save a little space for the delectable desserts that are on display in the house.

1 Chang Moi Soi 2. ℂ **05323-2328.** Main courses 220B–450B. MC, V. Daily 11am–2pm and 6–10pm.

The Whole Earth ★ 🍃 VEGETARIAN/INDIAN   Featuring Asian foods, mostly Indian and Thai, prepared with light, fresh ingredients in healthy and creative ways, this 30-year-old Chiang Mai institution is a real find. The restaurant is set in a traditional Lanna Thai pavilion and has an indoor air-conditioned nonsmoking section, and a long open-air veranda with views of the gardens. The menu is extensive, and everything on it is good. Try the spicy house vegetarian curry with tofu, wrapped in seaweed, and finish with a fresh mango lassi.

88 Sri Donchai Rd., A. Muang. ℂ **05328-2463.** Main courses 250B–420B. MC, V. Daily 11am–10pm.

INEXPENSIVE

Just Khao Soi NORTHERN THAI   If you'd like to try Chiang Mai's signature dish, *khao soi*, but don't trust those hole-in-the-wall places where they sell it, then head for this place, which elevates the dish to fine-dining status. You might be paying several times the going rate, but it's still reasonably cheap, and you get to choose from different strengths of broth and a wide range of accompanying side dishes, all served on a giant artist's palette. Add the spotless, smart surroundings and attentive staff, and you have the perfect setting in which to enjoy this memorable dish.

108/2 Charoen Prathet Rd. (1 block east of the Night Bazaar). ℂ **05381-8641.** Main courses 99B–249B. MC, V. Daily 11am–11pm.

The Riverside ★★ THAI/INTERNATIONAL   Casual and cool is what Riverside is all about. It is split into two parts: An old wooden building overlooking the river and a smart new place across the road. It is hugely popular among both Thais and foreigners, so make sure you get there before the dinner rush to get your pick of tables. There's live music, from blues to soft rock, great Thai and Western food (including burgers), and a full bar. Even if you just stop by for a beer, it is a jovial place that always has a jolly crowd of travelers, locals, and expatriates. Riverside also operates a dining cruise at 8pm (boards at 7:15pm) for just 90B per person (drinks and dining a la carte). Call ahead.

9–11 Charoenrat Rd. (east side of river, north of Nawarat Bridge). ℂ **05324-3239.** www.the riversidechiangmai.com. Main courses 90B–330B. AE, MC, V. Daily 10am–1am.

Around the Old City

EXPENSIVE

The House ★★★ PACIFIC RIM/MODERN ASIAN   This wonderful supper-only bistro was established by a resident Dane who immediately upped the culinary standards in Chiang Mai. Set in an old 1960s edifice that's been lovingly restored, the main dining room has large windows with gorgeous drapes, silk cushions, and candlelit tables; upstairs there are two rooms that are even cozier. An internationally trained Thai chef works his magic on a constantly evolving menu of regionally influenced classical dishes, a medley of grilled items and imported steaks, and lamb and seafood when available—there are fabulous desserts to boot. For good value, order the four-course set dinner (with a free glass of wine) for 900B. Outside is a Moorish souk-styled lounge bar with lights in the trees, and a separate tapas bar for snacks. This refined dining spot, with its romantic nooks and funky furnishings, caters to the discerning traveler.

199 Moon Muang Rd. (north of Thapae gate on the inside edge of the city moat). ⓒ **05341-9014.** Main courses 450B–850B. MC, V. Daily kitchen 6–10:30pm. Bar 6pm–1am.

MODERATE

Ruen Tamarind ★ THAI/INTERNATIONAL Part of Tamarind Village (see "Where to Stay," earlier in this chapter), Ruen Tamarind offers a fine selection of northern Thai cuisine with a couple of international favorites thrown in for the less adventurous. A must-try is the *tort mun pla*, or fried fish cakes, a common dish with a unique twist: The cakes are marinated with small chunks of banana and are served with peanut sauce. Delicious. In the evenings, the restaurant's candlelit tables spread onto the hotel's lovely pool deck.

At the Tamarind Village, 50/1 Ratchadamnoen Rd., Sriphum (a short walk toward the center of the Old City from Tha Pae Gate). ⓒ **05341-8896.** Main courses 180B–480B. MC, V. Daily 7am–11pm.

INEXPENSIVE

Aroon Rai Restaurant NORTHERN THAI For authentic northern food, adventurous eaters should try this nondescript garden restaurant, one of the city's longest-running eateries. Their *khao soi*, filled with egg noodles and crisp-fried chicken bits and sprinkled with dried fried noodles, is spicy and coconut-sweet at the same time. Chiang Mai sausages are served sliced over steamed rice; puffed-up fried pork rinds are the traditional cholesterol lover's accompaniment. Dishes are all made to order in an open kitchen, so you can point to things that interest you, including the myriad fried insects and frogs, for which this place is famous. You can even get prepackaged spices and recipes for make-it-yourself dishes back home.

45 Kotchasarn Rd. (2 blocks south of Thapae Gate, outside Old City). ⓒ **05327-6947.** Main courses 50B–110B. No credit cards. Daily 9am–10pm.

Art Café THAI/INTERNATIONAL This cheery corner cafe has black-and-white tile floors and cozy booths with picture windows overlooking the busy terminus of Thapae Road and the square beside Thapae Gate. That makes it a good spot for people-watching, resting from city touring, or picking up free maps and city guides and meeting other travelers. The menu is ambitious and offers tasty Thai food as well as familiar fare, from steaks and delicious thin-crust pizzas to Mexican dishes, meat-loaf, cake, and coffee.

291 Thapae Rd. (just opposite Thapae Gate). ⓒ **05320-6365.** Main courses 100B–370B. MC, V. Daily 8am–11pm.

Huen Phen ★★ 🏠 NORTHERN THAI Just south of Wat Chedi Luang, Huen Phen is not only a convenient spot for lunch when temple touring, but also probably the best place in town to sample authentic Northern Thai food. Lunch is served from a simple, open kitchen by the street, though there is an air-conditioned room, too. There's fabulous *khao soi* here, Chiang Mai's famed Burmese curry with noodle, and another tasty (but fiery) dish is *khanom jeen nam ngua*, a beef stew in a hearty broth over rice noodles. In the evening, the quaint, antique-strewn house out back provides a classier setting for a feast of Northern Thai cuisine, including *kaeng haeng lay*, a thick pork and ginger curry, and *nam phrik ong*, a delicious ground pork and chili dip served with raw vegetables and pork crackling.

112 Rachamankha Rd. ✆ **05327-7103.** Main courses 40B–160B. No credit cards. Daily 7:30am–4:30pm and 5–10pm.

La Villa Pizzeria ★ ITALIAN   La Villa is a friendly Italian-run operation. Light snacks, such as imported *prosciutto* and sardines, are a treat, and main courses include *fegato alla veneziana* (beef liver fried with onions and butter) and tasty pasta. The wood-fired thin-crust pizzas, with authentic tomato sauce and vegetable or meat toppings, are light and delicious.

Pensione La Villa, 130 Ratchapakinai Rd. (north of Rachamankha Rd.). ✆ **05327-1914.** Main courses 120B–280B. No credit cards. Daily 11am–11pm.

Pulcinella Da Stefano ★★ ITALIAN   Da Stefano's is in a narrow lane off Tha Pae Road; it's a lively and popular place with an extensive catalog of northern Italian cuisine, from steaks to excellent pizzas and pastas. Portions are big, the wine list is deep, and there are good daily set menus and specials. The boss is often on hand to advise, if you can't make up your mind, and it's very popular so reservations are a good idea. Meet lots of young backpackers splashing out after long treks around the northern hills.

2/1–2 Chang Moi Kao Rd. (just to the east of Tha Pae Gate). ✆ **05387-4189.** Reservations recommended. Main courses 150B–320B. AE, MC, V. Daily 11:30am–10:30pm.

Ratana's Kitchen ★ THAI/INTERNATIONAL   This cozy, cafe-style eatery on busy Thapae Road has become extremely popular for its fantastic range of well-prepared Thai dishes, as well as steaks, sandwiches, and yummy shakes, all at rock-bottom prices. There are books and magazines to browse and board games to play. It's a great place to watch festival parades go past, but, for such events, reservations are essential.

320-322 Thapae Rd. (150m/492 ft. east of Thapae Gate). Reservations recommended. ✆ **05387-4173.** Main courses 40B–170B. No credit cards. Daily 7:30am–11:30pm.

Westside/Huai Kaeo Road

The Amazing Sandwich CONTINENTAL   The recipe is simple here: Create your own "amazing" sandwich for eat-in or take-away. The palette for your masterwork is a list of ingredients, and you simply tick the appropriate boxes to your heart's delight. Even if you are more interested in local food, this is a great place to get a packed lunch for a self-guided day trip. As popular among expat locals as travelers, it also serves all-day breakfasts, burgers, salads, and pies.

20/2 Huay Kaew Rd. (across from Central Kad Suan Kaew). ✆ **05340-4174.** www.amazing sandwich.com. Main courses 85B–190B. No credit cards. Mon–Sat 8:30am–8pm; Sun 8:30am–4pm.

Hong Tauw Inn 🍴 THAI   Located in a parade of shops opposite the Amari Rincome Hotel at the northern end of Nimmanhaemin Road, this homey restaurant is cluttered with grandfather clocks and antiques. It makes for an unusual but pleasant ambience in which to taste some delicious Thai dishes; the menu also features several Northern specialties, and there's a good range of drinks.

95/17–18 Nantawan Arcade, Nimmanhaemin Rd. ✆ **05322-8333.** Main courses 80B–220B. MC, V. Daily 11am–11pm.

Snacks & Cafes

Kalare Food & Shopping Center, 89/2 Chang Klan Rd., on the corner of Soi 6, opposite the Night Bazaar (℃ **05327-2067;** 6pm–midnight), is where you'll find a small food court next to the nightly Thai culture show, which starts around 8:30pm (buy coupons at a booth and then pick what you want from vendors).

Bake & Bite (3/7, Kaew Nawarat Soi 3/2; ℃ **05324-9689;** Mon–Sat 7am–6pm and Sun 7am–3pm) is on a side street to the east of the Ping River and has tasty baked goods, fine bread, and good coffee.

The Kafe (127–129 Moon Muang Rd.; ℃ **05321-2717;** daily 8am–midnight) is just north of Thapae Gate and it's a good traveler's crossroads where you can pick up handy information, have a great meal of Thai or basic Western food, and throw back a few cold ones.

If you're looking for a break while looking at the temples in the Old City, a good choice is **Elliebum Café** (114/3–4 Ratchamankha Rd.; ℃ **05381-4723;** Mon–Sat 7:30am–6pm & Sun 7:30am–1pm), which offers sandwiches, smoothies, and a small range of Thai dishes.

For anyone with a sweet tooth, it's worth hunting down **Love at First Bite** (28 Soi 1, Chiangmai-Lamphun Rd.; ℃ **05324-2731;** 8am–6pm) for its scrumptious cakes that you can enjoy in a pleasant garden. It also serves a limited number of set dishes at lunchtime.

All along Nimmanhaemin Road, new, trendy eateries and coffee shops are springing up next to little juice bars and ice-cream parlors; take a stroll and pick your place.

EXPLORING CHIANG MAI

The Wats

Chiang Mai has more than 700 temples, the largest concentration outside of Bangkok, and unique little sites are around every corner. You can hit the highlights in Old Chiang Mai by tuk-tuk, but even more fun is to arm yourself with a map and wend your way from one side of the Old City to the other, weaving in and out of temple compounds.

Wat Chedi Luang ★★★ TEMPLE   Because this temple is in the heart of the Old City, most visitors begin their sightseeing here, where there are two *wats* of interest. This complex, which briefly housed the Emerald Buddha (now at Bangkok's Wat Phra Kaew; p. 106), dates from 1411 when the original *chedi* (stupa) was built by King Saen Muang Ma. The already-massive edifice was expanded to 84m (276 ft.) in height in the mid-1400s, only to be ruined by a severe earthquake in 1545, just 13 years before Chiang Mai fell to the Burmese. Some of the elephants around its base were restored in the 1990s, but the spire was never rebuilt. Buddhas sit in niches facing the cardinal points, and it is not unusual to spot a saffron-robed monk bowing to them as he circles the *chedi*. The huge *chedi* is especially atmospheric during the *puja* festivals, when monks and laymen circumambulate it carrying candles, flowers, and incense.

Wat Phan Tao, in the northeast corner of the same compound, has an impressive wooden *viharn* (assembly hall) that once served as a royal residence and is adorned with a striking mosaic of a peacock and dog above the main door. After leaving the temple, walk around to the monks' quarters on the side, taking in the traditional teak northern architecture and delightful landscaping.

Prapokklao Rd., south of Ratchadamnoen Rd. Suggested donation 20B. Daily 6am–8pm.

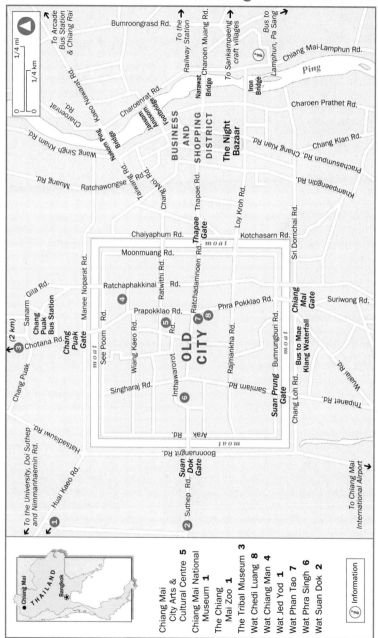

Chiang Mai
City Arts &
Cultural Centre **5**
Chiang Mai National
Museum **1**
The Chiang
Mai Zoo **1**
The Tribal Museum **3**
Wat Chedi Luang **8**
Wat Chiang Man **4**
Wat Jed Yod **1**
Wat Phan Tao **7**
Wat Phra Singh **6**
Wat Suan Dok **2**

ⓘ Information

Wat Chiang Man ★ TEMPLE   Thought to be Chiang Mai's oldest *wat*, this was built during the 14th century by King Mengrai, the founder of Chiang Mai, on the spot where he first camped. Like many of the *wats* in Chiang Mai, this complex reflects many architectural styles. Some of the structures are pure Lanna. Others show influences from as far away as Sri Lanka; notice the typical row of elephant supports around the small stupa behind the *viharn*. Wat Chiang Man is most famous for its two Buddhas: Phra Sae Tang Khamani (a miniature crystal image also known as the **White Emerald Buddha**) and the marble **Phra Sila Buddha.** Unfortunately, the small *viharn* that safeguards these religious sculptures (to the right as you enter) is almost always closed.

Ratchapakinai Rd., south of the Sri Phum Rd. moat. Suggested donation 20B. Daily 6am–6pm.

Wat Jed Yod ★★ TEMPLE   Also called Wat Maha Photharam, Wat Jed Yod ("Temple of the Seven Spires") is one of the city's most elegant sites, though it is located northwest of the center, beside the Superhighway. The *chedi* was built during the reign of King Tilokkarat in the late 15th century (his remains are in one of the other *chedis*), and, in 1477, the World Sangkayana convened here to revise the doctrines of the Buddha.

The unusual design of the main rectangular *chedi* with seven peaks was copied from the Maha Bodhi Temple in Bodhgaya, India, where the Buddha first achieved enlightenment. The temple also has architectural elements reflecting Burmese and early Chinese influences supposed to date back to the Yuan and Ming dynasties. The extraordinary proportions; the angelic, levitating *devata* (Buddhist spirits) bas reliefs around the base of the *chedi*; and the juxtaposition of the other buildings make Wat Jed Yod a masterpiece.

Superhighway, near the Chiang Mai National Museum (north of the intersection of Nimmanhaemin and Huai Kaeo rds., about 1km/⅔ mile on the left). Suggested donation 20B. Daily 6am–6pm.

Wat Phra Singh ★★★ TEMPLE   This compound was built during the zenith of Chiang Mai's power and is one of the more venerated temples in the city. It is still the focus of many important religious ceremonies, particularly the Songkran Festival. More than 700 monks study here and you will probably find them especially friendly with tourists.

King Phayu, of Mengrai lineage, built the *chedi* in 1345, principally to house the cremated remains of King Kamfu, his father. As you enter the grounds, head to the right toward the 14th-century library. Notice the graceful carving and the characteristic roofline with four separate elevations. The sculptural *devata* figures, in both dancing and meditative poses, are thought to have been made during King Muang Kaeo's reign in the early 16th century. They decorate a stone base designed to keep the fragile *saa* (mulberry bark) manuscripts elevated from flooding and vermin.

On the other side of the temple complex is the 200-year-old **Lai Kham (Gilded Hall) Viharn,** housing the venerated image of the Phra Sihing or **Lion Buddha,** brought to the site by King Muang Ma in 1400. The original Buddha's head was stolen in 1922, but the reproduction in its place doesn't diminish the homage paid to this figure during Songkran. Inside are frescoes illustrating the stories of Sang Thong (the Golden Prince of the Conchshell) and Suwannahong. These images convey a great deal about the religious, civil, and military life of 19th-century Chiang Mai during King Mahotraprathet's reign.

Samlarn and Ratchadamnoen rds. Suggested donation 20B. Daily 6am–6pm.

Monk Chat

What do you say to these tonsured men in orange robes one sees piously padding barefoot around Thailand? The answer is: "Hello. How are you?" Monks, especially seniors, deserve a special level of respect, of course, but are quite human, and the best way to find out is to stop by Mahachulalongkorn University (adjoining Wat Suan Dok—see above—west of town on Suthep Rd.). Every Monday, Wednesday, and Friday, from 5 to 7pm, they welcome foreign visitors for "monk chat," a classroom venue of small, informal discussion groups where visitors and monks come to connect, share culture, and learn about Buddhism from novices, eager to explain and, of course, practice their English. It is a mostly informal discussion about one's own country or sports (young novices are nuts about English Premier League soccer (football), but the more senior monks can give you some insights into Buddhist practice and monastic life.) They also meet for meditation groups and retreats. Call 🕾 **05327-8967** or visit www.monkchat.net for info.

Wat Suan Dok TEMPLE   This complex is special, less for its architecture (the buildings, though monumental, are undistinguished) than for its contemplative spirit and pleasant surroundings. The temple was built amid the pleasure gardens of the 14th-century Lanna Thai monarch, King Ku Na. Like several of Chiang Mai's other *wats*, Wat Suan Dok functions as a study center for monks who have isolated themselves from the distractions of the outside world.

Among the main attractions in the complex are the *bot*, with a very impressive **Chiang Saen Buddha** (one of the largest bronzes in the north) dating from 1504 and some garish murals. Also of interest is the *chedi*, built to hold a relic of the Buddha, and a royal cemetery with some splendid shrines. An informal "monk chat" is held here each week (see the box, above).

Suthep Rd. (from the Old City, take the Suan Dok Gate and continue 1.6km/1 mile west). Suggested donation 20B. Daily 6am–6pm.

Museums

Chiang Mai City Arts & Cultural Center ★ MUSEUM   In a well-preserved, colonial building behind the Three Kings Monument in the heart of the Old City, this museum houses a permanent exhibit that walks visitors through a tour of prehistory to the present. Another section houses short-term local exhibits of all types. This is a popular place to visit for those looking for some historical insights. It sometimes gets crowded with school trips in the morning, so visit in the afternoon to avoid crowds.

Phra Pokklao Rd. 🕾 **05321-7793.** Admission 90B for adults, 40B for children. Tues–Sun 8:30am–5pm.

Chiang Mai National Museum MUSEUM   While its collection of historical treasures is not nearly as extensive as that of Bangkok's National Museum, this place does provide something of a historical overview—and the highlights—of the region and the city. The Lanna kingdom, Thai people, and hill-tribes are highlighted in simple displays with English explanations. It's quite a way from the center, so best combined with a visit to Wat Jed Yod.

Just off the Superhighway, northwest of the Old City, near Wat Jed Yod. www.thailandmuseum.com/thaimuseum_eng/chiangmai/main.htm. 🕾 **05322-1308.** Admission 100B. Wed–Sun 9am–4pm.

The Chiang Mai Zoo ★★ ZOO ☺ One of Chiang Mai's most popular attractions for locals are the pandas, **Chuang Chuang** and **Lin Hui,** and their cub **Lin Ping,** born in 2009, who are the stars of Chiang Mai's extensive zoo. There's an extra admission fee to see the pandas (100B adults, 50B children), as there is for other new attractions—the **snow dome** (adults 150B, children 100B) and the **aquarium** (adults 450B, children 330B). Open-sided buses and elevated trams are on hand to run visitors around—the site is too large to see everything by walking. It makes for a good day out with kids who may be wilting from temple overdose (not to be underestimated).

100 Huai Kaeo Rd. (west of town, on the road to Doi Suthep). ✆ **05335-8116.** Admission 100B adults, 50B children. Daily 8am–5pm.

The Tribal Museum ★ MUSEUM Formerly part of Chiang Mai University's Tribal Research Institute, this small exhibit showcases the cultures and daily lives of the hill-tribe people of Thailand's north. It is recommended as a good introductory course for those who plan to visit many northern villages. Apart from its content, the octagonal building that houses the museum is attractive in itself, set in the middle of a lake in a large park.

In Ratchamankhla Park, on Chotana Rd. ✆ **05321-0872.** Free admission. Mon–Fri 8am–4:30pm.

Cultural Activities
THAI COOKING SCHOOL
If you love Thai food and fancy yourself as a chef, consider taking a cooking class in Chiang Mai. The priciest cookery classes are offered at top resorts like the **Mandarin Oriental Dhara Dhevi** and **Four Seasons** (covered earlier), but very reasonable courses abound in town as well, such as those offered at **Chiang Mai Thai Cookery School ★**, the oldest establishment of its kind in Chiang Mai. They have 1- to 5-day courses, each teaching basic Thai cooking skills, but daily menus feature up to seven new dishes—over a week you can learn a lot. You'll have hands-on training and a lot of fun. Classes start at 10am, last until 4pm, and cost 1,450B for the day. Contact them at their main office at 47/2 Moon Muang Rd., opposite the Thapae Gate (✆ **05320-6388;** www.thaicookeryschool.com).

For foodies who don't want to spend their time learning how to cook Thai food, it's worth joining a **guided food walk** around the Old City organized by the owner of **Elliebum Guesthouse** (114/3-4 Ratchamankha Rd.; ✆ **05381-4723;** www.elliebum.com). Tours, costing 700B per person, last about half a day and take in backstreet temples, markets, food stalls, and noodle shops most tourists never see.

MASSAGE SCHOOL
The **Thai massage schools** in Bangkok and Phuket teach the southern style of Thai massage, which places pressure on muscles to make them tender and relaxed. Northern-style Thai massage is something closer to yoga, where your muscles are stretched and elongated to enhance flexibility and relaxation. There are a number of schools in Chiang Mai, and many are no more than small storefronts where, for very little, you'll get individual instruction of varying quality. It is best to go with a more established school: **International Training Massage (ITM)**, has popular courses (conducted in English) for anyone from first-timers to experts. Each 5-day course is 5,000B. Contact them at 59/9 Chang Puek Rd., Tambon Si Phum (✆ **05321-8632;** fax 05322-4197; www.itmthaimassage.com).

MEDITATION

The **Northern Insight Meditation Center,** at Wat Rampoeng (Kan Klongchonpra-than Rd.), is a well-respected center for learning Vipassana meditation. "Are you ready?" is all they'll ask you upon arrival, because the daily schedule means rising early and spending many hours practicing meditation. The monks, nuns, and lay volunteers who run the center invite only men and women who bring a certain resolve—sufficient to see them through the 26-day course. Volumes have been written about the practice of Vipassana, but the main idea is to develop mindfulness and observe one's body, mind, and emotions—to eventually gain "insight" and to see things as they are, without delusion. Come prepared to "peel the onion" of the ego. Participants are assigned very sparse private rooms and are asked to wear white, loose-fitting clothes (available at the temple store), and basic meals are served at 6 and 10:30am only (there isn't an evening meal). Rules are drawn from the monastic precept and, thus, are rigid. There is no charge for the course, but you will be asked to make a contribution to the temple of whatever amount you see fit. Retreats for experienced meditators are ongoing, but they try to consolidate first-timers' start dates for orientation purposes. The temple also welcomes day visitors, and it might be a good idea for those considering a course to have a look. Located on a rural road south and west of town (past the airport), the temple is best reached by tuk-tuk, *songtaew,* or rented motorbike. For information on Wat Rampoeng, visit www.watrampoeng.net or call ✆ **05327-8620.**

CHIANG MAI ACTIVITIES

Tours, Treks, & Outdoor Adventure

TREKKING TOURS

There are so many tour groups in Chiang Mai that specialize in trekking that it can seem impossible to choose one. Below are some of the better options—and most reputable operators—for each type of trip. Most of the smaller companies have offices along Thapae Road, in guesthouses, and all along the major tourist routes in the city, and they are always happy to talk about what's on offer. Many adventure tours mix mountain biking or motorcycling with tribal village tours. See chapter 12 for more information on the hill-tribes themselves, descriptions of what to expect on tours and how to select a good operator.

For **jungle trekking,** one of the most efficient and reliable organizations is **Contact Travel.** Combining treks and village stays with multisport adventures by jeep, bicycle, and kayak, the folks at Contact can cater a tour to any need and price range. They also offer more traditional itineraries with elephant treks, visits to caves, and relaxing bamboo-raft river trips, and their English-speaking guides are the best in the area. Treks from Chiang Mai stop at Lisu, Lahu, and Karen villages. A 2-day/1-night trip is 4,600B per person if you join their regular tour, or 5,600B per person for a private group trip. A 3-day/2-night trip, which takes you to a greater variety of villages, is 5,500B per person if you join their regular tour or 6,850B per person for a private group. Their office in Chiang Mai is at 54/5 Moo 2, Soi 14, Tambol Tasala (✆ **05385-0160;** fax 05385-0166; www.activethailand.com).

Another company with lots of experience specializing in customized trekking tours (with a focus on bird-watching or rare orchids, for example) is the **Trekking Collective**

(℃ 05320-8340; 3/5 Loy Kroh Soi 1; www.trekkingcollective.com). Expect to pay around 3,000B to 5,500B per person per day, depending on the group size and itinerary.

BOAT TRIPS

Within the city, a **boat trip** along the Mae Ping River is a fun diversion. Head for the boat landing beside Wawee Coffee on the east bank of the Ping River just north of Nawarat Bridge to join a 90-minute tour on a rice barge, starting at 9am, 11am, 1pm, 3pm, or 5pm (minimum 2 people, 250B per person), operated by **Mae Ping River Cruise Co.** (133 Charoen Prathet Rd.; ℃ 05327-4822; www.maepingrivercruise. com). They also run private tours, including hotel pickup, which start at **Wat Chaimongkol,** on Charoen Prathet Road (opposite Alliance Française). These tours follow a similar route (heading about 8km/5 miles north of town before heading back). They last about 2 hours and cost 450B per person with fruit and drinks included. You'll get great views of old teak riverside mansions, behind which rises the tall skyline of this developing burg. While on the outskirts of town, you'll see villages that offer scenes of rural living.

History buffs might prefer to cruise the river in a **scorpion-tailed boat** of the kind that used to be poled up and down the river in the late 19th century when first missionaries and later teak traders turned up to try their luck in this remote outpost. The modern version is propelled by an engine, but visitors can look forward to a running commentary on the historical significance of places passed along the route. Tours are by arrangement and rates depend on numbers of passengers in the group. Call ℃ 05324-5888 or visit www.scorpiontailed.com for more information.

ELEPHANT ENCOUNTERS ★

One of Thailand's greatest treasures, the domesticated Asian elephant, has worked alongside men since the early history of Siam, and these gentle giants are an important symbol of the kingdom. Elephant training culture is strongest in parts of Isan (the northeast) and the far north. In and around Chiang Mai alone, there are a growing number of elephant camps that try to cash in on the popularity of these gentle giants. Not all elephant camps are pleasant: At shoddier camps, creatures are drugged to keep them placid, and conditions are grim, so choose your elephant camp wisely. Fortunately camp owners are finally realizing that visitors would much rather get up close and personal with the elephants than watch them performing in a show. Resort-run elephant camps, such as that shared by the **Anantara** (p. 354) and **Four Seasons' Tented Camp** (p. 355), north of Chiang Rai in the Golden Triangle, are among the most humane. Another popular place nearer Chiang Mai is the **Patara Elephant Camp** (℃ 08199-22551; www.pataraelephantfarm.com), located on the Samoeng Road to the southwest of town, which runs a pricey (5,800B) but enjoyable program called "Elephant owner for a day," in which you spend a day feeding, caring for, and riding your own elephant bareback. If you don't want to spend a fortune to interact with the animals, a visit to the **Thai Elephant Conservation Center** in Lampang (see the "Lampang" section in "Side Trips from Chiang Mai," later in this chapter) is highly recommended. Just north of town in the Mae Rim Valley, a number of camps offer shows lasting an hour or so (with rides to follow) that are fun, especially for kids. Some camps offer a few hours of hill trekking on elephant back with two or three passengers to a *howdah* (elephant seat), followed by ox-cart rides to so-called "primitive" villages and even bamboo rafting back to camp. **Maetaman Elephant Camp** (535 Moo 1, Tambol Rimtai, Mae Rim, Chiang Mai 50180; ℃ 05329-7060;

www.maetamanelephantcamp.com) is one such place. They charge 1,500B per person, which includes the show, an oxcart ride, bamboo rafting, an elephant ride, and a simple meal.

MOUNTAIN BIKING

In the fresh air in the hills outside of town, you can get a slower, closer look at nature, sights, and people. Many small trekking companies and travel agents offer day trips, but I recommend the folks at **Contact Travel** (54/5, Moo 2, soi 14, Tambol Tasala; ℂ 05385-0160) for their 1-day excursion cycling down Doi Suthep mountain, or for multiday adventures in the region. Day trips start at 2,000B.

Other Activities

Chiang Mai has a few noteworthy venues for adventure and extreme sports. This is the only place in Thailand where commercial **Hot-Air Ballooning ★★★** has been approved. **Earth Wind and Fire** (158/60 Moo 6, Cheungdoi, Doi Saket; ℂ 05329-2224; www.wind-and-fire.com) is a highly reputable and certified outfit with professional pilots operating predawn rides between November and March—depending on the weather. Prices are available on request.

Chiang Mai has also succumbed to **bungee jumping;** addicts can head north to the Mae Rim area to try out this sport. First-timers pay 1,500B, but thereafter it's 1,000B. For details, call the **X Center** at ℂ 05329-7700 or visit their website, http://chiangmai-xcentre.com.

One of the most popular activities around Chiang Mai is to spend a day on the ziplines at **Flight of the Gibbon** (ℂ 05301-0660-3; www.treetopasia.com). A day tour includes hotel pickup, a few hours on a zipline canopy adventure, and a 1-hour trek in the rainforest, and costs around 3,000B. Check out their website for information on all tours available.

Rock climbers can get their kicks at the north's main climbing area near Sankampaeng, about 35km (22 miles) east of Chiang Mai. Hundreds of routes have been pegged on the Crazy Horse buttress, and climbs are organized by **The Peak Adventure** (ℂ 05380-0567; www.thepeakadventure.com) for around 1,800B per day. If you're a beginner and you'd like to learn the ropes, so to speak, contact **Chiang Mai Rock Climbing Adventures** (ℂ 05320-7102; www.thailandclimbing.com), which organizes 1- to 3-day introductory courses for 2,795B and 8,995B, respectively.

Microlight flights are possible in Chiang Mai as well. A small but very organized operation, **Chiang Mai Sky Adventures,** flies from a private airstrip north of the city near Doi Saket. A 15-minute flight, more or less a piggyback ride on the pilot's shoulders, costs just 1,900B and takes you on a great loop out over a large dam and reservoir and past a spectacular hilltop temple. They also do flight instruction and certification. Call Mr. Chaimongkol, at ℂ 05325-5500, or visit www.skyadventures.info for info.

Hitting the Links

For Thais and Western retirees, golf is a favored hobby in Chiang Mai, especially in the cooler months. All courses below are open to the public and offer equipment rental. Call ahead to reserve a tee time.

○ **Chiang Mai Green Valley Country Club,** located in Mae Rim, 20 minutes north of town on Route 107, 186 Moo 1, Chotana Rd. (ℂ 05329-8220; fax 05329-7426), is in excellent condition with flat greens and fairways that slope toward the Ping River (greens fees: weekdays 1,800B, weekends 2,400B).

- **Lanna Golf Club,** on Chotana Road, 2km (1¼ miles) north of the Old City (© 05322-1911; fax 05322-1743), is a challenging, wooded 27 holes, and a local favorite with great views of Doi Suthep Mountain (greens fees: weekdays 1,200B, weekends 1,400B).
- **Royal Chiang Mai Golf Club,** a 30-minute drive north of town toward Phrao (© 05384-9301; fax 05384-931008), is a fine 18-hole course designed by Peter Thompson (greens fees: weekdays 1,400B, weekends 1,800B).

Spas & Massage

The spa industry is big business all over Thailand, and Chiang Mai is no exception. There are a few fine, full-service spas in and around town, and treatments come with a price but are worth it. Many hotels offer massage and beauty treatments, but some new "spa" areas are no more than converted guest rooms with subdued lighting and overpriced services. You can pay a fraction of the cost for the same treatment at one of the many small storefront massage parlors in and around any tourist area of the city. *Note:* The offer of an oil massage in a back room often covers for soliciting for sexual services.

Some of the most luxurious spas can be found in luxury resorts near Chiang Mai:

The Dhevi Spa ★★★ at the **Mandarin Oriental Dhara Dhevi** (51/4 Chiang Mai–Sankampaeng Rd., 5km/3 miles east of town; © 05388-8888; www.mandarin oriental.com) is an enormous complex built of teak to mimic a Burmese palace. The treatments and spa environment are extensive, with the unusual addition of a starlit sauna, or *rasoul,* and therapies that reflect local Lanna culture.

Oasis Spa ★ offers a good standard of service at its two locations in town: At 102 Sirimangkalajarn Rd. and 4 Samlan Rd. For reservations, call © 05392-0111 or visit www.chiangmaioasis.com. A luxury campus of private spa villas, Oasis Spa offers a long roster of treatments and provides free pickup and drop-off from hotels in Chiang Mai.

Ban Sabai (219 Moo 9, San Pee Sua; © 05385-4778; http://bansabaivillage. com) is the bridge between the expensive services of a five-star spa and the affordable street-side places. You get the best of both worlds here: A stylish facility and escape for a few hours at affordable rates. The spa is located in a rural setting 5km (3 miles) northeast of town.

Let's Relax, located in Chiang Mai Pavilion (on the second floor above McDonald's, 145/27 Chang Klan Rd.; © 05381-8498), and its sister, **Rarin Jinda,** just north of Nawarat Bridge (14 Charoenrat Rd.; © 05324-7000), have affordable massages and are perfect for a quick rest and recharge after wading through the Night Bazaar area.

SHOPPING

If you plan to shop in Thailand, save your money for Chiang Mai. Quality craft pieces and handmade, traditional items still sell for very little, and large outlets for fine antiques and high-end goods abound in and around the city. Many shoppers pick up an affordable new piece of luggage to tote their finds home and, if you find that huge standing Buddha or oversized Thai divan you've been searching for, all shops can arrange shipping—or look for the **UPS** office at 77 Sri Phum Rd. (© 05341-767-9; Mon–Sat 9am–5:30pm).

What to Buy

Thailand has a rich tradition of handicrafts, developed over centuries of combining local materials, indigenous technology, and skills from Chinese and Indian merchants. Drawing on such ancient technologies and the abundance of hardwoods, precious metals and stones, raw materials (for fabrics and dyes), and bamboo and clay, modern craftsmen have refined traditional techniques and now cater their wares to the modern market. Below is a breakdown of what you might find.

Tribal weaving and craft work is for sale everywhere in the Lanna capital and you can come away with some unique finds. Check out the highly innovative **Sop Moei Arts,** at 150/10 Charoenrat Rd. (www.sopmoeiarts.com), whose homegrown crafts and ceramics help sustain Pwo Karen hill-tribes, or the well-known **Mae Fah Luang** shops (a branch is at Chiang Mai airport), which is part of a different charity assisting hill-tribe communities and abused women.

These days, **hill-tribe embroidery crafts** are employed to produce more modern items; you'll find anything from chic shoulder bags and backpacks to pleated mini-skirts and appliqué shirts. The hill-tribes' **hand-woven textiles** are rich in texture and natural tones, and dyed with natural plant dyes. Cool, ready-made cotton clothing can also be found anywhere for a song.

Some of the city's best **art galleries** and **crafts stores** are all clustered along Charoenrat Road. Pop into **La Luna** at number 190 (© 05330-6678), for contemporary **Asian art, ceramics,** and **art photography,** while a few minutes' walk away toward the Nawarat Bridge at numbers 30 and 36 are **Vila Cini** (© 05324-6246) and **Oriental Style** (no phone); both have racks of stunning **silk** collections and tasteful **souvenirs,** with some truly outstanding **hand-loomed silk furnishings.**

For books, Backstreet Books (© 05387-4143) and Gecko Books (© 05387-4066) are neighbors on Chang Moi Kao, a side street north of eastern Thapae Road just before it meets the city wall. Both have a good selection of new and used books, and do exchanges at the usual rate (two for one, depending on the condition).

Fine **silver** works are synonymous with Chiang Mai, and the silversmiths working around Wua Lai Road occupy Chiang Mai's last remaining artisan's quarter. Early smiths are believed to have emigrated from Myanmar (Burma) with the coming of Kublai Khan, and skills have been passed from generation to generation. While silver is not a local resource, early raw materials were acquired from coins brought by traders. Traditional bowls feature intricate raised (*repoussé*) floral designs—the deeper the imprint, the higher quality the silver (some up to 92.5%). Some hill-tribe groups are known for their fine **silver jewelry**—necklaces, bangles, and earrings—in unusual traditional ethnic designs or more ordinary Western styles. For all hill-tribe handicrafts, the best place to shop is at the Night Bazaar.

Modern **jewelry** can be found in strikingly original designs at **Nova Collection,** 179 Tha Pae Rd. (© 05327-3058; www.nova-collection.com), while farther up the road, **Shiraz Jewelry** (170 Tha Pae Rd.; © 05325-2382) offers more traditional designs. For the biggest selection head for **Gems Gallery** at 80/1 Moo 3 (© 05333-9307; www.gems-gallery.com) on the Sankampaeng Road, to the east of town.

The lords of Lanna commissioned carvers to produce wood furnishings for use in palaces, thrones, temple doors and adornments, carriages, pavilions, *howdahs* (seats for riding elephants), and royal barges. The excellent quality of hardwoods in Thailand's forests allowed these items to be adorned with grand and intricate woodcarvings. The skills survived, and talented craftspeople still produce furniture, boxes, and all varieties of gift items imaginable. **Woodcarving** today is perhaps more influenced by foreign preferences, and most pieces are mass-produced.

Lacquer skills came from China with early migrants. Sap is applied in layers to bamboo items and can be carved, colored, and sometimes inlaied with mother-of-pearl for a very elegant finished product. Today it is acknowledged as a traditional Chiang Mai craft, having been perfected over centuries by the Tai Khoen people who live in communities outside the city. **Lacquerware** vases, boxes, bangles, and traditional items are lightweight gifts, practical for carrying home. Larger tiered boxes and furnishings can be shipped.

Celadon pottery is elegantly simple in tones of the palest gray-greens. The distinctive color of the glaze comes from a mixture of local clay and wood ash. Chiang Mai has some of the largest and best celadon factories in the country. The best places to purchase celadon are at the beautiful Lanna-style compound of Baan Celadon (www.baanceladon.com), 10km (6¼ miles) out of town, or at the large factory outlets.

Authentic antiques, except for furniture, are virtually extinct in the tourist areas of Chiang Mai. Most furniture is from China. Some shops may offer certificates of authenticity, but as anywhere, the rule is "buyer beware." If you do get your hands on the genuine article, you may have a problem getting it home (see "Customs," in chapter 2).

Markets

The **Night Bazaar** ★ has traditionally been regarded as the city's premier shopping location, and it's still a good place to find a wide range of souvenirs, but with the success of the Saturday and Sunday **Walking Streets** in recent years, the Night Bazaar has waned in popularity and many vendors are moving out. Located on Chang Klan Road, between Thapae and Sri Dornchai roads, the market starts around 6pm each night and winds up at about 11pm. The actual Night Bazaar is a modern three-story building, but the street-side stalls extend south for several blocks. Inside the Night Bazaar building, there are mass-manufactured Chinese goods such as low-cost fashions and souvenirs. More interesting are the tribal bric-a-brac stalls or items sold by wandering vendors dressed in hill-tribe get-up.

The **Anusarn Night Market,** which runs between Chang Klan and Charoen Prathet roads south of Suriwongse Road, features more hill-tribe goods in authentic traditional styles as well as several dining options. It's easy to combine a walk round here with a visit to the Night Bazaar.

The **Warorot Market,** on Chang Moi and Wichayanon roads, opens every morning at 7am and stays open until 6pm. This central indoor market is geared to locals rather than tourists and is the city's largest market. Produce, colorful fruits, spices, and food products jam the ground floor. On the second floor, things are calmer, with dozens of vendors selling cheap cotton sportswear, Thai-made shoes, and some hill-tribe handicrafts and garments: It's fun and inexpensive.

The **Walking Streets** take place on Saturday along Wualai Road (directly south of the Old City) and on Sunday along Ratchadamnoen Road (between Tha Pae Gate and Wat Phra Singh, in the Old City); both streets are closed to traffic from midday to midnight on the appointed day, rain or shine. The **Sunday market** ★★ is a bit bigger and is a great place to mingle with locals and other tourists (as long as you don't mind crowds—it can get packed sometimes) as well as pick up a few cheap but unique gifts.

City Center & Old Town

Small shops and boutiques line the tourist streets such as Tha Pae and Loy Kroh and there are many local designer boutiques on Nimmanhaemin Road (see "West Side of the Old City," below). **Ginger ★★** (199 Moon Muang Rd. Soi 7; ✆ **05341-9014** and 6/21 Nimmanheimin Rd., ✆ **05321-5635**) is a Thai-Danish affair selling gorgeous contemporary day wear (large European sizes are sadly limited), fun accessories, and fabulous twinkly costume jewelry. **Nova Collection** (see above) carries a unique line of decorative jewelry in contemporary styles with Asian influences. They make custom pieces and even offer courses in metalwork and jewelry making. **Princess Jewelry** (147/8 Chang Klan Rd., near the Night Bazaar; ✆ **05327-3648**) offers customized and ready-made jewelry, and good personalized service. **Mengrai Kilns ★** (79/2 Arak Rd., Soi Samlarn 6; ✆ **05327-2063;** www.mengraikilns.com) is in the southwest corner of the old city and specializes in fine celadon and decorative items. There are lots of silk dealers and tailors in and around town of varying quality. Try **City Silk** (336 Thapae Rd., one block east of the gate; ✆ **05323-4388**) among the many for its good selection and affordable tailoring.

West Side of the Old City

On the lanes off **Nimmanhaemin Road ★★** and along the street itself are boutiques selling crafts and designer wear. These make for good one-stop shopping, if your time is short. Soi 1 is especially good for textiles, homewares, and candles. Look for **Gong Dee Gallery** (✆ **05322-5032;** www.gongdeegallery.com), which has an extensive collection of gifts and original artwork. **Wit's Collection ★** (✆ **05321-7544**) is a truly sublime, all-white boutique featuring a treasure-trove of fantastic contemporary furniture, ceramics, and homewares. Opposite Soi 1, at 6/23–24 Nimmanhaemin Rd., **Gerard Collection ★★** (✆ **05322-0604;** www.gerardcollection. com) features beautifully made bamboo furniture.

Wulai Road

Chiang Mai's silver industry is just south of Chiang Mai Gate. **Siam Silverware** (5 Wua Lai Rd., Soi 3; ✆ **05327-4736**) tops the list of many offering fine crafted jewelry and silver work.

Sankampaeng Road

Shopaholics will be thrilled by the many handicraft outlets along the Chiang Mai–Sankampaeng Road (Rte. 1006, aka the Handicraft Hwy.), particularly since you can wander around the workshops, watch the craftsmen at work, and take some interesting photos of the processes, too. There are several shops, showrooms, and factories extending along a 9km (5⅔-mile) strip here. Talk to any concierge or travel agent about a full- or half-day shopping tour. *Important:* Do not arrange a day of shopping with a tuk-tuk or taxi driver, as they will collect a commission and drive up the price of your purchases.

The many shops along Sankampaeng feature anything from lacquerware to ready-made clothes, and from silver to celadon pottery. Among the many, try **Laitong Lacquerware** (140/1 Moo 3, Chiang Mai–Sankampaeng Rd.; ✆ **05333-8237;** www.thailacquerware.com), which carries a host of fine lacquer gifts (among other items). Some of the smaller items, such as jewelry boxes, can be quite lightweight, so you won't have to lug tons home with you. *Saa* (mulberry bark) paper cards with pressed flowers, stationery, notebooks, and gifts are not only top quality, but perfect for traveling light. There are plenty of outlets along the Handicraft Highway, with a particular concentration in Bor Sang village, also known as the **Umbrella village** since most people who live here are involved in the production of umbrellas made with *sao* paper.

To view a large selection of olive-green celadon, for which North Thailand is renowned, in traditional Thai as well as modern designs, head for **Baan Celadon,** which has an attractive rustic compound at 7 Moo 3, Chiang Mai–Sankampaeng Road. (© **05333-8288;** www.baanceladon.com). Smooth and lustrous vases, jars, bowls, and decorative objects spring to life, and even the salt and pepper shakers catch the eye.

Jolie Femme Thai Silk, 8/3 Sankampaeng Rd. (© **05311-6777;** www.jolie femme.com), weaves traditional silks in rich colors and they style much of their stock into modern ready-to-wear creations. But for truly exquisite woven silk, head to **Vila Cini's ★★** branch at Mandarin Oriental Dhara Dhevi (on Sankampaeng Rd.); a bigger selection is available at the Charoenraj Road shop (see above). Though focusing less on fashions and more on silk furnishings, this homegrown silk merchant outdoes even Jim Thompson's (p. 109) for creativity and sumptuously stylish designs, all following traditional Lanna hues and inspiration.

Nearby Villages

Many of the handicrafts you'll find in town—and out at Sankampaeng Road—are the fine work of local villagers around Chiang Mai. They welcome visitors to their villages to see their traditional craft techniques that have been handed down through generations. Purchase these items directly from the source, and you might save, though you'll need a guide to find some of them as they're off the beaten track.

East of Chiang Mai, **Sri-pun-krua** (near the railway station) specializes in bamboo products and lacquerware. On the Sankampaeng Road, **Bor Sang** (10km/6 miles outside the city) is a nationally renowned center for painted paper umbrellas and fans made of *saa* paper. Just west of Bor Sang, the village of **Ton Pao** (about 8km/5 miles outside the city) also produces *saa* paper products. Just to the south, **Pa Bong** (about 6km/3¼ miles down Superhighway 11) manufactures furnishings and household items from bamboo.

South of the city, **Muang Kung** (along Hwy. 108) is a center for clay pottery, while **Ban Tawai** (14km/8⅔ miles south near Hang Dong) is the north's capital for woodcarvings and wooden furniture.

ENTERTAINMENT & NIGHTLIFE

Pick up a copy of any free magazine—such as *Welcome to Chiang Mai & Chiang Rai, Guidelines,* or *Citylife*—at your hotel or in restaurants, for listings of special events and concerts in town during your stay. Most folks will spend at least one evening at the Night Bazaar (see above). For an impromptu bar scene, you can duck into one of the back alleys behind the Night Bazaar mall that are lined with tiny bars.

If you get tired and hungry during shopping or barhopping at the Night Bazaar, you could stop at **Kalare Food & Shopping Center,** 89/2 Chang Klan Rd., opposite the main Night Bazaar building (© **05327-2067**). Free nightly traditional Thai folk dance and musical performances, beginning around 8:30pm, grace an informal beer garden, where shoppers can stop for a drink or pick up inexpensive Chinese, Thai, and Indian food from the stalls there.

For a more studied **cultural performance,** the **Old Chiang Mai Cultural Center ★**, 185/3 Wua Lai Rd. (✆ **05320-2993;** www.oldchiangmai.com), stages a good show starting at 8pm every night for 420B, which includes dinner. Live music accompanies male and female dancers who perform traditional dances, such as a rice-winnowing dance and a sword dance, while dressed in lavish costumes. A dinner is served on a *khan toke* (low table on the floor) and, despite the crowds, the wait staff is attentive. Yes, it is touristy—busloads find their way here—but the quality of the food and entertainment are worth it. Call ahead and they'll plan transportation from your hotel.

For **live music,** one of the best hunting grounds is along the east bank of the River Ping, north of the Nawarat Bridge. Here you'll find three of the city's most popular bar/restaurants that are regularly packed with a mix of locals and tourists. **Good View** (13 Charoenrat Rd.; ✆ **05324-1866**) and **The Riverside ★★** (9/11 Charoenrat Rd.; ✆ **05324-3239**) both feature live music after 7pm with the beat getting progressively faster as the evening wears on. Blues and reggae fans should head straight for **Le Brasserie ★★** (37 Charoenrat Rd.; ✆ **05324-1665**), where resident guitarist Took gets everyone in the groove from around 10pm.

In the Old City just north of Tha Pae Gate, there are lots of bars and restaurants along Ratwithi Road, among which the **UN-Irish Pub** (✆ **05321-4554**) has regular events such as quiz nights and live music nights, and serves imported beers and shows sports on TV, too. Jazz fans should head to the **North Gate Jazz Co-op ★** (Sri Phum Rd.; no phone), just a few steps east of Chang Puak Gate inside the north moat of the Old City, to listen to local talent or to join in the Tuesday jam sessions.

The bars at the western end of Loy Kroh Road constitute the town's red-light district, with many hostess bars doubling up as brothels or pickup joints. Several hotels host discos, such as **Horizon** in the basement of the Duangtawan Hotel on Loy Kroh Road near the Night Bazaar, though they tend to attract more Thais than foreigners. If you're curious to see how the students from Chiang Mai University spend their evenings, head along to **Warm Up** (40 Nimmanheimin Rd. ✆ **05340-0676**), where various DJs compete for the attentions of the crowds. When everywhere else is closed at around 1am, the place to head for is **Spice** (✆ **05387-4011**), which is open from 9pm till dawn, at 311 Chang Moi Rd. near the junction with Chaiyaphum Road.

SIDE TRIPS FROM CHIANG MAI

The most popular out-of-town trip is to Wat Phra That Doi Suthep, Chiang Mai's famed mountain and temple; however, don't miss the charming allure of nearby Lampang or Lamphun, both sleepy rural towns with old teak homes and some exquisite Lanna temples—you can pop into the Elephant Training Camp in Lampang en route.

Wat Phra That Doi Suthep ★★★

The jewel of Chiang Mai, Wat Phra That Doi Suthep, glistens in the sun near the summit of the mountain known as Doi Suthep. One of four royal *wats* in the north, at 1,300m (4,265 ft.), it occupies an extraordinary site with a cool refreshing climate, expansive views over the city and the mountain's densely forested slopes, which form part of the Doi Suthep–Doi Pui National Park.

In the 14th century, during the installation of a relic of the Buddha in Wat Suan Dok (in the Old City), the holy object split in two, with one part equaling the original size. A new *wat* was needed to honor the miracle. King Ku Na placed the new relic on a sacred white elephant and let it wander freely through the hills. The elephant climbed to the top of Doi Suthep, trumpeted three times, made three counterclockwise circles, and knelt down, choosing the site for Wat Phra That Doi Suthep.

The original *chedi* was built to a height of 8m (26 ft.). Subsequent kings contributed to it, first by doubling the size and then by adding layers of gold and other ornamentation to the exterior; it now measures 16m (52 ft.) tall. The slender, gleaming *chedi* and the gilded-copper decorative umbrellas around it provide one of the most iconic images of North Thailand.

Other structures were raised to bring greater honor to the Buddha and various patrons. The most remarkable is the steep *naga* (sacred riverine snake) staircase, added in 1557, leading up to the *wat*—one of the most dramatic approaches to a temple in all of Thailand. To shorten the 5-hour climb from the base of the mountain, the winding road was constructed in 1935 by thousands of volunteers under the direction of a local monk.

Visitors with exposed legs are offered a sarong at the entrance. Most Thai visitors come to make an offering—usually flowers, candles, incense, and small squares of gold leaf that are applied to a favored Buddha or to the exterior of a *chedi*—and to be blessed. Believers kneel down and touch their foreheads to the ground three times in worship. Some shake prayer sticks to learn their fortune.

Wat Phra That Doi Suthep (admission 30B) is open daily 7am to 5pm; come early or late to avoid the crowds. To get here, take a *songtaew* from in front of the zoo, at the western end of Huai Kaeo Road. The ride can get cool, so bring a sweater or jacket in the cool season. If you'd rather not climb the 306 steps, a special part of the experience, there's a funicular railway to the top for 20B. You can simplify matters by booking a half-day trip though any tour agency for around 600B, including a stop at Phuping Palace (when it's open).

Phuping Palace is the summer residence of Thailand's royal family, which is 4km (2½ miles) beyond Doi Suthep, 22km (14 miles) west of the Old City off Route 1004. When the royal family isn't present (usually January to March; ask hotel staff to check for you), visitors are allowed to enter and stroll through its beautiful gardens. The hours are Friday to Sunday 8:30–11:30am and 1–4pm, and admission is 50B. You really have to dress conservatively for this one; military guards at the gate act like the fashion police.

Lamphun ★★

The oldest continuously inhabited city in Thailand, just 26km (16 miles) south of Chiang Mai, Lamphun was founded in A.D. 663 by the Mon Queen Chamadevi as the capital of Nakhon Hariphunchai. Throughout its long history, the Hariphunchai Kingdom, an offspring of the Mon Empire, was fought over and often conquered; yet it remained one of the powers of the north until King Mengrai established his capital in neighboring Chiang Mai. Like Chiang Mai, it is surrounded by crumbling walls and a moat.

The best way to get there is by car, taking the old highway, Route 106, south to town. Superhighway 11 runs parallel and east of it, but you'll miss the tall *yang* (rubber) trees, which shade the old highway until Sarapi, and the bushy yellow-flowered *khilik* (cassia) trees. Buses to Lamphun and Pasang leave from the **Chang Puak Bus**

Station (© 05321-1586), while *songtaews* leave regularly from just south of the TAT office on the Chiang Mai–Lamphun Road.

The town is legendary for its beautiful women. There are some historical *wats*, including excellent Dvaravati-style *chedis*, and a fine museum. Longan (*lamyai*), a native fruit that resembles clusters of fuzzy brown grapes—which peel easily to yield luscious, crisp white flesh—are popular here. The trees can be recognized by their narrow, crooked trunks and long, droopy oval leaves. On the second weekend in August, Lamphun goes wild with its **Longan Festival,** with a parade of floats decorated only in longans and a beauty contest to select that year's Miss Longan. Lamphun and Pasang (to the south) are also popular with shoppers for their excellent cotton and silk weaving.

The highlight of Lamphun is **Wat Phra That Hariphunchai ★★**, one of the most striking temples in all of Thailand. (Wat Phra That Doi Suthep was modeled after it.) The central *chedi*, in Chiang Saen style and said to house a hair of the Buddha, is more than 45m (148 ft.) high and dates from the 9th century, when it was built over a royal structure. The nine-tiered umbrella at the top contains 6,498.75g (229 oz) of gold, and the *chedi's* exterior is of bronze. Also of interest in the temple complex are an immense bronze gong (reputedly the largest in the world), and several *viharn* (rebuilt in the 19th and 20th c.) containing Buddha images. According to legend, the Buddha visited a hill about 16km (10 miles) southeast of town, where he left his footprint; the site is marked by Wat Phra Phuttabat Tak Pha. During the full-moon day in May, there's a ritual bathing ceremony for the Phra That.

The **Hariphunchai National Museum ★**, Amphur Muang (© 05351-1186; www.thailandmuseum.com/thaimuseum_eng/haribhunchai/main.htm), is across the street from Wat Phra That Hariphunchai's back entrance. It is worth a visit to see the many bronze and stucco religious works from the *wat*. The museum also contains a fine collection of Dvaravati- and Lanna-style votive and architectural objects. It's open Wednesday to Sunday from 9am to 4pm; admission is 100B.

Wat Chamadevi (Wat Kukut) ★ is probably one of the most unique temple complexes in the country, located less than 1km (⅔ mile) northwest of the city center. The highlights here are the superb examples of late Dvaravati-style (pyramid) *chedis*, known as Suwan Chang Kot and Ratana, built in the 8th and 10th centuries, respectively, and thought to be modeled on those in Sri Lanka's ancient capital Polonnaruwa. The larger one is remarkable for the 60 standing Buddhas that adorn its niches. The original temple was built by Khmer artisans for King Mahantayot around A.D. 755. The relics of his mother, Queen Chamadevi, are housed inside, but the gold-covered pagoda was stolen, earning this site its nickname Kukut (topless).

Lampang ★

The sprawling town of Lampang (originally called Khelang Nakhon) was once famous for its exclusive reliance on the horse and carriage for transportation, even after the "horseless carriage" came into fashion. These often florally adorned buggies can still be rented near the center of town next to the City Hall or arranged through any hotel for about 300B per hour; it's an enchanting mode of transport and a pleasant (and more eco-friendly) way to see some of the city's sights.

Lampang is graced with some of the finest Burmese temples in Thailand and supports the celebrated Thai Elephant Conservation Center (see below). Because of the region's fine kilns, there are dozens of ceramics factories producing new and reproduction "antique" pottery. For visitor information, contact the **Lampang Tourist**

Office, Thakhrao Noi Road, near the central clock tower (© **05423-7229;** Mon–Fri 8am–4:30pm, Sat–Sun 10am–4pm). The easiest way to reach Lampang from Chiang Mai is by car, taking Route no. 11 southeast for about 100km (62 miles). Buses to Lampang leave throughout the day from **Chiang Mai's Arcade Bus Terminal** (© **05324-2664**). The 1½-hour trip costs about 67B.

For an overnight sojourn, the atmospheric **Riverside Guest House** (286 Talat Kao Rd.; © **05422-7005;** www.theriverside-lampang.com) is the best place to lay your head; it's a lovingly maintained old wooden house and some rooms have great river views. Rates range from 300B for a small fan room to 1,800B for a luxurious suite. The best hotel as such in town is **Wienglakor Hotel** (138/38 Phaholyothin Rd.; © **05422-4470;** www.wienglakor.com), with a few stylish Thai touches in the rooms, which start at 1,400B.

Lampang's *wats* are best toured by car or horse and carriage, as they are scattered around. **Wat Phra Kaew Don Tao ★** is 1km (⅔ miles) to the northeast of the town center on the other side of the Wang River. For 32 years, this highly revered 18th-century Burmese temple housed the Emerald Buddha that's now in Bangkok's Wat Phra Kaew. Legend has it that one day the prince of Chiang Mai decided to move the Emerald Buddha from Chiang Rai to Chiang Mai. His attendants traveled there with a royal elephant to transport the sacred icon. But when the elephant got to this spot, it refused to go on to Chiang Mai with its burden, and so a *wat* was built here to house the image. There's an impressive carved wooden chapel and Buddha: A 49-m (161-ft) high pagoda houses a strand of the Buddha's hair. Poke around in the dusty **Laan Thai Museum** toward the back of the compound; it contains some fine woodwork and an old *sarn phra phum* (Spirit House).

Wat Phra That Lampang Luang ★★★ is in Koh Kha, 18km (11 miles) southwest of the center of Lampang. This impressive temple complex is considered one of the finest examples of northern Thai architecture. If you mount the main steps, you'll see a site map, a distinguished *viharn* (inspired by Wat Phra That Hariphunchai in Lamphun), and, behind it to the west, a *chedi* with a fine seated Buddha. Go back to the parking area and pass the huge Bodhi tree—whose stems are supported by dozens of bamboo poles and ribbons—and you'll see signs for the Emerald Buddha House. The small Phra Kaew Don Tao image wears a gold necklace and stands on a gold base; it's locked behind two separate sets of gates and is difficult to see.

The **Thai Elephant Conservation Center ★★★** (on the Lampang Hwy.; © **05482-9333;** www.thailandelephant.org) is 37km (23 miles) west of Lampang. They have elephant shows at 10am, 11am, and 1:30pm, and the cost is 170B for adults, 120B for children. The center is open to visitors from 8:30am to 3:30pm and elephant rides cost 1,000B per hour. This place has nothing like the pony-ride atmosphere of most elephant camps; instead, the focus is on the animals, and the country's only elephant hospital is on-site, caring for abused and injured elephants. They also offer mahout training courses, but these need to be booked in advance through the website. This was the first elephant camp to include a musical performance in its elephant show, and its accomplished Elephant Orchestra is still much more impressive than any of its imitators.

Doi Inthanon National Park ★★★

The turnoff for Thailand's tallest mountain, **Doi Inthanon**—2,565m (8,415 ft.)—is 55km (34 miles) southwest of Chiang Mai along H108. It crowns a 482-sq.-km (186-sq.-mile) national park filled with impressive waterfalls and wild orchids. A good, sealed road climbs 48km (30 miles) to the summit. At the base of the climb is the 30-m (98-ft.) high **Mae Klang Falls,** a popular picnic spot with food stands. The road to the top of the mountain features fine views and three more falls, **Wachirathan, Sirithan,** and **Siriphum,** all worth exploring. At the end of the park road, you are at the highest point in Thailand. There is a small visitor's center and a short trail into a thick wooded area of mossy overhanging trees called the **Ang Khang Nature Trail,** which makes for a short but picturesque walk.

Admission to **Doi Inthanon National Park** is 200B (children 100B). It's open daily from sunrise to sunset. Tents and bungalows are available to rent—contact the **Department of National Parks** at ✆ **02561-0777** or visit www.dnp.go.th.

The area is a popular day-trip destination for residents of Chiang Mai, particularly in the cool season when occasionally frost (an alien concept in the tropics) can be seen near the summit. Day trips organized by Chiang Mai tour companies will cost around 1,000B, including lunch and a few other stops for sightseeing. You can always use your own rented car, too—as long as you are confident driving on switchbacks and steep slopes; take Route 108 south through San Pa Tong, then turn right after 55km (34 miles), and follow the signs to the top of the mountain. You can take a 13-km (8-mile) side trip to Lamphun on Route 1015.

Mae Sa Valley ★

The pleasant Mae Sa Valley area is about 20km (12 miles) northwest of Chiang Mai. A rash of condo construction and the sprouting of roadside billboards all indicate that Mae Sa Valley is being developed as a rural tourist resort, but it still has an unhurried feel. Attractions include elephant shows (with rides), a tiger camp, a snake show, a monkey show, bungee jumping, the **Queen Sirikit Botanic Gardens** (✆ **05384-1000;** www.qsbg.org; daily 8:30am–4:30pm; admission 40B adult, 10B child, 100B car), and orchid nurseries. Some of these attractions are packaged by Chiang Mai tour operators as a half-day trip costing about 700B.

Chiang Dao ★★

The town of Chiang Dao, 72km (45 miles) north of Chiang Mai, and its environs offer several small resort hotels and a few fun activities, but if you don't have a car, the easiest way to sightsee is by joining a day trip organized by Chiang Mai operators, which costs about 1,500B per person (half-day trips are also offered). The **Elephant Training Center Chiang Dao** (www.chiangdaoelephantcamp.com; ✆ **05329-8553**), close to kilometer 56, on H107 from Chiang Mai, is rather touristy and not as good as that in Lampang (p. 321), but it's still a nice treat for kids. The adventure begins as you cross a swaying rope bridge on the way to the camp. After the elephants bathe in the river (showering themselves and their mahouts), they demonstrate log hauling and log rolling. After the show, you can climb into a *howdah* and take a safari across the Ping River to a Lisu village.

Sixteen kilometers (10 miles) north of the Elephant Training Center is the **Chiang Dao Cave (Wat Tham Chiang Dao),** one of the area's more fascinating sites. Two caverns are illuminated by electric lights, and you can see a number of Buddha statues, including a 4-m (13-ft.) long reclining one. The row of five seated Buddhas in the first cavern is particularly impressive. The cave and two connected caverns extend over 10km (6¼ miles) into the mountain, but you'll have to hire a local guide with a lantern to explore the unlit areas. It is open daily from 8:30am to 4:30pm, and a stop here can be included with any itinerary that brings you to the elephant camp.

The peak of Chiang Dao, called **Doi Luang** (2,240m/7349 ft.), is Thailand's second-highest mountain, and also its most dramatic, with sheer sides rearing up from the rice paddies. The summit can be reached by an arduous but scenic day-long trek that is one of North Thailand's top experiences, best done between November and February. Local guesthouses such as **Chiang Dao Nest** (*C* **05345-6242;** www. chiangdao.com) arrange guides and put you up before and after the trek.

EXPLORING THE NORTHERN HILLS

12

B eyond Chiang Mai and its satellite cities, travelers enter a lush, mountainous region replete with opportunities for adventure. Rugged landscape, proximity to Myanmar (Burma) and Laos, and the diverse ethnic hill-tribe groups living here distinguish northern Thailand from the rest of the country.

Connected by highways that undulate through forested mountains, descend into picturesque valleys, and pass through quaint farming villages, the country's northern points are best explored overland, with a rented vehicle (motorbike or car, with or without driver). There are lookout viewpoints along the way, and plenty of places to stop and eat, refuel, relax, and stay. Travelers can choose from a number of routes: The classic route is the rugged area northwest of Chiang Mai, encircled by the Mae Hong Son Loop; from Chiang Mai to Chiang Rai, and north from Chiang Rai to the Myanmar/Laos/Thai border at the Golden Triangle. Any trip in the region means mountain scenery and the opportunity to visit with unique ethnic groups; trekking by foot, jeep, elephant back, or boat through the forested hill-tribe homelands is very popular.

THE LAND & ITS PEOPLE
The Region in Brief

Northern Thailand is composed of 17 provinces and borders Myanmar (Burma) to the northwest and Laos to the northeast. This verdant, mountainous terrain, which includes Thailand's largest mountain, 2,565-m (8,415-ft.) Doi Inthanon, supports nomadic farming, teak plantations on the hillsides, and systematic agriculture in the valleys. The hill-tribes' traditional poppy crops have largely been replaced with rice, coffee, tea, soybeans, corn, and sugar cane. In the fertile Chiang Mai valley, lowland farmers also cultivate seasonal fruits such as strawberries, longan (*lamyai*), mandarin oranges, mango, and melon. The lush fields and winding rivers make sightseeing—particularly in the cool season—a visual treat. Textiles, mining, handicrafts, and tourism-related industries also contribute to the growing northern economy.

A Look at the Region's Past

In the late 13th century, King Mengrai united several Tai tribes that had migrated from southern China and built the first capital of the Lanna kingdom in Chiang Rai. Mengrai, whose rule was characterized by strategic alliances, was threatened by Mongol emperor Kublai Khan and his incursion into Myanmar (Burma). He quickly forged ties with the powerful kingdom of Sukhothai in the south. The Lanna king vanquished the vestiges of the Mon Empire in Lamphun and, in 1296, moved his new capital south to what is now Chiang Mai. There is a shrine to King Mengrai, around the corner from Chiang Mai's Wat Phan Tao, in the geographical heart of the Old City, where, it is said, he was struck by lightning and killed in 1317.

For the next century, Chiang Mai prospered and the Lanna kingdom grew, absorbing most of what now comprises the Northern provinces. In cahoots, Chiang Mai and Sukhothai were able to resist significant attacks from Khmer and Mon neighbors. After the Lanna dynasty absorbed Sukhothai, forces from Ayutthaya tried repeatedly to take Chiang Mai, but the city refused to yield. Instead, Chiang Mai grew in strength and prospered until the mid-16th century, when it eventually fell to the Burmese in 1558.

For the next 2 centuries, the Lanna kingdom was a Burmese vassal—Burmese culture is still in evidence today, especially with regard to clothing and cuisine. After Lampang's Lord, or "Chao" Kavila, recaptured Chiang Mai from the Burmese in 1775, the city was so weakened that Kavila moved its surviving citizens to nearby Lampang. For 2 decades, Chiang Mai was akin to a ghost town. Though the city was still nominally under the control of local lords, their power continued to decline, and, in 1932, Chiang Mai was formally incorporated into the modern Thai nation.

A Portrait of the Hill-Tribe People

The north is a tapestry of the divergent customs and cultures of the many tribes that migrated from China or Tibet to Myanmar (Burma), Laos, and Vietnam and ultimately settled in Thailand's Northern provinces such as Chiang Rai, Chiang Mai, Mae Hong Son, Phayao, and Nan. The six main tribes are the Karen, Akha (also known as the E-Kaw), Lahu (Mussur), Lisu (Lisaw), Hmong (Meo), and Mien (Yao), each with subgroups that are linked by history, lineage, language, costume, social organization, and religion.

Hill-tribes in northern Thailand are subdivided into Sino-Tibetan speakers (Hmong, Mien) and Tibeto-Burman speakers (Lahu, Akha, Lisu, and Karen), though most now speak some Thai.

In addition, tribes are divided geographically into lowland, or valley, dwellers, that grow cyclical crops such as rice or corn, and high-altitude dwellers, that traditionally grew opium poppies. The so-called indigenous tribes, who have occupied the same areas for hundreds of years, are those that tend to inhabit the lower valleys in organized villages of split-log huts. The nomadic groups generally live above 1,000m (3,280 ft.) in easy-to-assemble bamboo and thatch housing, ready to resettle when required.

Highland minorities believe in spirits, and it is the role of the village shaman, or spiritual leader, to understand harbingers and prescribe appeasing rites.

KAREN   An estimated 400,000 Karen make up the largest tribal group in Thailand, accounting for more than half of all tribal people in the country. In nearby Myanmar

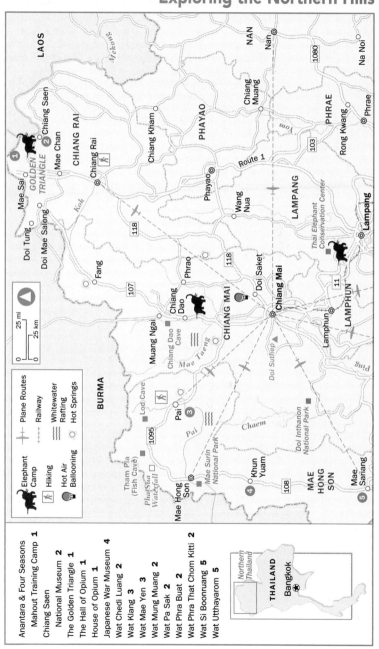

Exploring the Northern Hills

Anantara & Four Seasons
Mahout Training Camp **1**
Chiang Saen
    National Museum **2**
The Golden Triangle **1**
The Hall of Opium **1**
House of Opium **1**
Japanese War Museum **4**
Wat Chedi Luang **2**
Wat Klang **3**
Wat Mae Yen **3**
Wat Mung Muang **2**
Wat Pa Sak **2**
Wat Phra Buat **2**
Wat Phra That Chom Kitti **2**
Wat Si Boonruang **5**
Wat Utthayarom **5**

LAOS

BURMA

THAILAND
Bangkok

Northern
Thailand

Elephant Camp
Hiking
Hot Air Ballooning
Plane Routes
Railway
Whitewater Rafting
○ **Hot Springs**

0   25 mi
0   25 km

(Burma), it is estimated that there are more than four million people of Karen descent (who are practicing Buddhists and Christians). For years, the Burmese government has been suppressing Karen independence fighters who want an autonomous homeland. Many Burmese Karen have sought refuge in Thailand, ranging from Chiang Rai to as far south as Kanchanaburi. Practicing either Buddhism or an amalgamation of Christianity absorbed from missionaries and ancient animism, Karen can be easily identified by their method of greeting one another: An exaggerated, hearty handshake.

The Karen is among the most assimilated of Thailand's hill-tribes, making it difficult to identify them by any outward appearance. However, the most traditional tribespeople wear silver armbands and don a beaded sash and headband, while unmarried women wear white shift dresses.

HMONG (MEO)   The Hmong are a nomadic tribe scattered throughout Southeast Asia and China. About 160,000 Hmong live in Thailand, with the greatest number residing in Chiang Mai, Chiang Rai, Nan, Phetchabun, and Phrae provinces; there are approximately four million Hmong living in China. Within Thailand, there are several subgroups; the Hmong Daw (White Hmong) and the Hmong Njua (Blue Hmong) are the main divisions. The Hmong Gua Mba (Armband Hmong) is a subdivision of the Hmong Daw.

Hmong live in the highlands, cultivating corn, rice, and soybeans, which are grown as subsistence crops. Their wealth is displayed in a vast array of silver jewelry. Women are easily recognized by the way they pile their hair into an enormous bun on top of their heads and by their elaborately embroidered, pleated skirts. The Hmong are also excellent animal breeders, and their ponies are especially prized.

Hmong are pantheistic and rely on shamans to perform spiritual rites. Hmong place particular emphasis on the use of doors: Doors for entering and exiting the human world, doors to houses, doors to let in good fortune and to block bad spirits, and doors to the afterlife. The Hmong also worship their ancestors—a reverberation of their Chinese past. Because they're skilled entrepreneurs, Hmong are increasingly moving down from the highlands to ply trades in the lowlands.

LAHU (MUSSUR)   The Lahu people (pop. around 100,000) are composed of two main bands: The Lahu Na (Black Lahu) and the Lahu Shi (Yellow Lahu), with a much smaller number of Lahu Hpu (White Lahu), La Ba, and Abele. Most Lahu villages are situated above 1,000m (3,280 ft.), in the mountains around Chiang Mai, Chiang Rai, Mae Hong Son, Tak, and Kamphaeng Phet, where "dry soil" rice, corn, and other cash crops are grown.

The lingua franca in the hills is Thai, but many of the other groups can speak a little Lahu. The Lahu are skilled musicians, and their bamboo and gourd flutes feature prominently in their compositions—flutes are often used by young men to woo the woman of their choice.

Originally animists, the Lahu adopted the worship of a deity called G'ui sha (possibly Tibetan in origin), borrowed the practice of merit-making from Buddhism (Indian or Chinese), and ultimately incorporated Christian (British/Burmese) theology into their belief system. G'ui sha is the Supreme Being who created the universe and rules over all spirits. Spirits inhabit animate and inanimate objects, making them capable of benevolence or evil, with the soul functioning as the spiritual force within people. In addition, they practice a kind of Lahu voodoo, as well as following a messianic tradition. The Lahu warmly welcome foreign visitors.

YAO (MIEN)   There are now estimated to be 50,000 Yao living in Thailand, concentrated in Chiang Rai, Phayao, Lampang, and Nan provinces. The Yao are still numerous in China, as well as in Vietnam, Myanmar (Burma), and Laos. Like the Hmong, tens of thousands of Yao fled to northern Thailand from Vietnam and Laos after the end of the Vietnam War.

Even more than the Hmong, the Yao (the name "mien," also used to refer to the Yao, is thought to come from the Chinese word for "barbarian") are closely connected to their origins in southern China. They incorporated an ancient version of southern Chinese into their own writing and oral language, and many Yao legends, history books, and religious tracts are recorded in this rarely understood script. The Yao people also assimilated ancestor worship and a form of Taoism into their theology, in addition to celebrating their New Year on the same date as the Chinese, using the same lunar calculations.

Yao farmers practice slash-and-burn agriculture (cutting and burning to create fields) but do not rely on opium poppies, choosing instead to cultivate rice (grown in soil, not paddy fields) and maize. The women produce rather elaborate and elegant embroidery, which adorns their baggy pants, while their black jackets have scarlet, fluffy lapels. Their silver work is intricate and highly prized, even by other tribes, particularly the Hmong. Much of Yao religious art appears to be strongly influenced by Chinese design, particularly Taoist (Daoist) motifs, clearly distinguishing it from other tribes' work.

LISU (LISAW)   The Lisu represent less than 5% of all hill-tribe people. They arrived in Chiang Rai province in the 1920s, migrating from nearby Myanmar (Burma), and, in time, some intermarried with the Lahu and ethnic Chinese. The Lisu occupy high ground and, traditionally, grew opium poppies as well as other subsistence crops. Their traditional clothing is vibrant, with brightly colored tunics punctuated by hundreds of silver beads and trinkets. In a region of flamboyant dressers, the Lisu still steal the show.

The Lisu live well-structured lives; everything from birth to courtship to marriage to death is ruled by an orthodox tradition, with much borrowed from the Chinese.

AKHA (E-KAW)   Of all the tradition-bound tribes, the Akha, accounting for only 10% of all hill-tribe people living in Thailand, have probably maintained the most profound connection with their past. At great events in one's life, the full name (often more than 50 generations of titles) of an Akha is proclaimed, with each name symbolic of a lineage dating back more than 1,000 years. All aspects of life are governed by the Akha Way: An all-encompassing system of myth, ritual, plant cultivation, courtship and marriage, birth, death, dress, and healing.

The first Akha migrated from Myanmar (Burma) to Thailand in the beginning of the 20th century, originally settling in the highlands above the Kok River in Chiang Rai province. Today, they are increasingly migrating to the lower altitudes within China and Indochina in search of more arable land. They are "shifting" cultivators, depending on subsistence crops planted in rotation and raising domestic animals for their livelihood.

The clothing of the Akha is regarded as one of the most attractive of all the hill-tribes. Simple black jackets with skillful embroidery are the everyday attire for men and women alike. Women often also wear stunning silver headdresses, with different subgroups sporting different designs. Akha shoulder bags—woven with exceptional skill—are adorned with silver coins, cowrie shells, and all sorts of baubles and beads.

WHEN TO GO

THE CLIMATE Northern Thailand has three distinct seasons. The **hot season** (Mar–May) is dry, with temperatures up to 97°F (36°C). At this time of year, there is little difference between the north and other regions. The **rainy season** (June–Oct) is cooler, with the heaviest daily rainfall in September (predictably heavy daily afternoon downpours). While trekking and outdoor activities are still possible, mud and leeches should be taken into consideration. The **cool season** (Nov–Feb) is brisk and invigorating, with daytime temperatures as low as 50°F (10°C) in Chiang Mai town, and 41°F (5°C) in the hills. Bring a sweater and some warm socks, and a jacket if you plan to head for the hills. November to February is the best time for trekking, with December and January drawing a peak of visitors. In October and November, after the rains, the forests are lush, rivers swell, and waterfalls are more splendid than usual.

FESTIVALS Northern Thailand celebrates many festivals—even the nationwide ones—in different ways than the rest of the country. Many Thais travel to participate in these festivals, and advance booking in hotels is a must.

Northern Thailand Calendar of Events

Many of these annual events are based on the lunar calendar. Contact the **Tourism Authority of Thailand** (TAT; ✆ 02250-5500; www.tourismthailand.org) in Bangkok for exact dates and www.whatsonwhen.com for other events.

JANUARY

Umbrella Festival, Bo Sang. Held in a village of umbrella craftspeople and painters, about 9km (5⅔ miles) east of Chiang Mai, the Umbrella Festival features handicraft competitions, an elephant show, and a local parade. Third weekend of January.

FEBRUARY

Flower Festival, Chiang Mai. Celebrates the city's undisputed accolade as the "Rose of the North," with a parade, concerts, flower displays, and competitions. A food fair and a beauty contest take place at Buak Hat Park, on the first weekend in February.

King Mengrai Festival, Chiang Rai. Known for its special hill-tribe cultural displays and a fine handicrafts market. Early February.

Sakura Blooms Flower Fair, Doi Mae Salong. Sakura (Japanese cherry trees) were imported to this hilly village 50 years ago by fleeing members of China's Nationalist, or Kuomintang, party (KMT). Their abundant blossoms bring numerous sightseers. Early to mid-February.

MARCH

Poy Sang Long. A traditional Shan ceremony ordaining Buddhist novices—particularly celebrated in the northwestern town of Mae Hong Son, but can also be seen in Chiang Mai. Late March or early April.

APRIL

Songkran (Water) Festival. Thai New Year is celebrated at home and in more formal ceremonies at *wats* (temples). Presents and merit-making acts are offered, and water is "splashed" over Buddha figures, monks, elders, and tourists to encourage the beginning of the rains and to wish good fortune. Those who don't want a good soaking should avoid the streets. The festival is celebrated in all Northern provinces and throughout the country, but Chiang Mai's celebration is notorious for being the longest (up to 10 days) and the rowdiest. The climax comes April 12 to April 14, days that are official holidays.

MAY

Visakha Bucha. Honors the birth, enlightenment, and death of the Lord Buddha. Celebrated nationwide, it is a particularly dramatic event in Chiang Mai, where residents walk up Mount (Doi) Suthep in homage. On the first full moon day in May.

Lychee Festival, Kho Loi Park, Chiang Rai. This festival honors the harvest of lychees, a small, fragrant fruit encased in bumpy red skin. There is a parade, a lychee competition and display, a beauty contest to find Miss Lychee, and lots of great food. Mid-May.

Mango Fair, Chiang Mai. This fair honors mangoes, a favorite local crop. Second weekend in May.

AUGUST

Longan *(lamyai)* Fair, Lamphun. Celebrates North Thailand's most dearly loved fruit and one of the country's largest foreign-exchange earners. There is even a Miss Longan competition. First or second weekend of August.

OCTOBER

Lanna Boat Races. Each October, Nan Province holds 2 days of boat racing, with wildly decorated, long, low-slung crafts zipping down the Nan River. The Lanna Boat Races are run 7 days after the end of the Buddhist Rains' Retreat, which generally marks the beginning of the dry season. In mid- to late October.

NOVEMBER

Loy Krathong. Occurs nationwide on the full moon in the 12th lunar month. Small *krathongs* (banana-leaf floats bearing candles, incense, and garlands) are sent downriver to carry away the previous year's sins. In Chiang Mai, the waterborne offerings are floated on the Ping River. In the city, enormous 1-m (3¼-ft.) tall paper lanterns *(khom loy)* are released in the night sky, and there's a parade of women in traditional costumes. Late October to mid-November.

DECEMBER

Day of Roses, Chiang Mai. Exhibitions and cultural performances are held in Buak Hat Park. First weekend in December.

THE MAE HONG SON LOOP

The Mae Hong Son Loop covers more than 600km (373 miles) and sweeps around almost 2,000 bends as it heads through the rugged hills northwest of Chiang Mai to the well-loved tourist destinations of **Pai** and **Mae Hong Son,** then continues south to out-of-the way **Mae Sariang** and returns to **Chiang Mai** via Hot and Chom Thong on H108. For anyone wary of Thai traffic, going by organized tour or a hired car with driver is recommended—but a self-guided tour means freedom to take side trips and explore at one's own pace. Give yourself at least 4 days to do it, preferably more, staying 1 night at least in each town. The road, especially on the northernmost points, is serpentine and precipitous, particularly dangerous after rain, and calls for good driving skills. Traffic is normally not too heavy, but drivers must be on the alert for everything from water buffalo to slow-moving, smoke-belching trucks and buses.

The most useful resource for a self-guided tour by car or motorbike is the map titled *Mae Hong Son, The Loop* (published by Golden Triangle Rider and priced at 250B; www.gt-rider.com). The GT-Rider map gives exact details of even the smallest dirt track as well as useful site maps of each town. You can pick it up in many bookstores, guesthouses, and restaurants in Chiang Mai (see the website for outlets). The TAT offices in Chiang Mai (p. 288) or Mae Hong Son (p. 337) are also good resources for maps and advice on side trips.

Getting There & Getting Around

BY PLANE   Regular flights by **Nok Air** (© 1318 or 02627-2000; www.nokair. com) and **Kan Air** (© 02551-6111; www.kanairlines.com) link Mae Hong Son, Pai, and Chiang Mai daily.

BY CAR   This is certainly the best option for doing the "loop" or even just touring the hills around Pai and Mae Hong Son. See "Getting Around," in chapter 14. Travel agents and hotels can arrange a car with driver for about 2,000B per day.

BY MOTORCYCLE Though an increasingly popular option, this mode of transport is recommended only for experienced riders. Motorcycle travel around the Mae Hong Son Loop means less traffic than your average Thai highway, but the same warnings apply as anywhere: Wear a helmet, be defensive, and remember that there's not much between you and the road. A variety of good rental bikes is available in Chiang Mai. See the "Getting Around" section, in chapter 11, "Chiang Mai," for info.

BY BUS Regular public buses ply the winding tracks between all towns on the loop (Chiang Mai, Pai, Mae Hong Son, and Mae Sariang), but bus travelers are limited in their exploration of the countryside.

Pai ★

831km (516 miles) NW of Bangkok; 135km (84 miles) NW of Chiang Mai

Halfway between Chiang Mai and Mae Hong Son, the mountain road makes a winding descent into a large green valley carpeted with rice paddies and fruit orchards. Mountains rise on all sides, and on warm afternoons, butterflies flit along the streets. Here you'll find a village called Pai, named after the river that runs through the valley. Pai is a speck of a place with main roads (all four of them) littered with homegrown guesthouses, laid-back restaurants and bars, local trekking companies, and small souvenir shops. It has changed from being unknown a decade ago into one of the most popular destinations in North Thailand, known more as a place to kick back and relax than run around looking at temples and museums. It attracts mostly New Agers and gap-year students doing the Southeast Asian circuit (Thailand, Laos, Vietnam, and Cambodia). It can get very crowded in the cool season, when it's not such a relaxing place.

The **Pai River** itself is one of the main attractions here. Outfitters organize rafting adventures on some pretty raucous rapids from July to January. Trekking is also popular, with 2- and 3-day treks to **Karen, Lahu,** and **Lisu villages.** The adventurous can find a local map for self-guided hikes to nearby waterfalls and caves, but quite a few wayfarers just lounge in town living simply and enjoying the nightlife. In Pai, it seems every day is a lazy Sunday. Many local business owners are foreigners, or bohemian Thais, who come here for a slower pace than bustling Bangkok or Chiang Mai.

ESSENTIALS
Getting There

BY AIR The only air link to Pai is from Chiang Mai on **Kan Air** (✆ **05328-3311; www.kanairlines.com**), which flies light aircraft here; check online for current prices and schedules.

BY BUS Several public buses leave each day for Pai from Chiang Mai (trip time 3–4 hr.; fare 100B) and continue on to Mae Hong Son (trip time 3 hr.; fare 100B). The **Chiang Mai Arcade Bus Terminal** is off Kaew Nawarat Road, northeast of the Old City across the Ping River (✆ **05324-2664**). The **bus terminal** in **Mae Hong Son** is on Khunlumprapas Road (the main street), about 1km (⅔ mile) south of the town center.

BY MINIVAN Frequent minivans (called *rot too*) make connections between Chiang Mai, Pai, and Mae Hong Son for about 150B for each leg. These can be quicker than regular buses but may not be a good idea if you are prone to carsickness (because of all the bends). Contact any storefront travel agent or Arcade bus station for details.

The Mae Hong Son Loop

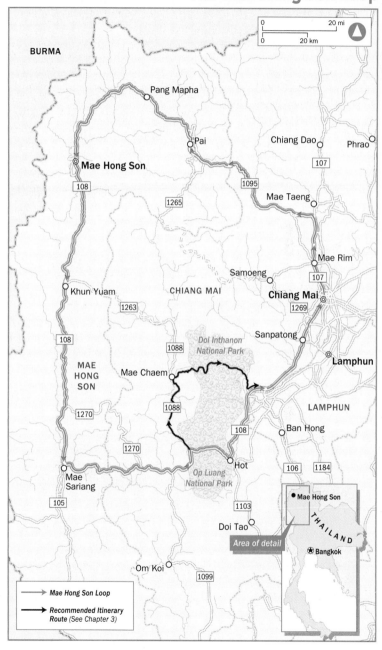

BY CAR The scenic route is long, with steep winding roads that make for some very pretty rural scenery: Take Route 107 north from Chiang Mai, and then Route 1095 northwest to Pai.

Orientation & Getting Around

You won't find a formal tourist information booth in Pai, but restaurateurs, bungalow owners, and fellow travelers are usually happy to share their knowledge and experience. Most guesthouses and restaurants offer photocopied maps of town and the surrounding areas. Tiny Pai consists of four streets: Route 1095, or the Pai–Mae Hong Son Highway (colloquially known as Khetkelang Rd.), runs parallel to Rangsiyanon Road, which is the main commercial street; Chaisongkhram and Ratchadamnoen roads run perpendicular, and many guesthouses and restaurants are in or around this central grid (with many more guesthouses in the surrounding countryside). You can walk the town in 5 minutes; renting a motorcycle is the best way to explore the hills around Pai. Mountain bikes and motorcycles are available at guesthouses or shops along the main streets for about 50B and 200B per day, respectively. Motorcycles can be rented at **Aya Service** (22/1 Moo 3, Chaisongkhram Rd.; ✆ 05369-9940); 100cc scooters start at just 100B for 24 hours, and 250cc motocross numbers go for around 500B.

Fast Facts

There's an **ATM** at the Krung Thai Bank, and another at the Bank of Ayudhaya, both on Rangsiyanon Road; they also offer money-changing services. There are **Internet cafes** along central Chaisongkhram Road.

TREKKING & ADVENTURE

Small trekking companies, operated by locals, are at every guesthouse and all along the main streets. It is hard to choose from the many options, but **Duang Trekking** (at Duang Guesthouse, across from the bus terminal; ✆ 05369-9101) has a good reputation, as does **Back Trax** (17 Chaisongkhram Rd.; ✆ 05369-9739). Expect to pay in the region of 700B per day per person.

The **Pai River** is really the most exciting attraction going. Overnight **white-water rafting** trips take you through some exciting rapids as well as more scenic lazy spots, through canyons walled with prehistoric fossilized lime and shell, and through a **wildlife sanctuary.** A pioneer of the rafting business here, longtime resident Guy Gorias runs **Thai Adventure Rafting ★★** (16 Moo 4, Rangsiyanon Rd., in the town center; ✆ 05369-9111; www.thairafting.com). There are regular trips from June to January. Two-day adventures begin and end in Pai, at a cost of 2,500B per person. There are many imitators in town, but Thai Adventure is the best outfitter by far, with high safety standards and quality equipment. They can also help arrange accommodation in Pai or make the necessary arrangements for pickup and drop-off in Mae Hong Son.

You can also go on **elephant treks** out of Pai, from where there are a number of hourly, all-day, and multiday programs to choose from. In addition, a number of elephant camps are on the ridge overlooking town; the best is **Thom's Pai Elephant Camp** (5/3 Moo 4, Rangsiyanon Rd.; ✆ 05369-9286; www.thomelephant.com).

EXPLORING PAI

There's little in the way of tour sites in Pai (most people simply come to put their feet up), but it is a great place to stroll along country lanes or even rent a motorbike and buzz around the countryside. There are a few small temples: **Wat Klang** is next to the bus station and has several small pagodas surrounding a central stupa, and **Wat**

Mae Yen sits on a low rise about 1km (⅔ mile) east of the town, across the Pai River. It's approached by a long stairway and features some interesting carvings on its solid, wooden doors. There's a **waterfall** about 7km (4⅓ miles) west of town past the hospital, and a **hot spring** about 7km (4⅓ miles) to the southeast, past the Pai High School.

Tiny Pai boasts quite a few traditional massage places. The best option is **Mr. Jan's Massage** (no phone), where you'll get a Burmese-style massage. Ask around for directions to Mr. Jan's—it's on the narrow Soi Wanchaloem, off Chaisongkhram Road.

WHERE TO STAY

There are now several posh resorts both outside and in town, though in the town center you'll find mostly guesthouses. You have your choice of some pretty rough little dives starting at 200B, but I've listed some comfortable options for people on any budget. Many midrange places are on the outskirts in Ban Mae Yen, Ban Mae Hi, and Ban Juang.

Note: Pai was hit with devastating flash floods in September 2005, when several riverside bungalows were swept away. Keep this in mind if considering riverside accommodation near the height of the rainy season.

Moderate

Belle Villa Resort ★★ 🎒 A swish, out-of-town resort consisting of pretty bungalows, built along a quiet, rural stretch of the Pai River, the Belle Villa has no rival anywhere along the Mae Hong Son Loop. Large, clean bungalow rooms boast contemporary conveniences such as digital safes and cable TV without sacrificing the rustic charm of thatched roof and bamboo walls. The yellow polished concrete bathrooms are resplendent. Spacious shower areas are surrounded by small rock gardens and have windows with views to the river. The restaurant is cozy and overlooks a small pool and the riverside beyond. The peace, quiet, scenery, and friendly service of this burgeoning little idyll are matchless.

113 Moo 6, Huay Poo-WiangNua Rd., Tumbol WiangTai, Amphur Pai, Mae Hong Son 58130 (down a small *soi* off the Mae Hong Son Rd., 2km/1¼ miles north of Pai). www.bellevillaresort.com. ✆ **05369-8226.** Fax 05369-8228. 47 units. 2,850B double; 3,900B cottage. MC, V. **Amenities:** Restaurant; outdoor pool; Wi-Fi (free). *In room:* A/C, satellite TV/DVD, minibar, fridge, hair dryer.

Pai River Corner ★★ Having lost its budget riverside bungalows to flash floods in 2005, Pai River Corner has been left with only its finest rooms set in two-story, four-unit villas right in the center of town. Interiors are lavish, decorated in a modern Thai style with lots of color and local flair. Even more unique are their oversized suite and spa rooms, one with an indoor Jacuzzi the size of a duck pond. The property boasts a cozy riverside perch for drinks and dining, and the location is the best in town.

94 Moo 3, Viengtai, Pai, Mae Hong Son 58130. www.pairivercorner.com. ✆ **05369-9049.** Fax 05306-4408. 9 units. 2,950B deluxe; 3,850B suite; 5,750B spa. **Amenities:** Restaurant; bar. *In room:* A/C, satellite TV, minibar, hair dryer, Wi-Fi (free).

Rim Pai Cottages Though billed as cottages, this property comprises an unassuming cluster of bungalows. You'll find little in the way of luxury, but lots of character in rooms that range from tiny, fan-cooled sheds to spacious rustic pavilions on stilts, with air-conditioning, small balconies, and riverside views. There are a few choice amenities: A welcoming restaurant pavilion, a helpful tour desk, and a spa. It's set apart from the rougher budget accommodation by virtue of its airy campus and good location—it occupies some of the best real estate in the center of Pai Town proper, with a large river frontage.

99 Moo 3, Viengtai, Pai, Mae Hong Son 58130 (right in town at riverside). www.rimpaicottage.com. ℂ **05369-9133.** Fax 05369-9234. 37 units. 1,200B–3,500B double; 4,000B suite. MC, V. **Amenities:** Restaurant, Wi-Fi (free). *In room:* A/C (some), no phone.

Inexpensive

Cheap and cheerful little **Charlie's House** is in the middle of town (9 Rangsiyanon Rd.; ℂ **05369-9039**), with basic rooms that have a fan and shared bathroom from 200B or air-conditioning units from 600B.

The Sun Hut   Located across the river from town (about a 10- to 15-minute walk), the Sun Hut occupies a plot peppered with bamboo and bananas, through which runs the Mae Yen stream. All the bungalows, named after planets and zodiac signs, are individually designed and made of brick and teak, with relaxing balconies. There's also a vegetarian restaurant and communal lounging area, and a 50% discount on rates during the low season (Mar–Oct).

28/1 Mae Yen, Pai, Mae Hong Son 58130. www.thesunhut.com. ℂ **05369-9730.** 13 units. 900B–1,900B double. No credit cards. **Amenities:** Restaurant. *In room:* Wi-Fi (free)

WHERE TO EAT

Little Pai plays host to a bevy of expatriate restaurants and bars as well as a whole range of street-side dining. The most popular spots in town for partying are **Ting Tong** and **Be Bop ★**, which both feature live music and are on the southern side of town on Rangsiyanon Road. At Be Bop, there's an excellent house band, and a young party crowd keeps the place hopping late into the night (about 1am). Live music starts at 9:30pm. Below are the other best restaurants in town.

Baan Benjarong ★ THAI   As you overlook mountain rice paddies from this friendly and casual open-air restaurant, you can choose from a poster-sized menu of delicious Thai dishes. Any of the many hearty stir-fries and spicy soups will do the trick. But I most recommend the savory curry made with crabmeat dipped in a sweet-and-sour sauce and the *tam long krop:* A unique dish of crispy, deep-fried gourd. This is a great place to fill up cheaply after trekking.

179 Moo 8, Rangsiyanon Rd. (adjacent to Be-bop Bar). ℂ **05369-8010.** Main courses 70B–150B. No credit cards. Daily 11am–10pm.

Burger House ★ INTERNATIONAL   Right in the center of town, Burger House serves up a range of delicious home-made burgers, such as chili burgers, using imported Australian beef, and many patrons consider them to be the best in Thailand. They also have veggie burgers and a good range of international favorites. It's a good place for people-watching while enjoying a long, slow breakfast or leisurely dinner.

14 Moo 4, Rangsiyanon Rd. (about halfway along the main street). ℂ **05369-9093.** Main courses 80B–180B. No credit cards. Daily 7am–11pm.

Between Pai & Mae Hong Son

Either as a day trip from Pai or as a stop on the way to Mae Hong Son, the best little detour going is the *lod,* or **Spirit Cave,** off Route 1095 (about 30km/19 miles north-west of Pai on Route 1095 in the town of Soppong, and then about 8km/5 miles north of the highway). This large, awe-inspiring cave filled with colorful stalagmites, stalac-tites, and small caverns will keep you exploring for hours. The cavern was discovered in the 1960s jam-packed with **antique pottery** dating from the Ban Chiang culture. There are three caves. The first chamber is a magnificent grotto and the second contains a prehistoric cave painting of a deer (which unfortunately has been largely blurred by curious fingers). The third cavern contains **prehistoric coffins** shaped like canoes.

A guide to all three caves costs 100B, with lantern rental included. Be sure to take the canoe ride to the third cave (the ferryman will hit you up for an extra 100B), where, especially in the late afternoon and evening, you can see clouds of bats and swallows vying for space in the cave's high craggy ceiling (the boat ride is fun, too). Pay again to get back by boat or you can follow the clear jungle path a few kilometers back to the parking lot. Bring your own flashlight for self-exploration as well.

There are lots of little guesthouses along the road near the entrance to the Spirit Cave in Soppong; the best is the **Soppong River Inn** (356 Moo 1, T. Soppong; ✆ 05361-7107; www.soppong.com) on the main road to the west of town. It offers a variety of room types, all oozing character, with rates ranging from 700B to 1500B a night.

As the road curves south heading into Mae Hong Son, **Tham Pla Park** (17km/11 miles north of Mae Hong Son on Rte. 1095) is a small landscaped park leading up to the entrance of Tham Pla, or Fish Cave. It is a small grotto crowded with carp (legend says there are 10,000 of them) that mysteriously prefer the cave to the nearby streams. You can buy fish food in the parking lot, but the fish don't eat it. Have a look—it is meant to be good luck (and is also a good leg stretch after the long drive). The grotto, once unsuccessfully explored by Thai Navy divers, is said to be several meters deep and extends for miles.

In the Tham Pla Park interior 10km (6¼ miles) away is the huge **Pha Sua Waterfall,** which tumbles over limestone cliffs in seven cataracts. The water is at its most powerful after the rainy season in August and September. The Hmong hill-tribe village of Mae Sou Yaa is beyond the park on a road suitable for jeeps, just a few kilometers from the Burmese border.

MAE HONG SON ★

924km (574 miles) NW of Bangkok; 355km (221 miles) NW of Chiang Mai via Pai; 274km (170 miles) NW of Chiang Mai via Mae Sariang

Not far from the Burmese border, Mae Hong Son, the provincial capital of Mae Hong Son province, is the urban center of this large patch of scenic woodlands, waterways, and unique hill-tribe villages. The town's surrounding hills, famed for their eerie morning mist, burst into color each October and November when *tung buatong* (wild sunflowers) come into bloom. The hot season (Mar–Apr) has temperatures as high as 104°F (40°C), and the rainy season is longer (May–Oct), with several brief showers daily.

The mountains around Mae Hong Son are scarred by slash-and-burn agriculture and evidence of logged teak forests from departed hill-tribe settlements. Roads, airfields, and public works projects have since opened up the scenic province, as poppy fields gave way to terraced rice paddies and garlic crops. At the same time, the surge in tourism brought foreigners trekking into villages where automobiles were still unknown. Although the busy town of Mae Hong Son continues to grow and develop, its picturesque valley setting and lovely Burmese-style *wats* (temples) are still the star attractions here, and it's a lot less crowded than Pai in the cool season.

ESSENTIALS

Getting There

BY PLANE Two daily **Kan Air** flights connect Mae Hong Son to Chiang Mai (flight time: 45 min.). During the July to August and December to January peak seasons, book in advance as flights fill up early, and, in low season, check to see if the flights are actually running (flights cancel often due to fog). Kan Air have an office in Chiang Mai at the airport (✆ **05328-33110;** www.kanairlines.com), and another at Mae Hong Son airport (✆ **05361-3188**). **Nok Air** (✆ **05392-2183** or 1318; www. nokair.com) runs flights (daily during the high season) from Chiang Mai as well.

The **Mae Hong Son Airport** (airport code HGN) is in the northeast section of town, about 10 minutes from the town center. Tuk-tuks and *songtaews*, or pickups, are always waiting for passengers outside the airport.

BY BUS Non-air-conditioned buses connect with Pai (trip time 4 hr.; fare 72B) or beyond to the **Chiang Mai Arcade Bus Terminal** (trip time 8 hr.; fare 150B; ✆ **05324-2664**). Bus service to Mae Sariang to the south leaves in the morning (trip time 4 hr.; fare 110B). The bus terminal in Mae Hong Son is on Khunlumprapas Road (the main street), about a kilometer south of the main intersection.

BY CAR The 8-hour journey to Mae Hong Son from Chiang Mai is a pleasant mountain drive with spectacular views and some fun attractions (see "Between Pai & Mae Hong Son," above). The road is winding but paved and safe, with places to stop for gas, food, and toilets, as well as scenic pull-offs. Take Route 107 north from Chiang Mai to Route 1095 northwest through Pai. For car-rental info, see chapter 11, "Chiang Mai."

Visitor Information

The **TAT** office (✆ **05361-2982**), Khunlumprapas Road, opposite the post office, has helpful staff. The **Tourist Police** office (✆ **05361-1812** or 1155), Singhanat Bamrung Road, is open daily from 8:30am to 5pm.

Orientation

Mae Hong Son is small and easy to navigate. Khunlumprapas Road, part of the Pai–Mae Sariang Highway (Rte. 108), is the town's main street and home to travel agents, most hotels listed below, and restaurants. The main sights are **Jong Kham Lake,** just east of the main street, and **Wat Phra That Doi Kong Mu,** which overlooks town from the west.

Getting Around

You can walk to most places in town, but there are a few tuk-tuks parked outside the market for longer trips. At some guesthouses, you'll find bicycle rental for 50B or 100cc motorbikes for rent at 150B to 200B per day.

FAST FACTS

There are major **banks** with ATMs and currency exchanges along Khunlumprapas and Singhanat Bamrung roads. In addition, several banks are open for each flight arrival at the airport. The **Sri Sangawan Hospital** is east of town on Singhanat Bamrung Road (✆ **05361-1378**). The **post office** is opposite the King Singhanat Rajah statue. There are a few **Internet cafes** along Khunlumprapas, near the Bai-yoke Chalet, most with good DSL for 40B per hour.

EXPLORING MAE HONG SON

Wat Jong Klang and **Wat Jong Kham** are reflected in the serene waters of Jong Kham Lake, in the heart of town. Their striking white and gold *chedis* (stupas) and

Mae Hong Son

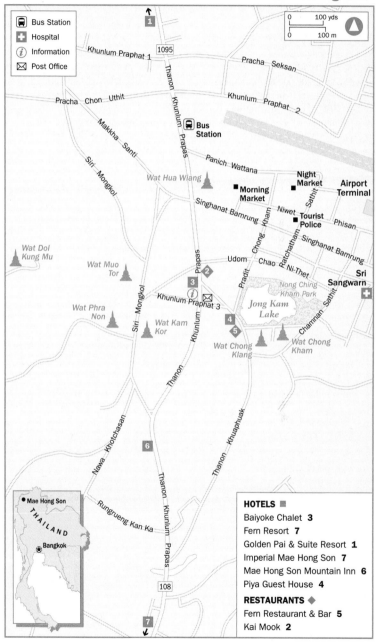

Legend:
- 🚌 Bus Station
- ➕ Hospital
- ⓘ Information
- ✉ Post Office

0 — 100 yds
0 — 100 m

Khunlum Praphat 1
1095
Pracha Seksan
Khunlum Praphat 2
Pracha Chon Uthit
Makkha Santi
Siri Mongkol
Thanon Khunlum Prapas
🚌 Bus Station
Panich Wattana
Wat Hua Wiang
Morning Market
Night Market
Airport Terminal
Singhanat Bamrung
Chong Kham
Niwet
Sathit
Tourist Police
Phisan
Wat Dol Kung Mu
Wat Muo Tor
Prapas
Udom
Chao
Pradit
Ratchatham
Ni-Thet
Singhanat Bamrung
Sri Sangwarn
Wat Phra Non
Siri Mongkol
Wat Kam Kor
Khunlum Praphat 3
Nong Ching Kham Park
Jong Kam Lake
Chamnan Sathit
Wat Chong Klang
Wat Chong Kham
Thanon Khunlum
Thanon Khuaphuak
Nawa Khotchasan
Rungrueng Kan Ka
Thanon Khunlum Prapas
108

THAILAND
● Mae Hong Son
✹ Bangkok

HOTELS ■
Baiyoke Chalet **3**
Fern Resort **7**
Golden Pai & Suite Resort **1**
Imperial Mae Hong Son **7**
Mae Hong Son Mountain Inn **6**
Piya Guest House **4**

RESTAURANTS ◆
Fern Restaurant & Bar **5**
Kai Mook **2**

dark teak *viharn* (assembly hall) reflect Burmese influence. Wat Jong Klang was constructed from 1867 to 1871 as an offering to Burmese monks who made the long journey here for the funeral of Wat Jong Kham's abbot. Inside is a series of folk-style glass paintings depicting the Buddha's life and a small collection of dusty Burmese wood carvings and dolls. The older Wat Jong Kham (ca. 1827) was built by King Singhanat Rajah and his queen, and is distinguished by gold-leaf columns supporting its *viharn*. Don't miss the colorful Burmese-style donation boxes; they're like musical arcade games with spinning discs and cups to drop your change in, only the end result is not "game over" but "make merit."

Wat Phra That Doi Kong Mu (also known as Wat Plai Doi) dominates the western hillside above the town, particularly at night when the strings of lights rimming its two Mon pagodas are silhouetted against the dark forest. The oldest part (ca. 1860) of this compound was constructed by King Singhanat Rajah, and a 15-minute climb up its *naga* (snake) staircase rewards one with grand views of the mist-shrouded valley, blooming pink cassia trees, and Jong Kham Lake below. Below Wat Phra That Doi Kong Mu, there's a 12-m (39-ft.) long **Reclining Buddha** in Wat Phra Non.

For short **1-day hill-tribe treks** in the region, **Rose Garden Tours** (86/4 Khunlumprapas Rd. in the center of town; ℂ/fax **05361-1681;** www.rosegarden-tours. com) offers many options including stops at local Lahu, Shan, and Karen villages, and adventure activities such as elephant trekking and bamboo rafting.

There are two **Padaung villages** close to Mae Hong Son populated by the famed **"long-neck Karen" people,** so called because their women wear layers of brass rings around their necks, constantly adding to them to give them elongated necks. However, visits to these villages tend to upset sensitive souls when they see the plight of these people who have been driven out of their homeland (Myanmar) and are treated like zoo exhibits by their neighbors (Thailand). If you must go, Rose Garden Tours (see above) includes village visits in its all-day tours or can arrange special half-day trips. **Nai Soi** village is about 35km (22 miles) northwest of town and easily reached by car or minivan (entrance is 250B), and **Nam Phiang Din** village is accessible by boat for 750B (including entrance fee to the village). Unfortunately, these fees do not filter down to the villagers, who receive little more than a plate of rice for smiling at the cameras.

WHERE TO STAY

The early '90s brought large-scale development to Mae Hong Son, so today there are a few decent hotel options downtown and a few rustic resorts in the surrounding hills.

Moderate

Fern Resort ★★★ 🏨   Out in the sticks some 8km (5 miles) south of town and just next to the Mae Surin National Park, the Fern Resort rests in a quiet valley along a rushing stream and is a dream come true for anyone wanting to stay in a genuine eco-resort. Tai Yai (Shan)-style bungalows have simple but comfortable local-style furnishings such as leaf roofs, glass windows, and doors; bathrooms offer slate-tiled showers with hot water. As you might expect in a bona fide eco-resort, there are no TVs or phones in the rooms, but this only adds to the appreciation of sounds from the jungle around. They have good trail maps of the immediate area, and experienced guides are available for more extensive treks.

64 Moo 10, Bann Hua Num Mae Sakut, T. Pha Bong, Mae Hong Son 58000 (8km/5 miles south of town). www.fernresort.info. ℂ **05368-6110.** Fax 05368-6111. 30 units. 2,500B–3,500B bungalow. MC, V. **Amenities:** Restaurant; outdoor pool; Wi-Fi (free). *In room:* A/C, no phone.

Imperial Mae Hong Son ★★   The Imperial is the top choice for the upscale traveler in Mae Hong Son. Though it's some 2km (1¼ miles) south of town, the hotel's style, service, many amenities, and upkeep set it far above the rest. Guest rooms overlook a teak forest, garden, and stream. All furnishings are in blond wood and wicker on bowling-alley-shined floors. Most rooms have spacious balconies, and suites are large and luxurious. The serpentine free-form pool is surrounded by a wooden deck, and the open-air restaurant has views of the grounds and garden. The staff is very professional and can help with any eventuality, from day tours to flat tires.

149 Moo 8, Tambon Pang Moo, Mae Hong Son 58000 (2km/1¼ miles south of town). Ⓒ **05368-4444.** Fax 05368-4440. 104 units. 2,464B double; from 3,653B suite. AE, DC, MC, V. **Amenities:** Restaurant; 2 bars; lounge; outdoor pool; health club; sauna; room service. *In room:* A/C, satellite TV, minibar, fridge, hair dryer, Wi-Fi (free).

Mae Hong Son Mountain Inn   You can't miss the dynamic angular spire of the oversized Thai Yai-style peaked roofs marking the entrance to this compound. The place has lots of charm and is in a good location just south of the town center. Comfortable guest rooms are arranged in two stories around lush central gardens. The hotel is a bit light on amenities, and you won't find many English speakers on staff, but they're helpful. Opt for a deluxe room with parquet floors (instead of old carpeting), more local accents, and a bit more panache. Deluxe bathrooms are large and done up using terra-cotta tiles and granite.

112/2 Khunlumprapas Rd., T. Jong Kham, Mae Hong Son 58000 (on the southern end of the main drag). www.mhsmountaininn.com. Ⓒ **05361-1802;** fax 05361-2284. 69 units. 2,400B–2,800B double; from 4,500B suite; seasonal rates and Internet discounts always available. AE, MC, V. **Amenities:** Restaurant. *In room:* A/C, satellite TV, minibar, fridge, Wi-Fi (free).

Inexpensive

Baiyoke Chalet   With an ideal location on the main street—and in walking distance of everything in town—this hotel offers simple, midsized rooms with high ceilings, hardwood floors, and clean guesthouse-style bathrooms. Rooms overlooking the back are quieter; the place is often overrun by adventure groups—a young and rowdy crowd sometimes. The hotel bar and restaurant, **Chalet,** looks over the main street in town, hosts live bands, and is where it's at for locals in Mae Hong Son.

90 Khunlumprapas, Jong Kham, Amphur Muang, Mae Hong Son 58000 (midtown, across from post office). www.baiyokehotel.com. Ⓒ **05361-3132.** Fax 05361-1533. 38 units. 1,280B–1,600B double. AE, MC, V. **Amenities:** Restaurant. *In room:* A/C, satellite TV, minibar, fridge, Wi-Fi (free).

Golden Pai & Suite Resort   Here's one for folks who are traveling with their own car—the Golden Pai is 5km (3 miles) north of town (toward Pai) and not accessible by public transport. Deluxe rooms (the best value) are large and cozy, with spacious balconies overlooking a small central pool. Mid- and low-end rooms are basic bungalows. They have a good riverside restaurant and offer some spa treatments, as well as local adventure tours. The very friendly staff ensures that this place stays popular with groups of visiting Thais.

285 Moo 1, Ban Pangmoo, Mae Hong Son 58000. www.goldenpairesort.com. Ⓒ **05306-1114.** Fax 05362-0417. 70 units. 1,500B–2,500B. MC, V. **Amenities:** Restaurant; bar; outdoor pool, Wi-Fi (free). *In room:* A/C, TV, minibar, fridge.

Piya Guest House   This is the best budget choice on beautiful Jong Kham Lake, easily the nicest part of town—and a short walk to the two lakeside temples. Piya is a one-story wooden house with a garden courtyard. Basic rooms have private bathrooms, hot-water showers, and air-conditioning, but aren't particularly nice (be sure to check first, because many are musty).

1/1 Khunlumprapas, Soi 3, Jong Kham, Mae Hong Son (east side of Jong Kham Lake). © **05361-1260.** 14 units. 600B bungalow. No credit cards. **Amenities:** Restaurant. *In room:* A/C, Wi-Fi (free), no phone.

WHERE TO EAT

The local **Night Market,** on central Khunlumprapas, is the busiest venue in town for budget travelers. There you can sample noodle soups, crisp-fried beef, dried squid, roast sausage, fish balls, and other snacks sold by vendors for very little. It's open until late daily.

Also look for a little Italian storefront pizza joint, **La Tasca** (88/4 Khunlumprapas Rd.; © **05361-1344;** daily 10am–10pm; main courses 80B–180B; no credit cards), in the town center. It's a great place for a real coffee and to watch the world go by.

Fern Restaurant & Bar ★★ THAI/INTERNATIONAL   The biggest and best restaurant in town serves an especially wide variety of food for this part of the country—all of it well prepared and pleasantly served. The bar at the entrance has an inviting quality, and behind it an open-air deck stretches back toward an entertainment area with live music and a karaoke bar. If you come in the early evening, head for the far back to get a view of the mountaintop temple, Wat Phra That Doi Kong Mu, in the evening glow.

87 Khunlumprapas Rd. (1½ blocks south of traffic light, on left). © **05361-1374.** Main courses 80B–250B. AE, MC, V. Daily 10am–10pm.

Kai Mook ★ THAI/CHINESE   This is a tin-roofed pavilion with more style than most: Overhead lights are shaded by straw farmer's hats, and Formica tables are interspersed between bamboo columns. The Thai and Chinese menu includes Kaimook salad (a tasty blend of crispy fried squid, cashews, sausage, and onions), and a large selection of light and fresh stir-fried dishes.

23 Udom Chaonitesh Rd. (one block south of traffic light, turn left). © **05361-2092.** Main courses 60B–190B. No credit cards. Daily 9:30am–2pm and 5:30–11pm.

Mae Sariang: Completing the Mae Hong Son Loop

180km (112 miles) W of Chiang Mai; 130km (81 miles) S of Mae Hong Son

The tiny town of Mae Sariang proper boasts no grand museums or shiny hilltop temples, though it does have a couple of eye-catching Burmese-style temples in the town center—Wat Utthayarom and Wat Si Boonruang. It is just a cozy river town along the border with Myanmar and the best halfway stopover on the long southern link between Mae Hong Son and Chiang Mai. Driving in the area, along Route 108, takes you past pastoral villages, scenic rolling hills, and a few enticing side trips to small local temples and waterfalls. Mae Sariang offers basic but adequate places to stay.

GETTING THERE

BY AIR   **Kan Air** (www.kanairlines.com; © **05328-3311**) operates a weekly flight on Saturdays between Chiang Mai and Mae Sariang.

BY CAR   Navigation is a cinch, but watch out for bends (there must be a thousand between Mae Hong Son and Mae Sariang). Just follow Route 108 between Mae Hong Son, Mae Sariang, and Chiang Mai. Carry a good road map for following the side roads, and set aside at least a day for travel time.

BY BUS Standard and air-conditioned buses connect Mae Hong Son, Mae Sariang, and **Chiang Mai Arcade Bus Terminal** (✆ 05324-2664) along the southern leg of Route 108. Several daily non-air-conditioned buses depart Chiang Mai for the 8- to 9-hour journey and cost 178B to Mae Hong Son and 95B to stop in Mae Sariang (4 hr.). Two air-conditioned buses make the same trip and depart Chiang Mai at 11am and 9pm (319B to Mae Hong Son; 171B to Mae Sariang).

EXPLORING MAE SARIANG

The road is good and the scenery is lush on the long stretch of Route 108 west of Chiang Mai. Don't forget to stop and smell the fertilizer or take side trips wherever possible. Roadside dining and service facilities are limited, but adequate.

In the village of **Khun Yuam,** 63km (39 miles) south of Mae Hong Son, you'll come to a junction with a road that no longer exists: A ghost trail remembered as "The Road of Japanese Skeletons," the path of retreat for Japanese soldiers fleeing what was Burma (now Myanmar) at the end of World War II. The road lives only in the memory of those who met the starved and dying troops, an estimated 20,000 of whom lie in mass graves in the surrounding area. The **Japanese War Museum** (just south of the junction of Rte. 108 and Rte. 163; 50B; daily 8am–5pm) commemorates this sorry chapter in history and is worth a visit. The museum features rusting tanks and weaponry, photos, personal effects, and written accounts (in Japanese, English, and Thai) of soldiers' struggles and the kindness of the locals.

Mae Sariang has a few outfits offering day treks and rafting (stop in any of the riverside cafes or hotels), but most people just spend a night here before making their way to Chiang Mai. It's worth a stroll around the small town center, particularly for the atmospheric, Burmese-style temples of **Wat Si Boonruang** and **Wat Utthayarom** on Wiang Mai Road.

Between Mae Sariang and **Hot,** you'll pass a turning on the left to **Mae Chaem** (H1088), a route that leads into **Doi Inthanon National Park** from the west. It is possible to return to Chiang Mai by this extremely scenic route, going over Thailand's highest peak (well, near the top anyway), though the more straightforward alternative (with less bends!) is to keep on H108 to Hot, where the road turns north and passes through Chom Thong en route to Chiang Mai.

WHERE TO STAY & EAT

There is lots of budget accommodation along the Mae Yuam River in the town center. The best choice is the **Riverhouse Resort** (6/1 Moo 2, Langpanich Rd., Mae Sariang; ✆ 05368-3066; fax 05368-3067; www.riverhousehotels.com), a small resort of cozy wooden pavilions overlooking the Yuam River. Doubles start at 1,800B. Riverhouse is also the best bet for dining in their riverside *sala* (open pavilion), but a short stroll through town will take you past any number of local greasy spoons, where the adventurous can find one-dish noodle or rice meals for next to nothing.

CHIANG RAI ★

780km (485 miles) NE of Bangkok; 180km (112 miles) NE of Chiang Mai

Chiang Rai is Thailand's northernmost province. The Mekong River marks the country's borders with Laos to the east and Myanmar to the west. The smaller yet scenic Mae Kok River, which supports many hill-tribe villages along its banks, flows right through the provincial capital of the same name.

Chiang Rai City lies some 565m (1,854 ft.) above sea level in a wide fertile valley, and its cool, refreshing climate, tree-lined riverbanks, and popular but more subdued Night Market and Walking Street lure travelers weary of traffic congestion and pollution in Chiang Mai. Chiang Rai also has some good places to stay, and many travelers use the city as a base for trekking and trips to Chiang Saen and the Golden Triangle.

Just over 100km (62 miles) north of Chiang Mai on the way to Chiang Rai, look for little **Suanthip Vana Resort** (49 Chiang Mai–Chiang Rai Rd., Tambon Takok; ✆ **05372-4226;** www.suanthipresort.com), a semiluxe property with cool honeymoon bungalows that overlook a river valley. Because the journey from Chiang Mai takes only 3 hours, it is possible to see Chiang Rai and the Golden Triangle in a day trip, but you'll need to get an early start and allot a very full day, spent mostly in a vehicle.

Essentials

GETTING THERE

BY PLANE   **Thai Airways** (870 Phaholyothin Rd.; ✆ **05371-1179;** www.thaiair. com) has daily flights to Chiang Rai (flying time: 85 min.) and **Kan Air** (✆ **05379-3339;** www.kanairlines.com) operates three flights a week. Budget carriers **Air Asia** (✆ **02515-9999** in Bangkok; www.airasia.com) and **One-Two-GO** (✆ **1126;** www.flyorientthai.com) also make regular connections.

Chiang Rai International Airport (✆ **05379-8000**) is about 10km (6¼ miles) north of town. There is a bank exchange, open daily 9am to 5pm, and a gift shop. Taxis hover outside and charge 200B to town.

BY BUS   Three air-conditioned VIP 24-seat buses leave daily from Bangkok's **Northern Bus Terminal** (✆ **02936-2841**) to Chiang Rai (trip time 11 hr.; fare 859B). Buses leave hourly between 6am and 5:30pm from **Chiang Mai's Arcade Bus Terminal** (✆ **05324-2664;** trip time 3½ hr.; fare 106B non-A/C; 191B A/C; 263B VIP). Chiang Rai's **Khon Song Bus Terminal** (✆ **05371-1224**) is near the night market in the center of town, though most buses, including those from Bangkok, now stop at a new bus station (✆ **05377-3989**) 6km (3½ miles) south of town. A shuttle service (10B) operates between the two stations, and tuk-tuks and *samlor* (motorized pedicabs) connect to hotels for 30B to 100B, depending on which station you arrive at.

BY CAR   The fast, not particularly scenic, route from Bangkok is Highway 1 North, direct to Chiang Rai. The direct route from Chiang Mai is along Route 118. A slow, attractive approach on blacktop mountain roads is on Route 107 north from Chiang Mai to Fang, and then Route 109 east to Highway 1.

VISITOR INFORMATION

The **TAT** (✆ **05374-4674**) is located at 448/16 Singhaklai Rd., near Wat Phra Singh on the north side of town; and the **Tourist Police** (✆ **1155**) are located on Phaholyothin Road, by the junction with Wisetwiang Road. Either the TAT office or your hotel can provide you with a map of the town.

ORIENTATION

Chiang Rai is a small city, with most services grouped around the main north–south street, Phaholyothin Road. There are three noteworthy landmarks: The striking clock tower in the city's center; the statue of King Mengrai (the city's founder), at the

Chiang Rai

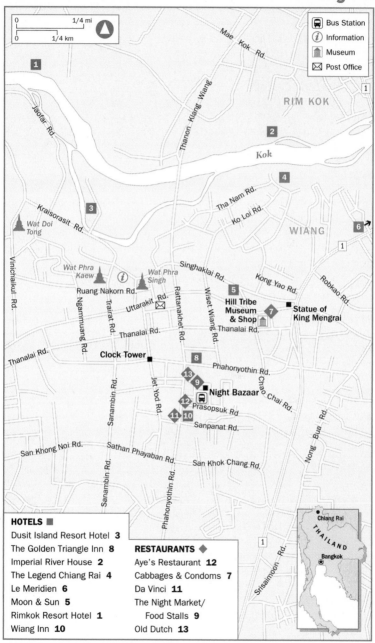

Bus Station
Information
Museum
Post Office

RIM KOK

Mae Kok Rd.

Thanon Klang Wiang

Jaofar Rd.

Kok

Kraisorasit Rd.

Wat Doi Tong

Tha Nam Rd.

Ko Loi Rd.

WIANG

Wat Phra Kaew

Vinichaikul Rd.

Wat Phra Singh

Ruang Nakorn Rd.

Singhaklai Rd.

Kong Yao Rd.

Robkao Rd.

Uttarakit Rd.

Wiset Wiang Rd.

Rattanakhet Rd.

Hill Tribe Museum & Shop

Statue of King Mengrai

Ngammuang Rd.

Trairat Rd.

Thanalai Rd.

Thanalai Rd.

Thanalai Rd.

Clock Tower

Phahonyothin Rd.

Sanambin Rd.

Jet Yod Rd.

Night Bazaar

Chao Chai Rd.

Prasopsuk Rd.

Nong Bua Rd.

Sanpanat Rd.

San Khong Noi Rd.

Sathan Phayaban Rd.

San Khok Chang Rd.

Phahonyothin Rd.

Sanambin Rd.

Srisaimoon Rd.

Chiang Rai

THAILAND

Bangkok

HOTELS

Dusit Island Resort Hotel **3**
The Golden Triangle Inn **8**
Imperial River House **2**
The Legend Chiang Rai **4**
Le Meridien **6**
Moon & Sun **5**
Rimkok Resort Hotel **1**
Wiang Inn **10**

RESTAURANTS

Aye's Restaurant **12**
Cabbages & Condoms **7**
Da Vinci **11**
The Night Market/
  Food Stalls **9**
Old Dutch **13**

northeast corner of the city, on the Superhighway to Mae Chan; and the Mae Kok River, at the north edge of town.

Singhaklai Road is the main artery on the north side of town, parallel to the river. The old bus station is on Prasopsuk Road, 1 block east of Phaholyothin Road, near the Wiang Inn Hotel. The Night Market is on Phaholyothin Road, next to the bus station, and the Saturday walking street is on Thanalai Road, running east to west from just south of the Mengrai statue.

GETTING AROUND

BY SAMLOR OR TUK-TUK   You'll probably find walking to be the best way to get around town as the center is so small. However, there are *samlors* parked outside the Night Market and on the banks of the Mae Kok River; they charge 30B to 40B for in-town trips. During the day, there are tuk-tuks, which charge 60B to 100B for in-town trips.

BY BUS   Chiang Rai's frequent local buses are the easiest and cheapest way to get to nearby cities. All leave from the bus station on Prasopsuk Road, near the Wiang Inn Hotel.

BY MOTORCYCLE   Motorcycling is another good way to get out of town. **Soon Motorcycle,** 197/2 Trirat Rd. (✆ **05371-4068**), charges 150B for a 100cc motor-bike.

BY CAR   Budget has a branch at the Golden Triangle Inn (see "Where to Stay," below), 590 Phaholyothin Rd. (✆ **05374-0442**), offering the standard rate beginning at 1,500B for a Honda Jazz.

FAST FACTS

Several **bank** exchanges are located on Phaholyothin Road in the center of town and are open daily from 8:30am to 10pm. The **post office** is on Utarakit Road, two blocks north of the Clock Tower. There are a few **Internet cafes** along the main drag, Phaholyothin Road, with service for as little as 40B per hour.

Exploring Chiang Rai

Wat Phra Kaew, on Trairat Road, on the northwest side of town, is the best known of the northern *wats* because it once housed the Emerald Buddha, now at Bangkok's royal Wat Phra Kaew. Near its Lanna-style chapel is the *chedi*, which (according to legend) was struck by lightning in 1436 to reveal the precious green jasper Buddha. There is now a green jade replica of the image on display in a pavilion behind the *viharn*.

Wat Phra Singh is two blocks east of Wat Phra Kaew. The restored *wat* is thought to date from the 15th century. Inside is a replica of the Phra Sihing Buddha, a highly revered Theravada Buddhist image; the original was removed to Chiang Mai's Wat Phra Singh.

The Burmese-style **Wat Doi Tong** (Phra That Chomtong) sits atop a hill above the northwest side of town, up a steep staircase off Kaisornrasit Road, and offers an overview of the town and a panorama of the Mae Kok valley. It is said that King Mengrai himself chose the site for his new Lanna capital from this very hill. The circle of columns at the top of the hill surrounds the city's new *lak muang* (city pillar), built to commemorate the 725th anniversary of the city and King Bhumibol's 60th birthday. It is often criticized for its failure to represent local style. (You can see the old wooden *lak muang* in the *viharn* of the *wat*.)

You can't miss the elaborately adorned **clock tower** at the junction of Banphap-rakan and Jet Yod Roads. The work of contemporary artist Chalermchai Kositpipat, it is a gold monument sprouting projections all over that certainly catches the eye. If it intrigues you, make the 13km (8 mile) journey south on Highway 1 to visit **Wat Rong Khun,** aka The White Temple, another work by the same artist that is constantly in progress. The dazzling white structure also sprouts countless twirling projections, and curious ponds full of hands clutching begging bowls and skulls flank the entrance.

The **Population and Community Development Association (PDA)**, 620/1 Thanalai Rd., east of Wisetwiang Road (*C* **05374-0088**), is an NGO responsible for some of the most effective tribal development projects in the region. The popular Cabbages & Condoms restaurants, with several branches countrywide, carry their important message of safe sex and family planning.

On the top floor of this office is a small **Hill-tribe Museum** (no phone) that's heavy on shopping and light on museum exhibits, but the admission goes to a good cause. It's open Monday to Friday 9am to 6pm, Saturday and Sunday 10am to 6pm, and admission is 50B.

The **Mae Kok River** is one of the most scenic attractions in Chiang Rai. You can hire a longtail boat to ferry you up and down the river. You'll have the option of stop-ping at the Buddha cave (a temple within a cavern), an elephant camp (for trekking), a hot spring, and a riverside Lahu village. Trips are about 2,000B per person for a group of three to five people. The ferry pier is beyond the bridge, across from the Dusit Island Resort. Contact **Maesalong Tours,** 882–4 Phaholyothin Rd. (*C* **05371-2515;** fax 05371-1011; www.maesalongtour.com), or ask at your hotel.

If you're in town on Saturday evening, don't miss the chance to meet some locals and pick up a few gifts at the **Walking Street** along Thanalai Road.

Trekking & Hill-Tribe Tours

Most of the **hill-tribe villages** within close range of Chiang Rai have long ago been set up for routine visits by group tours; a clear example is the "Union of Hilltribe Vil-lages," located just north of Chiang Rai airport, where members of various tribes are herded together for the convenience of tourists who don't have time to go farther. The vibe in such villages is more like a human zoo than an insight into a disappearing lifestyle. If your time is too limited for a trek, in-town travel agencies offer day trips to the countryside and areas less traveled. Guided tours with transport are priced on a two-person minimum basis and greater discounts are available for groups of three or more.

The best operation in Chiang Rai is **Golden Triangle Tours ★**, 590/3 Phaholyo-thin Rd. (*C* **05371-3918;** fax 05371-3963; www.goldenchiangrai.com). They are professional and experienced, offer an array of tours, and cater to personal interests. For hill-tribe treks, choose anything from a day trip to a week of adventure. **Day trips** to surrounding villages begin at 1,600B for a group of 8 to 15 people and can include light trekking to villages as well as elephant trekking for groups of two or three people (private tours cost a bit more). **Longer treks** range in price from 4,100B to 6,200B for a 2- to 4-day sojourn among Akha, Hmong, Yao, Karen, and Lahu tribes.

Where to Stay

This city of 40,000 has an impressive 2,000 hotel rooms, but group tours fill them up in high season. Most hotels are within walking distance of the sights and shopping, though an increasing number of fancy resorts are located by the river or out of town.

EXPENSIVE

Imperial River House ★★ The River House, recently taken over by the Imperial group, is a luxurious campus just across the river from town (near Rimkok Resort; see below). Set around a large pool flanked by laughing elephant sculptures, the resort has a full-service spa and dining area. Rooms are all a very high standard, similar almost to a stylish city hotel, with elegant built-in wooden cabinetry and fine furnishings. Second-floor rooms flank a large veranda overlooking farmers' fields at the riverside—they're a great place to watch the dragonflies at dusk. There are also a few more basic cottages in the grounds, surrounded by greenery. River House caters mostly to high-end Thai travelers and an increasing number of European and North Americans. They have regular evening shuttles to town, and the front-desk staff is very friendly and helpful.

482 Moo 4, Tambon Rim Kok, Chiang Rai 57100. www.imperialhotels.com. ✆ **05375-0829-34.** Fax 05375-0822. 39 units. 4,500B cottage; 6,300B deluxe; 8,900B suite. AE, MC, V. **Amenities:** Restaurant; bar; outdoor pool; health club; room service. *In room:* A/C, satellite TV, minibar, fridge, Wi-Fi (free).

Le Meridien ★★ ☺ In an idyllic setting by the Kok River, a few kilometers from the town center, Le Meridien is a clever blend of contemporary chic and traditional design. Spread out over five wings, the resort's rooms enjoy views of a private lake, lush lawns, and the river. The rooms themselves are spacious with pine floors, stylish furnishings in black and white, walk-in closets and desks, and high-speed Internet access. There are plenty of activities on-site, such as spa treatments, yoga classes, and a well-equipped gym, and trekking, boat tours, or biking tours in the hills around. There's also a shuttle service into town to see the sights or go shopping.

221/2 Moo 20, Kwaewai Rd., Tambon Robwieng, Chiang Rai 57000. www.lemeridien.com. ✆ **05360-3333.** 159 units. 5,000B–7,500B double; 20,000B suite. AE, MC, V. **Amenities:** 2 restaurants; 2 bars; outdoor pool; health club; spa; kids' club. *In-room:* A/C, satellite TV/DVD, minibar, high-speed Internet (530B per day).

MODERATE

Dusit Island Resort Hotel ★★ One of Chiang Rai's best resorts occupies a large delta island in the Kok River. The resort offers international comfort at the expense of local flavor and homeyness. The dramatic lobby is a soaring space of teak, marble, and glass, as grand as any in Thailand, with panoramic views of the Mae Nam Kok. Rooms are luxuriously appointed in pastel cottons and teak trim. The Dusit Island has manicured grounds, a pool, and numerous facilities, making the resort quite self-contained. The hotel's most formal dining room is Peak, on the 10th floor, with sweeping views and a grand terrace overlooking the river; the food is pricey but good. Chinatown is a more casual Cantonese restaurant serving a great dim sum lunch.

1129 Kraisorasit Rd., Chiang Rai 57000 (over bridge at northwest corner of town). www.dusit.com. ✆ **05360-7999.** Fax 05371-5801. 268 units. 2,700B–3,000B superior/deluxe double; from 4,700B suite. AE, DC, MC, V. **Amenities:** 4 restaurants; lounge; pub; outdoor pool; lit tennis courts; health club; sauna; steam room; Jacuzzi; room service; babysitting; executive floor. *In room:* A/C, satellite TV, minibar, fridge, Wi-Fi (535B per day).

The Legend Chiang Rai ★★ 🛍 The Legend is a unique and attractive rural boutique resort. Rooms are private sanctuaries with rustic, unevenly plastered walls and stone floors; the furnishings and canopy beds give them a crisp, modern look, with many natural touches. Pricier rooms overlook the river, others line a narrow garden pond, and all have great indoor and outdoor sitting areas, which allow for a constant connection with your surroundings. There are a few different configurations, but all include large shower areas, some with a Jacuzzi bathtub. One highlight is the inviting infinity-edge pool at the center of the resort. They have a great spa with outdoor *salas* on the riverbank and indoor treatment rooms. There are also two excellent restaurants. The Legend may not have the reputation, or all the facilities, of the international chain hotels, but it has endless charm.

124/15 Moo 21, Kohloy Rd., Chiang Rai 57000. www.thelegend-chiangrai.com. (✆ **05391-0400.** Fax 05371-9650. 78 units. 3,900B–5,900B studio; 8,100B pool villa. AE, MC, V. **Amenities:** Restaurant; bar; outdoor pool; spa; room service; babysitting. *In room:* A/C, satellite TV, minibar, fridge, Wi-Fi (500B for 7 hr. 30 min.).

Rimkok Resort Hotel ★ Everything is done on a large scale at the Rimkok. Public spaces are capped with high-peaked Thai roofs and are grand, featuring Thai decor and artwork. Lushly planted lawns surround the large central pool. Guest rooms are airy, with high ceilings/balconies and some Thai touches—the end result is an overall bland but comfortable setup. Though the resort is rather distant from town, it's thoroughly self-contained enough that you may not need to venture out, and if you do, there's a shuttle service to town (to visit the market). Because it's popular with group tours, the place sometimes gets overrun. Discounts are frequently available.

6 Moo 4, Tathorn Rd., Chiang Rai 57100 (on Kok River, about 2km/1¼ miles north of town center). www.rimkokresort.com. (✆ **05371-6445.** Fax 05371-5859. 256 units. 1,950B double; from 6,000B suite. AE, DC, MC, V. **Amenities:** 2 restaurants; bar and lounge; large outdoor pool; Jacuzzi; room service; babysitting. *In room:* A/C, satellite TV, minibar, fridge, Wi-Fi (free).

Wiang Inn ★ Wiang Inn has a convenient location (just around the corner from the bus station and Night Market), and is just a notch better than the Wangcome Hotel, which is also in the town center. Large rooms are trimmed in dark teak, with pale teak furniture and Thai artwork—including Lanna murals over the beds and ceramic vase table lamps. It is very well maintained, despite the steady stream of group tours, which makes an early booking advisable.

893 Phaholyothin Rd., Chiang Rai 57000 (center of town, south of bus station). www.wianginn.com. (✆ **05371-1533.** Fax 05371-1877. 260 units. 2,800B–3,200B double; from 6,000B suite. AE, DC, MC, V. **Amenities:** Restaurant; bar and karaoke lounge; outdoor pool; room service; babysitting. *In room:* A/C, satellite TV, minibar, fridge, Wi-Fi (100B for 50 hr.).

INEXPENSIVE

The Golden Triangle Inn ★ 🍴 A charming little hotel that offers lots of style and character, Golden Triangle is set in its own quiet little garden patch—once inside you'd never believe bustling Chiang Rai is just beyond the front entrance. Large rooms have wood or terra-cotta tile floors, traditional-style furniture, and reproductions of Lanna artifacts and paintings. The owners and management are very down to earth and extremely helpful. There's an efficient travel agency, **Golden Triangle Tours,** located right in front, which is the best choice in town for arranging travel in the area. The attached restaurant is excellent, too.

590 Phaholyothin Rd., Chiang Rai 57000 (2 blocks north of bus station). www.goldentriangleinn. com. (✆ **05371-1339.** Fax 05371-3963. 31 units. 800B double (breakfast included). MC, V. **Amenities:** Restaurant; Wi-Fi (free). *In room:* A/C, no phone.

Moon & Sun ★ Located to the north of the town center but still south of the river, Moon & Sun is Chiang Rai's smartest budget accommodation, well worth considering if you need to economize. The smallish rooms are well-equipped, with fridges, TVs, and simple, tiled bathrooms with shower stalls. Rates include breakfast. Ask for a room out back as the road in front gets busy in the rush hour.

632 Singhaklai Rd., Chiang Rai 57000 (just east of the TAT office). www.moonandsun-hotel.com. ℰ **05371-9279.** Fax 05374-4906. 28 units. 500B–600B double; 800B family room (breakfast included). MC, V. **Amenities:** Tea room; parking. *In room:* A/C, Satellite TV, fridge, Wi-Fi (free).

Where to Eat

The Night Market is the best for budget eats here, but beyond that there are a few good restaurants from which to choose. Be sure to sample some northern dishes, such as the *kaeng hang lay* or Burmese-style pork curry, the lychees which ripen in April, and the sweet pineapple wine.

Cabbages & Condoms ★ THAI   A sister restaurant to Cabbages & Condoms in Bangkok, this northern branch was opened by the Population & Community Development Association to promote their humanitarian work in the region. The extensive Thai menu is excellent and features local catfish. They play host to lots of events and live bands, and it is a popular stop for tour groups, which also come for the exhibit upstairs (see "Exploring Chiang Rai," above). It gets very busy on Saturdays when the Walking Street is in full swing in front.

620/25 Thanalai Rd. ℰ **05371-9167.** Main courses 80B–200B. MC, V. Daily 10am–11pm.

The Night Market/Food Stalls ★ THAI   Every night after 6pm, the cavernous, tin-roofed Municipal Market at the town center comes alive with dozens of chrome-plated food stalls that serve steamed, grilled, and fried Thai treats. This is where locals meet, greet, and eat. It's really the heart of the town (and a busy mercantile market as well), so don't miss a wander here even if you're not into street-eats. Just outside the main entrance to the market on the main drag is **Aye's Restaurant** (869/170 Phaholyothin Rd.; ℰ **05375-2534**), serving some familiar, if not all that exciting, European fare. Also try **Da Vinci** (879/4–5 Phaholyothin Rd.; ℰ **05375-2535**), an Italian restaurant with good fresh salads, thin-crust pizzas, and pasta.

Old Dutch ★★ INTERNATIONAL/THAI   Conveniently located on Phaholyothin Road near the bus station and Night Market, this stylish place, decked out with chunky furniture, is an ideal choice for a group when some want to eat Thai and others prefer Western food. They serve up some great steaks and salads, and several Indonesian dishes are on the menu too. Thai dishes are tasty, but toned down for Western tastes, so if you like it spicy, just say, "*Ow phet.*" Service is efficient and attentive, and there's draught beer on tap as well.

541 Phaholyothin Rd. (no phone). Entrees 90B–320B. MC, V. Daily 8am–11pm.

Shopping

The arrival of regular busloads of tourists has made Chiang Rai a magnet for hill-tribe clothing and crafts. You'll find many boutiques in the Night Market, near the bus terminal off Phaholyothin Road, as well as some fine shops scattered around the city.

Chiang Rai: Entertainment & Nightlife

The main activity is wandering the **Night Market,** which is really just a more toned-down version of the raucous Night Bazaar in Chiang Mai. On Saturday evenings, Thanalai Road is closed to traffic and becomes a **Walking Street** with stalls selling quirky items aimed at both locals and tourists. As in Chiang Mai, you can find a few bars and clubs (a bit seedy but fun). In Chiang Rai, there are the standard "beer bar" storefronts with such names as **Cat Bar, Lobo,** and **Butterfly** lining Jed Yod Road, which runs parallel to Phaholyothin Road a block to the west.

Chiang Rai to Mae Sai

This is a popular "visa run" route, where many resident expats go to renew their visas. You can cross the border at Mae Sai to Myanmar and reenter Thailand for another 30 days (as long as you have not been in Thailand for 60 consecutive days previously; you'll have to pay 500B). Most visitors coming from Chiang Rai give the dusty little border town of Mae Sai a miss and head instead for Chiang Saen and the Golden Triangle, but the town is worth a look. It is the northernmost point in Thailand.

Just to the right of the border gate to Myanmar (the end of the highway), you'll find a busy market area with rows of tacky souvenirs—and silver jewelry brought from Myanmar. There is also a busy hotel used mostly by Thai tourists and gem traders, the **Wang Thong Hotel** (299 Phaholyothin Rd.; ✆ **05373-3389;** from 900B double). It's getting a bit run-down these days, but has spacious rooms, a pool, a pub, and a dance club, and is almost hidden behind lanes of souvenir stalls. **Warning:** Don't be tempted by the offer of cheap rubies or sapphires, as such offers are almost certainly a scam.

CHIANG SAEN ★ & THE GOLDEN TRIANGLE

935km (581 miles) NE of Bangkok; 239km (149 miles) NE of Chiang Mai

The small village of Chiang Saen, the gateway to the Golden Triangle area, has a sleepy, rural charm, as if the waters of the Mekong carry a palpable calm from nearby Myanmar and Laos. The road from Chiang Rai (59km/37 miles) follows the small Mae Nam Chan River past coconut groves and lush rice paddies. Poinsettias and gladioli decorate thatched Lanna Thai houses with peaked rooflines that extend into Xs like buffalo horns. This elaborately carved roof decoration, called a *galae*, is a defining aspect of Lanna architecture.

Little Chiang Saen, the birthplace of expansionary King Mengrai, was abandoned for the new Lanna capitals of Chiang Rai, then Chiang Mai, in the 13th century, but the ruins of the old city remain, spread across a wide area. Today, the slow rural pace, decaying regal *wats*, crumbling fort walls, and overgrown moat contribute to its appeal.

Once upon a time, the Golden Triangle was the center point of many illicit activities. The name was given to the area where Thailand, Laos, and Myanmar come together—a proximity that facilitated overland drug transportation of opium and heroin in its first steps toward international markets. Thai authorities have mounted a concerted effort to stop the drug traffic here and, while some illegal activity goes unchecked, the area is hardly dangerous. Rather, Sob Ruak, the Thai town at the junction of the Kok and Mekong rivers, is a long and disappointing row of souvenir stalls, with a few "Golden Triangle" signs for photo souvenirs. Still, if you stand at the crook of the river, you can look to the right to see Laos and to the left to see Myanmar (Burma). When the river is low, a large sandbar appears that is apparently unclaimed by any authority.

A common route here is to leave from Chiang Rai by car (or motorbike) and travel directly north to the Burmese border town of **Mae Sai,** a great stop for souvenir shopping. Then follow the Mekong River going east along the border, making a stop at **The Hall of Opium,** and the town of **Sob Ruak,** before catching the museum and many temples of Chiang Saen. If you're overnighting in the area, the fanciest places are in the Golden Triangle proper (west of Chiang Saen).

Essentials

GETTING THERE

BY BUS Buses from **Chiang Rai's Bus Terminal** (p. 344) leave every 15 minutes from 6am to 6pm (trip time 1½ hr.; fare 35B). The bus drops you on Chiang Saen's main street, where the museum and main temples are within walking distance.

BY CAR Take the Superhighway Route 110 north from Chiang Rai to Mae Chan, and then route 1016 northeast to Chiang Saen.

ORIENTATION

Route 1016 is the village's main street, also called Phaholyothin Road, which terminates at the Mekong River. Along the river road there are a few guesthouses, eateries, and souvenir, clothing, and food stalls.

The Golden Triangle and the town of Sob Ruak are just 10km (6¼ miles) north of the town of Chiang Saen, and the choicest accommodations (the Anantara and the Four Seasons) is just a few clicks west from there. Mae Sai is some 30km (19 miles) west of the Golden Triangle.

GETTING AROUND

ON FOOT There's so little traffic, it is a pleasure to walk around here; the main temple ruins are within a 15-minute walk of the town center, though you'll need transport for the more far-flung sites.

BY BICYCLE & MOTORCYCLE It's a great bike ride (45 min.) from Chiang Saen to the prime nearby attraction, the Golden Triangle. The roads are well paved and pretty flat, though you should keep an eye out for speeding vehicles. Bicycles are also ideal for exploring Chiang Saen's more remote temples. Several places on the main road have bicycles for 50B per day, and 100cc motorcycles for 200B per day, as does **Gin's Guest House** (© **05365-0847**), 2km (1¼ miles) north of the center beside the river.

BY SONGTAEW Public *songtaews* make frequent trips between Chiang Saen and the Golden Triangle for about 50B. They leave from the eastern end of Phaholyothin Road, near the river.

BY LONGTAIL BOAT Longtail boat captains down by the river offer Golden Triangle tours for as little as 800B per boat (seating eight) per half-hour. Many people enjoy the half-hour cruise, take a walk around the village of Sob Ruak after they've seen the Golden Triangle, and then continue by bus.

FAST FACTS

A **Siam Commercial Bank** is in the middle of the town's main street, Phaholyothin Road, Route 1016. It's close to the **bus stop,** the **post and telegram office** (with no overseas service and few local telephones), the **police station,** and such attractions as the Chiang Saen National Museum. There are **currency exchange** booths at the Golden Triangle.

Exploring Chiang Saen & the Golden Triangle

Allow half a day to see all of Chiang Saen's historical sights before exploring the Golden Triangle. To help with orientation, make the museum your first stop. There is a good map about local historical sites on the second floor.

The **Chiang Saen National Museum** (702 Phaholyothin Rd.; ✆ **05377-7102;** Wed–Sun 8:30am–4:30pm; admission 100B) houses a small but very fine collection of this region's historic and ethnographic products. The ground floor's main room has a collection of large bronze and stone Buddha images dating from the 15th to the 17th century. Pottery from Sukhothai-era kiln sites is displayed downstairs and on the balcony. The handicrafts and cultural items of local hill-tribes on display here are fascinating, particularly the display of Nam Bat, an ingenious fishing tool. Burmese-style lacquerware, Buddha images, and wood carvings scattered through the museum reinforce the similarities seen between Chiang Saen and its spiritual counterpart, Pagan (in Myanmar). Allow an hour to carefully go through the museum.

Wat Pa Sak, the best preserved *wat* here, is set in a landscaped historical park that contains a large, square-based stupa and six smaller *chedis* and temples. The park preserves what's left of the compound's 1,000 teak trees. The *wat* is said to have been constructed in 1295 by King Saen Phu to house relics of the Buddha, though some historians believe its ornate combination of Sukhothai and Pagan styles dates it later. The historical park is about 200m (656 ft.) west of the Chiang Saen Gate (at the entrance to the village). It is open daily 8am to 6pm; admission is 50B.

The area's second-oldest *wat* is still an active Buddhist monastery, and is located right next to the National Museum. **Wat Chedi Luang** has a huge brick *chedi*, often draped in moss, that dominates the main street. The *wat* complex was established in 1331 under the reign of King Saen Phu and was rebuilt in 1515 by King Muang Kaeo. The old brick foundations of the *viharn*, now supporting a very large, plaster seated Buddha flanked by smaller ones, are all that remain. Small bronze and stucco Buddhas excavated from the site are now in the museum. It is open daily from 8am to 6pm. Admission is free.

There are several other *wats* of note in the town center. **Wat Mung Muang** is the 15th-century square-based stupa seen next to the post office. Above the bell-shaped *chedi* are four small stupas. Across the street, you can see the bell-shaped *chedi* from **Wat Phra Buat.** It's rumored to have been built by the prince of Chiang Saen in 1346, though historians believe it is of the same period as Mung Muang.

If you're exploring by bicycle or motorbike, head for **Wat Phra That Chom Kitti,** in the northwest corner of the Old City. Its main feature is a slender, slightly leaning, 25-m (82-ft.) *chedi*, but the site is also worth visiting, as it sits on a small hill and offers great views of the town and across the river to Laos.

The Golden Triangle

The infamous Golden Triangle (10km/6¼ miles north of Chiang Saen) is the point where Thailand, Myanmar, and Laos meet at the confluence of the broad, slow, and silted Mekong and Ruak rivers. They create Thailand's northern border, separating it from overgrown jungle patches of Myanmar to the west and forested, hilly Laos to the east. The area's appeal as a vantage point over forbidden territories is quickly diminishing, as there is now a legal crossing into Laos from nearby Chiang Khong.

Nonetheless, a look at the home of ethnic hill-tribes and their legendary opium trade is still interesting, and there are some good sites to see. In fact, the appeal of this geopolitical phenomenon has created an entire village—Sob Ruak—of thatch souvenir stalls, cheap riverview soda and noodle shops, and large, fancy hotels. In addition, the two attractions below are worth visiting.

The Hall of Opium ★★★ MUSEUM   Sponsored by the late Princess Mother as part of a larger effort to educate and find alternatives to opium cultivation for hill-tribe peoples of the north, this museum complex covers some 16 hectares (40 acres) of garden overlooking the Mekong. You enter the museum and follow a long corridor through a mountain. In the dark, all you can see are a few murals that portray the pain and anguish of addiction, and then emerge in a grand atrium with a large glowing golden triangle (the irony is a bit much). From there a multimedia romp of films and light-up displays tell of the growth of the poppy, its vital importance in British and international trade with China, the many conflicts over opium, the drug's influx into Thailand, and recent efforts to suppress international smuggling and address rampant addiction throughout the region.

Media-savvy exhibits are in both Thai and English. The "Hall of Excuses" at the end highlights (or lowlights?) many of the world's most well-known addicts, and the museum ends in the "Hall of Reflections," where guests are invited to ruminate on their experience. And it *is* an experience (taking about 1½ hr. to go through). There's nothing like it anywhere else in Thailand.

11km/6¾ miles north of Chiang Saen. ✆ **05378-4444.** Admission 200B. Tues–Sun 8:30am–5:30pm (last ticket sale 4pm).

House of Opium MUSEUM   The hand-painted description and battered old display cases here pale in comparison to the multimedia extravaganza that is the Hall of Opium (see above), but it's more convenient for travelers and you can find much of the same info about opium's cultivation, distribution, and place in global trade. There's lots of paraphernalia and a certain battered charm to the place (plus there's a good little souvenir shop and toilet stop for those on the way to Chiang Saen).

212 House of Opium, Chiang Saen (just opposite the golden Buddha, at the very heart of the Golden Triangle). ✆ **05378-4060.** www.houseofopium.com. Admission 50B. Daily 7am–8pm.

Where to Stay

There are a few cozy guesthouses in Chiang Saen and some fine resort hotels in the Golden Triangle area. The area is scenic and relaxing.

VERY EXPENSIVE

Anantara Resort & Spa Golden Triangle ★★★ 🎁   The superbly swish Anantara is a triumph of upscale, local design. Every detail reminds you that you're in the scenic hill-tribe region; and the resort's elegance and style depend on locally produced weavings, carved teak panels, and expansive views of the juncture of the Ruak and Mekong rivers. The balconied rooms have splendid views and are so spacious and private that you will feel like you're in your own bungalow. Tiled foyers lead to large bathrooms, and bedrooms are furnished in teak and traditional fabrics. The hotel supports a small elephant camp, and its busy tour desk can arrange any number of trips. Rooms are a luxurious city hotel standard, many with windows connecting large bathrooms with the main room area. This and the neighboring Four Seasons Tented Camp are the top choices in the far north hills.

ONWARD to laos

Many make Chiang Rai or Chiang Saen their last port of call in Thailand and head overland to rugged but inviting Laos. Travel downriver 70km (43 miles) to Chiang Khong, a small border town (buses and local *songtaews* also make the connection from either Chiang Rai or Chiang Saen). Most travelers head right across the border, but if you are stuck in Chiang Khong, try **Ban Tammila** (☏ **05379-1234**), with basic rooms overlooking the river, from 400B; or **Reuan Thai Sophaphan** (☏ **05379-1023**), right next door. You'll need to arrange a visa to get over the border to Laos, best done in Bangkok or Chiang Mai at any travel agency.

229 Moo 1, Chiang Saen, Chiang Rai 57150 (above river, 11km/6¾ miles north of Chiang Saen). http://goldentriangle.anantara.com. ☏ **05378-4084.** Fax 05378-4090. 77 units. From 10,500B double; from 15,000B suite. AE, DC, MC, V. **Amenities:** 2 restaurants; lounge and bar; outdoor pool; outdoor lit tennis courts; health club; spa; bike rental; room service; babysitting. *In room:* A/C, satellite TV w/in-house movies, minibar, fridge, hair dryer, Wi-Fi (475B per day).

Four Seasons Tented Camp ★★★   If you want to imagine that you're a 19th-century explorer in the wilds of Asia, but with all modern comforts, here's the place to indulge yourself. To call them "tents" does not do justice to these palatial lodgings set on a hillside above the Golden Triangle. This resort is all-inclusive, so the high rates include everything, from fantastic gourmet meals to spa treatments, and boat trips on the river to mahout training classes at the elephant camp that it shares with the Anantara (see above). The all-inclusive nature of the place also means there's a minimum stay of 2 nights. The huge tents, all enjoying total privacy, have large balconies, huge soft beds, and period furnishings such as brass bathtubs and ancient telephones. It is overwhelming and memorable.

P.O. Box 18, Chiang Saen P.O., Chiang Rai 57150 (next to Anantara on the Ruak River). www.fourseasons.com/goldentriangle. ☏ **05391-0200.** Fax 05365-2189. 15 units. 79,000B tent (2-night minimum). AE, DC, MC, V. **Amenities:** Restaurant; bar; outdoor pool; spa. *In-room:* A/C, minibar, hair dryer, Wi-Fi (free).

MODERATE

The Imperial Golden Triangle Resort ★   This five-story hotel block stands in the western corner of the tiny souvenir village of Sob Ruak. Modern, spacious guest rooms with pastel and rattan decor have large balconies, and the more expensive rooms overlook the Golden Triangle. It is a fine, comfortable choice if you're passing through, but pales in comparison to the nearby Anantara and Four Seasons (see above).

222 Golden Triangle, Chiang Saen, Chiang Rai (in Sob Ruak, 11km/6¾ miles north of Chiang Saen). www.imperialhotels.com. ☏ **05378-4001-5.** Fax 05378-4006. 73 units. 2,464B–2,719B double; from 5,862B suite. AE, MC, V. **Amenities:** Restaurant; bar; lounge; outdoor pool; high-speed Internet. *In room:* A/C, satellite TV, minibar, fridge, Wi-Fi (free).

INEXPENSIVE

Chiang Saen River Hill Hotel   This is the best place to stay in Chiang Saen, located about 1km (⅔ mile) south of the main drag. Guest rooms are concrete-block rooms with simple tile floors but are dressed in northern finery, with woodcarving details and funky little Lanna-style seating arrangements (axe cushions around low tables under regal umbrellas). The large and colorful coffee shop is open for breakfast, lunch, and dinner, with good selections and a relaxed and refreshing atmosphere.

714 Moo 3, Sukhapibansai 2 Rd., Tambon Viang, Chiang Saen, Chiang Rai (5-min. *samlor* ride from bus stop). www.chiangsaenriverhillhotel.com. © **05365-0826.** Fax 05365-0830. 60 units. 1,500B double. MC, V. Rates include complementary breakfast. **Amenities:** Restaurant, Wi-Fi (free). *In room:* A/C, TV.

EXPLORING ISAN: THAILAND'S FRONTIER

The 20 provinces of northeastern Thailand are collectively called Isan (e-sahn) and account for roughly one-third of the country's landmass, and a third of the population. Bordered by Laos to the north and east (along the Mekong) and by Cambodia to the south, the region suffers from a stagnant rural economy. Life is hard on the scorched plains of Isan, but the friendly people of this region welcome travelers warmly—you'll experience something along the lines of America's southern hospitality. There are a few tourist attractions, mostly off the beaten track, including some important archaeological sites (mostly dating from the Khmer period), lovely river towns, finely made crafts, and fiery food. The areas in the far north and along the Mekong Valley are particularly worth the trip.

The weather is especially hot in Isan but follows a pattern much like the rest of Thailand: It's coolest from November to February; hot and dry from March to May; and rainy from June to October. Windswept and infertile in parts, but verdant along the Mekong, the region is attracting more international tourists who like to explore remote provinces, but also because Isan is a good jumping-off point for trips to Laos.

Indeed, much about Isan, from the weather to the local dialect and culture, resembles Laos and is quite distinct from mainstream Thai culture. As a result, many joke about *Prathet Isan*, or "the Nation of Isan," for its unique language, culture, and stubbornly snail-like pace. As the poorest region of Thailand, with little opportunity for its young populace, Isan is experiencing an ever-increasing drain on people as young folks move to the area's larger cities. A few learned phrases of the Isan dialect will endear you to a large part of the Bangkok cab driver population, for example. You are sure to meet kind folks from Isan in every region of Thailand, including staff in resorts in the south, and the fact that you know the name of their town, much less have been there, will be a source of wonder.

INFORMATION & TOURS

Airlines covering this region include **Thai Airways** (📞 **02356-1111;** www.thaiair. com), **Nok Air** (📞 **1318;** www.nokair.com), **Air Asia** (📞 **02515-9999;** www.air asia.com) and **Thai Regional Airlines** (📞 **02134-7152;** www.thairegionalairlines. com). There are also regular bus and train connections throughout Isan. In more remote parts, buses are slow and won't stop near sights, so try to arrange a tour, or go by your own rented vehicle with a driver. The latter is a relatively affordable proposition; expect to pay about 2,000B per day, plus fuel. Contact **Isan Discovery Travel** in Khon Kaen (311/15 Klang Muang Rd., 3rd Floor, Room 305, Khon Kaen 40000; 📞 **04332-1268;** fax 04322-5196; www.thaitraveldreams.com), a small, expat-owned tour company; they can arrange a private itinerary covering the region.

There are **Tourist Authority of Thailand (TAT)** offices in bigger towns in the region (though few are conveniently located). Check out www.tourismthailand.org, or call 📞 **1672** for assistance.

NAKHON RATCHASIMA (KHORAT)

259km (161 miles) NE of Bangkok; 150km (93 miles) W of Buriram; 305km (190 miles) S of Udon Thani

Nakhon Ratchasima, popularly known as Khorat, isn't a wildly interesting city, but it is close to Bangkok and makes a good base for excursions to beautiful **Khao Yai National Park** (see "Side Trips from Bangkok," in chapter 6) and the Khmer temple at **Phimai.** It is a rapidly developing industrial city and is called the "Gateway to Isan" because it is located in the southwest corner of the region and all train lines, bus routes, roads, and communications from Bangkok pass through it. There is some comfortable accommodation in Khorat and a few temples and city monuments worth seeing. The city also gives its name to the Khorat Plateau, which occupies most of Isan. The plateau is made of sandstone, which accounts for the region's lack of fertility, and stands about 200m (656 ft.) above sea level.

Getting There

Thai Regional Airlines (📞 **02134-7152;** www.thairegionalairlines.com) operates three flights a week from Bangkok to Khorat. There are numerous daily trains from Bangkok's **Hua Lampong Station** (📞 **1690**), and frequent bus connections from Bangkok's Northern Bus Terminal, **Mo Chit** (📞 **02936-2841**). It's about a 3-hour journey by train or bus.

Exploring Khorat

A trip to **Pimai,** 60km (37 miles) northeast of town, is highly recommended to appreciate the wonders of Khmer archaeology, particularly if you have not visited Angkor Wat, in Cambodia. **Prasat Hin Pimai ★★** temple complex (daily 7:30am–6pm; 100B) has been beautifully restored by the Fine Arts Department, and there is a large museum on-site as well. In Khorat, the most interesting temple houses a sandstone image of Phra Narai (Vishnu), a sacred Hindu deity, at **Wat Phra Narai Maharat** (daily 8am–8pm), along Prajak Road, where you'll also find the **City Pillar.**

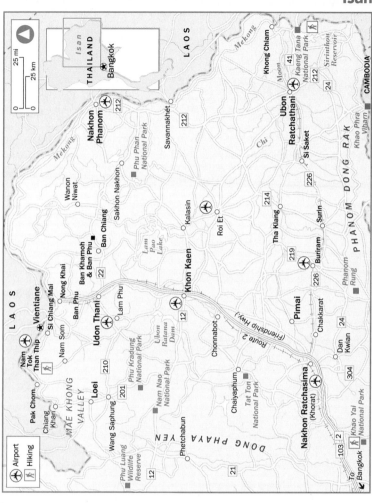

Where to Stay & Eat

The best hotel in town is the **Dusit Princess Khorat** (1137 Suranarai Rd., northeast of town near the stadium; www.dusit.com; ✆ **04425-6629**), with fair amenities and rooms starting from 1,500B. A close second is **Sima Thani** (2112/2 Mittraphap Rd., next to the TAT office, west of town; www.simathani.com; ✆ **04421-3100**), with similar rates. **Thai Inter Hotel** (344/2 Yommarat Rd., inside the old walled city; ✆ **04424-7700**) is a smart, newish place with basic rooms from 650B.

When it comes to dining, you can't do better than head for the reliable **Cabbages & Condoms** (86/1 Seub Siri Rd.; ✆ **04425-3760**), a branch of the Population &

Community Development Association-run chain that is located just west of the train station. With a shady terrace, an extensive menu of such Thai classics as *tom kha kai* (chicken in coconut soup), and a decent wine list, it's an ideal spot to while away a lazy evening. If you're hankering for Western food, head for **Chez Andy** (5–7 Manat Rd.; ✆ 04428-9556) in the southwest corner of the Old City, where you can order up a steak or fondue.

KHON KAEN

449km (279 miles) NE of Bangkok; 190km (118 miles) N of Nakhon Ratchasima; 115km (71 miles) S of Udon Thani

Though Khon Kaen is Isan's most heavily populated and busiest city, for most travelers it is just a stopover en route to places like Udon and Nong Khai. The town is along Route 2, connects by rail with Bangkok and Nong Khai, and has a large commercial airport.

Getting There

Thai Airways (✆ 02356-1111; www.thaiairways.com) has several flights a day from Bangkok. There are also three trains running daily from Bangkok, and bus services abound.

Exploring Khon Kaen

The town's most striking monument is the nine-tiered **Wat Nongwan Muang Kao,** located at the southern end of Klang Muang Road. Supposedly inspired by the Shwedagon Pagoda in Myanmar, its white, red, and gold coat glows in the early-morning and late-afternoon sun, making it great for photos. Conveniently located to the east of the temple is **Beung Kaen Nakhon,** a large lake that attracts walkers, joggers, and cyclists to its perimeter path (bikes can be rented for 20B) in the mornings and evenings, and diners to eat at restaurants overlooking the water. **Bua Luang,** situated at the northern end of the lake, is a good choice (see below).

Recently, the town has become a kind of "Dinosaur City," with models of these creatures everywhere. This is due to the discovery in 1996 of a small (6-m/l20-ft. long) fossil of a 120-million-year-old dinosaur at **Phuwiang,** about 90km (56 miles) northwest of Khon Kaen. Phuwiang has now been protected as a national park, but, in truth, there is little to see there apart from a few dusty old bones.

Where to Stay & Eat

You'll find many room options in Khon Kaen, as it's a busy regional convention center. The top choice is the **Pullman Khon Kaen Raja Orchid** (9–9 Prachasamran Rd.; www.pullmanhotels.com; ✆ 04332-2155), with stylish rooms from 2,800B. Almost as classy, but much cheaper is the **Charoen Thani Princess** (Srichan and Na-Muang roads; www.charoenthanikhonkaen.com; ✆ 04322-0400-14), a popular meeting and convention address with doubles from 1,400B. On a smaller scale, the **Bussaracam** (68 Pimpasut Rd.; www.bussarakamhotel.com; ✆ 04333-3666) has clean and comfortable rooms from 900B.

Because eating options in Thailand always increase in relation to the population, Khon Kaen has plenty of places for the culinary curious to explore. **Bua Luang,** at the north end of Beung Kaen Nakhon Lake, has an extensive menu with lots of seafood and generally efficient service, and is a favorite spot for locals to take guests for a feast. Nearer the center of town, **Didine,** on Prachasamran Road (near the train station), serves some imaginative Western dishes, such as chicken with tarragon sauce, as well as several Thai favorites; there's also a good selection of drinks and a pool table. Isan is famous for its **marinated grilled chicken,** so if you pass a roadside stall giving off a smoky, appealing aroma, don't hesitate to stop and buy a sample.

UDON THANI & BAN CHIANG

564km (350 miles) NE of Bangkok; 305km (190 miles) N of Nakhon Ratchasima

"No sweat, man," was once a common saying among tuk-tuk drivers here. The use of 1960s slang reminds tourists that Udon Thani (or Udon) was home to a large contingent of U.S. armed forces during the Vietnam War and memories of that time still linger. Today you might see a few retired U.S. servicemen around, and each year the area welcomes a contingent of the U.S. military for joint training with Thai forces (mostly the Air Force).

Udon itself has few attractions, but it is a good jumping-off point to such small towns as Loei, to the west (p. 362), and Ban Chiang, a well-known archaeological site, to the east.

Getting There & Getting Around

Thai Airways (℡ **02356-1111;** www.thaiair.com) offers daily flights to the area, as do budget carriers **Nok Air** (℡ **1318;** www.nokair.com) and **Air Asia** (℡ **02515-9999;** www.airasia.com). Numerous trains (best as an overnight in a second-class sleeper) connect from Bangkok's **Hua Lampong Station** (℡ **1690**) daily via Khon Kaen; and there are bus connections from Udon to anywhere in the region. *Note:* **Budget Car Rental** has an office at the airport (℡ **04224-6805**). It is a good idea to fly to Udon and rent a car here to explore the Mekong Valley to the north (see the following sections).

The hub of this town is the **Charoensri Shopping Complex,** around which you'll find many services. With a population of around 200,000, Udon is quite sprawling, so the best way to get around is by tuk-tuks, which, oddly, are called "skylabs" here.

Exploring Udon Thani & Ban Chiang

BAN CHIANG NATIONAL MUSEUM ★ The tiny hamlet of Ban Chiang, approximately 50km (31 miles) east of Udon on the Sakon Nakhon highway, boasts a history of more than 5,600 years, and, as such, the area was declared a UNESCO World Heritage Site in 1992. It was—quite literally—stumbled upon in 1974 and, since then, has been excavated by an international team. The findings at Ban Chiang prove the existence of a distinct and very sophisticated Bronze Age culture in Southeast Asia, long before any earlier findings. The museum was funded by the Kennedy Foundation and houses a fine collection of early statuary as well as pottery and ritual implements. The site is open Tuesday to Sunday from 8:30am to 4:30pm; admission is 150B. Ban Chiang is close to the main highway between Udon and Nakhon Phanom. It's best visited by private vehicle, but you can also ask local buses to stop at the Ban Chiang junction and take a tuk-tuk to the site. Along the main road to the site, look for the many villages producing replica Ban Chiang ceramic ware, with its distinctive spiral design.

The Mekong Valley Loop

This loop takes you from **Udon**, to the west, and the little town of **Loei**, then along the Mekong, the natural Thai–Laos border, through **Nong Khai**, and on to **Nakhon Phanom**. With a side trip to **That Phanom** (and a possible stop at Ban Chiang), you return to Udon, from where you can fly back to Bangkok. You could also follow the Mekong all the way south from Nakhon Phanom to **Ubon Ratchathani**, from where you can also hop on a flight back to Bangkok. This is adventurous off-the-track travel, and it's not a bad idea to hire a car and driver (see "Information & Tours," at the beginning of this chapter). The bigger companies like Budget will deliver a car (with or without driver) to you in one town and pick it up in another.

Where to Stay & Eat

Udon's best choice hotel, the **Centara** (277/1 Prachak Silpakorn Rd., west of the railway station and adjacent to the mall; ✆ **04234-3555;** www.centarahotelsresorts. com), was closed for renovations at the time of this update but should re-open by early 2012; it's in a central location with cozy rooms from around 1,800B. Your next best bet is the **Charoen Hotel** (549 Phosri Rd., near the train station; ✆ **04224-8155**), which has basic rooms from 900B.

For a range of choice, the best bet for eating in the evening is at the **Night Market**, on Prajak Road, just west of the train station. If you prefer something more relaxed and romantic, try **Rabiang Patchani,** at 53/1 Suphakit Janya Rd., on the east side of a lake called Nong Prajak. The menu here features an extensive range of unusual Isan dishes, and diners can choose between an air-conditioned interior and a breezy deck.

LOEI

520km (323 miles) NE of Bangkok; 344km (214 miles) N of Nakhon Ratchasima

Cool and often rainy because of its higher elevation (the town is reputedly the coldest spot in the kingdom), little Loei is a lazy riverside town worth an overnight stop, but this route is more about the beautiful road journey and nearby national parks rather than the town of Loei itself. Dan Sai, 80km (50 miles) southwest of Loei, hosts the annual **Pi Tha Khon Festival** (June/July), a Thai-style Mardi Gras in which young men dress as spirits and go crazy in the streets. "The devil made me do it!" is the excuse for all kinds of outlandish behavior; it's lots of fun. South of Loei town is **Phu Kradung National Park** (admission 400B adults, 200B children), one of Thailand's most dramatic sights: a bell-shaped, tabletop mountain of 1,300m (4,265ft.) that can be climbed in around 3 to 4 hours (porters can be hired to carry bags) and has rustic log-cabin huts (900B–3,600B double) for visitors to stay on the summit. The park is 82km (51 miles) from Loei and well worth the trip, especially in December and January when the scarlet maple leaves are falling, though it's closed during the rainy season (June–Sept).

Getting There

There is neither a train line nor an airport in Loei, but regular buses connect the town with Udon Thani and Khon Kaen. See p. 60 for information.

Where to Stay & Eat

Loei Palace Hotel (167/4 Charoenrat Rd.; ✆ **04281-5668;** www.oamhotels.com) is by far the best choice in town; it's a huge courtyard hotel with lots of amenities, including a pool and affordable rooms (from 1,300B per double). **King Hotel** (11/9–12 Chumsai Rd., in the town center; ✆ **04281-1701**) is an even more affordable choice with smart rooms and free Wi-Fi for 500B.

A good restaurant is **Ban Thai** (✆ **04283-3472**) at 22/58-60 Chumsai Rd., because it can satisfy a craving for Western food with steaks, pizzas, good beer, and coffee, but also turns out a good range of tasty Thai dishes—it's ideal for a group of diners with different tastes.

ALONG THE MEKONG FROM LOEI TO NONG KHAI

One of the most scenic areas in Thailand—and delightfully secluded—the north-western perimeter of Isan runs along the wide Mekong River, which forms the border with Laos. The terrain is relatively flat, the road is only lightly trafficked and in a good state of repair, and you can stop at a number of villages. Buses and *songtaews* don't make all of these connections, so you'll need to have your own transport.

The loop begins in Loei and ends in Nong Khai. Directly north of Loei, you'll reach the riverside town of **Chiang Khan,** where you'll find a few riverside guesthouses, and temples worth visiting, such as **Wat Si Khun Muang** with its Lao-style stupa, interesting murals and topiary. You can take a trip to the rapids at **Kaeng Kut Khu** by longtail boat for around 1,000B for a couple of hours (contact any riverside guesthouse).

From Chiang Khan, Route 212 follows the Mekong east to **Pak Chom, Sangkhom,** and **Si Chiang Mai** before arriving in Nong Khai. The route passes lush banana plantations, terraced fruit farms, and wonderful river views. Cotton and tomato fields fan out along the verdant flood plains of the Mekong basin. Farther inland are attractive waterfalls, such as **Than Thip** (between Pak Chom and Sangkhom), which are fun for hiking and ideal for picnics.

If you're looking for a stopover along this route, your best bet is the **Poopae Ruenmaithai Resort** (✆ **04244-1088;** www.poopaeresort.com), about a mile (1.6 km) east of Sangkhom on Route 211, which has some smart riverfront rooms at 500B to 1,500B in stylish stone buildings connected by wooden walkways. It's about halfway between Chiang Khan and Nong Khai.

As you head east from Sangkhom beside the river, don't miss **Wat Hin Mak Peng,** a meditation temple some 30km (19 miles) west of Si Chiang Mai, which occupies a glorious site overlooking the Mekong, or the unique gold tower of the **Prasutham Chedi,** just before you reach Si Chiang Mai, beside the main road.

Si Chiang Mai is opposite Vientiane, the Laos capital, and is but 58km (36 miles) due west of Nong Khai. The town is just a quiet Thai backwater. Walks along the long concrete pier or relaxing and watching Laos and Thai longtail boats load and unload or chug up- and downriver is about all that's going on here. In the evenings, join in a game of badminton or a circle of people juggling a *takraw* (a small rattan ball). There are lots of little open-air eateries at the riverside and a few small guesthouses along the quay at the town center. On the final stretch along Route 211 to Nong Khai, keep your eyes open for some amazing topiary at the roadside. Actually, you can't miss these huge hedges carved into the shape of elephants, kangaroos, and even Thai boxers—a great photo op!

NONG KHAI

615km (382 miles) NE of Bangkok; 51km (32 miles) N of Udon Thani

The little border town of Nong Khai is nothing special but its sprawling riverside market **Tha Sadet** is full of interesting goods from Laos and China, and the place has a palpable calm with some good, laid-back riverside guesthouses. Nong Khai is a popular jumping-off point for travel to Laos.

Getting There

The nearest airport is in Udon Thani (p. 361), but Nong Khai is the terminus of the Northeast train line from Bangkok and is an enjoyable, if rocky, overnight journey. Regular buses connect with points throughout the region, too.

Exploring Nong Khai

Tha Sadet, or the **Indochina Market** (daily 8am–6pm), located at the heart of town at the riverside, is the main attraction in Nong Khai and it is certainly worth a wander. Also check out **Sala Kaew Ku Sculpture Park** ★ (about 4km/2½ miles east of town, on Rte. 212), where you'll find concrete Buddhas, Hindu deities, and other fantastic statues of enormous proportions in an attractive garden setting—all the brainchild of the eccentric Mr. Luang Phu Boonlua Surirat. He studied with an Indian guru in Vietnam and later taught in Laos, and his mummified body can be viewed on a tour of the main temple building (he also built a similar sculpture garden just across the river near Vientiane, Laos). Entry is 20B, and the site is open daily from 8am to 6pm.

Good day trips from Nong Khai include a day (or overnight) across the border to **Vientiane** (visas are available at the border), or head out to **Phu Phrabat Historical**

GOODNESS gracious! GREAT BALLS OF . . . FIRE?

In October, when the moon is full, heralding the end of the Buddhist Lent, a ghostly phenomenon occurs that is, as yet, unexplained. From the waters of the Mekong rise glowing balls of red fire that ascend high into the night sky. This mystical event attracts thousands from all over Thailand. The explanation? Some say it is the rising *Naga*, or river dragon, coming to greet Lord Buddha. On the other hand, scientists claim it is bubbles of gas originating from rotting organic matter in the riverbed being released into the air. Whether believer or nonbeliever, superstitious Thais love to flock to the venue, and hotels are usually full this time of year. Be warned, however, that the spectacle is not guaranteed; when I visited, there were no fireballs to be seen. ***Note:*** There is little or no public transport available on these nights, so you'll need your own transport, and be prepared for traffic jams along the riverside road.

Park, some 70km/43 miles southwest of Nong Khai; the site is a unique grouping of natural sandstone towers that were fashioned into rudimentary cave dwellings.

Where to Stay & Eat

Budget accommodation lines the small streets all over town. **Mutmee Guesthouse** (1111/4 Kaeworawut Rd.; ✆ **04246-0717;** www.mutmee.com) is foreign-run, and a comfortable budget choice (from 150B for dorm beds; from 170B per double). It's also a great place to get good local info (and great food), and they can try to help with transport options on Naga Fireball nights. The best hotel in Nong Khai is the **Grand Paradise Hotel** (589 Moo 5, Nong Khai–Poanpisai Rd., just south of town; ✆ **04242-0033;** www.nongkhaigrand.com), with comfortable air-conditioned rooms from 1,400B.

For good local dining, try **Daeng Namnuang** (on a small side street just off the central market; ✆ **04241-1961**), serving a popular do-it-yourself Vietnamese pork spring roll. Alternatively, stop by **Café Thasadej** (✆ **04242-3921**), just round the corner at 387/3 Soi Thepbunterng, where you can choose from Thai favorites, German sausage, or spaghetti bolognese.

NAKHON PHANOM

740km (460 miles) NE of Bangkok; 252km (157 miles) E of Udon Thani; 481km (299 miles) NE of Nakhon Ratchasima

Travelers rarely make it out to these parts of Thailand; apart from a few good riverside hotels catering to Westerners, the place is pretty quiet. That's the allure. Walk riverside streets and look for the old Vietnamese clock tower—a gift from grateful Vietnamese Catholic refugees escaping Ho Chi Minh's Communists in North Vietnam. South of town is **That Phanom,** an important pilgrimage site for Thai Buddhists; from there, pass through Sakon Nakhon to return to Udon Thani (with a possible side trip to Ban Chiang) completing the loop. If you have more time, follow the Mekong south from Nakhon Phanom all the way to Ubon Ratchathani, where you can fly on Thai Regional Airlines or catch a train back to Bangkok. Each year, Nakhon Phanom hosts the famed "Lai Rua Fai," or **Fire Boat Festival,** where barges float downstream, twinkling with small candles in the night (also dragon boat races by day), all to celebrate the end of the rains in October.

Getting There

Though Nakhon Pathom has an airport, there are currently no flights serving the town. VIP buses from Bangkok take about 12 hours and cost around 1,000B.

Exploring Nakhon Phanom

The city's *wats* are built in a distinctive style, and the exterior bas-reliefs, attributed to the Laotian Lan Xang kingdom, are said to date back some 300 years. An hour to the south, **Wat That Phanom** is a temple built around a tall 9th-century stupa that collapsed in 1975 and was rebuilt in 1978. It's an important pilgrimage site for Thai Buddhists and makes for a pleasant trip. The 53-m (174-ft.) tall stupa itself is built in Laos style, with its tapering, curved sides decorated with gold patterns on a white background and topped off with a gold umbrella. There's always a reverential aura

Branching off on the eastern spur of the rail line at Khorat as you head north and east of Bangkok, you trace the edge of the Cambodian border on your way to Laos. First reach **Buriram,** a town with a few notable hilltop Khmer ruins, and then **Surin** (see below), an area famous for raising elephants, before reaching **Ubon Ratchathani.** There are few jaw-dropping sites—and few Western tourists—in this city.

around the place, particularly at the annual **That Phanom Festival,** usually in February, when it is crowded with pilgrims, both Thai and Lao, for 10 days.

Where to Stay

The Nakhon Pahanom River View Hotel (9 Nakhon Phanom—That Phanom Rd.; www.nakhonphanomriverviewhotel.com; ✆ **04252-2333**) has well-furnished rooms, some with glorious river views, starting at 1,500B.

SURIN

457km (284 miles) NE of Bangkok; 227km (141 miles) W of Ubon Ratchathani

Surin is elephant country and is justly famed for its annual roundup (in Nov), a nearly 200-year tradition; the city is also a good base for exploring far-flung Khmer ruins.

Getting There

Thai Regional Airlines (✆ **02134-7152;** www.thairegionalairlines.com) and **Nok Air** (✆ **1318;** www.nokair.com) both have a couple of flights a week from Bangkok to nearby Buriram. Ten trains connect daily to Surin from Bangkok via the spur line from Khorat (about 8½ hr.), and there are numerous buses; see p. 60 in chapter 5, "Settling into Bangkok," for details.

Exploring Surin

If you haven't come with your own guide, the best way to visit the sporadically scattered sites around Surin is to book a tour with friendly Mr. Pirom at the **Pirom Guest House** (✆ **04451-5140**). Mr. Pirom has been in the business for years and guiding is just an extension of his passion for the ancient history and culture of this rural region. The most popular tours are to the many secluded Khmer temples in the area, and he combines such visits with stops at elephant-training villages (such as Ban Tha Klang), Khmer cultural sites, handicraft villages, and even trips to the weekend market at the Cambodian border. Expect to pay from 1,000B per person.

The **elephant roundup ★** that takes place on the third weekend of November each year is one of Thailand's best-known festivals, so it attracts many Thais as well as foreign visitors. As a result, accommodation must be booked well in advance. Over the course of the weekend, the elephants parade in battle gear, play games of soccer, and test their strength with a tug of war. Don't miss the morning parade when locals lay out a spread for the pachyderms as they stroll through town. Tickets cost

UBON ratchathani

Tucked away between Thailand's borders with Cambodia and Laos, **Ubon Ratchathani** is one of Isan's largest urban centers with over 100,000 inhabitants. There is little to detain travelers in the town itself apart from a massive statue of a votive candle in **Thung Si Muang Park,** though it is a good base for trips to nearby national parks. The statue is a reference to the town's unusual annual **Candle Festival,** which takes place in July, when huge wax carvings are paraded round the town's streets.

Located a short stroll west of the town center at 251 Palochai Rd., the **Tohsang City Hotel** (www.tohsang.com; ☏ 04524-5531) provides a stylish spot to rest your head, with rooms starting at around 2,200B. For a more rural experience, go for the **Tohsang Khongjiam Resort** (www.tohsang.com; ☏ 04535-1174), which is situated on the banks of the Khong Chiam River, near the border with Laos, about 75 km/46 miles northeast of Ubon Ratchathani. Rates here are a little higher than at the City Hotel, but the picturesque views along the river make it worth it. Nearby are the national parks of **Pha Taem** (admission 200B adults, 100B children), which has some ancient rock paintings on a cliff overlooking the Mekong River, and **Kaeng Tana** (admission 100B adults, 50B children), where the attractions are waterfalls, caves, and unusual rock formations.

from 500B to 800B and can be reserved through the Tourist Authority of Thailand (www.tourismthailand.org). Outside of festival time, the best way to get up close and personal with the elephants is at **Ban Tha Klang,** to the north of Surin.

Outside of Surin

Buriram is about halfway between Surin and Khorat, and easily reached overland or by **Nok Air** (☏ 1318; www.nokair.com) or **Thai Regional Airlines'** (☏ 02134-7152; www.thairegionalairlines.com) flights from the capital. It's the best base (a little nearer than Khorat) to visit **Phanom Rung ★★** (daily 6am–6pm; admission 100B), a stunning Khmer ruin which was deserted in the late 13th century, rediscovered in 1935, and restored in the 1970s. This Khmer temple was built during the 11th century, and stands in a direct line between Angkor in Cambodia and Pimai, a little farther northwest. Like Pimai, it has benefited from a loving restoration by the Fine Arts Department, and is in some ways even more impressive than Pimai with its hilltop location and intricate carvings on the main *prang* (central tower). It's worth stopping by the **visitor center** (9am–4:30pm) to get an overview of the temple's most significant aspects.

An additional popular side trip from Surin is **Khao Phra Viharn,** another striking Khmer temple site, on the Cambodian border, with some wonderful lintel carvings, though not restored as meticulously as Pimai or Phanom Rung. However, at the time of this update (and for the last few years), it was closed to the public due to a border dispute, so check locally whether it has re-opened before setting out on the long journey. When it is open, it costs around 400B to get in—200B each for the Thai and Cambodian authorities.

Where to Stay

There are no stand-out hotels in Surin—your choice is between big, characterless places in the center of town, or a basic but welcoming guesthouse on the outskirts of town. **Thong Tarin Hotel** (60 Sirirat Rd., just east of the bus station and town center; www.thongtarinhotel.com; ✆ **04451-4281**) is a reasonable choice, with tidy rooms from 1,600B. Nearby **Phetchkasem Hotel** (104 Chitbumrung Rd., in the town center; ✆ **04451-1274**) is a basic business hotel, with rooms from just 1000B. **Pirom Guesthouse** (SoiArunee, Thungpo Rd., 1km/⅔ mile west of the station; ✆ **04451-5140**) is a very rustic but authentic guesthouse with rooms starting at 200B—you will feel as though you're a special guest of owners Pirom and his wife Aree when you stay here.

PLANNING YOUR TRIP TO THAILAND

GETTING THERE
Getting to Thailand
BY PLANE

When you plan your trip, consider that Thailand has more than one international airport. While most international flights arrive in Bangkok's **Suvarnabhumi International Airport** (airport code BKK; ℂ **02132-1888**), you can also fly directly to **Phuket** (airport code HKT; ℂ **07632-7230-7**), **Ko Samui** (airport code USM; ℂ **07724-5600**), and **Chiang Mai** (airport code CNX; ℂ **05327-0222-33**) from certain regional destinations such as Singapore or Hong Kong. Flight times from the U.S. to Thailand vary from 17 hours (from San Francisco or LA) to 22 hours (from New York). Stopovers add even more time, so it's worth opting for a direct flight if you want to avoid severe jet lag. Thai Airways' direct flights from Los Angeles or New York keep travel time to a minimum. Direct flights from London to Bangkok take around 11 hours. For information on how to get into the city from the airport, see the Arriving section in chapter 5.

BY TRAIN

Thailand is accessible via train from Singapore and peninsular Malaysia. **Malaysia's Keretapi Tanah Melayu Berhad (KTM)** begins in Singapore (ℂ **65/6222-5165**), stopping in Kuala Lumpur (ℂ **603/2267-1200**) and Butterworth (Penang; ℂ **604/323-7962**), before heading for Thailand, where it joins service with the State Railway of Thailand. **Bangkok's Hua Lampong Station** is centrally located on Krung Kasem Road (ℂ **02220-4334** or 1690). Taxis, tuk-tuks, and public buses wait outside the station and access to the MRT (subway) is a few steps away.

The *Eastern & Oriental Express* (www.orient-express.com) operates a 2-night/3-day journey between Singapore and Bangkok that makes *getting* there almost better than *being* there. The romance of 1930s colonial travel is joined with modern luxury in six Pullman cars, seven State cars, a Presidential car, plus two restaurant cars, a bar car, a saloon car, and an observation car. Along the way, stops are made in Penang (Georgetown) and Kanchanaburi (River Kwai) for light sightseeing. Current fares per person one-way are $2,440 for a Pullman superior double. At certain times of the year, promotions will include overnights at the Oriental Bangkok and its sister property, the Mandarin Oriental, Singapore. Call ✆ **800/393-5406** in the U.S., ✆ **65/6395-0678** in Singapore.

BY SHIP

Star Clipper Cruises run leisurely, week-long cruises stopping at several islands between Singapore and Phuket. For information contact ✆ **302810-300330** in Greece, or check the website, www.finesthotels.net/cruises-clippers2.php.

Getting Around

Thailand's domestic transport system is accessible, efficient, and inexpensive. If your time is short, fly. But if you have the time to take in the countryside, travel by bus, train, private car, or for the really adventurous, by rented motorbike. Read on for details about all your transport options.

For tips on deciphering Thai addresses, see p. 62 in chapter 5.

BY PLANE

Many domestic flights in Thailand depart from **Suvarnabhumi Airport,** though some flights use the former international airport at **Don Muang Airport** (airport code DMK; ✆ **02535-1111**), so make sure which one you're headed for, as they are a long way apart. Don Muang may not be as glitzy as the newer Suvarnabhumi, but it's certainly less stressful and works fairly well. Airports in other cities usually tend to be more basic but will have all the necessities such as money-changing facilities, information kiosks, and waiting ground transportation.

The majority of domestic flights are on **Thai Airways** (✆ **02356-1111;** www.thaiairways.com), with Bangkok as its hub. Flights connect Bangkok with several domestic destinations, including Chiang Mai, Chiang Rai, Ko Samui, Krabi, and Phuket. There are also some connecting flights between these cities.

The budget subsidiary of Thai Airways, **Nok Air** (✆ **1318;** www.nokair.com) has a head office in the Sathorn district. It operates on lesser-used routes, as does the no-frills carrier **Orient Thai** (✆ **1126;** www.flyorientthai.com), based at 18 Ratchadapisek Rd., in the Klong Toey district.

The growing fleet at **Bangkok Airways** (✆ **1177** or 02270-6699 for reservations; www.bangkokair.com) now covers 19 destinations across Asia and is the sole operator of the Phuket to Ko Samui, and Bangkok to Trat routes. It also has international flights to Singapore, Vietnam, Japan, Myanmar, Laos, China, and Cambodia, as well as to The Maldives.

Also check what's on offer from **Air Asia** (✆ **02515-9999** in Bangkok; www.airasia.com). They now fly between Bangkok and 10 Thai cities, as well as offering good-value fares internationally.

Several other less-well-known carriers serve destinations in the north, the northeast, and the southern peninsula. See individual chapters for details of the most convenient connections in different regions of the country.

BY CAR

Renting a car is easy in Thailand, but driving it is another matter. Driving in Bangkok is particularly hard; the one-way streets, poor and even misleading road signage, and constant traffic jams prove frustrating. Outside the city, it is a better option, although Thai drivers are unashamedly reckless—many never learned to drive, ignore basic rules, and have a total disregard for road safety. Foreign drivers must reorient themselves fast and Americans need to readjust to driving on the left.

Among the many car-rental agencies, both **Avis** (*C* **02251-2011;** www.avis thailand.com) and **Budget** (*C* **02203-9294-5;** www.budget.co.th) each have convenient offices around the country. All drivers are required to have an international driver's license. Self-drive rates start around 1,200B per day for a family-sized sedan, much more for luxury vehicles or SUVs.

Local tour operators in larger destinations, such as Chiang Mai, Phuket, or Ko Samui, will rent cars for considerably less money than the larger, more well-known agencies—sometimes up to 30%. All companies will need to see your international driver's license and a valid credit card, in case of damage. Check insurance coverage—if you are taken to court for an accident, you may be found guilty for not being properly covered. Don't sign unless it's included. If you're wary of driving yourself, ask about rates for a car and driver, which can be very reasonable.

Gas stations are conveniently located along highways and in towns and cities throughout the country. Esso, Shell, Caltex, and PTT all have competitive rates.

See p. 381, under "Safety," for tips on driving in Thailand.

BY TRAIN

Bangkok's **Hua Lampong Railway Station** (see "By Train," under "Getting There," above) is a convenient, user-friendly facility, though, as always in busy transport hubs, you should be on the alert for scams. Clear signs point the way to public toilets, coin-operated phones, the food court, and the baggage check area. A Post & Telegraph Office, information counter, police box, ATMs, and money-changing facilities are dotted around the main area. You'll find plenty of small convenience shops and a baggage check too.

From this hub, the State Railway of Thailand provides regular service to destinations as far north as Chiang Mai, northeast to Nong Khai, east to Pattaya, and south to Thailand's southern border, where it connects with Malaysia's *Keretapi Tanah Melayu Berhad* (KTM), with service to Penang (Butterworth), Kuala Lumpur, and Singapore. Complete schedules and fare information can be obtained at any railway station, or by calling **Hua Lampong Railway Station** directly at *C* **02220-4334,** or via their information hot line at *C* **1690.**

The State Railway runs a number of different trains, each at a different speed, and priced accordingly. First-class sleepers usually accord an air-conditioned, two-bunk compartment with wash basin; second-class sleepers are bunks with curtains and with a ceiling fan or air-conditioning, depending on the ticket price. The fastest is the Special Express, which is the best choice for long-haul, overnight travel. These trains cut travel time by as much as 60% (though they are still slower than buses) and have sleeper cars—which are a must for really long trips. Rapid trains (in reality, rather slow) are the next best option. Prices vary for class, from air-conditioned sleeper cars in first class to air-conditioned and fan sleepers or seats in second, on down to the straight-backed, hard seats in third class. See www.thairailways.com for schedules and prices.

Warning: On trains, pay close attention to your possessions. Theft is common on overnight trips.

BY BUS

Buses are the cheapest and fastest transportation to the farthest and most remote destinations in the country. However, the frequency with which wrecked buses appear on Thai news programs shows that taking the bus carries an inherent risk. If you go for it, the major choices are public or private and air-conditioned or non-air-conditioned. Longer bus trips usually depart in the evenings to arrive at their destination early in the morning. Whenever you can, opt for the **VIP buses,** especially for overnight trips. Some have 36 seats; better ones have 24 seats. The extra cost is well worth it for the legroom. Also, stick to government-subsidized buses operated by the **Transport Company** (© **1490**) from each city's proper bus terminal. Many private companies sell VIP tickets for major routes, but sometimes put you on a standard bus. Ideally, buses are best for short excursions. Longer-haul buses are excellent value (usually less than 30B per hour of travel), but can be scary if you get a reckless driver.

Warning: When traveling by long-distance bus, do not accept drinks or snacks from fellow Thai travelers; they can be spiked. And watch your possessions closely: Theft is common, particularly on overnight buses, when valuables are left in overhead racks.

BY TAXI, TUK-TUK, SONGTAEW & SAMLOR

By law, **taxis** must charge by the meter, with a typical ride costing 100B to 200B. However, outside Bangkok they rarely use them, so you'll need to negotiate a fare; ask staff at your hotel or guesthouse to help agree a reasonable fare. Even in Bangkok, if you look outwardly like a tourist, a driver may try to scam you into paying a hefty fare by refusing to use the meter. Get out and find a new taxi if that happens; and avoid stationary taxis (usually parked next to expensive hotels), as these tend to be the scam artists. Note that if you're journeying to a remote part of town, a taxi driver may refuse you, especially when it's coming up to a shift change (3–4pm) or if the traffic is bad.

If you don't speak any Thai, you'll be lucky to find a **tuk-tuk** ride for less than 50B, even for the shortest hops. Be sure to bargain hard with these guys, and don't let 'em take you for a ride (in other words, on shopping trips or to massage parlors). In most provincial areas and resort islands, small pickup trucks called *songtaews* cruise the main streets offering a communal taxi service at cheap, set fees. As with tuk-tuks, always remember to agree on your fare before engaging a driver.

The *samlor* (literally "three wheels") is a dying breed of pedal-powered transport—a bicycle taxi that is often referred to as a pedicab or trishaw; the rider pulls passengers along behind him in a covered seat, and this type of transport is most commonly seen laden with shopping from local markets. Some hotels organize sightseeing tours by *samlor*, but otherwise they are rarely used by visitors. Motorized three-wheel vehicles, such as tuk-tuks, are also sometimes called *samlors*.

Note: Few taxi, tuk-tuk, *songtaew*, or *samlor* drivers speak even basic English, so have a copy of your hotel's name, street address, and district written in Thai with you at all times.

A small tip is usually expected, though of course it is up to you. Because many taxi or tuk-tuk drivers claim to have no change, don't leave your hotel without some small bills.

TIPS ON PLACES TO STAY

The most visited parts of the country (meaning Bangkok, Phuket, Chiang Mai, Pattaya, and Ko Samui) offer the widest choice of accommodation. International chains, such as the Mandarin Oriental group, The Peninsula, Hilton, Accor, Sheraton, and

Marriott, have some of their finest hotels and resorts in these areas, while the Asian-based Dusit, Anantara, and Amari chains have numerous resort and city properties that can compete with the best.

Five-star hotels and resorts spare no detail for the business or leisure traveler, providing designer toiletries, plush robes, in-room DVD players, Jacuzzis, and Wi-Fi, plus many other creature comforts. At the other end of the scale, Thailand is famous for its good-value guesthouses; while they may lack fancy facilities, they do offer a friendly welcome and a comfy bed at rock-bottom prices. All expensive and some moderately priced hotels add a 10% service charge, plus 7% value-added tax (VAT), which can obviously make quite a difference, so check whether your chosen hotel adds them on. Air-conditioning is standard in most top-end and midrange hotels, while fans are the norm in most guesthouses. In some cases, such as in the north from November to February, air-conditioning is not a necessity.

Accommodation categories in this guide are calculated according to rack rates in high season, though keep in mind that prices may fall as much as 50% between March and October, especially on the beach. Categories also refer to the majority of rooms, so if a hotel has a few rooms for 9,800B but most are over 10,000B, it will fall into the "very expensive" category.

Price Ranges

Because they have more facilities, better activity options and services, and well-trained staff, luxury category hotels and resorts can charge more than 10,000B a night for a double room. These are listed as **very expensive,** and many hotels in this category have started quoting prices in U.S. dollars.

Most hotels that fall into the **expensive** category (5,000B–9,999B) also have lots of bells and whistles, and they may still offer such perks as silk bathrobes and DVD players, but feature less deluxe amenities. Room design and furnishings will not extend to the glamour of the higher categories, but all rooms will be well maintained and facilities tend to be of excellent quality.

Moderate hotels and resorts (2,000B–4,999B) are often quite modern and good value for your money. Most have swimming pools, good restaurants, toiletries, satellite television, in-room safes, and international direct dialing from your room. Small, personalized, boutique hotels, which are currently very much in vogue, fall into this category. One reason for their popularity is that they generally have more character than large, impersonal hotels.

Thailand offers a good range of **inexpensive** places (less than 2,000B) for the budget traveler. The many mom-and-pop guesthouses and cut-price hostels often allow for more authentic experiences. If you go really inexpensive (under 300B), expect to rough it. Cold-water showers or shared bathroom facilities, fan-cooled rooms, and dormitories are the norm. But sometimes, for 500B to 1,000B, you'll find accommodation that stands out from the pack—quaint beachside bungalow villages, city hotels with good locations, or small guesthouses with knowledgeable and helpful staff.

Warning: The thought of owning a vacation home in Thailand can be seductive, and private villas and timeshare properties are booming in places such as Ko Samui and Phuket. While many travelers fall for the sweet talk and buy right away, it pays to consult a reputable foreign law firm first. Many foreigners have lost their life savings in Thai real-estate scams.

HEALTH

Thailand poses a small risk to travelers, though the high standards of hygiene should reassure most visitors. The same precautions for visiting tropical climes apply to the more remote areas of the Thai kingdom, where some types of mosquito can transmit malaria or dengue fever. Ask healthcare professionals to supply you with the *latest* information about health risks specific to the region as well as global pandemics such as the H1N1 virus (swine flu).

It is recommended that travelers have current immunizations for hepatitis A, polio, and tetanus. Young people are advised to get a rubella vaccine to protect against the TB virus; check that you are protected. Wounds can be aggravated by heat and humidity, so watch out for infections; wash cuts promptly with iodine or saline solution, and keep them dry.

General Availability of Healthcare

Dispensaries and hospital facilities in Thailand, especially in urban centers, are generally excellent. In Phuket and Samui, hospitals are familiar with vacationers, especially victims of car and motorbike crashes. Smaller towns will usually have a basic clinic, but Bangkok is always the best bet. (See "Fast Facts," in individual destination chapters for info.) Throughout the country, there are many drugstores stocked with brand-name medications and toiletries, plus less expensive local brands. Pharmacists often speak some English, and a number of drugs that require a prescription elsewhere can be dispensed over the counter.

Common Ailments

STOMACH TROUBLE

Often the change in climate and diet will provoke **diarrhea** in travelers to Thailand. You can best avoid upset stomachs by sticking to bottled water at all times, and drinking lots of it. Also be sure canned or bottled drinks are unopened, and wash your hands regularly, especially before eating.

It's useful to keep good anti-diarrhea medicine, such as Imodium, handy in your travel bag, plus a fruit-flavored electrolyte powder to mix with water to prevent dehydration. *Note:* Carrying a roll of toilet paper or packet of tissues is a good idea too; Thai toilets do not always provide this. Pharmacies here, such as Boots or Watson's, have a wide range of Western brand drugs, including Imodium. 7-Eleven stores sell single toilet-paper rolls and ready-to-go electrolyte drinks, such as Gatorade, as well as the familiar items and brands such as Bayer, Tylenol, and Eno antacids.

While restaurant hygiene throughout the country is generally excellent, be wary of street-side food stalls in areas of heavy traffic where pollution might affect the cleanliness of ingredients. (See the "Overcoming a Fear of Food Stalls" box, on p. 27, for more info.) If you develop a condition that includes cramps and lasts more than 24 hours, find a doctor for possible antibiotic treatment.

TROPICAL ILLNESSES

Hepatitis A can be avoided using the same precautions as for diarrhea. Most Asians are immune through exposure, but people from the West are very susceptible. Consider starting a course of vaccine at least 3 months before your trip.

Major tourist areas, such as Bangkok, Phuket, Ko Samui, and Chiang Mai, are generally **malaria free.** However, malaria is still a problem in rural parts, particularly territories in the mountains to the north and near the borders with Cambodia, Laos, and Myanmar. When you're traveling to remote areas, start taking a malarial prophylaxis well in advance (most dosages start 4 weeks before travel and should continue for 4 weeks after travel), such as **Malarone** (a combo of Atovaquone and Proguanil) or **Doxycycline**—but see a travel medical specialist to confer, and have him or her advise you on the potentially harmful **side effects.** Note that **Mefloquine** (sold under the name Larium) is no longer recommended for Thailand.

The best way to prevent malarial transmission or catching any other diseases listed here is to cover up with light-colored clothing, and wear long pants and sleeves after dark. Sleep with **Permethrin**-treated mosquito netting well tucked in, and use repellents. And make sure your repellent contains a high percentage of DEET. If you do get bitten, apply a dab of **calamine lotion** to ease the itching, and avoid scratching, which only makes it worse. If you develop a fever within 2 weeks of entering a high-risk area, be sure to consult a physician.

Dengue fever is now a major problem throughout Southeast Asia. Recent years have seen epidemics in the region, including Thailand. Similar to malaria, the virus is spread by a mosquito, but this one can bite during the day as well as at night. Symptoms are similar to those of the flu, with high fever, severe aches, fatigue, and possible skin rashes or headaches, lasting about a week. Drink plenty of water and seek medical attention immediately if you experience these symptoms.

Japanese encephalitis is a deadly viral infection that attacks the brain and is spread by a mosquito bite. Outbreaks have been known to occur in the region, so stay abreast of the most up-to-date CDC information at www.cdc.gov. As for malaria and dengue, the best protection is to avoid being bitten, but seek medical attention if you develop symptoms such as fever, severe aches, and skin rashes.

BUGS & OTHER WILDLIFE CONCERNS

On jungle hikes in particular, wear long sleeves and trousers instead of shorts, which will protect against not just mosquito bites, but the ubiquitous ticks, leeches, nasty biting giant centipedes, and (rarely seen) snakes. In order to survive the heat and humidity, wear loose cotton pants, socks, and sturdy boots—natural fibers are perfect for this terrain. Always try to minimize the chance of getting cuts and scrapes (they can get infected 10 times faster than back home). When venturing into thick jungle terrain, do so with a qualified guide and follow his or her example. Don't pick or touch plants unless the guide says it's safe.

Rabies is a concern in Thailand, as are bites from any stray animals—infected or not. Temples house many mangy dogs because Buddhists believe their duty is to feed them. Such dogs are often members of a pack and can get aggressive toward strangers of any kind. Occasionally, a rabid animal makes its way into the mix. Stay clear of all stray animals; and seek medical attention immediately, if you've been bitten. If you find yourself cornered, look for a stick to keep these mutts at bay. Bangkok has a rabies and snakebite help desk at Chulalongkorn Hospital, © **02256-4214.**

Avoid **freshwater streams** or **lagoons,** as they can be contaminated by chemicals or parasites. Sadly, lack of environmental regulations means sewage outlet pipes often pour into the sea or freshwater streams. **Coral reefs** pose minor risks from such things as poisonous sea snakes, jellyfish, and sea urchins. You can alleviate Jellyfish burns simply by applying vinegar. In the case of any cuts or stings, try to clean with bottled water and apply an antimicrobial ointment or antihistamine, if you have an allergic response. If you catch an ear infection, ear drops are sold in pharmacies, or mild boric acid or vinegar solutions can help.

RESPIRATORY ILLNESS

The air in Bangkok at certain times of the year can be smog-laden and is especially bad on sidewalks (pavements), next to busy roads, or under the BTS. Chiang Mai can also be very hazy in March. Anyone with respiratory issues such as asthma should carry both regular and emergency inhalers, though brands such as **Seretide, Bricanyl,** and **Ventolin** are available without prescription. **SARS** and **H5N1 Flu (bird flu)** have caused problems here in the past; in 2009, **H1N1 influenza,** or swine flu, caused a global pandemic, though this has now abated. Check out the latest situation at **www.cdc.gov.**

COPING WITH THE HEAT

The symptoms for **sunstroke** or **heat exhaustion** are unbearable headaches, nausea, vomiting, dizziness, and extreme fatigue. Avoid these ailments by drinking mineral (*not* purified) water, electrolyte drinks, or soda water regularly, *but in small amounts,* to replace minerals and increase hydration. An aspirin or Tylenol can help lower body temperatures. Expose yourself gradually to the heat; wearing a high-SPF sunscreen and a hat will prevent sunburn but not heatstroke. Low alcohol consumption, light meals, and eating minimally spiced food will help you to acclimatize much faster.

Use talcum powder after showering to avoid incapacitating **heat rash,** and only use clean, dry towels to avoid pervasive fungal growths such as **tinea** or **candida.** Fast-acting antifungal powders, creams, or suppositories, such as **Canesten** (for tinea) and **Diflucan** (for yeast infections), are available in pharmacies without a prescription.

What to Do if You Get Sick in Thailand

Medical services in Thailand are good in cities, and high street dispensaries—though unregulated—sell most drugs, even those normally available only by prescription overseas. The pharmacist may have an almanac on the counter in English, where you can check the different brand names of generic pharmaceutical products in your country, but always seek professional advice.

In most cases, your existing health plan should provide the coverage you need. But double-check; you may want to buy **travel medical insurance** instead. Bring your insurance ID card (for hospital visits only) with you when you travel.

If you don't feel well, consider asking any hotel concierge to recommend a local doctor or clinic. Typically, doctors see patients on a first-come, first-served basis, unless there is an emergency. You may have to fill in a form telling of allergies or

SEX FOR sale

Prostitution in Thailand is illegal, and yet every day you will see foreigners picking up Thai hookers of both sexes. Selling sex is not so much tolerated as politely ignored. However, some travelers regard it as a tourist draw, especially when underage boys or girls are involved. These days, the international police are hard on their heels; high-profile arrests are now not just common, but actively sought.

It is hard to get exact numbers for Commercial Sex Workers (CSWs) in Thailand; the number fluctuates from 100,000 to 1,000,000, depending on the source. Due to the huge numbers involved and the dangers therein, Thailand has made significant steps to counter the spread of HIV/AIDS. Through education and the introduction of condoms, it has made efforts to stem the tide of new cases (though statistics are unreliable). A leading force in this effort is the **Population & Community Development Association (PCDA;**

www.pda.or.th/eng), led by the courageous and innovative public health crusader Senator Mechai Viravaidya.

The PCDA has enlarged the scope of its rural development programs from family planning and networks distributing condoms to running seminars for CSWs. In poor, uneducated, rural families, where sons provide farm labor, the sex trade has become an income-earning occupation for parents, who sell their daughters to urban criminal gangs, often saying they will "go to a good job." They don't. They end up as sex slaves. Under international statutes, many are still minors; having sexual relations with them is equivalent to rape. It is a sorely misplaced myth to believe that CSWs live a good life of fun and freedom. Addiction to drugs and alcohol or physical abuse is commonplace. Rape is even more frequent. Girls contract STDs or fall pregnant, and scores of unwanted children—many with HIV—are dumped on orphanages.

existing conditions before you see a physician. In only very grave cases will you be sent to the emergency room. I list **emergency numbers** under "Fast Facts," p. 378.

You'll need to get a taxi to the hospital (*rohng pha yaa baan*, in Thai), as Thailand does not normally offer ambulance services. In an emergency, some embassies or consulates can offer basic advice.

FAST FACTS: THAILAND

Area Codes   See "Telephones," on p. 384, for information on area codes.

ATMs   Most major banks throughout the country have ATMs. In general, you can get cash with your debit card at any Bangkok Bank, Thai Farmers' Bank, or Siam Commercial Bank – provided your card is hooked into the Mastercard/Cirrus or Visa/PLUS network.

Business Hours   Government offices (including branch post offices) are open Monday to Friday 8:30am to 4:30pm, with a lunch break between noon and 1pm. Businesses are generally open 8am to 5pm. Shops often stay open from 8am until 7pm or later, 7 days a week. Department stores are generally open 10am to 8pm. Most TAT visitor centers are open daily from 8:30am to 4pm.

Car Rentals   See "Getting Around Thailand," on p. 370.

Cellphones See "Mobile Phones," on p. 380.

Crime See "Safety," on p. 381.

Customs Tourists are allowed to enter the country with 1 liter of alcohol and 200 ciga-rettes (or 250g of cigars or smoking tobacco) per adult, duty free, and there is no official limit on perfume.

However, you should pay more attention to what you can take back with you to your home country. Thai export Customs is rather lax, but one exception is cultural treasures: It is forbidden to take antique Buddha images or Bodhisattva images out of the kingdom. Special permission is required for removing antique artifacts from the country, and the authorization process takes about 8 days. For further details, contact the **Department of Fine Arts, ((02628-5033)**, open weekdays 8:30am to 4pm.

Note: This is an issue only if the object in question is an antique. If you purchase a small Buddha image or reproduction, whether an amulet or a statue, you can ship it home or pack it in your bag. Any antique dealer will be able to notify you about which images require special permission.

Disabled Travelers Disabilities shouldn't stop anyone from traveling, but sadly Thai-land does not make it easy on the severely physically challenged. Visitors to Thailand will find that, short of the better hotels in the larger towns, amenities for travelers with disabili-ties are nonexistent, even in public places. Negotiating sidewalks in cities is hazardous even for the nimble-footed, and crossing roads is a nightmare, so itineraries need to be well-planned.

On the positive side, the Thais' warm-hearted and genuinely helpful nature means they go to great pains to make sure visitors are well looked after, and they will often find simple solutions to worrying problems. One way to guarantee a smooth trip if you have mobility problems is to sign up for a package tour with **Help & Care Travel Company ((02720-5395;** www.wheelchairtours.com), in Bangkok.

Doctors See "Health," on p. 374.

Drinking Laws The official drinking age in Thailand is 18, though you need to be 20 to enter a nightclub. You can buy alcohol at convenience stores and supermarkets from 11am to 2pm and from 5pm to midnight. On some public holidays and on the eve of elec-tion days, no liquor can be sold at all. Nightspots must close at 1am, and the rule is gener-ally policed vigorously, though you may find a few exceptions where bars are given "special dispensation" (in exchange for a bribe).

Driving Rules See "Getting Around," above.

Electricity All outlets—except in some luxury hotels—are 220 volts AC (50 cycles). Outlets have two flat-pronged or round-pronged holes, so you may need an adapter. If you use a 110-volt hair dryer, electric shaver, or battery charger for a computer, bring a transformer and an adapter.

Embassies & Consulates While most countries have consular representation in Bangkok, the United States, Australia, Canada, and the United Kingdom also have consul-ates in Chiang Mai. See chapter 5 for details. Most embassies have 24-hour emergency services. If you are seriously injured or ill, call your embassy for assistance.

Emergencies Throughout the country, the emergency number you should use is ((**1155** for the Tourist Police. Don't expect many English speakers at police posts outside the major tourist areas. For an emergency ambulance, call ((**1554.** You can also contact your embassy or consulate.

Family Travelers A visit to Thailand will certainly broaden the horizons of young visi-tors, and many families report great experiences in the kingdom, partly because most Thais dote on kids. Larger resorts and hotels have kid-friendly programs, kids' clubs, connecting rooms, sports equipment rentals, and kid-oriented group activities. Many of the larger hotels also offer special deals for families or young children. To locate places to stay, restaurants, and attractions that are particularly kid-friendly, refer to the "Kids" icons throughout this guide.

Some hotels allow kids under 12 to share their parents' room for free, especially if it has two double beds, but an extra bed can always be found at a small extra cost. There's not much point in looking for accommodation that includes kitchen facilities, as restaurants are generally inexpensive, but while the spiciness of Thai food appeals to most adults, you'll have to watch out for junior digging into a Thai salad laced with fiery chilies.

As in other countries, babysitting services are available in top hotels, but few consider this a chore in Thailand, and generally you can expect hotel and restaurant staff to be falling over each other to amuse the kids while you are eating or enjoying a snooze by the pool.

As to where to go for a family holiday, kids are as enthralled by tropical beaches and mountain landscapes as adults. Wildlife watching somewhere like Khao Yai National Park is a good idea, but you may want to give the ancient cities of Ayutthaya and Sukhothai a miss, as kids are likely to find the ruins a big bore.

Gasoline See "Getting Around," on p. 370.

Hospitals See "Health," on p. 374.

Insurance It's wise to take out travel insurance before heading to Thailand, particularly if you intend to go diving, ride a rented motorbike or participate in any other activity that entails an element of risk. For information on traveler's insurance, trip cancellation insurance, and medical insurance while traveling, please visit www.frommers.com/planning.

Internet & Wi-Fi Travelers have any number of ways to check their e-mail and access the Internet on the road in Thailand. These days, smart phones, Wi-Fi-enabled laptops, PDAs (personal digital assistants), or electronic organizers allow travelers to stay in touch almost anywhere. But bear in mind there's a very real risk while traveling in poor countries that any luxury electronic items, including the trendier cellphone models (unaffordable to poorer Thais) may get stolen. If staying wired isn't a major part of your holiday, it's better to leave the hardware at home and check e-mail at cybercafes, which are easy to find.

Thailand's **Internet cafes** stay open late, they're affordable, and you'll pretty much find them everywhere. Bangkok's Sukhumvit, Surawong, or Khao San Roads and the country's main beach destinations are all chock-full with Internet cafes. Many hotels have business centers that also offer Internet access, but they are much pricier.

Cybercafes charge around 30B to 80B per hour and most city connections now use high-speed lines (ADSL) and offer cheap overseas Internet calls on systems such as www. skype.com. Outside of the cities, look out for local cybercafes (usually full of school kids playing online shoot-'em-up games); most offer acceptable service.

More and more hotels, cafes, and retailers in Thailand offer free high-speed Wi-Fi access (or charge a small fee for usage). You'll find wireless services at Starbucks branches—or look out for signs marked with the Thai brand TRUE, in malls such as Siam Paragon and CentralWorld. A few luxury hotels offer Wi-Fi service free of charge, though in many you will have to buy a prepaid access card from around 400B per day. Contact your hotel in advance to see what your options are.

Major Internet Service Providers (ISPs) have **local access numbers** around the world, allowing you to go online by placing a local call. Check your ISP's website, or call its toll-free number to find out more. Thailand has its own popular ISPs, the biggest of which is **CS Loxinfo,** which offers dial-up and ADSL. You can buy handy prepaid cards at 7-Elevens.

Language Central (often called Bangkok) Thai is the official language. English is spoken in the major cities at hotels, some restaurants, and a few smart shops, and is the second language of the professional class. (For more information on the Thai language, see chapter 15.)

Legal Aid   As long as you do not break the law in Thailand, there is no reason that you should require legal aid. If, however, you feel you have been wrongly accused of, say, causing a road accident, you should consult your nearest embassy or consulate for advice. See "Embassies & Consulates," on p. 378.

LGBT Travelers   Thailand is famous for its seemingly gay-friendly attitudes, but homophobia certainly does exist. Lesbians are known as *tom dee*; they have their own hangouts and are usually less vocal and ostentatious than their male counterparts, or the theatrically inclined lady-boys *(katoeys)*.

There are occasional Gay Pride-style events, as well as regular cabaret shows and beauty competitions for lady-boys, throughout the country. The same kind of nightlife that caters to heterosexual males is offered in Bangkok, Pattaya, and Phuket's Patong Beach. Venues range from gay bars and dance clubs, men-only saunas (bathhouses), and "pay at the door" parties. In Bangkok, the most popular male-only joint is the opulent Babylon men's club, off Sathorn Road (www.babylonbangkok.com). Check **www.utopia-asia.com,** for gay-friendly information and plenty of travel tips for Thailand.

Mail   You can pick up mail while you travel by using a *poste restante*, which is simply a counter at a post office where your mail is kept for you until you pick it up; normally, 2 months is the maximum hold time. For those unfamiliar with this service, it is comparable to General Delivery in the United States. Mail is addressed to you, care of Poste Restante, GPO, Name of City. You'll need proof of ID, and must sign a receipt and pay 1B per letter received. Hours of operation are the same as those of the post office. (See individual chapters for local post offices and their hours.)

Airmail postcards to the United States usually cost 15B, but rates depend on the size of the card; airmail letters cost 19B per 10 grams (17B to Europe). Airmail delivery usually takes 7 to 20 days.

Air parcel post to the US costs 950B for up to 1kg. Surface or sea parcel post costs 550B for 1kg (3 or 4 months for delivery). International Express Mail (EMS) costs 598B from 1 to 250g, with delivery guaranteed within 7 days. Most post offices have a helpful packing service.

Shipping by air freight is quite costly, but most major international delivery services have offices in Bangkok and a network that extends to the provinces. These are **DHL Thailand,** 175 Sathorn City Tower, 8/1 and 7/1 Floor, South Sathorn Road (📞 **02345-5000**), and **Federal Express,** at Rama IV Road (📞 **1782**). **UPS Parcel Delivery Service** has a main branch in Bangkok at 16/1 Sukhumvit Soi 44/1 (📞 **02762-3300**).

Medical Requirements   See "Health," on p. 374.

Mobile Phones   Note that cellphones are referred to as "mobiles" or "handsets" in Thailand, which operates on the GSM system. If you have an unlocked phone, you can install a local, prepaid **SIM card** (sold at 7-Elevens and cellphone stores in Thailand). Show your phone to the salesperson; not all phones work on all networks. You'll get a local phone number—and much, much lower calling rates than using international roaming. Unlocking an already locked phone can be complicated, but it can be done; just call your cellular operator and say you'll be going abroad for several months and want to use the phone with a local provider. In Thailand, head to **Mah Boon Krong** (**MBK**), near the National Stadium BTS in central Bangkok, for assistance with unlocking cellphones at any cellphone vendor.

For trips of more than a few weeks spent in one country, buying a local SIM card becomes economically attractive, as Thailand has a number of cheap prepaid phone systems operated by **One-2-Call, True Move,** and **DTAC.** For around 800B, you will be given a starter pack, which includes a SIM card, an instant Thai cellphone number, plus some credit for free calls. Call costs depend on the package you choose; some systems offer free off-peak messaging (SMS). With most plans, though, incoming calls are free.

Newspapers & Magazines   The English-language dailies are *Bangkok Post* and *The Nation*. They cover the domestic political scene, as well as international news from Associated Press and Reuters wire services, and cost 30B. Both the *Asian Wall Street Journal* and *International Herald Tribune* are available Monday to Friday on their day of publication in Bangkok (in the provinces, it may be a day later). *Time, Newsweek*, and *The Economist* are sold in international hotels, as well as in a few of the major cities.

Packing   One of the great joys about visiting a tropical country like Thailand is that you don't need much more than a change of clothes in your bag, along with any other items you consider essential. Pack loose and light clothing, and make sure you have some long-sleeved shirts and pants, as well as a hat, for protection against the sun. Once you see the great deals in the country's markets, you'll want to pick up some new clothes anyway, so start with as little as possible.

Passports   All visitors to Thailand must carry a **passport** valid for at least 6 months, with **proof of onward passage** (a return or through ticket). Visa applications are not required, if you are staying fewer than 30 days and are a national of 1 of 41 designated countries including Australia, Canada, Ireland, New Zealand, the United Kingdom, and the United States (New Zealanders may stay up to 3 months).

Petrol   See "Getting Around," on p. 370.

Police   The **Tourist Police** (☎ 1155), with offices in every city (see specific chapters), speak English (and other foreign languages) and are open 24 hours. You should call them in an emergency rather than the regular police because there is no guarantee that police operators will speak English.

Safety   Though violent crime is rare in Thailand, it is unfortunately on the rise. Thankfully, foreign visitors are not usually targeted unless they have seriously upset a local. Tourists are more likely to encounter con artists, but a few basic precautions can help avoid problems.

Because **pickpockets** and scam artists work the tourist areas and pounce on friendly or naive travelers, keep an eye on valuables in crowded places, and be wary of anyone who approaches you in the street to solicit your friendship. However genuine the entreaty sounds, you will end up wasting precious time on "shopping tours," where your "guide" will collect a commission and keep you from getting where you'd like to go (or worse).

To report a lost or stolen credit card in Thailand, the following companies' services are available: **American Express** (☎ 02273-5544); **Diners Club** (☎ 02232-4100); **Mastercard** (☎ 800/11887-0663); and **Visa** (☎ 008/441-3485).

In general, even in big cities, single men and women are fairly safe as long as they stick to walking in brightly lit areas where there is plenty of activity. If, for whatever reason, you sense a confrontation developing, just walk away. The **tourist police hot line, ☎ 1155,** should bring a quick response but does not guarantee that the police will support the foreigner. Know you cannot win in any altercation: Every year a handful of gung-ho tourists injure themselves trying.

Thai police are some of the lowest-paid civil servants in the country, so it's not surprising that they have a reputation for harassment, intimidation, and bribery. Involving yourself in any way whatsoever (especially amorously) with a Thai cop is dangerous. There are many cases of lovelorn officers gunning down Thai and foreign girls (and/or their new boyfriends) who had previously flirted with their affections.

Thailand can offer illicit temptations that may seem harmless to naive travelers. Yet the Thai government has zero tolerance of drug trafficking and use. Many people who think they are being offered a casual puff on a joint don't realize they are being set up; every year a few will end up never leaving the kingdom, serving a life sentence in a Thai jail cell. Prostitution is also illegal; see the "Sex for Sale" box, above, for info on that.

Driving (See "Getting Around" p. 370) is another all-too-obvious danger here. Many drivers in the country have bought their licenses, and hence little attention is given to speed limits or other rules of the road. Driving a rental car here is not for the fainthearted; extreme caution should be taken and defensive driving skills are key. Every year Thai hospitals are full of banged, bruised, and mummy-wrapped travelers recovering from road accidents. For years, Thailand's annual road death statistics have defied belief, especially on the hilly islands of Phuket, Ko Samui, and Ko Chang, where a sense of exhilaration tempts drivers to their fates. Pedestrians in cities should be particularly wary of foot crossings operated by traffic lights, as many drivers ignore them completely.

If you do get in an accident, keep in mind that Thais don't normally have insurance. If they don't flee the scene, they might try to negotiate a settlement. Local officials may actually hinder the situation, especially if the culpable faction can persuade them you are to blame. If you find yourself in this situation, take photographs of the scene and ask to get a copy of the IDs of those involved.

Since the military coup d'état in September 2006, the **political situation** (See "Thailand in Depth" p. 9) in Thailand has become quite unstable and there has been much unrest as red-shirted supporters of the United Front for Democracy against Dictatorship (UDD), who would like to reinstate ex-Prime Minister Thaksin, rally against the yellow-shirted supporters of the People's Alliance for Democracy (PAD). Several clashes have occurred around Bangkok's Sanam Luang district and in front of Parliament House. Since the general election in July 2011, which brought Thaksin's sister, Yingluck Shinawatra into power, these color-coded political conflicts have thankfully subsided, but could re-appear at any time. The best advice is to steer well clear of any large groups, particularly if they are wearing red or yellow shirts.

If there is a hint of trouble, many shops will close; in extreme cases (such as the 2006 coup), local TV stations shut down. If you are unfortunate enough to be in the country at such a time, stay off the streets and watch overseas satellite news for the latest developments, but do not be tempted to be part of history by joining the protests. If you remain indoors, it's unlikely you'll be caught up in any violence.

The far southern provinces of Yala, Narathiwat, and Pattani, near the Malaysian border, are subject to ongoing sectarian violence between Thai Muslims and Thai military police. Thai institutions, schools, banks, and Buddhist temples have been targeted with small-scale bombs. Avoid this area, or travel through it with care.

Poor regulations and scheming between gangs and police do nothing to stop this. Though legislation coyly prohibits full nudity in most go-go bars, it just means the illegal backroom deals, kidnappings, rape, and the enslavement of children carry on behind closed doors, funded by the profits paid by the brothels' ignorant clientele.

If you choose to support prostitution, you are not only breaking the law, but also supporting the trafficking and abuse of women and men, including minors. You are putting your own life at risk from STDs and perpetuating a trade that ruins lives. It's not all one-sided play either: Numerous cases are known where tourists have been drugged in their hotel rooms by their sleeping partner. If they are lucky, they awake 2 days later to find all their valuables gone. There are a shocking number of stories about Western travelers found dead after a liaison with a CSW, but rarely will the newspapers report the full details.

Exercise caution in your dealings with any stranger. If, in spite of all these warnings, you decide to use the services of Thailand's CSWs, take proper precautions; carry condoms at all times, and check the person's ID. If you are in any doubt, walk away—it could save your life.

There is still a certain amount of institutionalized **racism** in old Siam, and much pride is taken in the fact that no foreign power colonized the kingdom. Thai people are, superficially at least, tolerant, but not always accepting of Western ways. Foreign men with young Thai girlfriends can be viewed with deep distrust, and even distaste.

Thais follow a codified hierarchy, with wealth and status going hand in hand. Therefore, the richer Thai-Chinese, who own and operate big businesses, top the scale, and people from Isan, the impoverished northeast of the kingdom, come way down in the ratings. Associating yourself with any Thai will, very often, put you at their level.

Caucasians are known as *farang* (a word that originally meant French, referring to the nation's earliest Western visitors). *Farang* is not necessarily a racist term, but, yes, foreign tourists are ritually overcharged and some take this personally as a form of discrimination. Look at this from a Thai, not Western, perspective. Thais believe if you have more, you are expected to give more; the rule applies to Thais as well, regardless of your budget. As a *farang* you are *automatically* seen as wealthy in Thailand. Skills in bargaining will come in time, if you practice. Just remember that Thais really appreciate generosity, rather than someone who makes a big deal about haggling over a baht or two.

Senior Travelers Senior citizens are highly revered in Thai society and are treated with deference and respect, which comes as a pleasant surprise to many first-time Western visitors. Unfortunately, this deference does not stretch to offering the kind of discounts on transport and admission fees that you might be used to back home. There are exceptions, however, and it's always worth asking politely if there are preferable rates for senior citizens, as Thais take pride in accommodating their guests' wishes.

Single Travelers Solo journeys in Thailand offer infinite opportunities to make friends and meet locals, and it's easy to change your plans without upsetting others. However, solo travelers are something of an oddity here. Thais love asking foreign visitors, "Are you married?" They themselves commonly marry quite young and start families early, so many assume single travelers to be sad or lonely. Be ready to be offered sympathy, if you're traveling alone, and don't take it personally. Show them photos of family and friends so they can see you're not alone in the world. Also be prepared to be pestered sometimes; Thais don't share Western notions of privacy, so they never think of "giving someone space."

As for expenses, some hotels offer discounts for singles. If, however, you like resorts, tours, or cruises, you're likely to get hit with paying a per-room rate regardless. Single travelers can avoid these supplements, of course, by agreeing to room with other single travelers on the trip. Another way to reduce costs is to find a compatible roommate before you go, from one of the many roommate locator agencies.

Smoking In Thailand, smoking is banned in air-conditioned public places such as restaurants and airports. Most hotel rooms are also nonsmoking, so you should specify when booking if you are a smoker. By and large the law is respected, though not in places like snooker halls. Some open-sided bars that don't serve food tolerate smokers, or have created smoker-friendly outdoor spaces, including upmarket private cigar bars. If in doubt, ask about nonsmoking sections. Shops are also prohibited from displaying cigarettes, so you'll need to ask for your brand in a shop like 7-Eleven.

Student Travelers Discounts for students in Thailand and the rest of Southeast Asia are better earned by the tenacity of the individual traveler's bargaining skills and tolerance for substandard accommodation rather than flashing a student ID—though showing one does help when buying mass transit tickets in Bangkok. The **International Student Identity Card (ISIC),** however, offers substantial savings on plane tickets and some entrance fees. It also provides you with basic health and life insurance and a 24-hour helpline. The card is available for $22 from **STA Travel** (📞 **800/781-4040** in North America; www. statravel.com), the biggest student travel agency in the world.

If you're no longer a student but are still under 26, you can get an **International Youth Travel Card (IYTC)** for the same price from the same people, entitling you to some discounts (but not on museum admissions). **Travel CUTS** (📞 **800/667-2887**; www.travelcuts.com) offers similar services for both Canadians and U.S. residents. Irish students may prefer to turn to **USIT** (📞 **01/602-1906;** www.usit.ie), an Ireland-based specialist in student, youth, and independent travel.

Taxes & Service Charges Hotels charge a 7% government value-added tax (VAT) and typically add a 10% service charge; hotel restaurants add 8.25% government tax. Most inexpensive and midrange hotels quote the price inclusive of these charges, while expensive places don't. This can make a big difference at top-end hotels, so check before you reserve a room.

Telephones Major hotels in Thailand feature convenient but pricey International Direct Dial (IDD), long-distance service, and fax services. They add a hefty surcharge to local and long-distance calls, which can add up to 50% in some cases. Note that 800 numbers, credit card numbers, or collect calls may not be readily available from your hotel phone; or if they are, a big fat service fee may be added. Check first.

Most post offices have special offices or booths for **overseas calls,** as well as **fax** and **telex service;** they're usually open Monday to Friday 8:30am to 4:30pm, though those in big cities may stay open later. There are also **overseas telegraph and telephone offices** (also called OCO, or overseas call office) open daily 24 hours throughout the country for long-distance international calls and telex and fax service. In addition, many Internet cafes, guesthouses, and travel agents offer long-distance calls using very affordable net-to-phone connections of varying quality.

Local calls can be made from any red or blue public pay telephone. Local calls cost 1B for 3 minutes; add more coins when the beeps sound. Blue public phones are for local and long-distance calls within Thailand.

Yellow TOT cards are sold in denominations of 100B, 300B, and 500B and are specific for domestic or international phones, which are clearly marked as such. **Hatari PhoneNet** offers a variety of phone cards that are a great value and are available at convenience stores everywhere. All cards can also be purchased at **Telephone Organization of Thailand** (TOT) offices.

To call Thailand: If you're calling Thailand from the U.S. or the U.K.

1. Dial the international access code: 011 (in the U.S.) or 00 (in the U.K.).
2. Dial the country code: 66.
3. Dial the number. So the whole number you'd dial for Bangkok would be 011-66-2-000-0000 (from the U.S.) or 00-66-2-000-0000 (from the U.K.).

Important Note: When making calls to Thailand, be sure to omit the "0" that appears before all phone numbers in this guide (thus you will dial only eight digits after the "66" country code). When calling within Thailand, you will need to add the two- or three-digit area code for the place you are calling, unless the number is a special four-digit hot line for an airline or tourist organization.

To make international calls: There are two ways to make international calls from Thailand—first, by IDD, for which the access number is 001; second, by Voice over Internet Protocol (VoIP), for which access numbers are 007, 008, and 009. The latter are much cheaper. After dialing the international access number, dial the country code (U.S. or Canada 1, U.K. 44, Ireland 353, Australia 61, New Zealand 64). Next, you dial the area code and number. For example, if you wanted to call the British Embassy in Washington, D.C., you would dial 001-1-202-588-7800.

For directory assistance: Dial 🕾 **1133,** or dial any hotel concierge or operator (even if you are not a guest, they can help).

Note: In smaller towns throughout this guide, I've left out phone numbers for bars/clubs that don't have permanent phone lines.

Time Zone   Thailand is 7 hours ahead of GMT (Greenwich Mean Time). During winter months, this means that Bangkok is 7 hours ahead of London, 12 hours ahead of New York, and 15 hours ahead of Los Angeles. Daylight saving time takes 1 hour off these times.

Tipping   Tipping is not an integral part of Thai culture but, unsurprisingly, Thais are willing to accommodate this generous Western habit, so feel free to reward good service wherever you find it. If no service charge is added to your check in a fine-dining establishment, a 10% to 15% tip is appropriate. Airport or hotel porters expect tips; 30B is acceptable. Tipping taxi drivers is also more or less expected. Carry small bills, as many cab drivers either don't have change or won't admit to having any in the hope of getting a tip.

Toilets   Most restaurants and hotels have Western toilets. Shops and budget hotels will have an Asian squat toilet, a ceramic platform mounted over a hole in the ground. Near the toilet is a water bucket or sink with a small ladle. The water is for cleaning yourself and flushing the toilet. Toilet paper is not usually provided.

VAT   See "Taxes & Service Charges," p. 384.

Visas   The **Immigration Division of the Royal Thai Police Department** recently moved to the Government Complex, B Building, Floor 2 (south zone), 120 Moo 3, Chaengwattana Road Soi 7, to the north of the city center (take a taxi from BTS Mo Chit); 🕾 **1111** or **02141-9889;** open Monday to Friday 8:30am to noon and 1–4.30pm. Visitors planning to stay for longer than a month can arrange a 60-day tourist visa at embassies overseas for a cost of 1,000B; this is renewable in Thailand for an additional 30 days for another 1,900B. If you overstay your visa, you will be charged 500B per day, which is payable when exiting the kingdom. Longer overstays are punishable by anything up to a 20,000B fine or a stay in jail. For more information, check www.thaivisa.com, but bear in mind that it may not be completely up-to-date.

Warning: Until they were outlawed in 2006, small travel agencies offered "visa services," wherein you paid for a courier to take your passport to a border post to get a new visa stamp. A police crackdown has put a halt to this illegal practice. Also, foreigners who take advantage of the free 30-day visa-on-arrival service must remember that they may do this only three times in a row (allowing them a cumulative stay of a maximum of 90 days). After that they will not be allowed to enter Thailand until they pay for a new visa issued by a Royal Thai Embassy overseas.

Visitor Information & Maps   **Tourist Authority of Thailand** (TAT; www.tourism thailand.org) is an extensive site with information on locations throughout Thailand. However, its listings are often incorrect or out-of-date. See the box "Online Traveler's Toolbox," below, for other options.

Water   Don't drink the tap water here, even in the major hotels. Most hotels provide bottled water; use it for brushing your teeth as well as drinking. Most restaurants serve bottled or boiled water and ice made from boiled water, but always ask to be sure. Purified water may not have the minerals you need to replace those lost in the heat and humidity, so check the label.

Wi-Fi   See "Internet & Wi-Fi," earlier in this section.

Women Travelers   Women travelers face no particular discrimination or dangers in Thailand. Women should, however, be very careful when dealing with monks: Never touch a monk, never hand anything directly to him (it should be set on the floor in front of the

ONLINE traveler's TOOLBOX

The following is a selection of handy online tools to bookmark for your trip to Thailand.

- For **transportation information,** try the following sites: **Thai Airways International** (www.thaiair. com), **Bangkok Airways** (www. bangkokair.com), **Nok Air** (www. nokair.com), and **Orient Thai** (www.flyorientthai.com). Out of the Southeast Asian hubs, there's the extensive **Air Asia** (www.air asia.com) and the smaller **Tiger Airways** (www.tigerairways.com), with **Jetstar** (www.jetstar.com) linking Asian cities with Australia. For train info, contact the **Thai State Railway** at www.railway. co.th. *Note:* The official Suvarnabhumi or Don Muang Airport websites are not updated regularly and could be misleading to travelers. Cross-check these sites with more reliable international travel sites or blogs.
- **Thai publications** in English are numerous. *Bangkok Post* (www. bangkokpost.com) and *The Nation* (www.nationmultimedia. com) are the only English-language dailies. The free *Where Magazine* lists lots of events and happenings, as does *BK Magazine,* which has a younger target audience.
- There are a few **blogs** and info sites on Thailand with (not always updated) info about upcoming events in the Bangkok area and tips on life in Thailand. Check the likes of **www.thaivisa.com, www. thaitravelblogs.com,** and **www. bangkokrecorder.com.**

monk or given to a man who will hand it to them directly), and don't sit next to monks on public transport or in the monk-only designated areas in waiting rooms. Some parts of temples do not allow women to enter; look for signs indicating this.

Thais are extremely modest, almost prudish, and though Thai bar girls dress in scanty fashions, that's not recommended if you want respect. Women should avoid wearing tank tops and short-shorts (the equivalent of wearing nightwear outdoors for Westerners, though strangely for Thais there is no taboo about this). Going topless on beaches is illegal in many areas and considered a public obscenity. At all temples and mosques, be sure to wear a long skirt or pants and have your shoulders covered. Your head should be covered in mosques, but headwear (caps, sun visors) must be removed in Buddhist temples.

When dressing for a night out, be very careful that you do not give the wrong message to Thai men. Wearing clothes that Thais would deem immodest (short skirts, low-cut shirts exposing cleavage, or bra tops) is regarded as a come-on.

MONEY & COSTS

THE VALUE OF THE BAHT VS. OTHER POPULAR CURRENCIES

Thai Baht	US$	Can$	UK£	Euro (€)	Aus$	NZ$
1	US$.03	C$.03	£.02	€.02	A$.03	NZ$.04

WHAT THINGS COST IN BANGKOK (THAI BAHT)

A taxi from Suvarnabhumi Airport to the city	250–300
Local call (pay phone) per minute	1
Double at the Oriental (very expensive)	13,000
Double at the Swiss Lodge (moderate)	2,800
Double at Bossotel (budget)	1,800
Dinner for one, without wine, at Sirocco (expensive)	1,500
Dinner for one, without wine, at Taling Pling (inexpensive)	150
Dinner for one, without wine, at a city food court (inexpensive)	100
Bottle of beer at a hotel bar	150
Bottle of beer at a local bar	80
Coca-Cola	25
Regular coffee at a mall cafe	100
Admission to the National Museum	200
Movie ticket	120

The Thai unit of currency is the **baht** (written B, Bt, Bht, or THB) and is divided into 100 **satang.** Tiny copper coins represent 25 and 50 satang; silver coins are 1B, 2B (rare), and 5B. The larger 10B coin is silver with a copper inset. Bank bills come in denominations of 20B (green), 50B (blue), 100B (red), 500B (purple), and 1,000B (brown).

Travel in Thailand is affordable and therefore attracts all types of travelers. In 2011, the average Thai income stood at around US$400 per person, per month, so standards of living and corresponding prices reflect this. Compared to home, many excellent hotels and restaurants cost a fraction of the price in Thailand, and, because of this, Thais consider any foreigner to be extremely well-off.

Always bear in mind that throughout Thailand, the baht will be the only acceptable currency, and foreign currency is rarely, if ever, accepted for everyday transactions.

There are no restrictions on the import of foreign currencies or traveler's checks, but you cannot export foreign currency in excess of 50,000B per person. Before the currency crisis in July 1997, one U.S. dollar could buy you 25 Thai baht. During the worst of the crisis, the value was 55B to the dollar. Though still prone to fluctuations, the exchange rate has recently steadied, and amounts listed throughout this book are calculated at **US$1=30B** and **£1=50B.** For the most up-to-date figures, see www.xe.com. The above box shows rough cross-values with major currencies.

Some travelers like to change a little money before leaving home, though it is not really necessary. You can sometimes buy Thai baht at your local American Express or Thomas Cook office or order baht at your bank; however, it is much easier to visit an airport exchange booth or ATM on arrival in Thailand. There are exchange kiosks at most international airport arrival halls in Thailand, which are generally open when flights arrive, but don't rely on them being open 24 hours.

Note: Though most prices in this guide are quoted in baht, some hotels quote their rates in U.S. dollars. Where that is the case, I provide $ rates in the listings.

If you have an ATM or a credit card, these can be used in 24-hour cash machines that dispense money in 100-, 500-, and 1,000-baht bills. Thai ATMs accept most international bank card systems. **Cirrus** (*C* 1-636-722-7111 for collect calls worldwide; www.mastercard.com) and **PLUS** (*C* 800/441-3485; www.visa.com) networks span the kingdom. Look at the back of your bank card to see which network you're on, and then call or check online for ATM locations in Thailand. Be sure you know your personal identification number (PIN) and daily withdrawal limit before you depart. You'll also need a 4-digit PIN in Thailand, so if yours is a 6-digit number, get it changed before you go.

The best banks to visit are **Bangkok Bank, Thai Farmer's Bank, Siam Commercial Bank,** and **Bank of Ayudhya,** as each has major branches in every city and many small towns. For specific locations of ATMs, see "Fast Facts" listings throughout this book.

There is an American Express office at S.P. Building, 388 Pahonyothin Rd., in Bangkok. You can reach the office at *C* 02273-5500; it's open Monday to Friday 9am to 5pm. For other Thai hot lines, visit www.americanexpress.com/thailand.

In Thailand, **traveler's checks** are seen less nowadays, having been largely replaced by ATMs. Given the fees you'll pay for using an ATM overseas, though, you might be better off with traveler's checks, if you're withdrawing money often. In Thailand, traveler's checks are best exchanged in a main branch of city-center banks or in a five-star international hotel. They may be accepted in Bangkok at the small exchange counters, but not always. (The best rates are at banks.)

International hotels and larger businesses in Thailand accept major **credit cards.** Despite protest from credit card companies, many establishments, such as supermarkets and department stores, add a 3% to 5% surcharge for payment by credit card (this is above and beyond any fees levied by your credit card company). Be sure to ask before handing over your card, and keep all receipts. When using your card in Thai department stores, also be aware that each section must ring up its receipt *separately*—so don't be alarmed if a clerk walks off a little way with your card to process the transaction, but still remain vigilant and take a common-sense approach.

MasterCard and **Visa** are the most widely accepted credit cards in Thailand, followed by **American Express.** Most hotels and restaurants accept all of these, especially in tourist destination areas. Discover and Diners Club are far less commonly accepted.

Never leave your cards with others for safekeeping (such as during a trek). If you don't want to carry them, put them in a hotel safe. There have been numerous reports of charges made while cards were left at guesthouses, or small shops running extra slips against a card. For tips and telephone numbers to call if your wallet is stolen or lost, see "Safety," on p. 381.

Beware of hidden **credit-card fees** while traveling. Check with your credit or debit card issuer to see what fees, if any, will be charged for overseas transactions. Recent reform legislation in the U.S., for example, has curbed some exploitative lending practices. But many banks have responded by increasing fees in other areas, including fees for customers who use credit and debit cards while out of the country—even if those charges were made in U.S. dollars. Fees can amount to 3% or more of the purchase price. Check with your bank before departing to avoid any surprise charges on your statement.

For help with currency conversions, tip calculations, and more, download Frommer's convenient Travel Tools app for your cellphone device. Go to http://www.frommers.com/go/mobile/ and click on the Travel Tools icon.

USEFUL TERMS & PHRASES

Thai is a tonal language, with low, mid, high, rising, or falling tones. There are five tonal markings:

low tone: `
falling tone: ^
middle tone (no marking)
rising tone: ˇ
high tone: ´

Most important, Thai also differentiates between the language used by a male and that used by a female. Thus, males use **Pǒm** for I, and females use **Deè-chǎn.** The suffix **khráp** is an affirmation used by men only, and **khǎ** is used similarly for women. It can be used as a lazy reply, such as "Uh-huh."

Though it's very difficult for Westerners to pronounce Thai sounds correctly, there are no problems with stress, as all syllables receive equal emphasis. A useful resource for self-study of Thai is **www.thai-language.com.**

BASIC PHRASES & VOCABULARY

English	Thai Transliteration	Pronunciation
Hello (male)	**Sà–wàt–dii–khráp**	sah-wah-dee-kup
Hello (female)	**Sà-wàt-dii-khâ**	sah-wah-dee-kah
How are you?	**Sà bai-dii mǎi?**	sah-bye-dee-my
I am fine	**Sà bai-dii**	sah-bye-dee
Do you speak English?	**Phûut phaa-sǎa ang rìt dǎi mǎi?**	poot pa-sah ang-krit dye my?
I do not understand	**Mǎi khǎo jai**	my cow jy
Excuse me/Sorry	**Khǎw thôht (-khráp, -khǎ)**	cor tort (-kup, -kah)
Thank you	**Khòp khun (-khráp, -khǎ)**	cop koon (-kup, -kah)
No, I do not want . . .	**Mǎi ao . . .**	my ow . . .
Yes, I want . . .	**Chǎi, ao. . .**	chai, ow . . .
Stop here!	**Yùt tîi nîi!**	Yut ti nee
Where is the (public) toilet?	**Hâwng nám yùu thîi nǎi?**	hong nam yutin nye?
I need to see a doctor	**Pǒm/Deè-chǎn tǎwng kaan hǎa mǎw**	pom/dee-charn tong-garn haa mor
Call the police!	**Rîak tam-rùat nàwy!**	reeyuk tamru-at noy

English	Thai Transliteration	Pronunciation
Never mind/No problem	**Mǎi pen rai**	my pen rye
Do you have . . . ?	**Mii . . . mǎi?**	mee . . . my?

Getting Around

English	Thai Transliteration	Pronunciation
I want to go to . . .	**Yàk jà pai . . .**	yark jar by . . .
Where is the . . .	**Yùu thîi nǎi . . .**	yutin nye . . .
taxi	**tháek-sǐi**	tak-see
bus station	**sà thǎa nee khǒn sòng**	sartarnee kornsong
train station	**sà thǎa nee rót fai**	sartarnee rot fye
airport	**sà nǎam bin**	sanam-bin
boat jetty	**thǎ reua**	taa ru-er
hotel	**rohng ra-em**	rorngrem
hospital	**rohng phá yaa baan**	roong-pye-aban
How much . . . ?	**Thǎo rai?**	tao-rye?
What time (does it depart)?	**(Jà àwk) kìi mohng?**	(jar ork) kee-mong?

In a Restaurant

English	Thai Transliteration	Pronunciation
coffee	**kaa–fae**	gar-fay
tea (hot)	**chaa–ráwn**	char-rawn
bottled water	**nám khuàt**	nam kwat
water	**nám**	nam
ice	**nám khǎeng**	nam keng
beer	**bia**	bee-ya
noodles	**kwǎy tǐaw**	kway tee-ow
rice	**khâo**	cow
fried rice	**khâo phàt**	cow pat
chicken	**kài**	guy
beef	**neúa**	nuhr
pork	**mǔu**	moo
fish	**plaa**	blar
shrimp	**kûng**	goong
mango with sticky rice	**khâo nǐaw má mûang**	cow neeow mar-mwang
Thai desserts (general)	**khà nǒm**	knom
I am a vegetarian	**Kin a hân jae**	gin aharn jae
I don't like it spicy	**Mǎi châwp phèt**	my chorp pet
I like it spicy	**Châwp phèt**	chorp pet
Delicious!	**Àh-ròy!**	ah-roy
Check/bill please	**Khǎw chék –bin**	gor chek-bin

Specific Menu Terms
BASIC INGREDIENTS

bread khà nŏm pan
cake/cookie khà nŏm
egg khài

salt kleua
sugar nám tan

COOKING METHODS

grilled pĭng
baked òb
barbecued yâng

boiled dôm
deep-fried tôrt
ground sĕe

roasted phăo
steamed nêung
stir-fried phàt

FRUITS

banana klûay
coconut máphráo
custard apple náwy nàa
durian thúrian
guava fà ràng
jackfruit khà nŭn

lime mánao
longan lam yài
mandarin orange sôm
mango mámûang
mangosteen mangkút
papaya málákaw

pineapple sàppàrót
pomelo sôm oh
rambutan ngáw
sapodilla lá mút
tamarind mákhăm
watermelon taeng moh

SEAFOOD

crab pu
lobster kûng yài
mussel hŏi maeng phû
oyster hŏi naang rom

scallop hŏi shell
shellfish hŏi
shrimp kûng fŏi

VEGETABLES

beansprouts thùa ngôk
cabbage phàk kà làm
cauliflower kà làm dàwk
corn khâo phôht
cucumber taeng kwa

eggplant mákhĕua mûang
garlic kràtiam
lettuce phàk kàat
long bean thùa fàk yao
mushroom hèt

scallions tôn hăwm
potato man fà ràng
spinach phàk khŏm
tomato mákhĕua thêt

Geographical Terms

bay ào
beach hàt
bridge sà phan
canal klong
cape lăem
city ná khon

district amphoe
hill khăo
island kò
lane soi
mountain doi
pier thâ

province changwàt
river mâe nám
street thà nŏn
town muang
village bân
waterfall nám tòk

Days of the Week & Time
DAYS OF THE WEEK

Sunday	wan aa thít
Monday	wan jan
Tuesday	wan ang kan
Wednesday	wan poót
Thursday	wan phá réu hàt
Friday	wan sòok
Saturday	wan săo

TIME

What is the time?	keè mohng láew?
Day	wan
Month	deuan
Year	pee
Evening	yen
Afternoon	bai
Morning	ton chaó
Now	deeo née
This evening	yen née
Today	wan née
Tonight	kern née
Tomorrow	prûng née
Yesterday	meûa wan née

Shopping

English	Thai Transliteration	Pronunciation
It's too expensive	**Phaeng kern pai**	peng kern pye
It's too big	**Yài kern pai**	yai kern pye
It's too small	**Lék kern pai**	lek kern pye
I don't like this one	**Mâi châwp an níi**	my chorp an nee
Do you have a (smaller/larger) size?	**Mii sai (lék /yài gwà) níi măi?**	mee sai (lek/yai gwa) nee my?
Do you have a black one?	**Mii sĭi dam măi?**	mee see dam my?
Can you give me a better price?	**Lót raa kah dâi măi?**	lot ra ka dai my?
How much is this?	**Nêe taô rai?**	Nee tao ray
Do you have anything cheaper?	**Toòk gwà nêe mii măi?**	Tuk gwa nee me my?

Numbers

Numbers	Thai Transliteration	Pronunciation
0	**sŭun**	soon
1	**nèung**	nung
2	**săwng**	song
3	**săam**	sam
4	**sìi**	see
5	**hâa**	hah
6	**hòk**	hork
7	**jèd**	jet
8	**pàet**	bet
9	**kâo**	gao
10	**sìp**	sip
11	**sìp-èt**	sip-ett
12	**sìp-săwng**	sip-song
100	**nèung ráwy**	nung-roy
1,000	**nèung phan**	nung-pan
10,000	**nèung mùen**	nung mwuen

To conjugate numbers like 30, 40, and so on, you simply say three-ten, four-ten, and so on. For example, 30 is *saam-sip*. Exceptions are:

○ Such numbers as 11, 21, 31, and so on use the suffix *et*, not *neung*, so 11 is *sip-et*.
○ Number 20 is *yee-sip* or simply *yip*, not *song-sip*.

Therefore, 21 is *yee-sip-et* or *yip-et*, not *song-sip neung*, as one might logically surmise!

Index

See also Accommodations index, below.

General Index

A

B

Accommodations